COMPUTER GRAPHICS

Volume 17 • Number 3 • July 1983
A quarterly report of ACM/SIGGRAPH

SIGGRAPH '83 Conference Proceedings
July 25-29, 1983, Detroit, Michigan
Edited by Peter Tanner

Sponsored by the Association for Computing Machinery's
Special Interest Group on Computer Graphics

ACM Order No. 428830

The Association for Computing Machinery, Inc.
11 West 42nd Street
New York, New York 10036

ISBN 0-89791-109-1

Sponsored by the Association for Computing Machinery's Special Interest Group on Computer Graphics in cooperation with the Engineering Society of Detroit, the IEEE Technical Committee on Computer Graphics and Eurographics

Additional copies may be ordered prepaid from:

ACM Order Department
P.O. Box 64145
Baltimore, MD 21264

Price:
Members $30.00
All others: $40.00

ACM Order Number: 428830

ACM/SIGGRAPH AWARDS

STEVEN A. COONS AWARD for OUTSTANDING CREATIVE CONTRIBUTIONS TO COMPUTER GRAPHICS

Dr. Ivan E. Sutherland

Dr. Ivan E. Sutherland became active in Computer Graphics over 20 years ago. He obtained his BSEE from Carnegie Mellon University (then Carnegie Tech) in 1959 and a MSEE a year later from the California Institute of Technology. At the Massachusetts Institute of Technology he studied under Claude Shannon and Steve Coons and completed his Ph.D. in 1963.

From 1964 to 1966, Dr. Sutherland served as Director of Information Processing Techniques for the Advanced Research Projects Agency (ARPA) of the Department of Defense. Following this, he was appointed Associate Professor at Harvard University. In 1968, he moved to Utah to found, with David Evans, the Evans and Sutherland Computer Corporation. Until 1973, he also taught part-time at the University of Utah. From 1974 to 1980 Dr. Sutherland worked at The RAND Corporation and served as Chairman of the Computer Science Department at the California Institute of Technology. He is currently Vice-president and Technical Director of Sutherland, Sproull, and Associates, which he and Robert Sproull founded in 1980, and Visiting Scientist at Carnegie Mellon University.

Dr. Sutherland is a Member of the Defense Science Board for the US Department of Defense, a Member of the National Academy of Engineering and the National Academy of Sciences and serves on the Boards of Directors of several corporations. He is also a partner in a venture capital investment group called Advanced Technology Ventures.

At this time Dr. Sutherland is the holder of five patents and has authored or co-authored over 45 publications. Of these, perhaps the most significant was his paper for COMPUTING SURVEYS (March, 1974), co-authored with Robert Schumaker and Robert Sproull, "A Characterization of Ten Hidden-Surface Algorithms".

In 1972, Dr. Sutherland was named the first recipient of the Zworykin Award presented to an outstanding young engineer by the National Academy of Engineering. Three years later, he received the Systems, Man, Cybernetics Society Award for Outstanding Accomplishment.

Sutherlands Ph.D. thesis, Sketchpad, was a truly seminal paper for computer graphics. It defined the first system to provide a quick, smooth interface for user interaction which allowed the user to see the results of his constructions and to test them on-line. In addition this system was the first to approach graphical problem solving through the use of a set of constraints, a technique that is still being developed, extended and applied to computer-aided design today, especially in VLSI design. More important, Sketchpad defined the Grail of computer graphics, providing a vision that sustained the field of computer graphics for over a decade while techniques and hardware matured.

At Harvard University, Dr. Sutherland started the first laboratory for computer graphics, concentrating on the display of three-dimensional objects, with particular effort being placed on the implementation of real-time clipping and perspective algorithms. While at Harvard, he also worked on the thorny issue of interaction, developing a head mounted three-dimensional display to study the requirements of user feedback.

As a co-founder of Evans and Sutherland, Dr. Sutherland was instrumental in the development of the LDS-1, a significant advance in display technology providing the first real-time display that incorporated clipping and perspective transformations and allowed for real-time simulation and modelling of moving objects within a defined environment.

At the University of Utah, Dr. Sutherland was a key player under David Evan's leadership in the research and development of real-time display of real images.

His greatest contribution to computer graphics has been his students. In the tradition of Steven Coons, he attracted a large number of talented individuals and encouraged and directed their efforts in the development of computer graphics technology. The techniques and capabilities resulting from the work of Sutherland and his students permeate current computer graphics technology and are being actively used in virtually all applications ranging from computer-aided design to motion pictures.

Dr. Sutherland presently divides his time between activities in his venture capital business and research in robotics where he is working with legged machines that walk.

COMPUTER GRAPHICS ACHIEVEMENT AWARD

Dr. James F. Blinn

Dr. James F. Blinn has been actively involved in computer graphics for the past 15 years. He obtained Bachelors and Masters degrees from the University of Michigan in 1970 and 1972, respectively and a PH.D. from the University of Utah in 1978. While a student at Utah he worked as a consultant for the Computer Graphics Lab of the New York Institute of Technology and for the Motion Picture Project at Information International Incorporated. He is currently at the Jet Propulsion Laboratory of the California Institute of Technology.

During the past six years, Dr. Blinn has made major and significant contributions to the advancement of image synthesis algorithms and systems. The technique for modelling textured surfaces and the use of reflectance maps, introduced by Blinn and Martin Newell, are two of the most widely used and most effective methods of producing highly realistic synthetic images. His model of light reflection from opaque surfaces is now the standard. He was the first to devise a scan-line algorithm for directly displaying bi-cubic surfaces. He has devised a variety of less spectacular but equally useful mathematical techniques for manipulating three dimensional objects. Moreover, this work has formed the starting point for numerous other projects by other researchers.

More recently, Dr. Blinn has published a method of describing nebulous objects whose geometry defies conventional representations. The model represents a complete departure from previous methods and promises to spawn a new class of useful geometric models.

SIGGRAPH'83

Preface

This issue of *Computer Graphics* (Volume 17, Number 3) contains the proceedings of the Tenth Annual Conference on Computer Graphics and Interactive Techniques (SIGGRAPH '83) held July 25-29, 1983 in Detroit, Michigan.

The organization of this year's technical program began with the publication of a Call for Papers and Guide for Authors in the May 1982 issue of *Computer Graphics*. These two items solicited papers in a wide variety of topics related to the field of computer graphics, while, at the same time describing how the papers were to be judged. Ninety-five papers were submitted. Each paper was then entrusted to a member of the program committee. These people did an enormous amount of work, soliciting reviews for each paper as well as reviewing the papers themselves. In this way each paper was reviewed by several top people in the field. The final selection of papers was made at a meeting of the program committee on March 4. We feel that the 34 papers published here represent the forefront of computer graphics research today. I am very grateful for the amount of time and energy put into the reviewing process by the committee. I believe that the SIGGRAPH program is a testament to their dedication.

As one can see from the list of reviewers, a great number of people were asked to review papers by the members of the program committee. These people gave thoughtful, well documented descriptions of their opinions. Not only are these reviews invaluable to the authors of accepted papers, but authors of rejected papers get valuable advice on improving their papers. I believe that many of the papers that were not accepted for SIGGRAPH '83 will be revised and accepted in the future, due in no small part to the effort of our reviewers.

Several outstanding papers selected for SIGGRAPH '83 were submitted to the editors of *Transactions on Graphics*. Of these, four were chosen to appear in the April 1983 issue of TOG. They are reprinted here for the benefit of SIGGRAPH members. A great deal of work by many people made this publication possible. Thanks to all who contributed so much.

Copper Giloth has been doing a tremendous job organizing the SIGGRAPH Art shows. One side benefit for the proceedings is our being able to select the pictures for the covers and title page from the Art show submissions as well as from the papers themselves. These images were chosen by Copper and the proceedings editor.

Thanks are also due to the many people at the National Research Council of Canada who helped in the preparation of the proceedings. SIGGRAPH '83 Technical Sessions Administrative Assistant Beth Haas, and NRC Electrical Engineering Division Editorial Office Head Evelyn Kidd and Theresa Tierney deserve special praise. Finally, I would like to thank Darlene Plebon for her work in putting together the cumulative ten year index. I am sure that this will prove most helpful for locating articles from years past.

Peter P. Tanner
Technical Program (Papers)
Proceedings Editor

The SIGGRAPH '83 Panels deal with a diverse set of important current issues in computer graphics, from theory to practice, from research to development to application.

Key research frontiers are represented by the panels on new display technology, on the simulation of natural phenomena, and on solid modelling.

The fundamental application of CAD/CAM, especially mechanical design, is represented by panels on solid modelling, on user experiences with solid modelling systems, and on the application of such systems to the automotive supplier community, a particularly pertinent topic for a meeting held in Detroit.

SIGGRAPH's ongoing interest in work outside the North American continent is reflected in the presence of two panels dealing with the state-of-the-art of Japanese computer graphics. We are particularly pleased to welcome a most distinguished group of individuals from Japan involved in computer graphics research, commercial production, and industry.

A fourth theme of our panels is the interface of computer graphics to the world of art, design, and animation. The relevant panels deal with workstations for visual designers, with artists interfacing with digital technology, and with Japanese commercial production.

Finally, ongoing concerns of SIGGRAPH are represented by a panel on standards, and by a panel on a variety of curricula for computer graphics.

The 11 panels were chosen from over 20 proposals that were submitted. A number of good proposals had to be rejected due to lack of time. Hopefully they will be refined and re-submitted next year.

I am grateful to all those who submitted proposals, and particularly to the Panel Chairmen. The result of their efforts is that we are able for the first time to include in the Proceedings a fairly detailed account of what is expected to transpire, including in a few cases detailed bibliographies of relevant readings.

I am also grateful to Pat Gall, my research associate, and Judith Allman, my secretary, for their significant contributions, and to Kellogg Booth and John Beatty for their support.

Ronald M. Baecker
Technical Program (Panels)

SIGGRAPH '83

Conference Committee

Conference co-chairs

John C. Beatty
University of Waterloo

Kellogg S. Booth
University of Waterloo

Committee chairs

Ronald Baecker
Technical program (panels)
Human Computing Resources Corporation

A. James Baroody Jr.
Preliminary and final programs
Xerox Corporation

Kathy Eastman-Hinrichs
Courses co-chair
Tektronix, Inc.

Hiram French
Exhibit co-chair
Megatek Corporation

John French
User groups
Exxon Production Research Corporation

Copper Giloth
Art show
Real Time Design, Inc.

Susan Hartwig-Hood
Exhibit co-chair
Megatek Corporation

Michael Herman
Merchandising
Dome Petroleum Limited

Doris Kochanek
Film and video shows
National Film Board of Canada

Cheryl Landman
Public relations
Seiko Instruments U.S.A., Inc.

Stephen MacKay
Student coordinator
National Research Council of Canada

Katherine Riordon
Treasurer
Ontario Science Centre

Baldev Singh
Conference poster
Schlumberger-Doll Research

Richard P. Sonderegger Jr.
Registration
Summagraphics Corporation

Tim Stevenson
Courses co-chair
Graphic Software Systems, Inc.

Peter Tanner
Technical program (papers)
National Research Council of Canada

Jane Veeder
Audio/Visual
Independent artist

Robert Whitton
Exhibitor Forum
Whitton Associate

Technical sessions committee

R. Daniel Bergeron
University of New Hampshire

Ingrid Carlbom
Schlumberger-Doll Research

Edwin Catmull
Lucasfilm Ltd.

Technical Sessions Reviewers

Steven Feiner
Brown University

Eliot Fiebush
IKONAS

Russell Fish
University of Utah

James Foley
The George Washington University

A. Robin Forrest
University of East Anglia

Alan Francis
Computercraft Ltd.

W. R. Franklin
Rensselaer Polytechnic Institute

Henry Fuchs
University of North Carolina at Chapel Hill

Don Fussell
University of Texas at Austin

Kicha Ganapathy
Bell Laboratories

William Gordon
Drexel University

Henri Gouraud
Centre Mondial

Leo Guibas
Xerox PARC

Satish Gupta
IBM Research Center

J. R. Gurd
University of Manchester

Samir Hanna
Cornell University

Marc Hannah
Silicon Graphics, Inc.

Robert Henry
University of New Hampshire

Don Herbison-Evans
University of Sydney

Gabor T. Herman
Hospital of the University of Pennsylvania

Robin Hillyard
Computer Vision

R.J. Hubbold
University of Manchester

Daniel H.H. Ingalls
Xerox PARC

David James
Hewlett Packard

Jim Kajiya
California Institute of Technology

Roger Kaufman
The George Washington University

Doug Kay
Marks and Marks

Stephan Keith
Atari Inc.

Myke Klucewicz
University of Utah

Lewie Knapp
University of Utah

Jeff Lane
Arrigoni Computer Graphics Inc.

John Lansdown
Turner, Lansdown, Holt and Paterson

Nelson Max
Lawrence Livermore National Laboratory

Scott A. McGregor
Xerox PARC

Donald Meagher
Phoenix Data Systems

David Meeker
University of New Hampshire

Gary Meyers
Cornell University

Jim Mohan
McDonnell Douglas

Tom Moran
Xerox PARC

Henry Moreton
Schlumberger-Doll Research

Timothy Mueller
University of Utah

Bruce Naylor
Georgia Institute of Technology

Course committee

Art show committee

Art show jury

Joanne Culver
Northern Illinois University

Copper Giloth
Real Time Design, Inc.

David Morris
Sculptor

Jessie Reid

Gene Youngblood
California Institute of the Arts

Film and video shows jury

Edwin Catmull
Lucasfilm Ltd.

Doris Kochanek
National Film Board of Canada

Bill Kovacs
Robert Abel and Associates

Art management

Cynthia Neal

Audio/visual management

Phil Morton
Video Research Consultants

Audio/visual consultant

Jack Coffman
Coffman, Coffman and Coffman, Inc.

Conference administration

Adele Newton

Conference management

Smith, Bucklin and Associates, Inc.

Sheila Hoffmeyer
Paul Jay
Joy Lee
Jodie Misch
Cynthia Stark
Lynn Valastyan

Decorator

Andrews-Bartlett

Bob Borsz
Betty Fuller
Ken Gallagher
Barby Patronski
John Patronski

Exhibition management

Robert T. Kenworthy, Inc.

Hank Cronan
Robert Kenworthy
Barbara Voss

Graphics design

Guenther Tetz
University of Illinois - Chicago

Panels assistance

Judith Allman
Human Computing Resources Corporation

Pat Gall
Human Computing Resources Corporation

Presentation visuals (courses)

Robin King
Sheridan College

Presentation visuals (technical program)

C-2 Computer Graphics Preparation
Service Computing Division
Los Alamos National Laboratory

Proceedings preparation

Evelyn Kidd
National Research Council of Canada

Theresa Tierney
National Research Council of Canada

Proceedings printing

Robert Kushner
K-Graphics

Technical program secretary

Beth Haas

SIGGRAPH'83

Exposition Exhibitor List

Adage, Inc.
Addison Wesley Publishing Co.
Advanced Color Technology, Inc.
Advanced Electronics Design, Inc.
Altek Corporation
AM Bruning
AMF Logic Sciences, Inc.
Analog Technology Corporation
The Anderson Report
Ann Arbor Terminals, Inc.
Apollo Computer, Inc.
Apple Computer
ARTEL Communications Corporation
Association for Computing Machinery
Auscom, Inc.
Aydin Controls
Aztek, Inc.
Bausch & Lomb
Bausch & Lomb, Houston Instruments Div.
Benson, Inc.
Business Computer Systems
CalComp
Cascade Graphics Development
Celco
Charles River Data Systems, Inc.
Computer Aided Engineering
Computer Decisions
Computer Design Magazine
Computer Graphics Lab, Inc.
Computer Graphics World
Computer Pictures Magazine
Computerworld
Comtal/3M
Conference Book Service
Cray Research, Inc.
CSP, Inc.
Cubic Systems
Cullinet Software, Inc.
Cybervision
Datacopy Corporation
Datacube, Inc.
Data Design Logic Systems, Inc., Div. of United Scientific
Data General Corporation
Datagraph, Inc.
Datamation
Data Sources
Data-Type, Inc.
Design Aids, Inc.
Dicomed Corporation
Digital Design
Digital Engineering, Inc.
Digital Equipment Corporation
Dimension Research Corporation
Dubner Computer Systems, Inc.
DYNAIR Electronics, Inc.
EIKONIX Corporation
Elector
Electrohome Limited
Electronic Engineering Times
Electronic News
Electronic Systems Products, Inc.
Elographics, Inc.
Engineering Automation Systems, Inc. (EASI)
Engineering Society of Detroit
Envision
EQS Systems, Inc.
European Software Contractors ApS
Florida Computer Graphics
Forward Technology, Inc.
General Electric Co./Projection Display Products Operation
Gould, Inc./DeAnza Imaging & Graphics Division
Goverment Data Systems Magazine
Graphic Controls Corp./Industrial Sales Div.
Graphic Software Systems, Inc.
Graphic Strategies, Inc.
Grinnell Systems Corporation
GTCO Corporation
GTI Corporation
Hewlett-Packard Company
Hitachi America Limited

Exhibitor List (continued)

IBM Corporation
ID Systems
IEEE Computer Society
Ikegami Electronics (U.S.A.), Inc.
Ikier Technology, Inc.
Imaging Technology, Inc.
ImagiTex, Inc.
Inmos Corporation
Intelligent Software Systems
Intelligent Systems Corporation
Intergraph Corporation
International Imaging Systems
ISSCO Graphics
C. Itoh Electronics, Inc.
Japan Radio Company, Ltd.
Jupiter Systems, Inc.
Kanematsu Electronics, Ltd.
KMW Systems
Lang Systems, Inc.
Lexidata Corporation
LogEtronics, Inc.
Lundy Electronics & Systems, Inc.
MacDonald Dettwiler & Associates, Ltd.
Machine Design
Marinco, Inc.
Matra Technology, Inc.
Matrix Instruments, Inc.
Matrox Electronic Systems, Ltd.
Measurement Systems, Inc.
Megatek Corporation
Metheus Corporation
Micro Control Systems, Inc.
Micro-Term, Inc.
Microtex Corporation
Mini-Micro Systems
Modgraph, Inc.
Moniterm Corporation
NEC Information Systems, Inc.
Nicolet Zeta Corporation
Nippon Computer Company, Ltd.
Nissei Sangyo America, Ltd.
Numonics Corporation
OCLI/Optical Coating Laboratory, Inc.
Omni Graphics Corporation
Optronics International, Inc.
Orcatech, Inc.
J. Osawa & Company, Ltd.
Panasonic Industrial Co./
The Electronic Component Div.
Panasonic Industrial Co./
The Industrial Sales Div.
Parallax Systems, Inc.
Peritek Corporation
Photonics Spectra
Photonics Technology, Inc.
Pick Computing Machinery, Inc.
Picture Element Limited
Polaroid Corporation
Precision Visuals, Inc.
PrintaColor Corporation
Quadram Corporation
Quality Micro Systems, Inc.
Quantex Corporation
Ramtek Corporation
Raster Technologies, Inc.
Recognition Concepts, Inc.
Ridge Computers
SAS Institute
Scientific Calculations, Inc.
Seiko Instruments U.S.A., Inc.
Graphic Devices & Systems Div.
Seillac Company Limited
Selanar Corporation
Sentry Database Publishing
SPSS Inc.
J.S. Staedtler, Inc./MARS CAD Div.
Sumitomo Corporation of America
Summagraphics Corporation
SUN Microsystems, Inc.
Superset, Inc.
Symbolics, Inc.
Symtec, Inc.
Systems Research Laboratories, Inc.
Technology & Business Communications, Inc.
Tektronix, Inc.
Terak Corporation
3M Company/Audio Visual Div.
Three Rivers Computer Corporation
Totoku Electric Company, Ltd.
Trillium Corporation
Universal Technical Graphics/
Graphic Resources Corporation
Vector Automation
Vectrix Corporation
Vermont Microsystems
Versatec, A Xerox Company
Via Video, Inc.
Vicom Systems, Inc.
Watanabe Instruments Corporation
Westward Micro Systems
Wicat Systems
Xerox Corporation/Printing Systems Div.
Zentec Corporation

SIGGRAPH '83

Contents

Wednesday, July 27, 1983 (cont'd)

THURSDAY, July 28, 1983

Thursday, July 28, 1983 (cont'd)

FRIDAY, July 29, 1983

Friday, July 29, 1983 (cont'd)

Pyramidal Parametrics

Lance Williams

Computer Graphics Laboratory
New York Institute of Technology
Old Westbury, New York

Abstract

The mapping of images onto surfaces may substantially increase the realism and information content of computer-generated imagery. The projection of a flat source image onto a curved surface may involve sampling difficulties, however, which are compounded as the view of the surface changes. As the projected scale of the surface increases, interpolation between the original samples of the source image is necessary; as the scale is reduced, approximation of multiple samples in the source is required. Thus a constantly changing sampling window of view-dependent shape must traverse the source image.

To reduce the computation implied by these requirements, a set of prefiltered source images may be created. This approach can be applied to particular advantage in animation, where a large number of frames using the same source image must be generated. This paper advances a "pyramidal parametric" prefiltering and sampling geometry which minimizes aliasing effects and assures continuity within and between target images.

Although the mapping of texture onto surfaces is an excellent example of the process and provided the original motivation for its development, pyramidal parametric data structures admit of wider application. The aliasing of not only surface texture, but also highlights and even the surface representations themselves, may be minimized by pyramidal parametric means.

General Terms: Algorithms.

Keywords and Phrases: Antialiasing, Illumination Models, Modeling, Pyramidal Data Structures, Reflectance Mapping, Texture Mapping, Visible Surface Algorithms.

CR Categories: I.3.3 [Computer Graphics]: Picture/Image Generation--display algorithms; I.3.5 [Computer Graphics]: Computational Geometry and Object Modeling--curve, surface, solid and object representations, geometric algorithms, languages and systems; I.3.7 [Computer Graphics]: Three-Dimensional Graphics and Realism--color, shading, shadowing, and texture.

1. Pyramidal Data Structures

Pyramidal data structures may be based on various subdivisions: binary trees, quad trees, oct trees, or n-dimensional hierarchies [17]. The common feature of these structures is a succession of levels which vary the resolution at which the data is represented.

The decomposition of an image by two-dimensional binary subdivision was a pioneering strategy in computer graphics for visible surface determination [15]. The approach was essentially a synthesis-by-analysis: the image plane was subdivided into quadrants recursively until analysis of a subsection showed that surface ordering was sufficiently simple to permit rendering. Such subdivision and analysis has been subsequently adopted to generate spatial data structures [5], which have been used to represent images [9] both for pattern recognition [13] and for transmission [10], [14]. In the field of computer graphics, such data structures have been adopted for texture mapping [4], [16], and generalized to represent objects in space [11].

The application of pyramidal data to image storage and transmission may permit significant compression of the data to be stored or transmitted. This is so because highly detailed features may be localized within an otherwise low-frequency image, permitting the sampling rate to be reduced for large sections of the image. Besides permitting bandwidth compression, the representation orders data in such a way that the general character of images may be recalled or transmitted before the specific details.

Pattern recognition and classification often require the comparison of a candidate image against a set of canonical patterns. This is an operation the expense of which increases as the square of the resolution at which it is performed. The use of pyramidal data structures in pattern recognition and classification permits the comparison of the gross features of two-dimensional functions preliminary to the minute particulars; a good general reference on this application is [12].

In computer graphics, pyramidal texture maps may be used to perform arbitrary mappings of a function with minimal aliasing artifacts and reduced computation. Once again, images may be represented at different spatial bandwidths. The concern is that inappropriate resolution misrepresents the data; that is, sampling high-resolution data at larger sample intervals invites aliasing.

2. Parametric Interpolation

By a pyramidal parametric data structure, we will mean simply a pyramidal structure with both intra- and inter-level interpolation. Consider the case of an image represented as a two-dimensional array of samples. Interpolation is necessary to produce a continuous function of two parameters, U and V. If, in addition, a third parameter (call it D) moves us up and down a hierarchy of corresponding two-dimensional functions, with interpolation between (or among) the levels of the pyramid providing continuity, the structure is pyramidal parametric.

The practical distinction between such a structure and an ordinary interpolant over an n-dimensional array of samples is that the number of samples representing each level of the pyramid may be different.

3. Mip Mapping

"Mip" mapping is a particular format for two-dimensional parametric functions, which, along with its associated addressing scheme, has been used successfully to bandlimit texture mapping at New York Institute of Technology since 1979. The acronym "mip" is from the Latin phrase "multum in parvo," meaning "many things in a small place." Mip mapping supplements bilinear interpolation of pixel values in the texture map (which may be used to smoothly translate and magnify the texture) with interpolation between prefiltered versions of the map (which may be used to compress many pixels into a small place). In this latter capacity, mip offers much greater speed than texturing algorithms which perform explicit convolution over an area in the texture map for each pixel rendered [1], [6].

Mip owes its speed in compressing texture to two factors. First, a fair amount of filtering of the original texture takes place when the mip map is first created. Second, subsequent filtering is approximated by blending different levels of the mip map. This means that all filters are approximated by linearly interpolating a set of square box filters, the sides of which are powers-of-two pixels in length. Thus, mapping entails a fixed overhead, which is independent of the area filtered to compute a sample.

Figure (1)
Structure of a Color Mip Map
Smaller and smaller images diminish into the upper left corner of the map. Each of the images is averaged down from its larger predecessor.

(Below:)
Mip maps are indexed by three coordinates: U, V, and D. U and V are spatial coordinates of the map; D is the variable used to index, and interpolate between, the different levels of the pyramid.

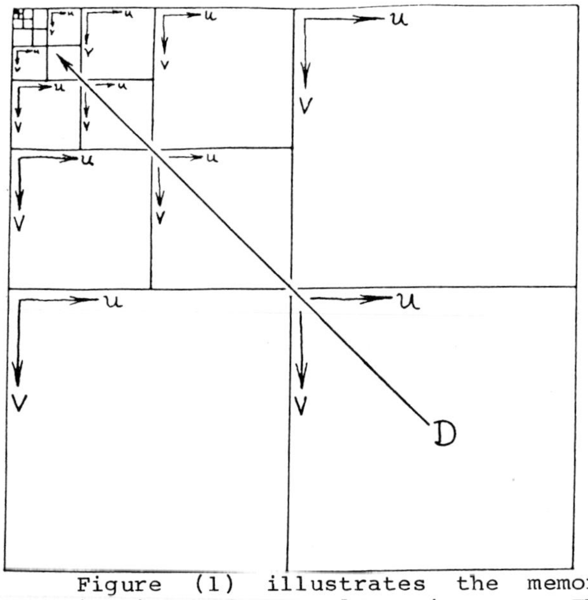

Figure (1) illustrates the memory organization of a color mip map. The image is separated into its red, green, and blue components (R, G, and B in the diagram). Successively filtered and down-sampled versions of each component are instanced above and to the left of the originals, in a series of smaller and smaller images, each half the linear dimension (and a quarter the number of samples) of its parent. Successive divisions by four partition the frame buffer equally among the three components, with a single unused pixel remaining in the upper left-hand corner.

The concept behind this memory organization is that corresponding points in different prefiltered maps can be addressed simply by a binary shift of an input U, V coordinate pair. Since the filtering and sampling are performed at scales which are powers of two, indexing the maps is possible with inexpensive binary scaling. In a hardware implementation, the addresses in all the corresponding maps (now separate memories) would be instantly and simultaneously available from the U, V input.

The routines for creating and accessing mip maps at NYIT are based on simple box (Fourier) window prefiltering, bilinear interpolation of pixels within each map instance, and linear interpolation between two maps for each value of D (the pyramid's vertical coordinate). For each of the three components of a color mip map, this requires 8 pixel reads and 7 multiplications. This choice of filters is strictly for the sake of speed. Note that the bilinear interpolation of pixel values at the extreme edges of each map instance must be performed with pixels from the opposite edge(s) of that map, for texture which is periodic. For non-periodic texture, scaling or clipping of the U, V coordinates prevents the intrusion of an inappropriate map or color component into the interpolation.

The box (Fourier) window used to create the mip maps illustrated here, and the tent (Bartlett) window used to interpolate them, are far from ideal; yet probably the most severe compromise made by mip filtering is that it is symmetrical. Each of the prefiltered levels of the map is filtered equally in X and Y. Choosing a value of D trades off aliasing against blurring, which becomes a tricky proposition as a pixel's projection in the texture map deviates from symmetry. Heckbert [8] suggests:

$$d = \max\left(\sqrt{\left(\frac{\partial u}{\partial x}\right)^2+\left(\frac{\partial v}{\partial x}\right)^2}\ ,\ \sqrt{\left(\frac{\partial u}{\partial y}\right)^2+\left(\frac{\partial v}{\partial y}\right)^2}\right)$$

where D is proportional to the "diameter" of the area in the texture to be filtered, and the partials of U and V (the texture-map coordinates) with respect to X and Y (the screen coordinates) can be calculated from the surface projection.

Illustrations of mapping performed by the mip technique are the subject of Figures (2) through (10). The NYIT Test Frog in Figure (2) is magnified by simple point sampling in (3), and by interpolation in (4). The hapless amphibian is similarly

Figure (2)
Mip map of the flexible NYIT Test Frog.

compressed by point sampling in (5) and by mipping in (6).

The more general and interesting case -- continuously variable upsampling and downsampling of the original texture -- is illustrated in (7) on a variety of surfaces. Since the symmetry of mip filtering would be expected to show up badly when texture is compressed in only one dimension, figures (8) through (10) are of especial interest. These pictures, created by Ed Emshwiller at NYIT for his videotape, "Sunstone," were mapped using Alvy Ray Smith's TEXAS animation program, which in turn used MIP to antialias texture. As the panels rotate edge-on, the texture collapses to a line smoothly and without apparent artifacts.

Figure (7)
General mapping: interpolation and pyramidal compression.

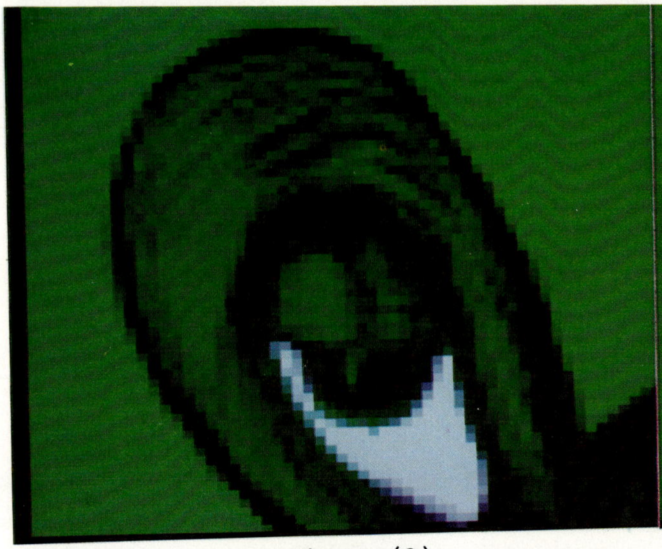

Figure (3)
Upsampling the frog: magnification by point sampling.

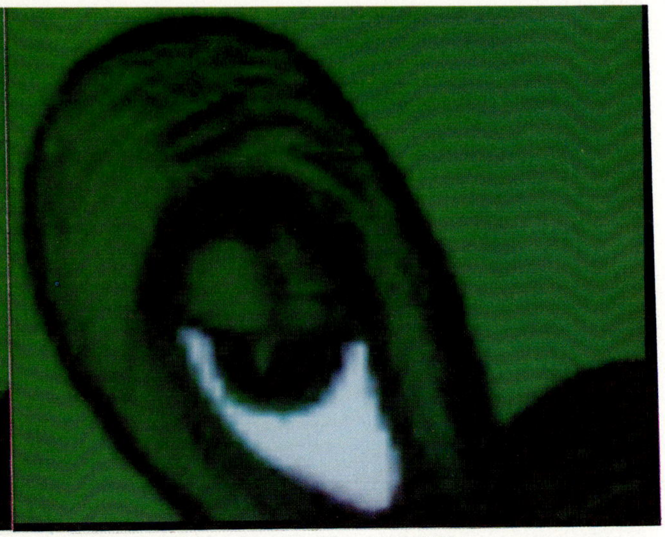

Figure (4)
Upsampling the frog: magnification by bilinear interpolation.

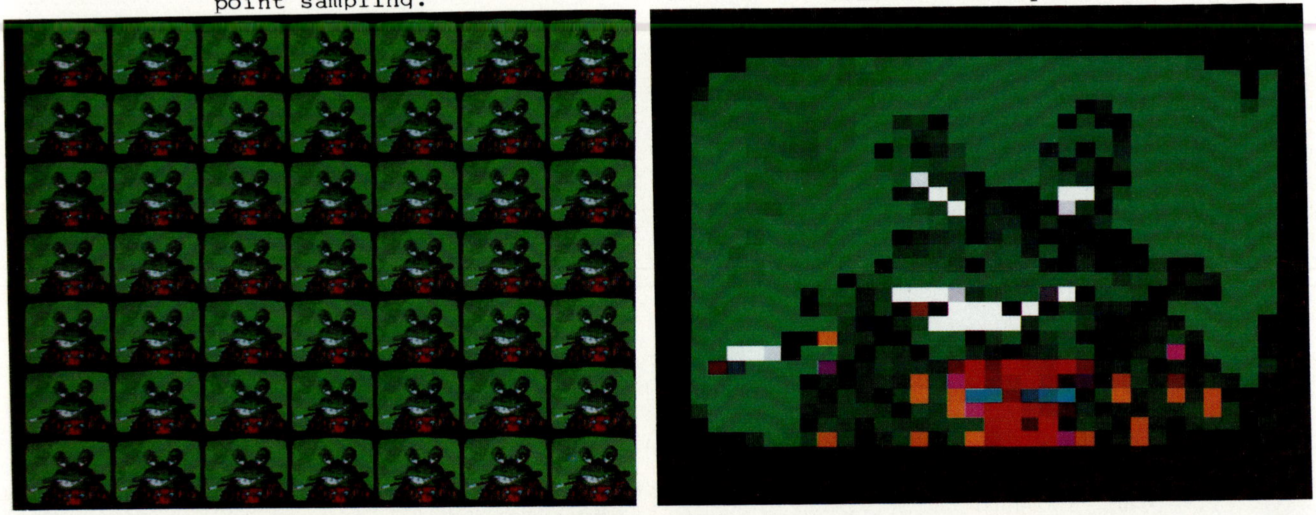

Figure (5)
Downsampling the frog: compression by point sampling (detail, right).

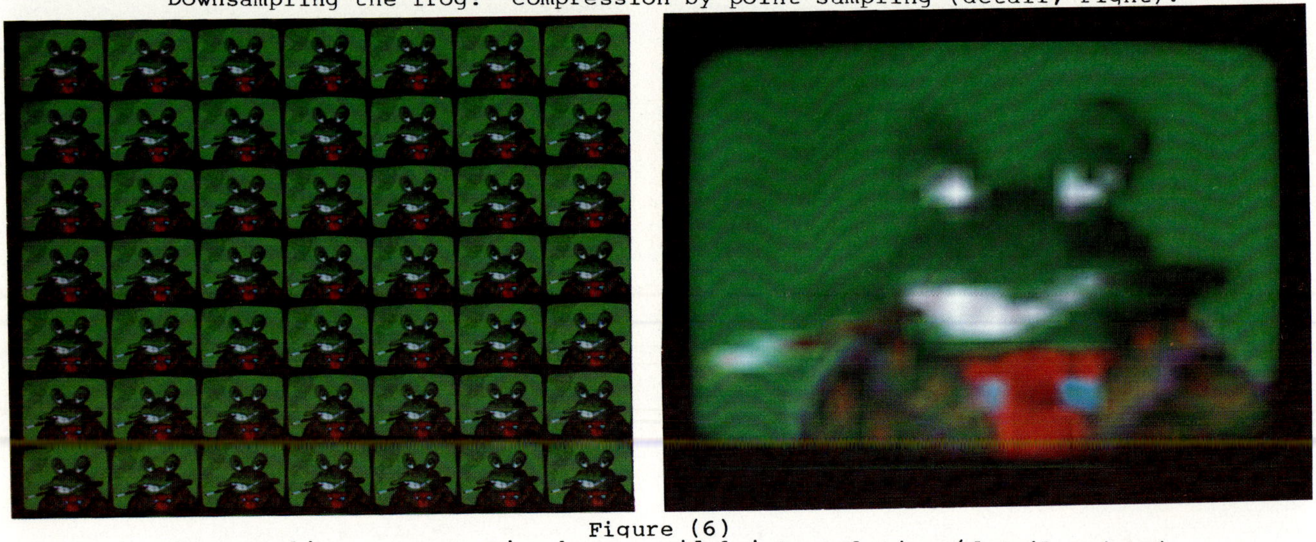

Figure (6)
Downsampling: compression by pyramidal interpolation (detail, right).

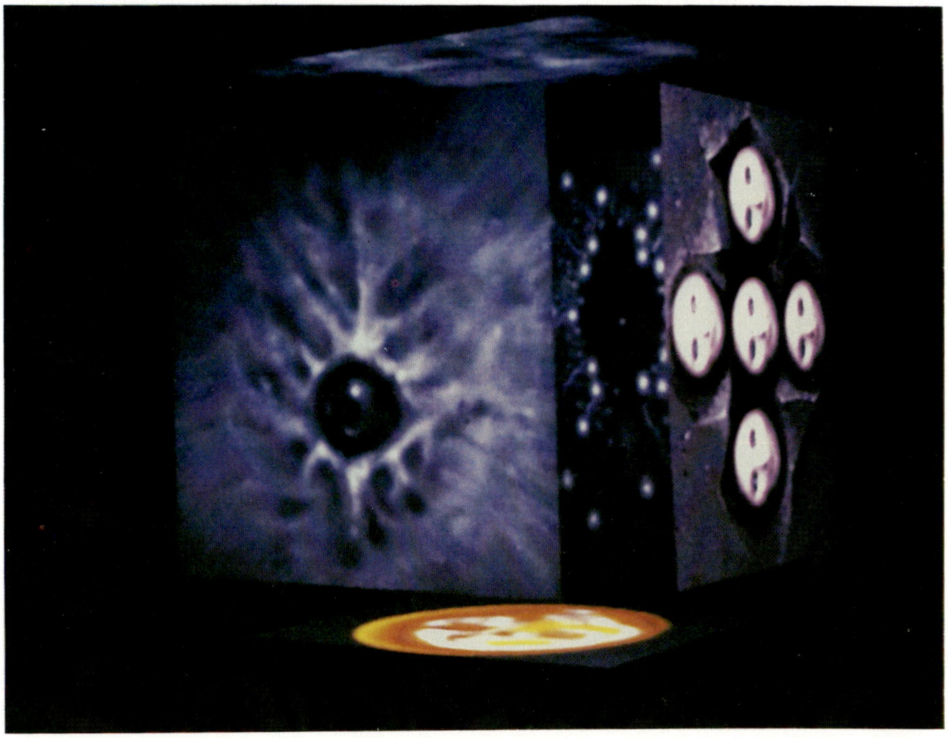

Figures (8)-(9)
"Sunstone" by Ed Emshwiller, segment animated by Alvy Ray Smith
Pyramidal parametric texture mapping on polygons.

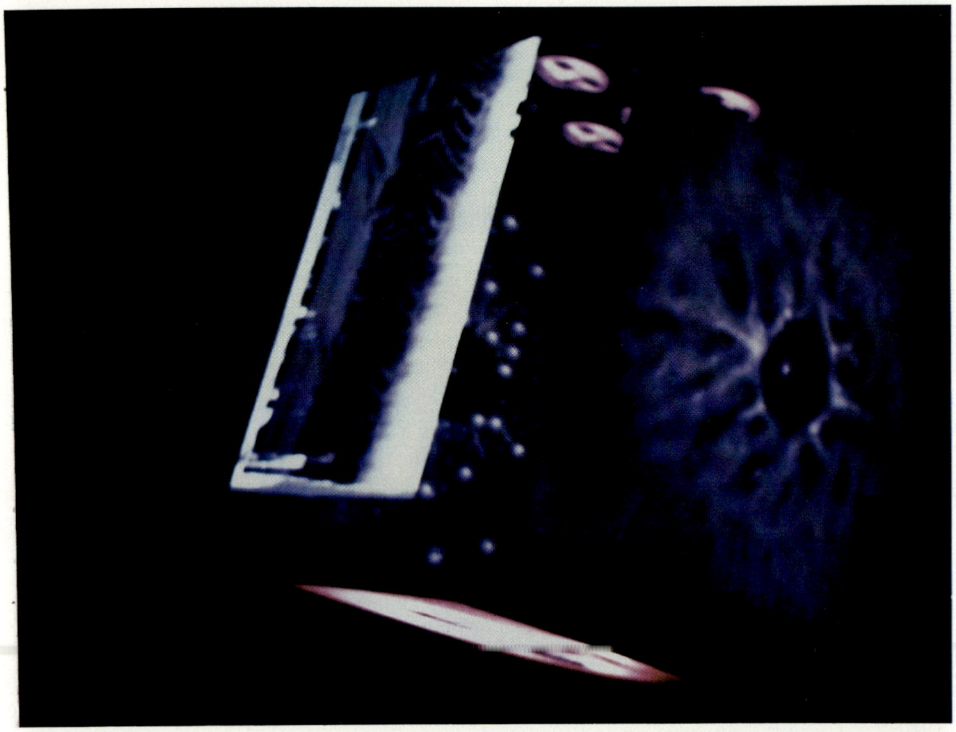

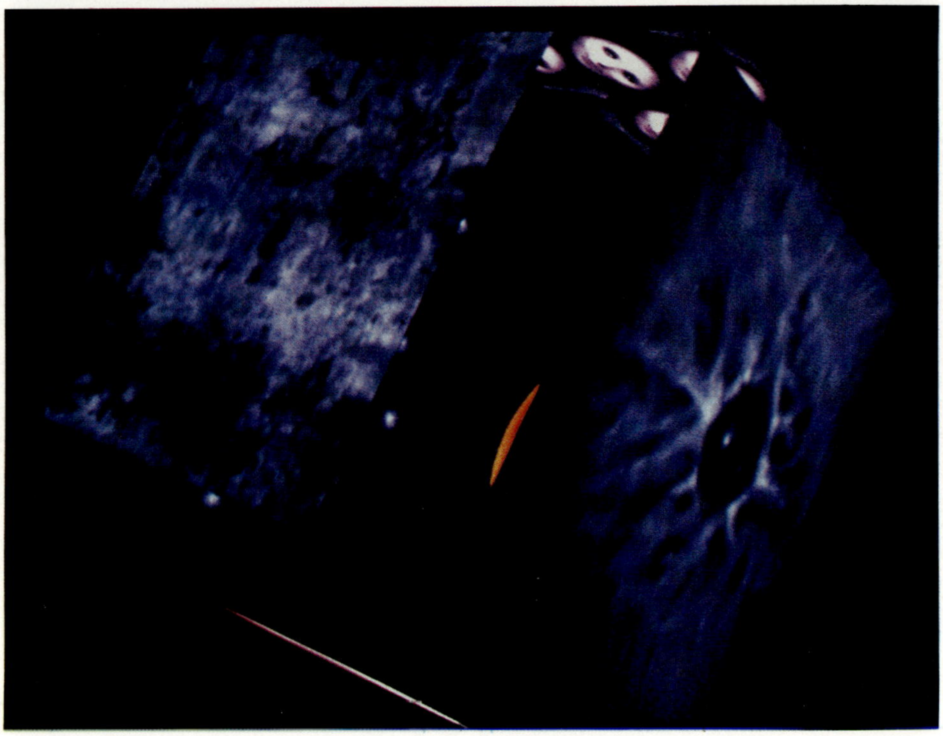

Figures (10)-(11)
"Sunstone" by Ed Emshwiller, segment animated by Alvy Ray Smith
Pyramidal parametric texture mapping on polygons.

4. Highlight Antialiasing

As small or highly curved objects move across a raster, their surface normals may beat erratically with the sampling grid. This causes the shading values to flash annoyingly in motion sequences, a symptom of illumination aliasing. The surface normals essentially point-sample the illumination function.

Figure (12) illustrates samples of the surface normals of a set of parallel cylinders. The cylinders in the diagram are depicted as if from the edge of the image plane; the regularly-spaced vertical line segments are the samples along a single axis. The arrows at the sample points indicate the directions of the surface normals. Depending on the shading formula invoked, there may be very high contrast between samples where the normal is nearly parallel to the sample axis, and samples where the normal points directly at the observer's eye.

Figure (12)

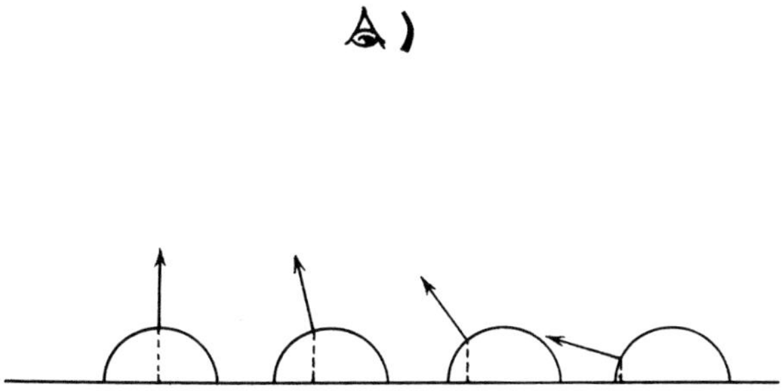

The shading function depends not only on the shape of the surface, but its light reflection properties (characterized by the shading formula), the position of the light source, and the position of the observer's eye. Hanrahan [7] expresses it in honest Greek:

$$\int_x \int_y \varphi(E,N,L) \frac{\partial(u,v)}{\partial(x,y)} \, dxdy$$

where the normal, N, the light sources, L, and the eye, E, are vectors which may each be functions of U and V, and the limits of integration are the X, Y boundaries of the pixel.

Figure (13) illustrates highlight aliasing on a perfectly flat surface. The viewing conventions of the diagram are the same as in Figure (12). "L" is the direction vector of the light source; the surface is a polygon at an angle to the image plane; the dotted bump is a graph of the reflected light, characteristic of a specular surface reflection function. The highlight indicated by the bump falls entirely between the samples. (Note that this is only possible on a flat surface if either the eye or the light is local, a point in space rather than simply a direction vector. Some boring shading formulae exclude the possibility of highlight aliasing on polygons by requiring all flat surfaces to be flat in shading.)

Figure (13)

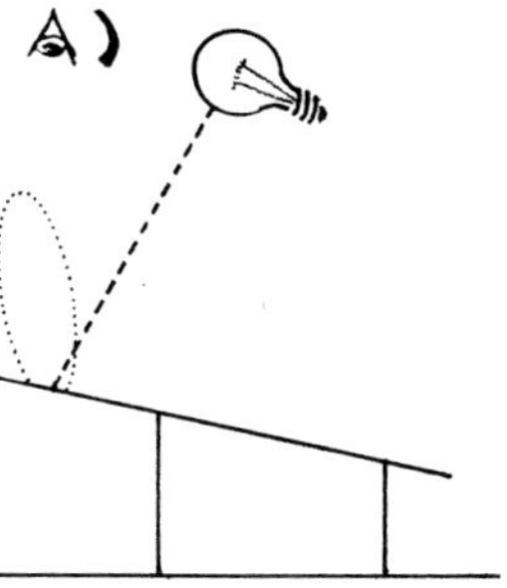

Figure (14)

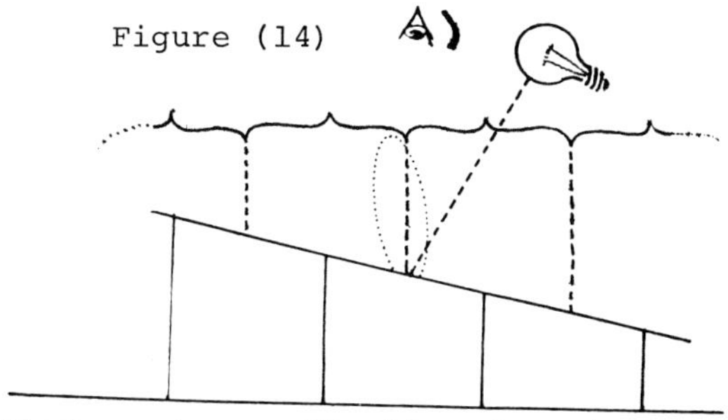

A first attempt to overcome the limitations of point-sampling the illumination function is to integrate the function over the projected area represented by each sample point. This approach is illustrated in Figure (14). The brackets at each sample represent the area of the surface over which the illumination function is integrated. This procedure is analogous to area-averaging of sampled edges or texture [3].

In order to generalize this approach to curved surfaces, the "sample interval" over which illumination is integrated must be modified according to the local curvature of the surface at a sample. In Figure (15), the area of a surface represented by a pixel has been projected onto a curved surface. The solid angle over which illumination must be integrated is approximated by the volume enclosed by the normals at the pixel corners. The distribution of light within this volume will sum to an estimate of the diffuse reflection over the pixel. If the surface exhibits undulations at the pixel level, however, aliasing will result.

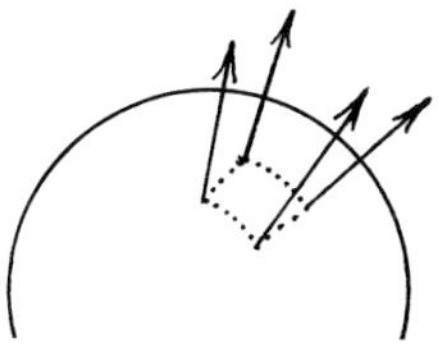

Figure (15)

Figure (16)
Michael Chou (right) poses with an imaginary companion. Reflectance maps can enhance the realism of synthetic shading.

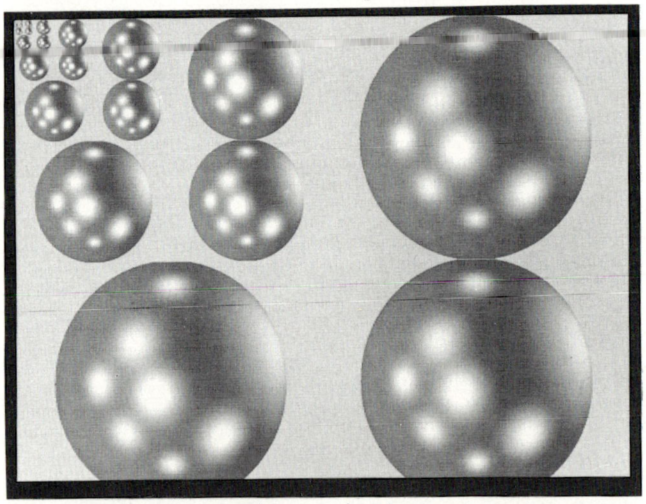

Figure (17)
A pyramidal parametric reflectance map, containing 9 light sources. The region outside the "sphere" is unused.

We might divide the surface up into regions of relatively low curvature (as is done in some patch rendering algorithms), and rely on "edge antialiasing" to integrate the different surfaces within a pixel. Alternatively, we may develop some mechanism for limiting the local curvature of surfaces before rendering. This possibility is explored in the next section.

If we represent the illumination of a scene as a two-dimensional map, highlights can be effectively antialiased in much the same way as textures. Blinn and Newell [1] demonstrated specular reflection using an illumination map. The map was an image of the environment (a spherical projection of the scene, indexed by the X and Y components of the surface normals) which could be used to cast reflections onto specular surfaces. The impression of mirrored facets and chrome objects which can be achieved with this method is striking; Figure (16) provides an illustration. Reflectance mapping is not, however, accurate for local reflections. To achieve similar results with three dimensional accuracy requires ray-tracing.

A pyramidal parametric illumination map permits convenient antialiasing of highlights as long as a good measure of local surface curvature is available. The value of "D" used to index the map is proportional to the solid angle subtended by the surface over the pixel being computed; this may be estimated by the same formula used to compute D for ordinary texture mapping. Nine light sources of varying brightness glint raggedly from the test object in Figure (18); the reflectance map in Figure (17) provided the illumination. In Figure (19), convincing highlight antialiasing results from the full pyramidal parametric treatment.

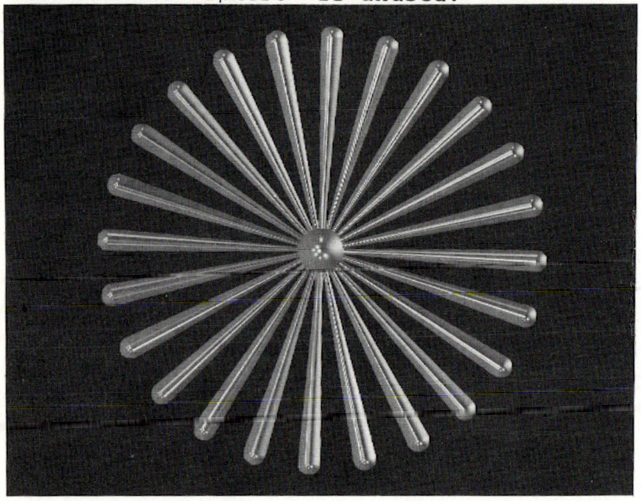

Figure (18) Before

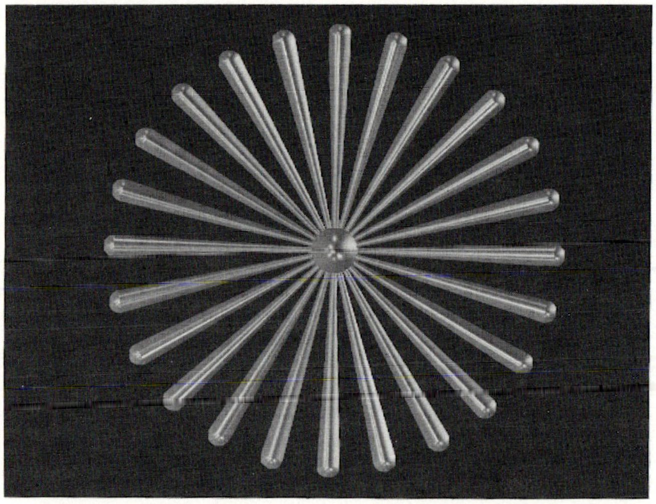

Figure (19) After

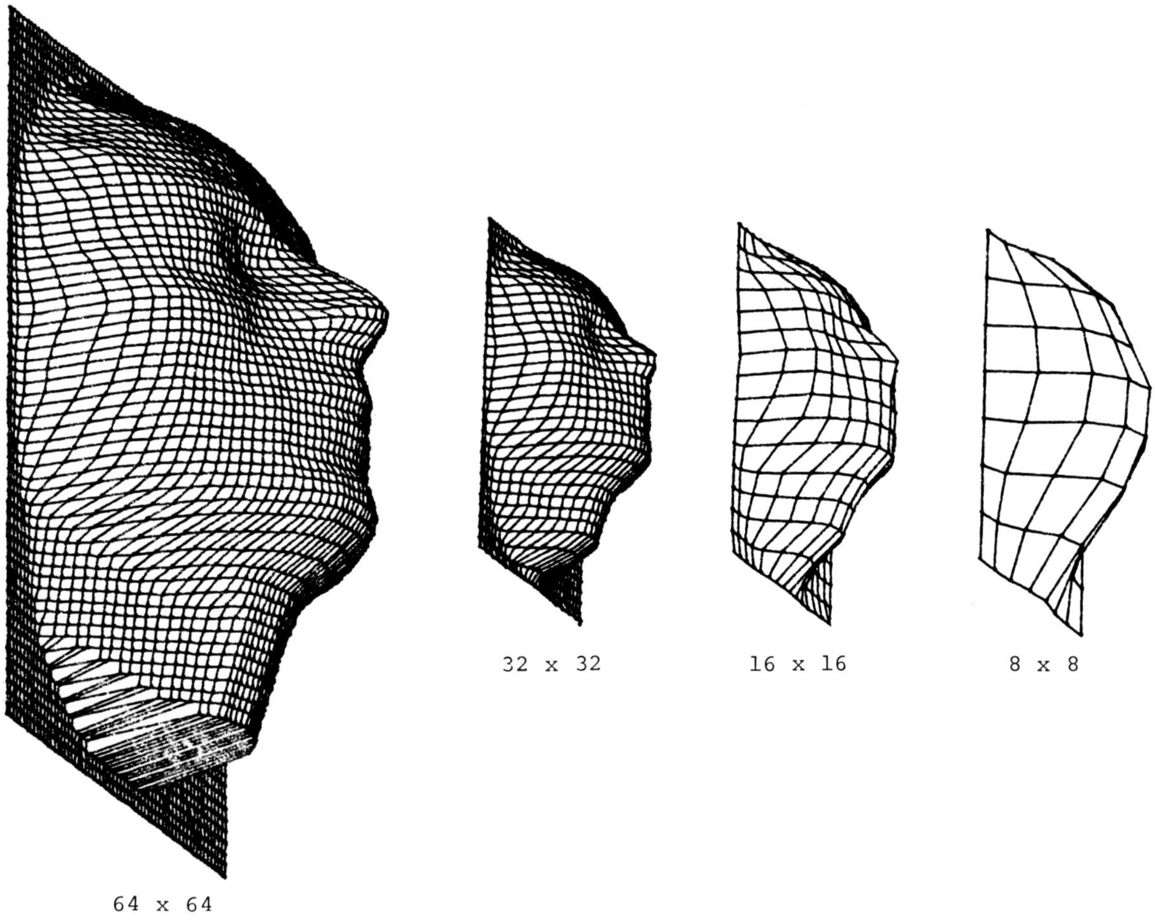

Figures (20-23) Different resolution meshes.

5. Levels of Detail in Surface Representation

In addition to bandlimiting texture and illumination functions for mapping onto a surface, pyramidal parametrics may be used to limit the level of detail with which the surface itself is represented. The goal is to represent an object for graphic display as economically as its projection on the image plane permits, without boiling and sparkling aliasing artifacts as the projection changes.

The expense of computing and shading each pixel dominates the cost of many algorithms for rendering higher-order surfaces. For meshes of polygons or patch control points which project onto a small portion of the image, however, the vertex (or control-point) expense dominates. In these situations it is desirable to reduce the number of points used to represent the object.

A pyramidal parametric data structure the components of which are spatial coordinates (the X-Y-Z of the vertices of a rectangular mesh, for example, as opposed to the R-G-B of a texture or illumination map) provides a continuously-variable filtered instance of the surface for sampling at any desired degree of resolution.

Figures (20) through (23) illustrate a simple surface based on a human face model developed by Fred Parke at the University of Utah. As the sampling density varies, so does the filtering of the surface. These faces are filtered and sampled by the same methods previously discussed for texture and reflectance maps. Pyramidal parametric representations such as these appear promising for reducing aliasing effects as well as systematically sampling very large data bases over a wide range of scales and viewing angles.

6. Conclusions

Pyramidal data structures are of proven value in image analysis and have interesting application to image bandwidth compression and transmission. "Pyramidal parametrics," pyramidal data structures with intra- and inter-level interpolation, are here proposed for use in image synthesis. By continuously varying the detail with which data are resolved, pyramidal parametrics provide economical approximate solutions to filtering problems in mapping texture and illumination onto surfaces, and preliminary experiments suggest they may provide flexible surface representations as well.

7. Acknowledgments

I would like to acknowledge Ed Catmull, the first (to my knowledge) to apply multiple prefiltered images to texture mapping: the method was applied to the bicubic patches in his thesis, although it was not described. Credit is also due Tom Duff, who wrote both recursive and scan-order routines for creating mip maps which preserved numerical precision over all map instances; Dick Lundin, who wrote the first assembly-coded mip map accessing routines; Ephraim Cohen, who wrote the second; Rick Ace, who translated Ephraim's PDP-11 versions for the VAX assembler; Paul Heckbert, for refining and speeding up both creation and accessing routines, and investigating various estimates of "D"; Michael Chou, for implementing highlight antialiasing and high-resolution reflectance mapping on quadric surfaces.

I owe special thanks to Jules Bloomenthal, Michael Chou, Pat Hanrahan, and Paul Heckbert for critical reading and numerous helpful suggestions in the course of preparing this text. Photographic support was provided by Michael Lehman.

8. References

[1] Blinn, J., and Newell, M., "Texture and Reflection on Computer Generated Images," CACM, Vol. 19, #10, Oct. 1976, pp. 542-547.

[2] Bui-Tuong Phong, "Illumination for Computer Generated Pictures," PhD. dissertation, Department of Computer Science, University of Utah, December 1978.

[3] Crow, F.C., "The Aliasing Problem in Computer Synthesized Shaded Images," PhD. dissertation, Department of Computer Science, University of Utah, Tech. Report UTEC-CSc-76-015, March 1976.

[4] Dungan, W., Stenger, A., and Sutty, G., "Texture Tile Considerations for Raster Graphics," SIGGRAPH 1978 Proceedings, Vol. 12, #3, August 1978.

[5] Eastman, Charles M., "Representations for Space Planning," CACM, Vol. 13, #4, April 1970.

[6] Feibush, E.A., Levoy, M., and Cook, R.L., "Synthetic Texturing Using Digital Filters," Computer Graphics, Vol. 14, July, 1980.

[7] Hanrahan, Pat, private communication, 1983.

[8] Heckbert, Paul, "Texture Mapping Polygons in Perspective," NYIT Computer Graphics Lab Tech. Memo #13, April, 1983.

[9] Klinger, A., and Dyer, C.R., "Experiments on Picture Representation Using Regular Decomposition," Computer Graphics and Image Processing, #5, March, 1976.

[10] Knowlton, K., "Progressive Transmission of Gray-Scale and Binary Pictures by Simple, Efficient, and Lossless Encoding Schemes," Proceedings of the IEEE, Vol. 68, #7, July 1980, pp. 885-896.

[11] Meagher, D., "Octree Encoding: A New Technique for the Representation, Manipulation, and Display of Arbitrary 3D Objects by Computer," IPL-TR-80-111, Image Processing Lab, Electrical and Systems Engineering Dept., Rensselaer Polytechnic Institute, October 1980.

[12] Tanimoto, S.L., and Klinger, A., Structured Computer Vision, Academic Press, New York, 1980.

[13] Tanimoto, S.L., and Pavlidis, T., "A Hierarchical Data Structure for Picture Processing," Computer Graphics and Image Processing, Vol. 4, #2, June 1975.

[14] Tanimoto, S.L., "Image Processing with Gross Information First," Computer Graphics and Image Processing 9, 1979.

[15] Warnock, J.E., "A Hidden-Line Algorithm for Halftone Picture Representation," Department of Computer Science, University of Utah, TR 4-15, 1969.

[16] Williams, L., "Pyramidal Parametrics," SIGGRAPH tutorial notes, "Advanced Image Synthesis," 1981.

[17] Yau, M.M., and Srihari, S.N., "Recursive Generation of Hierarchical Data Structures for Multidimensional Digital Images," Proceedings of the IEEE Computer Society Conference on Pattern Recognition and Image Processing, August 1981.

LIGHTING CONTROLS FOR SYNTHETIC IMAGES

David R. Warn

Computer Science Department
General Motors Research Laboratories
Warren, Michigan 48090

ABSTRACT

The traditional point source light used for synthetic image generation provides no adjustments other than position, and this severely limits the effects that can be achieved. It can be difficult to highlight particular features of an object. This paper describes new lighting controls and techniques which can be used to optimize the lighting for synthetic images. These controls are based in part on observations of the lights used in the studio of a professional photographer. Controls include a light direction to aim a light at a particular area of an object, light concentration to simulate spotlights or floodlights, and flaps or cones to restrict the path of a light. Another control relates to the color of the light source and its effect on the perceived color of specular highlights. An object color can be blended with a color for the highlights to simulate different materials, paints, or lighting conditions. This can be accomplished dynamically while the image is displayed, using the video lookup table to approximate the specular color shift.

CR Categories and Subject Descriptors: I.3.3 [Computer Graphics]: Picture/Image Generation - display algorithms; I.3.7 [Computer Graphics]: Three-Dimensional Graphics and Realism - color, shading, shadowing, and texture;

Additional Key Words and Phrases: light controls

INTRODUCTION

The lighting model and controls described in this paper are part of GMR AUTOCOLOR, a system developed at the General Motors Research Laboratories for automatic generation of color synthetic images. The major application for this capability within GM is design evaluation, to view a realistic image prior to or in place of building a physical model in wood or clay. It can be used both to display automotive body surfaces to aid in their aesthetic evaluation and to display automotive parts constructed with the GMSolid [8] modeling system to aid in visualizing complex geometric shapes. GMR AUTOCOLOR can also be used to display color coded scalar values such as stress [14], pressure, or curvature [11] on the surface of an object.

The geometric shape of an object is approximated by a mesh of three or four sided planar polygons. The polygonal representation was selected both for its availability within GM and for its efficiency. Polygons can be grouped to form parts. For a car body there might be separate parts for the door, hood, roof, fender, etc. Each part is assigned a surface type such as body or glass, and each type of surface has associated color and reflectance properties. The entire data structure is stored in tables using the GMR developed REGIS interactive relational data base [12]. The polygonal mesh is defined by two tables: a node table containing the Cartesian coordinates of the node points and a polygon table containing the node numbers to be connected to form each polygon. Auxiliary tables containing the part, surface, and lighting parameters can be supplied as input or created automatically by the system as they are needed. The tables are stored in virtual memory files [20] and are all directly addressable during image generation. This data organization is very efficient because it eliminates all I/O other than paging.

GMR AUTOCOLOR is a completely interactive system using menus and screen selection to define parameters and options, select a viewing orientation, or mix a color. A Watkins based scan line algorithm [3,21] is used for hidden surface elimination to determine which point on the object is visible at each pixel location. This algorithm is well suited for the polygonal representation. See [19] for a survey and comparison of other hidden surface algorithms.

The system is implemented in PL/I and runs on a VAX 11/780 computer under VMS. A RAMTEK 9300 is used to display the generated color images.

THE LIGHTING MODEL

The lighting model determines the intensity of the reflected light that reaches the eye from a given point on the object. It takes into account the reflectance properties of the surface as well as the physics of light reflection. This lighting computation is performed scan line by scan line as the hidden surface algorithm determines which portion of a polygon is visible.

A great deal of research has been reported on lighting models for synthetic images. See [17] for a good summary of early work with historical perspective and Newman and Sproull [18] for a general discussion of the issues involved. The Phong [15] model was the first to achieve realistic highlights using interpolation of surface normals and an approximation of specular reflection. This model has been extended and modified by others to incorporate improved highlights [5] and global scene illumination (multiple reflections) [22]. Other related work affecting the realism of synthetic images includes shadows [1,10], texture [4,6], transparency [13], clouds [7], a camera model [16], and surface reflection color [9].

The lighting model used in GMR AUTOCOLOR is based on the original Phong approach. The extensions which are described in this paper relate to providing controls and adjustments on individual lights and not to the particular method used to model light reflection. They could be applied to any lighting model. Using the Phong model to determine the intensity contribution from each light and with the additional controls described in the following section, it is possible to generate very realistic images of automotive body surfaces and parts. To provide a framework for discussing these extensions, the Phong lighting model will first be reviewed.

The geometry of light reflection is illustrated in Figure 1 for a light illuminating a point P on the surface of an object.

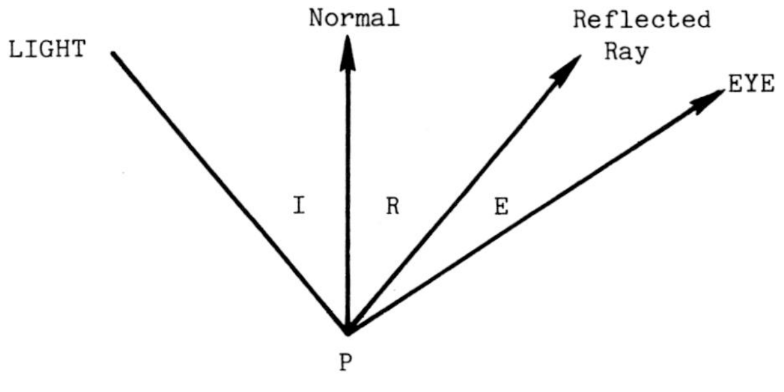

Figure 1. Geometry of Light Reflection

The positions of the EYE and each of the lights are specified by the user. The angle of incidence I is the angle between the ray from the light source and the surface normal at the point P. The angle of reflection R is equal to the angle of incidence. The direction of the surface normal vector is computed from the node normals using bilinear interpolation.

The intensity contribution for each light is modeled as the sum of diffuse and specular components multiplied by the intensity of the light source as shown in Figure 2. Diffuse reflection is light which is reflected uniformly in all directions. It depends only on the position of the light source, not on the position of the viewer and is modeled as the cosine of the angle of incidence, obeying Lambert's law. Specular reflection makes the object appear shiny by generating highlights in the mirror direction, taking into account the position of the viewer and the surface finish. The effect of specular reflection is approximated by a cosine raised to a power. This value will peak when the reflected ray points directly at the EYE so that the angle E is zero. It will fall off either gradually or quickly depending on the value of the exponent N which corresponds to the glossiness of the surface. Dull surfaces have a small value of N and shiny surfaces have a high value.

light(j) = intensity(j)*(diffuse + specular)

where: diffuse = D(cos(I))

specular = $S(\cos^N(E))$

intensity(j) = intensity of light j

D is the diffuse coefficient,
S is the specular coefficient,
N is the specular exponent,
I is the angle of incidence,
E is the angle between the reflected ray and the ray to the eye.

Figure 2. Phong Intensity Computation for each Light

D, S, and N are the reflectance properties associated with each type of surface to be displayed. The coefficients D and S control the proportion of diffuse and specular reflection. For a more accurate rendering, the specular coefficient S should be a function of the angle of incidence I as well as the type of surface (material) [18]. The values of cos(I) and cos(E) can be easily computed using the dot product of normalized unit vectors [18]. The intensity must be calculated for each light source and every point on the object which corresponds to a visible pixel in the image. The intensity at each point is the sum of the contributions from all lights plus an ambient term. The ambient intensity indicates the general level of illumination for the entire scene.

The method used for computing these intensities is the first departure from the basic Phong model. The light intensity at each pixel is computed as an unscaled floating point value in a virtual picture array. If an object is composed of multiple surfaces, the surface number being displayed at each pixel is stored in an auxiliary picture sized array. As the image generation proceeds, the maximum and minimum unscaled intensity values for the entire image and for each surface type are determined. The unscaled intensities are then mapped into integer intensities for the display. This rescaling process can be based on the unscaled intensity range for each surface or for the entire object. This approach places no restrictions on the range of values for the diffuse and specular coefficients D and S or on the number and intensity of light sources. It also permits experimentation with nonlinear mappings of the unscaled values.

LIGHT CONTROLS

The traditional point source light used for synthetic image generation provides no controls or adjustments other than position, and this severely limits the effects that can be achieved. The light controls described in this section were developed for GMR AUTOCOLOR after observing the lighting used to photograph a car in a studio. Cars are not photographed with a bare 100 watt light bulb (the analogy of a point source light). Many lights are used and each is carefully adjusted to produce a very specific highlight.

The light controls described below are implemented as modifiers of the intensity value determined at each point by the Phong lighting model and therefore could be applied to any other lighting model.

Light Direction and Concentration

The two most basic lighting controls are direction and concentration. These controls make it possible to aim the light and to adjust the distribution over an area. Point source lights are very difficult to position in order to produce highlights in a particular area of an object, and they can cause unwanted highlights in other areas. Each time a light is moved, the entire image must be recomputed which takes 1 to 5 minutes, depending on the number of polygons and the area of the screen covered by visible surfaces. This makes experimentation with lighting very tedious. Light direction and concentration controls make it possible to isolate the effect of a light to a particular area and achieve a desired highlight more quickly. This is not because the lighting model computations are any faster, but because the lights behave in a more "natural" way. A different approach to make lights easier to adjust is suggested in [2], using the lookup table to store surface normal information to permit dynamic lighting changes.

On real lights, direction and concentration are produced by reflectors, lenses, and housings. It would be possible to model these components directly, but that would introduce considerable overhead to the lighting computation. A simpler approach is to model the overall effect of such a system rather than the individual causes.

A directed light can be modeled mathematically as the light emitted by a single point specular reflecting surface illuminated by a hypothetical point source light. Think of the point labelled "Light" in Figure 3 as a surface which reflects light onto the object. The normal orientation of this single point surface is controlled by the light direction vector. A hypothetical point source light located along this vector illuminates the reflector surface which, in turn, reflects light onto the object.

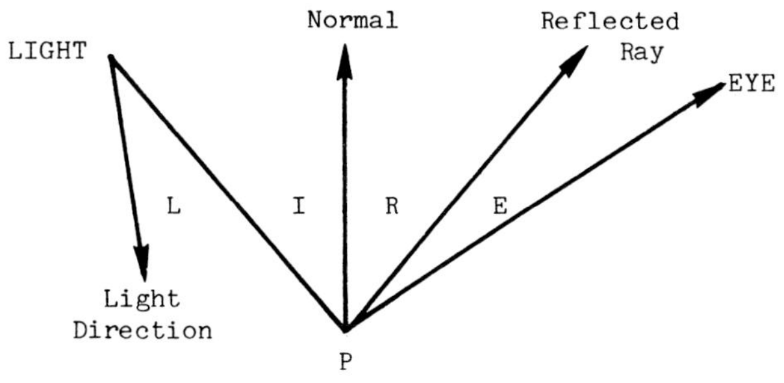

Figure 3. Light Direction

We can compute the intensity of the reflected light at a point P on the object using the model in Figure 2 and treating P as the eye position. Because the hypothetical point source light illuminating the reflector (but nothing else) is located on the surface normal, the angle of incidence is 0 and the reflected ray coincides with the light direction vector. The angle between the reflected ray and the ray to the eye (the point P) is then the angle labelled L in Figure 3, between the light direction and the ray from the light position to the point P. Since we are considering the light to be a specular reflecting surface, we will use a diffuse coefficient of 0 and a specular coefficient of 1. The intensity at the point P from the directed light source is then:

$$\text{intensity}(j)*\cos^{C}(L)$$

where C is the specular exponent of the light reflector surface. The exponent C provides control over the concentration of the light. By increasing the value of C, the light becomes more concentrated around the primary direction. This can be used to simulate the effect of a spot light or a flood light. The light can be aimed by adjusting the orientation of the light direction vector.

The above expression for the directed light intensity at a point can then be used to compute the intensity seen at the actual eye position from that point, again using the model in Figure 2. The intensity contribution from a directed light can then be expressed as:

$$(\cos^{C}(L))*\text{light}(j)$$

for cos(L) > 0 and light(j) computed as shown in Figure 2. Notice that when the concentration exponent C = 0 the directional multiplier becomes 1 and we have a point source light.

The effect of directed light can be seen in Figure 4. Figure 4.A shows a scene without directed lights. There is one point source light located about half the height of the pyramid above the plane. Specular reflection causes a highlight on the plane, which may not be desired. In Figure 4.B the same light has been aimed at the side of the pyramid, and the concentration exponent C is set to 1 for a floodlight effect. This eliminates the bright spot on the plane. In Figure 4.C the concentration exponent C has been increased to 40 for a spotlight effect. Obviously, additional lights are needed to provide general illumination in this scene.

The user can position and aim the lights using the interactive display shown in Figure 5. Three views of the object are shown: top, side, and front. Each view shows the eye position and view direction as well as the position and direction of each light. Point source lights would be shown with only a cross at the light position. To change any of these locations, the user selects the current position in one of the three views and then selects the new position in that view. By changing a position or direction in two of the three views, all three coordinates can be quickly changed without having to enter numeric coordinate values.

By moving the eye position or view direction, the view orientation can easily be changed. A small mesh image of the current view can be generated by selecting DISPLAY VIEW. This can be used to quickly verify that the desired orientation has been achieved. RESCALE can be selected to move closer or farther away. This control automatically rescales the three views based on the maximum coordinate values to leave a reasonable amount of space on all sides. ANGLE is used to select a rotation angle for the horizontal axis of the image plane.

Figure 6 shows the image generated for a 1983 Chevrolet Camaro using the lights and view from Figure 5. The polygonal mesh was generated from the actual design data base for the vehicle. The mesh has 9619 node points, 8136 polygons, and 17940 distinct edges. Figure 7 shows the same image with a single point source light located at the eye. Figure 8 shows the effect of each of the lights individually.

Light Flaps and Cones

Two additional light controls can be used to generate special effects by limiting the area illuminated by a light. Studio lights are equipped with large flaps called barndoors which can be used to restrict the path of a light. They can emphasize a crease line by lining up the flap with the crease to put all the light above or below the line.

Light parameters provide flaps in the X, Y, and Z directions to restrict light to a particular range of object coordinates. A minimum and maximum value can be specified for each coordinate, and a separate switch controls whether the flap is on or off.

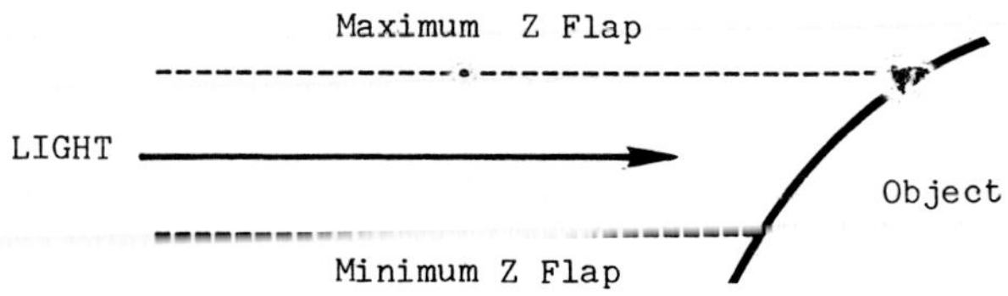

Figure 9. Light Flaps

The implementation of flaps is really quite simple. If any of the flap switches are on for a particular light, the object coordinates of the point being displayed are compared with the flap maximum and minimum values. If the point lies within the range, the lighting model is evaluated for that light. Otherwise, that light has no effect. Z flaps are illustrated in Figure 9. The light has no effect below the Z minimum flap or above the Z maximum flap. This implementation could easily be extended to provide general flaps which are not parallel to the coordinate axes.

It is possible to use flaps to produce effects which have no physical counterpart, for example, to drop an invisible curtain beyond which a light will have no effect. Using an X or Y maximum flap, the light would not illuminate any portion of an object which extended beyond the flap setting.

Another light control is a variable sized cone surrounding the light direction. This feature is not found on studio lights, but it can be used to produce a sharply delineated spotlight (as opposed to the tapering off which occurs using the concentration exponent) or to isolate a light on a single object in a scene composed of several objects. The cone size is specified by a cone angle, A, about the light direction as shown in Figure 10. The light has no effect if the angle L between the light direction ray and the ray to the point P on the surface is greater than the cone angle A.

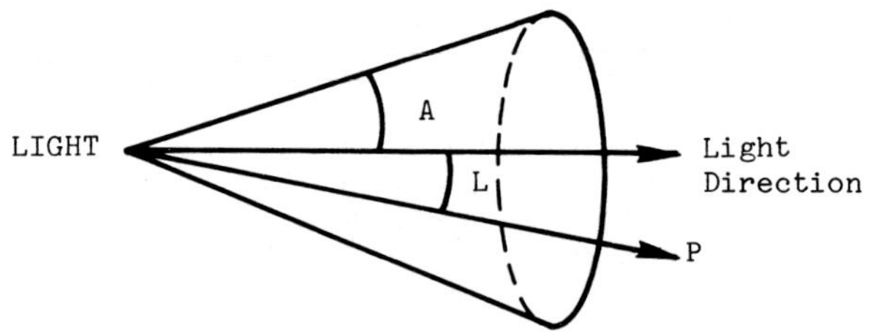

Figure 10. Light Cone Angle

The cone can be easily implemented as an extension of the light direction. Cos(L) is already being computed so it is only necessary to test if cos(L) < = cos(A) to determine if the point lies within the cone. If the point is outside the cone, the intensity contribution is zero, and no further evaluation of the lighting model is required for that light.

All of these controls -- direction, concentration, flaps, and cones -- can be used together or separately to produce the desired effect on the image. They are provided as lighting model parameters and can be selected from a menu by the user.

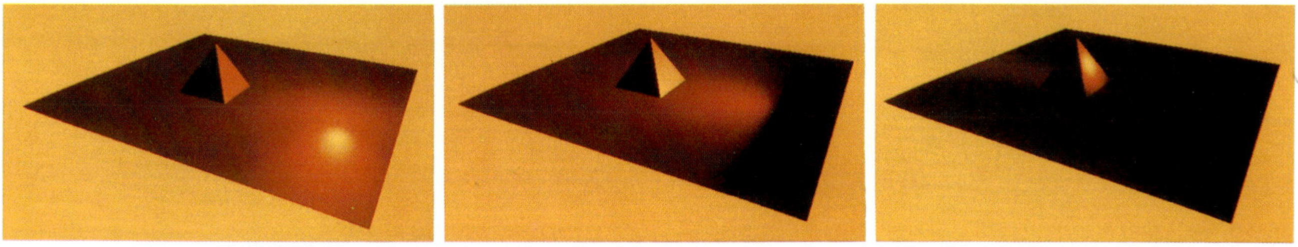

A. Point Source B. Directed Flood C. Directed Spot

Figure 4. Light Direction and Concentration.

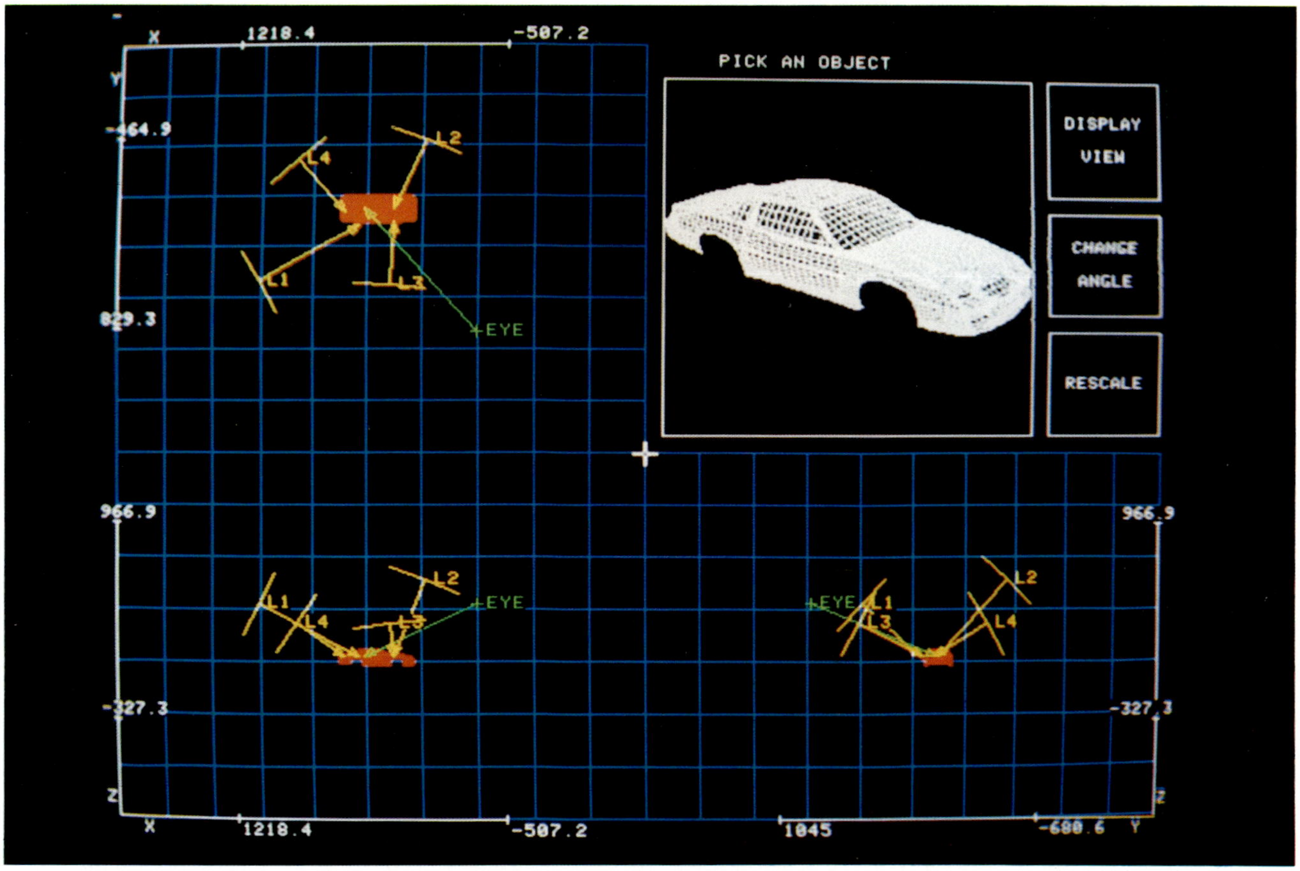

Figure 5. Light and View Selection.

Figure 6. Four Lights.

Figure 7. Light at Eye.

Figure 8. Individual Lights.

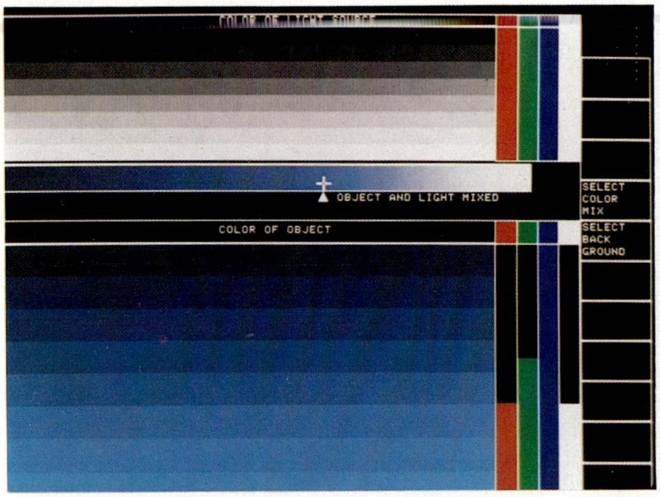

Figure 13. Color Mixing.

Figure 14. Blended Image.

A B C

Figure 15. Dynamic Light Blending.

Light Source Color Blending

At SIGGRAPH 81 Cook and Torrence [9] described a model for surface reflection. Their paper discusses in detail the importance of modeling the color of the specular reflection to realistically portray different materials. They show that non-homogeneous materials such as painted objects and plastics have specular and diffuse components that do not have the same color. For metals, the diffuse component is negligible and the color of the specular component is determined by the light source and the reflectance properties of the metal.

The color blending technique described below and implemented in GMR AUTOCOLOR uses the video lookup table to control the color of specular reflection. A user can dynamically blend an object color with a color for the specular highlights to simulate different materials or paints under variable lighting conditions. It is important to note that this method does not compute or predict the color of the specular component. It does provide a means of generating realistic effects without adding overhead to the lighting model.

The key to this approach is the method used to map the intensity values into video lookup table entries. The image intensities computed by the lighting model are mapped into separate sequential ranges of video lookup table entries for each surface type as shown in Figure 11. The value stored in the frame buffer is then logically equivalent to intensity for each surface type. By replacing the video lookup table values in one of the ranges, the corresponding surface color can be changed without recomputing the image. This approach requires a parallel lookup table which defines all three color components from a single value in the frame buffer. It cannot be used with three independent eight bit lookup tables.

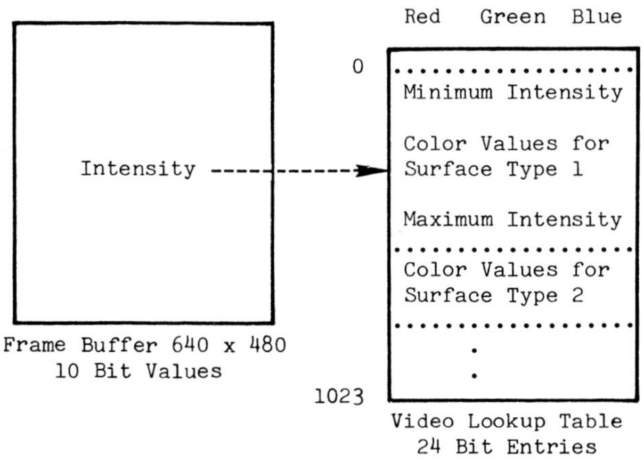

Figure 11. Intensity Mapping

Two colors are specified for each surface type, one for the diffuse component and the other for the specular component. As noted in [9], the color of the specular component may be the color of the material, the color of the light source, or a color derived from the light source and the material. For example, simulating plastic requires a colored diffuse component which is added to a white specular component. The relative amount of diffuse and specular intensity determines the resulting color. If we assume that each intensity level in the image corresponds to exactly one combination of diffuse and specular intensities, then we can store a fixed set of colors in the lookup table so that each intensity is associated with a particular combination of the diffuse and specular colors. This is an obvious simplification since many different combinations of diffuse and specular intensities could produce the same total intensity, but it works quite well.

The lookup table color values for a surface are obtained by combining the diffuse and specular colors. A blend intensity level determines the point at which the color begins to shift from the diffuse color to the specular color. All intensities below the blend intensity are assumed to be purely diffuse. In the intensity range from the blend intensity to the maximum intensity the color shifts from diffuse to specular as shown in Figure 12. The blending is done by determining the number of intensity levels N in the range and then reducing the diffuse color contribution and increasing the specular contribution by 1/N for each intensity increment.

Video Lookup Table Range for One Surface Type

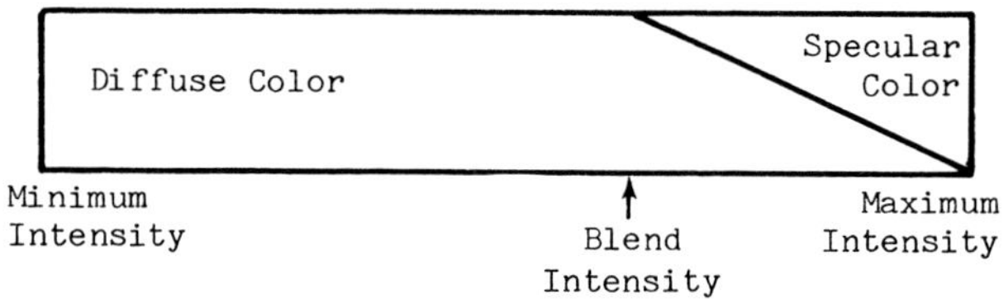

Figure 12. Color Blending

This blending method assumes that the highest intensity values for a surface correspond to specular reflection and that as the intensity reaches the maximum, the specular color dominates. The brightest points are assumed to be 100% specular. Since the diffuse component never really goes away, another control should be added to adjust the percentage of the specular color at the maximum intensity. Even with the simplifications and assumptions inherent in this approximation, the resulting images appear realistic.

The colors of the diffuse and specular components for each surface type are assumed to be known. Interactive color mixing permits the user to experiment with different color combinations without recomputing the image. The frame buffer image intensities are computed in a virtual memory array by the lighting model. This array is simply retransmitted to the display after color mixing is completed.

The interactive display used for mixing and blending colors for a surface is shown in Figure 13. Here the diffuse and specular colors are labelled object and light source for the benefit of users. The object (diffuse) color is displayed in the lower portion of the screen with all intensity values shown in the area to the left of the color bars. By selecting proportions on the red, green and blue bars, any color can be mixed and immediately displayed in the area to the left. The white bar can be used to quickly increase or decrease all three color components equally to generate tints or shades. The light source (specular) color is displayed similarly in the upper portion of the screen. Here it is shown as white but any color can be mixed. The horizontal bar in the middle of the display is used to select the blend intensity and shows the resulting color shift. Intensity values increase from left to right across the bar and the color shifts from the object color to the light source color in the intensity range to the right of the blend intensity.

For a given combination of object and light source colors, the user can interactively adjust the blend intensity and watch the image change dynamically on the screen to achieve a desired effect. This feature is illustrated in Figure 14. The vertical bar indicates intensity with the highest intensity at the top and lowest at the bottom. By selecting a new blend intensity on this bar, the image is redisplayed instantly with the new light blend. The sequence in Figure 15 shows the effects that can be generated using the same colors without recomputing the image. Only the body color is being changed. Figure 15.A uses only the object color. As the blend intensity point is reduced, the light source color is introduced at lower intensities as shown in Figure 15.B and 15.C. With the blend intensity at the lowest point in Figure 15.C, it gives the appearance of metallic paint.

CONCLUSIONS

The addition of controls on lights makes it possible to produce synthetic images with optimized highlights and special effects. Because they behave more like the actual lights used in studio photography, controlled lights are easier for users to position and adjust. With directed lights, undesirable side effects can be eliminated and a particular highlight can be obtained much faster than with point source lights. Adjustable concentration provides control over the distribution of light from an isolated spotlight to a general floodlight. The flap and cone angle controls provide special effects similar to studio lighting. Interactive, dynamic control over object and light source color blending makes it possible to simulate different materials or paints. Not all of these controls are used with every image, but by providing them as an integral part of the lighting model, they are available when the need arises.

ACKNOWLEDGEMENTS

This work has been accomplished in cooperation with GM Design Staff. I would particularly like to thank John Tuckfield and Tom Boswell for providing the polygonal mesh data for the Camaro using the GM Corporate Graphic System.

REFERENCES

1. Atherton, Peter, Weiler, Kevin, and Greenberg, Donald, "Polygon Shadow Generation," SIGGRAPH 1978 Proceedings, Computer Graphics, Volume 12, Number 3, pp.275-281.

2. Bass, Daniel H., "Using the Video Lookup Table for Reflectivity Calculations: Specific Techniques and Graphic Results," Computer Graphics and Image Processing, Volume 17, pp. 249-261, 1981.

3. Beatty, J. C., Booth, K. S., and Matthies, L. H., "Revisiting Watkins Algorithm," CMCSS, University of Waterloo, Ontario, Canada, 1981

4. Blinn, J. F., and Newell, Martin E., "Texture and Reflection in Computer Generated Images," Communications of the ACM, Volume 19, Number 10, pp. 542-547, October, 1976.

5. Blinn, J. F., "Models of Light Reflection for Computer Synthesized Pictures," SIGGRAPH 1977 Proceedings, Computer Graphics, Volume 11, Number 2, pp. 192-198.

6. Blinn, J. F., "Simulation of Wrinkled Surfaces," SIGGRAPH 1978 Proceedings, Computer Graphics, Volume 12, Number 3, pp.286-292.

7. Blinn, J. F., "Light Reflection Functions for Simulation of Clouds and Dusty Surfaces," SIGGRAPH 1982 Proceedings, Computer Graphics, Volume 16, Number 3, pp.21-29.

8. Boyse, John W. and Gilchrist, Jack E., "GMSolid: Interactive Modeling for Design and Analysis of Solids," IEEE Computer Graphics and Applications, Volume 2, Number 2, pp. 27-40, March 1982.

9. Cook, Robert L. and Torrance, Kenneth E., "A Reflectance Model for Computer Graphics," SIGGRAPH 1981 Proceedings, Computer Graphics, Volume 15, Number 3, pp. 307-316.

10. Crow, Franklin C., "Shadow Algorithms for Computer Graphics," SIGGRAPH 1977 Proceedings, Computer Graphics, Volume 11, Number 2, pp.242-248.

11. Dill, John C., "An Application of Color Graphics to the Display of Surface Curvature," SIGGRAPH 1981 Proceedings, Computer Graphics, Volume 15, Number 3, pp. 153-161.

12. Joyce, J. D. and Oliver, N. N., "REGIS - A Relational Information System with Graphics and Statistics," Proceedings of the AFIPS National Computer Conference 1976, Volume 45, pp. 839-844.

13. Kay, Donald Scott, and Greenberg, Donald, "Transparency for Computer Synthesized Images," SIGGRAPH 1979 Proceedings, Volume 13, Number 2, pp. 158-164.

REFERENCES

14. Oliver, N. N., "COLORSTRESS - A System for Superimposing Stress Patterns in Color on Three Dimensional Structures," General Motors Research Publication GMR-3712, November, 1981.

15. Phong, B. T., "Illumination for Computer Generated Pictures," Communications of the ACM, Volume 18, Number 6, pp. 311-317, June 1975.

16. Potmesil, Michael, and Chakravarty, Indranil, "A Lens and Aperature Camera Model for Synthetic Image Generation", SIGGRAPH 1981 Proceedings, Computer Graphics, Volume 15, Number 3, pp. 297-305.

17. Newell, Martin E., and Blinn, James F., "The Progression of Realism in Computer Generated Images," ACM 77, Proceedings of the Annual Conference, pp. 444-448.

18. Newman, William M. and Sproull, Robert F., Principles of Interactive Computer Graphics, Second Edition, McGraw-Hill, Chapter 25, 1979.

19. Sutherland, I. E., Sproull R. F., and Schumacker, R. A., "A Characterization of Ten Hidden Surface Algorithms," ACM Computing Surveys, Volume 6, Number 1, pp. 1-55, March 1974.

20. Warn, David R., "VDAM - A Virtual Data Access Manager for Computer Aided Design," Proceedings of the ACM Workshop on Databases for Interactive Design, pp. 104-111, September 1975.

21. Watkins, G. S., "A Real-Time Visible Surface Algorithm," Computer Science Department, University of Utah, UTECH-CSC-70-101, June 1970.

22. Whitted, Turner, "An Improved Illumination Model for Shaded Display," Communications of the ACM, Volume 23, Number 6, pp. 343-349, June 1980.

Artificial Texturing: An Aid to Surface Visualization*

Dino Schweitzer

Computer Science Department
University of Utah
Salt Lake City, Utah 84112

Abstract

Texture is an important surface characteristic which provides a great deal of information about the nature of a surface, and several computationally complex algorithms have been implemented to replicate realistic textures in computer shaded images. Perceptual psychologists have recognized the importance of surface texture as a cue to space perception, and have attempted to delineate which factors provide primary shape information. A rendering algorithm is presented which uses these factors to produce a texture specifically designed to aid visualization. Since the texture is not attempting to replicate an actual texture pattern, it is called "artificial" texturing. This algorithm avoids the computational limitations of other methods because this "artificial" approach does not require complex mappings from a defined texture space to the transformed image to be rendered. A simple filtering method is presented to avoid unacceptable aliasing.

CR Categories and Subject Descriptors: I.3.3 [Computer Graphics]: Picture/Image Generation – display algorithms; I.3.7 [Computer Graphics]: Three–Dimensional Graphics and Realism – color, shading, shadowing and texture

General Terms: Algorithms

---

*This work was supported in part by the National Science Foundation (MCS–8004116 and MCS–8121750), the U.S. Army Research Office (DAAG29–81K–0111 and DAAG29–82–K–0176), and the Office of Naval Research(N00014–82–K–0351).

1. Introduction

Almost all physical surfaces contain some microstructure or texture visible to the human eye. This texture gives us information such as the type of material which composes the object and the relative smoothness or coarseness of the surface. Computer generated images which portray such texture provide the same types of information and appear extremely realistic. Unfortunately, the algorithms for generating such images are generally time consuming and require knowledge of how to map the texture onto the surface.

Perceptual psychologists have analyzed a different type of information provided by texture: that of space perception [7] [3] [8]. The microstructure of a surface provides a somewhat regular pattern for visualization. The changes in this pattern, or texture gradient, give strong cues as to the orientation and depth of the surface. Extensive studies and experiments have shown that there are three characteristics of texture which provide this perceptual information: size, shape, and density. Changes in these components due to standard perspective and projective transformations provide knowledge about surface depth and changes in the orientation of the surface.

To avoid confusion in terminology, "texture" in this paper will not refer to the intuitive meaning of changes in the normal direction due to the surface microstructure. Rather, it is the pattern on the surface which is of interest. This pattern may be caused by different colors as in a tiled floor, or different intensities because of changing normals such as the skin of an orange. As will be discussed, it is the changes in this pattern which provide a basis for perception.

This paper describes a texturing technique which approximates the texture changes caused by distance from the viewer and orientation of a surface without attempting to exactly render a realistic texture. This approach supplies several of the same visualization cues as provided by exact texture rendering algorithms without the complexity of generating a realistic texture. Thus, "artificial" texturing is a means for providing an inexpensive aid to visualizing the shape of a shaded surface.

2. Background

To understand the objectives and advantages of this approach, some background will be provided on the role of textures in perception and conventional algorithms to simulate such texture.

2.1. Texture in Perception

Visual perception has been studied by different groups over many centuries. Early artists were interested in making paintings appear realistic, and thus developed the concepts of perspective, shading, and several other "cues" which could be used to imply depth. Physiologists and psychologists have studied vision and perception in an attempt to understand the workings of the eye and the brain. The results of these studies have been applied to computer generated images producing very realistic results.

The classic paradox in the study of perception is how one perceives depth from a two-dimensional retinal image. Cue theory attempts to explain this dilemma by suggesting that it is additional pieces of information, or cues, which when combined with the flat image provide the depth knowledge. Traditional primary cues were attributed to the physiological effects necessary to focus on an object while the cues used by painters such as perspective, occlusion, and relative size were termed secondary [3]. More recently, texture and movement have been studied as important visual cues [7].

Surface texture provides a fairly regular pattern over a large surface. For example, the size of individual blades of grass in a field may be random, but taken as a whole, creates a constant textural pattern. There are also textures which are created regularly such as bricks in a wall or a checkerboard. As a surface is slanted away from the eye the texture pattern gradually changes due to perspective and projection. This gradual change is called the texture gradient [8]. Perception researchers isolate three separate gradients which influence perception: texture size, shape, and density. Several experiments have shown that each of these gradients strongly influence the perception of surface depth and slant [3]. Figure 2–1 is a simple example of a textured surface, and illustrates the effects of texture size, shape, and density to perception.

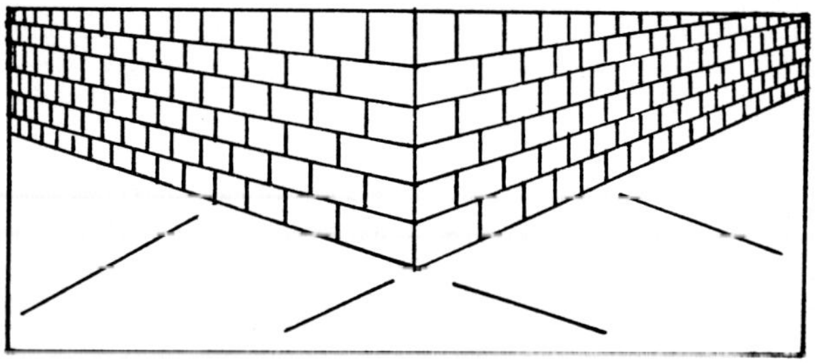

Figure 2–1: Simple texture

2.2. Conventional Algorithms

In an ever increasing struggle for realism, computer graphics researchers have developed different approaches to modeling surface texture. Catmull suggested one of the earliest techniques for mapping a defined texture onto subdivided patches [4]. His rendering algorithm subdivided parametric patches down to the pixel level for display. As a patch was subdivided, the parametric boundaries of each subpatch were carried along down to the pixel. Once at the pixel level, the (u,v) coordinates of the pixel corners specified an area in a texture definition array defined in (u,v) space. The color of the pixel was determined by averaging the values in this texture definition area.

Blinn and Newell took Catmull's technique a step further by introducing a more sophisticated filtering method [1]. The quadrilateral formed in texture definition space by the (u,v) corners of the pixel was used as the base for a square pyramid to weight the texture values. Their paper also discussed different techniques for creating texture patterns such as (u,v) functions, hand drawings, and scanned photographs.

Blinn also suggested a more novel approach to creating actual bumps in the surface via normal perturbation [2]. In this method, a perturbation function was mapped onto the surface to modify the normal vectors giving the illusion of wrinkles. This technique produced extremely realistic images, but at about twice the time of standard texture mapping.

Because of the amount of detail involved, textured images are extremely vulnerable to aliasing. More recent approaches have concentrated on the filtering aspect of the texture mapping [5] [10].

In each approach to creating texture the same two general functions must be performed: some sort of mapping is required from texture space to image space, and filtering is necessary to create acceptable images. Both of these increase the computation time of image rendering. Additionally, the mapping procedure is extremely data texture dependent, and is not always easy to define. For example, if one had a collection of polygons representing a surface and wanted to simulate bricks, it is not obvious how to map each polygons' coodinates to the brick texture definition. Although both of these functions are necessary to create realistic texturing, a simpler approach can be used to obtain the perceptual benefits of texture: artificial texturing.

3. Artificial Texturing

Artificial texturing is a means of applying a pattern to a surface in order to obtain the perceptual benefits of texture gradients. The goal of this approach is not to produce realistic textured images, but rather to aid the visualization of rendered surfaces. No knowledge of the type of object space data is required, but it is assumed that depth and normal information is available at each pixel as is required for z–buffer hidden surface rendering with normal interpolation for shading. Each of the perceptual characteristics of texture discussed earlier will be presented with a look at the information required to generate each.

3.1. Texture Size

Psychological experiments have shown that the texture pattern most effective in aiding perception is one of equally sized elements positioned on the surface at a regular density [3]. An example would be a set of equally spaced grid lines. As mentioned earlier, the problem with projecting such lines on an arbitrarily warped surface is that some mapping knowledge is required to know how such lines continue from surface element to surface element. However, a type of pattern which avoids this problem is one composed of individual texture elements, or "texels", such as a pattern of disjoint squares on a piece of cloth. The same texture gradients apply to individual texels: their changing size, shape, and density.

Along with the advantage of not requiring mapping knowledge, the use of individual texels also lends itself to a simplifying assumption: that each texel is only a function of the center of the individual element. Although this assumption does not imitate realism, it allows for a significant decrease in computation time. This simplification will be used in the calculation of all three texture gradients.

The size of each individual texel is strictly a function of the depth of the element from the projecting plane. The idea of perspective projections is well understood in the field of computer graphics and has been addressed by many authors [6]. Using the same simplifying assumption as previously stated, the size of the texel can be determined as a function of the depth of the center of the element using a standard perspective transformation.

3.2. Texture Shape

When equally shaped texels are used, the shape gradient is a strong cue as to the surface orientation [11]. The shape will be a function of the surface orientation over the texel as well as the orientation of the texel itself. For example, square elements will not necessarily be aligned with all edges parallel, and would appear unnatural if so forced. To avoid this problem, symmetric texels are used in this algorithm, specifically circles, or polka dots.

The shape as a function of surface orientation can be simplified using the same assumption as before, that it is strictly based on the orientation of the element's center. This will not result in exact realism since individual texels will not follow the surface curvature over the area of the element. However, as a visualization aid, this assumption allows for a simple texture generating method which produces perceptually helpful gradients. The shape of individual polka dots on the surface can be determined by projecting a circle perpendicular to the normal at the circle's center onto the display screen. Figure 3–1 shows a graphic description of this projection. The projection of the circle will be an ellipse whose eccentricity depends on the direction of the normal.

3.3. Texture Density

Another texture gradient providing perceptual information is the density gradient. When the texture pattern has regular density, the changes in the distance between elements, or density gradient, on the textured surface give clues to the depth and orientation of points on the surface. Researchers have distinguished two types of density gradients, compression and convergence [3]. Compression is a decrease in distance between texels due to the perspective transformation of elements at a greater depth from the viewer. Convergence is a result of elements being projected closer together when the surface is at a slant to the viewer. Thus, compression is a function of depth while convergence is based on normal information. As in the other two gradients, the approximation of using only the element's center simplifies the texture density calculations at any given point on the surface.

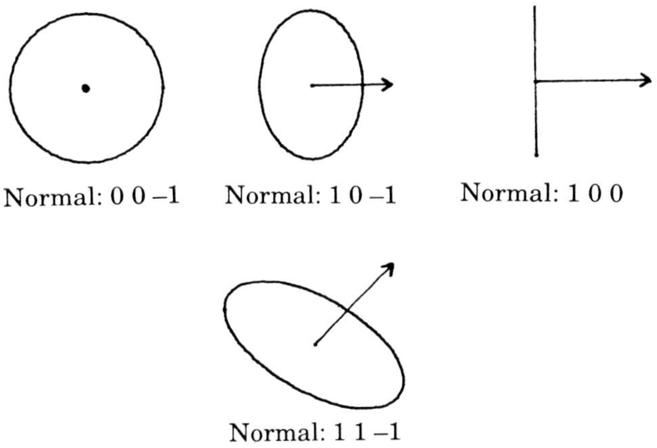

Figure 3–1: Circle projections for different normals

Algorithmically, the density information is required to determine where to put each texel. If only a density change is desired in either the horizontal or vertical direction, a simple solution is possible. The normal information available at each pixel during rendering can be used to estimate the surface distance between pixel centers. For a given density, the rendering process can determine where the next element goes by accumulating the distances across a scan line. Similarly, images could be scanned in a vertical fashion to create a vertical density change. Although either of these density techniques may provide perceptive information, the images they produce appear awkward and off balance.

To produce density information in both directions requires more detailed computation than simple horizontal or vertical distances. One solution is to approximate areas covered by each pixel's boundaries rather than distances between pixel centers. For a given normal at the center of each pixel, an approximation can be derived to the area bounded by the projection of the pixel boundaries onto the surface. This approximation can be modified by a perspective factor based on the depth of the surface at the pixel center. For a specified texture density, the placement of texels can be determined by summing surrounding pixel areas until enough area is found to place one element. Because the area calculation encompasses both depth and normal information, both compression and convergence density results. Figure 3–2 illustrates the difference in images using the variable density calculation.

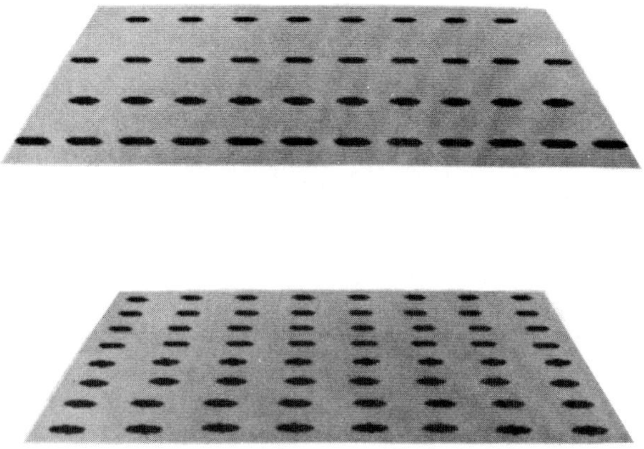

Figure 3–2: Static versus variable density

4. Implementation

The implemented version of artificial texturing uses a modified z–buffer image file as input. Rather than the standard r, g, b components at each pixel, the input z–buffer contains normal and intensity information. This data is readily available to the rendering program and can be encoded into the same size fields for compatability. For this implementation, input was obtained from a standard rendering program which contained a modified shading routine to return spherical normal coordinates in the r and g values, and an intensity in the b. It requires no additional computation time to generate such input files beyond normal rendering time.

4.1. Texel Projection

The shape of each texel is determined by projecting pixels surrounding the texel center onto the plane defined by the center normal. The distance from the projected point to the texel center is compared to the element radius to decide which pixels lie within the projected texel. Given a normal (N_x, N_y, N_z) and point (P_x, P_y) relative to the texel center, the equation for the z–component of the projected point, P_z, and distance to the texel center, D, are:

$$P_z = (P_x N_x + P_y N_y) / N_z$$

$$D = (P_x^2 + P_y^2 + P_z^2)^{1/2}$$

The texel radius is specified by the user and modified by the z depth of the texel center to reflect changes in the element's size due to perspective as described earlier.

A simple filtering mechanism is incorporated during texel projection. For each surrounding pixel, the corners of the pixel are projected and compared rather than the pixel centers. Thus, each surrounding pixel will have an associated count of 0 – 4 corners inside of the projected texel. This count can be used to weight the color of the texel with the surface to provide a simple filter. The weighted color is then modified by the intensity at each pixel. This is important to ensure that dots appearing in darker shaded portions of a surface are similarly darkened. Figure 4–1 shows the different shapes and sizes of projected dots caused from a variety of normals at different depths.

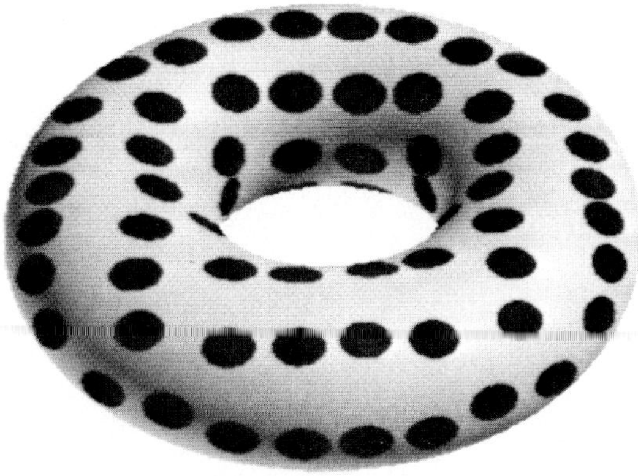

Figure 4–1: A textured torus

4.2. Texel Density

The algorithm as described could be implemented using a simple density function for texel positions such as placing them at equal x, y screen intervals. Although this provides size and shape information, it tends to appear awkward as in Figure 3–2, because the density is not changing as our intuition tells us it should. To provide for the density gradient the input file is preprocessed to determine positions for texel centers. As described earlier, this involves computing areas under each pixel in the image. To approximate these values the area cosine principle is used to determine the area on the surface bounded by the projected pixel. This approximation assumes that the surface bounded by the projected pixel is a plane defined by the normal at the pixel. The equation for this area is:

$$\text{Surface Area} = \text{Pixel Area} / \cos(\, pa \,)$$

where pa is the angle between the pixel plane and surface plane. The cosine is determined by taking the dot product of the surface normal with the screen normal and is simply the z–component of the surface normal, N_z. Thus,

$$\text{Surface Area} = 1 / N_z$$

To account for perspective, this area is further modified by the z depth of the sampled point similar to the texel radius.

Once individual pixel areas are found, it is necessary to group them into cohesive sections of equal area. This implementation uses a simple approach to this grouping by building an "area binary tree" from the individual areas. At the top level is the bounding box for the entire image. This image is divided into two subareas by a horizontal or vertical line with approximately equal areas on either side of the line. Each of these subareas are further subdivided into two equal segments, and so forth down to some specified level. At each level n, 2^n rectangular sections are defined of approximately equal areas. The direction of division for each area is determined by the longest side of the bounding box in an attempt to keep the subareas relatively square. The area center of each rectangle can be determined by weighting the pixel locations within the rectangle by their individual areas. This area center is stored as a texel location for the density defined by this level. Figure 5–2 shows a level of bounding boxes and texel centers for the surface in figure 5–1. Using these texel centers, figure 5–3 shows the resulting textured image.

The z–buffer input file is preprocessed to build an "area binary tree" of several levels (usually around 6). The resulting tree consists solely of texel locations for each level and becomes an input to the artificial texture rendering program. The user specifies a desired density level, and the appropriate level of the tree is loaded which specifies texel locations to be projected. Figure 5–4 shows the difference between static and variable density at different levels of the area binary tree. The upper two cylinders have a static density (texel centers equally spaced in x and y directions in screen space.) The lower cylinders were textured using different levels of the area binary tree, and do not demonstrate the "gaps" along the edges apparent in the upper cylinders.

5. Conclusion

Artificial texturing provides simple visualization enhancement at a low computation cost. Figures 5–1 and 5–3 are an example of the information available using artificial texturing. The lower left portion of the shaded image in figure 5–1 contains very little shading information to help interpret the shape of the surface in that area. It appears from the shading to be relatively flat. The artificially textured image, figure 5–3, gives a visual impression of the curvature of the surface.

The information provided can be compared to the "hedgehog" technique (displaying normal vectors attached to the surface) [9]. In fact, projected polka dots can be viewed as sort of "flattened hedgehogs". However, they provide a much more natural means of visualizing shape information since textures are interpreted in our everyday visual experiences. Also, additional information, such as depth, is more readily interpreted from texture gradients. One enhancement to artificial texturing which was found to be effective is to combine hedgehogs and texture. Projected polka dots are ambiguous in that they can represent one of two possible normals. By overlaying hedgehogs, the ambiguity is reconciled. Figures 5–5 through 5–8 show a warped surface with hedgehogs, texture, and both. Although the combined picture may not appear natural, it is easier to interpret than strictly hedgehogs and resolves the ambiguity of the texture elements.

Because of the number of assumptions and simplifications made, textures are sometimes generated which do not appear realistic. For example, on a surface with a sharp corner, if a texel is centered close to the edge of the corner, it will not "bend" around the corner as would seem natural. Another example is that because of the simple means of generating regions of equal surface area, densities at times will not look aligned exactly as they should. However, as stated at the outset of this paper, the goal is not extreme realism, but to simulate the texture gradients which provide strong perceptive information. To this goal, artificial texturing provides a fast, inexpensive approach to enhance surface visualization.

References

1. Blinn, James F. and Newell, Martin E. "Texture and Reflection in Computer Generated Images", *Communications of the ACM*, Vol. 19, No. 10, October 1976, pp. 542–547.

2. Blinn, J. F. "Simulation of Wrinkled Surfaces", *Computer Graphics*, Vol. 12, No. 3, August 1978, pp. 286–292.

3. Braunstein, M. L. *Depth Perception through Motion*, Academic Press, New York, 1976.

4. Catmull, E. "A Subdivision Algorithm for Computer Display of Curved Surfaces", Tech. Report No. UTEC–CSc–74–133, University of Utah, December 1974.

5. Feibush, E. A., Levoy, M., and Cook, R. L. "Synthetic Texturing using Digital Filters", *Computer Graphics*, Vol. 14, No. 3, July 1980, pp. 294–301.

6. Foley, J. D. and Van Dam, A. *Fundamentals of Interactive Computer Graphics*, Addison–Wesley, Reading, Mass., 1982.

7. Gibson, J. J. . *The Perception of the Visual World*, The Riverside Press, Cambridge, Mass, 1950.

8. Haber, Ralph N. and Henderson, Maurice. *The Psychology of Visual Perception, 2nd ed.*, Holt, Rhinehart and Winston, New York, 1980.

9. Newman, William F. and Sproull, Robert F. *Principles of Interactive Computer Programming, 2nd ed.*, McGraw–Hill, New York, 1979.

10. Norton, A., Rockwood, A. P., and Skolmoski, P. T. "Clamping: A Method of Antialiasing Textured Surfaces by Bandwidth Limiting in Object Space", *Computer Graphics*, Vol. 16, No. 3, July 1982, pp. 1–8.

11. Phillips, R. J. "Stationary Visual Texture and the Estimation of Slant Angle", *Quarterly Journal of Experimental Psychology*, Vol. , No. 22, 1970, pp. 389–397.

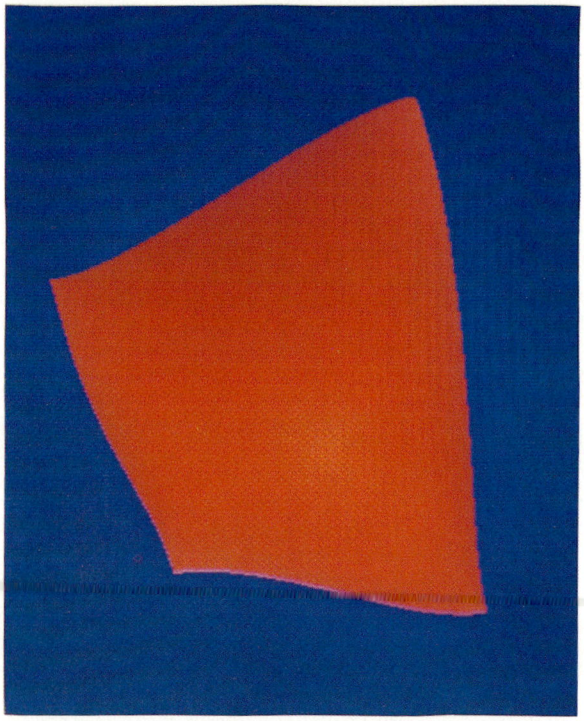

Figure 5–1: Arbitrarily warped surface

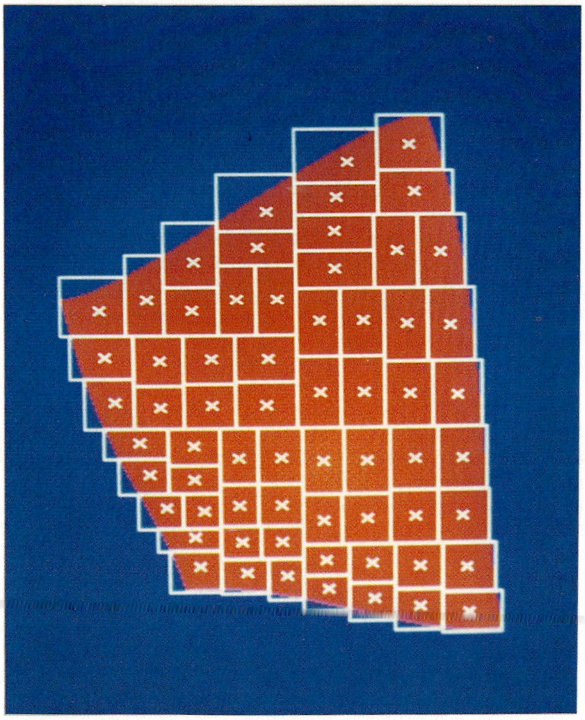

Figure 5–2: Equal area decomposition

Figure 5–3: Surface with artificial texture

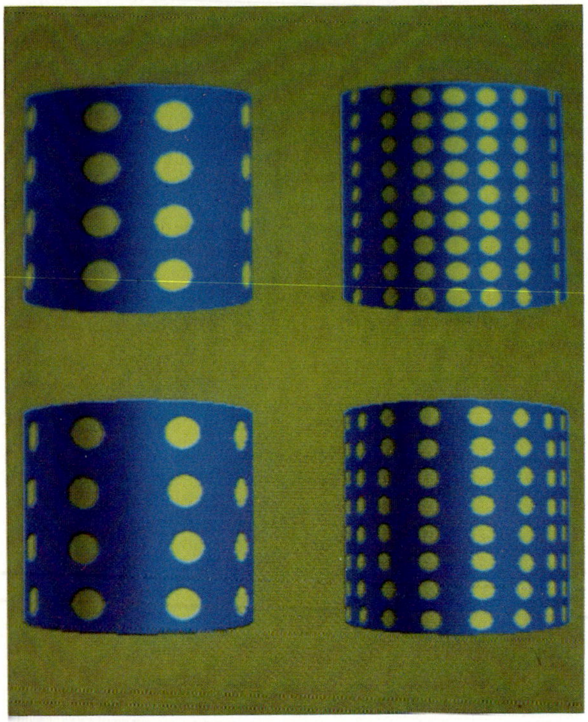

Figure 5–4: Different static and variable densities

Figure 5–5: Shaded surface

Figure 5–6: Surface with hedgehogs

Figure 5–7: Surface with artificial texture

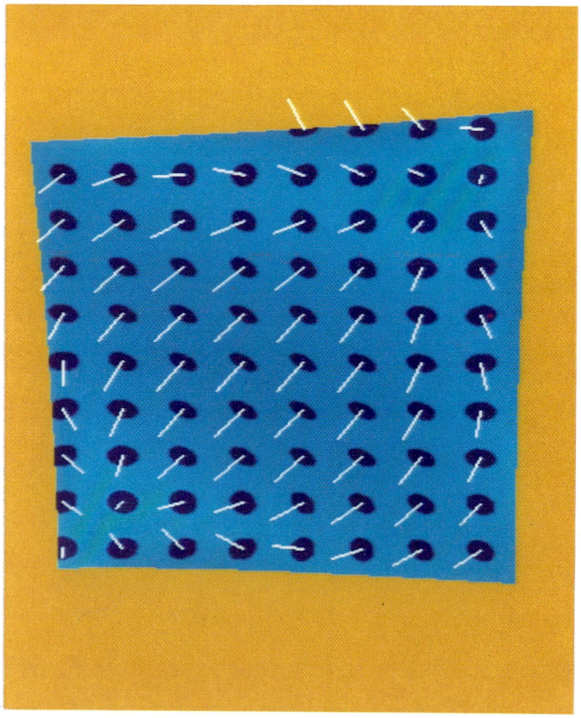

Figure 5–8: Combined hedgehogs and texture

PANEL

COMPUTER GRAPHICS IN HIGHER EDUCATION

CHAIR: James D. Foley, The George Washington University

PANELISTS: Al Bork, University of California - Irvine
Maxine Brown, Digital Productions
Robin King, Sheridan College
Andries van Dam, Brown University
Mike Wozny, Rensselaer Polytechnic Institute

CHAIRMAN'S INTRODUCTION:

Computer graphics is becoming an integral part of many educational curricula in colleges and universities. Four individuals who have developed successful curricula will describe both the form of the curricula as well as the process of building the curricula, so that others who wish to undertake such activities can benefit from their experience.

Panelists will address two areas. The first is how computer graphics integrates into the curriculum: how graphics is used, how often it is used, objectives for its use. The second area is a retrospective on how the program was developed: the resources needed, the administrative structures put in place to support the development, the delivery of graphics-oriented instruction, the overall development process, problems encountered, and lessons for those who would repeat the process.

Five areas are represented on the panel: science education, graphics design education, engineering education, computer science education, and SIGGRAPH.

Professor Alfred Bork of the University of California, Irvine, is Professor of Physics, Professor of Information and Computer Science, and Director of the Educational Technology Center. The Center's work concentrates on personal computers in education. Projects are proceeding in public libraries, middle schools, and universities. Bork was one of the four American speakers to the World Conference on Computers in Education. He was a co-director and keynote speaker at a NATO Advanced Study Institute. He was a consultant to the United Kingdom National Development Program in Computer Aided Learning. He is on the editorial board of Computers and Art and THE Journal - Technological Horizons for Education. He served as chair of the Special Interest Group on Computer Uses in Education of the Association for Computing Machinery. He is Physics Series Editor for CONDUIT.

The Educational Technology Center is involved in research and development of highly interactive graphics computer-based learning material. Professor Bork will describe briefly (1) a beginning physics quarter for science-engineering majors; and (2) scientific literacy material for non-science students. This material was developed using a production system which has been under development for many years at the Educational Technology Center. The facets of the system are shown in S.A.D.T. diagrams. The system begins with very competent teachers and completely separates pedagogical design from technical implementation, as with current textbook production. For the past several years the implementation language has been UCSD Pascal. Textual and graphic software has been developed to ease the task.

Mr. Robin King is coordinator of the one-year program in computer graphics at Sheridan College of Applied Art and Technology, Toronto, Canada. He has been at Sheridan since 1971 as a full-time faculty member in the School of Visual Arts, and has just recently developed their computer graphics program. Born and educated in England, Mr. King previously did research work in both chemistry and physics. His M.A. is in interdisciplinary studies, with his thesis work focusing on the Application of General Systems Theory to an Analysis of the Creative Process in Visual Art.

Mr. King will discuss some departures from traditional educational methods which have been taken in order to provide a balance between the need to establish a theoretical and practical groundwork and a strong desire to stress the importance of maintaining personal visual integrity. The most difficult obstacles encountered appeared during the initial transition from traditional skills and working methods to productive application of graphics technology as a tool for solving visual problems.

A wide variety of graduate students with different visual arts specialities were chosen in order to provide a wide range of expertise and to encourage exchange and collaboration. Several were trained on a variety of commercial turnkey graphics systems such as the Dicomed D39, Genigraphics 100C, and Norpack IPS2 and then, during the academic year, employed to teach a small group of workshops on a rotating basis. In addition to technical training, each student contracts a self-directed research program. A full-time program director and a programmer are the only full time staff, providing direction and continuity. Part-time specialists (an animator, a graphic designer and a videotext specialist) are available on a regular basis for individual consultation, and a production seminar focuses on group problems on a weekly basis. A large number of local, national and international guest speakers and lecturers are then used as a resource chosen by staff and students to match the particular needs and interests of the program participants and the group as a whole.

Michael Wozny is a director of the Center for Interactive Computer Graphics at Rensselaer Polytechnic Institute, in Troy New York. As an engineering educator, he feels his primary goal is to provide students with a solid grounding in fundamentals and an ability to use them for productive results. Computer graphics plays an important role in both areas. The inherent motivational aspects of a graphics display, coupled with appropriate interactive software strengthen students' understanding of concepts and improve their ability to make engineering judgments. Industry's widespread acceptance of computer graphics, integrated with CAD/CAM software, for increasing an engineer's productivity also means that most graduates will use this technology and methodology throughout their careers.

The RPI Center for Interactive Computer Graphics was originally established to address such graphics related educational issues. Today, five years later, the Center has evolved into a comprehensive instructional and research program, comprising of significant industrial and NSF research support, extensive graphics equipment, and a strong research and operations staff. The instructional laboratory, which now represents about a third of the Center's activities, handles more than 1,500 engineering students in 48 courses each semester. During the Fall, 1982 semester, for example, the faculty and students spent approximately 19,000 terminal hours in front of graphics displays working on classroom assignments and materials.

The success of the Center is based on many factors, including: (1) strong high-level administrative backing; (2) significant faculty interest and a commitment to attract faculty; (3) a major initial investment in hardware; (4) a charter to promote and coordinate instruction across the entire School of Engineering; and (5) a strong industrially sponsored research program which trickles ideas down into, and shares certain equipment with, the instructional program.

Andries van Dam is Chairman of the Department of Computer Science at Brown University where he has been teaching since 1965. His research has concerned software engineering in general and computer graphics, text processing, mini and microcomputers and microprogramming in particular. He has recently been working on the design of "computer books" based on color graphics displays, both for teaching purposes and for use by maintenance and repair technicians instead of paper documentation. Van Dam received the B.Sc. degree from Swarthmore College in 1960 and the MS and PhD from the University of Pennsylvania in 1963 and 1966, respectively. A member of Sigma Xi IEEE Computer Society, and ACM, he helped to found and was an editor of <u>Computer Graphics and Information Processing</u> for the last decade, and has now become an editor of ACM's new <u>Transactions on Graphics</u>. He was also the co-founder of ACM's SIGGRAPH Society for Computer Graphics in 1967. The book <u>Fundamentals of Interactive Computer Graphics</u>, co-authored with J. D. Foley, was published by Addison-Wesley in December of 1981.

Brown University has started an ambitious program to put networks of high resolution, graphics-based professional workstations across the entire campus for teaching and research. A report will be given on the first year's operational experience of an experimental teaching lab with a ring of twenty Apollo computers used in teaching introductory programming and computer science. The experiment and the experimental software and courseware will be very briefly described.

Maxine Brown is Secretary of SIGGRAPH and is director of documentation at Digital Productions, an animation studio specializing in computer imaging and simulation. She was formerly with ISSCO Graphics, working in the documentation, development and marketing areas. She has also worked at Hewlett-Packard, in both their research and development groups and in marketing. Maxine holds an M.S.E. degree in Computer Science from the University of Pennsylvania.

Ms. Brown will describe how SIGGRAPH serves as a forum for the promotion and dissemination of current computer graphics research, technologies and applications. The latest computer graphics achievements are communicated to members through publications, slide sets, fiche, video tapes and the annual conference. The SIGGRAPH conference includes technical presentations, tutorials and seminars, a large exhibition of hardware and software products, a formal art exhibit, and extensive film and video presentations.

SIGGRAPH encourages active participation from academia and industry to develop course curricula, prepare audio/visual materials, compile information source books and further its educational goals. An Education Committee is currently being organized to compile, develop and distribute high quality written and visual materials describing fundamental computer graphics concepts. Counselling information, detailing educational institutions, career requirements and application areas, is being prepared to inform students, counsellors, artists, technicians, and computer professionals of opportunities in the computer graphics field. Other activities are under discussion and will be given greater consideration when the Education Committee is in full operation. SIGGRAPH has a strong commitment to its membership to provide educational materials and programs...to heighten awareness and encourage interest...and to further the enhancement of the exploding computer graphics industry.

TOWARDS A COMPREHENSIVE USER INTERFACE MANAGEMENT SYSTEM

W. Buxton, M. R. Lamb,
D. Sherman & K. C. Smith

Computer Systems Research Group
University of Toronto
Toronto, Ontario
Canada M5S 1A4

ABSTRACT

A UIMS developed at the University of Toronto is presented. The system has two main components. The first is a set of tools to support the design and implementation of interactive graphics programs. The second is a run-time support package which handles interactions between the system and the user (things such as hit detection, event detection, screen updates, and procedure invocation), and provides facilities for logging user interactions for later protocol analysis.

The design/implementation tool is a preprocessor, called MENULAY, which permits the applications programmer to use interactive graphics techniques to design graphics menus and their functionality. The output of this preprocessor is high-level code which can be compiled with application-specific routines. User interactions with the resulting executable module are then handled by the run-time support package. The presentation works through an example from design to execution in a step-by-step manner.

CR Categories and Subject Descriptors: D.2.2 [Software] Tools and Techniques - User Interfaces; H.1.2 [Information Systems] User/Machine Systems - Human Information Processing; I.3.4 [Computer Graphics] Graphics Utilities - Software Support; I.3.6 [Computer Graphics] Methodology and Techniques - Interactive Techniques.

General Terms: Human-Computer Dialogue, Interaction Management.

Additional Keywords and Phrases: Dialogue Design and Specification, and Dialogue Run-Time Support.

1. INTRODUCTION

Traditionally, interactive graphical programs have been written using conventional programming languages, low-level tools, and often *ad hoc* techniques. The cost of doing so has been time, frustration, and quality of end product.

A *user interface management system* (UIMS) is intended to reduce this cost. The objective is to free the applications programmer from low-level details so as to be able to concentrate on higher applications-specific aspects of the user interface. A UIMS typically consists of a package of tools which support the implementation, debugging and evaluation of interactive human-computer dialogues.

An analogy can be drawn between a UIMS and a data base management system (DBMS). The DBMS mediates between programmer and data, enforcing a consistency of technique among all programmers in accessing that data. It provides portability because only the lowest-level DBMS routines are hardware-dependent. Similarly, the UIMS mediates between the applications programmer and the input events, encouraging a consistency both of graphical layout representation and of input processing mechanisms.[1]

This paper presents a UIMS developed at the Computer Systems Research Group, University of Toronto. The system comprises a set of tools for designing and implementing menu-based dialogues and for providing run-time support for more general event-driven interactive programs. The module for designing/implementing menu-based dialogues has the property of permitting hand-written programs to be integrated with code automatically synthesized from the programmer's specifications.

1.1 The Need for a UIMS

Our current understanding of human-computer interaction is extremely limited. We cannot sit down and design an interface for an application and know, *a priori*, how well it will perform. We must accept at the outset, therefore, the inevitable intertwining of specification, design, and implementation (Swartout & Balzer, 1982). Design then becomes an iterative process, each iteration consisting of three phases: *design*, *implementation* and *evaluation* (Buxton & Sniderman, 1980). The motivation to develop improved tools can therefore be seen as a desire to increase the number of iterations that we can afford to pass through in this loop. The hoped-for consequence will be an improvement in the quality of the user interfaces which we produce.

The UIMS presented herein aids in the *design* and *implementation* phases by providing the following set of tools: a graphics package; sketch editors; a standardized graphics communications protocol; table-driven run-time support of the user dialogue; and, most recently, a graphical layout and interaction specification preprocessor which generates C language programs. Underway are the development of interaction analysis tools to aid in the *evaluation* phase of the cycle.

1. This is not to imply that data-base management is independent of the user interface. Rather, the tools applied to each of these free the applications programmer so that their mutual influence can be better taken into consideration.

Each of the modules of the existing system has limitations. However, when viewed together, the various pieces begin to shed some light on what would comprise a comprehensive set of tools for the user interface designer. In presenting our experience in a longitudinal way, it is hoped that we will make some contribution towards the realization of such a comprehensive set of tools.

1.2 U of T UIMS Structure

In its current state, our UIMS consists of two main modules. The first is a preprocessor which enables the program designer, using interactive graphics techniques, to design and specify the graphical layout and functionality of menu-based user interfaces. It is with this module that the applications programmer establishes the relationships between what the user sees, does, and hears, and the application-specific semantics underlying the program being implemented.

The second main module is the run-time support package. It handles things such as event and hit detection, procedure invocation, and updating the display - all according to the schema specified using the preprocessor. An important aspect of this implementation is that the code executed by the run-time module can be generated automatically (complete with comments) from the data specified to the preprocessor.

The applicability of the current implementation of the preprocessor is restricted to menu-based interaction. Within this domain, however, it is quite flexible, and supports various types of displays (colour or monochrome) and sound output. The run-time support package is more general and does not depend upon the preprocessor. It is designed for supporting event-driven software and a variety of input devices. These two packages do not stand alone. They are just two components in a more general "kit" of prototyping tools to support iterative and experimental programming (Deutsh & Taft, 1980). In discussing these tools, we find it useful to distinguish between *general design tools* and *programmers' packaged units*.

The general design tools facilitate the specification of graphical information and functional relationships, the writing of application-specific code and the debugging of successive versions of applications programs. Many of these tools are standard components in modern operating systems. Besides the two modules mentioned above, our inventory of such tools includes: (1) the UNIX[2] operating system, with its highly sophisticated command interpreter, C language compiler, hierarchical file system and many utilities; (2) the GPAC device-independent graphics package (Reeves, 1975); (3) routines to save and retrieve pictures stored as standard format metafiles; (4) text editors; (5) graphical sketch editors; and (6) interactive symbolic debuggers.

Programmers' packaged units are ready-made modules which can be integrated into applications software. They are documented and tested *building-blocks*. They are generally packaged versions of blocks of code which are observed to be reccuring and of general utility. Our library of such modules, therefore, is continually expanding. Representative of such packaged units are: (1) specialized iconic cursors which can be used as meaningful tracking symbols; (2) directory windows which permit graphical user reference to any file of a given type; (3) a graphical potentiometer with a "knob" which the user can "slide" up and down to change the value of a program parameter; (4) a graphical piano keyboard which audibly plays the notes pointed to; (5) routines to manipulate lightbuttons within the above menu-driven system (e.g, to flash, deactivate and highlight individual menu items); and (6) an audio support package, which drives a digital sound synthesizer (Buxton, Fogels, Fedorkow, Sasaki & Smith, 1978). Many of these modules will be illustrated in examples which follow.

2. UNIX is a trademark of Bell Laboratories.

2. EVOLUTION OF OUR UIMS

Our UIMS has evolved over several years, in parallel with the development of innovative software for graphics applications. It is implemented in the C programming language on a PDP-11/45, which was acquired in 1975 and runs UNIX version 6.

First came GPAC, a device-independent graphics package (Reeves, 1975), onto which successively higher levels were built. Interaction techniques, specialized cursors and directory windows followed, in 1976-78. As part of the Structure Sound Synthesis Project, the table-driven run-time support package of the UIMS was put together in 1979. Finally, in 1982, MENULAY, the graphical menu layout and function specification preprocessor was built.

2.1 Table-driven run-time support system

With the development of a number of menu-based interactive programs in the late 1970's, it became apparent that the user interfaces all had a large number of common features, but that each programmer implemented them with a "personal" touch. So personal, in fact, that the code was difficult for others to understand or support. Accordingly, we began to develop a more uniform methodology which not only captured the best ideas of these various approaches, but also made them available in a fully-documented and well-supported environment. The basis of our new methodology was an externally-controlled, table-driven system which supported event-driven interactions. The programmer supplied the system with the applications-specific routines and information about what types of events were active when, and what and how such events were to affect the program's behaviour. At run-time, then, responses to user interactions (such as event and hit detection, display updates, and procedure invocation) were handled by this package.

The present package, an extension of that developed in 1979, is primarily oriented towards screen and menu-based systems. It is capable of supporting event-driven interactions that go well beyond simple light-button selection (examples are: Buxton, Sniderman, Reeves, Patel & Baecker, 1978; and Buxton, Patel, Reeves & Baecker, 1982). The tables used by the system have nine user-specified fields per entry. These fields include:

- the name of a user-specified procedure which is to be invoked upon the detection of a specified input event;
- the input event which is to trigger that procedure;
- fields to contain (variable) parameters of that procedure;
- the x and y hit area for procedures triggered by pointing events;
- any text (or the name of a graphics file containing a picture) to be displayed;
- the x and y co-ordinates of the item to be displayed;
- the item's size and colour.

The system also supports dummy table entries for setting various parameters, such as whether subsequent hit-areas are to have boxes drawn around them or not. As well, it provides for functions to be invoked in special cases arising in menu-based systems: (1) if the user misses all of the light-buttons, (2) when entering or (3) when exiting from the menu.

Finally,the package provides easy to use routines for setting-up and switching among the menus, or "states" of the application-defined system.

While this package was of value, it was still a tedious task to specify the data which made up the tables. This was especially true during the early stages of development, when the graphic design, functionality, and syntax of the user interface were continually being revised due to experimentation. Consequently, we were motivated to develop another tool which would facilitate the specification and modification of these data. The result was the preprocessor, MENULAY, described in the next section.

3. MENULAY AND MAKEMENU

3.1 Concept

The preprocessor which serves as the front end of our UIMS is known as MENULAY. The package is designed to enable the user interface designer (who is not necessarily the applications programmer) to specify rapidly and naturally the graphical and functional relationships within and among the displays making up a menu-based system. Specifications made using the package are converted into the C programming language and compiled through the use of a companion program MAKEMENU. The resulting code can be linked with application-specific routines.

MENULAY enables the designer to define user interfaces which are made up of networks of menus. These may be structured in a hierarchic manner, or in an arbitrary fashion. Furthermore, the method of interacting with these menus is open, and up to the designer. A prime objective of the tool is to minimize the bias imposed by the path of least resistance, which may favour one interaction technique over another. MENULAY is a product of itself. It therefore gives the user interface designer a feel for the nature of the interaction sequences being specified, while at the same time indicates the range of tools available.

3.2 Functional Flow

The entire sequence as set out in Figure 1 can be performed by the

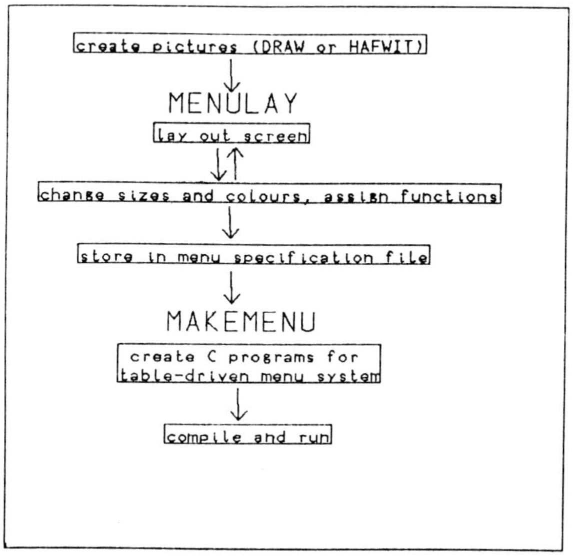

Figure 1. A typical Sequence for Constructing an Interactive Dialogue

applications designer in an interactive graphics environment. A graphics tablet and four-button puck are used for all input to MENULAY (except for such character-oriented input as the typing of the names of application-specific functions to be called upon hit detection). The MAKEMENU program creation and compilation options are also specified graphically.

3.3 Automatic Code Generation

MENULAY's elegance lies in the automatic conversion into C language programs of the graphical interface specified by the applications designer. This conversion is performed by MENULAY's companion program, MAKEMENU. The programs generated from MENULAY's compact specification files are syntactically correct, complete and internally documented with liberal comments. They are designed for compilation with the same table-driven support system on which MENULAY itself is built. Because these programs are in C, however, they can be adapted when required by using a text editor. Where necessary, these changes can be recorded automatically, and repeated whenever the menu specification files are changed[3].

Where the applications designer specifies names of application-specific functions, the programs generated by MAKEMENU contain unresolved external references ("hooks"). By writing functions with the required names and referencing the appropriate file names when MAKEMENU is called, the applications programmer can add any amount of application-specific programming to the layout and sequence information specified by the designer. The two sets of code (computer-generated and programmer-authored) are completely compatible, and can share global variable names, external function references, and so on.

Work is presently underway on a decompiler which will be able to reverse the MAKEMENU process. This decompiler, called UNEMEKAM, will convert a C program which makes use of the table-driven menu software into a menu specification file which can be edited graphically using MENULAY.

3.4 Command Hierarchy

MENULAY has one main command level, containing seven basic commands. These are *layout*, *size*, *colour*, *function*, *get save*, *tryout* and *exit* These are illustrated in Figure 2.

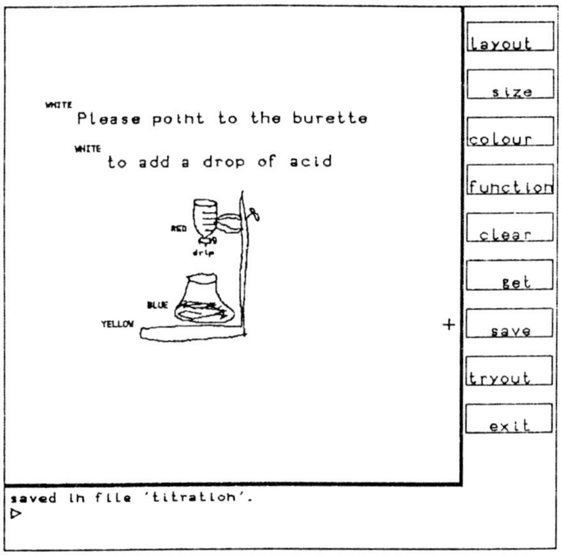

Figure 2. MENULAY Commands

Layout allows the designer to create textual items (e.g., light buttons) on the screen; add pictures either taken from the system library of graphical icons or created by the user with a sketch editor; change the position of any item; and delete items from the screen (see Figure 3).

Size enables the designer to change the scale of any item on the screen, either by "sliding the knob" on a graphical potentiometer or by typing in a scale factor, as shown in

3. Hand-coding changes to MAKEMENU output obviously causes problems in "unmaking" menus. Using the facility is a concession to reality: the state-of-the-art does not yet permit us to make a totally comprehensive UIMS.

Figure 4.

Colour allows one to specify (or change) the colour of any item on the end-user's screen (see Figure 5). This is independent of the device on which the designer is using MENULAY; the high-resolution display we most commonly use, for example, does not support colour graphics.

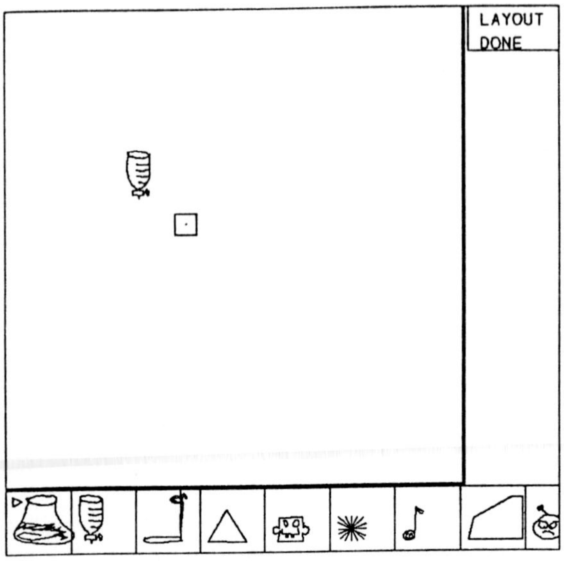

Figure 3. MENULAY - Laying Out the Display Graphics

Figure 4. MENULAY - Changing the Size of an Item (the stand) with a Graphical Potentiometer

Function enables the designer to specify what will happen when the end-user points to light buttons. The light buttons may be text or pictures. The designer may also specify a function to be invoked if the user activates an input event without pointing to any one light button. In addition, it is possible to specify functions to be called when the menu being designed is entered and exited. This is shown in Figure 6.

The function names may be taken from MENULAY's library of utility functions or be written by the applications

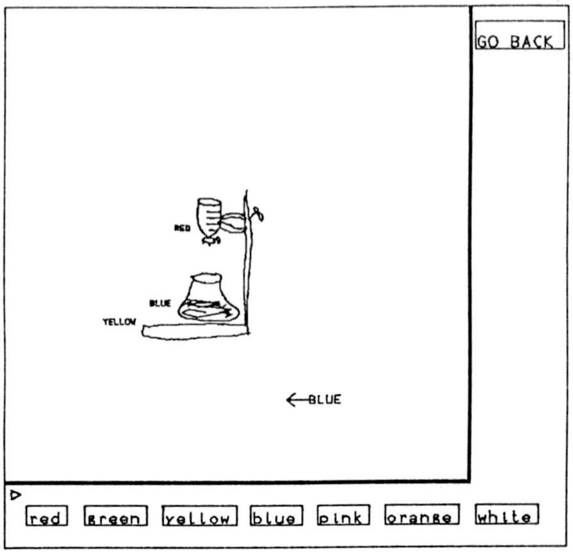

Figure 5. MENULAY - Assigning Colours to the Items on the Screen

programmer before compilation of the program. The writing of these functions is done entirely independently of (and either before or after) the creation of the menu specification file with MENULAY.

Function also allows programs of up to 50 characters - such as short *print* statements - to be typed directly into MENULAY. MAKEMENU takes care of creating a new function name for the function table to enable the code typed in by the user to be loaded.

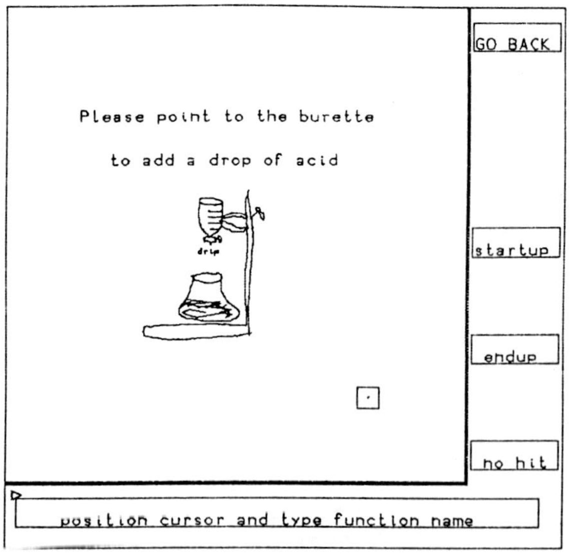

Figure 6. MENULAY - Assigning Function Names to the Active Items (Light-Buttons)

Get (and *save*) allow the user to retrieve from (and store into) a menu specification file the details of the layout and functional relationships which the designer has specified. The menu specification file is extremely compact and is thus a very efficient storage format. Each item of the menu screen is referenced by x and y coordinates, hit area, size, colour, function, text (if a textual item) or standard graphics format file name (if a graphical icon).

Tryout gives the user the opportunity to invoke *makemenu*, the code generation program, by specifying graphically the options and files he wishes to access (see Figure 7).

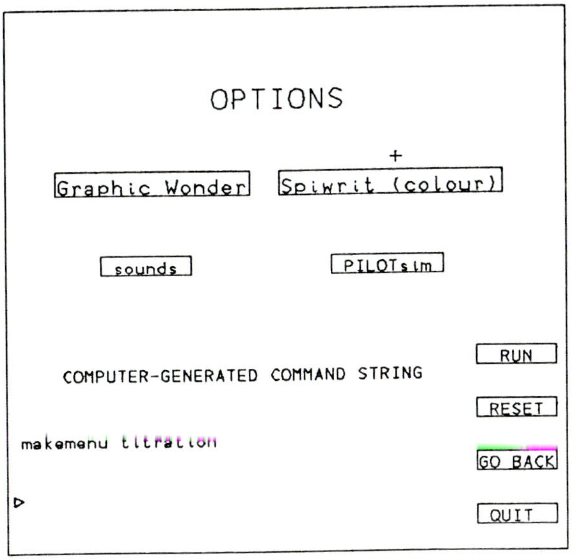

Figure 7. MENULAY - Generating 'C' Code to Implement Specified Interface (by Invoking MAKEMENU)

Once the program has been compiled, *tryout* then runs it for the user.

Exit is used to exit the program. The user is given a new menu with "YES" and "NO" options to confirm that he does indeed wish to exit.

MENULAY has levels of use: "novice" and "expert". In *novice* mode, only the basic commands (as set out above) are accessible. All input is done through one button on the cursor puck, and instructions are given at various points in the program. In *expert* mode, the other three buttons on the puck can be used to perform special functions (e.g., displaying a grid while positioning items; flipping from one menus of pictures or colours to another; assigning a function name which is identical to the text in the menu item), and fewer instructional diagnostics are displayed. The system maintains on disk a profile for each user (a file called "userpro"), initially tagging each person as "novice" and upgrading them based on experience with the system and on specific request.[4]

From any point within MENULAY (except during *layout*, where typing text causes the creation of light buttons containing the text typed), the user can access the UNIX shell (command interpreter) by typing at the terminal. (When this happens, the MENULAY screen fades and the user's scroller is reset to the full screen until the user returns to MENULAY.) This means that the full range of terminal-based commands can be accessed instantly without leaving MENULAY. For example, any calculations which the designer wishes to make in the course of the graphical layout specification can be made by invoking the on-line desk calculator. Similarly, the applications designer who is also a programmer may compose a function by invoking the text editor. Or the designer may send the programmer comments about the implementation by electronic mail before there's a chance to forget them.

3.5 Applications

MENULAY has already been used to construct the user interface for each of the following programs: (1) MENULAY itself; (2) the DRAW sketch editor, which is used to generate light-button graphics; (3) a computer-assisted instruction (CAI) program which teaches children about birds and their nests[5] (see Figure 8);

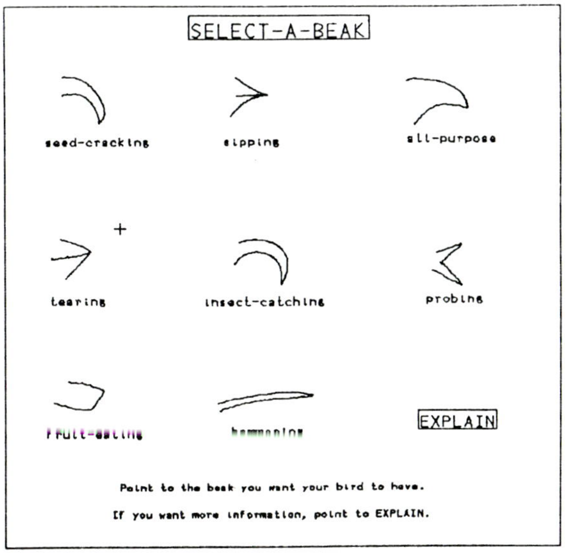

Figure 8. Beak Selection Sequence from 'Land Birds and Their Nests'

and (4) a graphical piano keyboard and musical notation editor (Kuzmich, in preparation: see Figure 9).

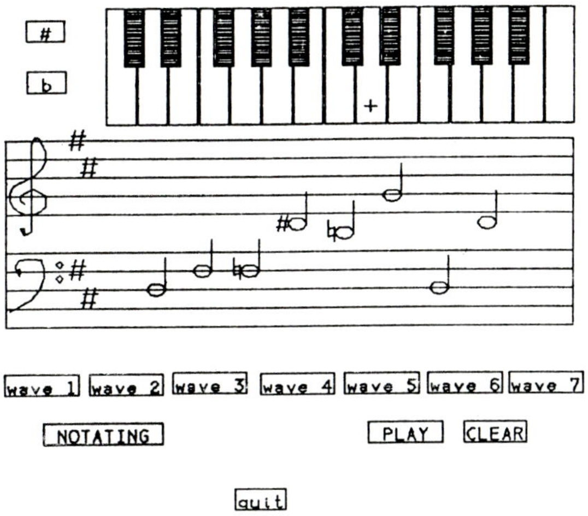

Figure 9. 'Melody Manipulations' music notation editor and teaching tool

It can be used to assemble, in minutes, sequences of frames for CAI in virtually any area of instruction where graphics is helpful. It has also proven useful for laying out

5. "Land Birds and Their Nests", designed by Young Naturalist Foundation, Toronto, Canada, and programmed by CSRG (in press).

figures such as Figure 1 of this paper. Appendix I presents a walk-through of a CAI example.

It is notable that since graphical icons for the user's screen are referenced by file name, these pictures can be changed without even having to recompile the applications program. Thus, a program could be fully constructed by an applications designer who is not a graphic artist, and an artist brought in later to revise the pictures.

4. UNIFORMITY AND PORTABILITY

It is important that a UIMS be portable in a number of senses. The system described satisfies these criteria theoretically and we are in the process of proving its portability in practice.

4.1 Output Device Independence

At the most primitive level, a user interface management system must support a number of different output devices with different characteristics. In the case of MENULAY and MAKEMENU, for example, the device independence is achieved by using the GPAC graphics package with such varied devices as a high-resolution vector display with 16 intensity levels and a low-resolution 16-colour raster display. The run-time support package (without MENULAY as of yet) has also been made to run on various alphanumeric terminals.

4.2 Input Device Independence

The UIMS must also be able to support alternative input techniques. The primary input device used in MENULAY at present is a graphics tablet with a four-button puck and the typewriter keyboard. A set of Allison sliders[6] are also used, but are only available through pre-programmed packages. Other pointing devices (such as mice, light-pens, or touch-screens) could be used in place of the tablet with the provision of the appropriate GPAC device driver. The run-time support package, however, can be driven by virtually any event-generating device that has a GPAC driver.

4.3 Language Independence

At a further level of portability, the UIMS should be structured to facilitate the ability to generate code in different programming languages. The output of MENULAY is a metacode which is translated into high-level language by MAKEMENU. To output code in a different language would involve rewriting this program and providing run-time support in a compatible format.

4.4 Machine Independence

At a higher degree of portability is the capacity to transfer a system such as MENULAY either to a more powerful machine than the PDP-11/45 (e.g., a VAX-11/780) or a less powerful one (e.g. an APPLE microcomputer).

As has been noted, MENULAY and MAKEMENU are written in C (a standardized language which is relatively portable) and use GPAC, a device-independent graphics package (which is itself written in C). Provided the necessary hardware drivers are available, GPAC and thus MENULAY/MAKEMENU could be transferred at reasonable cost to any system which will support UNIX and C.

4.5 Applications Program Portability

In contrast with MENULAY, the applications programs generated by MAKEMENU can be ported even to systems which do not support UNIX. With a cross-compiler and a basic graphics package, for example, applications programs such as computer-assisted instruction frames could be compiled to run on many microcomputers.

6. This device is a continuous belt slider. It is a treadmill with a 9 by 1.5 cm surface exposed which is used as a motion-sensitive input device. The mechanical section was developed by Allison Research Inc., 2817 Erica Place, Nashville, Tenn. 37204. The electronics used here were developed in house.

5. COMPARISON WITH OTHER SYSTEMS

Other UIMSs do exist, and have had an influence on the evolution of our system. The most distinguishing feature of MENULAY is its natural way of integrating graphical design specification with human-written applications programming. By way of comparison, we review briefly three systems: TRW's FLAIR; Olsen's automatic code generation design; and Kasik's TIGER.

5.1 FLAIR

FLAIR (Functional Language Articulated Interactive Resource) (Wong & Reid, 1982), is a user interface dialogue design tool which enables a system designer to construct graphically a user dialogue for an applications program. It is largely driven by voice input and incorporates text picture construction and editing (at the graphical primitive level) as well as dynamic frame layout. Its high-level features include the ability to define and control a menu hierarchy, graph and map generation, an on-line calculator and relational data base access for graphical entity storage and retrieval.

FLAIR is more advanced than MENULAY in its use of multiple input techniques and in its ability to permit the applications designer to specify a wide range of end user interactions. However, we are in the process of extending MENULAY's capabilities to permit the specification of a much wider range of user interactions.

FLAIR contains a powerful set of internal utilities, but appears to be rather limiting in its integration with application-specific code. FLAIR is a language and package unto itself, with no apparent "hooks" into other programming languages. This suggests that if the FLAIR "language" does not permit the applications programmer to program a certain algorithm conveniently, then that algorithm will be inaccessible. MENULAY, on the other hand, creates menu specification files that are converted into fully-documented C programs which, as noted earlier, are automatically integrated with any code the programmer may have written for the specific application.

5.2 Olsen's Model for Automatic Code Generation

Olsen (1982) describes research into the automatic generation of interactive graphical systems to facilitate faster and cheaper generation of interactive user interfaces. This work has not yet progressed beyond the design stage.

Olsen points out the useful distinction between these *design* of the application program interface and thes *writing* of the program itself. He observes that it is the design aspect of the program creation which is suited to automatic program generation. This is because of the high cost in time and effort of hand-coding and the increased reliability of automatically generated software.

Olsen envisages the use of Pascal procedure definitions for the characterization of interactive commands in the applications program. We feel that MENULAY is a significant improvement over this idea in that the command menus and interaction relationships are specified in the very way in which the end user will interact with the applications program, i.e. by pointing. Olsen does not address the possibility of having the specification technique use the same devices and interfaces as those the end-user will ultimately face.

5.3 TIGER

Kasik (1982), describes a UIMS which, like our UIMS, takes care of the bookkeeping associated with screen layout, interrupt handling and the definition of interactive dialogue sequences. This UIMS, called TIGER, has as its core the language TICCL, which permits the applications programmer to concentrate on the logical functions which he wishes to perform rather than the physical, low-level steps which must be taken to accomplish the task.

TICCL can be used to describe algorithms which combine graphical primitives in response to user interactions as well as to define user interaction sequences. TICCL code operates at a higher level than the Pascal code which is used for the non-graphical portion of the applications programming.

TICCL is useful as a mechanism for specifying user interaction at a higher level than is otherwise available to its designers. Such a language combined with a higher level package such as MENULAY would permit even more flexibility in user interface prototyping. While TIGER does not currently incorporate a module comparable to MENULAY, TICCL is a powerful language, and could support such a tool.

To the extent TICCL is used for constructing graphical primitives from user interactions, it is more advanced than our table-driven menu system for which MENULAY acts as preprocesor. On the other hand, we feel that our programmers' packaged units, together with the flexibility of GPAC and its integration into programmers' C code, provide a useful alternative set of interaction response tools.

6. FUTURE DIRECTIONS

6.1 Protocol Analysis

The recording of sequential data about end-user interactions is essential to the evaluation of the interaction techniques used in an applications program. With a menu-driven system based on cursor and tablet, this data consists of a time-stamped record of each user input, recording the x and y tablet co-ordinates of the cursor and the input event which was activated.

We are in the process of developing tools for the analysis of this data, stored in a so-called "dribble file". As part of the process of developing the interaction sequences for an applications program, the designer will ask an end-user to spend a session with the program. Afterwards the new tools will facilitate the analysis of the "dribble file" for that session in a number of ways. First, they will allow the designer to "play back" the user interactions in real time, so as to get a feel for the flow of the user-computer dialogue. Second, they will draw for the designer a "spiderweb" which superimposes graphically all of the hand motions of the user in his interaction with the program (see Figure 10). The spiderweb makes it easy to spot the

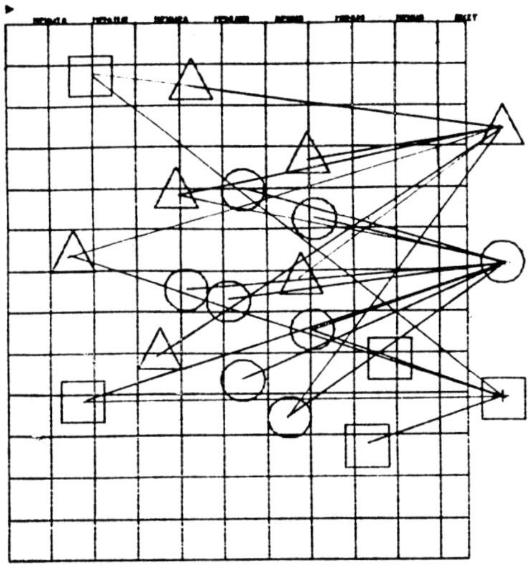

Figure 10. Tracing of Coordinates of Events Recording a User's Session

points at which the user is being forced to repeatedly make hand motions that are uncomfortable or excessively long.

To function properly, the dribble file data must be recorded at every user input. This implies that the recording be done at the level of event recognition, and that the information always be available unless the programmer has specified otherwise. To do so, however, requires special support in the event-detection mechanism of the graphics package used. Furthermore, the event recognition routines themselves should be able to function in a mode which permits input from sources other than the physical input devices. The stored data files should be able to be used as the source of input events.

6.2 Window Management

MENULAY presently generates code which operates within a single window on the screen. While multiple *frames* or *levels* within a program can be created very easily, multiple *windows* can not.

It is intended to expand the capabilities of the table-driven menu system (and therefore of MENULAY) to permit the designation of multiple windows by the applications designer. Windows would have attributed to them specific cursor tracking symbols, background colours, and input events. As at present, specific light buttons (text or graphical) will be locatable at any place within a particular window.

7. ACKNOWLEDGEMENTS

MENULAY and MAKEMENU are the highest level of a user interface management system which is built on years of work at the Computer Systems Research Group. We acknowledge with thanks the contributions of Ron Baecker and Leslie Mezei, former directors of the Dynamic Graphics Project; Bill Reeves, author of the GPAC graphics package; and other major contributors to our inventory of graphical tools and techniques: Tom Duff, Greg Hill, Tom Horsley, Sanand Patel, Rob Pike, David Tilbrook, Mike Tilson and Martin Tuori.

We also gratefully acknowledge the helpful comments made by the referees and by Dave Kasik.

Interactive graphics research at the Computer Systems Research Group has been funded for many years by the National Sciences and Engineering Research Council, and more recently by the Social Sciences and Humanities Research Council.

8. REFERENCES

Buxton, W., Fogels, A., Fedorkow, G., Sasaki, L. & Smith, K. C. (1978). An Introduction to the SSSP Digital Synthesizer. *Computer Music Journal* **2(4)**, 28 - 38.

Buxton, W., Patel, S., Reeves, W. & Baecker, R. (1982). Objed and the Design of Timbral Resources. *Computer Music Journal* **6(2)**, 32 - 44.

Buxton, W., Sniderman, R., Reeves, W., Patel, S. & Baecker, R. (1978). The Evolution of the SSSP Score Editing Tools. *Computer Music Journal* **3(4)**, 14 - 25.

Buxton, W. & Sniderman, R. (1980). Iteration and the Design of the Human-Computer Interface. *Proceedings of the 13th Annual Meeting of the Human Factors Association of Canada*, pp 72 - 81.

Deutsh, L & Taft, E. A. (1980). Requirements for an Experimental Programming Environment. *Technical Report CSL-80-10*, XEROX PARC.

Kasik, D. (1982). A User Interface Management System. *Computer Graphics*, **16(3)**, 99 - 106.

Kuzmich, N. (in preparation). Melody Manipulations. Music

Dept., Faculty of Education, University of Toronto.

Olson, D. (1983). Automatic Generation of Interactive Systems, *Computer Graphics* **17(1)**, 53 - 57.

Reeves, W. (1975). *A Device-Independent Interactive Graphics Package* M.Sc. Thesis, Dept. of Computer Science, University of Toronto.

Swartout, W & Balzer, R. (1982). An Inevitable Intertwining of Specification and Implementation. *Communications of the ACM* **25(7)**, 438 - 440.

Wong, Peter C.S., and Eric R. Reid (1982). FLAIR - User Interface Dialog Design Tool, *Computer Graphics*, **16(3)**, 87 - 98.

APPENDIX 1: A Walkthrough of a CAI application

The following is a brief account of an applications designer's use of MENULAY to create a lesson to help teach chemistry titration. The time taken in this instance was less than ten minutes.

The designer begins by typing "draw" to invoke the DRAW program and then uses the graphics tablet to input free-hand pictures of a burette, a beaker and a stand. Each picture is scaled down in size by pointing to the command "SIZE" and then sliding the "knob" on the displayed potentiometer (like that in Figure 4). The "knob" is slid by positioning the cursor over it and holding down the main button on the cursor puck while sliding it up or down. Each picture is stored in a disk file (by pointing to the command "SAVE", and typing in or pointing to the file name).

Next, MENULAY is invoked (by selecting "EXIT" and then "MENULAY" from a new menu), whereupon an explanation is displayed together with MENULAY's command menu. The user selects "LAYOUT" and sees the newly created pictures in a menu at the bottom of the screen. Selection of the burette causes a copy of it to be tracked as the cursor. It is anchored in the work area by pressing or releasing the main button on the cursor puck (see Figure 3). The same is done to the beaker and the stand. Typing at the keyboard causes that text to be displayed at the current cursor position. Any item in the work area (whether text or graphics) can be repositioned by pointing to it and dragging it to a new position, again anchoring it either by releasing the button or, if it was released immediately upon pointing, by pressing the button again.

To change the scale of any item, the user selects "SIZE" in the main menu (displayed in Figure 2), selects the item, and then changes its size, again with a graphical potentiometer (see Figure 4). To set or change the colour of any item, the user selects "COLOUR" in the main menu and chooses a tint from the menu at the bottom of the screen. This tint is tracked (as shown in Figure 5) until another tint is selected. Any items pointed to are assigned the currently tracked colour. The colour of each item is displayed next to the item if the hardware device does not support colour graphics.

The designer specifies that the function named *drip* is to be invoked when the end-user points to the burette (by selecting "FUNCTION", selecting the burette, and typing "drip": see Figure 6). The entire set of interface specifications is now stored in a file (by pointing to "SAVE" and typing a file name.

Finally, the user selects "TRYOUT" and then chooses Spiwrit (a colour raster screen) as the display device (see Figure 7) and references "drip.c", an application-specific C source file. This causes the interaction specifications to be automatically converted into C language programs which are compiled and linked with the application-specific code. The resulting binary file is then executed (see Figure 11).

Figure 11. Running the Titration Simulation

Here is the source code for the *drip* routine - the only code which the programmer had to write:

```
#include "/u0/dave/master/menuglobal.h"
#define beaker picture("beaker");
int drops 0;

drip()
{
        type("Added a drop of liquid...");
        sound(DRIPPING);
        drops = drops + 1;

        if(drops == 3)
        {
                type("Wow! It changed colour!");
                resetcolour(beaker, PINK);
                sound(BUZZING);
        }
}
```

SYNGRAPH: A Graphical User Interface Generator

Dan R. Olsen Jr.
Elizabeth P. Dempsey

Computer Science Department
Arizona State University

Abstract

The SYNGRAPH system automatically generates graphical user interfaces. It generates interactive Pascal programs from a description of the input language's grammar. From the grammar it deduces information about how to manage both physical and simulated devices, and how prompting and echoing are performed. Input errors are detected, and can be corrected using automatically provided rubout and cancel features. The natural integration of application specific semantics into the system is also shown including appropriate semantic recovery from input errors.

CR Categories and Subject Descriptors:

I.3.4 Computer Graphics: Graphics Utilities - software support; I3.6 Computer Graphics Methodology and Techniques - interaction techniques

Additional Keywords: user interface management

1. INTRODUCTION

The SYNGRAPH (SYNtax directed GRAPHics) user interface generator was designed and implemented as part of the AHI (Automated Human Interfaces) project at Arizona State University. The purpose of the AHI project is to generate graphical user interface programs from a description of the user interface.

As computing hardware becomes cheaper an increasing amount of emphasis has been placed on making software systems interact directly with human users. A major stumbling block, however, is the high cost of producing a quality user interface even if one knows exactly how such an interface should be designed. It has been the goal of our research to produce tools which will automate the production of such human interface software and thus make quality human interfaces more economical. SYNGRAPH is the first such tool which has been actually implemented on the project.

Formal languages and automata have long been a part of user interface design. One of the earliest of these was Newman's Reaction Handler [Newm68]. More recently a great deal of work has been done in using formal languages to characterize and analyze user interfaces [Bles82, Jaco82, Wass81]. Our specification language most closely resembles that of Bleser and Foley [Bles82]. Our research, however, has concentrated on the use of formal languages for implementation rather than specification.

Hanau and Lenorovitz[Hana80] have already shown the use of parser generation techniques for implementing prototypes of user interfaces. Our work goes beyond simply using the grammar to perform the input parsing. We perform additional analysis of the grammar to support other user interface management functions. In addition, our work is closely related to the TIGER system [Kasi82] which uses menu trees instead of grammars as its control structure.

The fact that a user interface is expressed grammatically rather than scattered throughout the program makes automatic analysis of the interface possible. Among the features that are automatically supplied by this analysis are menu management, simulated device management, prompting, echoing, error handling, backing up over erroneous inputs and canceling a sequence of interactive inputs to return to some known home state.

The key to this analysis lies in the parser automaton generated from the grammar. This automaton contains complete information about the syntax of the user interface. In order to perform much of this analysis it is necessary to stratify the user interface into "levels of interaction". Levels of interaction are in some sense the global modes or states of the generated user interface. From a user's point of view a level of interaction is characterized by the set of commands that can be performed within it. From the interface specifier's point of view, levels of interaction are characterized by certain non-terminals within the grammar. This additional information allows interactive resources to be allocated based not only on the current state but on the resource needs of a given level of interaction.

One side effect of such automation is that the application no longer has explicit control over the interactive devices and their management. In the current implementation all lexical input techniques are predefined by the system. This loss of explicit control over input devices is in some sense analogous to the loss of control over specific registers when one moves from assembly to a high-level language. It is hoped however that, as with compilers, these techniques will improve to the point that their other advantages will outweigh the loss of control in all but very specialized applications. It is also hoped that, as with high-level languages, the use of automatic user interface management will lead to a more disciplined and consistent approach to human interface design.

As described by Foley and Van Dam [Fole82], a user interface is decomposed into conceptual, semantic, syntactic and lexical levels. A SYNGRAPH interface specification fits naturally into this model. The conceptual level guides implementation rather than being part of it and is therefore only indirectly part of such a specification. The interaction semantics of SYNGRAPH are defined in a fashion similar to that used by Feldman [Feld82]. The semantics are viewed as a set of procedures and data types written in the implementation language. It is important to the semantic interface that a language supporting user-defined data types be used as the implementation language so that the semantic objects can be modeled using data types suitable to the application. The syntactic level is where the greatest contributions of SYNGRAPH are made. The syntax is described using an extended version of BNF which includes the names of logical input tokens, semantic actions and information about how the user interface is organized. The lexical level binds the logical token names to actual input devices and techniques.

The remainder of this paper will discuss how a user interface is expressed to SYNGRAPH and what services are performed automatically by the system. These will be discussed in terms of the lexical and syntactic specifications and it will be shown how the semantic interface is integrated with the syntax. The techniques for actually generating the interface are the subject of another paper and will not be discussed here.

2. Lexical Specifications

In the lexical portion of the specification, various input devices and techniques are bound to logical token names. These token names will then be used in the syntactic specification. There is no conceptual limit to the number of such tokens that can be created. The mapping of this potentially infinite token set to a finite set of interactive resources is handled syntactically. It should be noted that these tokens represent individual logical input devices. More complex input methods can be built up as non-terminals in the syntactic specification.

2.1. Device Configuration

Even though the user can specify input devices without limit there is a physical limit to the interactive resources available. This includes screen space as well as physical buttons and knobs. It will be shown in the next section how syntactic knowledge is used to organize and allocate these resources. Wherever there are insufficient physical devices to accommodate the specification, virtual devices are automatically provided.

The one exception to the unlimited number of logical devices is that only one locator is allowed. This is not an inherent restriction but is rather a limitation of the implementation.

2.2. Device Properties

All primitive input devices supported by the system are characterized in a fashion similar to that proposed by Rosenthal et. al. [Rose82]. Each primitive has the following properties:

- The type of value that it returns.
- Whether it is an event or sampled input.
- The display action required when it is enabled.
- The prompt required when it is a legal input in the current parse state.
- The acknowledgment required when it has been selected.
- What effect it has on the choice of parse transitions.

Note that all of the above properties are predefined and managed automatically by the system without need for programmer intervention. In SYNGRAPH a device is enabled when it is eligible for use within the current level of interaction. A device can be enabled without being a legal input in the current parse state.

2.3. Primitive Inputs

There are seven primitive input devices supported by SYNGRAPH. They are: menu items, the locator, valuators, function buttons, keys, characters, and picks.

Menu items are defined simply by giving a name without any further specification. All such tokens are automatically organized into menus as defined by the syntax specification. If desired an icon can be specified to be used in place of the textual name of the menu item. The name of a menu item or its icon is displayed in the menu space whenever the item is enabled. Whenever that token would be valid as the next input, the menu item is highlighted. The enabling and highlighting are performed under syntactic control.

A token can also be associated with a function button number. If no such button exists then the token is automatically converted to a menu item. This allows various physical device configurations to be handled automatically.

At present only one logical button can be bound to a given physical button. In future implementations this restriction will be lifted in all cases except where two or more logical buttons, which are mapped to the same physical button, are simultaneously acceptable inputs in some parse state.

The difference between key and character tokens is that a key token refers to a specific character and returns no value, whereas a character token refers to any character and returns the character as its value. The key token's primary purpose is to construct keywords and delimiters to control the parse. The purpose of a character token is to input textual material.

The valuator token is a sampled device that does not control the parsing actions. That is, it has no effect on which transition should be taken from a given parse state. It simply inquires as to the current value of the device's measure. As with buttons, if there are insufficient physical valuators then simulated ones are created. The creation and organization of simulated valuators is syntactically controlled in a fashion similar to menus.

2.4. Picking

Pick tokens are a special case in that the type of value that they return is not predefined. The notion that a pick token returns an integer pick identifier is really not suitable for effectively characterizing an interaction. Instead a pick token returns a value of a particular user-defined type[Bles82]. Unique pick tokens are defined in the lexical specification for each type of object that can be selected from the application's display space. This means that the graphical output routines return a pointer to a data value, along with an indication of its type, instead of a simple integer. The SYNGRAPH system automatically generates a routine for each pick type. The application can then use such routines to specify pick values when displaying images.

This use of typed picking instead of generic identifiers not only improves the interaction specification but also eases the semantic interface. In addition, it also helps solve some picking ambiguity problems [Suth66]. When an object is selected which is part of a hierarchy of objects, the intended level of the hierarchy is ambiguous. The syntactic knowledge of the expected type of object, coupled with the type information in the pick definition, can remove this ambiguity in most cases. In those cases where it cannot be solved, the system will automatically query the user for the intended object.

Pick tokens are also somewhat difficult to classify in terms of their event or sampled nature. The logical concept of a pick token is modeled after a light pen which is normally viewed as an event device. In many cases, however, logical pick devices actually use a tablet or other locator. Sampled devices are not suitable for controlling parse transitions because they do not specify when the transition should be taken. Pick tokens, unlike valuator or locator tokens, have a role in controlling the parse transitions. This is contrary to their sampled nature. The use of sampled input devices to control parser actions requires the association of a trigger with the device's measure process. This association is defined syntactically as will be shown later.

2.5. Example

The following example shows the association of logical token names with their input specifications. The use of "m" and "d" in the icon definition signifies moving to a point and drawing a line to a point.

```
TERMINALS
    loc locator;
    pick_point  button 1;
    scale valuator R 0.0,10.0;
    angle valuator I 0, 360;
    draw;
    move;
    new_house;
    new_window icon
         m(0,0) d(1.0,0) d(1.0,1.0)
         d(0,1.0) d(0,0)
         m(0.5,0) d(0.5,1.0)
         m(0,0.5) d(1.0,0.5);
    house pick house_type;
    window pick window_type;
```

Figure 1
Sample token declarations

In the above example the token LOC refers to the locator and PICK_POINT the stylus tip switch. The SCALE and ANGLE tokens are real and integer valuators. Since no physical valuator is specified they will both be simulated. The tokens DRAW, MOVE and NEW_HOUSE are all menu items that will be represented by their textual names. The NEW_WINDOW token will be represented in menus as a picture of a window. The HOUSE and WINDOW tokens each specify that a picture of the specified type is to be picked.

3. Syntactic Specification

The syntactic specification not only specifies the sequence of tokens which constitute valid input streams but also the organization and arrangement of their prompts and echos. Standard techniques from compiler construction are available for handling the valid sequencing of inputs. These techniques must be extended for interactive purposes to allow organization of prompting, echoing and device simulation. In addition, the error handling strategies used in compilers are inadequate in an interactive environment. The special problems caused by sampled devices must also be handled.

3.1. Grammar

The syntax of the dialogue is expressed in terms of a modified BNF which uses the logical token names defined in the lexical specification as well as non-terminals declared in the grammar. The use of non-terminals allows either a bottom-up design where primitive tokens are collected together to form more complex input sequences or a top-down approach where the user interface is decomposed into successively less complex sub-dialogues. The hierarchical arrangement of non-terminals within a grammar fits naturally the kinds of hierarchies found in many interactive systems.

The grammar used by SYNGRAPH allows for optional phrases, repeating phrases zero or more times (curly braces {}) as well as alternation (vertical bar |). These extensions beyond BNF allow non-terminals to be used to organize the dialogue rather than as a recursive control structure.

```
cmnd ::= move ( house | window )
      pick_point { loc pick_point }
```

Figure 2
Sample syntax specification

The above example is not the actual syntax used by SYNGRAPH because it lacks the semantic interface information.

3.2. Levels of Interaction

As mentioned before it is the syntax processing which controls the management of display and input resources. In complex interactions the logical resources required are much larger than those actually available. It is therefore necessary to decompose the user interface into smaller sub-dialogues. The resources are then allocated within each such sub-dialogue. The appropriate choice of such an organization must be application dependent so that functionally similar activities can be grouped together. This cannot therefore be done automatically. This organization is expressed by designating certain non-terminals as defining new levels of interaction.

A level of interaction extends from the non-terminal which is specified as its head through all non-terminals invoked by it either directly or indirectly which are not new levels themselves. When a new level of interaction is entered all of the tokens which are used within that level become enabled. In the case of menu items, simulated buttons and simulated valuators, this means that they are allocated screen space and displayed. A level therefore defines a specific configuration of virtual input devices. The following examples show how a change of level effects menus.

```
interaction [newlevel] ::=
      edit_mode | draw_mode

edit_mode [newlevel] ::= EDIT
      ( CHANGE | INSERT | DELETE )

draw_mode ::= DRAW ( LINE | CIRCLE )
```

Figure 3
Sample use of levels

```
menu for interaction =  EDIT
                        DRAW
                        LINE
                        CIRCLE

menu for edit_mode   =  CHANGE
                        INSERT
                        DELETE
```

Figure 4
Menu sets for levels of interaction

Note that the menu set for the INTERACTION level included the starting tokens for both edit_mode and draw_mode because those tokens are necessary to be able to enter those non-terminals. LINE and CIRCLE are also included because draw_mode is not a new level. Note however that CHANGE, INSERT and DELETE are not included since they are exclusively part of EDIT_MODE which is a level of interaction of its own.

At present the allocation and organization of menus and virtual devices is performed automatically by SYNGRAPH and is outside of the user's control. The placement of these objects on the screen can be defined by tables generated by SYNGRAPH. In the future there will be the capability of interactively repositioning these items simply by editing these tables. This will allow the human factors of the user interface to be fine-tuned without altering its functionality or correctness.

3.3. Prompting

Most of the prompting of the user is performed automatically by SYNGRAPH. This is done by examining the set of input tokens that are acceptable for a given state. Menu tokens and simulated valuators are highlighted and function buttons and physical valuators are lighted or labeled (if possible) whenever they are acceptable as the next input. Feedback is also performed automatically when a particular input has been selected.

In addition to the automatic prompting, it is possible to add additional help and prompting information to the grammar. Help items can be added as special transitions which do not effect the parse. These transitions, when taken, cause a message to be placed on top of a help stack. Whenever a new non-terminal is entered, the top of the help stack is marked. When the non-terminal has been completely recognized the help stack is popped down to the mark. The top message on the help stack is continuously displayed by the system. Additional levels of help can be obtained by a special HELP menu item which steps the user up through the help stack.

The management of help information on a stack allows an interactive user access at all times to information about the global environment. Many times, in complex or deeply nested interactions, the user will lose track of where he is. The constant availability of this help stack can help him relocate himself. The fact that this service is performed automatically means that it is not dependent on the programmer to insure that it is available in all circumstances.

3.4. Error Correction

Error detection is relatively easy in a table driven input parser. It is simply a matter of reporting an error whenever an input is found for which there is no valid transition. The interactive handling of errors is much easier than in a compiler because the erroneous input is simply ignored and the user is prompted for a correct entry. In a generated interface this is always handled correctly and consistently.

3.4.1. Graphical Rubout

A special problem arises in interactions when a legal input is entered by the user but the user is not pleased with it. In textual interactions it is possible to rubout or backup over undesired inputs. This is usually done by deferring any processing on an input line until a carriage return is entered. Because no processing has been done, the rubout is simply a matter of removing the undesired characters from the input line.

In a graphical interaction there are two problems with performing rubouts. The first is that there is no concept of a current line and no generally accepted terminator. The second is that even though the execution of a command can be deferred, the processing of prompts and echos must proceed concurrently with the input process.

Rubout processing can be performed either by deferring semantic processing of a command until closure is reached or by some method of undoing the semantics of the input to be removed. In SYNGRAPH both methods are used. Because SYNGRAPH controls all of the prompting, menu management and echoing all of these functions are undone when a rubout is requested. The application semantics however are not controlled by SYNGRAPH and cannot be undone. These actions are deferred until closure is reached.

Because there is no concept of an end of line to specify when closure is reached, we use certain non-terminals in the grammar to specify complete commands. Certain non-terminals in the syntactic specification are identified as rubout non-terminals. When the parsing process enters such a non-terminal, the SYNGRAPH input process begins saving all of the inputs. None of the application semantic actions are performed during this phase. The prompting and syntactic feedback, however, are performed using the information in the automaton which defines the user interface.

When a rubout is encountered, the last input is removed from the saved inputs and the parse is restored to the state that it was in before the input was entered. When the parse state is restored, the prompting and feedback are also restored to the appropriate status for that state. Rubout actions cannot be performed past the beginning of the current rubout non-terminal. Rubout processing also extends to all non-terminals that appear in the production of a rubout non-terminal.

Closure occurs when a complete input string for the rubout non-terminal has been recognized. When an input is entered which indicates that the rubout non-terminal has been completely recognized, a semantic parse of the saved inputs is executed without performing any of the prompting or echoing. This evaluates all of the deferred semantic actions.

3.4.2. Returning to a Known State

In very involved interactions a user may, on occasion, get lost or otherwise determine that he would like to dispose of some portion of what has been entered and return to some known state. For this purpose a CANCEL operation is provided. Cancel operations, to be effective, must be enterable at any point in the input and behave correctly when entered. They also frequently require a more global recovery than can be appropriately handled by rubout. The CANCEL operation must therefore provide for semantic recovery.

In order to accomplish this semantic recovery, the application must be notified that CANCEL processing is being performed so that appropriate steps can be taken to undo the semantic actions. In order to handle the CANCEL action each non-terminal has an ESCAPE production, in addition to its normal parse production.

Whenever CANCEL is entered, the parse immediately branches to the beginning of the ESCAPE production for the current non-terminal and begins executing whatever actions are found there. When the ESCAPE production is completed, the parse terminates the non-terminal and returns to where the non-terminal was called from. The ESCAPE production for the non-terminal that was returned to is then initiated. This process continues until a HANDLED action is encountered in an ESCAPE production. The HANDLED action indicates that the CANCEL has been completely processed. When the ESCAPE production in which HANDLED appears is completely recognized, the parse can continue normally.

The following example, although somewhat simplistic, will show how the CANCEL action would be performed. Given the grammar and input stream in figure 5, the parse would perform the action to undo_object and return to the command non-terminal. Because the CANCEL has not yet been handled it would perform the action undo_command, mark the CANCEL as handled and return to INTERACTION at the point indicated in figure 6.

```
interaction ::= { command } QUIT

command ::= MOVE object TO loc
          | DRAW

     ESCAPE ::=  undo_command) HANDLED

object ::= HOUSE pick_house
         | WINDOW pick_window
         | DOOR pick_door

     ESCAPE ::=  undo_object)


input stream

     MOVE HOUSE CANCEL
```

Figure 5
Processing of CANCEL operations

```
interaction ::= { command } QUIT
                          ^
                          |
```

Figure 6
Parse state after performing CANCEL

3.5. Picking

As stated previously, a pick token has a specific data type associated with it. When a pick input is performed all pick identifiers which can possibly be associated with the pick operation are collected. Multiple identifiers can either occur because of a picture hierarchy or because the picking mechanism is inexact, as when a locator with gravity fields [Newm79] is used. Each of these pick identifiers is compared against the legal transitions for the current parse state. Any pick identifier whose data type does not match one of the pick transitions is eliminated. If more than one such identifier remains, then the system automatically prompts the interactive user to resolve this ambiguity.

3.6. Sampling

Sampled devices such as locators and valuators require two kinds of additional information. The first is that a trigger must be associated with them to specify when the sampling is to take place. Second there must be in most cases, a discrete input such as a pick or button to act as a selector to differentiate a state transition on a sampled device from other transitions. The association of sampled devices with their triggers and selectors (which may be the same device) as well as associating triggers with pick devices is defined syntactically.

In the following grammar segment the trigger event for picking a house is the key H, for a window it is the key W and for simply inputing a point it is the pick_point button.

```
cmnd ::= ( house 'H'
         | window 'W'
         | loc pick_point)
```

Figure 7
Trigger Specification

For trigger associations pick and sampled devices are handled in a similar fashion. The trigger(s) for an instance of a sampled token are the set of event devices that follow the sampled token in the parse string. As the example shows, this association of a trigger event with a pick input token also allows the use of syntactic context to further resolve any ambiguities in picking. Such an ambiguity would occur between all three alternatives when pointing at a window which is part of the house.

The association of selectors with sampled tokens requires a special second pass in order to calculate the parse transitions. The first pass propagates event devices through the grammar to associate triggers with sampled and pick devices. The second pass propagates picks and their associated triggers through the grammar to act as selectors for sampled tokens.

3.7. Summary of Syntax

At the syntactic level the SYNGRAPH system deduces a substantial amount of information from the grammar. The prompting of legal input tokens is automatically derived from the state machine. The acknowledging of inputs is handled by the supplied devices. A general organization of dialogues into levels allows menu and simulated device setup to be performed automatically by examining the grammar. A rubout facility is automatically provided with automatic prompting even though the semantics have been deferred until closure. A CANCEL operation which returns the interaction to some known state allows for explicit semantic recovery.

4. Semantics

The SYNGRAPH system is written in PASCAL and the interaction semantics are handled using PASCAL statements. Each non-terminal is generated as a recursive PASCAL procedure whose control structure is the syntax tables produced from the grammar. Each non-terminal in the grammar can have a parameter string and a header string associated with it. The parameter string must be a PASCAL parameter specification and the header string a set of PASCAL declarations. This allows complete flexibility in the type and organization of the semantic attributes. Within the production for the non-terminal, semantics are expressed either as symbol attributes or semantic actions.

Each non-terminal in the grammar can be viewed as a PASCAL procedure whose control structure is the syntax of the input grammar. Each such non-terminal can have parameters and local declarations. Interspersed in the production, PASCAL statements can be inserted to perform semantic actions. When the parse reaches the state where such an action appears, it is executed. Symbol attributes are associated with both non-terminals and terminals as PASCAL argument lists.

This procedure view of semantics which is clearly tied to the implementation language makes it much easier for the average programmer to produce a complete practical system. Even when rubout is present the deferring semantic actions until closure is masked from the application programmer leaving only the problem of extracting and processing information from the inputs. It has been felt from the outset that the semantics of the user interface must be a natural extension of the specification rather than an awkward add-on.

5. Conclusions

The SYNGRAPH system has shown how a grammatic specification can be used to automatically generate graphical interactions. SYNGRAPH has demonstrated the automation of prompting, menu and device management as well as error detection and handling. Inference of resource allocations for menus and virtual devices using the specification grammar have been demonstrated using levels of interaction to partition the user interface. A rubout facility has been automatically generated which allows prompting and feedback while deferring actual semantic actions until closure is reached. A CANCEL operation is provided which allows semantic recovery to a known state. Lastly the semantic actions of the interface have been integrated with the input specification in a manner which is consistent with the implementation language.

The generation of these features automatically from the specification should reduce the cost of implementing interactive systems as well as greatly enhance the ability to modify them. This modifiability will ease the process of iteratively producing a user-friendly interface. In addition, because rubout, cancel and error detection are all performed automatically they will be much more reliable and consistent than most hand-coded systems.

References

Bleser, T. and Foley, J. "Towards Specifying and Evaluating the Human Factors of User-Computer Interfaces." Proceedings: Human Factors in Computer Systems, (March 1982).

Hanau, Paul R. and Lenorovitz, David R. "Prototyping and Simulation tools for User/Computer Dialogue Design." Computer Graphics 14,3 (Aug 1980).

Feldman, M. and Rogers, G. "Toward the Design and Development of Style-Independent Interactive Systems." Proceedings: Human Factors in Computer Systems, (March 1982).

Foley, James D. and Van Dam, Andries. Fundamentals of Interactive Computer Graphics. Addison-Wesley Publishing Company, (1982).

Jacob, R. "Using Formal Specifications in the Design of a Human-Computer Interface." Proceedings: Human Factors in Computer Systems, (March 1982).

Kasik, David J. "A User Interface Management System." Computer Graphics 16. 3 (July 1982).

Newman, William M. "A System for Interactive Graphical Programming." Spring Joint Computer Conference, (1968).

Newman, William M. and Sproull, Robert F. Principles of Interactive Computer Graphics. New York: McGraw-Hill, (1979).

Rosenthal, David S. H., Michener, James C., Pfaff, Gunther, Kessener, Rens and Sabin, Malcolm. "Detailed Semantics of Graphics Input Devices." Computer Graphics 16. 3 (July 1982).

Sutherland, Ivan E. "Computer Graphics: Ten Unsolved Problems." Datamation 12, 5 (May 1966).

Wasserman, A. I. "User Software Engineering and the Design of Interactive Systems." Proceedings of the Fifth International Conference on Software Engineering, (March 1981).

A Graphics Editor for Benesh Movement Notation

Baldev Singh
Schlumberger-Doll Research
Old Quarry Road — P.O. Box 307
Ridgefield, Conn 06877
(203) 431-5000

John C. Beatty
Kellogg S. Booth
Computer Graphics Laboratory
University of Waterloo
Waterloo, Ontario N2L 3G1
(519) 886-1351

Rhonda Ryman
Department of Dance
University of Waterloo
Waterloo, Ontario N2L 3G1
(519) 885-1211 ext 3665

This paper describes an interactive computerized editor for *Benesh Movement Notation* that aids in the preparation of dance scores on a medium resolution colour display. Benesh Movement Notation is a two-dimensional system for recording human movement in three dimensions of space which has been successfully used in the preparation of scores for a wide repertoire of dances. The preparation and revision of Benesh scores is a lengthy and error-prone process which interactive editing techniques can greatly facilitate. We describe the current state and future extensions of a prototype editing system in which all user interaction is based on a menu-driven scheme using a graphics tablet. Extensive visual cues including iconic trackers and semantic information are provided at all times. Both user and system initiated dialogues are supported. This system has served as a testbed for a variety of man-machine interaction studies, allowing us to transfer the wealth of experience with interactive text editing to a related task: the preparation of dance scores. The project has given us a better understanding of the issues involved in implementing an effective user-interface.

CR Categories and Subject Descriptors: I.3.4 [**Computer Graphics**]: Graphics Utilities — *application packages*; I.3.4 [**Computer Graphics**]: Methodology and Techniques — *ergonomics; interaction techniques*; J.5 [**Arts and Humanities**] — *arts, fine and performing*

General Terms: Design, Human Factors

Additional Key Words and Phrases: Dance, menu-driven, movement notation, system-initiated dialogue, user-initiated dialogue

1. INTRODUCTION

Today we take for granted the existence of a suitable notation in almost all fields of human study. Notation is the primary means by which inventors communicate with those who will implement their ideas. Without a concise and precise notation system, the world as we know it would be unimaginable. Our knowledge of the past and present would be limited by memory and prone to error in oral transmission. Any comparison of past and present works would be virtually impossible, limiting the depth and breadth of our knowledge to what we can carry in our minds.

The field of human movement exhibits these limitations, but has no universal notation system. The problems are especially apparent in ballet — a classical style of expressive dance. Most ballets from the past have been completely lost, leaving behind only memories. The losses have been enormous even among the most recent ballets.

This problem has been widely recognized by professionals in the area and a number of notation systems have been developed to capture human movement. Some of these mark the steps of each dancer with lines superimposed over a sketch of a floor plan, while others use small skeleton figures drawn in dance positions. Still others adapt musical notation, using the conventional signs to represent space instead of pitch. There have been many individualized systems too — some very ingenious. But most fail to be practical under rigorous professional conditions. Among the few that have enjoyed substantial interest are *Labanotation*, developed by Rudolf Laban in 1928 [16,17], *Eshkol-Wachmann notation* devised by Noa Eshkol and Abraham Wachmann during 1951-56 [10], and *Benesh notation*, a system invented by Rudolf Benesh in 1947 [3,8].

Human movement is very complex; movement notation systems are inherently complicated and difficult to master. However, we can use a computer to provide tools that simplify the use of these notations. Such tools have been developed at the University of Pennsylvania [2,6,11,29], the University of Waterloo [26], the University of Iowa [27], Simon Fraser University [7], Sydney University [15,21] and elsewhere [18]. With the exception of the Sydney University project and Lansdown's work, which use Benesh notation, almost all of these projects deal exclusively with the interpretation of Labanotation.

The Computer Graphics Laboratory and the Dance Group at the University of Waterloo, in consultation with the National Ballet of Canada, are currently investigating the computerized editing of Benesh Movement Notation. Our aim is to provide state-of-the-art computer tools for creating, editing, and verifying records of human movement, similar to the tools commonly available for interactive text editing. This paper describes the design and implementation of a graphical editor for a subset of Benesh Movement Notation. Professional choreologists have tested a prototype system based on these ideas. Our primary interest here is in describing the techniques for man-machine interaction. We view this work as a significant testbed for a number of ideas, some new, incorporating a systematic methodology for man-computer dialogue. The interactive tools developed for the Benesh editor have been successfully integrated into a VLSI layout editor and an interactive Beta-spline surface modeling system.

2. Problem Description

Many movement notations seem similar to musical notations at first glance. Both serve as a communication medium between composers and performers. However, they are used differently. Musicians learn a composition from musical manuscripts, whereas dancers learn their parts directly from the *choreographer* (a dance composer) through verbal and visual communication; dance requires direct interaction between the choreographer and the dancers. In music, notation is the means by which a performer realizes the creator's conception of a composition [6]. In contrast, movement notations are mainly used to record the finished product for historical preservation. They can also be used for comparative analysis and reconstruction at a later date, without the choreographer's presence or the need to repeat the entire creative process. While musical notations are well standardized, dance notations are still evolving.

The process of recording dance using Benesh Movement Notation begins with a *choreologist*, a specialist in Benesh notation, who attends rehearsals and makes rough notes which are refined gradually during subsequent rehearsals. This score is later checked for errors in the movements recorded and in the notation's usage. Once the score has been checked, it is put into finished form by an *autographer*, who composes and inscribes each page by hand. Upon completion of this process the score is ready for printing.

During rehearsals dancers learn complete movements: all parts of the body move simultaneously. However, the notation must record changes in each body part individually. If there are many dancers learning complex movements, it becomes difficult to capture all the details. The recording process is limited by the speed at which the choreologist can write. Therefore the choreologist usually notes only the key positions, filling in the details at later rehearsals. In a large ballet company, where many hours each day are devoted to teaching new steps, the choreologist works with different groups of dancers throughout a ten to twelve hour period. This makes filling in details after rehearsal virtually impossible. The task becomes even more difficult when the choreographer decides to add or drop parts of the dance or revise steps and sections. The choreologist has to struggle constantly with the organization of notes, filling in the missing details during *cleanup rehearsals* conducted after all the dancers have learned their parts.

Under these conditions the choreologist is often unable to work on the final draft of the score as the rough notes accumulate. There is often not enough time until after the dance is in performance. Then many hours must be spent laboriously copying the rough notes, laying out the pages and refining the notation.

It should be apparent that the basic problem facing a choreologist is one of information overload which worsens from rehearsal to rehearsal. Improvements to this process might involve a faster means for recording movements (ideally at the speed of performance), an efficient mechanism for storing and retrieving this information for editing or verification, or a means for producing the finished score in hardcopy form.

One possible approach would be to store the rough score in a computer system by scanning it with a video input device at the end of each rehearsal. The time between rehearsals could be devoted to editing and verifying this information through a graphical editor and producing medium quality hard-copy output that could be used for further refinements at subsequent rehearsals. Alternatively, movement information could be directly entered into a computer system using goniometers [7,31] or three-dimensional imaging techniques [19,25], although this is difficult in a rehearsal situation.

The inverse process of producing movement from notation has proven to be a very useful tool for verifying the recorded movement. Labanotation has been used to animate Calvert's *stick-figure* model and Badler's *Bubble-Man*, while Herbison-Evans used Benesh notation to animate *Sausage-Woman*.

Although substantial progress has been made in recording and analyzing movements, tools for editing scores, especially in Benesh Movement Notation, are virtually non-existent. Much more research is needed to make editing movement scores as easy and convenient as editing text. The work presented here deals with the issues involved in editing dance scores based on the Benesh Movement Notation system. Another Benesh editor is being developed at Sydney University [15]. Earlier editors based on Labanotation have been designed at the University of Pennsylvania [6] and at the University of Iowa [27].

3. Benesh Movement Notation

Benesh Movement Notation records movements using marks on a matrix representing a human figure. The five line music *stave* serves conveniently as a matrix dividing the human body at the feet, knees, waist, top of the shoulder and top of the head (see Figure 1). Two horizontal dashed *leger lines* are added to cover all possible body positions. A leger line above the stave lines represents the maximum reach of the hands when the arms are fully extended upwards. Locomotor transitions such as jumps, slides, turns and skimming movements are shown by lines drawn between the first stave line and a leger line below it. Because the span of horizontally extended legs is approximately equal to the body height with the arms fully extended upward, all possible body positions can be enclosed in a square. Therefore the stave is divided into square *frames*, each representing a body position [14]. All this makes the notation visual and avoids the need for a large number of signs.

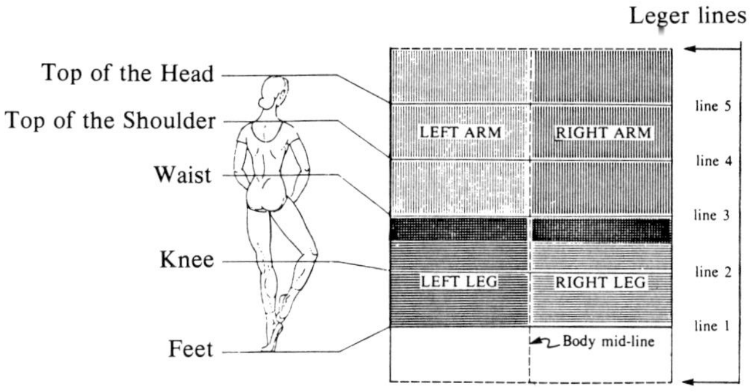

Fig. 1. The Benesh stave.

NOTE: The doubly hashed region is the overlap for hands and feet

Movements are recorded as they would be observed from behind the performer. Positions are recorded by noting the projection of the four *body extremities* (hands and feet) and the *bends* (in knees and elbows) onto the *cardinal coronal plane* (see Figure 2). This projection is not a true projection of the whole body figure. Rather, it is the projection of body segments in relation to the *body centre line* onto the corresponding areas on or between the stave lines. The projections provide two-dimensional information. For three-dimensional information it is necessary to know whether a limb is in front of or behind the cardinal coronal plane, which is considered to be as thick as the body. This is recorded using the following basic signs for the four extremities:

level (with the cardinal coronal plane)

in front (of the cardinal coronal plane)

behind (the cardinal coronal plane)

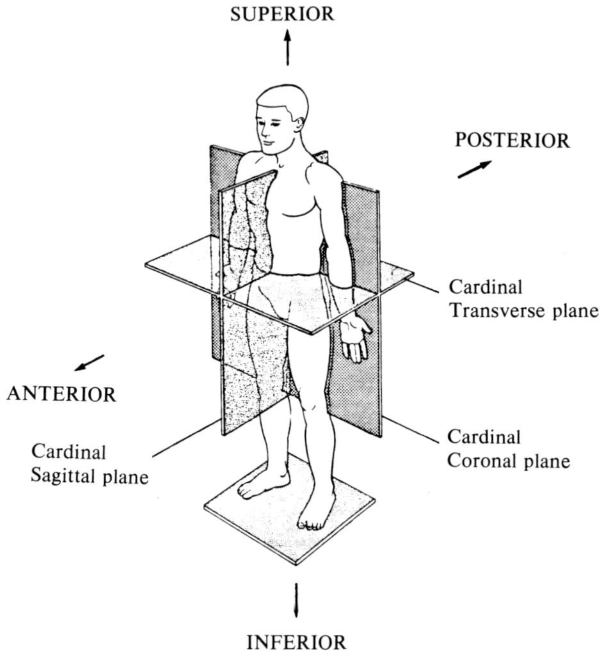

Fig. 2. Human body in anatomic position.

It is not necessary to state how far in front or how far behind the cardinal coronal plane the extremities lie. Figure 3 illustrates the use of basic signs. Only one position is physically possible as the limbs are of fixed length, although there is the possibility of bending the limbs. The basic signs for bends (in knee or elbow) are:

level (with the cardinal coronal plane)

in front (of the cardinal coronal plane)

behind (the cardinal coronal plane)

The signs for all four limbs are identical and thus do not identify the limb (right leg, left arm, *etc.*) to which they refer. This information is inferred from the location of the sign. Figure 1 shows the domains for the four body limbs. Whenever a limb sign moves out of its domain it is lightly crossed with a diagonal stroke known as the *crossover* (see Figure 3). There are two types of crossovers: a *lateral crossover* in which an extremity or bend is positioned to the other side of the body; and a *vertical crossover* in which a foot or bent knee is positioned above the waist line, or a hand or bent elbow moves below the thigh. The crossover signs are:

lateral crossover

vertical crossover

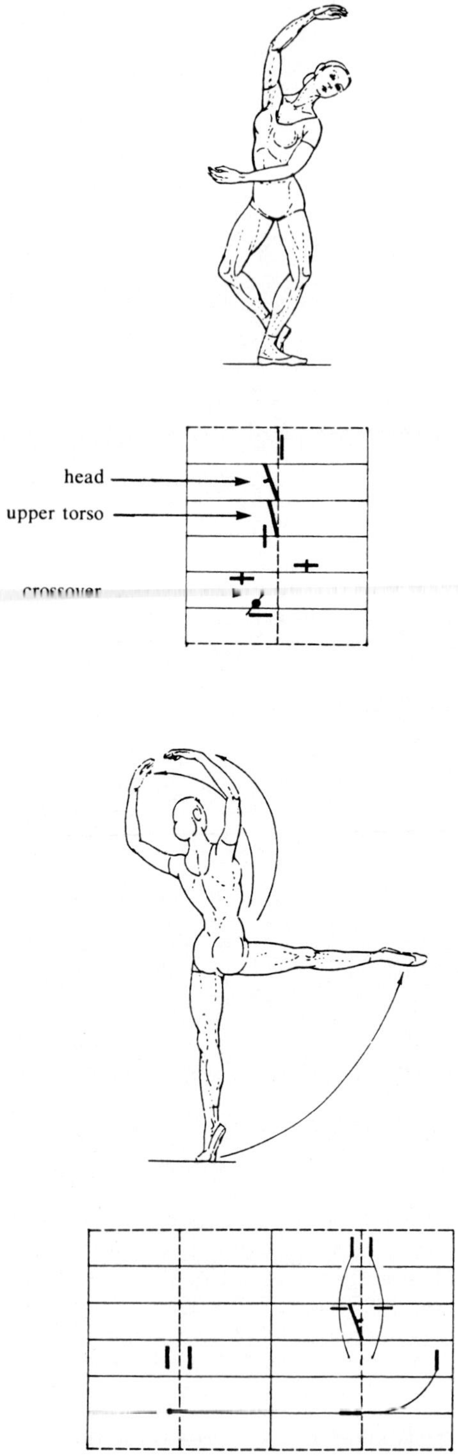

Fig. 3. Use of basic signs.

The *head* is represented by a straight line drawn between the fourth and the fifth stave lines. The bottom end of this head line is normally fixed to the intersection point of the fourth stave line with the body centre line while the top end always touches the fifth stave line. The angle between this head line and the body centre line specifies the degree of tilt. A shorter straight line drawn perpendicular to the head line represents the chin position. The length and location of this chin line indicates the degree of turn in the head. The intersection point between the head and chin lines specifies the extent of backward or forward bend in the head (see Figure 4). Intersection above this midpoint represents a backward bend and intersection below the midpoint indicates a forward bend.

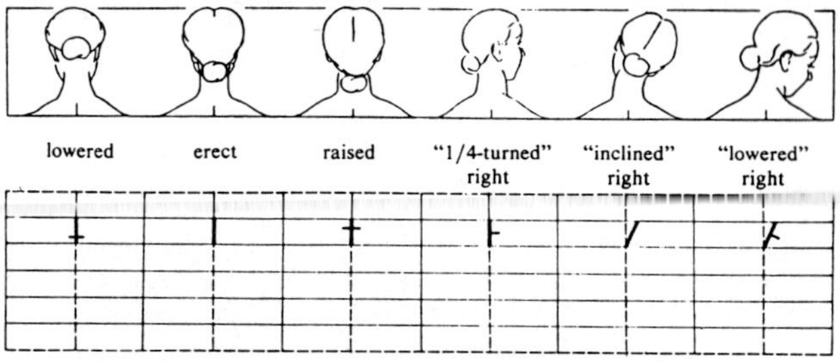

Fig. 4. Various head positions.

The third stave line represents the waist. Therefore all body bends and turns from the waist up *(upper torso)* are recorded between the third and fourth stave lines. The signs used and their manipulation are identical to those used for the head. *Hip (pelvic)* movements are similarly recorded between the second and the third stave lines. Figure 3 illustrates the method for recording these main body parts.

In Benesh one typically records only the *changes* in posture; constant data is not shown, but is inferred from previous frames. Furthermore, positions for *main body parts* (head, torso and hips) are recorded only if they are *not* in or returning to their normal anatomic position.

4. The Benesh Editor

The basic unit of information in Benesh Movement Notation is the *frame.* Unlike a line of text, which is made up of symbols (characters) written at discrete points in a one-dimensional space, the Benesh frame records body information by means of signs in a continuous two-dimensional rectangular space. Benesh frames are ordered sequentially within a score, but the positioning of signs within a frame is more complex than the placement of characters in a line of text.

Three levels of basic operations are necessary for editing a text document: editing lines, editing words within a line and editing characters within a word. Similarly, the editing operations required for Benesh scores are manipulation of an entire frame or a set of frames, manipulation of sign positions within a frame and construction of the signs themselves. A complete score corresponds to an entire text document. High level operations such as *print*, *copy* and *archive*, are analogous to those for text. The techniques for implementing text editors are well developed and a number of very good editors such as *Ed*, *Emacs*, *Ex*, *Fred*, *Qed*, *Vi* and the *Xerox Star editor* are available. The Benesh editor described in this paper uses many techniques derived from the analogy between editing text documents and Benesh scores.

As in most text editors the primary data structure used here is a doubly linked list, in which each node represents a Benesh frame. Each node contains complete body information for a frame even though only changes are displayed.

Benesh notation uses a basic set of pre-defined signs. Other signs are built from a combination of these basic signs, for example, by adding a *crossover*. Still others, like main body signs, are constructed whenever necessary. This last approach is used for highly variable signs. An example is the sign which captures the degree of tilt, turn and backward or forward bend of the head. In this case it would be very difficult to provide a fixed set of predefined signs covering all possible combinations. Thus a new sign is constructed whenever a new head position must be specified.

A moving *display window* is superimposed on the linked list structure of frames. At any given time, the editor displays all the frames within the current display window. Other frames are displayed by moving the window over the desired frames in the linked list. The window displays the score as it would normally be written on a piece of paper, except that the first frame in the window always shows the complete body position for readability, irrespective of the frame immediately preceding it in the score. In addition, the editor provides a working frame in which all frames are first constructed before posting them to the display window.

The editor is based on a *menu-driven* scheme and provides *abort* and *undo* facilities for error recovery. *Abort* cancels the current action and backs up to the next higher level in the menu hierarchy. Thus a sequence of *abort* requests will eventually return the editor to its initial state.

Two types of *undo* requests are supported by the editor. The first undoes the previous step in a sequence of actions comprising an editing operation, while the second undoes the entire last editing operation that was successfully completed. In both cases *undo* acts like a toggle switch; a second application undoes the last *undo*, thus restoring the original action.

5. User Interface

The most important single consideration in designing any computer system, hardware or software, is the design of the interface between computer and user. It is the most visible aspect of the editor and the only channel of communication between the system and the choreologist. The success of a system is entirely dependent on the success of its user interface. However, user interfaces are the most difficult and the least understood part of interactive systems. Our design process was highly iterative and thus very time consuming.

The interactive techniques used by the Benesh editor have evolved through a careful task analysis and prototyping process. A choreologist was closely observed at work under rehearsal conditions and later interviewed. The results of this study formed the problem description described earlier. Careful analysis of user behaviour and a trace of interactions during editing sessions helped to isolate problem areas and devise alternate techniques. The resulting design adheres to a small set of principles that have been adapted to make the editing environment familiar and friendly to the user, to simplify the man-machine interaction, and to unify all editing functions so that any experience gained in one situation can be easily applied to similar situations. In designing the user interface, two primary issues of concern were:

- an *interaction language*, the medium through which the user expresses commands to the system, and
- a *display representation*, showing the system's state and the options currently available to the user.

The first is expressed as actions applied to the input devices, while the latter is expressed through the output devices. This section discusses these principles.

5.1. Hardware and Software

Before describing the user interface of the Benesh editor, several essential characteristics of the hardware and software used should be pointed out. Without these it would have been difficult to design an interface such as the present one.

The editor uses an Ikonas RDS 3000 *frame buffer* attached to a *colour display monitor* and a Summagraphics Bit Pad *tablet* with a *puck*. The frame buffer's bit planes are divided into two sets called the *foreground* and *background*, as shown in Figure 5. The background planes contain static display information, such as the menus. Each item of static information is written into the frame buffer memory using a different seven-bit colour value. The item can then be made visible or invisible by manipulating *colour lookup table* entries. To display an item written in the background planes, the corresponding colour lookup table entry is set to a colour different from the background colour.

The foreground plane contains dynamic information. A microprocessor based support package is used to display all foreground information [5]. This package is organized around a segmented display file which is interpreted by a high speed bit-slice microprocessor. It provides facilities to *create*, *delete*, *move*, or *pick* segments and to make them visible or invisible.

A *write-mask* is used to access only the single foreground bit-plane and an *auto-clear* feature in the display hardware causes that bit-plane to be erased after every display cycle. This combination of clearing and re-writing provides the illusion of dragging a symbol as its display position changes between one display cycle and the next. Since all of this is done in the microprocessor, the redisplay appears to be instantaneous as long as the number of segments is kept small enough to allow rewriting in every display cycle.

All code for the editor is written in the C programming language and runs on a VAX 11/780 minicomputer under the Unix operating system.

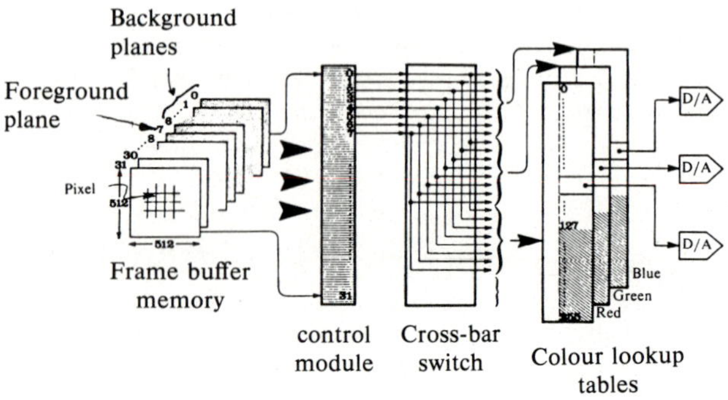

Fig. 5. Ikonas video chain.

Fig. 6. Display screen with tablet and puck.

5.2. Interaction Language

As the user moves the puck across the tablet surface, its position is determined and a *tracker* sign is displayed at an equivalent position on the display screen (see Figure 6).

A list of options (the *current menu)* is displayed, from which the user chooses an action by moving the puck until the tracking sign is aligned with the desired menu option on the display screen. Pressing one of the puck buttons selects the action. The displayed items can specify actions or they can request a different menu. A menu-based scheme offers several advantages [24]. For example, it displays the full range of options available to the user. This avoids the problem of erroneous commands by preventing the user from selecting options outside that range. It also helps the user to remember commands which he does not use frequently. It is very flexible: a menu label can be easily changed to suit the user's terminology.

Conceptual Model

A user's *conceptual model* is the set of ideas by which he explains the behaviour of the system, the picture in his mind which enables him to understand and interact with the system. Developing a suitable conceptual model was a very important step in the design of the interaction language. It is almost identical to that of Benesh Movement Notation. A few new approaches have been added to aid in the editing process. The use of a five line musical stave to record movements is further enhanced by a body figure menu. The finished score is displayed as a choreologist would write it on a piece of paper. The terminology used for editor functions is adapted from Benesh.

Instead of asking the user to explicitly draw Benesh signs, the editor presents a set of neatly drawn signs. The user need only select a sign and position it at the desired location. The rules and conventions for positioning the signs are those of the Benesh notation and are strictly observed by the editor. All frames are composed or modified in a *working frame,* which is displayed at twice the size of a normal frame in the score. This allows for more accurate positioning and manipulation of signs.

Recognition versus Recall

Learning to use any system requires the memorization of information. An important consideration in designing a user interface is the nature of the *dialogue* between the system and its user. The aim is to minimize the amount of information a user must memorize in order to initiate and carry out a dialogue with the system.

There are two approaches to the design of man-machine dialogues [20]. One is *system-initiated dialogue,* in which the system displays everything relevant to a task and then prompts the user for his next action. The system guides the user. All "conversational" and menu oriented systems belong to this category. The other approach is *user-initiated dialogue,* in which the user requests an action by issuing the necessary commands. Here the user must remember the commands and their order of execution to perform a particular task.

During conscious thought the brain utilizes several levels of memory, the most important being *short-term memory.* Many studies have analyzed short-term memory and its role in thinking. The following conclusions stand out:

- conscious thought deals with concepts in short-term memory [1], and
- the capacity of short-term memory is limited [22].

When all relevant information is visible, the display eases the load on short-term memory by acting like a "visual cache". Thinking becomes easier and more productive. A well designed dialogue can actually improve the quality of user thinking. The conversational nature of a system-initiated dialogue implies a truly interactive form of communication. It enables the system to give instantaneous positive or negative feedback to the user in response to his previous action, in addition to prompting the user for the next step.

By contrast, user-initiated dialogues are generally easier to implement and more efficient in executing a particular task *once the user has gained some experience.* They are usually more flexible, and shortcuts are often available for performing a particular task. The ordering of dialogue steps is not fixed and this can be more efficient for an experienced user, although the opposite is true for a casual user or novice. User-initiated dialogues also place an additional burden on the user's memory.

Command Set

In designing the man-machine dialogue for the Benesh editor, the user's problem space has been broken into tasks which are in turn partitioned into two different forms of dialogue. Commands like *abort, undo,* and *help* (which is not yet implemented) can be invoked at any time and have a user-initiated dialogue. The commands in this group have been restricted to a very small number and are structured to fit the user's normal way of thinking and working, thus reducing the burden on short term memory. These commands can be invoked at any time during an editing session by pressing the puck buttons shown in Figure 7. The assignment of these commands to the puck buttons is always displayed on the screen as an aid to the novice or occasional user. The remaining commands are grouped appropriately within the system-initiated dialogue and implemented using menus.

Buttons allow a very convenient and efficient way of specifying functions, but they distract the user, causing a shift of attention from the display to the buttons. With experience a user learns the button locations and activates them without looking, just as a touch typist no longer looks at the typewriter keys but instead concentrates on the manuscript. This is especially true if there are only a few buttons to remember.

The puck used for the prototype editor (see Figure 7) has four buttons that are located close together in a diamond pattern. Each button has been colour coded for easy recognition. However, the user doesn't normally look at these buttons, but instead uses tactile memory to locate them. In our experience users have consistently had trouble selecting the appropriate button for actions other than the *do* function (yellow button). The colour coding is obviously of no help. The problem has to do with the structure of the hand and the layout of the puck buttons. Our finger tips move comfortably in the vertical direction but not in the horizontal direction. Thus the user has no problem selecting the *do* and *undo* buttons, but has difficulty in selecting the *help* and *abort* buttons. These observations suggest that pucks be designed with a single button, or at most two vertically positioned buttons per finger. Many mice and some tablet pucks have taken this into consideration.

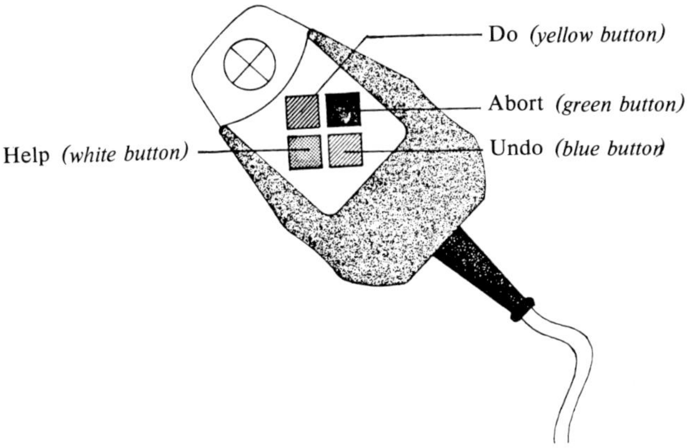

Fig. 7. Tablet puck.

A menu can have a very large number of options. The discussion in the previous section argued that short-term memory is the most important level utilized in conscious thought. Miller's experiments [22] show that the capacity of our short-term memory is limited to "the magical number seven plus or minus two" for absolute judgement of unidimensional stimuli. He explains that this capacity can be increased by increasing the dimensions of the stimuli. However, the increase in capacity is not linear. Instead it asymptotically approaches a fixed limit as the dimensionality of the stimulus is increased [22]. One way to increase this capacity is by grouping [4]: thus telephone numbers are divided into groups to help in remembering them. Similarly, commands for manipulating frames have been sub-divided into five groups according to their function, each group containing a maximum of five commands. Figure 8 illustrates this grouping within the *root menu,* which is the menu for manipulating frames.

Text versus Iconic Labels for Menu items

Natural language is an excellent medium for communicating propositions intended for people. A picture can also be thought of as conveying a proposition, but the problem with a picture is that it often conveys a large number of propositions [13]. Without some constraining context it is difficult to know the intended proposition. Mills explains that the problem of multiple meanings in a picture has its roots in the very nature of the human conceptual apparatus, which uses a finite set of general cognitive frameworks or schemata to form definite descriptions of specific inputs [23]. Even in purely visual perception, the same input can give rise to many different descriptions by drawing on different combinations of schemas depending on changes in context. This flexibility can create problems for the use of *icons* if they are not designed properly.

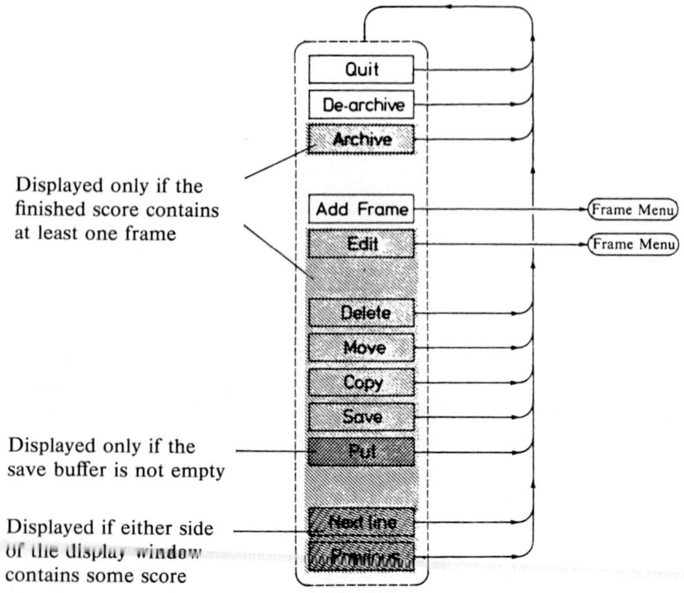

Fig. 8. Root menu.

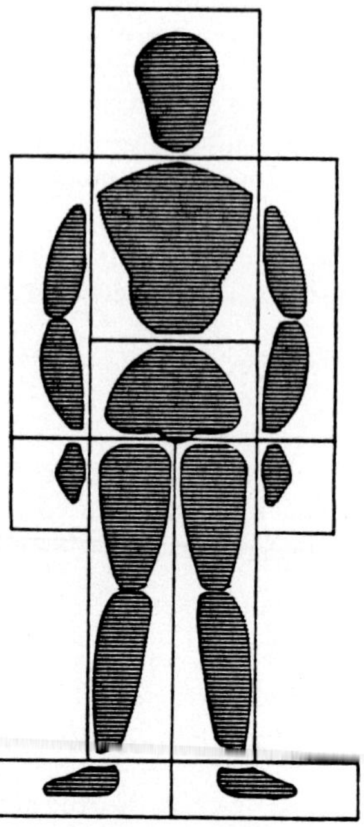

Fig. 9. Body menu.

The design of iconic representations is a specialized area of study that draws on many other disciplines, such as art and psychology. A good icon needs simultaneously to be a *symbol* — representing something else by convention or association, and a *picture* — a visual representation. It must use abstract graphical elements to highlight generic qualities, yet must be recognizable as a visual representation of a specific kind of object, situation or event. Poor icon design will inhibit communication rather than help. Dreyfuss presents a collection of standard symbols used internationally [9]. These symbols can be easily adopted for icons in man-machine dialogues.

Translating a verbal statement into an equivalent pictorial description is often not easy. In fact, it is difficult to form pictorial propositions about past, future and conditional events or to form logical chains of inference [23]. However, in an appropriate combination pictures and text can function together in directing the user towards the intended meaning of a message.

These ideas have been used in labeling menu items for the Benesh editor and in defining the iconic cursors explained in a later section. Abbreviated words from the Benesh terminology have been adopted to label most menu items. *Benesh signs* have been used whenever available. The body menu in Figure 9, showing the body limbs and main body parts, is an excellent example of pictorial labeling of menus. This combination of icons and abbreviated text labels is intended to constrain label meanings to avoid ambiguity.

Dynamic versus Static Menus

Menus that are always displayed at a fixed location are known as *static menus.* The user becomes accustomed to their display locations and habitually looks for and expects them to appear at the same position. This provides visual continuity and maintains a sense of "place" in the interaction dialogue. A drawback of static menus is that the user has to move his eyes (and his hand for controlling the puck) from their current position on the display screen to the location at which the menu is displayed. In contrast, a *dynamic menu* appears at the user's current position on the display screen, thus avoiding additional eye or hand movements. The assumption is that the user's centre of attention is near the *tracker,* his current position on the display screen. Thus a dynamic menu minimizes overall hand and eye movement. Static menus allow the use of tactile memory to pre-position the tablet puck, while dynamic menus minimize visual search [12].

Dynamic menus are more flexible; they can overlay existing data and so can be displayed anywhere on the display screen. Static menus use fixed display regions that cannot be used for displaying any other data. The total number of static menus that can be displayed is thus limited by the available area on the display. An important feature of static menus is their natural display of the current system state.

The Benesh editor uses both types of menus. All sign menus are dynamic, minimizing hand and eye movement for sign selection. The remaining menus are static, highlighting the *closure* [12] of each operation by requiring the user to return to the menu display area. The layout of the static menus is also designed to minimize hand and eye movements and to show the system state, as explained below.

5.3. Display Representation

The display is the most visible part of any system and must be carefully designed to be both appealing and informative. It should always reflect the user's conceptual model and should hide all implementation details. Our design goal was to minimize the short-term memory required for system operation, to relieve it for more important user tasks. This is achieved by displaying all the information necessary for the user to perform a task at any given time. The editor provides this information by immediate feedback to user requests, by displaying the system state at all times, and by always displaying the current status of the finished score as well as that of the frame being composed. This section describes the methods used for displaying this information.

Feedback

Feedback is an essential part of any conversation, whether with a machine or with a person. In a normal conversation several forms of feedback are exchanged automatically without any conscious action by the participants. This feedback includes gesture, body language, facial expression and eye contact. Foley explains the psychological blocks that occur in the absence of adequate feedback [12]. Typical symptoms are boredom, panic, frustration, and confusion. Immediate feedback not only avoids these psychological blocks but also provides continuity in the dialogue.

Originally the editor provided feedback at the lexical, syntactic and semantic levels. *Lexical* feedback consists of changing the cursor icon to the icons shown in Figure 10, depending on the puck button pushed. *Syntactic* feedback differs depending on the item being selected. Selecting a frame results in a change in its background colour. Selecting a sign from a sign menu replaces the cursor icon with the selected sign, as shown in Figure 11. *Semantic* feedback is provided by displaying the results of the selected operation.

This feedback hierarchy offers several advantages. Lexical feedback provides a placebo whenever the system is running slowly. However, this placebo can be annoying under normal system operation. When the transition from the lexical to the syntactic level takes a very short time, the lexical feedback turns into an irritating flash. These flashes are especially annoying for the *do* button, the most frequently used. To avoid this effect, lexical feedback for the *do* button has been suppressed and for consistency all lexical feedback was removed. Thus the current version of the editor provides feedback at the syntactic and semantic levels only. This has proven satisfactory for most operations.

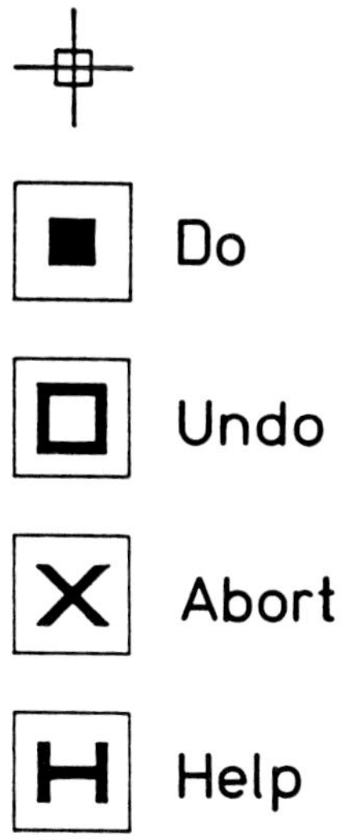

Fig. 10. Icons for lexical feedback.

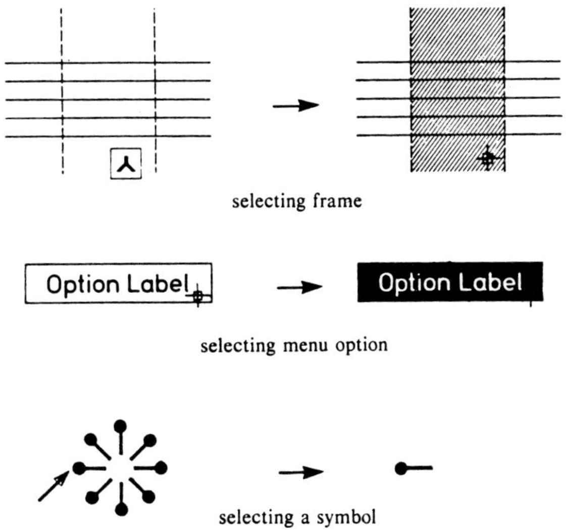

Fig. 11. Syntactic feedback.

Some form of placebo is still necessary for time-consuming operations such as archiving and dearchiving finished scores. All editor operations were analyzed and a placebo is provided for such operations. The placebo used is a *Buddha* icon adopted from Newswhole [30], as shown in Figure 12.

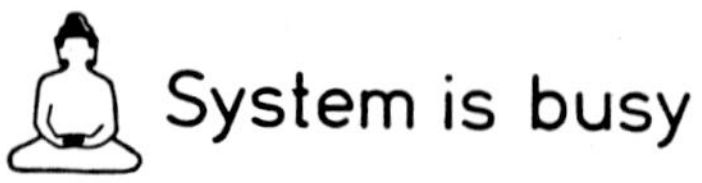

Fig. 12. Buddha icon.

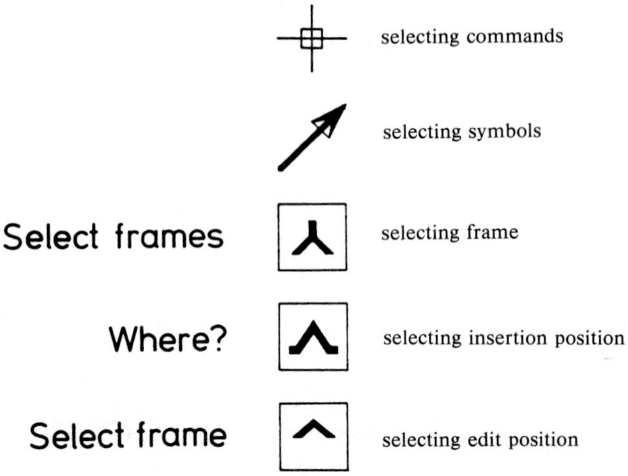

Fig. 13. Tracker icons.

System State

A very important aspect of the display representation is showing the system state at all times. Most systems reserve an area of the display screen for displaying this information. However, there are some drawbacks to this approach. During an interactive dialogue, the user's centre of attention is generally focussed on the object that he is manipulating. Anything appearing outside his centre of attention, especially outside his peripheral field of vision, will not register. Therefore the problem with displaying the system state in a fixed location is that if this location falls outside the user's centre of attention but within his peripheral field of vision, it will distract his attention. The user's curiousity will move his centre of attention to the location where the system state is displayed. After reading the state information, the user will return his attention to the original position. This eye movement every time the system state is changed can be very tiring and very annoying, especially if the system state changes quite frequently. A better way to present this information is to display it within the user's centre of attention, thus avoiding eye movement and providing visual continuity.

The system state referred to here is not the internal program state, but the current mode of the editor within the user's conceptual model. Selecting an option in a non-sign menu inverts the option label and all other options are switched off. As the user moves along the menu hierarchy selecting menu options, he leaves behind a trail of reverse video menu labels, the most recent of which is always at the centre of attention.

The editor also indicates the action in progress by changing the tracker icon, as shown in Figure 13. The inverted labels and the iconic tracker together define the complete state of the system at a given time.

The Current Status of the Score

The editor displays the finished score in the display window. While editing a frame, the selected frame is left highlighted to indicate its context within the score. When adding new frames to the finished score, the editor displays the current insertion position, which is updated each time a new frame is added. All frames added during the current *add frame* operation remain highlighted until the end of the operation. This always shows the current status of the finished score.

When editing a frame or composing a new frame, the working frame shows three types of information. Firstly, a body part may not have been defined yet. Secondly, a body part may have been carried over from the previous frame. Thirdly, a body part may have been newly defined for this frame. All body information is shown using signs. One way to show the different types of information is to use signs of different colour. However, this might imply an ordering of signs by their importance and thus change the semantics of the signs. Instead the editor displays this information for each body part by using different background colours for the corresponding menu items, as shown in Figure 14. A black background means that the menu item has not been selected. Colour association is used for the remaining types of information. If the background colour of a menu item is the same as the highlight colour of the last frame added to the finished score, this implies that the corresponding sign has been carried over from the previous frame and selection of this item will result in replacement of the existing sign. A background colour which is the same as that of the working frame implies that the corresponding body part has been newly defined. This colouring scheme provides checklists of body information that has already been defined and that still need to be defined.

6. Future Extensions

The major problem in designing interactive computer systems is the development of man-machine communication mechanisms suited to the particular task. Most of the design effort for the current system has been directed towards the construction of a user interface which is both powerful and easy to use. Some additional functions will

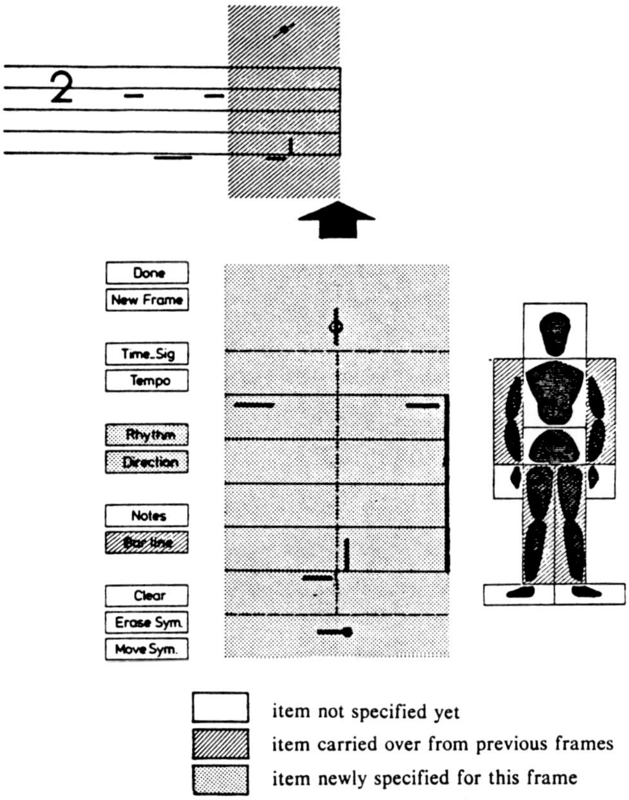

Fig. 14. Status information display.

be incorporated into the system in the near future. These include specification of movement lines and enforcement of body model constraints (neither are in the current implementation). Full screen display of the score with facilities to scroll backward and forward will also be incorporated. This will enable the user to read through a score more easily by examining an entire screenfull at one time.

We plan to add a means for producing a medium quality copy of the composed score on a 200 dots per inch electrostatic printer/plotter. The aim is to eventually produce high-quality copies of the score on a digital typesetter for reproduction purposes. Because a Benesh score consists of a limited set of basic signs, it is possible to define a specialized Benesh type font. Several manufacturers of phototypesetting equipment allow for the incorporation of such user-defined fonts into their systems.

In the long term there is a need for extending the system to verify body position, to score multiple dancers and to detect collisions. Further error checking could be performed in the following manner. Each frame in a Benesh score defines what is know by film animators as a *key-frame*. An animation system with a suitable interpolation method could be used to calculate the intermediate positions between Benesh frames. The sequence of Benesh frames and intermediate frames could then be used to produce a stick-figure animation of the Benesh score, enabling us to verify the movement.

Another area of research is the translation of data between various notation systems. Three dimensional body information calculated from the Benesh score could be used for this translation. Similar information is collected by other systems based on Labanotation, and the reverse mapping from body information into notation also exists. For example, a project at Simon Fraser University collects body information using goniometers and then maps this data into Labanotation scores [7].

7. CONCLUSION

The importance of achieving literacy in dance is very well recognized. The notational systems which have been developed are often difficult to master or cumbersome to use. The computer assisted editing system described in this paper is designed to facilitate the learning, teaching and use of the Benesh Movement Notation. Its particular value to the professional dance community lies in the ability to facilitate the production and revision of master scores. Its value to the computer graphics community is an increased understanding of the issues involved in the implementation of effective user interfaces.

ACKNOWLEDGEMENTS

It is especially important in a project such as this to elicit the evaluations of skilled choreologists concerning the ease and naturalness with which the system can be used. We would like to thank Monica Parker (director, Institute of Choreology, London, England), Robyn Hughes (then choreologist with the National Ballet of Canada), Wendy Walker (choreologist with the American Ballet Theatre), Sandy Caverly Lowery and Joan Mallet of York University, and the dancers who attended the First International Summer School in Benesh Movement Notation, held at the University of Waterloo in August 1982. We would also like to thank the other members of the Computer Graphics Laboratory at the University of Waterloo for providing the tools and environment in which this work could be carried out. The Ikonas software written by Paul Breslin [5] was especially valuable.

Our work was supported by the Natural Sciences and Engineering Research Council of Canada, the Province of Ontario under its BILD Program, and the University of Waterloo.

REFERENCES

[1] ARNHEIM, R. *Visual Thinking.* University of California Press, Berkeley, Calif., 1969.

[2] BADLER, N.I., J. O'ROURKE, and B. KAUFMAN. Special problems in human movement simulation. *Computer Graphics 14*, 3 (July 1980), 189-197.

[3] BENESH, R. and J. BENESH. *Reading Dance, The Birth of Choreology.* Souvenir Press (E&A) Ltd., 1977.

[4] BOURNE, L.E. and B.R. EKSTRAND. *Psychology: Its Principles and Meanings* (3rd edition). Holt, Rinehart and Winston, 1979.

[5] BRESLIN, P., and J.C. BEATTY. A powerful interface to a high performance raster graphics system. Tech. Rep. CS-82-45, Computer Graphics Laboratory, Department of Computer Science, University of Waterloo, Dec. 1982.

[6] BROWN, M.D. and S.W. SMOLIAR. Preparing dance notation scores with a computer. *Computers and Graphics 3*, 1 (1978), 1-7.

[7] CALVERT, T.W., J. CHAPMAN, and A. PATLA. The simulation of human movement. *Proceedings Graphics Interface '82*, NCGA of Canada, Toronto, Ontario (1982), 227-234.

[8] CAUSLEY, M. *An Introduction to Benesh Movement Notation*, Man Parrish, London, 1967.

[9] DREYFUSS, H. *Symbol Sourcebook*. McGraw-Hill Book Company, New York, 1972.

[10] ESHKOL, N. *Right Angled Curves*. Movement Notation Society, 1975. (For the Research Centre for Movement Notation, Faculty of Arts, Tel Aviv University, Israel)

[11] FEDAK, J. F. An initial design specification of a syntactic analyzer for Labanotation. Movement Project Report No. 10, Department of Computer and Information Science, University of Pennsylvania, Philadelphia, Pa., Jan. 1978.

[12] FOLEY, J.D. The design and implementation of user-computer interfaces. *Siggraph '82 Tutorial Notes 7*, ACM, New York, N.Y., July 1982.

[13] GOMBRICH, E.H. The Visual Image. *Scientific American 227*, 3 (Sep. 1972), 82-96.

[14] GRATER, A. *private correspondence*. Institute of Choreology, London, England, 1982.

[15] HERBISON-EVANS, D. A human movement language for computer animation. *Language Design and Programming Methodology*, ed. Jeffrey M. Tobias, (Sep. 1979), 117-128. (Proceedings of the Symposium on Language Design and Programming Methodology, Sydney, Australia)

[16] HUTCHINSON, A. *Labanotation* (3rd Edition). New York: Theatre Arts, 1977.

[17] LABAN, R. *Laban's Principles of Dance and Movement Notation* (2nd Edition). Macdonald & Evans Ltd., London, 1975.

[18] LANSDOWN, J. The computer in choreography. *IEEE Computer 11*, 8 (Aug. 1978), 19-30.

[19] MACKAY, S.A., R.E. SAYRE, and M.J. POTEL. 3D Galatea: Entry of three-dimensional moving points from multiple perspective views. *Computer Graphics 16*, 3 (July 1982).

[20] MARTIN, J. *Design of Man-Machine Dialogues*. Englewood Cliffs, N.J., 1973.

[21] MCNAIR, B. A language for notating human movement. M.Sc. Thesis, Basser Department of Computer Science, Sydney University, 1979.

[22] MILLER, G. The magical number seven, plus or minus two: Some limits on our capacity for processing information. *Psychology Review 63*, 2 (March 1956), 81-97.

[23] MILLS, M.I. Cognitive schemata and the design of graphics displays. *Proceedings Graphics Interface '82*, NCGA of Canada, Toronto, Ontario, (May, 1982), 3-12.

[24] NEWMAN, W.M. and R.F. SPROULL. *Principles of Interactive Computer Graphics* (2nd edition). McGraw-Hill Book Company, 1979.

[25] PERRYNOWSKI, M.R. *A Physiological Model for the Solution of Individual Muscle Forces During Normal Human Walking*. Ph.D. Thesis, Department of Kinesiology, Simon Fraser University, July 1982.

[26] SAVAGE, G.J., J.M. OFFICER, and G. MCDOUGALL. Computer graphics simulation of body movement language. *Proceedings 6th Man-Computer Communications Conference*, (1979), 209-217.

[27] SEALEY, D. Computers and Labanotation. *Proceedings of the Twelfth Biennial Conference, Columbus, Ohio*, International Council of Kinetography Laban, (Aug. 1981), 126-127.

[28] SINGH, B., J.C. BEATTY, K.S. BOOTH and R. RYMAN. A graphics editor for Benesh movement notation. Tech. Rep. CS-82-41, Computer Graphics Laboratory, Department of Computer Science, University of Waterloo, Waterloo, Ontario, Dec. 1982.

[29] SMOLIAR, S.W. and L. WEBER. Using the computer for a semantic representation of Labanotation. *Computing in the Humanities, Proceedings of the Third International Conference on Computing in the Humanities*, eds. Serge Lusignan and John S. North, The University of Waterloo Press, Waterloo, Canada, (Aug. 1977), 253-261.

[30] TILBROOK, D. A newspaper page layout system. M.Sc. Thesis, Department of Computer Science, University of Toronto, Toronto, Ontario, 1976.

[31] TOWNSEND, M.A., M. IZAK, and R.W. JACKSON. Total motion knee goniometry. *J. Biomechanics 10*, 3 (1977), 183-193.

PANEL

ADVANCES IN NEW DISPLAY TECHNOLOGY

CHAIR: Sol Sherr, Westland Electronics
PANELISTS: Ifay Chang, IBM Corporation
Thomas Maloney, PanelVision
Peter Pleshko, IBM Corporation
Elliot Schlam, Eradcom
Peter Seats, Thomas Electronics

CHAIRMAN'S INTRODUCTION:

New display technology has made some significant strides forward in the last few years. Although the CRT remains the most prevalent display device, accounting for over 85% of all installations, flat-panel matrix displays are becoming an increasingly significant factor in this area. The most important advances have been in thin film electroluminescence, gas discharge panels, and liquid crystal displays. In addition, light emitting diodes have shown improvements in light output and efficiency, and some recent work in electrophoretics give some promise that this technology will lead to viable display devices. Also, older technologies such as incandescent, vacuum flourescent, and electromechanical are still with us, and continue to be useful in many applications, the first where very high luminance is required, the second in such applications as automobile dashboards, and the third in various outdoor and large board installations. Finally, the CRT, not to be outdone by its rivals, has come up with improvements in performance, and with the flat tube versions in form factors that compete with those offered by the matrix displays. All of these advances will be discussed by the members of this panel.

The participants in this panel are all eminently qualified to deal with the various technologies. Dr. Peter Pleshko of IBM is in charge of their plasma panel activity, which has taken on added importance with the recent announcements that IBM is offering both the panel and terminals using the panel on an OEM basis. Dr. Ifay Chang, who is a staff member at the IBM Yorktown Laboratories, has been active in the display field for many years, and has contributed numerous articles and papers on advances in display technology to various publications. He is Vice President of the Society for Information Display, (SID) and has been Guest Editor for several issues of the Proceedings of the SID. Dr. Pleshko has also been a Guest Editor of the Proceedings, is a Regional Director of SID, and has been a co-Chairman of the Biennial Display Conference. He has contributed many articles to various publications, including the seminal one with P. M. Alt on "Scanning Limitations of Liquid Crystal Displays". Both he and Dr. Chang are Fellows of SID.

Thomas Maloney is President of Panelvision, a company that is in the forefront of developments in liquid crystal displays using thin-film transistors for switching matrices. Prior to his joining Panelvision, he was associated with the Burroughs Corporation for many years, and was intimately involved with the development and production of SelfScan and other display products of that company. He is a Fellow of SID, and has been actively involved in that society at both the local and national level, as well as being co-chairman of the Biennial Display Conference.

Peter Seats is President of Thomas Electronics, one of the few remaining manufacturers of CRT's left in the U.S. He has been active in CRT design and manufacture for many years and has lectured extensively on the subject at seminars and other forums. He is one of the outstanding authorities in the world on CRT's and is intimately familiar with all advances in that technology.

Dr. Elliot Schlam is Chief of the Display Devices Branch at Eradcom, a Fellow of SID, and has been Guest Editor of the SID Proceedings. In addition, he has contributed important articles on electroluminescent display devices to the IEEE Proceedings and other publications. He has also been an Editor of the Transactions on Electron Devices, and most recently has been closely associated with the latest advances in thin-film electroluminescence.

Finally, Sol, Sherr, the Chairman of this panel, is President of Westland Electronics, Ltd., a consulting firm that specializes in computer graphics and display technology. He is a charter Member and Fellow of SID, has written three books on display devices, equipment and systems as well as numerous articles, and is Editor of the SID Proceedings.

Sherr, Sol, "Video and Digital Electronic Displays - a User's Guide", John Wiley, N.Y. 1982.

Sherr, Sol, "Electronic Displays", John Wiley, N.Y. 1979.

Kmetz, A.R. and F. K. Willisen, Eds., "Non-Emissive Electrooptic Displays", Plenum Press, N. Y. 1976.

Kazan, B. Ed., "Advances in Image Pickup and Display", Academic Press, N.Y.

Cakir, A., et al, "Visual Display Terminals", John Wiley, N. Y., 1980.

Morell, A.M., "Color Television Picture Tubes", B. Kazan Ed., Advances in Image Pickup and Display, Supplement 1, Academic, N.Y., 1974.

Cornsweet, T.N., "Visual Perception", Academic Press, N.Y., 1970.

Biberman, L.M., Ed., "Perception of Displayed Information", Plenum Press, N.Y., 1973.

Biberman, L.M., and S. Nudelman, Eds., "Photoelectric Imaging Devices", Plenum Press, N.Y., 1971.

Proceedings of the Society for Information display, all issues.

SID Symposia Digests, all issues.

IEEE Transactions on Electron Devices, selected issues.

Biennial Display Conference Record, all issues.

PANELISTS' ABSTRACTS

Dr. I. F. Chang, IBM

Evolutionary advances have always been made in various display technologies including CRT and several flat panel displays. However, advancements are expected to be accelerated due to the tremendous demand from exploding computer applications. The main thrust in display technology development today is to achieve good quality display from existing mature technology with emphasis on high resolution, ergonomics, portability and color capability. Thus, electronic integration, power, volume and weight reductions and ergonomic design are being pursued along with effort in achieving high resolution and color capability at a reasonable cost. Advances made in these areas for CRT and several competing display technologies will be the main discussion.

Peter Pleshko, IBM

AC Plasma Technology is emerging as the leading flat panel technology for large screens. Its inherent memory and fast pixel update time allow the screen to be updated fast and the image to be displayed without flicker, regardless of size. Monochromatic resolutions of up to 125 lines per inch have been demonstrated, which, practically speaking, eliminate "staircasing". Colour has also been shown feasible using dc plasma as a source of either ultra-violet radiation or for electrons to excite phosphors.

Pleshko, P., "AC Plasma Flat Panel Displays", Computer Graphics World, Vol.5, No.7, July 1982, pp.47-48.

Criscimanga, T.N., and P. Pleshko, "The AC Plasma Display", Chapter 3 of Vol.40, Topics in Applied Physics, Springer-Velaq, Berlin, 1980, J.I. Pankove, Editor. (A comprehensive, detailed treatment of both the processing technology and electro-optic characterization and behavior of the ac plasma display.)

Elliot Schlam, Eradcom

Thin film electroluminescent display technology offers the advantages of high definition computer graphics and fast response gray scale, making it television compatible. These capabilities, coupled with very low power consumption, small package size and light weight, create exciting potential for this technology. A brief description of operating principles and a live demonstration will be presented.

Peter Seats, Thomas Electronics

A review of CRT developments will be presented with emphasis on monochrome and color displays for use with portable computers. The progress of flat CRT techniques will also be discussed. CRT's are also being developed for high resolution (4000 x 4000) color slide recording, and their special capabilities will be described. If time permits, CRT developments for improved graphics displays, based on three-color voltage penetration screens and color wheel techniques will also be reviewed.

Near Real-Time Shaded Display of Rigid Objects

Henry Fuchs
Gregory D. Abram
Eric D. Grant

University of North Carolina
at Chapel Hill

Abstract

Described is a visible surface algorithm and an implementation that generates shaded display of objects with hundreds of polygons rapidly enough for interactive use -- several images per second. The basic algorithm, introduced in [Fuchs, Kedem and Naylor, 1980], is designed to handle rigid objects and scenes by preprocessing the object data base to minimize visibility computation cost. The speed of the algorithm is further enhanced by its simplicity, which allows it to be implemented within the internal graphics processor of a general purpose raster system.

CR Categories and Subject Descriptors: I.3.3 [**Computer Graphics**]: Picture/Image Generation - Display Algorithms; Viewing Algorithms; I.3.7 [**Computer Graphics**]: Three-Dimensional Graphics and Realism - Visible Line/Surface Elimination

1. Introduction

The generation of realistic, colored images of 3D scenes has been a subject of much study for nearly twenty years. Many visible-surface algorithms have been developed for a variety of applications and machine environments (see, eg., [Sutherland, Sproull and Schumacker, 1974] or [Foley and Van Dam, 1982]). However, for real-time interactive applications, very expensive special purpose hardware is needed. Even if a much lower image generation rate, of perhaps one or two per second, is acceptable, we know of no (previously published) algorithm which can accomplish this on a general purpose graphics system.

It is not surprising that the generation of rendered color images is computationally expensive. Not only do the usual transformation, clipping and perspective steps need to be performed (the ones independent of the particular type of display or image generation algorithm) but visibility and rendering calculations must also be performed for every pixel in the image. General purpose algorithms may take several seconds (or much longer) to generate these images because they require either many calculations at each pixel or have significant overhead at a higher level in order to minimize the pixel calculations.

Our own long-term goals are to have real-time 3D images generated in our laboratory, for use in a wide range of interactive applications. Although we are designing special purpose equipment for this [Fuchs, Poulton, Paeth and Bell, 1982], in the immediate future the images have to be generated with our current general purpose graphics system. To generate these images, we are willing to sacrifice update rate, down to even one or two per second. Further, we have found that many of our applications (as well as those of others) have the significantly simplifying property that the world model changes far less frequently than the viewing position [Schumacker, Brand, Gilliland and Sharp, 1969]. Our aim, then, is to cut image generation time by taking advantage of this simplification. We do so by by pushing much of the visible-surface overhead into a preprocessing phase, thereby greatly reducing the overhead at image-generation time. By doing so, we hope to make the generation of realistic, colored images for our class of applications fast enough to be useful in an interactive mode.

2. BSP-Tree Basics

This section briefly reviews the Binary Space Partitioning algorithm (BSP-tree) as introduced in [Fuchs, Kedem and Naylor, 1980].

2.1. Motivation

[Schumacker, Brand, Gilliland and Sharp, 1969] introduced the notion that the image generation can be simplified in situations where the world model changes less frequently than the viewpoint or direction of view of the observer. Many applications have this property: a biochemist studying a complex molecule, a physician examining an anatomical structure for signs of disease, an architect (or her client) walking through a planned house or subdivision, an engineer designing a mechanical part. However, the Schumacker approach's dependence on manual intervention in the building of the internal data structure made it difficult (and time consuming) to generate new databases, and thus limited its general usefulness.

Although the current implementation of the BSP-tree algorithm is limited to static world models (since whenever the world model changes, the preprocessing data restructuring step must be invoked) we hope to ease this restriction in the future.

* This work was supported in part by NSF grant MCS79-02593 and in part by NIH grant NS/HL 16759-01.

In order for the algorithm to run fast, the entire BSP-tree should be in local memory. Although this is not an inherent restriction in the algorithm, the overall performance would be significantly degraded if parts of the tree had to be swapped from backing store. Our implementation (detailed below) uses 8 bit-planes of a 24-bit frame buffer to store a BSP-tree data structure with up to approximately 5000 polygons.

2.2. Description of the basic algorithm

The algorithm consists of two components:

- a one-time preprocessing module ("Make_tree") that converts the input polygon list into the BSP-tree structure, and
- an image-generation module ("Traverse") which traverses this structure and generates the polygons in a back-to-front order. (Strictly speaking, the order is not back-to-front, but is functionally equivalent to it.)

2.2.1. Building the BSP-tree

The fundamental notion is one of a separating plane: that is, given a plane in the 3D scene and a viewing point, no polygon on the viewpoint side of the plane can be obstructed by *any* polygon on the far side. Of course, if the viewpoint should move to the other side of the plane, the obstruction priorities are reversed [Schumacker, Brand, Gilliland and Sharp, 1969].

The algorithm uses this simple notion to construct a binary tree of polygons from the original polygon list (see Fig. 1). A polygon is selected from the list and placed at the root of the tree. Each remaining polygon in the list is tested to determine the side of the root polygon in which it lies and is then placed in the appropriate descendent list. Any polygon which crosses the plane of the root polygon is split along that plane and each part put in the appropriate list (see polygon 5 in fig. 2). This procedure is repeated recursively in the following way: from each of these descendent lists, a polygon is selected to be the root of that subtree, and the remaining polygons in this list are split by the plane of the root of the new subtree (see polygon 2 fig. 3).

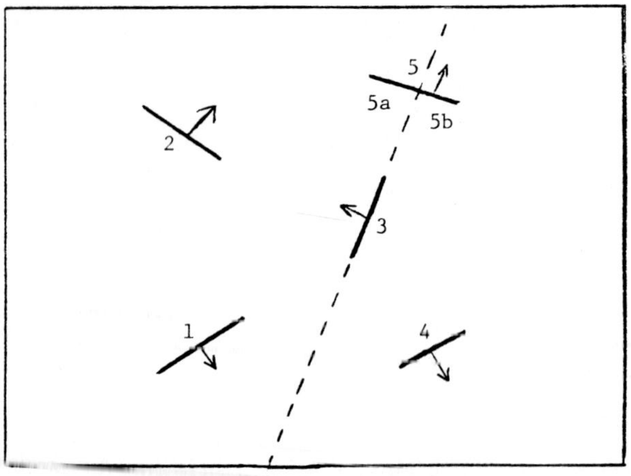

Figure 1: Top view of scene

```
PROC Make_tree (poly_list)
       returns (BSP_tree);

 if (poly_list is empty)
   return (NULL_TREE)

 else {
   root := select (poly_list);
   back_list := NULL;
   front_list := NULL;
   foreach (polygon in poly_list)
     if (polygon is not the root)
     {
       if (polygon in front of root)
          Addlist (polygon, front_list);
       else if (polygon is behind root)
          Addlist (polygon, back_list);
       else
          {
          Split_poly
            (polygon, root,
              front_part, back_part);
          Addlist (front_part, front_list);
          Addlist (back_part, back_list);
          }
     }

   return
     (Combine_tree (Make_tree (front_list),
             root,
             Make_tree (back_list)));
   }
END
```

The choice of the root polygon strongly influences the size of the tree. In the example illustrated in Figures 1-3, a better choice of the initial root would be a polygon *other* than 3, for example polygon 5. Figure 4 illustrates a BSP-tree with an initial choice of polygon 5. Note that the number of polygons in this tree is the same as the number in the input polygon list, while in the example of Figure 3, the tree is larger (6 polygons instead of the original 5). In reasonable-sized scene descriptions, the tree may grow substantially. In section 3.1 we discuss strategies to keep the tree small and give results. ([Naylor, 1981] develops bounds on the size of the BSP-tree and discusses many other related issues.)

2.2.2. Image generation

Once the BSP-tree has been constructed, generating an image from any point of view is simple. The tree is traversed in a special in-order fashion. At each node of the tree, we determine whether the eye is in front of or behind the node polygon. This result determines which subtree will be traversed first. The order is always the same: traverse the "other side" subtree, output and paint the node polygon, then traverse the "near side" subtree.

3. New Results

3.1. Tree size

When this algorithm was first introduced, there was concern that, in many cases, the tree would be significantly larger than the original polygon list. Indeed, there were fears that, given a list of N polygons, the BSP-tree may turn out to contain N^2 or more polygons! Although no tight bound has been yet been found, from our experience the trees derived from most world model databases are less than twice the size of the original

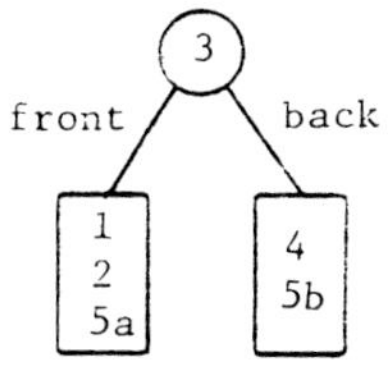

Figure 2:
After one level of recursion. Polygon 3 chosen as root.

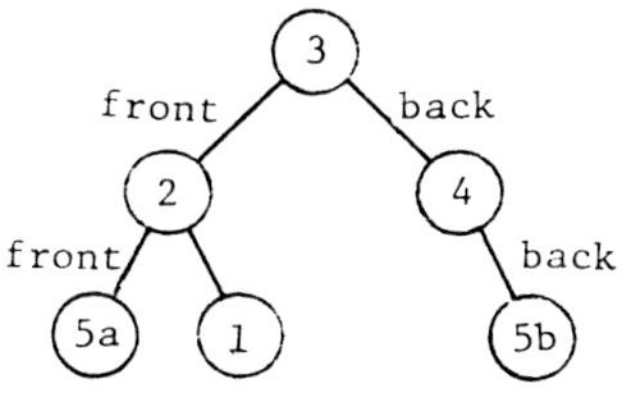

Figure 3:
A complete tree.

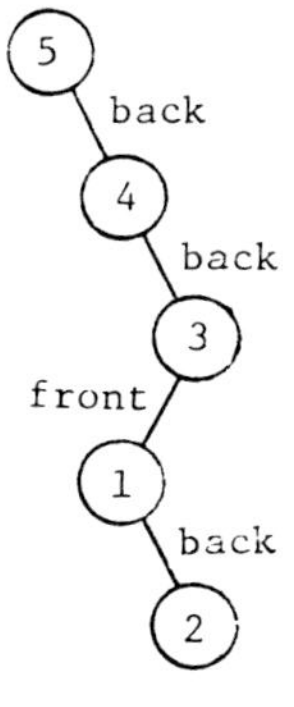

Figure 4:
An alternate tree with polygon 5 at root.

```
PROC Traverse_tree (tree)
/*
  Traverse an input BSP-tree and generate visible-
  surface image. The function Display handles
  transformation, clipping, perspective division,
  lighting and rendering. All but the rendering
  can be done elsewhere if deemed more efficient.
*/

  if (tree is empty) return
  else {
    if (eye is in front of tree.root.polygon) {
      Traverse_tree (tree.back_descendent);
      Display (tree.root.polygon);
      Traverse_tree (tree.front_descendent);
    }
    else {
      Traverse_tree (tree.front_descendent);
      Display (tree.root.polygon);
      /* if back-facing polygons are to
        be considered invisible,
       remove the previous line. */ ·
      Traverse_tree (tree.back_descendent);
    }
}
END
```

polygon list; the largest found was 2.33 times. It should be noted that the image generation time does not increase by nearly this factor of two since it is dominated by pixel-painting time and the total pixel area of a model does not change as the polygons within it are split. Table 1 indicates the input polygon list and BSP-tree sizes for the various objects illustrated in Figures 6 - 10.

We use the heuristic of selecting a root at each step whose plane cuts the fewest other polygons in the list. In our first experiments, we made the selection after examining every polygon in the list as a candidate for root. We have since found, however, that selecting just a few candidates at random from the list (originally suggested by Zvi Kedem) gives nearly as good results. These results are shown in table 1, which indicates that near-minimal trees can be found by examining only about 5 candidate polygons at each level. The most startling result in this table is the example of the "Old Well", (the longstanding symbol of UNC - Chapel Hill). In this highly non-convex model of 356 polygons, this heuristic produces a tree which is *exactly* the same size as the input polygon list.

3.2. Simple implementation in a graphics processor

Although it may be clear from section 2.2 that the algorithm can be simply expressed in a high level language with recursion, what may be less obvious is that the image generation component is simple enough to be implemented entirely within a programmable graphics processor. Our implementation runs on an Ikonas RDS3000 raster graphics system, which has a programmable AM2900-based internal processor. The run-time component consists of 1309 64-bit microcode words, of which only 218 words implement the BSP-tree part of the image generation algorithm, while the rest (1091 words) implement the transformations, clipping, perspective and polygon painting routines that are needed in any 3D image generation system.

Figure name (and number)	**Size of input polygon list**	**Output for varying number of candidates**			
		1	**3**	**5**	**15**
Carotid artery (Fig.s 6a,b)	915	2421	1843	1720	1633
Old Well (Fig. 8) (low detail)	356	1125	384	378	356
SkullCT (Fig. 9)	988	3341	2361	2255	2053
Old Well (high detail)	1000	2426	1304	1176	1032
Space Shuttle	418	2092	1201	1095	972
3cubes (Fig. 10)	216	402	279	263	240
Ribbon plot	368	1478	929	797	660
Klein bottle	450	1475	1118	1035	990
Robot arm	268	975	650	587	440

Figure name	**Treemaking time for 5 candidates (seconds)**
Carotid artery	116.3
Old Well (low detail)	45.0
Old Well (high detail)	448.2
SkullCT	225.8
Space Shuttle	144.2
3cubes	15.4
Ribbon plot	66.4
Klein bottle	272.7
Robot arm	52.7

Table 1: Tree making statistics. The implementation is written in C under UNIX on a VAX 11/780.

3.3. System speed

Table 2 indicates the time needed to generate the images illustrated in Figures 6 - 10. Because some of the speed of this implementation is due to a relatively fast graphics processor, it may be useful to analyze where the efficiencies are due to the algorithm itself (rather than the processor), to determine the utility of the algorithm independent of the processor on which it is implemented. To do this, we compare it with the most similar previous algorithm, the widely used Z (or depth) buffer algorithm (see, eg., [Foley and Van Dam, 1982]). The BSP-tree algorithm has a fixed per-polygon overhead of the tree traversal; this consists of a) the maintenance of a stack of tree return pointers for traversing the tree, and b) performing the inner product at each node to determine which way to turn next. The Z buffer, on the other hand, has none of this *polygon* overhead, but has the extra burden of calculating the Z, comparing, and possibly updating Z at *each pixel*. There is then a tradeoff between this per-polygon overhead and the per-pixel overhead, and it appears that until the average polygon size becomes very small (a few pixels) that the per-polygon overhead of the BSP-tree will be considerably less burdensome than the per-pixel

Figure name and number	Number of polygons in tree	Image generation rate (frames/second)
Carotid Artery (Fig. 6a,b)	1633	0.50 - 0.58
SkullCT (Fig. 9)	2255	0.40 - 0.48
3 atoms (Fig. 7)	1440	1.53 - 1.84
Old Well (Fig. 8) (low detail)	356	1.6 - 2.5
Space Shuttle	923	1.94 - 2.56
3 cubes (Fig. 10)	280	2.46 - 4.81
Old Well (high detail)	1005	1.05 - 1.58

Table 2: Image generation statistics.

course, is only valid for applications which can conform to the two limitations of the BSP-tree algorithm: a static world model and sufficient local memory to hold the BSP-tree.

4. Future Work

4.1. Removing static world model restrictions

In the present implementation of the algorithm, whenever the world model changes, the entire BSP-tree must be rebuilt. From table 1, one can see that it takes a minute or two for this process. We are working on various alternatives to allow relaxing this restriction. We are considering the situation in which there is only limited change in the world model. One such example might be when the *range of motion* of the moving objects is known; such as airplanes which always fly above the airport and land only on runways, or automobiles which remain on the road, or parts of molecules which only move in certain restricted ways, or doors which only swing on their hinges. With this knowledge, we might be able to construct a series of convex regions, which always contain the moving object. The BSP-tree of the world model could be constructed such that no root polygons cuts this region. This causes all the polygons of the moving object to end up in their own subtree, which may then be transformed independently from the rest of the scene by using a nested transformation matrix at the root of this object's subtree (see Figure 5).

4.2. Anti-Aliasing

We are currently experimenting with adding anti-aliasing to the image generation using a sub-pixel mask similar to the latest Evans and Sutherland digital scene generator, the CT-5 [Schumacker, 1980]. This technique involves maintaining a binary mask of, say, 4x4 subpixels at each pixel. The polygons are painted front-to-back, and are sampled at the subpixel resolution, with the binary mask indicating the subpixel areas which have already been covered by a polygon. We note that the BSP-tree can generate a front-to-back (equivalent) order of polygons simply by reversing the order of the traversal (i.e., instead of far side; node polygon, near side, the order becomes near side, node polygon, far side). The contributions of the current polygon to a particular pixel's color are determined by the number of subpixels within that pixel of which this polygon is visible. This contribution is accumulated in the RGB pixel value in the image frame buffer.

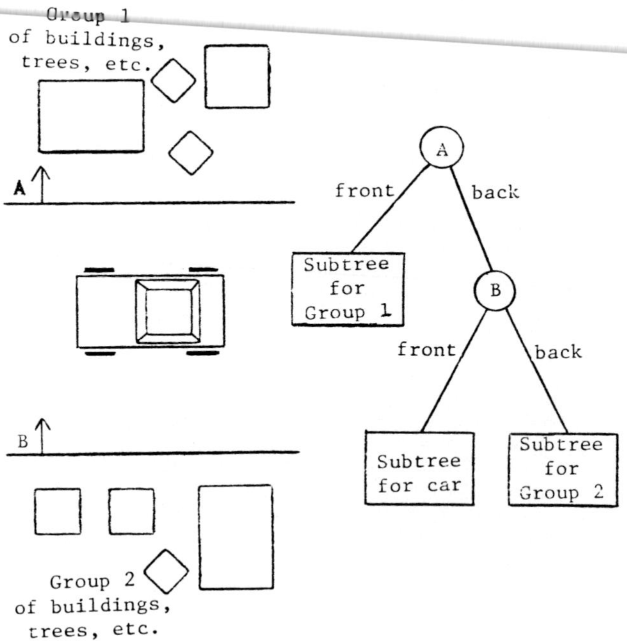

Figures 5a and 5b: non-static scene handling

5. Summary and Conclusions

We have shown that the BSP-tree visible-surface algorithm generates images rapidly enough to be useful in interactive applications and that it can be easily implemented in a programmable graphics processor. Further, we have shown that in all cases encountered so far, that the tree size stays within reasonable bounds. We are currently using the system to study reconstructed surfaces of human arteries and density distributions of organic molecules. Our experience indicates that it is a viable (and faster) alternative to the commonly used Z buffer in many situations.

Finally, we note that this algorithm may be increasingly attractive as new raster graphics hardware systems become available. At least one new commercially available system (Megatek 7200 [Foley and Van Dam, 1982]) and several experimental designs ([Clark and Hannah, 1980] and [Fuchs, Poulton, Paeth and Bell, 1982]) concentrate on fast rendering of lines and polygons. It appears that these systems will most easily and directly generate realistic images of 3D scenes from a back-to-front ordered list of polygons. Since many can be expected to have transformation and clipping hardware, all that remains to be done in software is to generate the ordered list of polygons, something which can be achieved quite handily by the BSP-tree algorithm.

Acknowledgements

We would like to thank the many people at UNC-CH and elsewhere who have assisted us with this research: Gregg Podnar and Yehuda Kalay (CMU), Mike Connally (Yale), James R. Smith (NASA-Johnson Space Center), Richard A. Weinberg (Cray Research), and Sandy Bloomberg and Frank Moore (UNC) all for kindly allowing us the use of their graphic databases, Gary Bishop (UNC) for programming tools, and Bo Strain and Mike Pique (UNC) for photographic assistance.

References

Clark, J.H. and Hannah, M.R. Distributed Processing in a High-Performance Smart Image Memory", LAMBDA, 4th Quarter (1980), pp. 40-50.

Foley, J.D. and Van Dam, A. *Fundamentals of Interactive Computer Graphics*, Addison Wesley, Reading, Mass. (1982).

Fuchs, H., Kedem, Z.M., and Naylor, B.F. On Visible Surface Generation by A Priori Tree Structures, Computer Graphics (Proc. SIGGRAPH '80), Vol. 14, No. 3, (July, 1980), pp. 124-133.

Fuchs, H., Poulton, J., Paeth, A., Bell A. Developing Pixel-Planes, A Smart Memory-Based Raster Graphics System, Proceedings, Conference on Advanced Research in VLSI, Cambridge, Mass. January 25-27, 1982.

Naylor, B.F. "*A Priori* Based Techniques for Determining Visibility Priority for 3-D Scenes", Doctoral Dissertation, University of Texas at Dallas (1981).

Newman, W.M. and Sproull, R.F. *Principles of Interactive Computer Graphics* (2nd. ed.), McGraw-Hill, New York, (1979).

Schachter B.J. Computer Image Generation for Flight Simulation, IEEE Computer Graphics and Applications, Vol. 1, No. 4, (October, 1981).

Schumacker, R.A. "A New Visual System Architecture, Proc. Second Interservice/Industry Training Equipment Conf., Salt Lake City, Utah, (Nov. 1980), pp. 94-101.

Schumacker, R.A., Brand, B., Gilliland, M., and Sharp, W. "Study for Applying Computer Generated Images to Visual Simulation", Tech. Report No. AEHRL-TR-69-14, (AD 700375), US Air Force Human Resources Lab (1969).

Sutherland, I.E., Sproull, R.F. and R.A. Schumacker, R.A. A Characterization of Ten Hidden-Surface Algorithms", Computing Surveys, Vol. 6, No. 1 (1974).

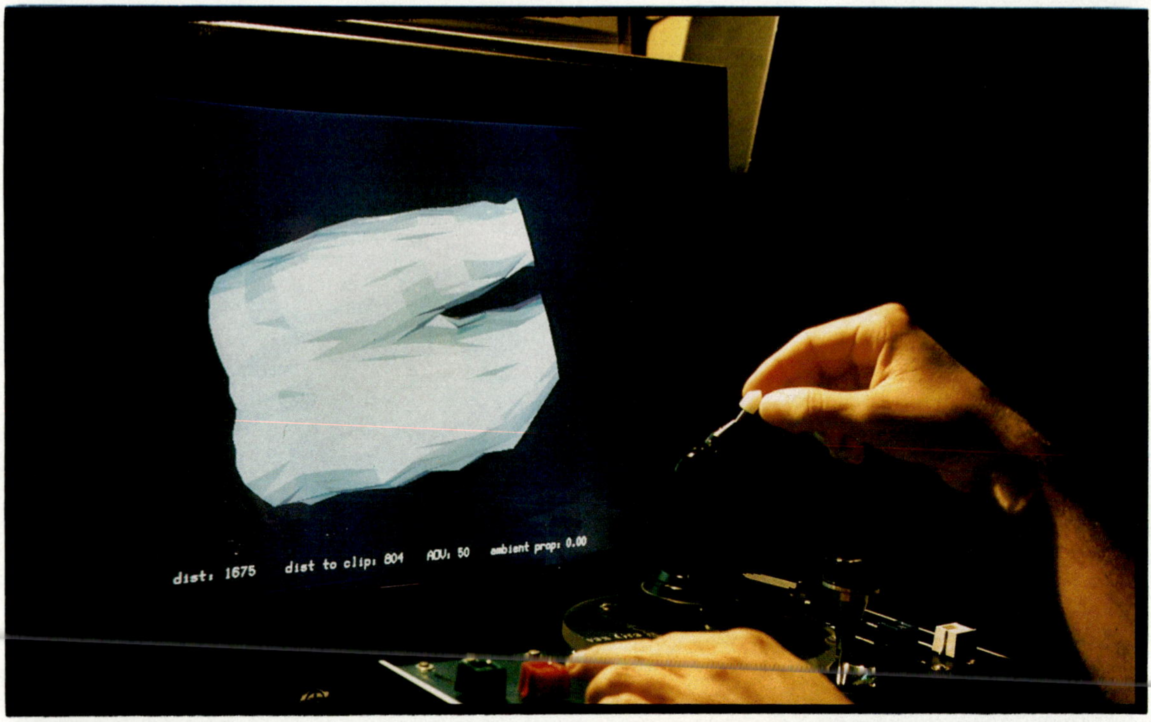

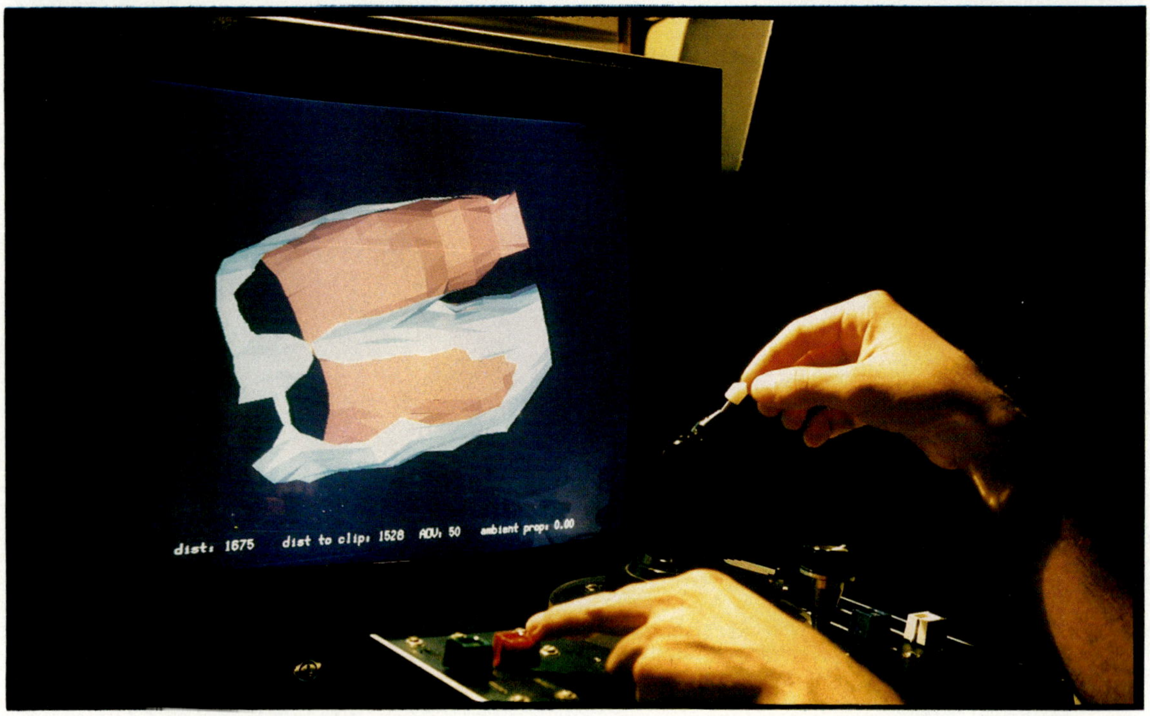

Figures 6a,b:
Two images of a carotid artery reconstructed from CT data. A 1.7 second update time is achieved from a BSP-tree of 1633 polygons. The three-dimensional "toothpick", used for rotation, and the slide-pot box, for controlling zoom, clipping, angle-of-view and lighting effects are visible. Note the use of the clipping plane for cross-sectioning.

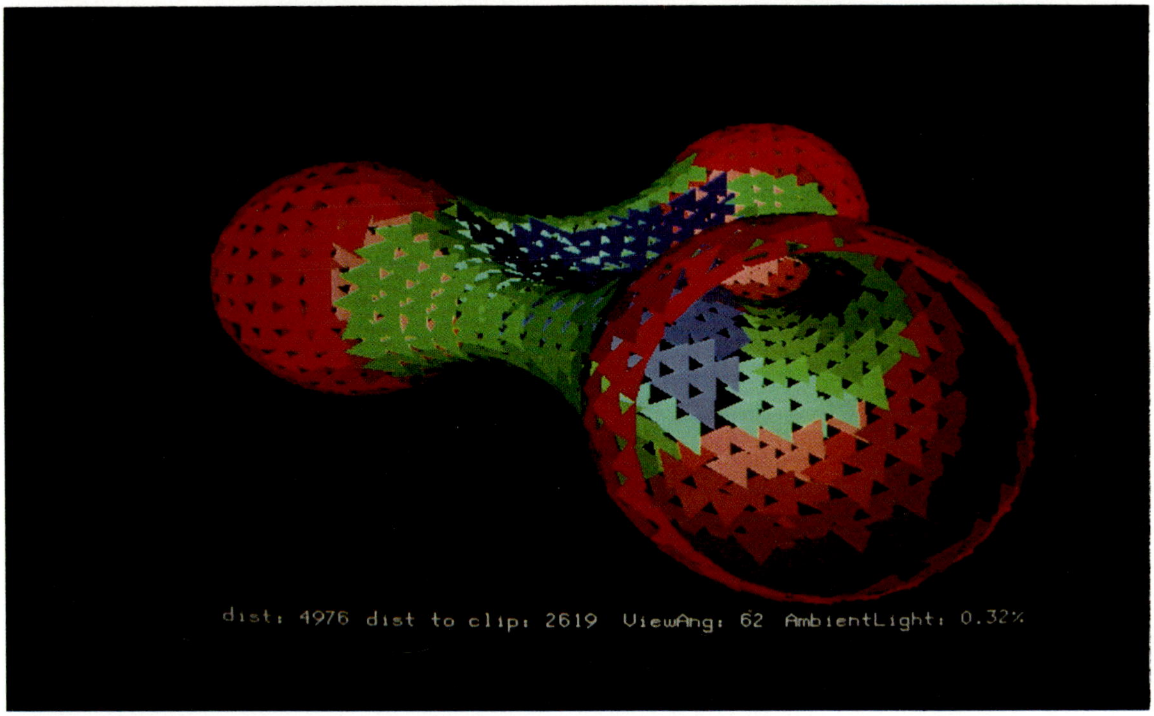

Figure 7:
Three simulated atoms, as created by Michael Connally of Yale. The BSP-tree has 1440 polygons, and we generate about 1.5-2 frames per second. The front of the object has been cut away by the interactive clipping plane.

Figure 8:
The small version of the Old Well. A BSP-tree of 356 polygons was created from 356 input polygons. We generate more than 2 images a second in most cases.

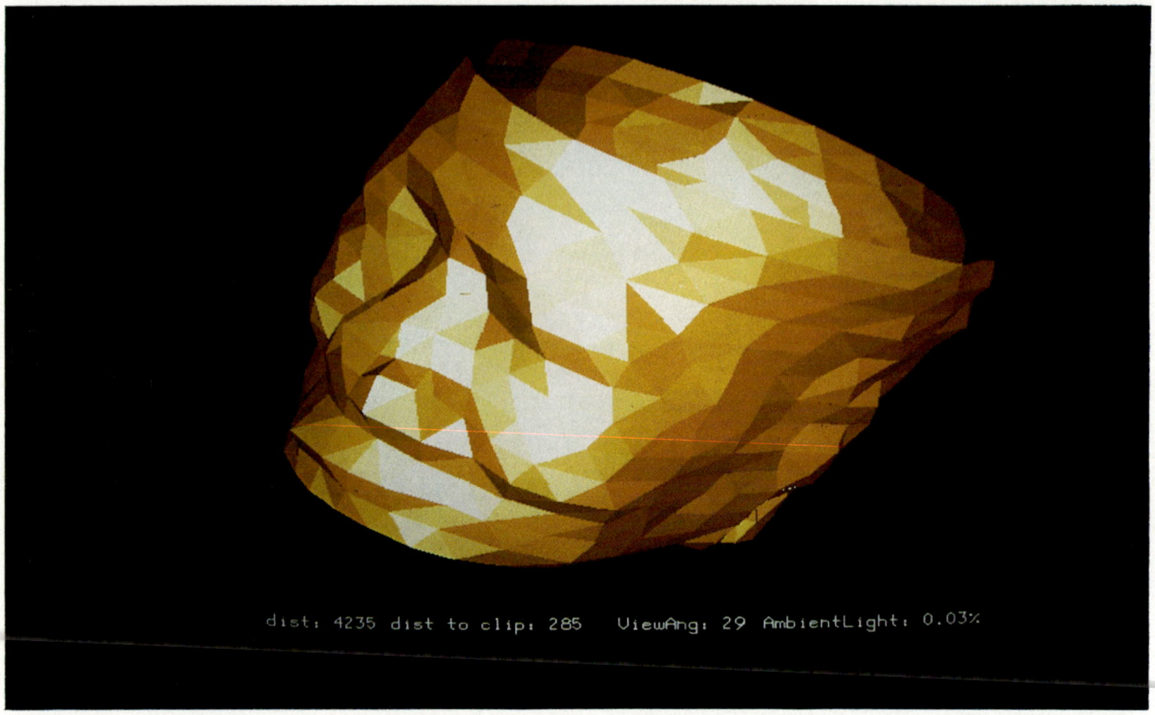

Figure 9:
A skull, reconstructed from CT scans. A single 8-bit intensity value is computed, rather than separate red, green and blue intensities as in the other images. This is then displayed using a heated object spectrum color map.

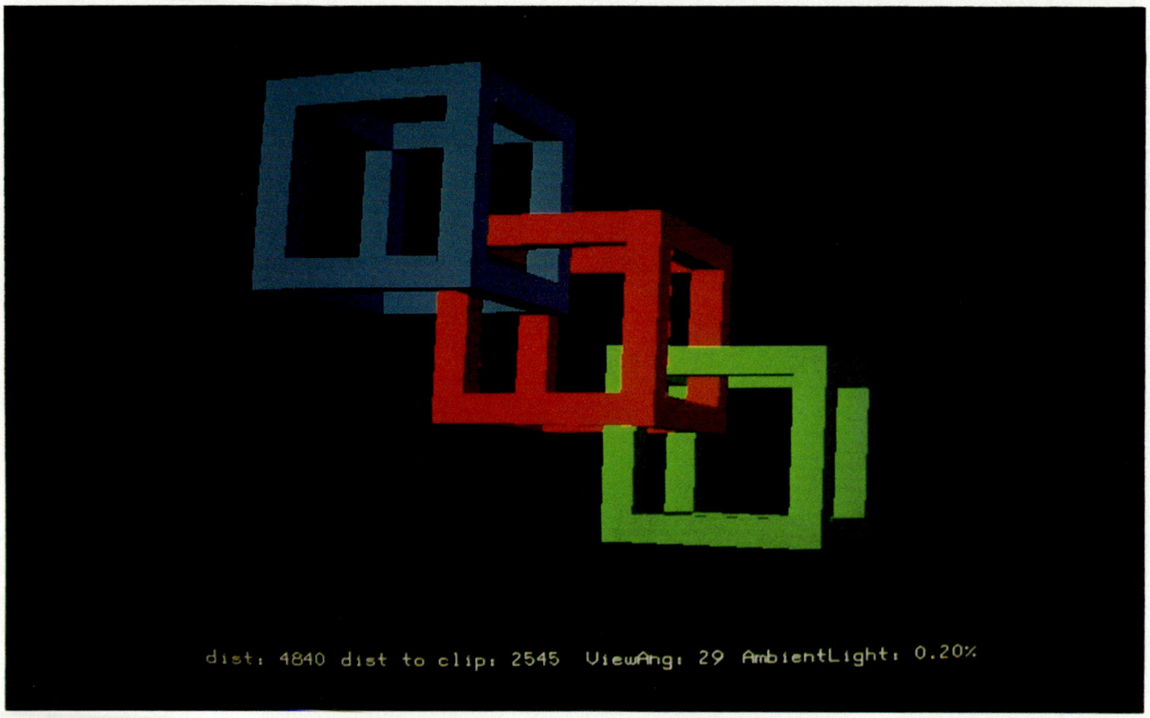

Figure 10:
3 interlocking cubes. The BSP-tree has 280 polygons. For this very simple object with low screen coverage we can generate up to 5 images per second.

A SCAN-LINE HIDDEN SURFACE REMOVAL PROCEDURE FOR CONSTRUCTIVE SOLID GEOMETRY

Peter R. Atherton

General Electric Company
Corporate Research and Development
Schenectady, New York 12345

Abstract

This paper presents a new methodology for resolving visible surface images of solid models derived from Boolean combinations of volumetric building blocks. The algorithm introduced here is an extension of well-established scan-line hidden surface removal procedures, and it integrates knowledge of a Boolean construction tree in the surface resolution process. Several hidden surface coherence properties are discussed in terms of their possible exploitation in the intricate solid model visualization process. While many of the earlier coherence techniques depend on a polygon environment in which surfaces and volumes do not intersect, the Boolean process can not afford that luxury because it is inherently required to handle intersecting volumes and surfaces. Initial tests indicate that substantial performance improvements over previous methods can be achieved with the algorithm described in this paper, and that these improvements increase as model complexity increases.

An underlying philosophy of a dual solid modeling system is proposed in this paper. It suggests that two solid modelers are necessary to successfully satisfy both analytical precision requirements and user interface visualization requirements. The visual solid modeling task addressed in this paper provides greatly improved response capabilities, as compared to other systems, by striving to optimize the constructive solid model (CSG) solid model computations specifically for display purposes.

CR Categories: I3.7 [Computer Graphics]: Three-Dimensional Graphics and Realism - Visible Line/Surface algorithm; **I3.5** [Computer Graphics]: Computational Geometry and Object Modeling — Curve, surface, solid and object representations; **I3.3** [Computer Graphics]: Picture/Image Generation — Display algorithms; **J.6** [Computer Applications]: Computer-aided Engineering — Computer-aided design (CAD), Computer-aided manufacture (CAM)

Key Words and Phrases: computer graphics, hidden-surface removal, hidden line removal, solid modeling, constructive solid geometry, computer-aided design

1. INTRODUCTION

In his book entitled *Emulation and Invention* [7], Brooke Hindle says of Samuel Morse

> "His great strength remained a quality of mind that permitted him to manipulate mental images of three-dimensional telegraph components as well as complete telegraphic systems, altering them at will and projecting various possibilities for change and development."

Few people possess the natural capability to mentally envision three-dimensional mechanical systems, particularly from someone else's description. Therefore, there is a very great opportunity for the application of computer graphics in solid modeling to assist the design, analysis, and manufacturing engineers with their spatial understanding of model structures. In concept, solid models can offer the designer more physically understandable building components, and computer graphics will afford him visual comprehension of the physical structures and the spatial relationships between those building blocks. In contrast to the views of some researchers in the solid modeling field [10, page 20], I feel that interactive graphics technology has a long way to go before it can offer all CAD/CAM users a tool that will provide three-dimensional visual insight equaling the natural abilities of someone like Samuel Morse.

The application of volumetric Boolean set operations to solid objects in order to represent more complex solid objects is commonly referred to as constructive solid geometry (CSG). The fundamental building blocks used in CSG are solid objects called primitives. Two primitives (for instance, A and B) can be combined to form a new solid object by applying one of the volumetric Boolean set operations defined as follows:

Union ($A \cup B$):	that volume of space found in either A or B
Intersection ($A \cap B$):	that volume of space found in both A and B
Difference (A-B):	that volume of space found in A but not found in B

The systematic application of the Boolean set operations is usually controlled by a binary tree data structure commonly referred to as a CSG tree (Figure 1). Each internal node of a CSG tree defines the Boolean set operation to be applied to

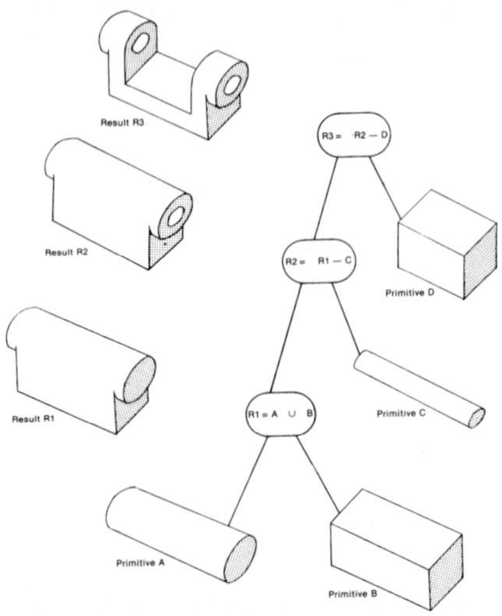

Figure 1. A CSG tree controls the systematic application of Boolean set operations

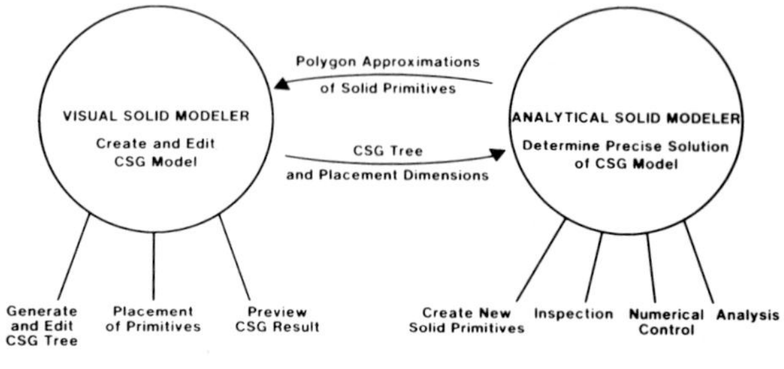

Figure 2. The Dual Solid Modeling Scenario

its two children. The leaves of the CSG tree contain information to indicate what solid primitives are to be used for Boolean processing. A CSG model includes both the CSG tree and the associated solid primitives. A new primitive can be created by geometrically evaluating the CSG model in order to produce a new solid object definition. A library of primitives can be built up from both original solid objects defined by some means other than CSG and the solid objects resulting from previous CSG evaluations.

For CAD/CAM applications, there are essentially two basic uses of a CSG model. In most manufacturing processes, a very precise evaluation of the CSG model is required. There is little concern for how much computing time is needed to derive this accurate definition as long as it is accomplished eventually. For example, numerical control engineers will normally refer to accuracy tolerances in terms of thousandths of an inch and run-times in terms of minutes or hours. On the other hand, most interactive visualization tasks such as design or robot programming need only enough accuracy and information about the CSG model to make a meaningful image of it. However, user interaction does require that images be generated rapidly in order to maximize user productivity. In the past, solid modelers have been developed with the intention of solving both the accuracy and interactive visualization tasks with essentially the same modeler. It is proposed here that these tasks can be better solved by deviating from the single modeler trend and analyzing each of these two tasks separately (Figure 2). Operating in the dual modeler scenario, a designer would create and edit a CSG model by interacting with the visual modeler at a design station. The analytical modeler would be invoked on a demand basis when exact model solutions are required for high-tolerance applications. The motivation behind this paper is to solve the visualization task efficiently, in order to provide informative shaded surface imagery of CSG models rapidly enough for effective interactive use.

As described in past literature there are two general approaches used to generate shaded surface images from CSG models:

1. Geometrically evaluate the CSG model in order to define the boundary surface model resulting from the application of volumetric Boolean processes to previously defined solid primitives. Subsequently, apply a hidden surface removal program to the resulting solid object boundary definition [1,4,5,8,13,14,17]. One class of hidden surface removal procedures that could be applied to boundary surface models is described in Section 3 of this paper.

2. Mathematically fire a ray through each image picture element into an environment composed of transformed primitives. For each ray, analyze the one-dimensional Boolean problem enough to resolve the first visible point along the ray [2,3,6,9,10,12,16,19]. The application of ray-firing is closely examined in Section 2.

Given that the "ultimate" user interface goal is real-time human interaction with the solid model, execution speed of the image generation task is a primary concern. In light of that goal, both approaches described above involve significant unnecessary computation. The first approach requires that a geometric solution to the CSG model be found before a display calculation can be made. As such, a great deal of the computation is wasted in resolving CSG results that the hidden surface removal process will hide. Also, calculation of the three-dimensional Boolean tasks (like surface intersections and data base changes) tends to be much more complex and time consuming than the subsequent hidden surface removal processing even for polygon based models or model approximations. Several commercial solid modelers do support polyhedral model approximations, but they utilize this time consuming two-step approach in order to generate CSG images. The ray-firing approach does simplify the Boolean calculations by operating in a one-dimensional space instead of three. It is significant to note that several CSG modelers that can produce a resultant boundary surface model from a CSG model use the ray-firing technique to produce shaded surface images [2,3]. Nonetheless, ray-firing does tend to be computationally expensive and time consuming in that distinct solutions are derived for every picture element. In other words, the general ray-firing approach is inefficient because it does not take advantage of coherence properties [12].

Based upon past analyses, shaded image generation of higher order surfaces can be made significantly faster by using polygonal approximation techniques [5]. In most engineering, manufacturing, inspection, and assembly applications, polygonal approximation of curved surfaces is either unacceptable in terms of accuracy or impractical in terms of the number of polygons necessary for reasonable tolerance limits. For a user display interface, however, the accuracy requirements are not nearly as rigorous. In addition, polygonal approximation computations of solid primitive surfaces can be performed as a preprocessing step to CSG interaction and need not be performed during the actual interaction process. Thus, interactive speed requirements seem to dictate that polygonal approximations be used for interactive image generation until superior methods are developed.

When the entire geometric model has been transformed into a polygonal form, a large body of existing hidden surface removal technology can be made available. To date, there is no publication known to the author that applies scan-line hidden surface removal techniques to the problem of generating shaded images directly from CSG models. The remainder of this paper will focus on the application of polygon-based scan-line techniques for visible surface processing of models composed of Boolean combinations of polygonal primitives. The next two sections provide a framework for the CSG scan-line hidden surface procedure by describing the fundamental ray-firing and scan-line hidden surface removal algorithms that will be applied. Following sections describe a specific CSG scan-line hidden surface procedure in detail, and how coherence techniques [14] can be applied to this more complex procedure. The paper concludes with a description of a CSG scan-line hidden surface implementation and a comparison to a corresponding ray-firing algorithm in terms of execution speed.

2. SOLVING ONE-DIMENSIONAL BOOLEAN TASKS USING RAY-FIRING

Ray-firing algorithms like those described by Roth [12] and Goldstein and Malin [6] apply a single procedure to every point on the viewing screen in order to resolve surface visibility while solving the required Boolean operations. This procedure determines the Boolean solution for a one-dimensional sample of the three-dimensional CSG model. A formalized classification of one-dimensional Boolean solutions in a polygon based environment has been proposed by Tilove [15]. The major significance of the ray-firing technique is that it does not require that a complete geometrical boundary surface solution of the CSG model be determined *a priori*. An iterative procedure for resolving the visible surface points from a CSG model using ray-firing might be structured as follows:

```
    For each scan-line
        For each pixel in the scan-line
1.          For each surface
                Determine surface intersections with the
                    visual ray
2.          Sort surface intersections by Z-depth
3.          Resolve the one-dimensional Boolean operations
                along the visual ray using the CSG tree
4.          Determine the first visible point along the
                ray from the Boolean solution
            Display point
```

Figure 3 illustrates the simplicity of solving Boolean operations in one dimension of the sampled space for two primitives. In addition to simplicity, this technique offers an attractive advantage for display — namely, the fact that the Boolean operations need only be solved as far as the first visible point. Unfortunately, that neat one-dimensional Boolean solution procedure must be precluded by expensive surface intersection and Z-sort computations. Furthermore, all four steps must be executed for every point on the screen. Roth does describe a culling procedure to somewhat reduce the number of surfaces to be considered for each picture element. The problem has changed little, however, because the surface intersection, Z-sort, Boolean, and visibility computations are still executed in the inner-most program loop for every pixel. Roth also describes a sampling/searching technique which will locate and display silhouette and surface intersection edges without having to analyze each display picture element. Unfortunately, that approach is not generalized for shaded surface display in that the higher level of sparseness of sampling that leads to speed improvement also leads to a higher potential for informational errors in the resulting image.

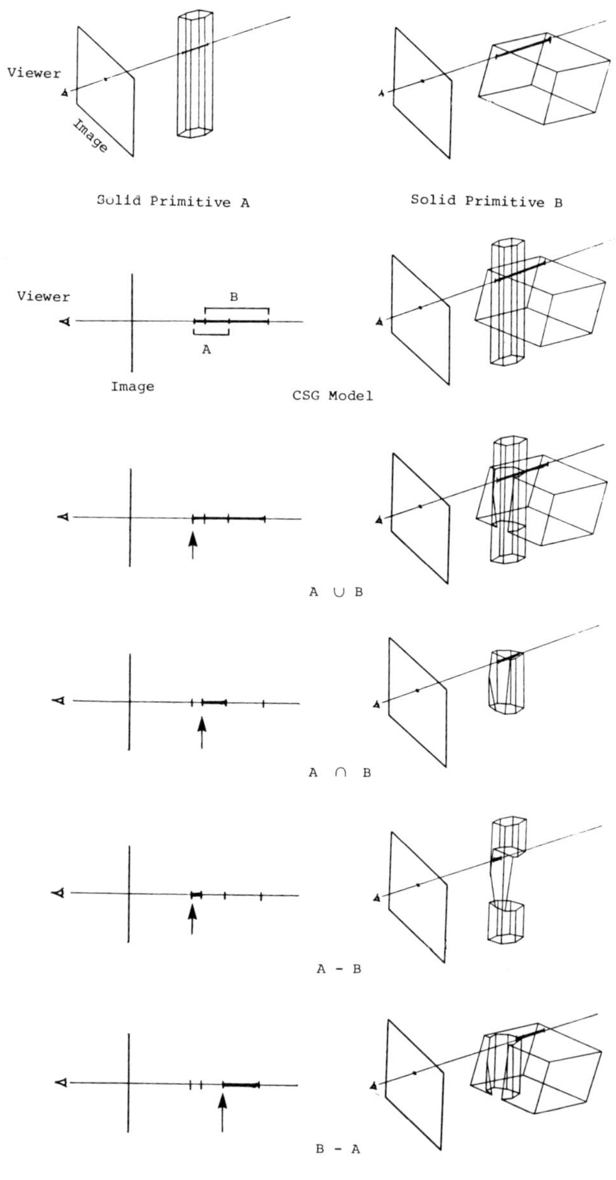

Figure 3. Ray-firing technique used to solve the one-dimensional Boolean problems for two solid primitives

3. OVERVIEW OF POLYGON SCAN-LINE HIDDEN SURFACE ALGORITHMS

A classification scheme for hidden surface removal algorithms was published in 1974 by Sutherland, Sproull and Schumacher [14]. Within this "taxonomy" of algorithms, Sutherland et al. classified three algorithms that sampled points in image space and resolved the visible surfaces based on depth priority. The three authors referenced by Sutherland et al. in this classification were Romney [11], Bouknight [1], and Watkins [17]. All three methods followed a similar sequence of operations that reflect an execution ordering of television-type raster devices. The four steps are described as follows:

1. Polygon edges are sorted by Y-vertex values typically using a bucket sort. For each scan-line, the Y-sorted list is utilized to determine which polygons should be considered for each scan-line, and where the associated scan-plane intersects each of those polygons. Sutherland et al. refer to the intersection of a scan-plane and a polygon as a segment.
2. For each scan-line that crosses one or more polygon surfaces in image space, an X-sorted list of related segments is determined in order to establish a sequential set of spans. A span is typically a continuous portion of a scan-line from which the visibility of a single segment can be resolved. Romney utilized a bucket sort to determine the X-ordering, whereas Bouknight and Watkins applied a bubble sort to update an X-sorted list between scan-lines, in order to capitalize on scan-line coherence properties.
3. In order to restrict further analysis to within the bounds of a span, all segments that enter the span are clipped to the span limits.
4. In most cases, visibility is then determined simply by searching for the segment portion that is closest to the viewer. Some additional complexity is encountered in the event that two visible segment portions cross within a span [1].

A typical scan-line program that utilizes the Y-X-Z order of sorting described above would have an iterative structure like the following:

```
1. For each polygon edge
      Bucket sort by the Y-vertex values
   For each scan-line
      For each active polygon
         Determine segment (intersection of
            scan-plane and polygon)
      Sort segments by X-vertex values
2.    Determine span boundaries
         For each span
3.          Clip active segments to span boundaries
4.          Resolve segment visibility within span by
               searching for the closest segment in Z
            Display segment
```

For each of the algorithms they studied, Sutherland et al. pointed out that the authors made crucial decisions in the selection of their sorting procedures and corresponding application of coherence properties. It is the judicious utilization of coherence that reduces the costly sorting computational requirements for these visible surface programs. The application of coherence becomes significantly more complex when a visible surface algorithm is extended to solve Boolean operations between solid primitives. Before the applications of coherence are dealt with in detail, it is appropriate to first describe a general scan-line hidden surface removal procedure for constructive solid geometry.

4. A GENERAL CSG SCAN-LINE HIDDEN SURFACE REMOVAL PROCEDURE

The hidden surface removal algorithm for CSG models that is to be presented utilizes a framework based on essentially the same four steps outlined by Sutherland et al. [14] for scan-line algorithms as described in the preceding section. The general CSG scan-line algorithm is achieved by integrating the efficient one-dimensional Boolean solution technique of the ray-firing approach into step (4) of the scan-line iterative structure. That is, for each span boundary, the one-dimensional Boolean problem is solved to the first visible point. Where the same surface is visible throughout a span, shading can be interpolated in between. The functional steps for the general CSG hidden surface removal procedure are structured as follows:

```
1. For each polygon edge
      Bucket sort by the Y-vertex values
   For each scan-line
      For each active polygon
         Determine segment (intersection of scan-plane
            and polygon)
      Sort segments by X-vertex values
2.    Determine span boundaries
         For each span
3.          Clip active segments to span boundaries
4.          Solve one-dimensional boolean operations
               to the first visible point as
               specified in the CSG tree
            If same Z-order of segments at boundaries
            Then
               Display segment
            Else
               Subdivide span at segment intersections
               and repeat steps (3) and (4) for each
               new span
```

Some complexity may be added where surface intersections take place between span boundaries. Note, however, that the image generation process need not have knowledge of those surface intersections that do not affect the resulting image.

A change in surface visibility within a span is detected by a difference in the order of segments encountered between the viewer and the first visible point at each span boundary. This order is determined as part of the one-dimensional Boolean calculation for both left and right sides of the span boundary. When needed, segment intersection decisions are made using this depth order with the understanding that all segments that fall within a span will completely traverse that span. After the intersection between two selected segments is determined, the X-component of the intersection is used to create another span boundary which subdivides the span under consideration. The two new spans formed by this subdivision are processed separately in a recursive manner. It is significant to recognize that in most practical cases, polygonal intersections are relatively rare occurrences. This characteristic is a coherence property which can be exploited to improve program efficiency and will be discussed further in the next section of this paper.

A simple example of this general scan-line procedure for generating visible surface imagery of a CSG model containing two primitives is illustrated in Figure 4. The two solid primitives found within the CSG model are a six-sided box (primitive A) and a four-sided pyramid (primitive B). A scan-plane that intersects each primitive and a volume of space common to both is illustrated in Figure 4-A. The seven end points of the resulting segments are sorted by their X-components and subsequently used to define six spans (Figure 4-B). Up to this point, the operations described are common to the scan-line hidden surface removal algorithms described earlier.

The ray-firing technique is applied to each span border in order to evaluate the one-dimensional Boolean problem up to the first visible point. Taken in Z-depth order, each segment intersection along the ray is examined to see if a CSG tree solution exists. If so, the first visible segment point is saved and all surface intersections encountered up to that point are maintained in a sorted list. The Boolean process must be solved on both the left and right sides of the span boundaries because a change in segment geometry may occur there. However, not all of the span boundaries are necessary to complete the processing for a scan-line because some do not represent any changes in surface visibility. Span boundaries that can be deleted from further consideration in the processing of a scan-line without affecting the resulting image exhibit one of the two following properties:

1. Boolean processing on each side of the span boundary resolves no visible points (as a result of subtraction or intersection operations).
2. Boolean processing resolves visible points from the same segment on both sides of the span boundary.

Figures 4-C through 4-F illustrate the four potential Boolean combinations of the two primitives. Pertinent span boundaries are labeled by the order of primitive surface intersections a visual ray would encounter on each side of the span boundary until the first visible point is found. Span boundaries that exhibit one of the two properties described above have been removed. Span boundaries that would be inserted as a result of segment intersections are included. Also illustrated are the outlines of the resulting images of each Boolean operation with the scan-plane intersections highlighted. Imagery can be produced for each scan-line in two forms. A hidden-line removed image can be produced on a sampled pixel basis by rendering each scan-line point that represents a visible segment endpoint or visible segment intersection. These points are produced as a result of the span boundary generation and deletion processes already described. If color and intensity information is maintained at each of the final span boundaries, shading values can be interpolated between in order to produce a faceted or smoothly shaded image. Examples of imagery produced in this manner can be found in Section 6 of this paper.

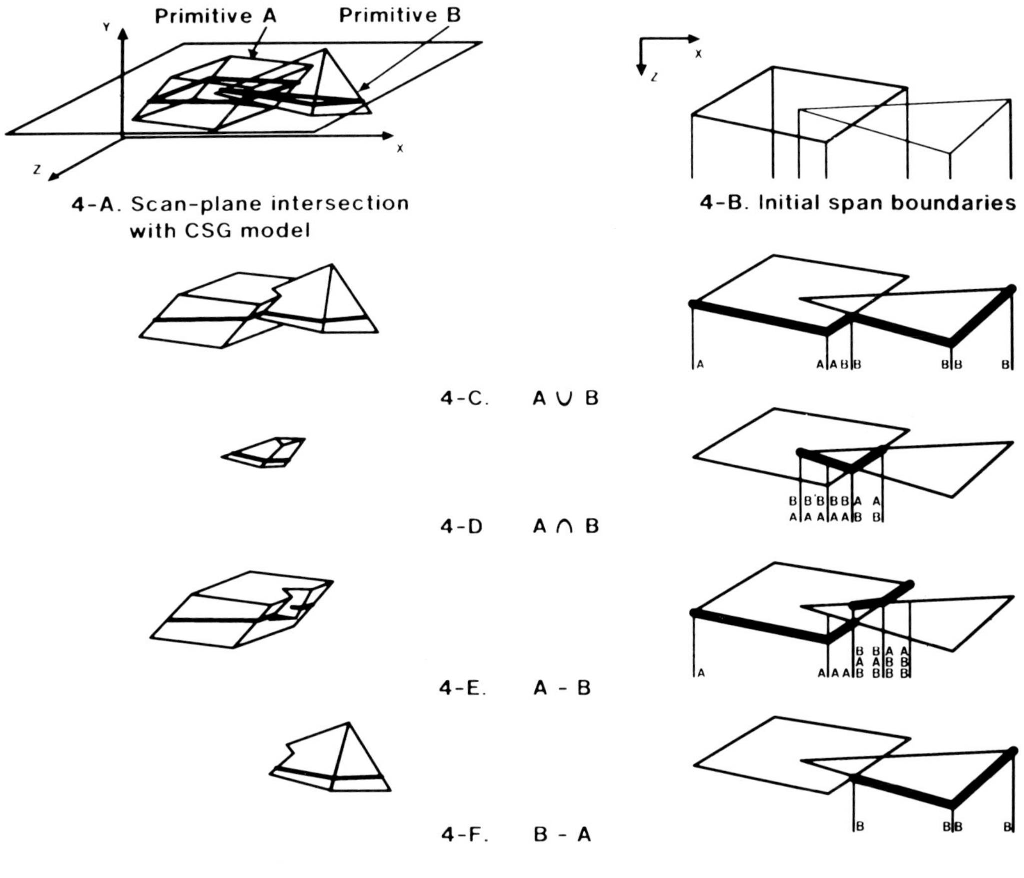

Figure 4. The CSG scan-line hidden surface removal process for two solid primitives

5. APPLICATION OF COHERENCE TECHNIQUES

Several coherence techniques for scan-line hidden surface removal algorithms have been previously published. Although the terminology may vary, the goal common to all is to reduce computation, particularly within inner program loops. The major categories of coherence techniques are listed below. Each of these will be examined for applicability to the CSG scan-line visible surface procedure.

A. *Span Coherence*: Only one surface is usually visible between initial span boundaries. The exception is necessary for intersecting surfaces.

B. *Visible Segment Coherence*: Where a segment is known to be visible across span boundaries, those boundaries need not be considered further [17].

C. *Scan-line Coherence*: There are relatively few changes between neighboring scan-lines.

   C.1 Intersections of adjacent scan-planes with a polygon model produce nearly the same set of segments [1,4,11,14,17].

   C.2 Sorted ordering of segments along the X-axis tends to be very similar for neighboring scan-lines [1,4,13,17].

   C.3 Sorted ordering of segments along the Z-axis tends to be very similar for neighboring scan-lines [4].

   C.4 Segment intersections have nearly the same X- and Z-components for neighboring scan-lines.

D. *Face Coherence*: The occurrence of intersecting surfaces is assumed to be relatively rare [4].

E. *Object Coherence*: Within its image space boundaries, the visibility status of a solid primitive changes little.

   E.1 Polygon connectivity can be applied to scan-line segments where no intersections exist [4,13].

   E.2 Where it is known that specific objects do not visibly intersect, silhouette boundaries of those objects can be used to determine visibility.

F. *Boolean Combination Coherence*: Simplifications can be devised from particular sequences of Boolean operations.

G. *Frame-to-frame coherence*: Image composition changes little between frames that are adjacent in time [8].

The coherence properties described in items (A) through (C) are specific to scan-line based algorithms whereas the properties represented by items (D) through (G) are more general in nature.

Several of these techniques were utilized to some extent in the general CSG scan-line algorithm described in the last section. Span coherence (A) can be considered as the first improvement over ray-firing algorithms. That is, where there is no change in surface visibility throughout a span, Boolean visibility computations need be executed only at the span boundaries. Shading can then be interpolated in between. Even when surface intersections require subdivision of an initial span, shading can be interpolated between the new subdivision span boundaries. Visible segment coherence (B) was established by a property that allowed for span boundaries where no visible point is resolved to be removed from further consideration in the processing of a scan-line. Note, however, that for both (A) and (B) to be applied in the CSG scan-line procedure, the depth order of all segments encountered up to the first visible point are necessary. Previous scanline hidden-surface algorithms need only be concerned with information relative to the single segment closest to the viewer since it would hide the other more distant segments.

Some applications of scan-line coherence property (C) can easily be added to the general CSG visible surface algorithm. Several people discovered that the straight polygon edges allow for a simplification of the scan-plane/polygon intersection calculation on successive scan-lines (C.1). That is, when each edge of a polygon is first encountered in the Y-bucket sorted list, the values dx/dy and dz/dy are found. While an edge remains active, segment endpoints for successive scan-lines can be determined using simple difference equations. Horizontal polygon edges are handled as a special case since they would result in a zero dy value. The X-sort scan-line coherence property (C.2) can be applied by maintaining the segment X-order information between successive scan-lines. Since the X-sort order generally changes very little between scan-lines, this coherence property can be utilized by applying a sorting algorithm that executes quickly on a list that is assumed to be nearly sorted. Several hidden surface program developers have found a bubble sort effective for maintaining the X-sort list from scan-line to scan-line [1,17].

Extension of other forms of scan-line coherence are not so easily applied to the CSG visible surface problem. The Z-sort coherence property (C.3) was first implemented by Hamlin and Gear [5] by combining the X- and Z-sort operations into a single "stack" procedure. Their execution statistics exhibited marginal improvement for geometric models that did not allow intersecting polygons. Extensions of the "stack" algorithm to handle intersecting polygons would increase program complexity, and execution speed could be adversely affected. The application of a segment intersection scan-line coherence property (C.4) appears to exhibit a similar efficiency weakness. For the application of constructive solid geometry, there is a potential for surface intersection at any screen location where primitives overlap. As such, the test for polygon intersection must be made at each span boundary where the visual ray penetrates more than one solid primitive regardless of the results from the previous scan-line.

Previous scan-line hidden surface algorithms that utilized face coherence (D) did so by providing a preprocessing step that would split up all intersecting polygons along their common borders. The major application for this approach would be for geometric models that were to be viewed from several positions, but whose internal components would not change relative to each other. In direct contradiction to that application, constructive solid modeling interaction demands relative movements between primitives be made with the potential of many surface intersections taking place. As Sutherland et al. pointed out [14], there is also a great probability of needlessly calculating intersections for portions of the model that would be hidden from view.

At least one form of object coherence, polygon connectivity (E.1), can easily be applied to the CSG hidden surface removal algorithm. For regions of image space where only one primitive resides, no Boolean or intersection solutions need be produced (Figure 5). For segments with visible points resolved from a single primitive, only the first point on each span boundary needs to be found, as in normal visible surface processing. Common span borders that resolve no visible points as a result of subtraction of intersection operations can be removed from further processing of a

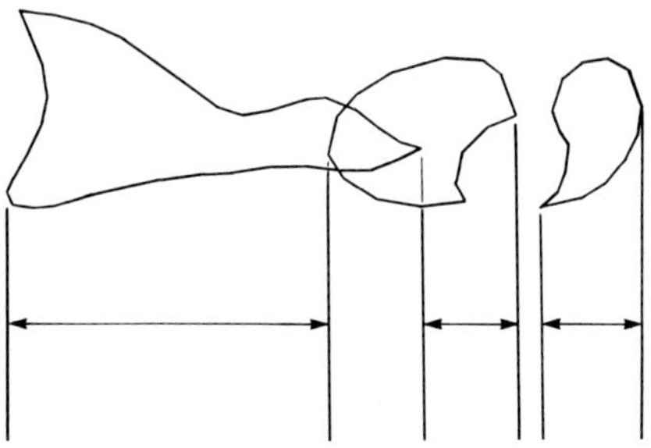

Figure 5. Object coherence properties can be used to define span boundaries where no Boolean operations need be resolved

scan-line. Uses of polygon connectivity coherence assume the common notion that surfaces bounding a primitive volume do not intersect. There appears to be potential for a similar application of polygon connectivity coherence at each level of the Boolean construction tree. At this point in time, the author has not found an efficient solution that compensates for the greatly increased complexity of this task.

There are several other potential areas of coherence application that could improve the efficiency of a CSG visible surface algorithm. Object coherence has often been applied to geometric models comprised of nonintersecting surfaces by determining visibility of primitives relative to each other using their visual silhouette border (E.2). Some extensions might be applied as special cases to the CSG model environment for nonintersecting primitives. An area not yet pursued is the application of rules characteristic to Boolean combinations that might provide some coherence benefits (F). An example of this would be where a region of the image space is covered by overlapping primitives that take part in only union operations. When this situation is detected in the Boolean tree, the visible surface task need only search for portions of the model nearest the viewer. This process is analogous to the standard scan-line hidden surface removal procedure (like that described in Section 3).

Perhaps the coherence techniques involving the most complicated application to the CSG visible surface problem are those that utilize knowledge maintained between image frames (G). This is because the CSG interactive editing process involves surface intersections and geometry changes which are not encountered in traditional frame-to-frame coherence applications. Several people have suggested local updating to only portions of an image that correspond to geometry changes. This approach is reasonable as long as the viewing transformations are consistent.

There remain several applications of coherence properties yet to be explored in the CSG visible surface task. The problems are significantly more complex than the traditional hidden surface removal problem; but the benefits to interactive solid modeling may result in significant future payoffs for CAD/CAM applications.

6. IMPLEMENTATION AND COMPARISONS

A Fortran implementation of the CSG scan-line hidden surface removal procedure described in Section 4 has been completed on a VAX 11/780 computer system. The CSG scan-line code is preceded by software that performs coordinate transformation, viewbox clipping, and perspective-divide operations. A transformation matrix can be allocated to each node of the CSG tree for relative scaling and placement of CSG model components.

The images in Figures 6 and 7 were generated by the CSG scan-line hidden surface removal program at 512 × 512 resolution. The images in Figure 6 were generated from simple CSG models, each containing the same three boxes. The top image in Figure 6 illustrates the relative placement of the three boxes before Boolean evaluation. The CSG model for the top image contained a single-node CSG tree for each primitive. The other two images represent CSG models with only one CSG tree apiece, utilizing all three primitives. New surfaces introduced by subtraction operations are highlighted in blue for better visualization.

The images in Figure 7 represent the two basic stages of a plastic coffee pot handle mold design, as produced using constructive solid modeling. During the first stage of design, solid primitives are either loaded from a library or created using in-house CAD systems. It is significant to point out that the coffee pot handle primitive was modeled using bicubic surface patches which have been approximated by polygons. Figure 7 illustrates some basic operations which a designer could use to create the bottom half of the mold cavity. In the first operation, a truncated cone is subtracted from the handle in order to provide space for a screw that will attach the handle to the rest of the coffee pot. This final representation of the plastic coffee pot handle is then subtracted from a metal block to form the bottom half of the mold.

In order to provide a basis of comparison in terms of program efficiency, a ray-firing CSG hidden-surface removal program has been implemented. The ray-firing program is a polygon-based implementation of the algorithm described in Section 2 of this paper, with extensions to use the culling-box technique suggested by Roth [12] in order to reduce computation. The CSG models depicted in Figures 6 and 7 were used as test cases and the results are summarized in Table 1.

Table 1

EXECUTION TIMING TEST RESULTS

Image	Number of Polygons	CPU seconds (Vax 11/780) Ray-Firing	CSG Scan-line
Figure 6:			
[(AuC) − B]	18	65.3	8.8
[(B − (AUC)]	18	64.6	9.1
Figure 7:			
[Handle − Cone]	1056	650.2	11.7
[Block − (Handle − Cone)]	1062	1143.6	18.8

The author found that the CSG scan-line program needed approximately 1/60th the CPU time required by the ray-firing program to derive shaded images from CSG models of similar complexity to the mold example. This is a very significant improvement when one considers the productivity increase a user might gain from waiting only 20 seconds for an image instead of 20 minutes. Initial tests indicate that the execution speed improvements exhibited by the CSG scan-line program over the ray-firing program increase with model complexity. In other words, the coherence techniques employed by the CSG scan-line program seem to dramatically improve relative performance with greater numbers of primitives and polygons.

It is significant to point out that existing CSG ray-firing programs normally do not use polygon approximations of primitive surface definitions. Rather, they typically restrict the user to a few relatively simple primitives (i.e., block, sphere, cylinder) for which straight-forward ray/surface intersections can be derived. The CSG scan-line hidden surface removal procedure described in this paper is intended to provide a general purpose solution for primitives bounded by any order of surface by using polygon approximations. For example, the coffee pot handle primitive shown in Figure 7 utilizes a third-order sculptured-surface definition that quadric level CSG modelers could not possibly duplicate. Approximation of curved surfaces with polygons may result in a significant increase in data space requirements, but that factor is becoming less pertinent each day as computer technology progresses; and the pay-offs in terms of geometric model generality and improved user interaction are great.

Work has begun on a workstation-based implementation of the CSG scan-line hidden surface removal procedure. It will utilize at least one microprocessor local to a frame buffer display system in order to improve user response, and will also serve to move some computational load from the host computer. This implementation will also provide a working tool for a dual solid modeling system as described in the Introduction of this paper.

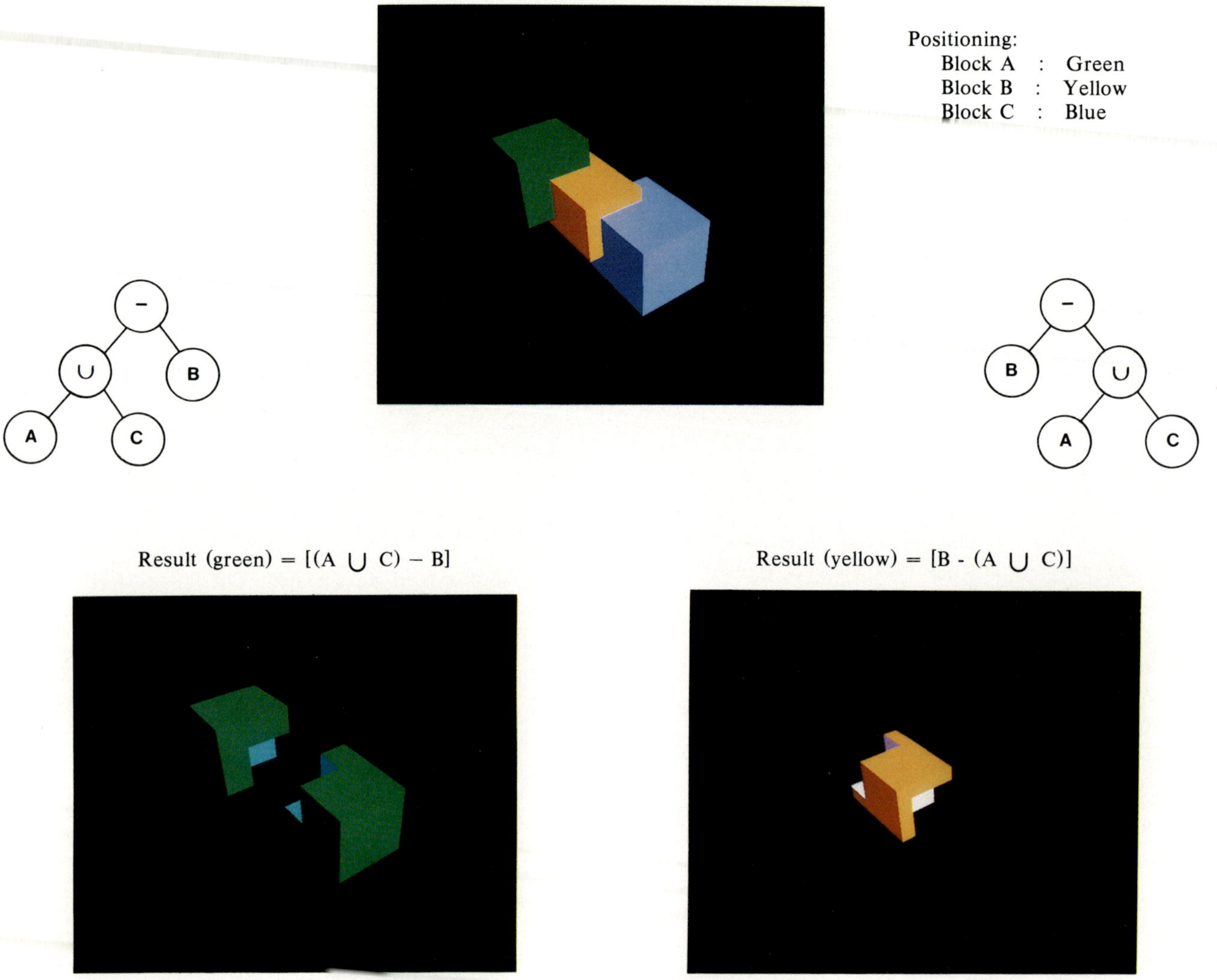

Figure 6. Three block example of output from the CSG scan-line hidden surface removal program

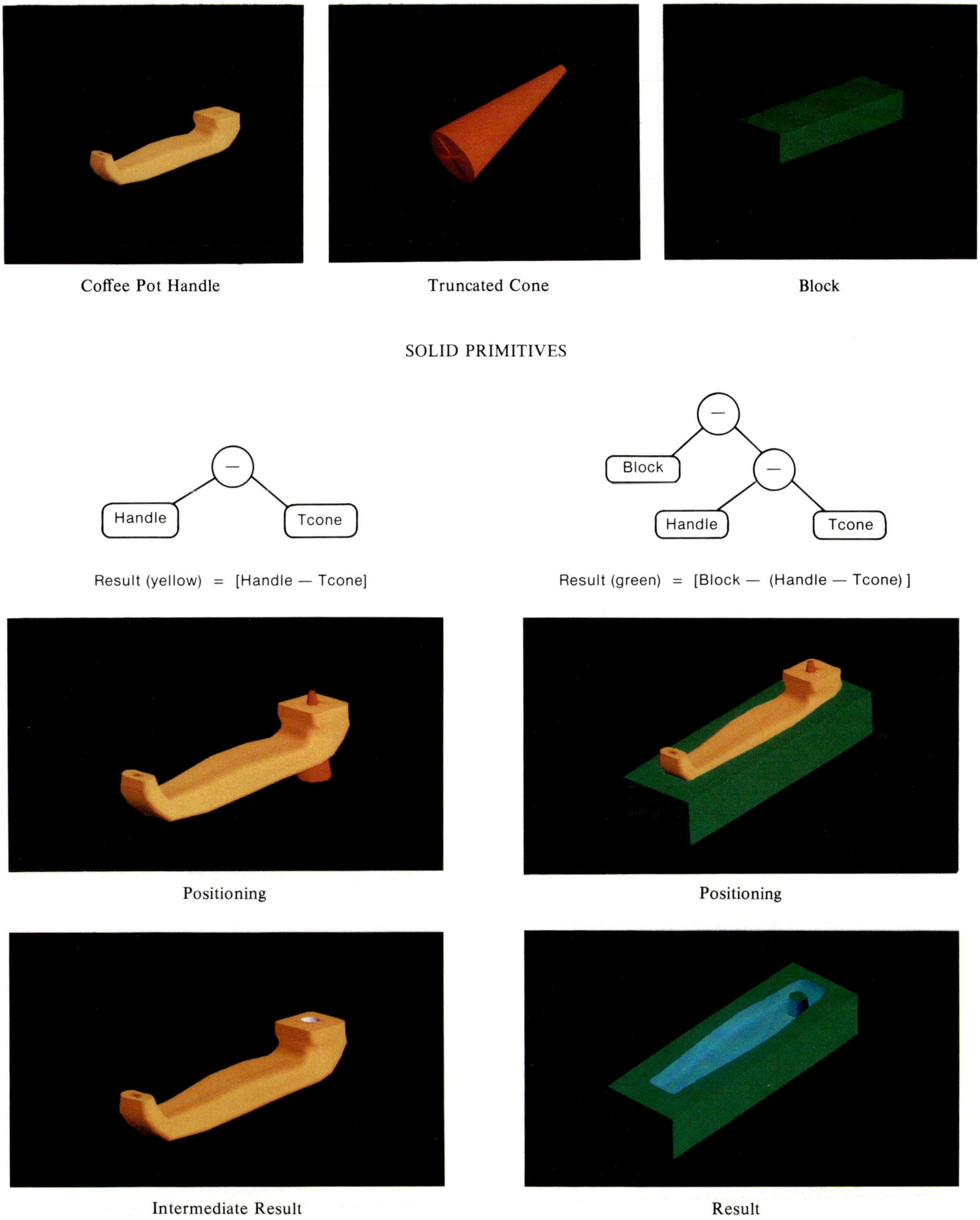

Figure 7. Mold design example of output from the CSG scan-line hidden surface removal program

7. CONCLUSION

A method for displaying visible surfaces of CSG models using a scan-line hidden surface removal procedure has been described. Implementations of this procedure demonstrate significant efficiency improvements over previous approaches. Initial tests indicate that these efficiency improvements increase with model complexity. These results indicate that a visual solid modeler based upon the CSG scan-line hidden surface removal procedure could be a truly interactive system. In addition to providing a vehicle for these dramatic speed improvements, the fundamental polygon basis of this procedure allows it to be a general purpose visualization tool for CSG model editing in that all higher order surfaces can be approximated to desired tolerances by polygons. There remain several coherence properties that could be further exploited in order to improve execution speed of the CSG hidden surface removal program even more. Further study is also necessary to understand what rendering techniques would provide the most information to the user at the least computational expense for the purpose of CSG model creation and editing.

A dual solid modeling system which serves to separate the functions of a "visual solid modeler" and an "analytic solid modeler" has been proposed. The CSG hidden surface removal algorithm presented in this paper is aimed at solving the interactive image generation requirements of the "visual solid modeler." A great deal of work remains in precisely defining the "analytical solid modeler" and the interrelationships between the analytical and visual solid modelers at a system level.

8. ACKNOWLEDGEMENTS

This paper incorporates a number of recommendations that were made by readers of earlier drafts. Of particular note were the comments made by Kevin Weiler who bathed my first draft with red ink. Recommendations by Lon Jones, Virg Lucke and three anonymous SIGGRAPH reviewers led to several clarifications and deletions of extraneous verbiage. The final proofreading, typesetting, photography and layout were accomplished by General Electric's Graphics Operation. The geometric models used for Figure 7 were provided by Jim Beck and John Hinds.

I would also like to thank Professor Wozny of Rensselaer Polytechnic Institute who is leading me in my Ph.D. effort of which this paper will play a major part.

9. REFERENCES

[1] Bouknight, W.J., "A Procedure for Generation of Three-Dimensional Half-Toned Computer Graphics Representations," *Comm. ACM*, Vol. 13, No. 9, September 1970.

[2] Boyse, J.W. and Gilchrist, J.E., "GMSolid: Interactive Modeling for Design and Analysis of Solids," *IEEE Computer Graphics and Applications*, Vol. 2, No. 2, March 1982, pp. 86-97.

[3] Brown, C.M., "PADL-2: A Technical Summary," *IEEE Computer Graphics and Applications*, Vol. 2, No. 2, March 1982, pp. 69-81.

[4] Hamlin, G. and Gear, C.W., "Raster-Scan Hidden Surface Algorithm Techniques," *Computer Graphics*, Vol. 11, 1977, No. 2, pp. 206-213.

[5] Foley, J.D. and VanDam, A., *Fundamentals of Interactive Computer Graphics*, Addison-Wesley, 1982.

[6] Goldstein, R.A. and Malin, L., "3D Modeling with the Syntha Vision System," First Annual Conference on Computer Graphics in CAD/CAM Systems, MIT, April 1979, pp. 244-247.

[7] Hindel, B., *Emulation and Invention*, New York University Press, 1981.

[8] Hubschman, H., and Zucker, S., "Frame-to-Frame Coherence and the Hidden Surface Computation: Constraints for a Convex World," *Computer Graphics*, Vol. 15, No. 3, August 1981, pp. 45-54.

[9] Myers, W., "An Industrial Perspective on Solid Modeling," *IEEE Computer Graphics and Applications*, Vol. 2, No. 2, March 1982, pp. 86-97.

[10] Requicha, A.A.G., and Voelcker, H.B., "Solid Modeling: A Historical Summary and Contemporary Asessment," *IEEE Computer Graphics and Applications*, Vol. 2, No. 2, March 1982, pp. 9-24.

[11] Romney, G.W., *Computer Assisted Assembly and Rendering of Solids*, Computer Science Department, University of Utah, TR-4-20, 1970.

[12] Roth, S.D., "Ray Casting for Modeling Solids," *Computer Graphics and Image Processing*, No. 18, 1982, pp. 109-144.

[13] Sechrest, S., and Greenberg, D.P., "A Visible Polygon Reconstruction Algorithm," *Computer Graphics*, Vol. 15, No. 3, August 1981, pp. 17-27.

[14] Sutherland, I.E., Sproull, R.F., and Schumacher, R.A., "A Characterization of Ten Hidden-Surface Algorithms," *ACM Computing Surveys*, Vol. 6, No. 1, March 1974, pp. 1-55.

[15] Tilove, R.B., "Set Membership Clarification: A Unified Approach to Geometric Intersection Problems," *IEEE Transactions on Computers*, Vol. C-29, No.10, October 1980.

[16] Voelcker, H.B., "Algorithms and Applications," Tutorial on Solid Modeling, SIGGRAPH '82 (ACM).

[17] Watkins, G.S., *A Real-Time Visible Surface Algorithm*, Computer Science Department, University of Utah, UTECH-CSC-70-101, June 1970.

[18] Wesley, M.A., Lozano-Perez, T., Lieberman, L.I., Lavin, M.A. and Grossman, D.D., "A Geometric Modeling System for Automated Mechanical Assembly," *IBM Journal of Research and Development*, Vol. 24, No. 1, January 1980.

[19] Wolfe, R., Fitzgerald, W., and Gracer, F., "Interactive Graphics for Volume Modeling," Procedings of the IEEE Eighteenth Design Automation Conference, pp. 463-470.

Ray Tracing Algebraic Surfaces

Pat Hanrahan

Computer Graphics Laboratory
New York Institute of Technology
Old Westbury, New York

Abstract

Many interesting surfaces can be written as polynomial functions of the spatial coordinates, often of low degree. We present a method based on a ray casting algorithm, extended to work in more than three dimensions, to produce pictures of these surfaces. The method uses a symbolic algebra system to automatically derive the equation of intersection between the ray and the surface and then solves this equation using an exact polynomial root finding algorithm.

Included are illustrations of the cusp catastrophe surface, and two unusually shaped quartic surfaces, Kummer's quadruple and Steiner's surface.

General Terms: Algorithms.

Keywords: Algebraic Surfaces, Curved Surface Display, Ray Tracing, Symbolic Algebra, Polynomial Roots.

CR Categories: I.3.3 [Computer Graphics]: Picture/Image Generation--display algorithms; I.3.5 [Computer Graphics]: Computational Geometry and Object Modelling--curve, surface, solid and object representations, geometric algorithms, languages and systems; I.3.5 [Computer Graphics]: Three-Dimensional Graphics and Realism--visible line/surface algorithms

1. Introduction

Underlying the most spectacular computer generated images is a precise geometric model of the scene. A very profitable line of recent research has been the development of display algorithms for a larger range of mathematical models. New display algorithms have been implemented that are capable of displaying curved surfaces, some for parametric surface patches, most notably the bicubic patch [Catmull, 1975; Blinn, Carpenter, Lane and Whitted, 1980] and implicitly defined surfaces, for example quadrics [Duff, 1980; Blinn, 1980], superquadrics [Barr, 1981] and exponential density distributions [Blinn, 1982]. The differences in these algorithms are primarily geometric; that is, for each type of surface equation different methods may be needed to transform the object into the viewing coordinate system, and to determine the relative priority between parts of an object or objects so that only the visible surface element will be drawn. Once a visible surface patch has been found it is rendered into a frame buffer. This can be done quite realistically using the normal of the surface element and a local lighting model [Blinn, 1977; Cook and Torrance, 1981].

Ray tracing [Goldstein and Nagle, 1971] is a very powerful general approach to rendering surfaces since it reduces the geometric calculations to that of solving for the intersection of a line with the surface. This has been done for the case of planar and quadric surfaces [Goldstein and Nagle, 1971; Potmesil and Chakravarty, 1981; Whitted, 1980] and more recently bicubic surface patches [Whitted, 1980; Potmesil and Chakravarty, 1981; Kajiya, 1982]. Generally there is no need to transform the surface since the view is encoded in the geometry of the light rays. This also has the advantage that rays can be recursively split [Whitted, 1980], to form new rays representing specular reflections and transmissions, without changing the nature of the calculations.

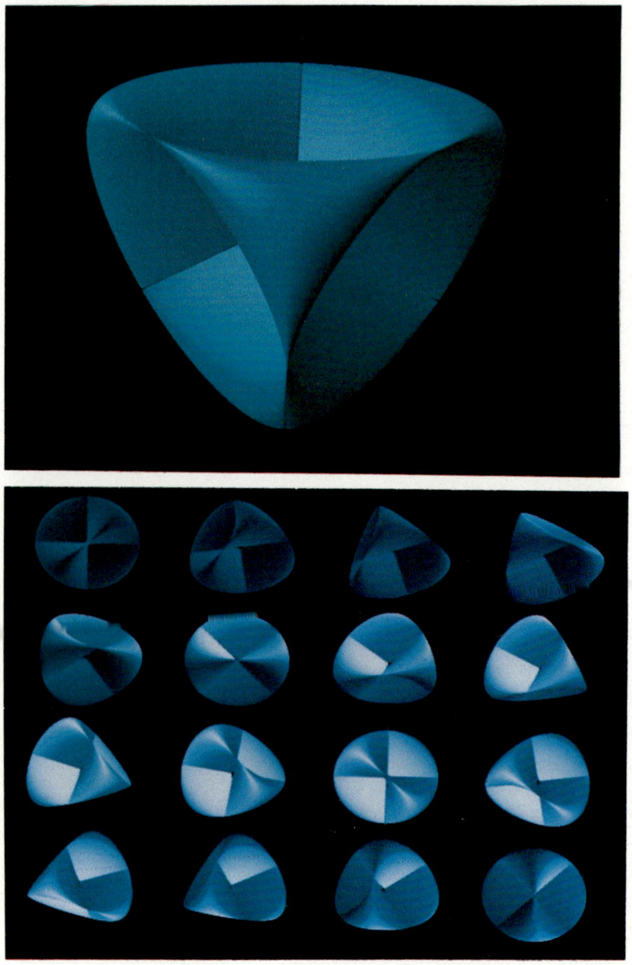

Figure 1. The Steiner Surface.

Figure 2. Kummer's surface.

In this paper we show how to use a ray casting approach to generate pictures of any polynomial function of position. Such surfaces are called algebraic surfaces. Common examples of algebraic surfaces are planes and the quadric surfaces. The main goal of this work is to enlarge the domain of curved surface algorithms while also generating pictures of many mathematically interesting surfaces that have never been properly drawn. Figure 1 shows the Roman or Steiner surface and Figure 2 shows a quadruple; one of the class of surfaces first investigated by Kummer [Hudson, 1905]. Other examples of polynomial surfaces are the catastrophe surfaces; an example is the "cusp" shown in figure 3. The catastrophe surfaces are particularly interesting since they represent a fundamental classification of the types of surfaces that can be formed from polynomials. They are also interesting in that they exist in an n-dimensional space and their display requires that the ray trace be capable of proceeding through more than three dimensions.

Figure 3. The Cusp Catastrophe.

2. Ray tracing implicit surfaces

Although we are concerned primarily with algebraic surfaces embedded in n-dimensional space, in this section we will outline the steps needed to display any analytic surface by means of a ray trace.

Each point in this space is represented by a vector, the n-tuple

$$(x,\ y,\ \ldots,\ z) \qquad (1)$$

and the surface by the n-1 dimensional subset satisfying the equation:

$$F(x,y,\ \ldots,z) = 0 \qquad (2)$$

The normal to the surface is in the direction of the gradient of F evaluated at a point on the surface,

$$\overline{N} = \left(\frac{\partial F}{\partial x},\ \frac{\partial F}{\partial y},\ \ldots,\ \frac{\partial F}{\partial z}\right)\Bigg|_{F=0} \qquad (3)$$

The major geometric calculation underlying all ray tracing algorithms is the intersection of a line, which represents a particular light beam, with a surface. The line equation can be written in the following parametric form:

$$\begin{aligned} x &= x_1 t + x_0 \\ y &= y_1 t + y_0 \\ z &= z_1 t + z_0 \end{aligned} \qquad (4)$$

If the parameter t spans the real numbers then the line extends infinitely in both directions; if instead we restrict t to take on only positive values then we are left with a ray anchored at the point, $(x_0,\ y_0,\ \ldots,\ z_0)$, and pointing in the direction $(x_1,\ y_1,\ \ldots,\ z_1)$, For each ray of light we must find which surface it intersects, if any, and for all the possible intersections (there may be more than one) the closest intersection along the path of the ray. The intersections can be found by substituting for the x,y,...,z coordinates of the surface equation the corresponding ray equations, (4), to yield the new equation in the single variable t,

$$F^*(t) = 0 \qquad (5)$$

The real zeros, $t_0,\ t_1,\ \ldots,\ t_k$, of this equation are simultaneous solutions to both the ray and surface equations and therefore intersections. If there are no real solutions then the ray does not intersect the surface; if there exists a solution $t<0$ then that intersection is behind the anchor point of the ray and therefore physically does not impede the path of the ray. The first physical intersection is the closest point to the anchor and corresponds to the lowest positive real solution to the above equation. Given the solution we can determine the coordinates of the point of the intersection by the original ray-equation (4). These in turn can then be substituted into equation (3) to find the surface normal. Depending on the illumination model, we can either split the incoming ray into additional rays and recursively trace them or immediately compute an intensity value using a local shading function.

To generate a complete frame buffer image a ray is cast at each picture element, sampling the surface. To do this we must determine the location of the image plane in space and the type of projection desired. The image plane can be parameterized by:

$$\overline{I} = \{\ \overline{R}+u\overline{U}+v\overline{V}\ :\ (u,v) \in [-1,1]\ \} \qquad (6)$$

where the vector

$$R = (x_r, y_r,\ \ldots,\ z_r)$$

is a point on the plane, and the two vectors,

$$U = (x_u, y_u,\ \ldots, z_u)$$

and

$$V = (x_v, y_v,\ \ldots, z_v),$$

are two orthogonal vectors contained in that plane. The parameters u and v are normalized frame buffer coordinates. The surface is projected onto this plane by passing a ray through that image point out into the object space. There are two common methods of doing this (i) by forcing all rays to pass through a common vantage point, or (ii) forcing all rays to travel in the same direction. The first method is called a perspective projection; the second method a parallel projection.

The method outlined above works for arbitrary functions provided we can (i) convert the function F to F*, and (ii) solve for the first positive real zero of

P*. The remainder of this paper will describe a system that performs both these operations for surfaces defined as polynomial functions of the space coordinates.

3. Ray tracing algebraic surfaces

An algebraic surface are those surfaces that can be written as a finite number of terms involving coordinates raised to a positive integral power. With this definition a surface defined using logarithms, exponentials or transcendental functions is not considered an algebraic surface. The general form is therefore:[1]

$$P(x,y,\ldots,z)=\sum_{i=0}^{l}\sum_{j=0}^{m}\ldots\sum_{k=0}^{n} a_{ij\ldots k}x^{i}y^{j}\ldots z^{k} \qquad (7)$$

The degree of the surface is equal to the maximum combined degree of the coordinates, $d=l+m+n$.

Upon substitution of the ray-equation into this equation a univariate polynomial in t is formed:

$$P^{*}(t) = \sum_{i=0}^{d} a_{i}t^{i} \qquad (8)$$

The line intersection with an algebraic surface has several properties not shared by the general analytic surface. First, notice that the maximum number of real roots is equal to the degree of the original polynomial. And, if all the coefficients of the univariate polynomial are zero then the equation is always satisfied, implying that the line lies on the surface.

The display system we have developed consists of two major parts, a surface compiler and the ray caster/intersector. The surface compiler reads the equation of the surface and generates the coefficients of the univariate polynomial P*. The same program calculates expressions for the normal to the surface. The output of the surface compiler is included in another program which casts the rays to generate the picture. The aspects of these programs unique to algebraic surfaces are (i) the symbolic processing in the surface compiler and (ii) the line intersection calculation in the ray casting program. These are described in the next sections.

---

[1]The symbol F is used to signify an analytic surface and the symbol P to denote a polynomial or algebraic surface.

3.1. Symbolic Methods

The surface compiler is a lisp program which accepts as input the equation of the surface, substitutes the ray equations into this equation to form expressions for the coefficients of the polynomial P* and outputs them as a series of statements in the programming language C. The symbolic algebra needed to manipulate polynomials in these ways is well understood, therefore we will only outline the methods used.

When the equation is read it is converted to the equivalent lisp expression (i.e., from infix to prefix). All the arithmetic operators from the original surface equation are replaced by operators which perform polynomial arithmetic and all the spatial coordinates are replaced with expressions from the right hand side of the ray equation (4) for that variable; these equations are linear polynomials in t. The resulting expression for the surface is evaluated by symbolically combining the polynomials in t. At each step the coefficients of the new polynomials are passed to an algebraic simplifier. When all the original arithmetic operators have been evaluated there remains a single univariate polynomial in t, the desired P*. Notice that the coefficients are represented by expressions containing the variables of the ray, the x_0 and x_1 etc., and any other constants which were part of the original surface equation.

The eventual evaluation of the coefficients can be further optimized while their equations are still in symbolic form. In particular, the resulting statements often contain common subexpressions which are repeated several times. The total number of arithmetic operations can be substantially reduced by evaluating these subexpressions only once. The optimizer accepts a group of statements, and from these creates a list of innermost expressions (that is, terminal nodes in the expression tree) which occur more than once. For each repeated subexpression a new statement is created which assigns that subexpression to a temporary variable and substitutes the temporary variable for the subexpression in the original set of statements. The entire process is then repeated until no common subexpressions have been found.

Finally from the original surface equation it is possible to symbolically differentiate the equation with respect to each spatial coordinate to form the normal to the surface.

Figure 4 contains the output of the surface compiler for the coefficients of Roman surface shown in Figure 1. The same figure also shows the final code generated

```
{
a[4]=y0*y0*z0*z0+z0*z0*x0*x0+x0*x0*y0*y0+x0*y0*z0;
a[3]=((((y1*y0+y0*y1)*z0*z0)+(y0*y0*(z1*z0+z0*z1)))+((((z1*z0+z0*z1)*x0*x0)+
(z0*z0*(x1*x0+x0*x1)))+((((x1*x0+x0*x1)*y0*y0)+(x0*x0*(y1*y0+y0*y1)))+(((x1*y0+x0*y1)*z0)
+(x0*y0*z1)))));
a[2]=((y1*y1*z0*z0+(((y1*y0+y0*y1)*(z1*z0+z0*z1))+y0*y0*z1*z1))+((z1*z1*x0*x0+
(((z1*z0+z0*z1)*(x1*x0+x0*x1))+z0*z0*x1*x1))+((x1*x1*y0*y0+(((x1*x0+x0*x1)*(y1*y0+y0*y1))
+(x0*x0*y1*y1)))+((x1*y1*z0)+((x1*y0+x0*y1)*z1)))));
a[1]=(((y1*y1*(z1*z0+z0*z1))+((y1*y0+y0*y1)*z1*z1))+(((z1*z1*(x1*x0+x0*x1))+
((z1*z0+z0*z1)*x1*x1))+(((x1*x1*(y1*y0+y0*y1))+((x1*x0+x0*x1)*y1*y1))+(x1*y1*z1))));
a[0]=y1*y1*z1*z1+z1*z1*x1*x1+x1*x1*y1*y1;
d=4;
}

{
double g26,g25,g24,g23,g22,g21,g20,g19,g18,g17,g16,g15,g14,g13,g12,g11,g10,g09,g08,g07;
g07=y0*y0; g08=z0*z0; g09=x0*x0; g10=x0*y0; g11=y1*y0; g12=y0*y1;
g13=z1*z0; g14=z0*z1; g15=x1*x0; g16=x0*x1; g17=x1*y0; g18=x0*y1;
g19=y1*y1; g20=z1*z1; g21=x1*x1; g22=x1*y1;
g23=g11+g12; g24=g13+g14; g25=g15+g16; g26=g17+g18;

d=4;
a[0]=g19*g20+g20*g21+g21*g19;
a[1]=g19*g24+g23*g20+g20*g25+g24*g21+g21*g23+g25*g19+g22*z1;
a[2]=g19*g08+g23*g24+g07*g20+g20*g09+g24*g25+g08*g21+g21*g07+
g25*g23+g09*g19+g22*z0+g26*z1;
a[3]=g23*g08+g07*g24+g24*g09+g08*g25+g25*g07+g09*g23+g26*z0+g10*z1;
a[4]=g07*g08+g08*g09+g09*g07+g10*z0;
}
```

Figure 4. The output of the surface compiler for the Steiner surface shown in Figure 1.

after subexpression optimization which in this case reduces the total number of arithmetic operations required by almost 50 percent.

3.2. Numerical Methods

Once the coefficients are determined several methods are used to solve for the real roots. We have opted for root finders which uses the properties of polynomials to increase the accuracy of the roots.

Many of the equations of interest have degree less than 5. For these equations there exist analytical solutions requiring the radical of a real number. Linear equations can be trivially solved; quadratic equations can be solved by the quadratic formula, requiring a square root. A method for solving cubics was discovered by Cardan and a method for solving quartics was discovered by his pupil Ferrari.[2] In these cases we generate all the roots, ignore the imaginary roots and negative real roots, and then finally sort the remaining real roots to find the lowest positive root. We have found that these methods are simple, fast and robust.

For polynomials whose degree is greater or equal to 5 we use a hybrid method which is guaranteed to give the exact answer to within some tolerance. It was originally described by Uspensky[1948] and then improved and modified by Collins for use in the SAC-2 computer algebra system [Collins and Akritas, 1976; see also Collins and Loos, 1982]. This algorithm allows one to separate the real roots within the interval, 0 to 1, into a set of disjoint intervals each containing a single root. The number of roots within an interval can be calculated using a theorem due to Descartes that states that the number of sign variations, that is, transitions in the coefficients from negative to positive or vice versa, is equal to the number of positive real roots or less than that by an even number. A corollary is, if the number of sign variations is 1 then there exists a single positive real root, and if the number of sign variations is 0 then there cannot be any positive real roots. To take advantage of this theorem the interval, 0 to 1, must be transformed to the positive real axis. This is done with the substitution,

$$p*' = (t+1)^n p*(1/(t+1))$$

[2]Other exact methods exist up to higher orders but involve complicated functions. It is well known that equations above degree five cannot be solved using only radicals; in fact equations of degree 3 also cannot be solved without the use of trigonometric substitution--this is the famous _causus irreducibilis_.

(which amounts to simply reversing the order of the coefficients and then expanding the polynomial in powers of t+1). If there is more than one sign variation we can bisect the standard interval, transform the two subintervals to the standard interval and repeat the above test. An elegant theorem due to Collins guarantees that this method isolates all the roots. A further remarkable fact is that if the coefficients are integers then all the operations described above can be done using only shifts and adds.

Since we need only the lowest positive real root we can always search the leftmost interval first, switching to the right interval only if no roots are contained in the first. This allows us to more quickly home in on the isolating interval containing the lowest positive root. Also once an interval containing a single root has been found other iterative root finding methods can be employed provided they guarantee that the root does not wander outside the interval. Experimentally, we have found that the method of regula falsi more rapidly converges to the root than either simple bisection or continual application of the Collins-Uspensky algorithm.

4. Results

To test the program we used Steiner's surface

$$x^2y^2+y^2z^2+z^2x^2+xyz = 0,$$

the quadruple Kummer's surface

$$(x^4+y^4+z^4+1)-(x^2+y^2+z^2+y^2z^2+z^2x^2+x^2y^2) = 0,$$

and the cubic cusp catastrophe

$$z^3+xz+y = 0.$$

These surfaces were generated at an effective resolution of 1024 x 972 on a Digital Equipment Corporation VAX 11/780. Since they have degree less than 5 the ray intersection can be calculated with either the classic method or the Collins-Uspensky algorithm. On the average a full screen image of the quartics took 6 minutes of CPU time with the exact solution and approximately 25 percent longer with the more general polynomial root finder.

5. Summary and Discussion

To reiterate, we have shown how to automatically perform the line-surface intersection for a general algebraic surface resulting in a univariate polynomial, P*, and how to solve for the first positive real root of this polynomial to within some specified tolerance. This root is the intersection of a ray with the surface and represents the visible surface element. The above methodology is very general placing no restrictions on the number of dimensions or the degree of the surface.

The symbolic surface compiler has been very valuable, especially since we are interested in displaying a variety of surfaces defined by quite different equations. To generate a picture of a new surface the user need only provide the equation of the surface and the view desired; there is no need to know any of the details of the ray tracing algorithm itself. Within a few minutes of entering the equation of a surface a custom program is created which is capable of displaying the surface. The surface compiler automatically performs the tedious and error prone task of generating the coefficients of the univariate polynomial and the normal to the surface.

Since the compilation is done once per surface, it is worth the extra time to simplify and optimize the evaluation of the various expressions generated. Execution time profiles show that over 90 percent of the time is spent in solving for roots of the polynomial P*, the substitution time being almost insignificant despite the complexity of the expressions. We strongly believe that the symbolic preprocessing significantly speeds the execution time of the resulting program but since the programming required to perform the ray substitution at every pixel has approximately the same complexity as that involved in the compiler we decided to only implement it as a preprocessor.

The importance of the polynomial root finder is very graphically illustrated by the catastrophe surfaces which contain sharp singularities susceptible to numerical imprecision. The polynomial root finder we have used was originally implemented as part of the SAC-2 computer algebra system and is exact, that is, if the coefficients of the polynomials are represented as multiple precision integers the calculated roots are guaranteed to lie within a prespecified tolerance of the true roots. Dennis Arnon has used this system to display algebraic curves [Arnon, 1981]. Unfortunately, generating a shaded image with multiple precision integers would be quite slow so we opted for ordinary floating point arithmetic. This introduces some error into the calculation but does not seem to effect the pictures we have generated. However, a systematic method of performing the computations with integers of fixed size would be very desirable.

When tracing a ray of light only the lowest positive solution need be calculated. An algorithm employing bisection, such as the Collins-Uspensky algorithm, can use this fact to reduce the number of roots calculated and save a significant amount of time.

Of considerable interest is the development of algorithms for other classes of analytical surfaces. As outlined above with a ray tracing approach the problem reduces to essentially that of finding positive real roots of the function F*. General purpose zero finding procedures either are too computationally expensive and/or lack the accuracy required. Unlike algebraic functions which have exact solutions other classes of functions require heuristics based on the qualitative properties of the function. For example, properly selected starting points followed by the application of an iterative root finding algorithm will often converge to the true root. Jim Blinn's blobby atoms display algorithm is excellent example of careful application of this paradigm.

One of the major advantages of ray tracing algorithms is that they provide a uniform geometric framework, the line-surface intersection, for displaying a variety of different surface types. Perhaps only Z-buffer algorithms are as flexible. Unfortunately this increased generality increases the computation time significantly. Therefore, it may be time to seriously consider implementing some part of the algorithms in hardware. One approach is to exploit the independence of the calculations from pixel to pixel and perform these calculations in parallel, perhaps on a multiprocessor architecture. But since the majority of the execution time is spent searching for line-surface intersections it might be more advantageous to employ special hardware to solve for these intersections. In this paper we have shown how this problem can be solved for algebraic surfaces. Jim Kajiya [Kajiya, 1982] has also very elegantly shown how the intersections of a piecewise polynomial surfaces with a line can also reduced to solving a univariate polynomial equation. A large class of surfaces could therefore be displayed if a polynomial root finder was embedded in hardware. The Collins-Uspensky algorithm would be a leading candidate for such a machine since it involves very simple operations on the coefficients of the polynomial.

6. Acknowledgements

I would like to thank Kevin Hunter for sparking my interest in display algorithms for implicitly defined surfaces. I also am greatly indebted to George Collins, for graciously providing me with his polynomial root finding algorithm, and Scott McCallum for helping me through the details. Michael Lehman provided invaluable photographic assistance.

7. References

Arnon, D. S., Automatic analysis of real algebraic curves. SIGSAM 15(4) pp 3-9, 1981.

Barr, A. H., Super quadrics and the angle preserving transformation. IEEE Transactions on Computer Graphics and Applications. 1(1) pp 11-23, 1981.

Blinn, J. F., Models of light reflection for computer synthesized pictures. SIGGRAPH 77 Proceedings, Computer Graphics 11(2) pp 192-198, 1977.

Blinn, J.F., Notes on geometric modelling. SIGGRAPH 1980 Tutorial.

Blinn, J. F., A generalization of algebraic surface drawing. ACM Transactions on Graphics 1(3) pp 235-236, 1982.

Blinn, J.F., Carpenter, L.C., Lane, J.M., and Whitted, T., Scanline methods for displaying parametrically defined surfaces. CACM, 23(1) pp 23-34, 1980.

Catmull, E., Computer Display of Curved Surfaces., Proc. IEEE Conference on Computer Graphics, Pattern Recognition, and Data Structures, pp 11-17, 1975.

Collins, G. E. and Akritas, A. G., Polynomial real root isolation using Descartes' rule of signs. Proc. 1976 ACM Symposium on Symbolic and Algebraic Computation. pp 272-276, 1976.

Collins, G. E. and Loos, R., Real zeros of polynomials. Computing, Suppl. 4 pp 83-94, 1982.

Cook, R. L., and Torrance, K. E., A reflectance model for computer graphics. SIGGRAPH 81 Proceedings, Computer Graphics 15(3) pp 307-316, 1981.

Duff, T., The soid and roid manual. New York Institute of Technology. 1980.

Goldstein, E. and Nagle, R., 3D visual simulation. Simulation 16(1) pp 25-31, 1971.

Hudson, R.W.H.T., Kummer's Quartic Surface. Cambridge University Press, 1905.

Kajiya, J. T., Ray tracing parametric patches SIGGRAPH 82 Proceedings, Computer Graphics 16(3) pp 245-254, 1982.

Potmesil, M. and Chakravarty, I., A lens and aperture camera model for synthetic image generation. SIGGRAPH 81 Proceedings, Computer Graphics 15(3) pp 297-306, 1981.

Uspensky, J.V., Theory of Equations McGraw-Hill, 1948.

Whitted, T. J., An improved illumination model for shaded display. CACM 23(6) pp 343-349, 1980.

NEW TECHNIQUES FOR RAY TRACING PROCEDURALLY DEFINED OBJECTS

James T. Kajiya
California Institute of Technology
Pasadena, Ca. 91125

ABSTRACT. We present new algorithms for efficient ray tracing of three procedurally defined objects: fractal surfaces, prisms, and surfaces of revolution. The fractal surface algorithm performs recursive subdivision adaptively. Subsurfaces which cannot intersect a given ray are culled from further consideration. The prism algorithm transforms the three dimensional ray-surface intersection problem into a two dimensional ray-curve intersection problem, which is solved by the method of strip trees. The surface of revolution algorithm transforms the three dimensional ray-surface intersection problem into a two dimensional curve-curve intersection problem, which again is solved by strip trees.

KEYWORDS: computer graphics, raster graphics, ray tracing, fractal surfaces, procedural modelling, strip trees, stochastic models, surfaces of revolution.

CR CATEGORIES: I.3.3, I.3.5, I.3.7

§1 Introduction

Of all synthetic images, those rendered by ray tracing stand above the rest in realism (Appel[1], Goldstein and Nagle[10], Whitted[16]). Many have disparaged its use because of its large appetite for floating point computation. However — even though ray tracing is conceded to be the slowest of all methods for rendering computer imagery — no other technique has a performance envelope quite as large. In ray tracing the combined effects of hidden surfaces, shadows, reflection, and refraction are handled with a simplicity and elegance unmatched by its competitors.

This paper is about novel ways of performing the key computational step in rendering procedural objects via ray tracing. We present new ways of computing the intersection between a ray and certain procedurally defined objects. The use of procedural objects is not new to ray tracing — Whitted[16] and Rubin and Whitted[15] have advocated their use. Indeed, one could make the claim that the natural organization for ray tracing programs is one using procedural objects.

In section two, we present a method which efficiently computes the intersection of a ray with a fractal surface. In the course of the development of this algorithm a number of results useful to other rendering techniques of fractals. We also analyze the complexity of the new technqiue.

In section three, we give an algorithm for intersecting a ray with a surface defined by translating a plane curve orthogonally. We call a surface of this type a ***prism***.

In section four, we treat surfaces of revolution. The algorithm works well even though the radius curve may be defined by thousands of points.

Algorithms for efficient rendering the above two objects are of immediate importance to CAD/CAM applications. Combined with well known methods for ray tracing Euler combinations of primitives (Goldstine and Nagel[10], Roth[14]), the above techniques facilitate rendering of models described by constructive solid geometry (CSG). Indeed, most of the objects in CSG are combinations of prisms and surfaces of revolution (Braid[4], Requicha[13]), the so called swept volumes.

In section five we present the results of our algorithms; and in section six, we discuss directions for further work.

It is likely that the locus of ideas exposed here will be

A revised version of this paper will appear in the July 1983 issue of **acm Transactions on Graphics.**

applicable to other types of objects exhibiting either a high degree of symmetry or a hierarchical organization or both. These ideas suggest a rich panoply of techniques applicable to many procedural objects which has heretofore gone unsuspected.

§2 Fractal Surfaces

The so-called method of fractals (Fournier, Fussell and Carpenter[9], Mandelbrot[11]) has generated models of startling realism. One would conjecture that applying a ray tracing rendering algorithm to objects modelled by this technique would yield very interesting images indeed. Unfortuately, practical considerations prevent one from doing this directly.

Though a simple algorithm, the fractal modelling technique generates models of visual interest through their great geometric complexity. A typical fractal surface may consist of polygons whose numbers may reach easily into the six figure range. As we shall see below, naive ray tracing is simply too slow to feasibly render a complex fractal surface.

The method we present here overcomes this problem. It does so by evolving the fractal surface in concert with the rendering of it. We generate only those parts of the surface which are likely to intersect the ray being traced. In this way, each ray need be compared with only a handful of polygons instead of the large collection of polygons making up the entire fractal surface. We compute a certain polytope, viz. an *extent*, which completely encloses the surface ultimately evolved with a high degree of certainty. If a ray intersects this extent we must inspect its contents more closely. If not, the extent is pruned from further consideration thus saving much computation.

We mention that this method is essentially the adaptive subdivision technique mentioned in (Fournier, Fussell, and Carpenter[9]) translated to the ray tracing context.

2.1 The Recursive Subdivision Method

We use the subdivision method for generating fractals (Carpenter[5], Fournier and Fussell[8], Fournier, Fussell, and Carpenter[9]). In what follows we give a brief review of the technique as presented in the references above.

The recursive subdivision technique proceeds as follows.[1] The surface is modelled as a large number of triangles. The x and y coordinates of the triangle vertices are set on an isometric grid (See figure 1), while their z-coordinates are generated recursively as follows:

> Once the displacements z_i, $i = 1,2,3$ for a given level of recursion are determined, generate three new independent random variables ξ_i, $i = 1,2,3$ with mean given by the equation
>
> $$E\xi_i = \frac{z_j + z_k}{2}$$
>
> and variance
>
> $$var(\xi_i) = \left(\frac{l_i}{2}\right)^{2H}$$
>
> where l_i is the length of the side of a triangle and H is the "fractal dimension". That is, z_i is the height of the vertex i of a triangle and the ξ_i is the displacement over the bisector of its opposite edge. These are summed to make z_i' the vertices of triangles at the next level of recursion.

2.2 The Rendering Algorithm

The rendering algorithm is very simple. Instead of instantiating the surface in its entirety, we evolve a piece at a time. There are several advantages to this.

In the ray tracing method, the intersection computation is the most time consuming step. If we were to fully evolve the fractal surface, we would need to determine the intersection point of the current ray with every polygon.[2] As a typical scene requires tracing on the order of a million rays and a fractal surface may contain the same order of magnitude of polygons, the intersection computation under the naive method would require a trillion ray-polygon intersections. Clearly this is impractical.

By evolving only a piece of the fractal surface at a time, we can cut down the number of intersections which must be computed.

The computation must intersect a ray r with a recursively defined surface. Suppose that we are able to enclose each part of the surface with an *extent*, viz. a volume which is guaranteed to contain a segment of

[1] We restrict ourselves to the case of triangularized surfaces. See Carpenter[5] and Fournier and Fussell[8], for other methods.

[2] One of the reviewers has pointed out that a fractal surface can never be *fully* evolved but only approximated to a certain level of detail

A revised version of this paper will appear in the July 1983 issue of acm Transactions on Graphics.

the fully evolved surface. The fractal surface is represented by a tree t of branching ratio four. At each node n of t we associate a pair (p, e) where p is a polygon, called a ***facet***, representing the surface at the level of recursion indexed by the depth of n, and e is an extent which encloses the surface given by the subtree at n. The leaf nodes of the tree correspond to the fully evolved fractal surface. The polygon corresponding to a leaf node shall be called a ***primitive facet***.

An an object A is said to ***shadow*** a node $n(p, e)$ with respect to a ray r if the ray intersects A at a point closer to the ray origin than the intersection with e. A node $n(p, e)$ is said to be ***active*** if its extent e intersects the ray and no primitive facet shadows it.

Note that an inactive node can never contain the closest intersection of the ray with the fully evolved surface.

The algorithm maintains a list of active nodes which are to be traced by the current ray r. With each node is associated a ***distance*** d from the origin of the ray to the closest intersection with its extent.

The algorithm proceeds as follows:

> Choose the closest node n and remove it from the active node list.
>
> Intersect with the four extents e_i, $i = 1, \ldots, 4$ associated with the children n_i, $i = 1, \ldots, 4$ of the node n.
>
> If no e_i intersects r then there are no new active nodes. Start over.
>
> Else, add the nodes whose extents e_i intersect the ray to the active node list.
>
> If the new nodes contain primitive facets p_i and the facets intersect the ray then cull from the active node list the nodes shadowed by the closest p_i. (Simply compare the distance of each node to the distance of the facet intersection point).

It may be conjectured that a node ought to be rendered inactive whenever it is shadowed by any facet (not necessarily primitive). Certainly this holds in the two dimensional case, see figure 2a. But figure 2b shows that this is false in the three dimensional case. The facet for node n shadows its neighboring extent but it contains no primitive facet doing so.

2.3 Computing Extents

The key to the performance of the above algorithm lies with the specification of extents. Beyond the necessary conditions for an extent—that they enclose the actual surface segment corresponding to a node—there are two additional desiderata which extents should satisfy. First, extents should be ***tight***, that is, they should enclose the actual surface snugly. Consider the case when extents do not, say when an extent is the whole of space. Then no pruning will ever take place: the algorithm degenerates to the naive method. As extents become more and more snug, opportunity to prune surfaces arises. Thus tight extents improve the asymptotic complexity of the algorithm. The second desideratum for an extent is that it be easily intersected with a ray. That is, one should not expend undue amounts of computation in determining whether a ray intersects an extent or not. This criterion determines the not insignificant multiplier in the complexity of the algorithm.

By the second criterion, an ideal extent for ray tracing is the sphere. Among all bounding surfaces it is the easiest to intersect with a ray. However, it fails with respect to the first criterion. Spheres do not contain fractal surfaces very snugly.

We have chosen an extent which is shown in figure 3. This extent is formed by taking the convex hull of the facet translated in z by a distance $\pm\eta$. Because of its shape we have called this object a ***cheesecake extent***. Given that η is of minimum value, this extent is relatively tight. Because it is formed from simple polygons, it is easy to determine ray intersections.

How can we determine the value of η? A fractal surface is stochastically defined. Thus it is not possible to predict with complete certainty how it will vary. On the other hand, because the statistical properties of the surface are well known, we can choose η so that there is an overwhelming probability that a cheesecake encloses the fully evolved surface.

There are two approaches we may take. The first uses the Chebyshev inequality (Chow and Teicher[6]):

Let X be a random variable with $E|X| < \infty$ and variance σ_X^2. Then

$$P\{|X - EX| \geq a\} \leq \frac{\sigma_X^2}{a^2}, \qquad a > 0$$

Now, if $S(x, y)$ is a generalized Levy surface, the variance of

$$\Delta S = S(x_1, y_1) - S(x_2, y_2)$$

is simply a function of the distance d between the points (x_1, y_1) and (x_2, y_2). Namely,

$$var(\Delta S) = d^{2H} V_H$$

A revised version of this paper will appear in the July 1983 issue of **acm Transactions on Graphics.**

where V_H is a constant depending on the fractal dimension H, (see corollary 3.4 of Mandelbrot and van Ness[12]).

The point of maximum distance from all the vertices of a triangle with sides of length l is the center. This distance is $\frac{l\sqrt{3}}{3}$ If we use the expression for unconditional variance, (it is clear that conditioning can only make the variance go down) then the variance is given by:

$$\sigma = \left(\frac{l\sqrt{3}}{3}\right)^{2H} V_H$$

Choosing η to be 10σ guarantees a .99 chance of the cheesecake enclosing the fully evolved surface.

If, as is usual, we know the surface follows a Gaussian distribution then one can do much better than the Chebyshev inequality. The probability that the center point extends beyond the cheesecake is then simply twice the tail of the distribution. For example, choosing η to be 3σ gives $P = .9974$. Carpenter has pointed out that if the random numbers ξ_i are generated via table lookup, then extents may be calculated with total certainty (Whitted[17]).

2.4 Analysis of the Algorithm

To analyze this algorithm we note that there are three cases of ray intersection: 1)the ray does not intersect the top level cheesecake; 2)the ray intersects the top level but not the surface; and 3)the ray intersects the surface.

If the ray does not intersect the top level cheesecake then one intersection computation is sufficient to prune the fractal. The number of rays which do not satisfy this criterion is roughly the number of pixels in which the fractal is visible (assuming extensive self shadowing does not occur).

The number of rays of the second kind is small if the extents are at all tight, to be conservative we treat these rays as if they were of the third kind.

The algorithm choses active nodes to process on the basis of distance. In the best case, only those nodes contained in the path from the root to primitive facet are chosen. At each step, new nodes are spawned and added to the active node list.

Each step computes intersections with 4 cheesecakes and may either discard or add the new nodes to the active node list. When the primitive facet is finally encountered the entire rest of the list is culled. Thus the number of intersection computations which must be done is:

$$4 \log_4 n.$$

The number of node generation steps is the same. Generating each new node is relatively cheap compared to the intersection computation.

Thus in the best case, the number of intersection calculations is

$$(\text{number of visible pixels}) \times 4 \log_4 n$$

In the worst case, the extents are able to do no pruning at all. Then we degenerate to the naive case: nm where n is the number of primitive triangles and m is the number of rays for the scene.

It has been our experience that the average case with real data possesses the same asymptotic complexity as the best case. We present some preliminary computations indicating why this should be so. In general, however, evaluating the average case complexity is problematical.

We would like to calculate the probability that a ray striking a triangular facet with a given set of angles will strike neighboring cheesecakes first, thus causing unnecessary intersection computations to be performed. In the following analysis we assume that ray strike points are distributed uniformly across a facet.

Let a ray strike a triangular facet with angle θ to the facet normal. (See figure 4). Then it must be a distance less than l' from the boundary to strike a neighboring cheesecake, where

$$l' = h \tan\theta$$

Now, projecting the ray onto the facet plane gives figure 5.

The ratio of the area of the entire triangular facet to the area of the shaded region gives the probability that a random ray will strike a neighboring cheesecake first.

This ratio may be computed by noting that the following equations hold:

$$c = l' \sin\phi$$
$$a = \frac{c}{\tan\frac{\pi}{3}} = \frac{c}{\sqrt{3}}$$
$$b = l' \cos\phi$$

A revised version of this paper will appear in the July 1983 issue of acm Transactions on Graphics.

The ratio of the areas is the ratio of $a + b$ to l or

$$Prob = \frac{l'}{l}(\cos\phi + \frac{\sqrt{3}}{3}\sin\phi)$$
$$= \frac{h\tan\theta}{l}(\cos\phi + \frac{\sqrt{3}}{3}\sin\phi)$$

Where h is determined as the cheesecake height of the previous section, say 4σ. So the probability of at least an extra intersection computation occuring given a certain set of angles for the incoming ray is:

$$P\{\text{Extra Computation}|\theta,\phi\} = 4\left(\frac{\sqrt{3}}{3}\right)^{2H} V_H \tan\theta$$
$$\times(\cos\phi + \frac{\sqrt{3}}{3}\sin\phi)\frac{l^{2H}_{\text{neighbor}}}{l_{\text{triangle}}}$$
$$= K l^{2H}_{\text{neighbor}}$$

The probability given a set of angles goes down exponentially for each level of recursion of the neighbors. Now, each level of recursion halves l_{neighbor}. We sum the geometric series to obtain the expected number of intersection computations required.

$$\text{Number of computations} = K\sum_{n=0}^{\text{max level}}\left(\frac{l_{\text{neighbor}}}{2^n}\right)^{2H}$$
$$\le K\sum_{n=0}^{\infty}\left(\frac{l_{\text{neighbor}}}{2^n}\right)^{2H}$$
$$= K l^{2H}_{\text{neighbor}}\sum_{n=0}^{\infty}(\tfrac{1}{2})^{2Hn}$$
$$= K\frac{(2l_{\text{neighbor}})^{2H}}{2^{2H}-1}$$

The key observation one should make about the above calculation is that the number of expected superfluous computations for small incidence angles is very small — much less than for the worst case. In fact, the geometric series sums to a small constant making the asymptotic complexity the same as for the best case.

To find the expected number of superfluous computations we use the theorem of total probability. But here the evaluation of the number of computations becomes problematical. The distribution of angles is not a simple uniform distribution. Figure 6 shows that a facet relatively far from the ray source sees a distribution of angles which is highly peaked about the viewing angle. When shadowing and reflection occur, the distribution is far from uniform.

We have observed in practice an average performance whose general character is very good. For example, when the level of recursion was increased from 5 to 6 — quadrupling the number of polygons from 1024 to 4096 — the runtime of the algorithm increased by some 12%.

No effort has been made to cache calculated subtrees. Each ray intersection must evolve the surface anew from the top node. Whitted has suggested that caching the subtree computations can be a very useful optimization. (Whitted[17]).

§3 Prisms

A box is formed by moving a rectangle orthogonally in space, and a cylinder is formed by so moving a circle. In general, we define a ***prism*** to be a volume formed by translating a plane curve along a vector n for a distance d. The curve is defined in a plane P whose normal vector is n.

Many objects can be defined as collections of ***prisms***. Among them include: block letters, machine parts formed by extrusion, simple models of urban architecture, surfaces with "ridges"– small vertical perturbations of a plane which embellish the texture of a surface with sharp edges.

All these objects can always be modelled as collections of polygons. We consider the case where the plane curves defining these surfaces are complex, e.g. having thousands of vertices. Ray tracing such prisms defined as collections of polygons would be extremely expensive.

The technique we describe here illustrates a general technique which will be used again later. We take advantage of the essential symmetries characterizing these surfaces to reduce the intersection problem from three to two dimensions. We then solve this two dimensional ray tracing problem by using a representation for plane curves known ***strip trees*** which is popular in computational geometry (Ballard[2]).

A prism is defined as the union of three parts. The first part is the set of *sides* of the prism given by the locus of points $tn + \gamma(s)$. Where $\gamma(s)$ is a curve embedded in a plane P known as the *baseplane*, n is the unit normal of P, and $0 < t < h$ where h is the *height* of the prism. The second and third parts of the prism are known as the *base* and *cap*. The base B is set of points interior to the curve $\gamma(s)$ in P, the cap is simply the set $B + hn$.

A revised version of this paper will appear in the July 1983 issue of **acm Transactions on Graphics.**

We now give the algorithm for intersecting a ray with a prism. First find the intersection point of the ray with base and cap planes and project these points down onto the base plane. The ray itself is then projected onto the base plane. We have now reduced the problem to a two dimensional one because of the following fact. (See figure 7.)

Proposition. To intersect a ray $r(t) = o + tv$ with a prism $(B, h, \gamma(s))$, let the ray-base plane strike point be at $t = t_0$. Let the base plane projection of the ray-cap plane strike point be $t = t_1$. Then r strikes the prism iff 1) the base plane projection $r'(t)$ of $r(t)$ intersects the curve $\gamma(s)$ at a point $t = t'$ and

$$0 < |t' - t_0| v \cdot n < h$$

where n is the unit normal of the baseplane B, or 2) $r'(t_0)$ or $r'(t_1)$ is in the interior of $\gamma(s)$.

This proposition then suggests the following algorithm:

> **Find the ray strike points $t = t_0$ and $t = t_1$ with the base plane B and with the cap plane $B + hn$, respectively.**
>
> **Project the ray r down into the base plane to give the two dimensional ray r'.**
>
> **Find all the intersections of the ray r' with $\gamma(s)$. (We discuss how this will be done later.)**
>
> **Sort the intersections by distance t from the ray origin o.**
>
> **Scan the sorted list and perform the actions conditioned by the following cases: 1) Cap plane strike point: if inside $\gamma(s)$ then stop else proceed. 2) Base plane strike point: if inside $\gamma(s)$ then stop else proceed. 3) A $\gamma(s)$ intersection: If the intersection point $t = t'$ is such that $0 < |t' - t_0| v \cdot n(B) < h$ then stop else proceed.**

How is the intersection of the two dimensional ray r' with an arbitrary plane curve $\gamma(s)$ to be done? We use the method of ***strip trees***. Strip trees are presented in (Ballard[2]) as generalizations of structures computed in a curve digitization algorithm invented by Duda and Hart[7]. A strip tree is a hierarchical structure which represents the curve at varying resolutions.

The strip tree associated with a curve $\gamma(s)$ is a tree t with nodes $n(e, c)$, where c is a portion of $\gamma(s)$ and e is an extent which completely encloses c. An extent e is shown in figure 8, it is a triple $e = (b, w_1, w_2)$ consisting a ***baseline*** b, two widths w_1, w_2. The baseline is a line segment of arbitrary orientation. Geometrically, the extent is a rectangle whose edges are determined by the baseline and widths. The extent rectangle is chosen in such a way as to enclose the minimum area containing the curve segment c. Thus each edge of e touches at least one point of c. See figure 9. The subtrees of node n subdivide c on a point which touches the edge.

> We now give an algorithm for generating a strip tree associated with any plane curve $\gamma(s)$.
>
> **Choose as a baseline the line segment connecting the first and last point of the curve. Now scan the curve for the maximum and minimum signed distance away from the baseline. These set the widths of the root triangle. Divide the curve at one of these points and compute the subtrees recursively.**

It is evident that this is an $n \log n$ computation. A linear time algorithm is also available (Ballard[2]).

It is now a simple matter to efficiently intersect a two dimensional ray with a plane curve defined by a strip tree. First intersect the ray with the root extent. If there is an intersection then intersect with each of the subtrees, if not, there is no intersection with the ray. Continue recursively.

Given the above algorithms we are now able to calculate the intersection point of the ray with the prism. Calculating the normal of the surface at the intersection point is simple. If the ray strikes either the base or cap planes then the normal is the plane normal. Otherwise, it strikes the sides. The three space normal is then a simple linear transformation of the two space normal which is given by the strip tree baseline equation. This linear transformation is determined by the base plane normal.

§4 Surfaces of Revolution

Polygon or patch methods may serve as approximations to the surfaces of revolution described in this section. However, this technique can model complex surfaces which would require dozens of patches or hundreds of polygons. The tracing time of such patches or polygon collections would be high. The method described here takes advantange of the high degree of symmetry available in the model. As ray tracing algorithms go, it is relatively fast.

A surface of revolution is defined via a 3-tuple $(b, a, \rho(s))$, where b is a point called the ***base point***, a is the ***axis vector***, and $\rho(s)$ is the ***radius function***. See figure 10.

Figure 11 shows the geometrical interpretations of the following definitions. We define the *cut plane* as the plane containing the current ray which is parallel to the axis of revolution. Let the ray be given as an origin

A revised version of this paper will appear in the July 1983 issue of **acm Transactions on Graphics.**

and direction vector:

$$r(t) = o + tv.$$

Then the cut plane normal c is given by

$$c = a \times v.$$

The plane contains the ray origin o. Define d to be the perpendicular distance of the base point b to the cut plane.

The algorithm first reduces the problem of intersecting a ray r with a surface of revolution to the problem of intersecting a two dimensional ray r' with two plane curves γ^1, γ^2 formed by intersecting the cut plane with the surface of revolution.

Define a coordinate system in the cut plane as follows. The origin of the plane is the projection b' of the base point. The y axis vector is the projection of the axis of revolution a, the x axis unit vector is given by $a \times c$.

The algorithm now attempts to intersect the two dimensional ray with the two curves γ^1, γ^2 representing the surface meeting the cut plane. But how are these two plane curves to be determined? Figure 12 shows how the curves depend on the radius function $\rho(s)$ and the distance d, namely:

$$\gamma^i_x = \pm\sqrt{\rho_x^2 - d^2}$$
$$\gamma^i_y = \rho_y.$$

If the quantitiy under the root is negative then the curve disappears altogether.

Now, the radius curve $\rho(s)$ may contain thousands of points: it would be extremely expensive to calculate the plane curves γ^i for every ray using the above relation. Even if we do, the question of which specific algorithm to intersect the curves with the ray remains unanswered. Of course, we intend to use strip trees. But if we do so directly then we would be forced to recalculate the bounding extents at each intersection computation. This is because the plane curves change radically for each different ray. Such a scheme would be impractically slow. Strip trees only yield advantages if their extents can be precalculated and reused for each ray trace.

The solution to this problem is to trace in a different space. Specifically, we trace not in (x, y)-space but in (x^2, y)-space. In this space the equation defining the two plane curves appears as:

$$\gamma_x = \rho_x - d^2$$
$$\gamma_y = \rho_y$$

The original radius curve ρ is defined as the square of the actual radius curve. The plane curve γ is simply translated by the square of d the distance of the cut plane from the base point.

Figures 13a,b show examples of this transformation. As the distance of the cut plane from the axis grows, more of the curve lies below the axis. Note that we are now tracing curved rays that bounce off the origin. Thus the parts of curves below the axis are inaccessible to the ray. To trace curved rays we use a slightly different ray equation. Instead of tracing rays defined as

$$r = o + tv$$

we now trace rays defined as

$$r_x = (o_x + tv_x)^2$$
$$r_y = o_y + tv_y$$

We are now charged with intersecting a curved ray defined as above with an arbitrary plane curve. Fortunately, this plane curve is translated by d so that now it is a simple matter to use strip trees. We recursively intersect the curved ray with an extent box. Each extent intersection is easily acomplished by straightforward solution of a polynomial with at most quadratic degree in t. Solving for t gives the distance from the ray origin. Substituting into the original vector form for the ray gives the exact intersection point.

The above algorithm then determines intersection point of a ray with a surface of revolution. To complete the ray tracing process we need to compute the surface normal. This is done in two steps.

The first step is to translate the slope of the plane curve in bent (x^2, y)-space back into a plane normal in flat (x, y)-space. This we do by using the following equations. Let i_x be the x-coordinate of the intersection (in flat two space), and l_x, l_y the components of the normal vector in bent two space given by the baseline line equation in the strip tree defintion, then the normal vector (n_x, n_y) expressed in flat two space coordinates is:

$$n_x = \frac{2l_x i_x}{\sqrt{(2l_x i_x)^2 + l_y^2}}$$
$$n_y = \frac{l_y}{\sqrt{(2l_x i_x)^2 + l_y^2}}$$

A revised version of this paper will appear in the July 1983 issue of **acm Transactions on Graphics.**

The second step is to translate the plane normal into space normal using the geometry shown in figure 14. The space normal is given by:

$$n = n_x i_x c \times a + n_x(-d)c + |x| n_y a.$$

We have now calculated the intersection point and the normal to the surface at that intersection point for a surface of revolution. This is all that is required for rendering the surface.

§5 Results

The above algorithms were coded in FORTRAN on a DECSYSTEM-2060. The actual fractal algorithm performed differs from the presented one in that no selection of closest extents occurs. The facets are expanded and pruned in a strict depth first manner with fixed ordering for the four subnodes. Evidently, the programmed algorithm is slightly simpler at the cost of increased computation time.

Figure 15 shows a sample output of the algorithm. A scene composed of a reflecting sphere placed above a fractal "valley" evolved from a single initial triangle with vertices $(-1, -\frac{\sqrt{3}}{3}, .5), (1, -\frac{\sqrt{3}}{3}, .5), (0, \frac{\sqrt{3}}{2}, 0)$. Note that in the reflection of the sphere the back side of the mountain can be seen to shadow itself.

This image, computed at a resolution of 256×256 pixels, consumed 190 minutes of CPU time.

Figure 16 shows an example of the prism algorithm. In this scene, an "E" shaped curve is translated along the z-axis. Two reflecting spheres are placed in proximity with the prism.

An example of the surface of revolution algorithm is shown in figure 17. This scene shows a wine glass resting on a single triangle. The wine glass is defined as a base point b on the surface of the triangle, an axis of revolution coincident with the z-axis, and a radius curve of only 9 points. This points out an interesting feature of the algorithm. Because the radius curve is defined in bent two space, straight lines translate into parabolas. Thus the curvature of the glass is due entirely to the curvature of the coordinate system. This image consumed 20 minutes of CPU time.

§6 Further Work

There are several obvious extensions of the above algorithms which allow for other primitives.

A modification of the fractal rendering algorithm will work for arbitrary ***deterministic*** height fields defined on triangular grids. Many objects in computer graphics may be so defined: human faces, digitized terrain, planar polygons with detailed surface features, injection molded objects, etc. In fact, this algorithm is applicable to scan-line rendering methods as well as ray tracing.

A ***subdivision tree*** is constructed by recursively subdividing the height field. Each node of the tree stores an extent enclosing a section of the field. Once such a tree has been constructed, we use the fractal rendering algorithm. The algorithm operates in exactly the same manner as above except that the tree is fully instantiated before rendering. Generating the subdivision tree is similar to the strip tree algorithm.

> **Recursively execute the following step:**
>
> **Scan the surface defined by the domain triangle, searching for the point of maximum and minimum distance η_1, η_2 to the triangle containing the vertices. Store the extent cheesecake with distances η_1, η_2. Subdivide the domain triangle into four subtriangles.**

Note that the complexity of constructing this tree is $n \log_4 n$ where n is the number of points in the height field. A linear time algorithm which computes somewhat larger cheesecake extents is also possible by constructing the tree in a bottom up fashion. Both these algorithms construct bivariate analogs of strip trees and essentially mimic the strip tree algorithms (Ballard[2]).

A further modification of the height field algorithm follows from the observation that objects other than polygons can serve as leaf nodes in the tree. Such a tree, with extents given by procedural definitions, is easily seen to be an elaboration of the well known method of Rubin and Whitted[15].

It may well be that extents other than cheesecakes would be more effective for the fractal rendering algorithm. For example, it is easy to argue that ellipsoids would be tighter extents than cheesecakes. The conditional variance of a fractal segment is maximum in the center of the fractal and diminishes as it approaches the vertex of a facet. Ellipsoids also exhibit this behavior but cheesecakes do not.

To construct an ellipsoid extent, one would choose two of the three ellipsoid principal axes to be in the plane of the triangle. The principal lengths would be set to cover the vertices. The third principal axis should be vertical with principal length sufficient to cover $\pm\eta$ in the center of the ellipsoid.

A revised version of this paper will appear in the July 1983 issue of **acm Transactions on Graphics**.

It should be easy to calculate intersection points between a ray and an extent. And, certainly, intersecting a ray with an ellipsoid is almost as easy as intersecting one with a sphere. Let the matrix A be formed using the principal axes as rows. Intersecting a ray r with an ellipsoid is equivalent to intersecting a ray $A^{-1}r$ with a sphere.

The prism and surface of revolution algorithms may be extended in a number of ways. One extension is to allow curves other than simple line segments to reside in the leaves of the strip tree. There are two requirements that such new leaf curves should satisfy. First, they should be completely enclosed by a suitable rectangular extent. Second, it should be relatively easy to intersect a ray with these primitive curves. Useful primitives are: circular arcs, parabolas, and algebraic curves.

Both algorithms may also be generalized by linearly transforming the incoming ray. In this way surfaces of revolution may have elliptical instead of circular cross sections. In addition, this technique can model skewed surfaces of revolution and skewed prisms.

Note also that the methods presented here may be applied in a mutually recursive manner to efficiently render objects of potentially high complexity. We can best explain what we mean by an example. Suppose the task is to model an office building. One way to do this would be to model it as a prism where each face of the prism is the base plane of a collection of smaller prisms each of whose faces is, say, a deterministic height field. The rendering of this building would recursively invoke the algorithms presented above.

Of course, the normal computation of the surface is subject to the now standard techniques of Phong smoothing, and Blinn perturbation mapping. The prism and surface of revolution algorithms also allow a cheaper version of these techniques to be applied to the two dimensional normals as well. Thus, it is possible to generate, say, smoothly reflecting and refracting prisms even though the boundary curves may be coarsly polygonal.

ACKNOWLEDGMENTS. I would like to thank Howard Derby for many discussions and much help during the course of this investigation. I also thank the SIGGRAPH and TOGS reviewers for suggesting many useful changes.

§7 References

1. APPEL, A. Some Techniques for Shading Machine Renderings of Solids. SJCC (1968) 37-45.

2. BALLARD, D.H. Strip trees: a hierarchical representation for curves. *Comm. ACM,* 24 (May 1981) 310-321.

3. BLINN, J.F. Simulation of wrinkled surfaces. *Computer Graphics* 12 (August 1978) 286-292.

4. BRAID, I.C. Designing with Volumes, Ph.D. Dissertation. Univ. Cambridge, England (1973).

5. CARPENTER, L.C. Computer rendering of fractal curves and surfaces. *SIGGRAPH80 Conference Proceedings Supplement* (August 1980).

6. CHOW Y.S., TEICHER, H. *Probability Theory: Independence, Interchangeability, Martingales.* Springer Verlag, Heidelberg (1978).

7. DUDA, R.O. AND HART,P.E. *Pattern Classification and Scene Analysis.* Wiley-Interscience, New York (1973).

8. FOURNIER, A., FUSSELL, D. Stochastic modelling in computer graphics. *SIGGRAPH80 Conference Proceedings Supplement* (August 1980).

9. FOURNIER, A., FUSSELL, D. AND CARPENTER, L. Computer rendering of stochastic models. *Comm. ACM,* 25 (June 1982) 371-384.

10. GOLDSTEIN, E. AND NAGLE, R. 3D visual simulation *Simulation* 16 (Jan 1971) 25-31.

11. MANDELBROT, B. *Fractals: Form, Chance, and Dimension.* W.H. Freeman, San Francisco(1977).

12. MANDELBROT, B. Fractional brownian motions, fractional noises and applications. *SIAM Review* 10,4 (October 1968) 422-437.

13. REQUICHA, A.A.G. Representations for rigid solids: theory, methods, and systems. *ACM Computing Surveys* 12 (December 1980) 437-464.

14. ROTH, S.D. Ray casting for modeling solids. *Computer Graphics and Image Processing* 18 (1982) 109-144.

15. RUBIN, S. AND WHITTED, T. A three-dimensional representation for fast rendering of complex scenes. *Computer Graphics* 14 (1980) 110-116.

16. WHITTED, T. An improved illumination model for shaded display. *Comm. ACM,* 23 (June 1980) 343-349.

17. WHITTED, T. *private communication* (1983).

A revised version of this paper will appear in the July 1983 issue of **acm Transactions on Graphics.**

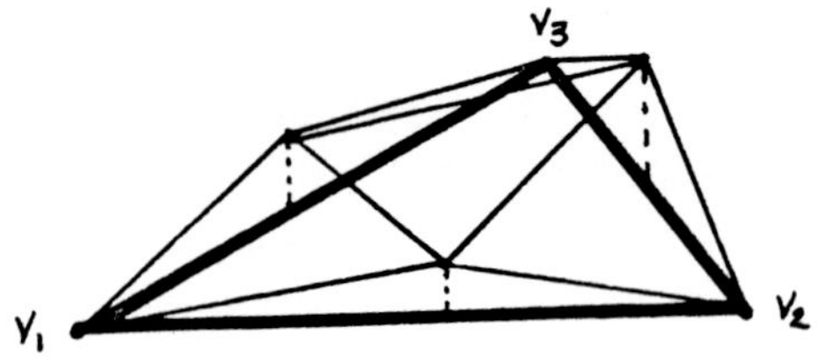

Figure 1. **Fractal subdivision.** The midpoint of each edge of the triangle is displaced in z by a random variable.

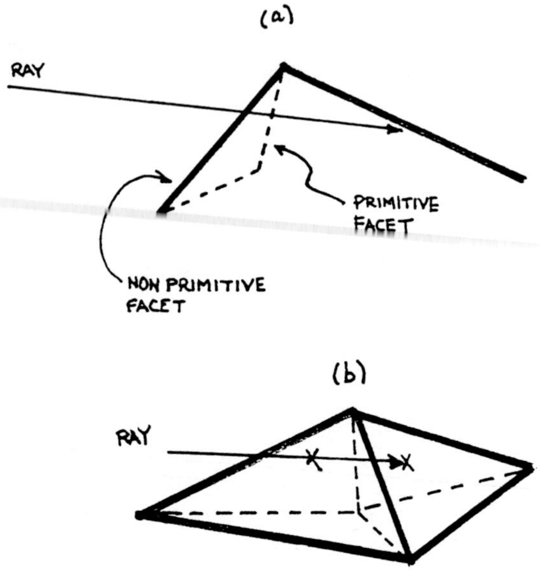

Figure 2. **Shadowing by nonprimitive facets.** (a) In the two dimensional case, non-primitive facets shadowing other facets is a sufficient condition to cull them from further consideration. (b) In the three dimensional case a non-primitive facet may shadow another at a given stage of evolution but later stages (shown as dotted lines) may uncover the shadowed facet.

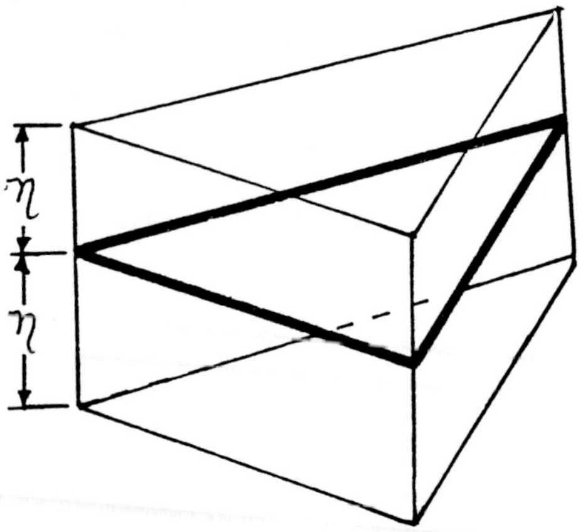

Figure 3. **A cheesecake extent.** This extent is formed by the volume swept out by translated a facet in z by $\pm\eta$.

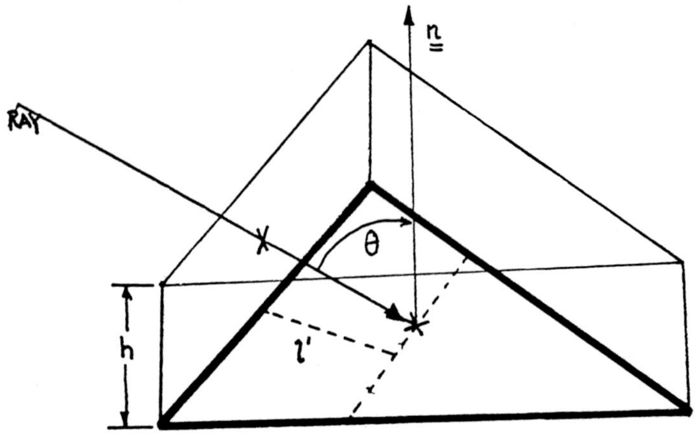

Figure 4. **Estimating wasted computations.** If an incoming ray strikes a facet at a small enough angle θ, it will miss the sides.

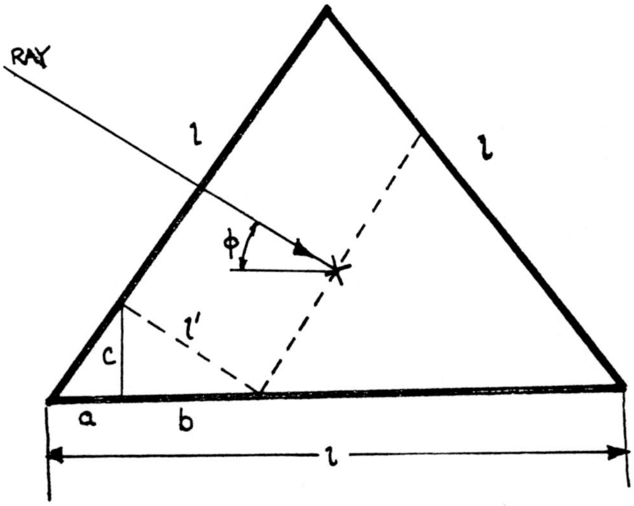

Figure 5. **Estimating wasted computations.** This figure shows a top view of figure 4. We use it to calculate the area of the shaded region.

A revised version of this paper will appear in the July 1983 issue of **acm Transactions on Graphics.**

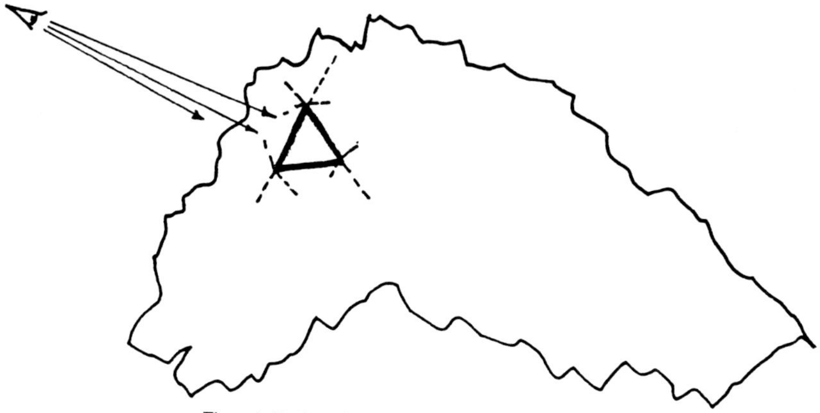

Figure 6. **Estimating wasted computations.** Under typical viewing conditions, the angle of ray-facet intersections is hardly uniformly distributed.

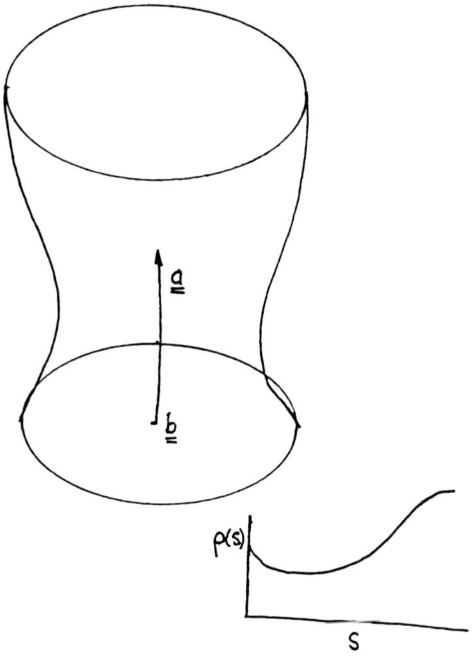

Figure 10. **A surface of revolution.** The surface is defined by a base point *b*, an axis vector *a*, and a radius function *ρ(s)*.

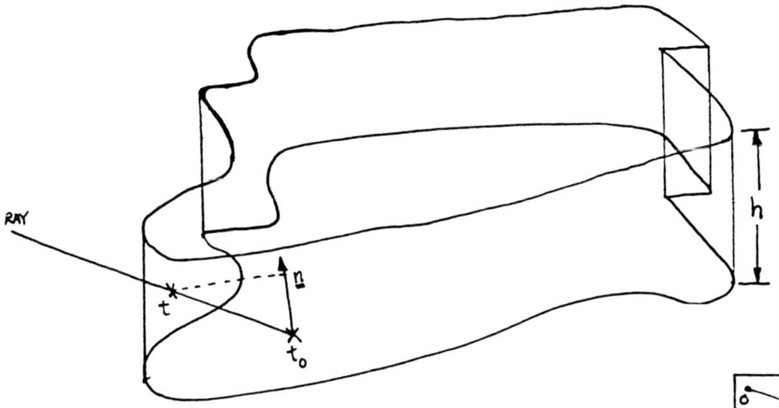

Figure 7. **A prism.** The ray is shown striking the side of a prism of height *h* with base plane normal *n*.

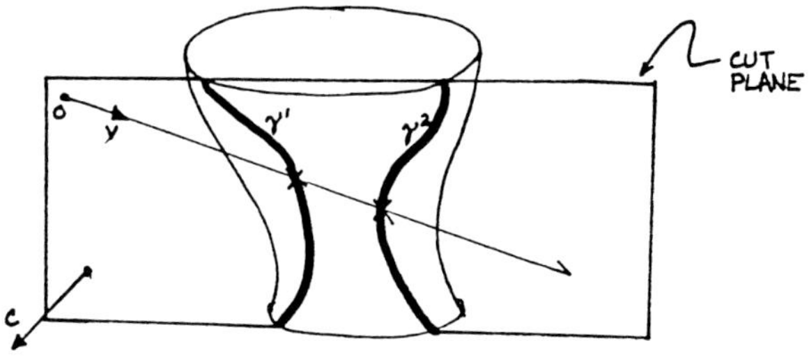

Figure 11. **Computing the intersection.** The cut plane contains the ray and is parallel to the axis of revolution. It cuts the surface in two curves.

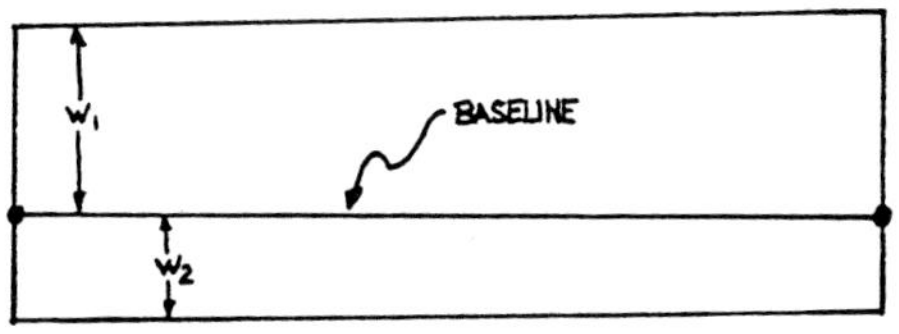

Figure 8. **A strip tree extent.**

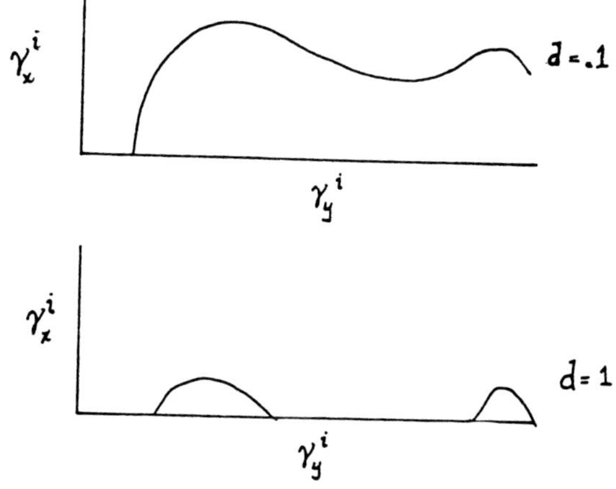

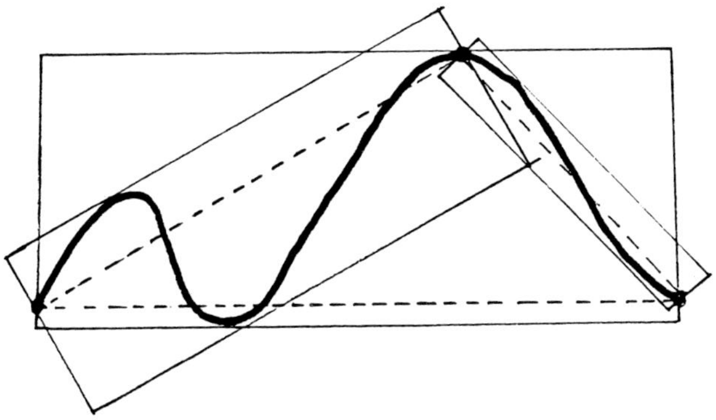

Figure 9. **A strip tree.** Rectangular extents completely enclose the bold curve.

Figure 12. **Intersection curves.** The cut plane intersection curves vary dramatically in shape with the cut plane to base point distance.

A revised version of this paper will appear in the July 1983 issue of **acm Transactions on Graphics.**

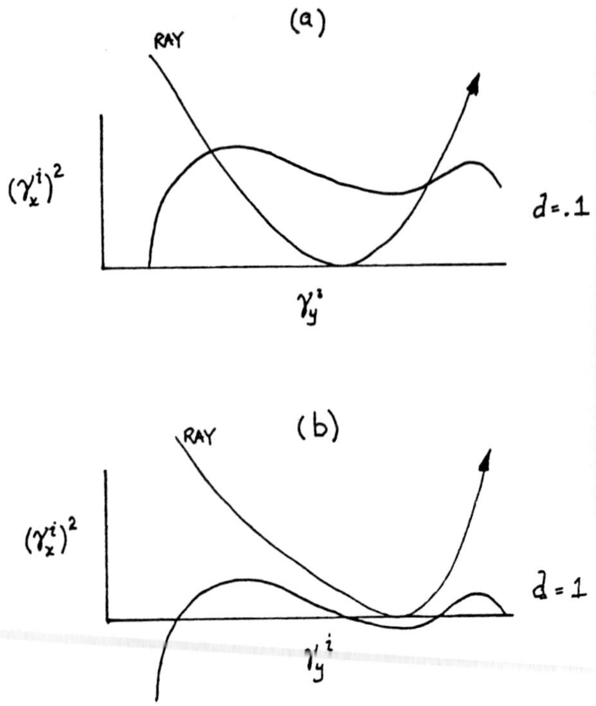

Figure 13 **Intersecting a ray in bent space.** (a) The bent space ray is now curved. The two intersection points represent intersections with the different γ_x^i. (b) Changing the cut plane to base point distance simply translates the radius curve.

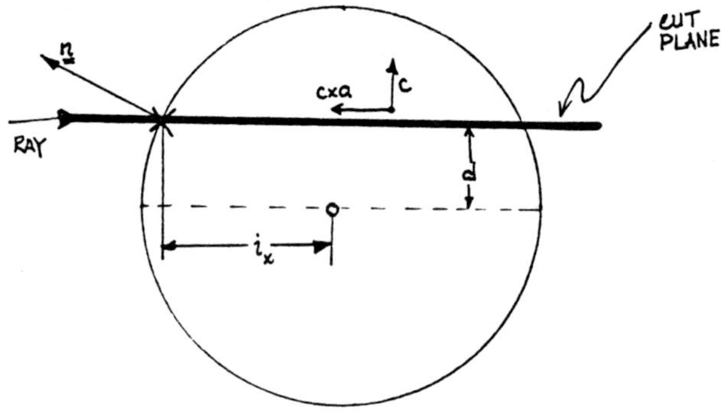

Figure 14. **Calculating the three space normal.** This is a top view looking down the axis vector.

Figure 15. **A fractal surface.** The surface is shadowed by and reflected in a mirrored sphere. Note that in the reflection, the surface can be seen to be shadowing itself.

Figure 16. **A prism.** The prism is surrounded by two mirrored spheres.

Figure 17. **A surface of revolution.** This glass is defined by only 18 real numbers.

A revised version of this paper will appear in the July 1983 issue of **acm Transactions on Graphics.**

PANEL

TECHNICAL IMPLICATIONS OF PROPOSED GRAPHICS STANDARDS

CHAIR: David Straayer, Tektronix, Inc.
PANELISTS: Peter Bono, Athena Systems
Richard Ehlers, Evans & Sutherland
Gunter Enderle, Karlsruhe Nuclear Research
Theodore Reed, Los Alamos National Laboratory
David Shuey, McDonnell Douglas Automation
Mark Skall, National Bureau of Standards
Elaine Sonderegger, SIGGRAPH
Tom Wright, ISSCO

CHAIRMAN'S INTRODUCTION:

This panel session is intended to present recent technical developments in the efforts to standardize computer graphics.

Several alternative approaches to 3-D standards will be presented and contrasted. The Virtual Device Metafile will be presented, as well as a proposed binding of the GKS standard to Fortran.

Presentations will be made by the following individuals:

Dr. Peter Bono is the chairman of the ANSI X3H3 technical committee developing standards for Computer Graphics Programming Languages, and will present the current status of the effort to adopt 2-D GKS as an International Standard and as an American National Standard.

Tom Wright will be available to respond to questions about the Programmer's Minimal Interface to Graphics (PMIG) proposal, and its current status as a new output level of the draft proposed American National Standard (dpANS) GKS.

Mark Skall will present a proposed binding of GKS to the Fortran Language. Mr. Skall will also discuss progress in the field of formal specification of graphics standards and developments in the establishment of conformance/certification procedures for implementations of GKS.

Theodore Reed will present the technical content of the Virtual Device Metafile (VDM) draft proposed American National Standard. Discussed will be the relationship of the VDM to GKS and to the yet to be proposed Virtual Device Interface. Specific functionality of the VDM will be discussed as will specific bindings of that functionality as a character set extension and as a binary format.

David Shuey will present an overview of the Programmer's Hierarchical Interface to Graphics (PHIGS) proposal. The PHIGS proposal is intended to support hierarchical structuring of graphics data, in contrast to the Core System and GKS proposals. This type of structure addresses highly interactive graphics applications which need to modify the presentation and the relationships within graphics data.

Richard Ehlers will present the attribute model of the PHIGS proposal and explore the relationship of attribute model to structured graphics data bases. Also, Mr. Ehlers will discuss the viewing and transformation implications of structured graphics data bases using examples.

Gunter Enderle is a member of the West German delegation to the International Standards Organization (ISO) Working Group on Computer Graphics. Herr Enderle will be discussing ISO proposals for the extension of the GKS standard from 2-D to 3-D functionality. Several such proposals have been made, including one by DIN (the official standards making body of the German Federal Republic) and a Norwegian proposal called IDIGS.

Elaine Sonderegger was a member of the ACM SIGGRAPH Graphics Standards Planning Committee, and is the ACM SIGGRAPH representative to ANSI X3H3. Ms. Sonderegger will contrast the 3-D functionality of the Core System, IDIGS, DIN proposed 3-D extensions, and PHIGS.

COMPUTER GRAPHIC MODELING OF AMERICAN SIGN LANGUAGE

Jeffrey Loomis
Seacoast Software
The Salk Institute for Biological Studies

Howard Poizner
Ursula Bellugi
Alynn Blakemore
The Salk Institute for Biological Studies

John Hollerbach
Massachusetts Institute of Technology

Abstract

The essential grammatical information of American Sign Language (ASL) is conveyed through changes in the movement and spatial contouring of the hands and arms. An interactive computer graphic system is described for the analysis and modeling of sign language movement. This system consists of four components. The first component reconstructs actual movements in three dimensions and allows the user to interactively segment and transform the data for later analysis. The second component allows a user to interactively create synthetic signs by specifying angle functions in a jointed model. The third component provides a novel technique for manipulating movement quality independently of spatial path. The fourth component allows the building of complex stimuli and real-time stimulus sequencing for psycholinguistic experiments. The emphasis is on interactive techniques and data structures that allow analysis and modeling of the complex hand and arm movements of American Sign Language.

CR Categories and Subject Descriptors: I.3.0 [Computer Graphics]: General; I.3.4 [Computer Graphics]: Graphics Utilities - Application packages; I.3.6 [Computer Graphics]: Methodology and Techniques - Interaction techniques; I.3.7 [Computer Graphics]: Three-dimensional Graphics and Realism - Animation; J.4 [Computer Applications]: Social and Behavioral Sciences - Psychology; J.5 [Computer Applications]: Arts and Humanities-Linguistics

General Terms: Computer graphics, modeling, simulation, interpolation

Additional Keywords and Phrases: American Sign Language, movement

I. INTRODUCTION

The general objective of our research is to study biological foundations of human language. In their surface forms, the languages of the world differ widely--in phonetic detail, in concepts symbolized, in word construction, in typology, and in sentence structure. Focusing on the surface, one might conclude that languages can differ in innumerable ways. Beneath the surface, however, there are striking similarities in terms of formal properties. A central question in the attempt to understand the human capacity for language has been to what extent these underlying similarities found across spoken languages are a product of their vocal-auditory transmission.

Our laboratory has undertaken the first indepth study of languages that have developed in alternative articulatory-perceptual channels--languages produced by highly articulated movement of the hands rather than the vocal apparatus, and perceived by the eyes rather than the ears. We have been specifying the ways in which the formal properties of languages are shaped by their modality of expression, sifting properties peculiar to a particular language mode from more general properties common to all languages.

A major finding of our research is that American Sign Language (ASL) has developed elaborate morphological devices in a form which is unique to a visual-gestural system. Signs undergo a wide variety of grammatical processes--regular changes in form resulting in systematic changes in meaning--each of which operates by imposing different dynamic changes in movement and spatial contouring. The existence of such a fully expressive system arising outside the mainstream of spoken languages affords a new vantage point for investigating biological constraints on linguistic form. Our research has focused on the special nature of the grammatical processes that have arisen in ASL; strikingly, the essential grammatical information is conveyed by the structured use of three-dimensional space and movement (Klima and Bellugi, 1979; Bellugi and Studdert-Kennedy, 1980; Bellugi, 1980).

That the inflectional level of structure in ASL is instantiated entirely in dynamic movement patterns has been shown by studies in which deaf signers are asked to identify inflectional processes from their extracted movement patterns alone. In order to isolate information about movement from information about form (e.g., handshape) in the language, we have utilized a technique developed by Johansson (1975) for studying perception of motion. Small incandescent lights are placed at selected points on the body of a signer corresponding to the major joints of the hands and arms (shoulders, elbows, wrists, index fingertips). Signing is recorded in a darkened room so that on the videotape, only the pattern of moving points of light appears against a black background. Even with such greatly reduced information, deaf signers are highly accurate at recognizing and identifying inflections presented in these dynamic point-light displays, demonstrating that these patterns of dynamic contours of movement form a distinct isolable (but co-occurring) layer of structure (Poizner, 1981, 1983; Poizner, Bellugi, and Lutes-Driscoll, 1981; Poizner, Newkirk, and Bellugi, 1983). In this paper we outline a method for computer-graphically visualizing, manipulating and analyzing movements of the hands and arms that convey both grammatical and lexical information in ASL.

We have begun to utilize a method for measuring ASL movement that allows three-dimensional measurement, with a digital readout of coordinates fed directly to a computer. Using two optoelectronic cameras, we track the positions of light-emitting diodes suitably placed on joints of the hand and arm. Three-dimensional coordinates are then calculated from the readouts of the two cameras. The ability to visualize and interactively manipulate these reconstructed movements in three dimensions is critical for analysis. Movement segmentation is an important linguistic aspect, with separate analyses applied to separate movement segments. The interactive control and three-dimensional visualization of a reconstructed movement makes segmentation and movement analysis a feasible and powerful tool. We couple this physical analysis of the sign signal with the computer synthesis of signs.

II. BACKGROUND

The system described in this paper is related both to motion analysis and human movement simulation. Recorded movements have been used to study human gait (Winter, Greenlaw, and Hobston, 1972) and to assist professional athletes in improving their performance (Donkoh, 1980). Computer graphic techniques are used to assist in the extraction of movement data from film or videotape. The earliest and most notable system of this type is GALATEA, designed and implemented by Futrelle, Potel, and others at the University of Chicago (Futrelle, 1974; Potel and Mackay, 1980). Baecker, Miller and Reeves (1981) describe a prototype laboratory instrument for the interactive motion analysis of videotape records, a system inspired by the success of GALATEA.

The primary thrust of our system for motion analysis is the visualization and analysis of data acquired automatically by optoelectronic means (Woltring, 1974), rather than assisting in the acquisition of the data from film or videotape. We use computer graphics to display the shape of three-dimensional time histories, to replay them, to segment and transform them for later analysis. The curves that we display are analogous to the p-curves described by Baecker (1969) in that the dynamics of the movement are captured in the spacing of the dots along the curve.

Our second emphasis is on movement simulation, which is a rapidly growing field as the recent special issue of IEEE Computer Graphics and Applications (Badler, 1982) attests. Badler and Smoliar (1979) provide a survey and taxonomy of techniques for digital representation of human movement, and provide an approach for animating a realistic human body in terms of a network of special-purpose processors. In addition, there has been some work in the area of modeling sign language. Platt and Badler (1981) describe an intergrated system for representing and simulating human facial movements, the face being one channel of ASL communication. Badler and Morris (1982) present a method for representing non-rigid articulated objects and apply it to modeling the shape of the hand used in ASL signs. Finally, Shantz and Poizner (1982) present a method for generating ASL signs based on a stick figure model.

The goal of much of the previous work in human movement simulation has been realism, either in the rendering of the human figure or in the underlying control mechanisms. Zeltzer (1981), for example, views the control of an animated figure as a problem of robotics. Our emphasis is on a simple stick figure model, manipuated directly. We emphasize simplicity for two reasons. First, we were interested in having a working model fairly quickly, and a simple abstraction is easier to implement. Second, movement is critical to sign language. Movement itself conveys the essential grammatical information of the language and this information is well conveyed when the display is reduced to only a few moving points of light (Poizner, Bellugi, and Lutes-Driscoll, 1981). A stick figure model, while conveying the configuration of the hand, allows focus on movement, and in particular, on the subtle and complex movements crucial to American Sign Language.

The model described in this paper is a direct descendant of a model implemented in BASIC on a Hewlett-Packard 9830-A microcomputer (Shantz and Poizner, 1982). The difficulty with the earlier system was the non-interactive and two-dimensional nature of the display. Functions defining how joint angles changed over time were input via a data tablet, but the resulting motion could not be viewed immediately, and then only in two dimensions. We found that the task of specifying positions and movements can be difficult even with a three-dimensional interactive display. We describe some techniques for improving procedures for analyzing and synthesizing three-dimensional movement. The capacity to synthesize ASL signs could well allow major advances in the experimental investigation of the perception of sign language.

III. COMPUTER ENVIRONMENT

The software described in this paper runs on a PDP-11/34 running Bell Laboratory's Unix operating system (Bell, 1978). The graphics hardware consists of an Evans and Sutherland Picture System II, along with three banks of sixteen function switches, a bank of eight dials and a data tablet. The availability of the function switches dictated the nature of the operater interface. Most programs are controlled via function switches rather than using the tablet and software generated menus.[1]

The flowchart in Figure 1 shows the relationship between the various data files and programs in the system. The double boxes represent areas which are outside the scope of this paper but are shown here for completeness. The large boxes represent interactive graphics programs. The small rectangular boxes represent filters, programs which map data from one format into another format. The circles represent data files, of which there are several different types. The abbreviations for the various data files are expanded in Table 1.

The system divides naturally into four subsystems, which we refer to as SELD, ASLSYN, DYNO, and STIM. SELD displays reconstructed sign language movements acquired using a Selspot movement monitoring system. This component allows the investigator to interactively segment and transform the data for later analysis. ASLSYN allows the user to interactively specify synthetic sign language movements by manipulating the angle functions of a jointed model. In addition to the action file editor there are programs for creating target files, which aid the synthesis procedure, and for compiling action files. Each frame in a compiled action is a list of points to be displayed, rather than the underlying joint angles. DYNO provides a technique for manipulating the temporal characteristics of sign language movements. STIM allows the building of complex stimuli and real-time stimulus sequencing. Stimuli can consist of a number of actions and objects, displayed for a specified number of frames. Stimuli are stored in a high performance swapping region of the disk, allowing real-time playback.

The various subsystems interact in several ways. Selspot data can be converted to compiled action files and can

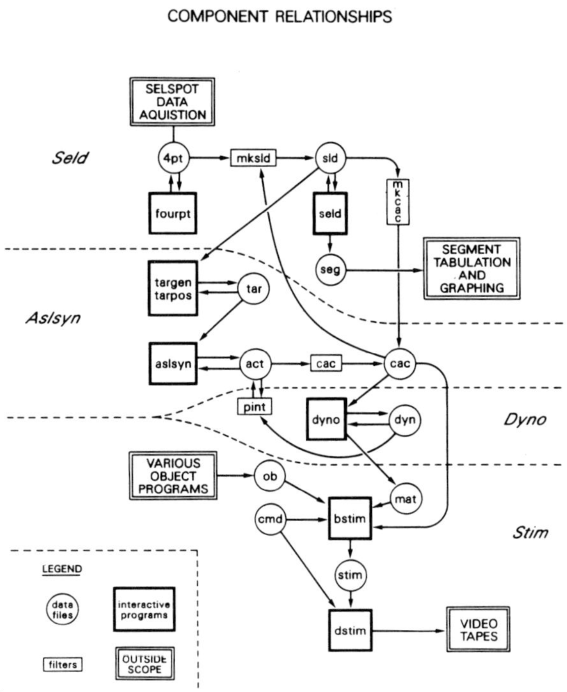

Figure 1. Relations among components of the analysis, synthesis and stimulus construction programs.

Table 1. Data File Definitions

4pt	Raw Selspot data for all four points (shoulder, elbow, wrist and finger).
sld	Selspot data for two points, plus velocity and acceleration graphs.
seg	Segment information; begin and end points, minimum, average and maximum velocities and accelerations, etc.
act	Action file. Consists of joint angle functions and static joint information.
cac	Compiled action file. Each frame consists of a list of vectors to be displayed.
mat	Transformation matrix files.
dyn	Dynamic functions, used to modify the temporal characteristics of sign language movements.
ob	Object definitions.
cmd	Command files for stimulus generation and sequencing.
stim	Stimulus files, composites of multiple action files and object files.

then be displayed as stimuli. Compiled actions can be converted to Selspot data format and analyzed using SELD. Selspot data can be converted to target point arrays, which are used to aid in the synthesis of sign language movement.

IV. COMPUTER-GRAPHIC THREE-DIMENSIONAL RECONSTRUCTION OF ASL--SELD

Actual sign language movement trajectories are acquired using the Selspot movement monitoring system. The components of this system are a control unit, two special cameras, and infrared LEDs attached to a small connector box. The LEDs are taped to limb segments, and the connector box is strapped to the body. The control unit pulses up to 30 LEDs at a rate of 315 Hz., and synchronizes the camera output with the pulsing. We record signing with four LEDs attached to the dominant arm of the signer, at the index fingertip, wrist, elbow, and shoulder. The Selspot cameras have special detector plates and electronics which locate the x/y position of an LED spot on the plate.

The Selspot control unit transmits data to a PDP 11/34 computer through a DMA interface, which automatically reads data into successive computer memory locations. At the same time, the computer memory buffer is emptied onto a disk to allow large amounts of data to be recorded. A special interface between the control unit and the DMA interface allows the computer to limit the data transmitted by transmitting only data for a specified number of LEDs and to skip entirely one Selspot cycle to obtain a form of frequency control.

The three-dimensional coordinates of an LED are calculated from two cameras by triangulation. First, the data from each camera are calibrated for lens and electronic distortions through a table lookup; the tables are specific to lens settings, and are formed by exhaustive placement of target LEDs at known locations. Second, the data are filtered and missing points are interpolated if desired (missing points occur when an LED goes out of view). Third, the three-dimensional coordinates are obtained with the knowledge of relative camera position and orientation.

The major advantage of the Selspot system over other movement monitoring techniques is the convenience of obtaining the camera coordinates of the LEDs. The movements are also unrestrained, with the proviso that the LEDs remain in view; this proviso could eventually be relaxed by the addition of more cameras. The accuracy of the system as a whole is fairly good: between 0.5-1.0 cm within a 1 cm^3 box at a camera distance of 3 meters. The resolution is 0.3 cm at this distance, corresponding to 10-bit resolution at the cameras.

SELD displays the movement trajectories in three dimensions. Trajectories for two points can be displayed simultaneously. The three-dimensional structure of the trajectories can be visualized using the depth-cueing capability of the Evans and Sutherland Picture System II, by viewing the trajectories while they are rotating and by viewing the trajectories in a stereo display mode. The stereo display mode consists of a split screen presentation and a stereo hood. For orientation a set of labeled axes can be displayed along with the trajectories. A rectangular solid can be drawn around the trajectory to delimit the maximum deviation of the movement along each of the three Cartesian dimensions. Finally, a three-dimensional calibration index, 50mm on a side, can by displayed to provide scale information.

The dynamics of the trajectory are captured in the spacing of the dots along the trajectory. It is also possible to "replay" the trajectory. In this mode a bar is displayed between the points on the two trajectories at a given time. When the time at which the bar is displayed is incremented steadily, it appears as if the bar is moving along the original trajectory. The rate at which the bar moves is controlled by varying the amount that time is incremented or by varying the number of frames that each time is displayed.

The velocity and acceleration along the path is determined by calculating the distance along path (by summing individual interpoint distances) as a function of time, differentiating this function to get velocity along path, and differentiating velocity along path to get acceleration along path. A five point Lagrangian interpolation polynominal is used to perform the numerical differentiation (Hildebrand, 1956). A graph of velocity and acceleration along path can be displayed for either trajectory on the right hand side of the screen. A sweeping axis is displayed at the time at which the bar in the trajectory display is being drawn.

By manipulating a dial the investigator can control one of two time pointers. In this mode, a bar is drawn on the trajectory display and the velocity/acceleration graph at the time selected by the active pointer. The nonactive pointer is shown by a dashed axis on the velocity/acceleration graph. The investigator selects which time pointer is active using a function switch. Once the investigator has identified an interval of interest he can make that interval a window by selecting a function switch. This alters ("blows up") the time scale on the velocity/acceleration graph and limits the movement of the time pointers. Function switches allow the operator to display the data in the current interval, in the window or to display all of the data for either trajectory. At any time the operator can create a file for the current interval containing a definition of the segment (begin and end points) and a number of calculated parameters (minimum, average and maximum velocity and acceleration, distance along path, etc.).

Another feature of the SELD program is the ability to transform the data using the "write back to memory" feature of the Picture System. The coordinates in which the data are acquired are often not the coordinates of interest to the investigator. The investigator can orient the data so that it is aligned along major planes of interest, and then transform the data to the new coordinate system.

We will illustrate aspects of this interactive display system in the computer graphics reconstruction of some American Sign Language grammatical inflections. In Figure 2, two grammatically inflected signs are shown together with their movement paths reconstructed in three dimensions. The left panels illustrate line drawings of the basic sign LOOK[2] and its form under two inflections for temporal aspect. The basic sign LOOK is made with a single outward movement (not shown). One inflected form of the sign is LOOK[Continuative], which changes the meaning to 'look for a long time.' The form of the sign under the Continuative inflection (shown in the upper left panel) is tense rapid outward movement with an elliptical slow return to the starting point. The reconstructed movement of the fingertip, along with associated velocity and acceleration curves is shown in the middle panel. The time pointers on the velocity and acceleration graphs were positioned to delineate the first of two movement cycles. Characteristics of this first cycle are shown in the upper right hand panel of the figure. In that panel, the time pointer was positioned at the point of maximum velocity. The correspondence of that point with the spatial path is indicated by the bar in the trajectory display.

A second inflectional form is illustrated in the lower left hand panel of the figure: LOOK[Durational]. Under this inflectional form, the meaning changes to 'look continously.' The form of the sign under the Durational inflection is a smooth circular even movement, which is repeated several times. The middle panel illustrates the movement of the Durational inflection. The right hand panel displays the first repetition cycle, corresponding to the time window established by the pointers in the middle panel. This procedure allows the segmentation of sign movements into relevant linguistic components.

In summary, the SELD program provides an extremely powerful tool for visualizing and analyzing the large volume of data generated by the Selspot movement monitoring system.

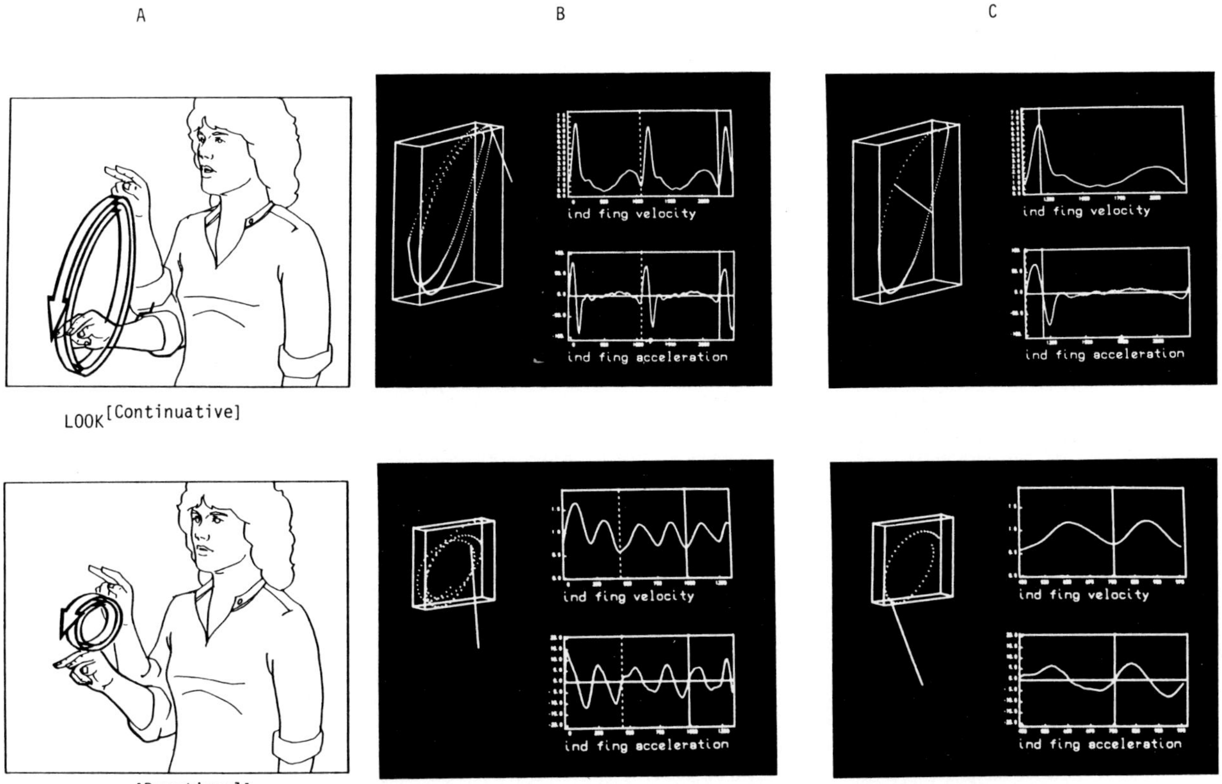

LOOK[Durational]

Figure 2. Three-dimensional reconstructions of two ASL inflections. A) line drawings; B) the entire reconstructed movement with time pointers 'windowing' one movement cycle; C) characteristics of one movement cycle.

V. COMPUTER SYNTHESIS OF AMERICAN SIGN LANGUAGE - ASLSYN, DYNO

In order to model certain linguistic processes, it is necessary to computer-synthesize ASL forms. A signer simply cannot produce forms that are exactly equal in trajectory shape, in duration, or in any other physical variable; neither can he produce a series of forms that are separated physically by exactly the same increment. However, such precise control over the form of stimuli is of crucial importance for many psycholinguistic experiments.

In synthesizing signs, we manipulate a representation of the skeletal linkages of the arms utilizing the interactive capacities of the Picture System. We can readily access our data on the physical characteristics of actually-occuring sign movement, and perform identical three-dimensional analyses (e.g., calculations of velocities, accelerations, etc.) on the sign movements that we generate. Thus, we work back and forth between motions that we synthesize and characteristics that we know are critical to the form.

ASLSYN is an interactive action file editor. An action file consists of a number of angle functions, although in the general case any degree of freedom could be represented in these functions. An action file has a fixed duration; independent utilities exist for rescaling and altering the "time scale." A user enters an action by specifying all of the angles at a number of key frames; the rest of each function is interpolated linearly. Any angle function can also be modified by drawing in a new function on a data tablet. For purposes of selecting angle functions, we divided the angles into a number of categories, each containing from two to four angles. The angle group is selected using function switches and all of the angles in an angle group can be manipulated using dials. Only one angle can be selected for tablet input with this angle selected by toggling a function switch.

The relationships among the various angle functions are specified in a skeleton definition. A skeleton definition is a table of skeleton operation codes and operands. By externalizing the structure of the model, we created a tool which is capable of modeling a number of different movements, of which upper arm motion is just a particular instance. This feature has been used to handle various types of arms; in one case we completely define the arm and hand, in another we model just the arm and index finger.

In some cases, particular angles are not dynamic, they remain the same throughout the movement. In these cases it is possible to eliminate the angle function, using instead a fixed value. This generality is implemented by including a map of what angles are represented as functions. When an action file is input, the skeleton definition is also input. The definition is scanned for operands which specify dynamic angles. If the dynamic angle is actually a static angle, the skeleton definition is changed from a dynamic operation to a static operation and the static value is inserted into the skeleton definition. Figure 3 shows the structure of action files.

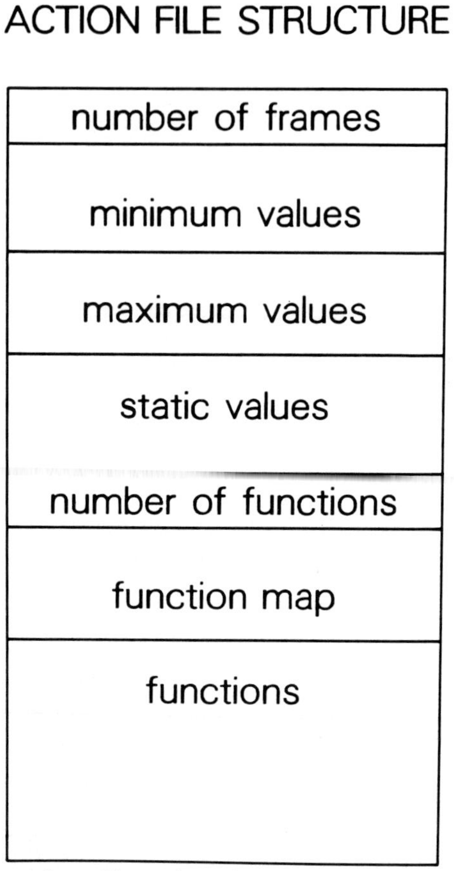

Figure 3. The structure of action files.

Skeleton definitions were designed so that a single action file could be played on either arm. This was done by having two types of rotation operations, mirrored and unmirrored. In a mirrored rotation the sign of the angle changes depending on the side that the action is being played on. ASLSYN is also capable of doing a different action on each arm.

While the three-dimensional interactive technique of specifying action files was an improvement over the two-dimensional system, the task was still a difficult one. It can be awkward to manipulate a three-dimensional stick figure using dials to control various joint angles, since it is often difficult to specify the various positions in a movement without some guidelines. Because of these problems, we developed two techniques to simplify the task.

The first of these techniques is target points. Target points are an array of fingertip positions, one for each frame in the action. Target points can be specified in one of three ways: the array can be drawn using a data tablet, elliptical arrays can be specified by entering an aspect ratio (many signs have elliptical paths), or actual sign data can be used from Selspot digitization. In the first two methods, the array must be planar. We have not found this to be too limiting a constraint.

After specifying the target point array, the user positions the array relative to the simulated signer. The array can be translated in x, y and z and rotated into correct orientation. We found that a rotate-by-90 degrees switch simplified the process of orienting the target array. It was also important to show the direction and starting point of the target array. This was done by drawing the first quarter and the third sixth of the points as solid lines (see Figure 4). The starting point in Figure 4 is at eleven o'clock and the direction of motion is clockwise.

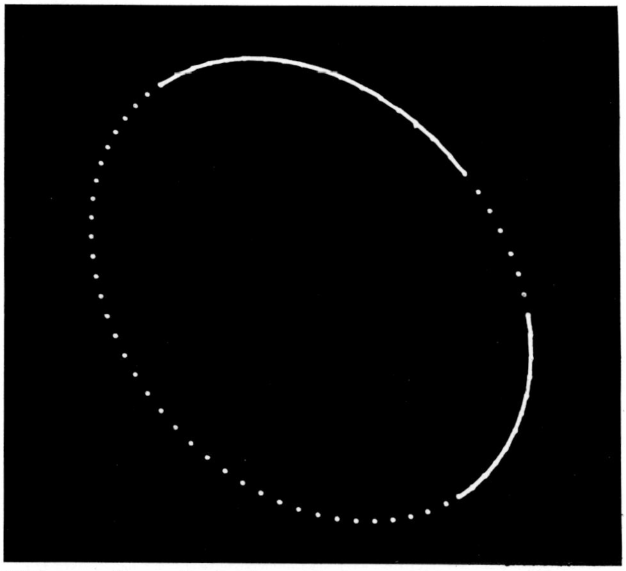

Figure 4. Target points with orientation lines.

Once the target array has been positioned correctly, the task of entering the angle functions is greatly simplified. To correctly position the figure at any point in time, the fingertip has to be moved to the target point. Without this constraint it is difficult to determine where the arm should be at any given time. The user has only to make sure that the arm is positioned "correctly," since there is more than one possible arm position when the fingertip is at the target point. In the future we hope that the tedious task of actually moving the fingertip to the target point will be done by the computer. The user would correctly position the arm while the computer would "hold" the fingertip to the target point (see also Badler, O'Rourke and Kaufman, 1980 for a working system with target capability).

The second technique for simplifying skeleton positioning was user-defined dials. We found that in order to position the fingertip, it was necessary to select the elbow group, tweak the elbow angle, select the shoulder group, tweak the shoulder angles, and so on, back and forth between the two angle groups. Since we had additional dials, we added a feature whereby the user could map any angle to one of the additional dials using a command. Being able to simultaneously tweak one of the elbow angles and one of the shoulder angles simplified the task of positioning the arm. Figure 5 shows stroboscopic photographs of synthesized movements of the hand along the target path together with a plot of how one angle function changes over time.

<u>Compiled Actions</u>. Because of the computation involved, we could only achieve a rate of 10 frames per second with a single fully articulated arm and hand. This rate was too slow for work in the DYNO program so an alternate representation was required. Using the "write back to memory" feature of the Picture System, it is possible to get the three-dimensional coordinates of the various joints and fingertips. Because the number of points and the number of frames is small, it is posible to store an entire motion in memory. Since there is essentially no computation involved, it is possible to achieve a rate equal to the update rate of the monitor, 30 or 40 frames a second. Thus, an action is specified using the angle function representation and then "compiled" for the high speed displays required for manipulating dynamics.

<u>Dynamic Functions (DYNO)</u>. A given linguistic movement can have different meanings depending on the dynamics of the motion, as indicated above. We use the concept of a dynamic function to manipulate this variable. An action is defined in the frame domain and displayed in the time domain. Dynamic functions map time domain into frame domain. That is, for a given time, a dynamic function specifies the frame to be displayed. A typical dynamic function is illustrated in Figure 6. By definition the function starts at (0,0) and ends at (f,t), where <u>f</u> is the number of frames in the action and <u>t</u> is the length of time the action is to be played. The dashed diagonal line represents the "null" dynamic function, where the actual playback rate is the rate at which the action is defined. The solid line is the dynamic function. Where the slope of the function is shallow the action is slow, where the function is steep the action is rapid. During a hold the dynamic function is perfectly flat. The dynamic function is used to determine what frame to display at each point in time. At time <u>a</u>, frame <u>b</u> is shown. At time <u>c</u>, frame <u>d</u> is shown. During a hold the same frame is shown over a number of time increments, and during rapid motion, frames are skipped.

We are interested in how signers perceive distinctions between ASL

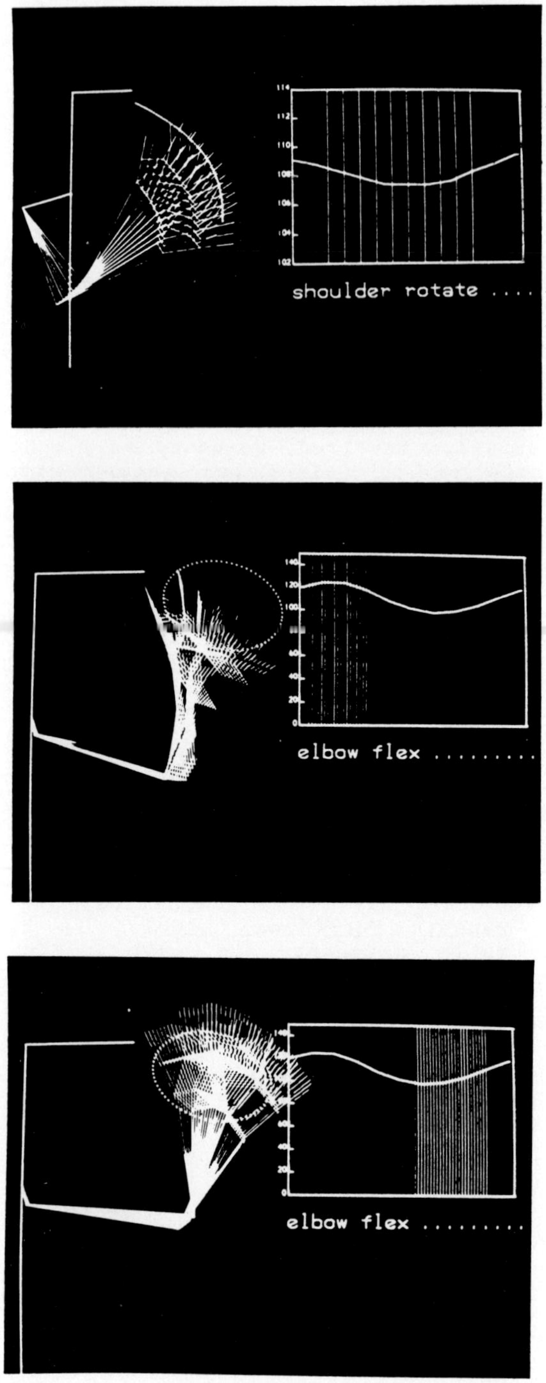

Figure 5. Stroboscopic photographs of synthesized signs showing the hand moving along target points.

inflections as the movement dynamics gradually change, in equal physical increments from that specifying one inflection to that specifying another. In order to investigate this perceptual phenomenon, we developed a program for interpolating dynamic functions. Given two dynamic functions, we are able to generate intermediate functions. This process was not just averaging the values of two frames at any given point in time, but rather involved the following technique. We vary the frame coordinate from 0 to f. At each step we find the corresponding times in the two functions and average them, generating a point on the interpolated function. by using a weighted average we can vary the interpolated function smoothly from one function to another. For functions with a hold at either end there is no unique time corresponding to the initial or final frame. For initial holds we average the time at which the hold terminates; for final holds, we average the time at which the hold begins. The generated points are connected to form the interpolated function.

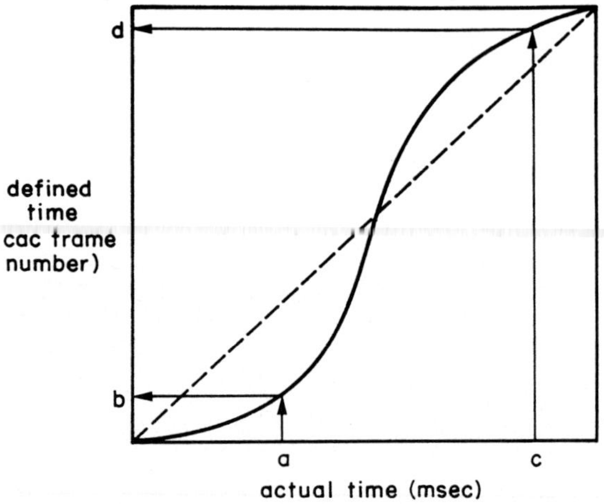

Figure 6. A typical dynamic function.

The dynamic function is used in two different ways. In the first, the dynamic function is used to select a frame from a static array of frames. If the dynamic function specifies frame 5.6, the program displays frame 5. This is adequate for previewing the effects of different dynamic functions on a given action. In the second, we use dynamic functions to modify actions, interpolating when the dynamic function specifies non-integral frame numbers. In this case a new action file is generated. We refer to this as "precise interpolation", and the filter which performs this function is called PINT. PINT can also be used with null dynamic functions to rescale action files, changing the number of frames which define an action.

Figure 7 illustrates a continuum of dynamic functions. The upper panel of Figure 7 presents seven dynamic functions equally spaced along a continuum. The left-most function produces a movement modification which conveys one particular grammatical inflection in ASL (the Intensive, meaning 'extremely'). The right-most function conveys a different inflection (the Resultative, meaning 'become fully'). The five intermediate functions produce movement modifications intermediate in form between the two. The lower panel illustrates the nature of the movement modifications produced by each of the seven functions. The upper (continuous) row of dots represents the movement without any dynamic function applied. The action starts at the left of each row and moves to the right, with each dot representing one frame. The second row of dots (int) reflects the nature of the action after the left-most dynamic function was applied. The first and final frames are held, only a few of the intermediate frames are displayed. The rest of the rows show the selection of frames dictated by the remaining dynamic functions. The movements produced by each of the dynamic functions will be used in psycholinguistic experiments that investigate how signers discriminate movement changes in ASL.

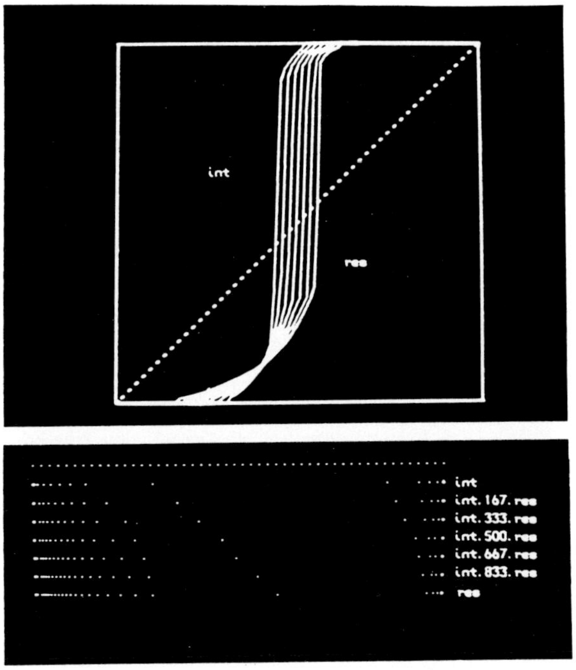

Figure 7. A continuum of dynamic functions and their effect on a single action.

Stimulus Generation and Display. The ultimate products of the simulation system are videotapes of objects and actions to be used as stimuli in perceptual experiments. Each stimulus is a composite of several different actions and objects. The same object or action can be instantiated in several different locations. Stimuli are built up using commands, either interactively or using scripts (batched commands). The program which builds stimuli is called BSTIM, and the program which displays stimuli is called DSTIM. There are also various utilities which store the stimuli in an area on the disk for high speed access, and for building the necessary directories for mapping stimulus name to disk address. These procedures are essential for the real-time generation of stimuli for psycholinguistic experiments.

VI. CONCLUSION

American Sign Language displays all the complex linguistic structure and organization found in spoken language, yet the mechanisms by which the essential grammatical information is conveyed are unique to the modality in which the language developed. This grammatical information is conveyed by changes in the movement and spatial contouring of the hands and arms. We have presented procedures for the three-dimensional reconstruction and manipulation of actual sign movements and techniques for synthesizing American Sign Language signs and grammatical processes. These procedures incorporate interactive techniques for the visualization and manipulation of signs. This system greatly enhances our ability to investigate the perception of sign language, much as computer synthesized speech has aided the investigation of speech perception. However, the study of sign language has the added advantage that the movements of the articulators are directly observable. The study of sign language thus provides an especially promising vehicle for investigating the relationship between the articulatory and perceptual properties that underlie linguistic structure.

REFERENCES

Badler, N. I., Ed. Modeling the human body for animation. (Special issue devoted to the topic). IEEE Computer Graphics and Applications, 2, 9, (November 1982).

Badler, N. I. and Morris, M. A. Modelling flexible, articulated objects. Proceedings of the ONLINE Conference, (1982).

Badler, N. I., O'Rourke, J. and Kaufman, B. Special problems in human movement simulation. Computer Graphics (Proceedings of SIGGRAPH 1980), 14, 3, (July, 1980), 189-197.

Badler, N. I. and Smoliar, S. Digital representation of human movements. ACM Computing Surveys, 11, (March 1979), 19-38.

Baecker, R. M. Picture-driven animation. Proceedings of the Spring Joint Computer Conference, (May 1969), 273-288.

Baecker, R. M., Miller, D. and Reeves, W. Towards a laboratory instrument for motion analysis. Computer Graphics, 15, 3 (August 1981), 191-197.

Bell System, UNIX time-sharing system (entire issue devoted to UNIX). The Bell System Technical Journal, 57, 6, Part 2 (July-August 1978).

Bellugi, U. The structuring of language: Clues from the similarities between signed and spoken language. In U. Bellugi and M. Studdert-Kennedy (Eds.), Signed and Spoken Language: Biological Constraints on Linguistic Form. Dahlem Konferenzen. Weinheim/Deerfield Beach, Fla.: Verlag Chemie, (1980), 115-140.

Bellugi, U. and Studdert-Kennedy, M. (Eds.). Signed and Spoken Language: Biological Constraints on Linguistic Form. Dahlem Konferenzen. Weinheim/Deerfield Beach, Fla.: Verlag Chemie, (1980).

Donkoh, S. Computer analysis helps train atheletes. CIPS Review., (July-August 1980), 14-15.

Futrelle, R. P. GALATEA: Interactive graphics for the analysis of moving images. Information Processing 74, Proceedings of the 1974 IFIP Conference, North-Holland Publishing Company, 712-716.

Futrelle, R. P. and Potel, M. J. The system design for GALATEA, an interactive real-time computer graphics system for movie and video analysis. Computers and Graphics, 1, Pergamon Press, (1975), 115-121.

Hildebrand, F. B. Introduction to Numerical Analysis. (1956).

Johansson, G. Visual perception of biological motion and a model for its analysis. Perception and Psychophysics, 14, (1973), 201-211.

Johansson, G. Visual motion perception. Scientific American, 232, 6, (1975), 76-89.

Klima, E. S. and Bellugi, U. The Signs of Language. Cambridge, Mass.: Harvard University Press, 1979.

Platt, S. M. and Badler, N. I. Animating facial expression. Computer Graphics, 15, 3, (August 1981), 245-252.

Poizner, H. Visual and 'phonetic' coding of movement: Evidence from American Sign Language. Science, 212, (1981), 691-693.

Poizner, H. Perception of movement in American Sign Language: Effects of linguistic structure and linguistic experience. Perception and Psychophysics, 33, (1983), 215-231.

Poizner, H., Bellugi, U. and Lutes-Driscoll, V. Perception of American Sign Language in dynamic point-light displays. Journal of Experimental Psychology: Human Perception and Performance, 7, (1981), 430-440.

Poizner, H., Newkirk, D. and Bellugi, U. Processes controlling human movement: Neuromotor constraints on American Sign Language. Journal of Motor Behavior, 15, (1983), 2-18.

Potel, M. J. and Mackay, S. A. Graphics input tools for interactive motion analysis. Computer Graphics and Image Processing, 14, (1980), 1-23.

Shantz, M. and Poizner, H. A computer program to synthesize American Sign Language. Behavior Research Methods and Instrumentation, 14, 5, (1982), 467-474.

Winter, D. A., Greenlaw, R. K. and Hobson, D. A. Television-computer analysis of kinematics of human gait. Computers and Biomedical Research, 5, (1972), 498-504.

Woltring, M. J. New possibilities for human motion studies by real-time light spot position measurement. Biotelemetry, 1, (1974), 132-146.

Zeltzer, D. Motor control techniques for figure animation. IEEE Computer Graphics and Applications, 2, 9, (November 1981), 53-60.

ACKNOWLEDGEMENTS

This work was supported in part by National Science Foundation Grant #BNS81-11479 and National Institutes of Health Grant #HD13249 to The Salk Institute for Biological Studies, and National Institute of Health Research Grant AM 26710, awarded by the National Institute of Arthritis, Metabolism, and Digestive Diseases to the Massachusetts Institute of Technology.

We are indebted to Dr. Robert Livingston for use of the Evans and Sutherland Picture System II.

FOOTNOTES

1. The graphics library was written by Tom Ferrin at the University of California, San Francisco.

2. Words in capital letters (e.g., LOOK) represent English glosses for ASL signs. A bracketed symbol following a sign gloss (e.g., LOOK[Continuative]) indicates that the sign is made with some change in form associated with a change in meaning from its unmodulated form, and thus indicates grammatical changes on signs.

INCENSE: A SYSTEM FOR DISPLAYING DATA STRUCTURES

Brad A. Myers*
Xerox Palo Alto Research Center, California

ABSTRACT

Many modern computer languages allow the programmer to define and use a variety of data types. Few programming systems, however, allow the programmer similar flexibility when displaying the data structures for debugging, monitoring and documenting programs. *Incense* is a working prototype system that allows the programmer to interactively investigate data structures in actual programs. The desired displays can be specified by the programmer or a default can be used. The default displays provided by Incense present the standard form for literals of the basic types, the actual names for scalar types, stacked boxes for records and arrays, and curved lines with arrowheads for pointers. In addition to displaying data structures, Incense also allows the user to select, move, erase and redimension the resulting displays. These interactions are provided in a uniform, natural manner using a pointing device (*mouse*) and keyboard.

CR Categories and Subject Descriptors: D.2.2 [**Software Engineering**]: Tools and Techniques - Structured Programming; User Interfaces; D.2.5 [**Software Engineering**]: Testing and Debugging - Debugging Aids; Monitors; D.3.3 [**Programming Languages**]: Language Constructs - Abstract Data Types; E.1 [**Data Structures**]; I.3.4 [**Computer Graphics**]: Graphics Utilities; I.3.6 [**Computer Graphics**]: Methodology and Techniques Interaction Techniques.

General Terms: Design, Human Factors, Languages.

*Author's current address: Three Rivers Computer Corporation, 720 Gross Street, Pittsburgh, Pennsylvania, 15224

I. Introduction

Many modern computer languages allow the programmer to define and use different data types. Few programming systems, however, allow the programmer similar flexibility when displaying these data structures in debugging, monitoring and documenting programs. *Incense*, a system written in and for the Pascal-like language *Mesa* [19], allows the programmer to design and use pictorial representations for the display of data structures.[1]

Strongly typed languages, such as Pascal [14] and Mesa, allow the programmer to define new types using the basic types supplied by the language. These new types can then be used to declare variables. Other languages, such as CLU [18] and Smalltalk [22], have the definition of types and their operations as the central programming paradigm. A data display system like Incense would be a great asset to programmers using a language of either type.

Modern Computer Science theory promotes the value of information hiding, where only the relevant information at a particular level should (or can) be accessed at that level. Most modern languages promote this method of programming. When debugging, however, the programmer is typically restricted to viewing the data at a very basic level. Just as the user of a real number does not want to have to examine the bit patterns used to represent the number, the user of a Ring Buffer or Hash Table generally does not want to see the records, arrays, and pointers used to implement them. Incense therefore allows the programmer to define the display for any type and have that display used whenever data of that type is shown. Since a programmer may not want to define displays for all (or possibly any) of the types used in his program, an extensive set of default displays is also provided.

[1] Incense was designed and implemented at the Xerox Palo Alto Research Center by the author. A full description can be found in [20].

While the importance and utility of user-defined displays is clearly evident for any computer environment, the ability to create genuine pictures enhances Incense's effectiveness considerably. The importance of pictures can be understood by looking at a typical programmer's bulletin board or note pad. When debugging a program or explaining it to another person. the programmer is likely to draw a plethora of pictures representing typical cases or those under consideration. These pictures allow the situation to be more easily understood. It is clear, for example, that Figure 1 is easier to understand than Figure 2, and that the programmer is more likely to visualize and draw the former. A guiding principle of Incense is to automatically create displays that would be similar to those the programmer might have drawn on paper.

Figure 1.
Pictorial representation of a POINTER TO INTEGER[2].

```
                @1275:  14
                @1276:  25
p: 1276↑        @1277:  37
                @1278:  85
```

Figure 2.
Typical display for a POINTER TO INTEGER in a character oriented system.

In some cases an even more pictorial representation than Figure 1 may be useful. For example, bar graphs, icons, tables and *analogical* pictures[3] are much more evocative than the numbers on which they are based. Frequently, these pictures will provide the right amount of detail and can be understood much more quickly. For example, a *percent-done thermometer* (Figure 3), as a representation for an iteration variable, allows instant recognition of how much of the loop has been completed.

With the progress in computer hardware, creating these pictures for debugging has become increasingly economical. Many personal computers, such as the Xerox Alto [24] and the Three Rivers PERQ [21], come with powerful graphic displays that can be easily used by all programs to make dynamic pictures.

[2] This figure and all others in this paper except 2, 3, 4 and 18 were created by Incense and taken directly from the screen.

[3] Pictures understood by *analogy* with the physical world.

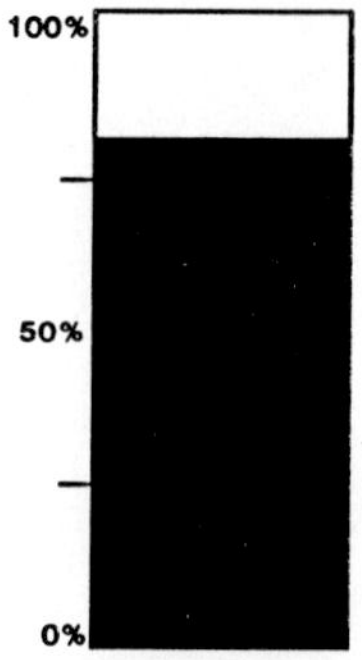

Figure 3.
"Percent-done thermometer" as an analogical representation for an iteration which is 80% complete.

The desired situation would be for the computer to create or verify programs automatically and thereby eliminate the need for debugging and for the displays of data structures. Dijkstra claims that good programmers could avoid all debugging if they would only use structured programming techniques [6]. Debugging, however, is still very much a problem for programmers. In fact, van Tassel claims that "a bug-free program is an abstract theoretical concept" [25, p. 117]. The programmer currently spends a great portion of his debugging time trying to understand the state of the machine. If the computer automatically produced pictures of the data structures, the programmer would be freed of one of the more laborious parts of the debugging process.

Thus, better tools for debugging are needed. Since the necessary support hardware is now generally available, the time is ripe for a development of systems that support pictorial, user-defined displays of data structures such as provided by Incense.

II. Previous work.

The utility of graphical representations for program concepts has long been known. Flow charts were an early attempt at representing computer information graphically. In addition, it was felt that they should be produced automatically by a computer since the hand made flowcharts were expensive and slow to produce, inaccurate when drawn, and hard to maintain [16][10].

A number of systems have been built which can create pictures for a program after the execution has finished. Usually, code must be added to the source program to define the output and then the program must be run through some sort of pre- or post-processor (examples are [4][26][3]). Some excellent algorithm demonstration movies have been produced using this technique [3][13], frequently at a fairly high cost. Other systems have produced high quality dynamic real-time displays for a limited set of types. For example, there have been a number of tree display programs (e.g. [23]) and LISP list displays [7][17], but these are typically restricted to a single, simple type of value at each node. Knowlton [15] describes a system for L-6 that displays the language's arbitrary field definitions.

III. The Environment for Incense.

Incense was written on the Alto personal computer at Xerox PARC. The Alto has a 875 by 603 pixel raster scan display and a "mouse" pointing device with three buttons. A cursor on the screen follows the mouse's movements. Incense was written for the Mesa language. The compiler for Mesa produces extensive symbol tables for each program that provide full type information for all constants and variables.

IV. The Incense system.

Unlike the systems described above, Incense can automatically generate pictures for *any* data type during the execution of an actual Mesa program. This is done in real time without modifications to the source program. The user need only specify at debug time the string name of a variable to get a full pictorial display. If desired, new, pictorial displays can easily be created and associated with data structures. These user-defined displays can eliminate unnecessary detail or more graphically depict the abstraction that the data structure is implementing. The pictures are then displayed in real time while the program is running. Monitoring ("animation") or static visualization of program execution at a high conceptual level is therefore possible. All input from the user is supplied in a similar high level by using the "mouse" pointing device to draw rectangles or select displays.

A unique feature of Incense is the ability to provide multiple displays, called *Formats*, for a single data structure. The user might provide both iconic and detailed representations so that detail can be eliminated when not needed but still be available to implementers. For each Format, the user can supply a number of *Subformats*, one of which is chosen automatically by Incense based on the amount of screen space given for the particular display.

V. Design Considerations for Incense.

In designing a system to implement the ideas mentioned above, two major problems had to be solved. First, an appropriate structure had to be designed that would be sufficiently powerful to allow very complex displays to be created and used. It was important, however, that this design make it easy to define and use simple pictures. Second, a design for the display of pointers had to be formulated. Pointers are a special problem since the space used to display the referent has to be specified. For records and arrays, the subpieces all fit neatly inside the box for the aggregate, but for pointers, the referent is displayed outside of the pointer's box.

As part of the solution to the first problem, *Artists* are used, as discussed below. *Layouts* were invented to solve the problems with pointers (discussed in section 7). A run-time type system, described in [20], allows Incense to discover the types of all variables in programs using the Mesa compiler's symbol tables. This makes it possible for Incense to automatically display any structure given only the name of the variable that holds it.

In order to have an element of data displayed in Incense, an *Artist* must be associated with it. An Artist is a collection of procedures and data that handles the display, erasure, and modification of the data. An Artist is created for each aggregate structure (such as a record) and for each data item, even if the data item is a field of an aggregate structure. The association between the data and the Artists to display them is maintained automatically by Incense. The memory address and type of the data, as well as other information, are stored as part of the Artist's internal data. Five classes of procedures are also stored in each Artist. There are procedures for displaying the data, drawing arrows, erasing pictures and arrows, selecting Artists, and editing the associated data structures. Each of these will be discussed below in a separate section.

VI. Display.

Although pictorial representations are easier to understand, they are not always appropriate. For example, the user of a Ring Buffer may want only to see the display of Figure 4, but the implementer may need to see the underlying basic types. Incense supports multiple views of the same data through the use of *Formats*. Each Artist has one or more Formats, each of which displays the data in a different manner. For example, an Artist for a Time record (Figure 5) might contain Formats for displaying itself as a record (a) or a clock (b). Formats are intended to be used for radically different ways of viewing a data structure. The implementer of the Artist defines the Formats, but the user specifies interactively which Format to use in a particular display. If an implementer wants to protect the internal representation of a data structure from the client, he can supply an Artist that only has a Format to display an iconic representation.

The caller of an Artist Format procedure specifies the area in which the display must fit. Thus the user[4] always specifies the size and position of the display, and Artists must be prepared to fit into any size rectangle. Other data display systems have used very different strategies. For example, in AMBIT/G, the displayed objects always take a constant amount of space [5], and in Smalltalk, the objects themselves decide how much space to take [9]. The advantage of the Incense approach is that the user's choice is never pre-empted, and aggregate structures, such as records and arrays, can accurately specify the position and size of subparts.

[4]In the case of nested Artists used by aggregates such as records and arrays, this is done by a procedure, as explained below.

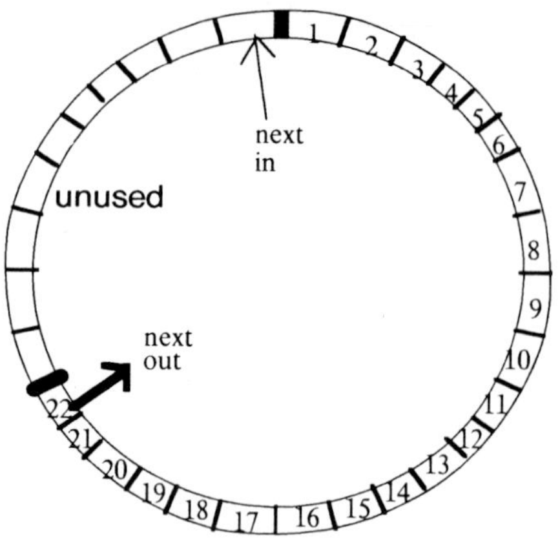

Figure 4.
Possible display for a ring buffer.
(This figure was not created by Incense).

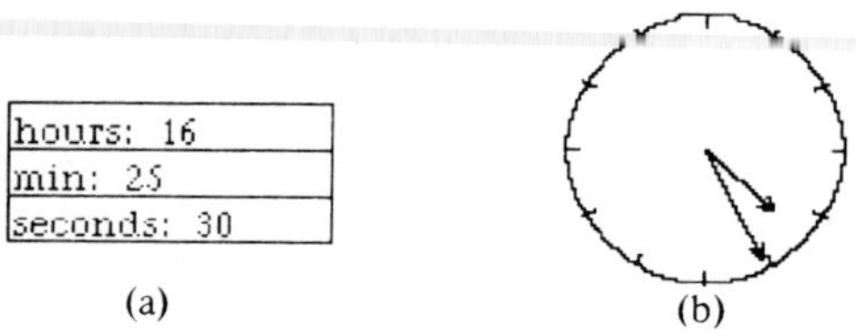

Figure 5.
Two Formats for the record Artist for:
Time: RECORD [hours, min, seconds: INTEGER];
holding the time of day:
(a) as a normal record and (b) as an analog clock.

To increase the flexibility of the displays and allow all control to be procedural, each Format contains one or more *Subformats.* Once the user specifies a Format, the system then chooses one of that Format's Subformats. This decision is based on various contextual information such as the size of the area in which the display is to fit. For example, the standard Artist Format for a Mesa record has two Subformats (Figure 6). The first displays the data at full size (a). If insufficient room for the display is provided, however, the second Subformat would be invoked. It scales the record display so that it will retain the same proportions as the original, yet still fit in the box (b). The client is not allowed to specify which Subformat should be used. Instead, the creator of the Artist associates a test with each Subformat. This test determines whether the Subformat is applicable in the current context. Since more than one of these tests may succeed, the designer also specifies an ordering of the Subformats. If none of the Subformat tests succeed, the data is simply not displayed. This may happen, for example, if the area in which the data is to be displayed is very tiny.

The basic types of Mesa, including STRINGS, INTEGERS, CARDINALS (positive INTEGERS), BOOLEANS, CHARACTERS, REALS, PROCEDURES, UNSPECIFIEDS, WORDS, and Enumerated Types (lists of names, *e.g.* {Mon, Tues, Wed, Thurs, Fri}), all have default displays which use text strings of the same form as the literals used by the programmer. These are fully interpreted as can be seen in Figure 7. Mesa uses a special representation for

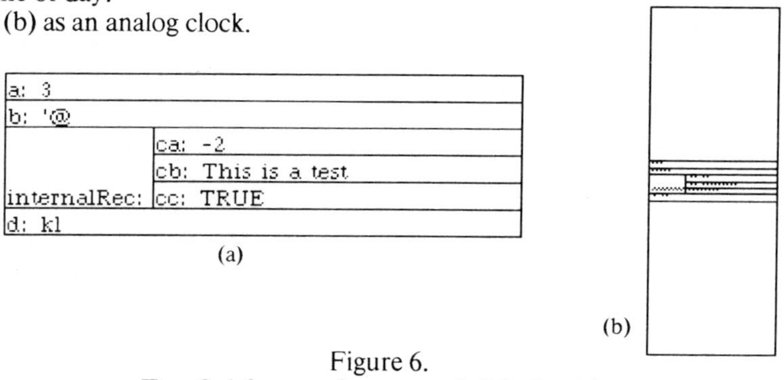

Figure 6.
Two Subformats for a record: full size (a),
and scaled proportionally and centered vertically inside a bounding rectangle (b).

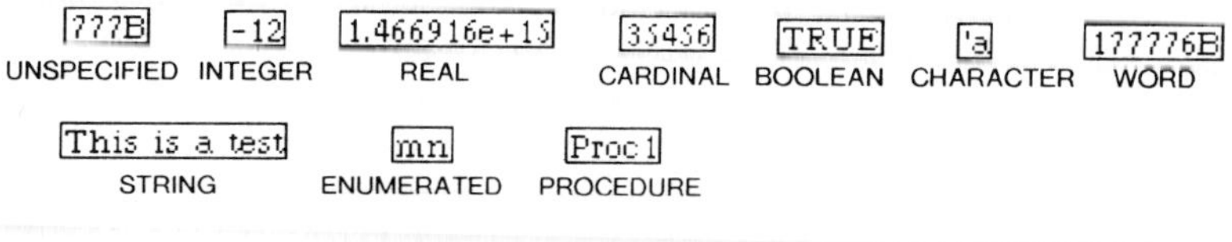

Figure 7.
Default boxed display for the basic types.

subranges of the above types. Incense hides this transformation so the programmer always sees the values he would have typed into the program. There are two Formats for Artists of each of the basic types. The first draws a box around the value (as in Figure 7). This is useful when the value is standing alone or when there is a pointer to it (see Figure 1). The other Format does not draw a box around the value. This is used in aggregate structures such as records and arrays when boxes are drawn around the entire field. For each Format of each of the basic types, there are two Subformats. One displays the value as a text string. This string is allowed to be clipped slightly (Figure 8 (a) and (b)). If there is not enough room for a meaningful portion of the value to be displayed, the second Subformat will be used which displays a grey area which has a size proportional to the string that would have been displayed (Figure 8 (c) and (d)).

(a) (b) (c) (d)

Figure 8.
Demonstration that clipped strings do supply information: (a) and (b) are values of BOOLEANS. Grey areas have different lengths proportional to the size of the string: (c) is for FALSE and (d) is for TRUE.

The Subformats of some Artists, such as those for records, arrays, and pointers, can cause the display of subordinate Artists. For example, the automatically supplied Artist Subformat for a record will iterate through the fields calling the appropriate Format in the Artist for each. The record Subformat divides the rectangle allocated for the display of the record among the fields giving an appropriate portion to each. Thus, the subordinate Artists are called with the same types of arguments as the top level Artist, and the record Subformat need not know, for example, whether the subordinate is an integer, pointer, or even another record (see Figure 9).

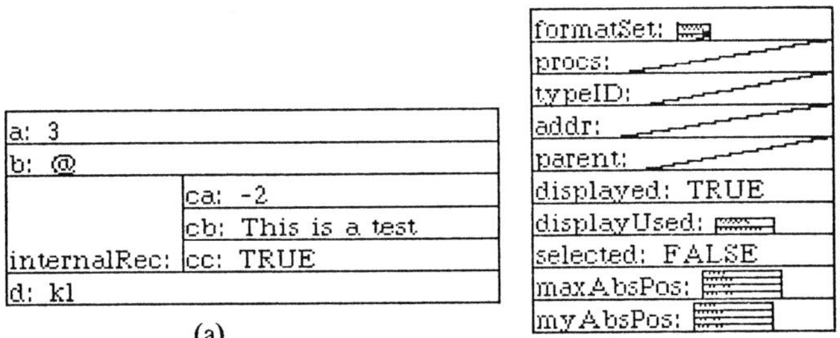

(a) (b)

Figure 9.
Two ways records can contain other records. Full size (a) and reduced (b). The diagonal lines in (b) represent the pointer value NIL.

Each record field actually consists of two Artists: one for the field's *name* and one for the field's *value*. The field's name and the value's type are discovered automatically using the information from the Mesa symbol tables [20]. The field name is displayed using an Artist to make the interface more consistent. This has the additional advantage that standard STRING Artists can be used for the names. The field names therefore become grey if the area is too small and can be selected and redisplayed in the same manner as all other values (see section 9). It has been suggested that the field names should have special Formats that center the name vertically in the area provided, or display it at the top of the field's value. This would be a trivial modification and could, in fact, be done by the user.

Arrays are handled in exactly the same manner as records, except, of course, that there are no field names. Special Artists could be created to provide the indices of the values and/or to allow scrolling so that large arrays could be easily handled. Both record and array Artists store, as part of their internal data, the set of rectangles used to specify the fields' positions. These rectangles are defined at Artist creation time based on the types of the values, and the length of the field name strings for records. Making arrays display vertically or horizontally is therefore accomplished simply by defining the rectangles with the appropriate offsets (Figure 10). Thus two-dimensional arrays are easily displayed (Figure 11).

The rectangles and other static information stored in the Artists are called *Form Data* since they describe the *form* of the picture. Other information stored in an Artist, called *Display Data*, is generated when the Artist's associated data structure is displayed. The Display Data includes such things as the current screen position of the the picture and whether or not it is selected.

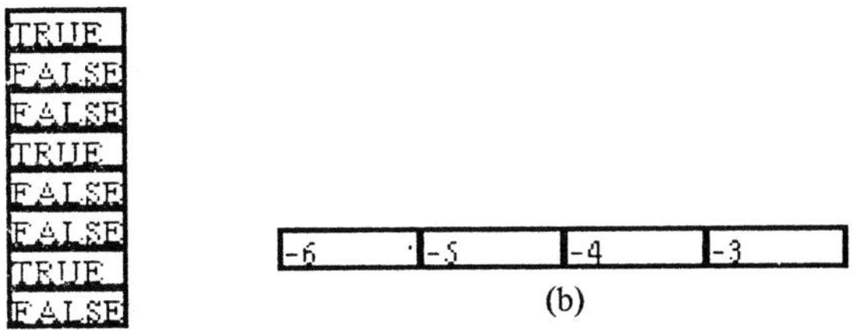

(a) (b)

Figure 10.
Arrays oriented vertically (a) and horizontally (b).

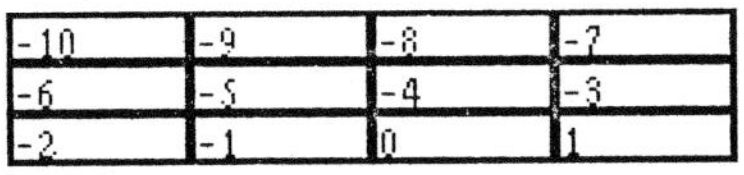

Figure 11.
Two dimensional array:
ARRAY [1..3] OF ARRAY [1..4] OF INTEGER;

VII. Displaying Arrows.

One of the most complex aspects of the Incense design was choosing the best method for displaying pointers. It was clear that they should be shown as arrows, but the difficulty was deciding where to put the data to which the pointer points (the *referent*). The simplest technique would have been to require the user to specify where each referent should go. For deep structures, however, this would be very tedious. The simplest automatic placement scheme was used by AMBIT/G where the referent simply appeared at a pre-determined, fixed position relative to the parent irrespective of what might have been there previously [11]. This method is not consistent with Incense's philosophy of hierarchical rectangles and user control. The most complex technique would be to treat the screen space like a heap memory and simply allocate and free rectangles of display area. This has the potential for maximal usage of the space. Unfortunately, this two-dimensional space allocation problem is very complicated and prone to poor performance. The specialized space allocation techniques used in tree and list drawing programs are also unworkable since they assume that all nodes will be the same size. This is certainly not necessarily the case in Incense.

The algorithm finally chosen for Incense is very general and fast, but it does not allocate the screen space as well as the general allocator described above. *Layouts* were invented to hold the pointer and its referents. When the user specifies a rectangle for the display of a Layout, that rectangle is subdivided into rectangles to be used by the arrow sources and all referents. Each component rectangle is managed by a *Layout Field*. For example, a Layout for a record containing two pointers would have three fields: one for the record and one for each referent (see Figure 12). Layouts and Layout Fields are implemented as special Artists that have no associated data; they exist solely to locate and manage the various components. A user of Incense need never know of the existence of Layouts and Layout Fields since they are created and managed automatically by the system. Of course, since Layouts are a special type of Artist, the user is free to create his own type of Layouts if desired.

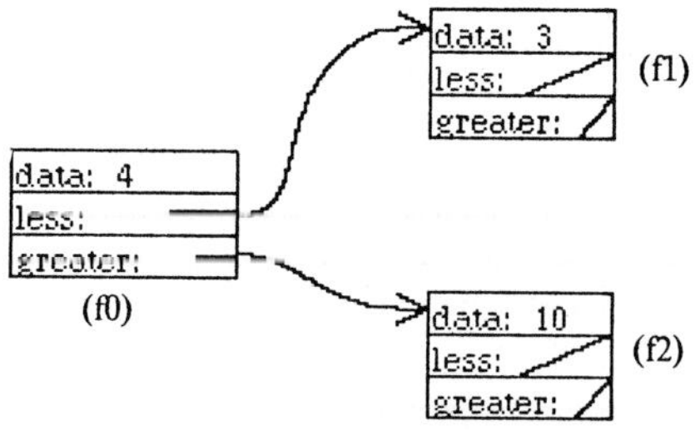

Figure 12.
Layout with 3 fields: one for record: (f0), and one for each referent: (f1) and (f2).

Currently, Layouts use a very simple scheme for assuring that all the subcomponents fit into the rectangle specified for the Layout. As with records and arrays, the rectangles for the various fields (the *Form Data*) are fully specified at Artist creation time. When the Layout is displayed, the subcomponents are simply instructed to fit into the appropriate Layout Field rectangle. In a deep recursive structure such as Figure 13, the displays get progressively smaller as the nesting level increases. This theoretically would allow an arbitrarily deep structure to be displayed in a finite space, but, in fact, display ceases after the pictures become smaller than a threshold size.

When a Artist Subformat for a pointer is called, it first checks to see if the pointer's value is NIL. If so, a diagonal line is drawn through the box for the pointer. This is consistent with the LISP community's usual pictorial representation of NIL. Otherwise, the Subformat checks every Artist on the screen to see if any are associated with the referent. If so, the pointer is referring to data that has already been displayed, and an arrow is simply drawn to this occurrence (Figures 14 and 15). This mechanism also handles the case where a pointer refers to values inside aggregates (Figure 16). If the referent is not currently displayed, the pointer Artist must arrange for the correct Layout Field's Artist to display the referent so an arrow can be drawn to it.

This process can best be explained by using an example. Suppose a record contains a POINTER TO CARDINAL and an integer (Figure 17). When the user requests a display for a record of that type, the system first notices that it contains pointers. A Layout is therefore created with two Layout Fields (Figure 18 gives the Artist hierarchy). The Layout is then ordered to display itself in the rectangle specified by the user. The Layout tells the first Layout Field to display. This Field, in turn, calls the appropriate Format in the record Artist. Now the record begins to display itself in the manner described earlier. When the pointer Artist is finally called, it will discover that its referent (the CARDINAL) has not yet been displayed. The Layout responsible for this pointer must therefore be found since only it knows where the referent should be placed. The pointer Artist will therefore send a message up the Artist hierarchy to find the Layout that will handle its referent. The message will go first to the record Artist, then to Layout Field 1, and finally to the Layout. The Layout, upon receiving this message, causes Layout Field 2 to be displayed which, in turn, causes an Artist for the CARDINAL to be created and displayed. If this had been a more complex structure, such as the recursive structure of Figure 13, more Layouts and Artists would have been created and displayed at this point. An Artist is not created for a data structure if the pointer to it is NIL. This is obviously important for recursive structures since otherwise an infinite number of Artists would be required.

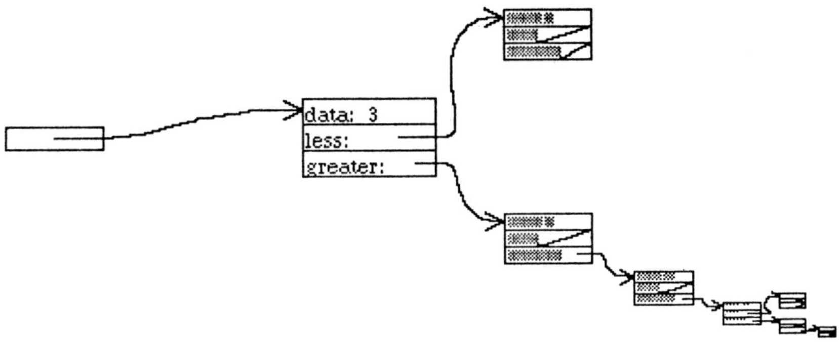

Figure 13. Deep recursive tree display demonstrating how elements get smaller. Overall structure, however, is easily understood.

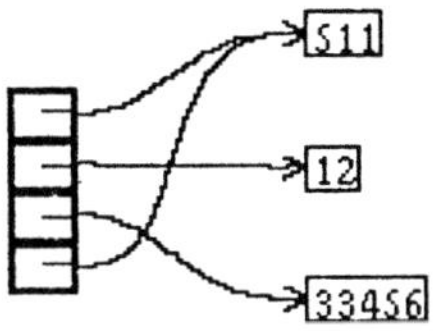

Figure 14.
ARRAY [1..4] OF POINTER with two POINTERs referring to the same value.

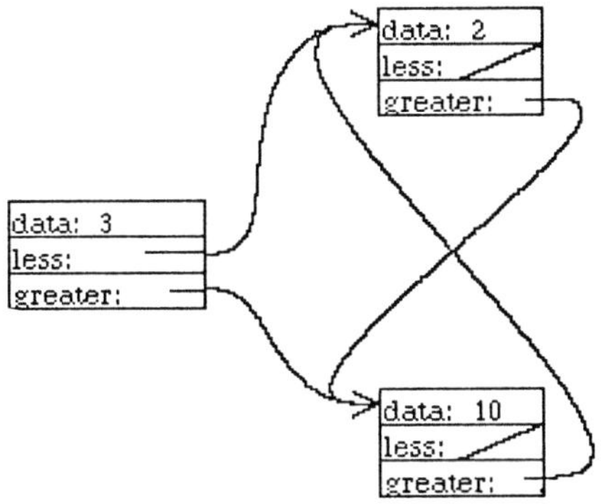

Figure 15.
This erroneous tree structure demonstrates that a pointer to previously displayed object does not generate a new copy. The second arrow is drawn to the first occurrence.

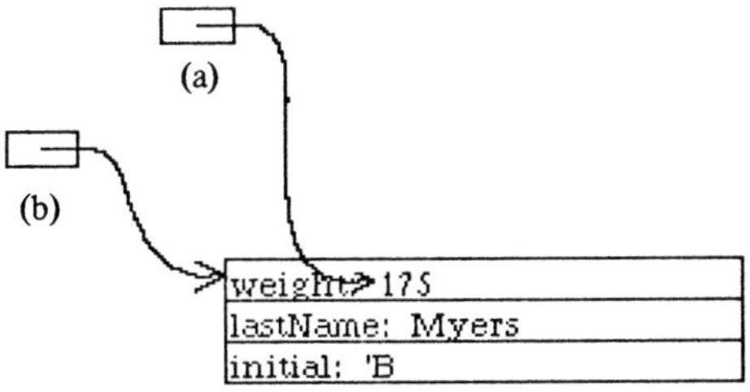

Figure 16.
Pointer to value inside a record (a) does not get confused with a pointer to the record itself (b).

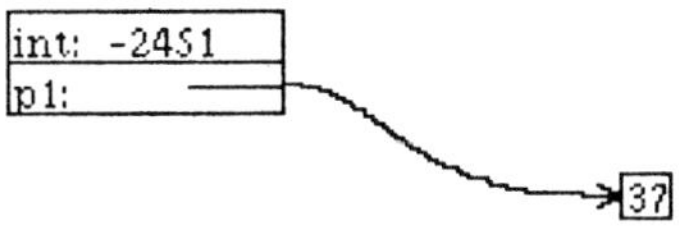

Figure 17.
Incense display for
RECORD [int: INTEGER, p1: POINTER TO CARDINAL].

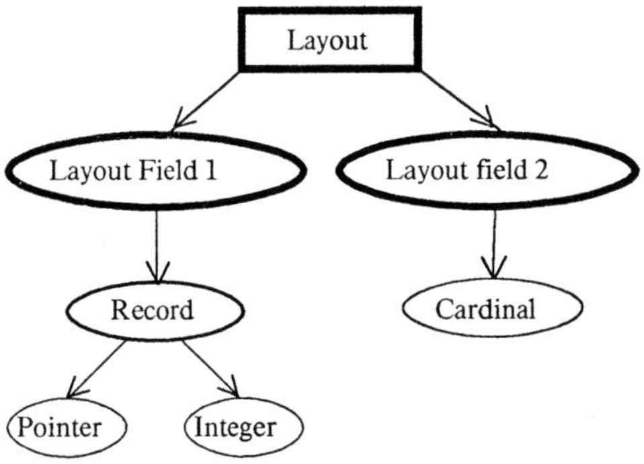

Figure 18.
Artist hierarchy that would be created for:
rec: RECORD [p1: POINTER TO CARDINAL, int: INTEGER];
(This figure was not created by Incense).

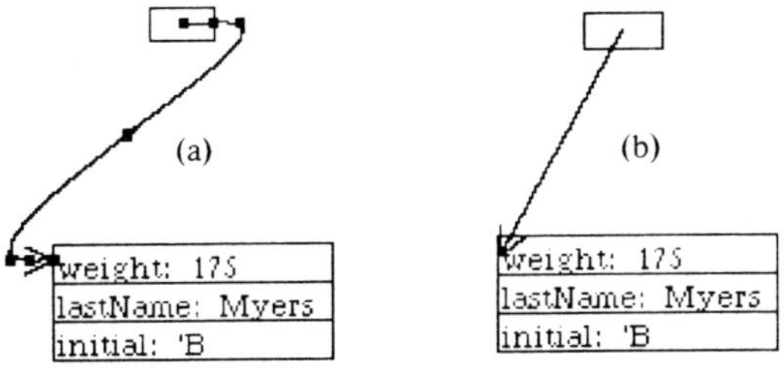

Figure 19.
Demonstration of the advantage of curved lines used in Incense (a) over straight lines (b). The control points used to specify the spline are shown as black squares in (a).

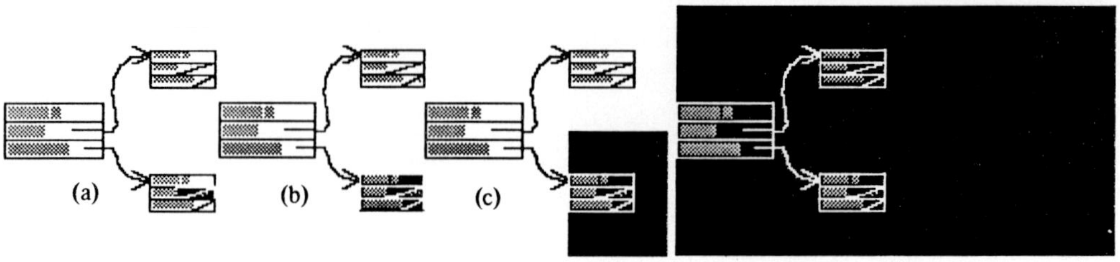

Figure 20.
Selections (shown by black areas) moving up the Artist hierarchy: from record field (a) to record (b) to Layout for record (c) to Layout for everything (d).

Upon completion of the display of Layout Field 2, the Layout returns control to the original pointer Artist with the Layout Artist as the return value. The pointer Artist now sends a different message to the Layout requesting the address of the actual Artist associated with the CARDINAL. This message is passed down the Artist hierarchy from the Layout to Layout Field 2 and finally to the CARDINAL's Artist. If there had been more Layouts, Layout Fields, and records under Layout Field 2, as there would be for recursive structures, this message would have had to pass through more levels. In any case, the POINTER now knows which Artist is associated with its referent and that the referent has been displayed. Finally, the POINTER Artist can find out where the referent is on the screen, and an arrow is drawn from the pointer's box to that of the referent.

The actual arrow itself is a curved line called a *spline* [1]. At the end of the spline, an arrowhead is drawn. The size of the arrowhead is adjusted to insure that it is never bigger than the destination box. The spline is defined by seven control points placed along the arrow's path. Three are placed in a straight horizontal line near the source and three near the destination (Figure 19). Three are needed at each end to insure that the curves approach the end points from the correct direction. Another control point is then placed between the ends to make the spline smoother. Splines were chosen rather than straight lines since they are more attractive and are less easily confused with other lines in the picture (see Figure 19).

The default destination points for arrows to Artists of the basic types are at the center of their left side. For records and arrays, however, the destination points are calculated as the center of the left side of the first field. Since the user is free to re-arrange the rectangles for the fields (see section 11), the arrow end points are stored as part of the Form Data. Thus if the fields are rearranged, the user can simply supply a new set of destination points for the arrow. When the record or array is displayed, the actual screen points for that instance are calculated. This is done before any of the fields are displayed in case a field contains a POINTER back to the record or array itself.

VIII. Erasure.

In addition to display, Artists support a number of other operations. One of these is erasure. An erased Artist[5] can be redisplayed with a new size, location, and Format. There is an erase procedure for each Subformat of an Artist since only the Subformat knows exactly how the data structure was displayed. The Artist's erase procedure therefore calls the internal erase procedure for the Format and Subformat with which the Artist was displayed. This internal erase procedure will first call the erase procedures in any subordinate Artists. Then, the screen area for the Artist will be painted white,[6] and then any arrows are erased by redrawing them with white. Arrows must be erased explicitly since they will lie outside of the rectangle for the POINTER.

IX. Selection.

Incense was designed to be used interactively. Therefore, the user needs to be able to refer to various displays on the screen to allow them to be erased, redisplayed or modified. Many systems require that the user *name* the display either by tracing from some root (*e.g.* First↑.greater↑.lesser↑.greater↑.greater↑.greater↑.value) or by using some arbitrary labels. Fortunately, Incense runs on a computer that provides a much more natural method for referring to displays. The *mouse* is a pointing device that moves a cursor around on the screen [8]. All the rectangles for the display are specified using the mouse. In addition, pressing one of the mouse buttons tells Incense to *select* the Artist to which the cursor points. The selected Artist is shown visually by video reversal (see Figure 20). There can only be one Artist selected at a time; however, due to the hierarchical nature of Artists, there are typically many Artists at any point on the screen. For example, with an integer in a record in a

[5]"Artists" here and in later sections will be used to refer both to the object that controls data display and the picture on the screen that the Artist creates.

[6]The pictures are drawn in black on a white background as shown in this paper.

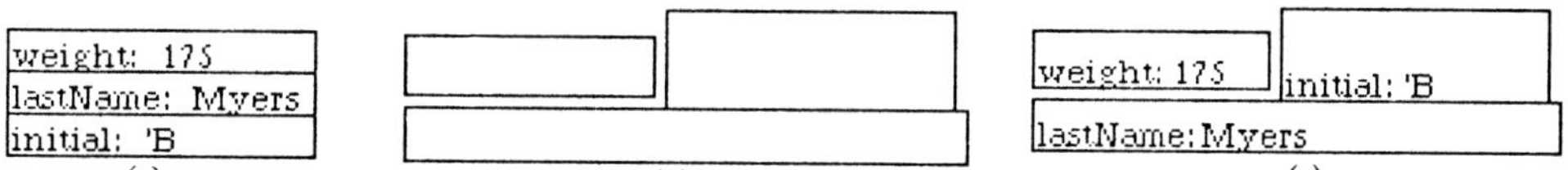

(a) (b) (c)

Figure 21.
Normal display for record (a), form defined by user (b), and resulting display (c).
Note that field order has been switched.

Layout, pointing to the integer could refer to the integer, the record, the Layout Field, or the Layout. Incense solves this problem by having the smallest (in screen area) Artist selected. In order to select a larger, enclosing Artist, it is simply necessary to re-select the Artist which is already selected. Thus, for example, a pointer value in a record field might be selected (Figure 20a). If some other field was then selected, the selection would simply move there. If the original pointer was selected again, however, the entire record that contained that pointer would be selected (Figure 20b). Next, the Layout containing the record would be selected (c), and finally, the Layout enclosing everything would be selected (d). If this outermost Layout was selected again, everything would be deselected.

Since Incense frequently displays values using grey areas, selection is very important. The user can display a large structure, select the part of it that he thinks is important, and then have that portion redisplayed using a larger area. Since it is so easy to select and redisplay Artists, the decision to use a simple, fast space allocation algorithm is shown to be justified.

X. Editing.

Once an Artist is selected, its value could be edited.[7] Unfortunately, editing is not yet supported by Incense. In a future version, the user might select the Artist associated with a BOOLEAN variable, type in FALSE, and have the value of the variable change. Type checking of the new values would be done along with the appropriate conversions. For pointers, it would be appropriate to allow the user to simply point to the display for the data that will be the new referent. The system would then discover the correct value for the pointer cell. Type checking would be done in this case also. Different styles for specifying new values other than type-in may also be appropriate for other specialized displays. It is the job of the edit routines in the Artist to handle these transformations, the modification of the actual memory, and the subsequent redisplay of the Artist.

[7] *Editing* is used here solely to mean modifying the *value* of some data and not for modifying its *display*.

XI. User-defined Artists.

The discussion of the previous sections has concentrated on the default displays provided by Incense. These are necessary for making the system usable and for demonstrating its feasibility and power. A major goal of Incense, however, is to make it easy for the user to specify his own Artist styles (called *Prototypes*). This can currently be done at two levels.

As was mentioned in section 6, aggregate Artists store the rectangles used for the pieces as part of the Form Data. It is very easy for the user to specify these rectangles using the mouse (see Figure 21). If desired, the user is asked to point with the mouse to the corners of each rectangle needed for the display. The rectangles define the relative size and position of the various fields. This technique can be used to eliminate some fields (by giving them rectangles of zero size) or to favor the more important fields. It would be useful to have a *Forms Editor* program to help in aligning and positioning the rectangles.

If a more radical change in display is desired (such as the clock display in Figure 5), the user simply writes a small program in Mesa defining the picture. Incense provides a rich variety of display primitives and parameterized procedures to aid in this process. Libraries of Artist Prototypes can be kept so that new Prototypes could be created through small modifications to existing Artists. It is felt that this is a better strategy than requiring the Artist designer to learn an entirely new language to define the desired pictures.

Once a Prototype has been created, the user can then associate it with a specific variable, a type, or a basic type. Thus, for:

```
Time: TYPE = RECORD [hrs, min, sec: INTEGER];
curTime: Time ← [3, 30, 14];
```

a Prototype can be associated with the variable curTime, the type Time, or the basic type RECORD. This gives the user complete control over all displays in Incense.

XII. Current Implementation and Plans for the Future.

The Incense system described here currently runs only on Xerox *Alto* mini-computers that have 128K of memory and special micro-code to handle floating point operations. Incense has successfully demonstrated the feasibility of user-defined and analogical displays for data structures. Default displays currently exist for all the basic types of Mesa, two-dimensional displays are used for records and arrays, and arrows are used for POINTERs. All of these displays are automatically created using the type of the variable, so that no matter how complex a variable is, the user need only type "Display X" and specify a rectangle using the mouse. The display of a basic type takes about 350 milleseconds, for a POINTER TO INTEGER, 1.9 seconds, and for the complex structure of Figure 13, 33.4 seconds. The mouse is used for specifying all rectangles and for selection. The selected Artist can be erased and redisplayed, but editing is not currently supported by Incense. Reasonable defaults are computed automatically for all field rectangles in aggregate structures, and the user is free to define these rectangles using the mouse if desired. The user can also define displays by writing programs in Mesa. Finally, it is easy to convert any display on the screen into a form that can be printed as was done for this paper.

There are some places in Incense where a reimplementation would allow a substantial decrease in execution time and memory usage. Also, certain parts of the system, such as the edit command, have yet to be implemented. The major aspect of Incense that remains unfulfilled, however, is the creation of special purpose Artists for various types. Designs have already been prepared for the displays of trees, list structures, stacks, processes, hash tables, ring buffers (Figure 4), large arrays and some other common data types. Iteration variables (Figure 3) and other special purpose data items could also have special displays. These would greatly enhance the attractiveness of Incense to potential users. Finally, Incense needs to be integrated with a full debugger that can take advantage of Incense's power and flexibility. The debugger would handle the specification of what data should be displayed, possibly by having the user point at the variable in a window holding the source text of the program. The debugger could call Incense frequently to incrementally monitor variables and thereby "animate" the program's execution. If this is not practical, Incense could simply be called to create static displays at breakpoints. The parameters to Incense would be the variable's string name, a symbol table context in which that variable can be found (found based on the run-time stack), and a rectangle for display. The rectangle might be supplied by the user or the debugger might have a standard window for data display. An integrated environment using Incense-style displays has been proposed in [12].

An Incense style display for data structures will be useful to programmers no matter how a debugger is organized. The pictures and the associated data structures can be dynamically rearranged and modified. The displays from Incense-like systems help the programmer monitor and understand the execution of complex programs. Since the user can specify the desired display, the pictures created can be used to provide documentation for the data structures themselves. Finally, debugging will probably be more enjoyable when using pictures rather than long strings of characters. This, combined with the higher conceptual level provided by the pictures, may make the debugging task easier and thereby increase programmer productivity.

Acknowledgments.

I would like to thank Xerox PARC CSL and the MIT Cooperative program for giving me the opportunity to work on this project. Special thanks go to Dan Swinehart and Butler Lampson of PARC for their design and implementation suggestions. John Warnock of PARC supplied the underlying graphic system that made this work possible and also helped with the design for Layouts. Ed Satterthwaite of Xerox SDD provided a great deal of support while I was creating the run-time type system needed by Incense. Finally, I would like to thank Dan Swinehart, Warren Teitelman, Ed Satterthwaite, David Reed, the referees, and many others for helpful and thorough comments on this paper.

REFERENCES

1. Ahlberg, J. H., Nilson, E. N., and Walsh, J. L. *The Theory of Splines and their Appli-cations.* New York: Academic Press (1967).

2. Baecker, Ron. Two Systems which Produce Animated Representations of the Execution of Computer Programs. *ACM SIGCSE Bul-letin.* Vol. 7, No. 1 (Feb. 1975). pp. 158-167.

3. Baecker, Ron. *Sorting Out Sorting.* 16mm color, sound, film. 25 minutes. Dynamic Graphics Project, Computer Systems Re-search Group, University of Toronto, Toronto, Ontario (1981). Presented at ACM SIGGRAPH Conference, Dallas, Texas (Aug., 1981).

4. Balzer, R. M. EXDAMS -- EXtendable Debugging and Monitoring System. *Proceedings AFIPS Spring Joint Computer Conference.* 34 (1969). pp 567-580.

5. Christensen, Carlos. An Example of the Manipulation of Directed Graphs in the AMBIT/G Programming Language. *Proceedings of the ACM Symposium on Interactive Systems for Experimental Applied Mathematics,* Washington, D.C. (August, 1967).

6. Dijkstra, Edsger W. The Humble Programmer. *Communications of the ACM.* Vol. 15, No. 10 (Oct 1972). pp 859-866.

7. Dionne, M. S. and Mackworth, A. K. ANTICS: A System for Animating LISP Programs. *Computer Graphics and Image Processing.* Vol. 7 (1978). pp. 105-119.

8. English, W. K., Engelbart, D. C. and Berman, M. L. Display Selection Techniques for Text Manipulation. *IEEE Transactions on Human Factors in Electronics.* Vol. HFE-8, No. 1 (March 1967).

9. Goldberg, A. and Robson, D. A Metaphor for User Interface Design. *Proceedings of the 12th Hawaii International Conference on System Sciences 1979.* Vol. 1 (1979). pp. 148-157.

10. Hain, G. and Hain, K. A general purpose automatic flowcharter. *Proc. Fourth Annual Meeting of UAIDE,* New York (Oct. 1965). pp. IV-i to IV-12.

11. Henderson, D. Austin. *A Description and Definition of Simple AMBIT/G--a Graphical Programming Language..* Wakefield, MA: Massachusetts Computer Associates CA-6904-2811 (April 28, 1969). 32 pages.

12. Herot, Christopher P., Brown, Gretchen P., Carling, Richard T., Friedell, Mark, Kramlich, David, and Baecker, Ronald M. An Integrated Environment for Program Visualization. *Proceedings of the IFIP WG 8.1 Working Conference on Automated Tools for Infor-mation System Design and Development.* New Orleans, LA (January 26-28, 1982). H. J. Schneider and A. I. Wasserman (eds). North Holland, Amsterdam, 1982.

13. Hopgood, F. R. A. Computer Animation Used as a Tool in Teaching Computer Science. *Proceedings of the 1974 IFIP Congress,* Applications Volume. (1974) pp 889-892.

14. Jensen, K. and Wirth, N. *PASCAL User Manual and Report.* Englewood Cliffs, N.J.:Prentice-Hall (1975).

15. Knowlton, K. C. *L6: Bell Telephone Laboratories Low Level Linked List Language.* Two black and white films, sound. Bell Telephone Laboratories, Murray Hill, New Jersey (1966).

16. Knuth, Donald E. Computer Drawn Flowcharts. *Commu-nications of the ACM.* Vol. 6 No. 9 (Sept, 1963). pp. 555-563.

17. Laaser, William. Private conversation with the author (Nov. 9, 1979). System was built using DLISP which is described in Warren Teitelman. *Display Oriented Programmer's Assistant.* Palo Alto: Xerox PARC CSL-77-3 (March 8, 1977).

18. Liskov, Barbara, Snyder, Alan, Atkinson, Russell, and Schaffert, Craig. Abstraction Mechanisms in CLU *Communications of the ACM.* Vol. 20, No. 8 (Aug, 1977). pp. 564-576.

19. Mitchell, James, *et al. Mesa Language Manual, Version 5.0.* Palo Alto: Xerox PARC CSL-79-3 (1979).

20. Myers, Brad A. *Displaying Data Structures for Interactive Debugging.* Palo Alto: Xerox PARC CSL-80-7 (June, 1980). 97 pages.

21. Rosen, Brian. PERQ: A Commercially Available Personal Scientific Computer. *IEEE CompCom Digest* (Spring, 1980).

22. Shoch, John F. An Overview of the Programming Language Smalltalk-72. *ACM Sigplan Notices.* Vol. 14, No. 9 (Sept 1979). pp. 64-73.

23. Sweet, Richard. Appendix B: Implementation De-scription. *Empirical Estimates of Program Entropy.* Palo Alto: Xerox PARC CSL-78-3 (1978). pp. 85-96.

24. Thacker, C. P., McCreight, E. M., Lampson, B. W., Sproull, R, F., and Boggs, D. R. *Alto: A Personal Computer.* Palo Alto; Xerox PARC CSL-79-11 (August 7, 1979). 50 pages. Paper also appears in Siewiorek, Bell and Newell, *Computer Structures: Readings and Examples,* second edition.

25. van Tassel, Dennie. *Program Style, Design, Efficiency, Debugging and Testing.* Englewood Cliffs, NJ: Prentice-Hall, Inc. (1974). 256 pages.

26. Yarwood, Edward. *Toward Program Illustration.* University of Toronto Computer Systems Research Group Technical Report CSRG-84 (M. Sc. Thesis) (October 1977).

Graphical Style

Towards High Quality Illustrations

Richard Beach and Maureen Stone
University of Waterloo and Xerox PARC

Abstract

If there is to be widespread acceptance of computer generated images in areas traditionally served by graphic artists, these images must meet a high standard of quality. Document preparation systems are an application area that is gaining maturity in providing high-quality computer typeset documents. These systems exhibit a trend towards specifying the formatting information for a document separately from the body of the text. The goal is to have the document format designed by someone with expert knowledge of typography. Writers can then apply a format to their own work simply by indicating the semantic content of their text, such as the headings, paragraphs, or footnotes. The result is that a writer can produce properly typeset documents without learning the esthetics of typography. This paper extends this idea to encompass the illustrations in the text. We have developed a prototype system that uses a set of graphical style rules to define the design guidelines for the illustrations. The rules, called a *graphical style sheet*, can be used to control a uniform "look" over a set of illustrations, or to change the appearance of a particular illustration to reflect different publishing styles or different media. The prototype coordinates with an existing document preparation system and the combined systems were used to produce this paper. We conclude that this is a viable method for controlling image style for at least one class of illustrations. This approach contributes to image quality by providing a method for capturing knowledge of graphic arts standards, and for ensuring a consistent appearance of related illustrations within technical documentation.

Categories and Subject Descriptors: I.3.3 **[Computer Graphics]:** Picture/Image Generation – *Display algorithms;* I.3.4 **[Computer Graphics]:** Graphics Utilities – *Picture description languages;* I.3.6 **[Computer Graphics]:** Methodology and Techniques – *Device independence;* I.7.2 **[Text Processing]:** Document Preparation – *Format and notation; languages; photocomposition;* J.5 **[Computer Applications]** Arts and Humanities – *Arts, fine and performing;*

Additional key words and phrases: Graphic arts, graphic design, graphical style sheet, illustration, integrated text and graphics

Introduction

If there is to be widespread acceptance of computer generated images in areas traditionally served by graphic artists, these images must meet a high standard of quality. Increasingly, we see examples such as chart-making systems or spectacular special effects where the quality is defined by the traditional graphic arts standards for print, video or film media. This paper describes the development of tools to improve the quality of technical illustrations.

The inclusion of graphic images into computer-typeset documents is an area of current research and development, for example, PIC [7], IDEAL [18], JANUS [5], Etude [12], and the Xerox Star [10,17]. Typical illustrations which we wish to include are line art and shaded images. Frequently the composition systems which create them are text formatters extended to handle the higher quality output and flexibility available with typesetters and laser printers.

Computer graphics has evolved along two fronts towards quality images: the introduction of new output devices and the development of new rendering algorithms. New devices have higher resolution and more color capability making it possible to render images more precisely. New algorithms that generate smooth curves and more realistic shaded surfaces provide a way to produce high-quality images. Now, artists and designers can expect to find opportunities for creative expression within such systems.

The *style of a document* is a phrase that conveys several meanings, all related to quality. The word *style* in a thesaurus refers to the ideas of fashion, method, beauty, class, and expression. To a graphic designer, the phrase *house style* refers to the customary way that a particular publishing house handles typesetting or illustrations.

Traditionally to a graphic designer, a style sheet communicates to the compositor how to render a document or image [16]. A style sheet, such as the one in Figure 1, provides typographic parameters for typesetting text and guidelines for achieving certain visual effects. The purpose of a style sheet is to ensure consistency and design discipline within a project, and to provide a rapid and effective means for specifying that discipline.

Content	Parameters	Typeface			Typesize		Type-weight					Slope		Leading		Lettering			Color		Column-width		Type-of-column			Indent
		1.	2.	3.	1.	2.	light	medium	bold	semi-bold	extra-bold	regular	italic	solid	points	all-caps	all-lower	initial-cap	black		pica	justified	unjustified	centred	flush-right	points
Title	main																									
	subtitle																									
Heading	1st level																									
	2nd level																									
	3rd level																									
	4th level																									
Text	quotations																									
	normal																									
	footnotes																									
	captions																									
Tables	captions																									
Numbering	folios																									
	illustrations																									
	footnotes																									

Figure 1. TRADITIONAL STYLE SHEET for specifying typographic parameters. The rows indicate the parts of the document to be treated specially. The columns indicate the typographic parameters which the compositor uses when typesetting this job. Entries in the matrix are either checkmarks or numeric values.

Computer typesetting systems have provided style mechanisms for text composition through formatting macros or style sheet databases. The '-ms' macro package supplied with TROFF is an example of formatting macros that implement document style [11]. SCRIBE uses *document types* to establish the formatting details for a variety of document styles [15]. The Xerox Star uses *property sheets* to select parameters to control the appearance of selected items of text and graphics in documents [10]. In each of these systems, some mechanism is provided to manipulate the content of a document separately from the appearance of the document. Thus consistency and design discipline can be achieved. This is accomplished without forcing the author to become a graphic designer while the graphic designer can supply specialized knowledge to create the document style.

Extending these formatting style techniques to include graphic images is a natural evolution. In the following sections we describe our concept of graphical style for illustrations and also the artwork-rendering prototype that we integrated with an existing text composition system. The illustrations we consider will be line drawings, although a provision for continuous tone images will also be described.

Examples of Graphical Style

To motivate our concept of graphical style, we present two examples taken from traditional graphic arts productions. The first example presents observations on some stylistic aspects of *Scientific American* illustrations. The second example describes how a consistent style was achieved in producing a book having many line drawings.

Scientific American Illustration Style

Scientific American has established a reputation for the clarity and effectiveness of its illustrations. In Figure 2 taken from the recent article, 'Artificial Intelligence,' in the October 1982 issue of *Scientific American* [19], we can observe several aspects of the *Scientific American* style. Lines are generally thin, although with different weights to convey detail, arrowheads are always the same open design, lettering is always 8-point Helvetica capitals, shades of grey and colors are used only when needed and then only to convey essential meaning, and the design is clean and carefully crafted. While the author supplies the concept sketch and the illustrator renders the image with great skill, it is the art department that ensures that the traditional style of *Scientific American* illustrations is maintained [4].

Traditional Illustrated Book Production

A recent textbook for introductory computer science co-authored and typeset by the first author of this paper [6] required a large number of illustrations. Many of the illustrations were listings of computer programs and their output. With a suitable typeface and the text files containing the original programs and computer output, these figures were easily composed directly into the main body of the book. In contrast, there were over 150 line drawings that were hand-drawn by a draftsman. The production of these illustrations presented a considerably different problem.

Illustration guidelines were written to establish the desired style. The authors and the book designer described how various details were to be handled by the draftsman for each type of illustration: mathematical graphs, Pascal syntax diagrams, data structure diagrams, and simple line drawings.

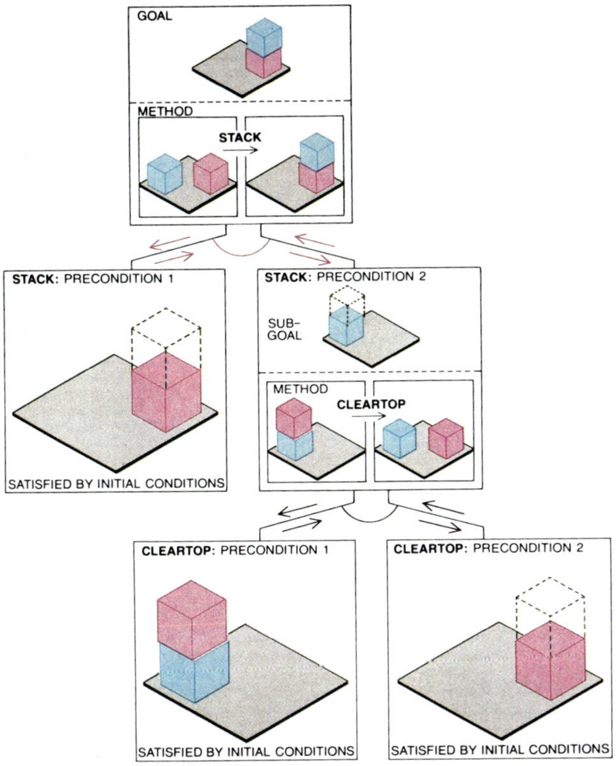

Figure 2. SCIENTIFIC AMERICAN STYLE for illustrations is evident in this one from David Waltz' article 'Artificial Intelligence' [19] in the October 1982 issue, page 122. Several stylistic aspects can be noted: the thin line weights, the open arrowhead design, the use of color and shading, and the caption typography. (Used with permission of W.H. Freeman & Co.)

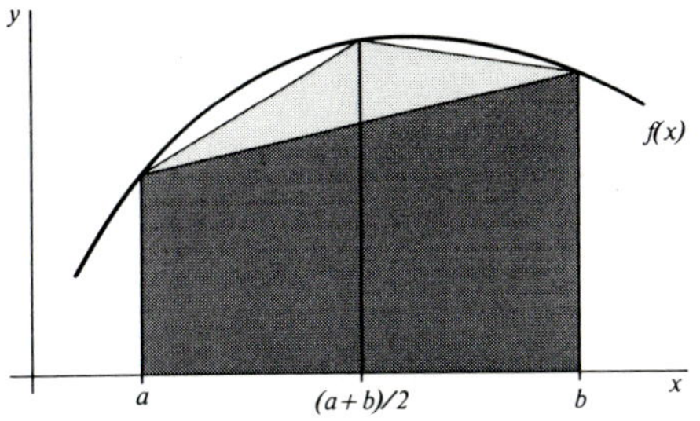

Trapezoidal Rule for n=1 and n=2.

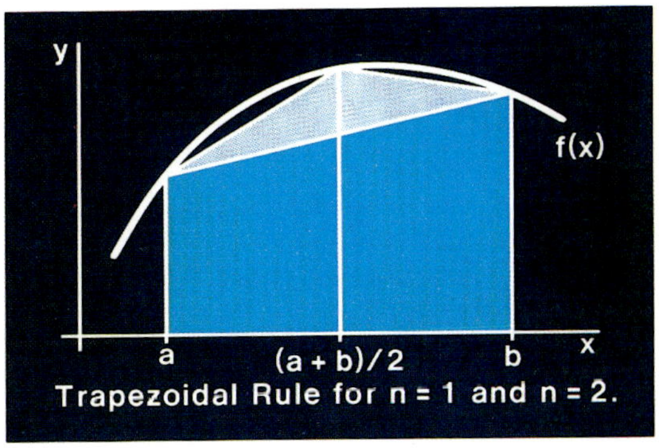

Figure 3. TRAPEZOIDAL RULE FIGURES demonstrate the use of graphical style to produce two very different visual effects. The top illustration is adapted from *Computing* [6] by redrawing it with the Griffin illustrator. The style is faithful to the hand-drawn original. The bottom illustration uses the same picture file but with a style appropriate for a 35 mm. color slide. The slide has the preferred format with light detail on a dark background, thicker lines in white, a larger, bolder and simpler typeface, and the caption is formatted to the slide width. (Used with permission from Reston Publishing Co.)

For instance, the guidelines specified the different line weights for the axes and curves in graphs, the typography for labels on graphs and syntax diagrams, the shading technique for areas in graphs and simple line drawings, and the treatment of arrows in syntax and data-structure diagrams. These guidelines were organized by illustration categories, and then by illustration components. Thus the guidelines for graphs specified the treatment of axes, curves, areas, intersection points, axis tick marks, axis labels, and curve functions; and the guidelines for syntax diagrams specified the treatment of terminal symbols, nonterminal symbols, and grammar rules. Unfortunately, there was no computer support available for drawing the illustrations that could produce sufficiently high quality output or that could implement the various guidelines.

The book's illustrations were also used to produce overhead transparencies for lectures. The computer programs and output could easily be reformatted with a larger type size suitable for projection by specifying a different text formatting style. The hand-drawn artwork had to be enlarged photographically. When an illustration was scaled to transparency size, much of the detail in the illustration was often too small to be read in a large lecture hall. A style substitution facility for graphical images, similar to the one available for text, with the ability to change the proportions of line weights, to use different shading, and to request larger, bolder, text captions would have been invaluable.

Graphical Style Sheets

A graphical style sheet is a way of describing the design guidelines for an illustration. A set of figures produced with the same style sheet should "look" related. It should also be possible to dramatically change the appearance of a figure by specifying different styles, as shown by the book style and transparency style for the Trapezoidal Rule illustration in Figure 3. This implies that there is some separation between the style sheet and the specifics of a particular illustration. The style sheet should contain rendering information specified in some semantic way. For example, there might be a rule that specifies how all axes for graphs should be rendered. We need to determine, therefore, how to separate an illustration into content versus format, and how to specify the format in terms of rendering attributes.

Content versus Format in Illustrations

To apply the *content versus format* discipline found in text composition systems to illustrations, it is necessary to define the content of an illustration separately from its format. The illustration's content is analogous to the author's rough sketch given to a draftsman, such as Figure 4, and its format is analogous to the appearance of the finished artwork rendered by the skill and craftsmanship of the artist, for example, Figure 3. The sketch is described by geometrical objects and their positioning, while the artwork rendering is described by design guidelines and drawing techniques.

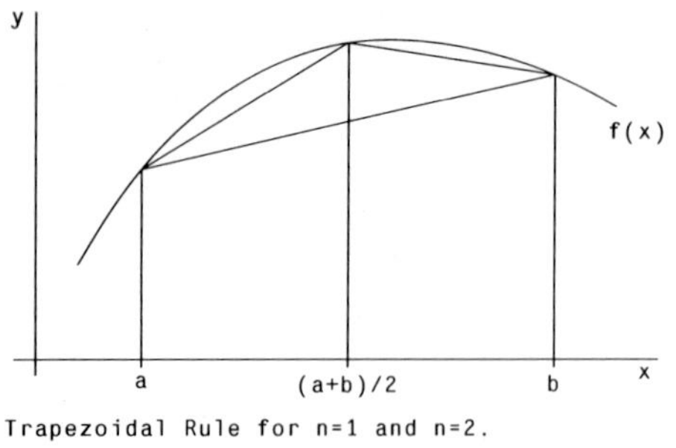

Figure 4. SKETCH OF THE ILLUSTRATION for Figure 3 represents the basic geomety of the picture. All the rendering information for the figure has been reduced to drawing thin lines and using a typewriter-like typeface. The three examples of the Trapezoidal Rule have all been produced by using the same TiogaArtwork file but with appropriate differences in the style rules.

In a manner analogous to the style mechanisms of text formatters, there must be an additional means of including semantic notions in an illustration. Just as not all three-space indentations are paragraph indents, not all thin lines are axes on a graph. Therefore, graphical style must include mechanisms for capturing the intent of the author/illustrator. One way to do this is to provide a level of indirection which names the semantic parts of the illustration. The rendering attributes and guidelines associated with these names are defined separately in a graphical style sheet. If this level of indirection is available, then it is possible to render the same illustration in quite different ways by changing only the graphical style definitions. For example, Figure 3 shows two graphical styles with thin, clean lines for a typeset book and with wider, bolder lines and colors for a color transparency.

Rendering Attributes

A graphical style sheet must express how an illustration is to be rendered. Basic drawing attributes supported in most graphics packages are obvious candidates for specifying how an artwork rendering program should produce an illustration. Examples of such attributes appear in the Griffin illustrator [3], the GKS standard workstation attribute model [2] and in the Xerox Star basic graphics feature [10]. These examples suggest that at least line weight, line patterns, color specification, and caption typography parameters be included in any graphical style sheet.

Graphic designers frequently rely on mechanical aids and transfer sheets to obtain consistent or special effects, suggesting other sources of rendering attributes. A standard reference for transfer sheet designs is the Letraset Catalog [1]. Additional rendering algorithms can be created to produce some of those effects. For instance, a line in an illustration sketch might be rendered by specifying an arrow design in the graphical style sheet to be drawn along that line. Similarly, borders or texture patterns might be rendered from details provided in graphical style sheets.

The Prototype System

Overview

To experiment with these ideas of graphical style we developed a prototype suitable for a class of technical illustrations The system, named TiogaArtwork, was designed to coordinate with the Tioga document preparation system and an interactive illustration program called Griffin [3]. The procedure for generating a figure is to make a draft using Griffin and then convert the figure to a special kind of Tioga document. Once the figure is in document form it is possible to adjust both the style and the content using a combination of Tioga and TiogaArtwork. All of the figures in this paper, except the published example in Figure 2, have been produced using this technique.

The TiogaArtwork system was developed in the Cedar programming environment [14], which is a research project at Xerox PARC. Cedar is both a language, derived from Mesa [13], and a computing environment. The hardware for this environment is a Dorado processor [9] with a 1024 by 808 pixel bi-level display and, optionally, a 640 by 480 pixel color display. A range of medium- to high-resolution printers is available. The highest-quality printers produce digitally half-toned images at phototypesetter-compatible resolutions either in black and white or as color separations.

The design of the prototype is based on features of the Tioga document preparation system, so it is necessary to briefly describe Tioga before going into the details of TiogaArtwork. The current implementation of Tioga consists of an interactive text editor and a batch-oriented typesetter. Documents in this system consist of two files: a file of text nodes and a file of formatting style rules. The text nodes in Tioga have a hierarchial structure similar to that of the NLS editor [12]. A document is a tree-structured hierarchy of nodes containing text, for example, in section, subsection, paragraph order. A normal tree-traversal results in the familiar form of the document. Each node in the document can possess certain *node properties.* The principal use of these properties is to associate the formatting style rules with the nodes. Figure 5 represents the Tioga document structure of some surrounding nodes of the document for this paper.

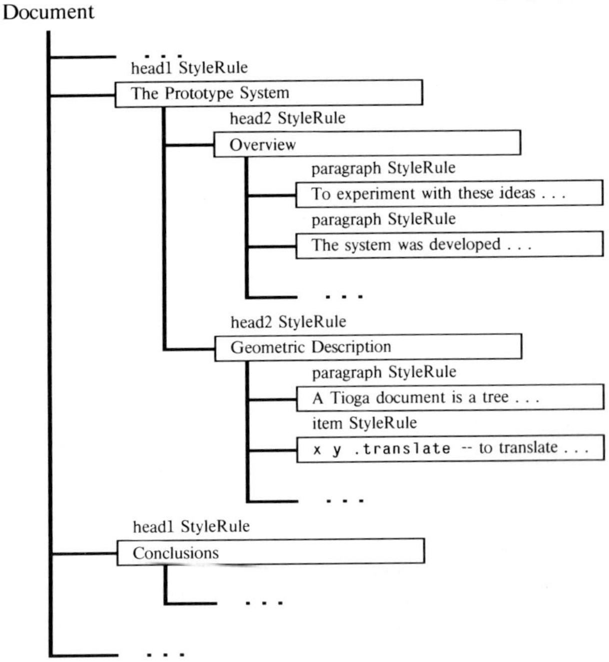

Figure 5. DOCUMENT STRUCTURE provides a hierarchy for organizing a text document. This illustration represents the Tioga document structure for the nearby sections and subsections of this paper. The boxes represent text nodes and the labels above each box represent the node properties. The StyleRule property indicates the formatting attributes for first-level headings, second-level headings, paragraphs, and items within a list.

The style concept in the Tioga formatter is similar to that in SCRIBE [15]. In Tioga, formatting styles are defined by a collection of rules contained in a separate file. The style rules specify formatting parameters such as type family, style, and size, indentation, interline leading, text justification mode, and composition layout parameters. The formatting rules are written in an interpreted language, so it is possible to compute parameters during the formatting process.

We have designed a way to include nodes containing graphics in a Tioga document. These nodes contain a textual representation of geometric attributes such as line coordinates, curve control points, positions, and transformations. The style rules associated with these nodes specify graphical parameters and rendering attributes. Tioga's node properties are implemented as named property lists, so we defined a new property, which we called `ArtworkClass`, for the illustration nodes. The style machinery for Tioga is extensible, so the current set of tools allows us to build on the existing mechanisms for manipulating styles and for adding graphical style attributes. It also means that our system can use Tioga facilities for text formatting.

A document in our system, therefore, is a tree of nodes arranged in a hierarchical structure. Some of the branches of the tree represent paragraphs of text and some represent illustrations. An illustration is a subtree in the document tree-structure with its root node possessing an `ArtworkClass` property. Nodes within the subtree structure may be either graphics or text. Nodes representing subpictures will have the `ArtworkClass` property, while text captions within an illustration will have only the standard Tioga properties. This recursive relationship is important; it means that our system can use all the text formatting features of Tioga for text inside of illustrations. Figure 6 represents the Tioga document node structure for portions of the Trapezoidal Rule illustrations in Figures 3 and 4.

TiogaArtwork is the part of the system that interprets the graphical nodes and style rules. The pictures can be previewed on a display screen using the Cedar graphics package [21] or converted for printing.

The combination of using the Tioga document structure and representing the graphics as text allows TiogaArtwork to interact easily with the Tioga editor and the Tioga typesetter. This is advantageous in a number of ways. One advantage is the ease of creating and editing figures. The Tioga editor does not react to the `ArtworkClass` property, so the text and style properties for a graphics node can be edited in the normal manner. This means that for the prototype experiment we did not have to write a special editor to manipulate the graphics, although we did write a conversion routine which translated from Griffin format to Tioga node structure and automatically generated style rule properties from the Griffin style attributes.

Another advantage of using the Tioga document structure for illustrations is that it permits us to typeset any text in the illustration. This is accomplished by setting up a call-back mechanism between the typesetter program and TiogaArtwork. As the document tree is traversed, the typesetter formats text nodes in the normal fashion. Whenever a node with the `ArtworkClass` property is encountered, that entire subtree is passed to TiogaArtwork. If TiogaArtwork subsequently encounters a text node while rendering the illustration, it passes the text branch back to the typesetter. This recursion is guaranteed to terminate at the end of the tree-path traversal.

Trapezoidal Rule Figure

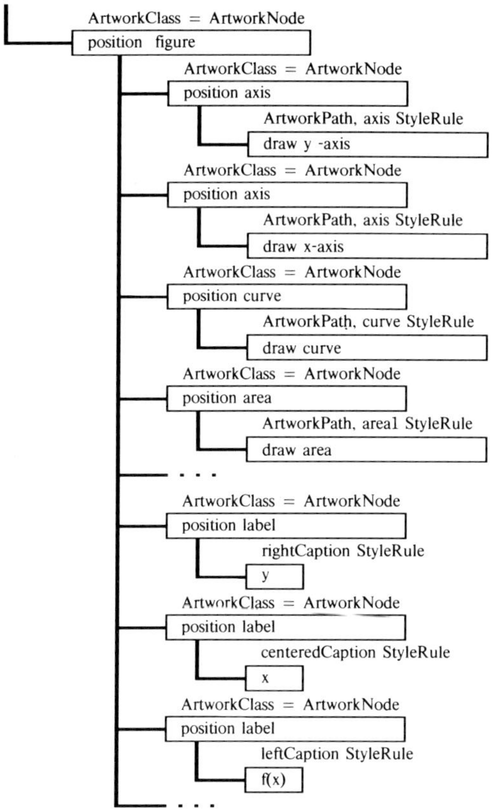

Figure 6. ILLUSTRATIONS in TiogaArtwork also use the Tioga document structure. The boxes represent the artwork nodes which contain the geometrical representation, and the labels above the boxes represent the node properties. Note that StyleRule properties exist on both text and artwork nodes. This structure can be extended to encompass pictures composed of many subpictures and text captions in a natural hierarchy.

The call-back mechanism is also used to pass dimensional information between the two programs. The typesetter provides the dimensional parameters for the formatted text with which TiogaArtwork can layout the caption within the illustration according to the style rule. TiogaArtwork generates the dimensions of the formatted graphics so the typesetter can layout the figures with the paragraphs on the page.

This document structure and system design gives us a great deal of flexibility for experimenting with the best way to represent illustrations in a document. The current structure puts only geometric information in the document body and puts all rendering parameters in the style rules. We found that this representation gives a good semantic description of the picture. The next sections will describe our current implementation in more detail.

Geometric description

A Tioga document is a tree of nodes. Some of the branches of the tree represent paragraphs of text, and some represent illustrations. For text, the levels of the tree represent the section-subsection-paragraph hierarchy of the document. For illustrations, the hierarchy represents a relative set of transformations for subpictures. Each subpicture in the illustration is drawn relative to the coordinate system established by its ancestors. An `ArtworkClass` node, therefore, may contain a set of coordinate transformations which establish the coordinate system for this node and all of its descendant subpictures:

`x y .translate` -- to translate the origin to <x,y>

`sx sy .scale` -- to scale by x,y scaling factors

`r .rotate` -- to rotate by r degrees

A geometrical shape can be composed of straight lines and curves, and a sequence of these lines and curves is called a *path* [21]. A path can represent a line, an area or a clipping region. The path definition is provided by commands to draw lines and curves:

`x y .moveto` -- establish the current path position <cx,cy> as <x,y>

`x y .lineto` -- draw a line from the current position to <x,y>, and reset <cx,cy> to <x,y>

`x1 y1 x2 y2 x3 y3 .curveto` -- extend the path with a curve which has the four Bezier control points <cx,cy>, <x1,y1>, <x2,y2>, and <x3,y3>, and reset <cx,cy> to <x3,y3>

For the kind of pictures we are working with, the paths and transformations are all that is specified in the nodes of an illustration document. The rest of the rendering information will be supplied by the style rules. Figure 7 is an extract from the geometric description used for the three instances of the trapezoid rule diagrams in Figures 3 and 4:

```
% TiogaArtwork figure for Trapezoid Rule
  % Cluster 1
  0 0 .translate 1 1 .scale 0 .rotate
    % y-axis
    11 31 .translate 1 1 .scale 0 .rotate
      1 1 .moveto 1 185 .lineto
    % x-axis
    3 39 .translate 1 1 .scale 0 .rotate
      1 1 .moveto 249 1 .lineto
    % curve
    27 87 .translate 1 1 .scale 0 .rotate
      1 1 .moveto
      8 17  15 33  25 49 .curveto
      43 78  71 106  105 113 .curveto
      131 118  161 110  185 97 .curveto
      194 92  201 87  209 81 .curveto
    % area from a to (a+b)/2
    51 39 .translate 1 1 .scale 0 .rotate
      1 1 .moveto 1 97 .lineto
      81 161 .lineto 81 1 .lineto
      1 1.lineto
    % area from (a+b)/2 to
    ...
    % y-axis label
    8 216 .translate 1 1 .scale 0 .rotate
      y
    % x-axis label
    247 36 .translate 1 1 .scale 0 .rotate
      x
    ...
```

Figure 7. GEOMETRIC REPRESENTATION of an illustration in a textual form consists of comments, transformations, and path definitions. The Trapezoidal Rule illustration was first drawn with the Griffin illustrator [3]. It was then automatically converted into a TiogaArtwork document generating the node structure and node properties from the Griffin illustration file. The indentation indicates the node structure. The comments, which begin with percent signs, were added manually by editing the document text.

For reasons which become apparent during the discussion of rendering algorithms, it is necessary to distinguish between transformations and path definitions in the contents of an `ArtworkClass` node. It is also convenient to create artwork nodes which specify the file name of a TiogaArtwork illustration. Continuous-tone images stored as files are another category of illustration that can be accommodated by the `ArtworkClass` property. The values of the `ArtworkClass` property are the following:

`ArtworkNode` -- node contains the textual representation of an illustration which is not a path, such as transformations

`ArtworkPath` -- node contains the geometric definition of a path

`ArtworkImage` -- node contains the name of a continuous-tone image file stored as an array of intensity samples

`ArtworkFileName` -- node contains the name of another TiogaArtwork file

Basic style parameters

Style rules are described in an interpreted language with each format rule expressed as a procedure definition. A typical rule describes a list of parameter-value pairs which will be stored in a global association list. The general format for this in the Tioga editor is:

```
(name-of-style-rule) "commentary
      describing the style" {
       value parameterName
       value parameterName
       ...
       value parameterName
       } StyleRule
```

The `name-of-style-rule` refers to some semantic aspect of the illustration such as axis, curve, or nonterminal. Values are either numbers or keywords and may be expressions. Values which are distances may be expressed in most convenient units. For instance, 2-point line weight can be expressed as `2 pt`, colors can be expressed by keyword color names such as `red`, `darkBrown`, or `lightBlue`, and relative colors can be evaluated as some percentage (such as `75 percent`) of the brightness or saturation of a named color.

The following basic set of drawing attributes were defined as graphical style parameters:

`lineWeight`	the line thickness
`pathType`	the path area/outline type: `filled`, `outlined`, `filled+outlined`
`penType`	the pen shape: `round`, `square`, `rectangular`, `elliptical`, `italic`
`penHeight`	the pen height as a proportion of `lineWeight`
`penWidth`	the pen width as a proportion of `lineWeight`
`penAngle`	the rotation of the pen, in degrees from horizontal
`areaColor`	the color of filled areas: hue, saturation, brightness
`outlineColor`	the color of outlines: hue, saturation, brightness

The following set of style attributes are supplied by the existing formatter but are interpreted by the artwork-rendering software for illustration captions and labels:

`family`	the type family, such as Helvetica or TimesRoman
`size`	the type size
`face`	the type style: `regular`, `italic`, `bold`, and `bold+italic`
`captionFormat`	the text justification mode: `flushLeft`, `flushRight`, `centered`, or `justified`
`captionAlign`	the vertical text justification mode: `flushTop`, `centered`, `baseline`, or `flushBottom`
`lineLength`	the length of caption lines
`leftIndent`	the left indent for captions
`rightIndent`	the right indent for captions
`leading`	the spacing between lines
`textRotation`	the rotation of the text line, in degrees from horizontal
`textColor`	the color of caption text: hue, saturation, brightness

To demonstrate both the style language and the graphical style attributes, Figure 8 shows the two style definitions necessary for Figure 3.

Rendering the illustration

TiogaArtwork translates our representation of an illustration into a set of calls on the Cedar graphics package [21] . The graphics package implements a full set of transformation and clipping operations. Shapes are described as a set of analytical outlines that are filled either with a flat color or an image.

The geometry in our documents consists of paths and transformations. The transformations translate one-for-one into calls on the graphics package. The path definitions are compatible with the outline description required by the graphics package. Thus, if a node contains a path with the `pathType=filled`, then the path represents a closed area to be colored with `areaColor` and can be easily rendered.

If the `pathType` is `outlined`, then it represents the center-line of a line or pen stroke. A thick line is drawn along this path as defined by the `lineWeight` and pen parameters. Predefined pen shapes are round, square, rectangular, elliptical, and italic. Other style parameters control the aspect ratio and rotation of the pen shapes. The graphics package does not currently support a pen semantic, so TiogaArtwork reduces this description to an outline. This definition of a thick line is similar to that of a stroke in Metafont [8].

Extended style semantics

This basic graphical style machinery can be extended to express more complicated style semantics. The following examples of shadows, arrows, and borders are based on common graphic arts practice.

Shadow Styles

Two-dimensional shadow effects can be created to emphasize an object. Two simple examples of shadow effects are drop shadows and offset shadows, shown in Figure 9. A drop shadow appears to give an object depth by extending a slanted shadow line away from the object. An offset shadow gives emphasis by showing an underlying copy of the object a short distance away. The style parameters for shadow effects are the following:

`shadowType`	the shadow effect: `drop` or `offset`
`shadowPathType`	the offset shadow path type: `filled`, `outlined`, `filled+outlined`
`shadowAngle`	the angle of the shadow from the object, in degrees
`shadowOffsetAmount`	the distance that the offset shadow is placed at `shadowAngle`
`shadowDirection`	the direction of the shadow from the object: `upLeft`, `upRight`, `downLeft`, `downRight`
`shadowWeight`	the weight of the drop shadow or outline of the offset shadow
`shadowAreaColor`	the color of the drop shadow or offset shadow area
`shadowOutlineColor`	the color of the offset shadow outline

```
% TrapezoidBook.Style

BeginStyle

(BasicGraphics) AttachStyle

(BasicText) AttachStyle

(axis) "x,y axes" {
  black outlineColor
  outlined pathType
  1 pt lineWeight
  } StyleRule

(area1) "dark areas" {
  grey areaColor
  filled pathType
  } StyleRule

(area2) "light areas" {
  lightGrey areaColor
  filled pathType
  } StyleRule

(curve) "function line" {
  black outlineColor
  outlined pathType
  2 pt lineWeight
  } StyleRule

(leftCaption) "..." {
  "TimesRoman" family
  8 bp size
  italic face
  flushLeft captionFormat
  flushTop captionAlign
  0 leftIndent
  } StyleRule

(centeredCaption) "..." {
  ...

(rightCaption) "..." {
  ...

EndStyle
```

```
% TrapezoidSlide.Style

BeginStyle

(BasicGraphics) AttachStyle

(BasicText) AttachStyle

(axis) "x,y axes" {
  white outlineColor
  outlined pathType
  2 pt lineWeight
  } StyleRule

(area1) "dark areas" {
  orange areaColor
  filled pathType
  } StyleRule

(area2) "light areas" {
  lightYellow areaColor
  filled pathType
  } StyleRule

(curve) "function line" {
  white outlineColor
  outlined pathType
  4 pt lineWeight
  } StyleRule

(leftCaption) "..." {
  "Helvetica" family
  12 bp size
  bold face
  flushLeft captionFormat
  flushTop captionAlign
  0 leftIndent
  white textColor
  } StyleRule

(centeredCaption) "..." {
  ...

(rightCaption) "..." {
  ...

EndStyle
```

Figure 8. GRAPHICAL STYLE SHEETS for the two Trapezoidal Rule illustrations in Figure 3 demonstrate the style language and the graphical style attributes. The style on the left produces a typeset book quality illustration and the style on the right produces a colored 35 mm. slide form. Note that the styles differ in the line weights, color selections, and typography parameters.

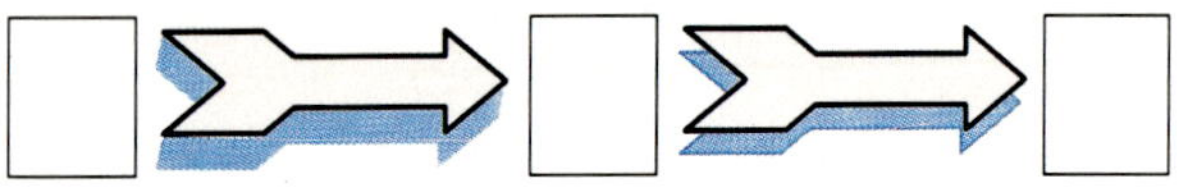

Figure 9. SHADOW EFFECTS can be rendered by a simple algorithm that reuses the geometric path definition several times. The arrow on the left has a drop shadow and the arrow on the right has an offset shadow. Several style parameters are available to control the weight, angle, color, and type of shadow.

Both shadowing techniques can be rendered by first drawing the shadow of the object and then drawing the intended object. Slightly darker shadow colors can be computed in a style rule, for instance, `shadowAreaColor` might be computed as `50 percent` of the brightness of the `areaColor`.

Arrow Styles

Arrows in drawings can be described as paths having a particular arrow style. The style must describe the shape of the arrowhead and tail. One approach is to define a prototype shape on a simple rectangular grid. This model resembles a transfer sheet system such as the one provided by Letraset [1]. To avoid cataloging a large variety of curved arrows, a mapping is used to stretch the prototype shape along any given path. The x-axis of the grid is mapped onto the path directly, and y-values are mapped into distances normal to the path [20]. This scheme permits considerable scope for creative designs by using a simple and easy-to-draw prototype, and then computing the hard-to-draw finished design as in Figure 10.

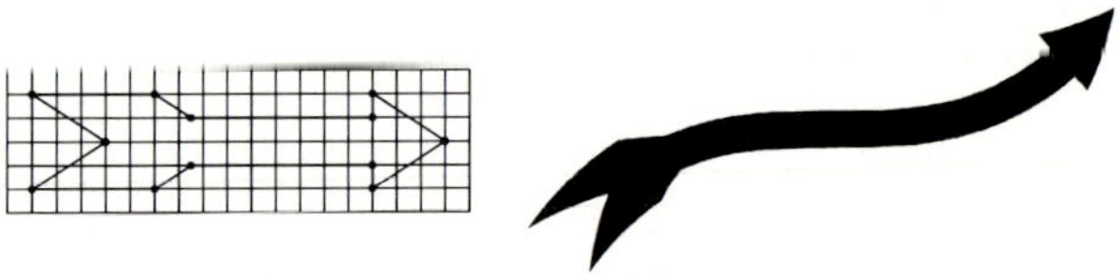

Figure 10. ARROW STYLES can be created by mapping a prototype design, developed on a rectangular grid, along a curved path. The mapping algorithm can be controlled to preserve the arrow head and feather shapes and only stretch the shaft of the arrow. The path can be any combination of lines or curves. The style of the mapped arrow can be filled or outlined in a similar way to other TiogaArtwork objects.

Border Patterns

Arbitrary patterns are a logical extension of the style for arrow heads. These border patterns are slightly more complicated to render because the prototype pattern must be repeated along the path like a wallpaper design. As only an integral number of repetitions is desired, the mapping algorithm must adjust scale factors to ensure an exact number of cycles. Again, the same simple prototype grid is mapped along the path, as shown in Figure 11.

Figure 11. BORDER PATTERNS can also be mapped along paths using the same technique as for the arrows, but using an integral number of repetitions. This Greek Key design consists of a white rectangular area and a blue spiral. The design was created to fit together end to end. The path is a cubic curve.

Conclusions

We conclude that a representation that explicitly specifies the stylistic properties of an illustration provides a powerful way to control document quality. Graphical style sheets can provide design discipline. Using a common style when designing a set of illustrations for a paper, for example, can guarantee a uniform specification of such parameters as color, line styles, and arrowhead shapes. Another benefit is that the additional semantic structure introduced by the style sheet makes it possible to produce those figures over a range of circumstances. Different style sheets can be designed to accommodate not only different publishing styles but also the restrictions inherent in different media, such as the difference between paper and 35 mm slide media. If it is easier to reuse figures, then perhaps more time will be spent producing good ones.

We have successfully implemented a prototype system for manipulating graphical styles which was built to coordinate with the Tioga document preparation system. We have used the combination of Tioga and TiogaArtwork to produce this paper. We conclude from working with this system that it is possible to control some of the stylistic aspects of illustrations using a set of style rules, and that this approach is a useful one for specifying pictures in documents. The particular representation we used was a convenient one for our environment. The important aspect is the separation of the geometry and the style properties, especially the level of indirection introduced by using named style rules. The flexibility inherent in the textual representation and the style language was important in an experimental system. We suspect that a style language is the correct level of abstraction for graphical styles even in fully developed systems.

Representing illustrations as styles plus geometry introduces some interesting issues with respect to rendering algorithms. For example, one natural specification for line style is to specify a uniform width. The specification should also describe the behavior of the line at joints and endpoints; for example, whether the corners are mitered or rounded off. An algorithm that produces an analytical description for the shape of an outline specified in this manner is nontrivial, especially if the path contains parametric cubic splines. This kind of example forces us as graphics system designers to pay attention to useful rendering algorithms, not just convenient ones.

Future Work

It is clear that for many applications one should use an interactive graphics system to design an illustration. For example, we used the Griffin system to generate the illustrations for our paper rather than manually calculate path descriptions. There are many interesting questions about how graphical style should be specified in such a system. Griffin assigns attributes to shapes, but there is little semantic content to the assignment; all objects with the same set of properties have the same style.

In general, we need to learn more about organizing style rules. Our current implementation has a different rule for each node that looks at all different. Often, however, the styles vary in only a few parameters. In fact, the actual semantics may really be: these nodes are the same except for these parameters. In the current TiogaArtwork system, it is possible to define *generic* style rules, that can be referenced in specific style rules to specify the common set of attributes. Tools are needed to provide an effective interface to this style machinery.

Illustrations are often produced by executing other graphics programs. Frequently these programs have little facility for providing graphical style. Many times the illustrations produced must be redrawn or the programs fine-tuned to generate publication-quality results. Some mechanism for capturing the images produced and for supplying graphical style semantics would be most helpful in incorporating such illustrations in documents.

Another interesting topic is style guidelines which apply to the layout and design of illustrations rather than to simple rendering parameters. It can be convenient, for example, to express box dimensions as a function of the size of the text in the box. The size of the text depends on its font style, so there needs to be some way of specifying this relationship between the style and the geometry. In another example, the actual endpoint of an arrow changes when it is pointing to something which is rendered with a thick line than a thin one. Style rules might also include document layout parameters. For example, the style of an illustration could control the layout so that the figure might have a horizontal orientation when the document is typeset with wide columns, a vertical one when narrow columns are used, or a fixed aspect ratio to suit videotape or slides. A dynamic reconfiguration capability would be helpful in making the illustrations look better in the chosen layout.

Acknowledgements

The sensitivity to graphic arts quality and design issues in this project is due in part to George Roth, a graphic designer who collaborated on a variety of typesetting projects, including the *Computing* text book [6]. With enthusiasm and insight, he often asked "Why can't you program it to do this?" while offering suggestions as to the appearance of the final result.

Both the design and implementation of Tioga document preparation system are critical to our work. Bill Paxton, Michael Plass and Scott McGregor are responsible for Tioga, and we would like to publicly thank them for their contributions to the graphical style project. We also thank John Warnock and Doug Wyatt for the Cedar graphics package and other graphical tools used in our prototype.

One of the principal features of Cedar is that it is an integrated environment. In other words, it is very easy to use pieces of the existing system in a new application. Our work uses this feature extensively, so we were able to build our prototype system in rather short time. Therefore, we will simply thank all of the Cedar implementors for their contributions.

References

[1] anon., *Letraset Catalog*, Letraset USA. (1980).

[2] anon., *Graphic Kernel System (GKS) Functional Description*, ISO TC97/SC5/WG2 N117 (1982).

[3] Baudelaire, Patrick and Stone, Maureen, Techniques for Interactive Raster Graphics, *Computer Graphics* **14**, 3, (1980).

[4] Bell, Edward, Personal communication regarding the production of illustrations within *Scientific American* (1982).

[5] Chamberlin, D., King, J., Slutz, D., Todd, S. and Wade, B., JANUS: An interactive System for Document Composition. *IBM Systems Journal* **21**, 3 (1982).

[6] Dyck, V.A., Lawson, J.D., Smith, J.A. and Beach, R.J., *Computing -- An Introduction to Structured Problem Solving Using PASCAL*, Reston (1982).

[7] Kernighan, Brian W., PIC - A Language for Typesetting Graphics, *Software Practice & Experience* **12**, 1 (Jan. 1982).

[8] Knuth, Donald E., *TEX and METAFONT, New Directions in Typesetting*, Digital Press (1979).

[9] Lampson, Butler W., Pier, Kenneth A., McDaniel, Gene A., Ornstein, Severo M. and Clark, Douglas W., *The Dorado: A High-Performance Personal Computer, Three Papers*, CSL-81-1, Xerox PARC (January 1981).

[10] Lipke, Daniel, Evans, Steven R., Newlin, John K., Weissman, Robert L., Star Graphics: An Object-Oriented Implementation, *Computer Graphics* **16**, 3 (1982).

[11] Lesk, Mike E., Typesetting Documents on UNIX and GCOS: Using the -ms Macros with Troff and Nroff, *Unix Programmer's Manual* **2A**, 7th ed., Bell Laboratories (1979).

[12] Meyerowitz, Norman and van Dam, Andries, Interactive Editing Systems, Parts I and II, *ACM Computing Surveys*, **14**, 3 (1982).

[13] Mitchell, James G., Maybury, William and Sweet, Richard, *Mesa Language Manual*, CSL-79-3, Xerox PARC (April 1979).

[14] Paxton, Bill, *The State of Cedar*, Xerox PARC videotape, V-163 (1982).

[15] Reid, Brian K., A High-Level Approach to Computer Document Formatting, *ACM Symposium on Principles of Programming Languages* (Jan. 1980).

[16] Ruegg, Ruedi and Frohlich, Godi, *Basic Typography*, ABC Verlag Zurich (1978).

[17] Smith, David Canfield, Irby, Charles, Kimball, Ralph and Verplank, Bill, Designing the Star User Interface, *Byte* (Apr. 1982).

[18] Van Wyck, Christopher J., *IDEAL User's Manual*, Computing Science Technical Report No. 103, Bell Laboratories (1982).

[19] Waltz, David, Artificial Intelligence, *Scientific American* **247**, 4 (1982).

[20] Warnock, John, Personal communication regarding the mapping of prototype rectangular grid designs on to curve paths (1982).

[21] Warnock, John and Wyatt, Douglas K., A Device Independent Graphics Imaging Model for Use with Raster Devices, *Computer Graphics* **16**, 3 (1982).

PANEL

THE SIMULATION OF NATURAL PHENOMENA

CHAIR: Charles A. Csuri, Ohio State University
PANELISTS: James Blinn, Jet Propulsion Laboratory
Julian Gomez, Ohio State University
Nelson Max, Lawrence Livermore National Laboratory
William Reeves, Lucasfilm Ltd.

CHAIRMAN'S INTRODUCTION:

This panel will discuss the issues and the problems associated with the simulation of natural phenomena. This is a difficult area of research since it generally involves complex data bases and in many instances time variant phenomena. The computational loads can become enormous as one considers the physics or the mathematical modeling of structures.

Most items in nature, trees, clouds, fire and comets being some examples, have not been displayed realistically in computer graphics. This lack stems from a few different problems, all of which are significant. The first is the fact that realistic portrayals require large amounts of storage and consequently large compute time. Nature is able to create diverse detail at the most minute levels within an object of grandoise scale. The second problem is that of diversity of design within a given framework. For example, if a scene requires two dozen poplar trees, how does the designer construct trees that look different but are undeniably poplars? Humans typically become tired after the first few iterations of such a design process, with a resulting degradation in the subsequent models. Clearly, this problem applies to all of the phenomena mentioned above. Finally, there is a lack of models. First, second and third order representations are commonly used in computer graphics to model various kinds of surfaces and their boolean combinations. However, their applications to objects, which do not lend themselves well to being described as surfaces has not been addressed sufficiently.

Previous attempts at realism have dealt with the appearances of the surfaces being modeled, in terms of their illumination or relief. More recently, fractal methods have introduced a new degree of realism into terrain modeling systems. However, it appears that natural phenomena will require more research into the fundamental way things occur in nature, and in terms of computer graphics, their representation will build on previous work, but will still require new modeling techniques.

Dr. Nelson Max of the Lawrence Livermore Laboratory has dealt with computer graphics simulations of mathematical concepts, molecular structure, water and clouds. He will present his recent work on the simulation of clouds.

Dr. William Reeves of Lucasfilm did his dissertation research in the area of motion control at the University of Toronto. He has done a simulation of fire for the science fiction film Star Trek II and he will discuss the techniques used to generate the data and the animation.

Dr. James Blinn of the Jet Propulsion Laboratory is well known for his basic research in computer graphics. He has produced numerous animated sequences of scientific phenomena. His presentation will focus upon smoke, clouds and soft structures.

Julian Gomez is a PhD candidate in computer graphics at the Ohio State University. He worked at the Jet Propulsion Laboratory for three years in computer graphics. His dissertation research is in the area of the simulation of natural phenomena and he will discuss smoke and fire.

Blinn, James F. and Martin E. Newell, "Texture and Reflection in Computer Generated Images", Comm. ACM, Vol 19 (10), pp. 542-547 (October, 1976)

Blinn, James F. "Computer Display of Curved Surfaces", PhD Thesis, University of Utah, (December 1978)

Blinn, James F. "Simulation of Wrinkled Surfaces", Computer Graphics, Vol. 12 (3), pp. 286-292 SIGGRAPH-ACM (August 1978)

Blinn, James F. "Light Reflection Functions for Simulation of Clouds and Dusty Surfaces", Computer Graphics, Vol 16 (3) SIGGRAPH-ACM, July 1982

Brooks, J., Murarka R.S., Onuoha, D., "An Extension of the Combinatorial Geometry

Technique for Modeling Vegetation and Terrain Features", NTIS Report AD-782-883, (August 1974)

Carpenter, Loren C. "Computer Rendering of Fractal Curves and Surfaces", Comm. ACM, to appear

Dungan W., A Terrain and Cloud Computer Image Generation Model, Proceedings SIGGRAPH'79, (August 1979), 143-150

Futrelle, R., "Galatea Project for Analysis of Moving Images", Department of Biophysics and Theoretical Biology, The University of Chicago, Technical Reports, 1973-74

Mandelbrot, Benoit B., Fractals - Form, Chance and Dimension, W. H., Freeman, San Francisco 1977

Marshall, Robert, Wilson, Rodger, and Carlson, Wayne, "Procedure Models for Generating Three-dimensional Terrain", Computer Graphics, Vol. 14, (3), pp. 154-162, Proc. SIGGRAPH 80 (July 1980)

Newell, M.E., The Utilization of Procedure Models in Digital Image Synthesis, Computer Science, University of Utah, UTEC-CSC-76-218 (1975)

PANELISTS' ABSTRACTS:

Julian E. Gomez, The Ohio State University

The basic problem with applying conventional modeling methods to the representation of natural phenomena is the intractability of the datasets. Objects such as clouds or fire are clearly difficult to model with polygons, bicubic surface patches, or quadric surfaces. The first two methods require large amounts of data, with a corresponding high computational cost. The third has the additional problem of creating surfaces which appear too regular. The problem is compounded by the fact that natural phenomena inherently change form with time, thus requiring large numbers of already large data bases.

Additionally, the objects under discussion are not even surfaces, so the addition of detail by, for example, surface normal pertubation or stochastic surface element subdivision is not applicable. Nevertheless, given recent demonstrations by Mandelbrot, Carpenter and Fournier, et. al., it is apparent that fractals will have major application to the representation of natural phenomena.

These phenomena can be simulated by massive systems of differential equations describing the motion of particles within the system. A situation like this is for the most part out of the range of a laboratory without access to large or "super" computing capability. One way around this is to "fake" the object, i.e., to find a method which reproduces the appearance of the object without actually simulating it.

It is difficult to separate the appearance of the object from the systems describing it, because of the illumination models required. Keeping in mind a particulate nature, smoke reflects light, fire emits and transmits light, and a cloud reflects, transmits and scatters light. High complexity illumination models, sometimes called ray tracing algorithms, are necessary to accurately portray the action of light in one of these situations.

Finally, a modeling technique should be hierarchical by screen complexity, i.e., generate enough detail as necessary to occupy the proper portion of screen space plus a little for antialiasing.

Nelson Max, Lawrence Livermore National Laboratory

If a cloud volume is defined by the region between two height fields, above and below a mean cloud plane, the heights may be computed by formulas involving trigonometric functions, polynomials, square roots and basic arithmetic operations. Since the cloud shape is specified by a small number of coefficients, rather than by random access to a large data base, these computations can readily be "vectorized" to run on modern supercomputers with parallel or pipeline architectures. Colour raster animation of these shapes will be shown, including semi-transparent 2-D clouds and opaque 3-D clouds.

Semi-transparent 3-D clouds will also be illustrated rendered by a new algorithm for efficiently integrating the "single-scattering" model of Jim Blinn [1] along a ray from the eye through the cloud. When the sun is directly overhead and the cloud has constant density, the intensity contributed by a segment where a ray intersects the cloud is approximated by a linear combination of the moments of the region where the cloud intersects a vertical plane containing the ray. The indefinite integrals for the moments up to a certain degree are precomputed, and reused for the various rays in the vertical plane.

An animated sequence simulating a laser fusion target implosion will show smoke produced when the ablator blows off after absorbing the incoming radiation. The smoke was made from thousands of small moving dots, as in Bill Reeves' method. Optical printing was used to blur them and combine them with the rest of the target image. This eliminates the need for motion blur and anti-aliasing and requires fewer dots.

Blinn, J., "Light Reflection Functions for Simulation of Clouds and Dusty Surfaces", Computer Graphics, Vol 16, No. 3 (1982) pp. 21-29.

William T. Reeves, Lucasfilm Ltd

Image synthesis of scenes containing natural phenomena is, as we all know, a difficult problem. Real objects do not have smooth or rectangular surfaces composed of bronze, chrome or plastic -- they are rough, pockmarked dirty, cracked, fluid, amorphous and very irregular. In natural images, the complexity and level of detail seems infinite. And yet, with proper anti-aliasing and the high resolution framebuffers and film recorders being manufactured today, we are capable of displaying very realistic and detailed images. The display-space bandwidth is there - all we have to do is generate and correctly filter the signal to be displayed. What follows are some directions in which I think graphics research needs to proceed in order to synthesize natural scenes.

Computer models of natural phenomena are too complex and detailed to be designed efficiently by an interactive user with access to only a simple set of building blocks such as polygons or patches. Instead, we must continue to research and develop procedurally based modeling domains, and, in particular, those based on stochastic processes (e.g., fractals [Mandelbrot 82] [Fournier 82] and particle systems [Reeves 83] . With such tools, the interactive user only specifies global constraints and parameters and the procedural and stochastic elements are responsible for generating the actual images. We need to develop systems in which to test, debug and experiment with procedural models.

Traditional modeling primitives, such as polygons, quadrics and patches are often inappropriate for modeling natural phenomena. We need new modeling primitives that are simple to render so that we can afford to compute millions of them to build up image complexity.

Texture mapping techniques are effective as a means of adding detail to an image. Photographing a real scene, scanning it in, and using it as a texture in a synthetic image might be called "cheating" by some people, but it works and is quite cost effective. We should continue to develop texture mapping and look into using procedural texture maps or writing systems and languages in which one can create new textures.

The knowledge needed to synthesize a particular natural phenomenon is domain dependent - what you need to know to draw trees is quite different from what you need to draw clouds. This information is often available in scientific literature. The problems are finding it and then deciphering what it says. Working with other researchers from the field in question is often a good idea.

Finally, making a natural scene look "right" is only two thirds of the problem. Making it move right is the other one third. Motion is often overlooked in image synthesis, especially in the motion of objects within the scene. Animated scenes containing natural objects will not look real until we are able to synthesize their motions. Procedurally and stochastically defined motions are interesting areas of research.

Fournier, A., D Fussel, L. Carpenter, "Computer Rendering of Stocastic Models", Comm. ACM 25, No. 6 (June 1982)

Mandelbrot, B.B., "The Fractal Geometry of Nature", W. H. Freeman, 1982.

Reeves, W.T., "Particle Systems - a Technique for Modeling a class of Fuzzy Objects", Proceedings of SIGGRAPH'83, July 1983.

A Parallel Scan Conversion Algorithm with Anti-Aliasing for a General-Purpose Ultracomputer

Eugene Fiume
Alain Fournier

Computer Systems Research Group
Department of Computer Science
University of Toronto
Toronto, Ontario, M5S 1A4

Larry Rudolph

Department of Computer Science
Carnegie-Mellon University
Pittsburgh, PA 15213

ABSTRACT

Popular approaches to speeding up scan conversion often employ parallel processing. Recently, several special-purpose parallel architectures have been suggested. We propose an alternative to these systems: the general-purpose ultracomputer, a parallel processor with many autonomous processing elements and a shared memory. The "serial semantics/parallel execution" feature of this architecture is exploited in the formulation of a scan conversion algorithm. Hidden surfaces are removed using a single scanline, z-buffer algorithm. Since exact anti-aliasing is inherently slow, a novel parallel anti-aliasing algorithm is presented in which subpixel coverage by edges is approximated using a look-up table. The ultimate intensity of a pixel is the weighted sum of the intensity contribution of the closest edge, that of the "losing" edges, and that of the background. The algorithm is fast and accurate, it is attractive even in a serial environment, and it avoids several artifacts that commonly occur in animated sequences.

CR Categories and Subject Descriptors: B.3.2 [**Memory Structures**]: Design Styles - *Shared Memory*; D.3.3 [**Programming Languages**]: Language Constructs - *Concurrent programming structures*; F.2.2 [**Analysis of Algorithms and Problem Complexity**]: Nonnumerical Algorithms and Problems - *Geometrical problems and computations*; I.3.1 [**Computer Graphics**]: Hardware Architecture - *Raster display devices*; I.3.3 [**Computer Graphics**]: Picture/Image Generation - *Display algorithms*; I.3.7 [**Computer Graphics**]: Three-Dimensional Graphics and Realism - *Visible line/surface algorithm.*

1. Introduction

The performance of a raster graphics system is strongly influenced by the inefficiency of scan conversion. Several recent papers have proposed speeding up scan conversion by employing special-purpose hardware. These systems exploit parallel processing in various ways, some of which are:

(1) "Intelligent" VLSI-based memory. This includes systems such as PIXEL-PLANES, by Fuchs *et al.* [FuPo81, FPPB82], the smart memory architecture by Gupta *et al.* [GuSS81], and the Rectangular Area Filling Display System Architecture by Whelan [Whel82].

(2) Hardware enhancements or graphics engines. Clark's geometry engine, although not a scan conversion system, illustrates the latter [Clar82], and Whitted's enhanced frame buffer is an example of the former [Whit81]. The proposed systems of Fussell and Rathi [FuRa82], and Weinberg [Wein81], are graphics engines.

(3) Special-purpose, multiple-processor systems. These systems incorporate special-purpose hardware to broadcast image descriptions to the processors. Image memory is often partitioned to enhance parallelism. Examples include Fuch's central broadcast controller [Fuch77], Parke's splitter tree, and Parke's splitter tree/broadcast controller hybrid [Park80].

Obviously, any parallel-processing scheme should demonstrably hasten scan conversion. The above proposals are no exception. Several issues remain open, however. First, few proposals address the aliasing problem. Indeed, anti-aliasing is difficult to perform on the systems of Fuchs *et al.*, Fussell and Rathi, Whelan, Fuchs, and Parke. Second, display systems exploiting parallelism should always exhibit subserial behaviour. Third, it is not clear that a special-purpose system is the best approach if similar computational power is required for other tasks. It is likely that the feasibility of large-scale display processors with special-purpose hardware will coincide with that of general-purpose parallel processors. The ultracomputer, described below, is one such processor. We wish to demonstrate that the ultracomputer can be a very effective "graphics engine" in its own right. This is illustrated by presenting a parallel scan conversion algorithm including anti-aliasing. The worst case behaviour of the algorithm is subserial.

Not all problems necessarily have faster parallel implementations. However, problems such as scan conversion, which naturally decompose into a large set of independent subproblems, are good candidates for parallel processing. The objective of a general-purpose parallel processor design is to maximise the degree of subproblem independence over a wide class of tasks. Otherwise, the major advantage of such a processor over special-purpose systems is lost. In our ultracomputer model, subproblem independence is facilitated by a small repertoire of powerful concurrent operations on shared memory. To each processing element (PE) of the ultracomputer, a concurrent operation appears to execute indivisibly. In fact, an intelligent, multistage network cleverly connects the PEs to shared memory, and combines all operations simultaneously directed at a variable into one operation. Programs thus appear to have a serial semantics, but parallel execution. Moreover, parallel programs are simply expressed, unlike the often more complicated techniques required to optimise computations on vector or pipeline processors. Because of this "serial semantics/parallel exection" property, the algorithms below can be implemented on any processor capable of simulating the concurrent operations, although the resulting programs may run more slowly.

Section 2 outlines the basic ultracomputer architecture. A scan conversion algorithm that utilises this parallel processing model is presented in Section 3. A novel anti-aliasing algorithm is given as an integral part of scan conversion. Lastly, the generality of the ultracomputer is illustrated by noting other problems to which it can be applied. This is discussed in Section 4, as are topics for future research.

2. Ultracomputer Architecture

An *ultracomputer* is a parallel processor composed of many processing elements (PEs), which have multiple-cycle access to shared memory. Ultracomputers are a good model of parallel computation. Schwartz has made an extensive survey of this field, summarising various upper and lower bounds for parallel sorting algorithms, set operations, matrix multiplication, etc. [Schw80]. Ultracomputers are more than just a theoretical model, however. Indeed, our ultracomputer model is based on the work done at New York University, at which a large-scale implementation is planned [GGKM81]. The model we propose is a very slight extension of the NYU model, incorporating additional concurrent instructions.

An NYU Ultracomputer is composed of $N = 2^D$ autonomous PEs and connected to N shared memory modules. Local memory for each PE is provided by means of a partitioned memory cache. PEs access shared memory via a $D = \log_2 N$-stage connection network composed of an N×D array of "intelligent" 2-input, 2-output switches[1]. Switch interconnection is based on Lawries's omega-network [Lawr75], illustrated in Figure 1.

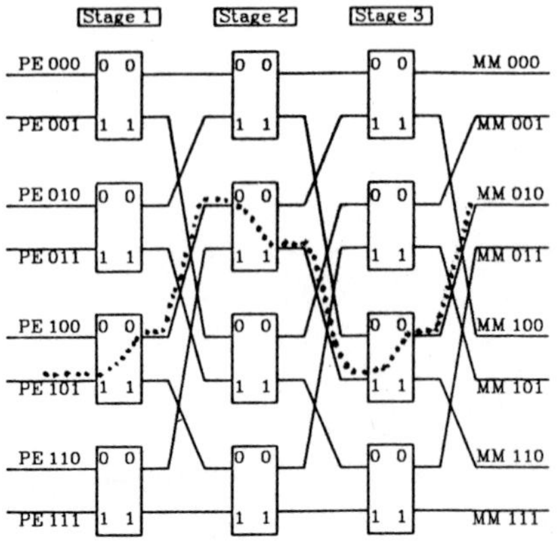

Figure 1. *Routing through an omega-network for 8 PEs.* Connections between PEs, switches, and MMs are by means of a *shuffle-exchange*: an object numbered $d_1 d_2 \cdots d_D$ in binary is connected to the object numbered $d_2 \cdots d_D d_1$ in the next stage of the network. A message transmitted from PE $p_D \cdots p_1$ to MM $m_D \cdots m_1$ uses output port m_i when leaving the ith switch. Similarly for travelling from MM to PE. The route from PE 5 (101_2) to MM 2 (010_2) is indicated.

The novelty of the NYU design rests in the intelligent switches, which implement concurrent access to variables in shared memory. The network easily realises concurrent fetch or store operations. Other more powerful concurrent operations can be implemented. Presently, one such instruction is supported: the ***replace-add***, which creates the illusion of indivisibly adding a value to a shared variable, and returning the sum to the requesting PE. Specifically, the format of the operation is **RepAdd**(V,e)[2], where V denotes a shared (integer) variable and e is an integer expression. Let V have value v. Suppose PE_i issues the command S_i =**RepAdd**(V,e_i), and PE_j issues the command S_j =**RepAdd**(V,e_j) simultaneously. Then, assuming V is not simultaneously updated by another PE, either

$$S_i = v + e_i$$
$$S_j = v + e_i + e_j,$$

or

$$S_i = v + e_j + e_i$$
$$S_j = v + e_j,$$

and in either case, the new value of V is $v + e_i + e_j$. Note that **RepAdd**(V,0) is a fetch instruction.

When operations on the same cell in shared memory meet at a switch, they are synthesised into a single instruction. This is sent to the next stage in the network in one cycle. Instruction combining can occur at any stage in the network. Hence of all the operations simultaneously directed at a single variable, V, only one cumulative operation actually "reaches" V. Thus memory traffic is reduced and network bandwidth is increased. Indeed, the processor has the following surprising property: it is

1. The entire architecture can be easily generalised to $N = k^D$ PEs and a $D = \log_k N$-stage network using k-input, k-output switches.

2. The semantics of this operation has recently been modified in the NYU design, and has since been renamed FetchAdd. Since RepAdd can be easily constructed from FetchAdd, we will continue to use RepAdd in our ultracomputer model.

particularly efficient when many operations are concurrently issued on a small set of variables. Simultaneous update of the same variable by all N PEs is resolved in O(log N) time, compared to O(N) time for typical parallel processors using semaphore-like mutual exclusion. This is a useful property which is often exploited. For example, RepAdd makes an effective synchronisation primitive [GoLR83]. Moreover, data structures allowing parallel access are conveniently implemented using RepAdd. A polygon display list can be nicely implemented as a parallel queue. Suppose the index NextPolygon is used as a subscript into a polygon list. Then every PE executing **RepAdd**(NextPolygon,1) is guaranteed to get a unique value for NextPolygon.

The standard NYU ultracomputer model supports the three concurrent instructions described above: fetch, store, and RepAdd. To realise these operations, a switch only needs a small amount of memory, and an adder. Implementation details, together with a network performance analysis, are found in [GGKM81]. Although these instructions have proved useful for constructing good parallel solutions to scientific and operating system problems, we believe a concurrent, flexible comparison instruction is needed. We propose a new concurrent instruction, *replace-minimum*, or RepMin, which is easily realised by adding a comparator to each switch. Its semantics is defined as follows. Let V denote a cell of shared memory having value v, and let e be an expression such that both v and e are pairs (intensity,depth) of values[3]. Then **RepMin**(V,e) causes all of V to be replaced by e iff e.depth < v.depth. The value returned by RepMin will be discussed presently. The utility of RepMin in scan conversion is obvious. Consider the following parallel version of the z-buffer algorithm found in [NeSp79]. Here, the entire z-buffer is assumed to be addressable as an nxm array of shared memory. Each PE executes the following.

```
while polygons remain do begin
    get P from polygon list (use RepAdd)
    ∀pixels (x,y) ∈ P do begin
        i := PolygonIntensity(P,x,y)
        z := PolygonDepth(P,x,y)
        RepMin( (x,y), (i,z) )
    end
end
```

Let us now discuss the value returned by a RepMin operation. We only consider the case where n PEs ($0 \le n \le N$) simultaneously issue a RepMin for cell V. Informally, of all the RepMin's simultaneously directed at variable V, the value returned to a PE is one which has "lost" in at least one comparison. Moreover, any value sent by a particular PE is returned exactly once. Perhaps surprisingly, this is achievable in the switches, and can be shown by induction on n.

The NYU ultracomputer also presently lacks concurrent logical bit operations. The scan conversion algorithm below makes use of another concurrent instruction, the RepAnd. This operation has the same format as the RepAdd, but performs a logical *and* of the arguments instead of an addition. Note that in principle, only a few Nand gates in each switch would be required to realise all 16 boolean operations as concurrent instructions.

In general, an instruction supported by the connection network must be associative. Thus concurrent floating point operations *cannot* be properly realised[4]. There exist inherently non-associative operations, such as the group (or Fourier) commutator. Defined as $[a, b] = aba^{-1}b^{-1}$, this operation is not associative for non-commutative groups; thus a "RepCom" instruction for matrices under multiplication is inherently unrealisable.

The *serialisation principle* is a necessary property of the connection network: The network ensures that the *effect* of simultaneous operations by the PEs is equivalent to some serialisation of the operations.

3. A Fast Parallel Scan Conversion Algorithm

3.1. Preliminaries

Our definition of scan conversion is the traditional one (e.g. [NeSp79]). Given a scene represented by P simple polygons, determine the set of pixels and their intensities that best approximates the scene. The solution, based on the conventional single-scanline z-buffer algorithm, performs hidden-surface removal and anti-aliasing. Serial scanline algorithms typically require a YX-sort of polygon spans intersecting with a given scanline [SuSS74]. However, RepMin allows us to drop the X sort. The shared memory storing ultimate scanline intensities is assumed to be available to a video controller, by dual-ported memory, for instance.

3.2. The Algorithm

First we briefly outline the major steps performed by each PE. As in traditional scanline algorithms, a Y-scanline bucket is employed to determine polygon segments that enter the scene at scanline y.

(1) Remove backfacing polygons.

(2) Convert remaining polygons into sets of *span-areas*, i.e. trapezoidal or triangular regions. Insert each span-area into the Y-bucket corresponding to its largest y-value.

(3) Scan convert span-areas:
for y := ymin **to** ymax **do**

(a) The span-areas from bucket y are inserted into the *active span list* (ASL).

(b) Process active spans for scanline y. Each PE takes a span from the ASL. If the span is large, only a fraction of it is taken at a time, thus permitting parallel processing of the span. For each pixel in its portion of a span, the PE computes intensity and depth values, and performs a table look-up to approximate the portion of the pixel covered by the span. The left and right endpoints of the span are then updated. If the span-area is exhausted, it is removed from the ASL.

(c) Anti-aliasing. For each non-empty pixel, an approximate anti-aliasing procedure is performed by

---

3. To make the replace-minimum instruction quite general, the extent of the intensity and depth subwords could be controlled by a modifiable bit-mask stored in each switch. Clearly, the names of the subwords, "intensity" and "depth", are illustrative. In practice, the subwords could be known by arbitrary names.

4. In most computers, $((10^{\alpha}-10^{\alpha})+1) \neq (10^{\alpha}+(-10^{\alpha}+1))$, for large α.

determining the intensity contribution of the closest span, and adding in the average contribution of the "losers". The coverage information computed in step (b) is used in these calculations.

3.2.1. Data Structures

For clarity, we only use static storage in shared memory. Assume there are P input polygons found in the array InputList. In what follows, let V_i be the number of vertices in input polygon P_i, and let V be the largest such V_i. Assume the PEs are programmed in a high-level language such as Pascal or Euclid which allows programmer-defined data types. Note that arrays in shared memory are possible, since their starting addresses can be stored in the local memory for each PE. The names assigned to variables in shared memory begin with an upper case letter. Local variables begin with a lower case letter.

```
{ Polygon display list }
 InputList: array 1..P of Polygon
 Ngon: array 1..P of Polygon
  - each polygon P_i contains an array 1..V_i of (x,y,z).

{ Y bucket. Yp gives next available position for scanline y }
 Y: matrix ymin..ymax 1..PV of SpanArea
 Yp: array ymin..ymax of 0..P

{ Active Span List. S reflects the number of spans. }
 ASL: array 1..PV of SpanArea
 S: 1..PV := 0

{ Some indices }
 PolyIn, PolyOut, CurrentSpan: Integer

{ Locks for synchronisation. Assume they are initialised to 0 }
 Lock1, Lock2: 0..P := 0

 SpanArea: type
   record of
     yt    { top y }
     dy    { height of span-area }
     xl    { current LHS }
     xr    { current RHS }
     xm    { multiplicity-see below; initially xm=xl-M}
     dxl   { Δx/Δy of LHS }
     dxr   { Δx/Δy of RHS }
     dyl   { Δy/Δx of LHS }
     dyr   { Δy/Δx of RHS }
     DepthInfo
     IntensityInfo
   end
```

3.2.2. Synchronisation, Initialisation, and Backfacing Polygon Removal

Since the code in this section is familiar, it is a good place to illustrate some principles of synchronisation and initialisation. Assume each PE has access to a unique identifier in the manifest constant PEid, which takes on a value between 1 and N. The following code initialises PolyIn and PolyOut, performs synchronisation, and removes backfacing polygons as in [NeSp79, Appendix III]. We assume the polygons in the input list have undergone perspective transformation. The reader may wish to verify that two locks are necessary to have fully reusable locks for synchronisation.

```
 i, j, p: integer
 InputList, Ngon, Lock1, Lock2, PolyIn, PolyOut: shared

{ The first PE in initialises PolyIn, PolyOut }
 if RepAdd(Lock1,1) = 1 then PolyIn := PolyOut := Lock2 := 0
 while Lock1 < N do {nothing}

{ The last PE out resets Lock1 for future use }
 if Lock2 = N-1 then Lock1 := 0
 RepAdd(Lock2,1)
 while Lock2 < N do {nothing}

 p := RepAdd(PolyOut,1)
 while p ≤ P do begin
   for polygon InputList[p], calculate c
   c := Σ_{i=1}^{V_p} (V[i].x-V[j].x)(V[i].y+V[j].y)
        where j=i+1 if i<V_p ; otherwise j=1
   if c ≤ 0 then {the polygon faces us, add it to Ngon}
     Ngon[RepAdd(PolyIn,1)] := InputList[p]
   p := RepAdd(PolyOut,1)
 end
```

In the average case, each PE processes about P/N polygons. This algorithm assumes that N<P, since otherwise those PEs with PEid>P do no work. The amount of memory traffic this algorithm would cause is suboptimal, since polygon definitions are moved around, rather than their pointers.

3.2.3. Decomposition of Polygons into Span-areas

As presented in this paper, the scan conversion algorithm presumes the input polygon list has been decomposed into span-areas: trapezoidal or triangular regions. This idea is not new (see [Lee81, Wein81, WhWe81]). Unlike polygons, span-areas have a bounded, concise specification in terms of left and right edges. Thus span-areas are useful in scanline-oriented algorithms. However, desirable properties of trapezoids such as planarity are not necessarily preserved after geometric transformations. Consequently, the input polygon list is preprocessed for each frame. This additional computation can be circumvented if polygons are triangulated once and for all, since triangles remain (trivially) planar after geometric transformations (see [FuRa82, Whit81]). The scan conversion algorithm easily adapts to triangles, but since span-areas are so simple to work with, the algorithm is presented using span-areas. Both triangles and span-areas can lead to fragmentation of very small (pixel-sized) polygons, making anti-aliasing critical.

A maximum of V-1 span-areas are generated for a polygon of V vertices. An O(V logV) serial algorithm to decompose a simple polygon into span-areas was recently published [Lee81]. A straightforward, polygon-per-PE parallelisation of this algorithm would yield an $O(\frac{PV}{N} \log V)$ average-case running time. As each span-area is generated, it is inserted into the Y-bucket corresponding to the largest y value of the span-area. This can be determined on-the-fly with no change in the order statistic.

3.2.4. Scan Conversion

Each PE performs the following scan conversion loop.

```
for y:=ymin to ymax do begin
    UpdateASL(y)
    InitialiseScanLine
    ScanConvert(y)
    <synchronise>
end for
```

UpdateASL places the contents of bucket Y[y] into the active span list. All PEs synchronise at the completion of scan conversion for each scanline. This is not necessary. If sufficient memory is available, the algorithm easily generalises to k-scanlines, k ≥ 1. We now consider the scan conversion process in more detail.

```
procedure InitialiseScanLine
  InitialiseXBucket
  CurrentSpan := 1
  <synchronise>
end InitialiseScanLine

procedure ScanConvert(y: ymin..ymax)
  span: SpanArea
  spansLeft: Boolean
  X: shared

  GetSpan(span,spansLeft)
  while spansLeft do begin
    ∀x ∈ span calculate pixelInfo:
        intensity, depth, and coverage mask
        UpdatePixel(x, pixelInfo)
    GetSpan(span,spansLeft)
  end while
  AntiAliasScanline(y)
end ScanConvert
```

The X bucket contains all required scanline information. It will be discussed shortly, as will the routines UpdatePixel and AntiAliasScanline.

GetSpan does the obvious: it returns an unprocessed span to the scan converter. However, the routine is complicated by the fact that we wish to get a subserial worst case behaviour. In particular, large spans should receive parallel treatment, for otherwise all PEs could wait for one PE to complete a long span. One approach is for PEs to recursively subdivide large spans so that each PE processes a smaller portion of the span. However elegant this solution appears, this approach is likely to increase memory traffic substantially. The approach we have taken avoids this problem. Assume there is a constant M which denotes the maximum number of pixels in a span that a PE is allowed to process at a time. This value may be empirically or theoretically determined, and represents a good balance between the overhead in GetSpan and the increased efficiency in parallel processing of large spans. Multiple copies of a span may be returned; the index xm is used to indicate the leftmost point of the unprocessed portion of the span[5]. The following is one possible implementation of GetSpan. It is somewhat tricky since it must cope with the unlikely event that two PEs simultaneously try to get an exhausted span.

5. See the definition of the SpanArea data type above.

```
procedure GetSpan(var span: SpanArea;
                  var spansLeft: Boolean)
  gotSpan: Boolean
  S, ASL, CurrentSpan: shared
  M: Constant
  newLHS: Integer

  spansLeft := CurrentSpan ≤ S
  gotSpan := false
  while ~gotSpan and spansLeft do begin
    span := ASL[CurrentSpan]
    with ASL[CurrentSpan] do begin
      { calculate new LHS of span, and see if LHS>RHS }
      newLHS := RepAdd(xm,M)
      gotSpan := newLHS ≤ xr
      if ~gotSpan then
        { if span is exhausted, the first PE advances CurrentSpan
            and processes the remaining span segment }
        if newLHS-xr ≤ M then
          RepAdd(CurrentSpan,1)
      spansLeft := CurrentSpan ≤ S
    end with/while
  if gotSpan then span.xm := newLHS
  spansLeft := gotSpan
end GetSpan
```

3.2.5. Anti-aliasing

The aliasing problem is immediately apparent to anyone who has seen synthesised raster images. Various aliasing artifacts are possible in both still and moving images. An abundant literature describes the problem and some of its solutions. See [Crow77, Crow81] for a start. It is thus of prime importance to examine whether anti-aliasing can be incorporated into our algorithm. Since we currently compute the picture scanline by scanline without backtracking over scanlines, we cannot use any scheme where the value at one pixel depends on the value of some of its neighbours, unless we arbitrarily privilege the x direction[6].

The best solution under the circumstances is what we can call the Exact Area Sampling solution, where the intensity for the pixel is $I = \frac{1}{A}\sum_i I_i A_i$. A_i and I_i are the areas and intensities of the visible surfaces within the pixel, and A is the total area of the pixel. If colour is used, this formula is used for the three primaries. As pointed out in [Catm78], and implemented there and in [FuBar79], this requires a hidden surface algorithm at the pixel level.

We can establish a more formal lower bound, by showing that any algorithm that computes the EAS can be used to determine the order of a list of n non-negative integers. The reduction is as follows. Given a list $N_1, N_2, \cdots, N_n$ of numbers, construct a scene with n rectangles of depth N_i, with the left, top and bottom edges coincident with the pixel left, top and bottom, and the right edge of rectangle i at N_i. Without loss of generality, assume that the pixel right edge is at max(N_i). Let the intensity I_i of each rectangle be D^{i-1} where D is a constant greater than max (N_i) - min (N_i).

The answer to the EAS problem is then:

6. The idea is not totally without merit, since as seen on broadcast television it produces decent images. Note, moreover, that a k-scanline version (k > 1) of the algorithm would permit a multiple-pixel anti-aliasing scheme.

$H \times \sum_i D^{i-1}(N_i - N_p)$ where H is the height of the pixel, and N_p is the predecessor of N_i in the sorted order. The predecessor of $\min(N_i)$ is 0. This transformation can be done in O(n) time. It is clear that the answer, when expressed as a base D number, contains $N_i - N_p$ in the i th digit (from the least significant), and that therefore in O(n) time one can find, for every number, its predecessor in the sorted order. Computing the answer to the EAS problem allows sorting with a O(n) time transformation, and therefore takes at least O(nlogn) time. While this does not prove that it is necessary to solve the hidden surface problem to solve the EAS problem, this shows that nothing easier than sorting will do it. For other results about the EAS, see [FoFu83].

In view of this result, we will aim for an approximate solution. Our approach will be to limit the amount of computation and to utilise parallelism as much as possible.

We subdivide the pixel into $n \times n$ subpixels. It is convenient to have n a power of 2, for example $n = 2^3 = 8$. For each line which intersects a pixel, the two intersection points along the boundaries of the pixel are used as an index into a lookup table, whose entries give the subpixels covered by the halfplane defined by this line. We will call this entry the *mask* for this halfplane. In our example, the mask would be a 64 bit number. Each intersection with the boundaries of the pixel is computed with k bits of fraction (where there are 2^k intervals, since the fraction n/n=1 in the current pixel is 0 on the next pixel). In our example, then, k=3. Thus each intersection can be fully described as a $k+2$ bit number, 2 bits to identify the boundary crossed, and k bits to give the crossing position along the boundary (see Figure 2). The total entry for a line is then a $2(k+2)$ bit number, which in our example is a 10 bit number. This gives a $1K \times 64$ bit table, which is small enough to allow a copy for each PE. Alternatively, several PEs could directly share such a read-only table.

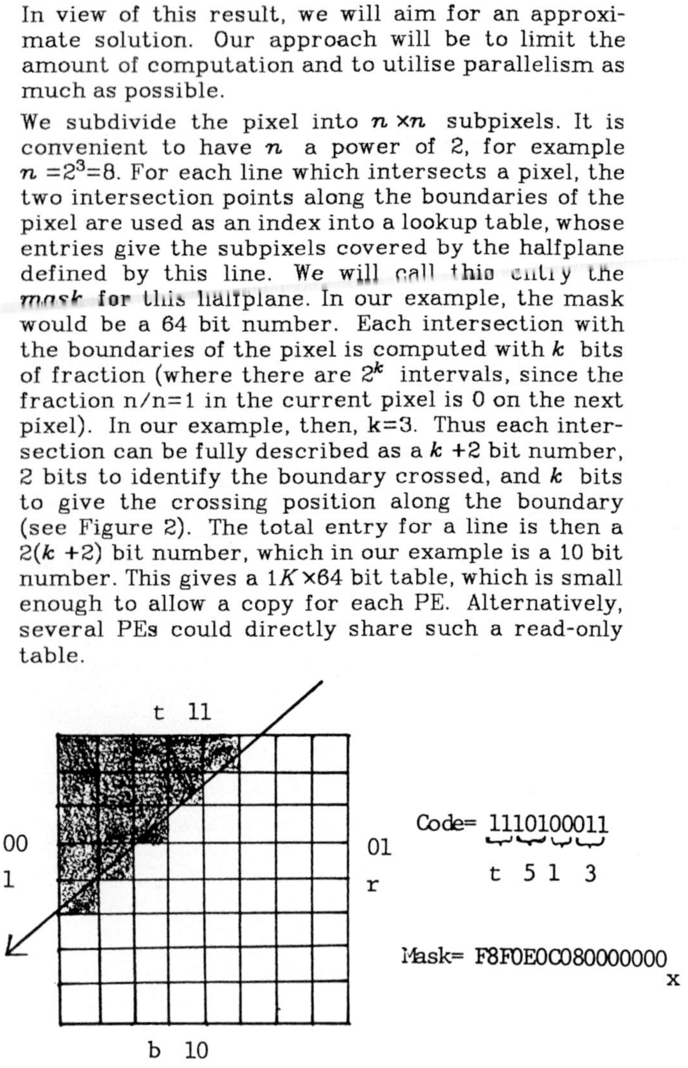

Figure 2. *Pixel-line intersection encoding.*

The order of the intersections is relevant, since the line should be oriented. We adopt a convention that the inside is to the right when going from the first intersection to the second. The size of the table can be reduced by making it into a triangular array, and using an extra bit to indicate the direction, which will tell whether to complement the mask or not. The table is of course precomputed, and each bit is on if the subpixel corresponding to it is more than half-covered by the halfplane described by the index.

Of the four edges of a normal span-area, two are horizontal, and are relevant only at the start and at the end of its scanning. For these, a small special lookup table can be used, with the y fraction used as the index. For the other two edges, updating the intersection information from pixel to pixel is fairly simple, and requires only additions and subtractions.

The coverage mask has interesting boolean properties. Indeed, the mask for the intersection of a span-area with a pixel is the ***and*** of the masks of the span-area's edges which cross the pixel. Thus we get an accurate representation of the subpixels covered by a given span-area. It is also easily seen that the mask for the background (indicating the subpixels where the background is seen) is the complement of the *or* of all the span-area masks for this pixel. It is unfortunately impossible to go much farther without making some approximations. The problem is that we do not want to compute the Z values at the subpixel resolution, since it would be tantamount to going to a higher resolution. Each span-area at a given pixel is then associated with only one Z value, namely its Z at the centre of the pixel. Given that, we cannot guarantee that the depth comparison allows the visible areas to be exactly determined, unless the planes of support of the span-areas do not intersect within the pixel (see Figure 3). We will give two approximation algorithms, and discuss where they succeed, and where they fail. Let ***weight*** (***mask***) be the fraction of the pixel covered by a mask (this can be easily computed by counting the number of one bits in the mask). The span-area with the smallest Z value is called the *winner;* the others are called *losers*.

There are two ways to compute the final pixel intensity. One way necessitates the use of an X-bucket to hold pixel information for each span-area intersecting with the current scanline; a pass over the content of this bucket would be performed at the end of the scanline, since the final intensity cannot be computed until the winner is known. The other approximation can be computed on-the-fly, and is almost as accurate as the first. The two methods calculate intensities I_1 and I_2, respectively, as follows.

$$I_1 = WinnerComp + LoserComp_1 + BackgroundComp$$
$$I_2 = WinnerComp + LoserComp_2 + BackgroundComp$$

$$WinnerComp = I_w \times weight\,(mask_w)$$
$$BackgroundComp = I_b \times weight\,(\wedge AllMasks)$$
$$LoserComp_1 = Cor_1 \times \sum_{all\ l} I_l \times weight\,(mask_l \wedge \overline{mask_w})$$
$$LoserComp_2 = Cor_2 \times weight\,(\overline{mask_w}) \times \sum_{all\ l} I_l \times weight\,(mask_l)$$
$$Cor_1 = \frac{weight\,(\overline{mask_b} \wedge \overline{mask_w})}{\sum_{all\ l} weight\,(mask_l \wedge \overline{mask_w})}$$
$$Cor_2 = \frac{weight\,(\overline{mask_b} \wedge \overline{mask_w})}{\sum_{all\ l} weight\,(mask_l)}$$

The subscripts w, l, and b, stand for "winner", "loser", and "background", respectively. The correction factors are ratios of the actual coverage by the losers compared to the sum of their individual coverage as computed by each algorithm. Therefore the correction factors give a measure of the amount of overlap of the losers, hence of the possible error.

3.2.5.1. First approximate anti-aliasing algorithm

This solution requires an X bucket. For each pixel, several additional pieces of information are kept: the current winner, background data, the losers' intensity, and their sum of coverage-mask weights. The following data structures are used.

```
{ X bucket. Xp contains list of number of span-areas per pixel }
 X: matrix xmin..xmax 1..PV of PixelInfo
 Xp: array xmin..xmax of 0..PV := 0

{ Additional pixel information }
 Pixels: array xmin..xmax of
             Winner, Back: PixelInfo
             LoserInt, SumOfWeights: Integer

 PixelInfo: type record of
         Depth
         Int           { intensity }
         Mask          { coverage mask }
 end PixelInfo
```

The ScanConvert routine above executes the following version of UpdatePixel and AntiAliasScanline. Recall that each PE executes ScanConvert.

```
procedure UpdatePixel(x: xmin..xmax, pix: PixelInfo)
    { Add pixel from this span into bucket }
    X[x,RepAdd(Xp[x],1)] := pix
    { pix may be a "winner" }
    RepMin(Pixels[x].Winner,pix)
    { Determine how much background is covered by pix }
    RepAnd(Pixels[x].Back.Mask, pix.Mask)
end UpdatePixel
```

```
procedure AntiAliasScanline(y: ymin..ymax)
    x: Integer
    winner,pix: PixelInfo

  Initialise Cx to xmin
  while Cx ≤ xmax do begin
     { Many PEs work on each pixel (i.e. X bucket) }
     x := RepAdd(Xp[Cx],-1) + 1         { get pixel info for span }
     winner := Pixels[Cx].Winner
     while x > 0 do begin
       pix := X[Cx,x]
       if pix ≠ winner then begin
         { pix is a loser, calculate its contribution }
         newMask := pix.Mask ∧ winner.Mask
         newInt := Weight(newMask) × pix.Int
         RepAdd(Pixels[Cx].LoserInt, newInt)
         RepAdd(Pixels[Cx].SumOfWeights, Weight(newMask))
       end if
       x := RepAdd(Xp[Cx], -1) + 1
     end while
     if x = 0 then begin
       { PE with x=0 adds background and losers' contrib }
       for Pixels[Cx], compute:
       c := Weight(Back.Mask∧Winner.Mask)/ SumOfWeights
       RepAdd(Winner.Int, c×LoserInt + Back.Int)
       RepAdd(Cx,1)
     end then
     else <synchronise> {all other PEs wait}
  end while
end AntiAliasScanline
```

3.2.5.2. Second approximate anti-aliasing algorithm

No X bucket is required in this solution. We only keep four pieces of information for each pixel, Winner, Back, SumOfWeights, and Losers. Winner, Back, and SumOfWeights are as in the first solution; Losers is used to keep track of the losers' coverage and intensity contributions on-the-fly.

```
procedure UpdatePixel(x: xmin..xmax, pix: PixelInfo)
    loser: PixelInfo

    loser := RepMin(Pixels[x].Winner, pix)
    intContrib := loser.Int × Weight(loser.Mask)
    RepAdd(Pixels[x].Losers.Int, intContrib)
    RepAnd(Pixels[x].Back.Mask, loser.Mask)
    RepAdd(Pixels[x].SumOfWeights, Weight(pix.Mask))
end UpdatePixel
```

```
procedure AntiAliasScanline(y: ymin..ymax)
    { each PE handles a pixel, so if N > X, some PEs are idle }
    x := PEid + xmin - 1
    while x < xmax do begin
      pix := Pixels[x]
      { compute background and losers' intensity contrib }
      backInt := pix.Back.Int × Weight(pix.Back.Mask)
      c := Weight(pix.Back.Mask∧pix.Winner.Mask)/ pix.SumOfWeights
      loserInt := pix.Losers.Int × Weight(pix.Winner.mask) × c
      RepAdd(Pixels[x].Winner.Int, backInt+loserInt)
      x := x + N
    end while
end AntiAliasScanline
```

3.2.5.3. Analysis of the approximations

These approximations, and indeed all approximations of this kind, should be characterised in three ways: when they are right (here right is to be understood exact within the subpixel resolution), when they are wrong and how wrong they can be, and when they are *consistently* wrong. The last is important, since aliasing is particularly noticeable in motion, by ***crawling***, ***scintillation*** and other annoying artifacts. If an algorithm computes a wrong shade, but is consistent as the polygons move, then these artifacts will be avoided.

Both solutions will be right when there is only one span-area within the pixel, whether it covers the whole pixel or not. As long as a span-area covers at least one subpixel (1/64 of a pixel in our example), it will contribute to the total intensity of the pixel. Both solutions are also right when none of the span-areas overlap. This is especially important, since we might have cut a polygon into numerous small span-areas. Fortunately we will not have to pay a heavy price in aliasing problems. In fact, the problems, if any, will be at the silhouette edges of the objects, and not against the background, but against each other. The first solution has the additional advantage of being right when the winner overlaps the losers, but the losers do not overlap each other. The second algorithm will be right in case of overlap by the winner if the loser coverage ratio is sensibly the same under the winner as in the rest of the pixel.

Figures 3 and 4 give examples of wrong cases, and the errors made by each algorithm. Figure 3 shows the worst case for both algorithms, where the amount of overlap of the losers and the area they cover is maximal. Figure 4 shows a case where the first algorithm is right and the second is wrong.

Figure 3. ***The worst case for both algorithms.*** Span 1, the winner, covers a sliver of the pixel. Losing span 2 obscures another loser, 3.

$Z_1 < Z_2 < Z_3$

Correct Answer $\simeq I_2$

Computed Answer $= \dfrac{I_2 + I_3}{2}$

Error $= \dfrac{I_2 - I_3}{2}$

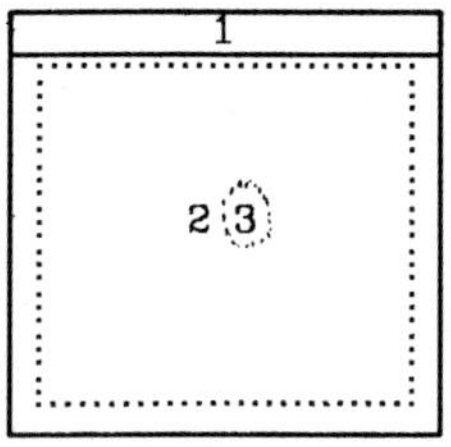

Figure 4. ***A bad case for algorithm 2 only.*** Winning span 1, covering half the pixel, obscures losing span 3. Losing span 2 covers half the pixel as well.

$Z_1 < Z_2 < Z_3$

Correct Answer $= \dfrac{I_1 + I_2}{2}$

Algorithm 1 $= \dfrac{I_1 + I_2}{2}$

Algorithm 2 $= \dfrac{I_1 + \frac{I_2 + I_3}{2}}{2}$

Error 2 $= \dfrac{I_2 - I_3}{4}$

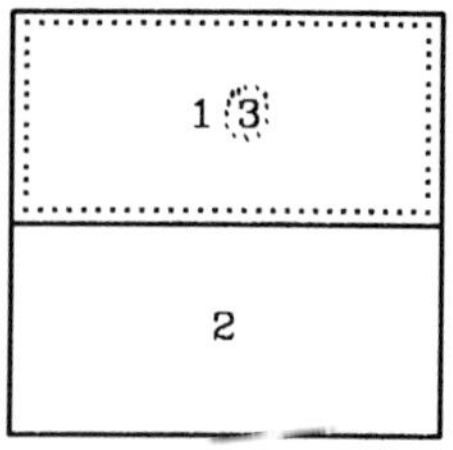

A gross estimate of the extent of the errors for 10^3 polygons, covering an average of 10^3 pixels each, and with 10^2 boundary pixels each, on a screen with 10^6 pixels, shows that less than 5% of the pixels would have an error, and that for these the average error would be less than 10% of the shade of the pixel.

As the polygons move with respect to each other, we avoid the numerous problems of point sampling. Since the wrong cases are computed from averages, the errors made will not exhibit large discontinuities, but will be consistent from frame to frame. In the example of Figure 3, as polygon 3 moves out of the pixel, its contribution to the pixel intensity will go smoothly from $\frac{I_3}{4}$ (which is wrong), to 0 (which is right).

3.2.6. Discussion

An implementation of this algorithm has been made, demonstrating that the approach works, and illustrating a realisation in a pseudo-concurrent language. The implementation is written in Concurrent Euclid, a language developed at the University of Toronto which supports processes and monitors. Concurrent operations such as RepAdd are simulated using monitors. The only relevant aspect in which our implementation differs from one on an ultracomputer is speed. The lack of "true" concurrency, and the O(N) performance of concurrent operations (compared to O(logN) on an ultracomputer), make our implementation somewhat slower than would be expected on an ultracomputer.

The algorithm above has several appealing properties. It is independent of N, the number of PEs in the ultracomputer. Indeed, the speed of the algorithm is inversely proportional to N, up to a lower bound constant when $N \geq \frac{XY}{M}$. A good serial algorithm is obtained when N=1. We emphasise the fact that the anti-aliasing techniques presented here easily transfer to serial environments, as illustrated here. Another property of the algorithm is that although it scan converts polygons, the general approach adapts to other scene representations (e.g. scanline methods for parametric surfaces as in [BCLW80]).

Several improvements could be made to the algorithm. An issue deserving of attention is space complexity and memory traffic. By using dynamically allocated shared memory and pointers, the amount of storage required would be drastically reduced; memory traffic would decrease, since pointers would travel through shared memory. However, indirect shared memory references require two passes through the connection network. A solution is to make greater use of the cache memory local to each PE. A copy of the static pointers may be placed in the local memory for each PE, thus saving the O(log N) connection network cycle time.

4. Other Ultracomputer Applications and Future Research

As the plethora of published parallel algorithms shows [Schw80], the ultracomputer is truly a powerful, general-purpose tool. Fast parallel algorithms exist for matrix multiplication, sorting, linear programming, fluid dynamics, etc. We hope to have demonstrated that the ultracomputer has great potential in the computer graphics field. Other applications would also significantly benefit from ultracomputer implementation. For instance, a parallel queue could be exploited to parallelise ray-tracing algorithms [Whit80]. Since the processing of one ray (or alternatively, one pixel) is an independent task, we believe significant speed-up in ray-tracing can be achieved on an ultracomputer. Similarly, we believe many problems in image processing, signal processing, and artificial intelligence are likely to benefit.

5. Acknowledgements

We wish to thank John Amanatides and Peter Schoeler for their suggestions, which have improved the clarity of this paper. The first two authors gratefully acknowledge the financial support of the Natural Sciences and Engineering Research Council of Canada.

References

BCLW80 Blinn, J.F., L.C. Carpenter, J.M. Lane, and T. Whitted, "Scan line methods for displaying parametrically defined surfaces", *Comm. ACM 23*, 1 (Jan. 1980), 23-34.

Catm78 Catmull, E., "A Hidden-Surface Algorithm with Anti-Aliasing", *Computer Graphics (ACM), 12*, 3, (Aug. 78), 6-11.

Clar82 Clark, J.H., "The geometry engine: a VLSI geometry system for graphics", *Computer Graphics (ACM) 16*, 3 (July 1982), 127-134.

Crow77 Crow, F.C., "The Aliasing Problem in Computer-Generated Shaded Images", *Comm. ACM 20*, 11 (Nov. 1977), 799-805.

Crow81 Crow, F.C., "A Comparison of Antialiasing Techniques", *IEEE Computer Graphics and Applications, 1*, 1 (Jan. 81), 40-49.

FPPB82 Fuchs, H., J. Poulton, A. Paeth, and A. Bell, "Developing PIXEL-PLANES, a smart memory-based raster graphics system", *1982 Conference on Advanced Research in VLSI, MIT*, January 1982, 137-146.

FoFu83 Fournier, A. and D. Fussell, "On the Power of the Frame Buffer", unpublished manuscript, 1983.

FuBar79 Fuchs, H. and J. Barros, "Efficient Generation of Smooth Line Drawings on Video Displays", *Computer Graphics, 13*, 2, (Aug. 79), 260-269.

FuPo81 Fuchs, H., and J. Poulton, "PIXEL-PLANES: a VLSI-oriented design for 3-D raster graphics", *CMCCS Conference Proceedings*, (June 1981), 343-348.

FuRa82 Fussell, D., and B.D. Rathi, "A VLSI-oriented architecture for real-time raster display of shaded polygons", *Graphics Interface '82*, May 1982, 373-380.

Fuch77 Fuchs, H., "Distributing a visible surface algorithm over multiple processors", *Proceedings of ACM 1977*, Seattle (Oct. 1977), 449-451.

GGKM83 Gottlieb, A., R. Grishman, C.P. Kruskal, K.P. McAuliffe, L. Rudolph, and M. Snir, "The NYU Ultracomputer--designing an MIMD shared memory parallel computer", *IEEE Transactions on Computers, C-32*, 2 (Feb. 1983), 175-189.

GoLR83 Gottlieb, A., B.D. Lubachevsky, and L. Rudolph, "Basic techniques for the efficient coordination of very large numbers of cooperating sequential processors", *Transactions on Programming Languages and Systems (ACM) 5*, 2 (Apr. 1983), 164-189.

GuSS81 Gupta, S., R.F. Sproull, and I.E. Sutherland, "A VSLI architecture for updating raster scan displays", *Computer Graphics (ACM) 15*, 3 (Aug. 1981), 71-78.

Lawr75 Lawrie, D.H., "Access and alignment of data in an array processor", *IEEE Transactions on Computers, C-24*, 12 (Dec. 1975), 1145-1155.

Lee81 Lee, D.T., "Shading of regions on vector display devices", *Computer Graphics (ACM) 15*, 3 (Aug. 1981), 37-44.

NeSp79 Newman, W.M., and R.F. Sproull, *Principles of Interactive Computer Graphics*, Second Edition, McGraw-Hill, New York, 1979.

Park80 Parke, F.I., "Simulation and expected performance of multiple processor z-buffer systems", *Computer Graphics (ACM) 14*, 3 (July 1980), 48-56.

Schw80 Schwartz, J.T., "Ultracomputers", *Transactions on Programming Languages and Systems (ACM) 2*, 4 (Oct. 1980), 484-522.

SuSS74 Sutherland, I.E., R.F. Sproull, and R.A. Schumacker, "A characterization of ten hidden-surface algorithms", *Computing Surveys (ACM) 6*, 1 (March 1974), 1-55.

Wein81 Weinberg, R., "Parallel processing image synthesis and anti-aliasing", *Computer Graphics (ACM) 15*, 3 (Aug. 1981), 53-62.

WhWe81 Whitted, T., and D.M. Weimer, "A software test-bed for the development of 3-D raster graphics systems", *Computer Graphics (ACM) 15*, 3 (Aug. 1981), 271-277.

Whel82 Whelan, D.S., "A rectangular area filling display system architecture", *Computer Graphics (ACM) 16*, 3 (July 1982), 147-153.

Whit80 Whitted, T., "An improved illumination model for shaded display", *Comm. ACM 23*, 6 (June 1980), 343-349.

Whit81 Whitted, T., "Hardware enhanced 3-D raster display systems", *CMCCS Conference Proceedings*, (June 1981), 349-356.

Figure 5. *Aliased cube. Enlarged view at 256×256 resolution.*

Figure 6. *Anti-aliased cube.*

Figure 7. *Aliased Italian tablecloth.*

Figure 8. *Anti-aliased Italian tablecloth.*

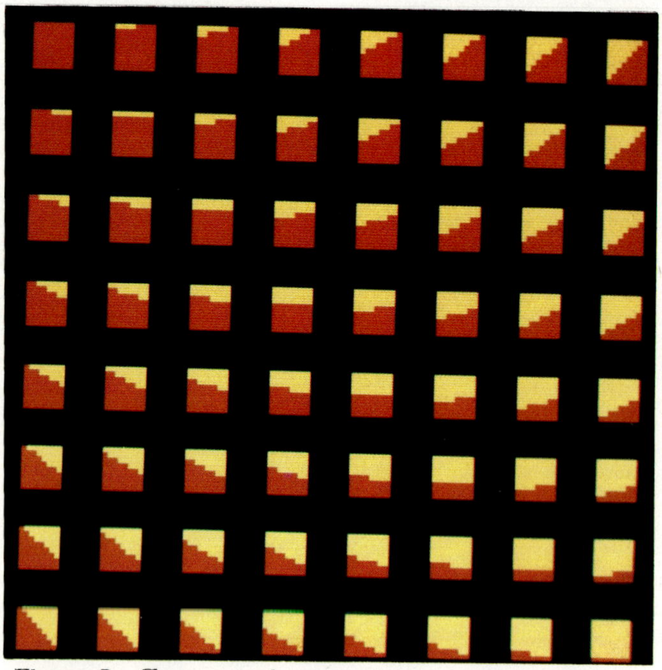

Figure 9. *Close-up of some coverage masks.* Each yellow area indicates the subpixel coverage of an oriented line.

Anti-Aliased Line Drawing Using Brush Extrusion

Turner Whitted

Bell Laboratories
Holmdel, New Jersey 07733

Abstract

This algorithm draws lines on a gray-scale raster display by dragging a "brush" along the path of the line. The style of the line is determined by the properties of the brush. An anti-aliasing calculation is performed once for the brush itself and thereafter only a trivial additional operation is needed for each pixel through which the brush is dragged to yield an anti-aliased line.

There are few constraints on the size, shape, and attributes of the brush. Lines can be curved as well as straight. It is possible to produce lines with a three dimensional appearance.

CR Categories and Subject Descriptors: B.3.2 [**Memory Structures**]: Design Styles-*cache memories*; I.3.3 [**Computer Graphics**]: Picture/Image Generation-*display algorithms*

General Terms: Algorithms

Key Words: Line Drawing, Anti-aliasing, Painting, Filtering, Raster Displays

Prior Work

This paper describes a method of displaying anti-aliased lines on a raster display by painting with an anti-aliased brush. It combines a painting technique developed by Smith [17] with an adaptation of an anti-aliasing technique described by Crow [7]. While there are several commercial anti-aliasing paint systems, the one described here is particularly flexible, yet simple to implement.

Line drawing on raster displays usually emulates plotters, i.e. the lines are narrow and have uniform shade. Unless the line drawing procedures take account of the sampling that is inherent in raster displays, lines will have the jagged appearance of a staircase caused by aliases in the sampled signal. According to the sampling theorem, graphical objects can be rendered faithfully on a sampled raster display only if a low pass filtering step is included in the display process prior to sampling. Existing anti-aliased line drawing algorithms fall into two classes: those which emulate plotters [7,10], and those more general polygon rendering algorithms which treat lines as long, thin polygons [5,2,9]. The latter class, which we shall call "skinny polygon" algorithms in this report, are more difficult to implement than the former class.

Raster displays are capable of a much richer variety of line styles than plotters. Paint programs illustrate one of the simplest methods of exploiting this versatility by allowing an artist to drag patterned brushes along the path of brush strokes to create patterned lines. Smith describes a technique called "z-paint" that allows users to create lines that appear to be glossy tubes by drawing with a brush that looks like a glossy sphere [17]. The algorithm described here is an extension of this technique.

There is no need to limit painting to artist drawn strokes. Brush extrusion paths can just as easily be specified by a vector display list. If alphanumeric characters are defined by strokes, then the technique can be applied to text as well. Although anti-aliased text can be more rapidly displayed by preparing an entire set of anti-aliased fonts [20,11], the ability to draw stroke drawn characters at arbitrary scales is a useful feature.

Painting and Brush Extrusion

The fundamental operation of paint programs is copying pixel data from a source image to a destination image,

$$dst \leftarrow src \ binop \ dst \ ,$$

usually called "bit-blt" or "raster-op" [14]. For images with one bit per pixel, the binary operation *binop* can be any one of 16 boolean functions of two variables. Paint software copies a small source pixel array, the brush, into a larger destination pixel array, usually a frame buffer memory, at locations which correspond to the position of a stylus on a tablet.

For gray-scale displays, the logical binary operator is replaced by an arithmetic operator. The most useful one is linear interpolation:

$$dst \leftarrow a*src + (1-a)*dst$$

or with one less multiplication

$$dst \leftarrow a*(src-dst) + dst. \tag{1}$$

Then in addition to the obvious effect of overwriting the frame buffer contents with the brush contents, advanced paint programs can simulate semi-transparent paints or fuzzy brushes. To produce a line, the brush is successively copied into each point along the path of the stroke.

Figure 1a illustrates the result of drawing with a uniformly shaded brush. Figure 1b, drawn with a glossy brush, fails to achieve the desired effect because at each position the brush completely overwrites the previous contents of the image. To solve this problem, a z-value (depth) is associated with each pixel of the brush and each pixel of the image. The brush then becomes a three dimensional hemisphere which overwrites only those pixels in the image whose depth is greater than the depth of the corresponding pixel of the brush,

$$dst \leftarrow \textbf{if } (\text{src.z} > \text{dst.z}) \textbf{ then } \text{dst} \textbf{ else } \text{src}$$

as shown in figure 1c. This technique is the well known "z-buffer" algorithm which has been used extensively in three dimensional computer graphics for hidden surface elimination [4]. The algorithm's most serious drawback is the need to store depth information for every pixel of the display. It is not necessary to accurately match the brush's z-value to the corresponding hemispherical brush surface. For the circularly symmetric brush used in figure 1, any depth that increases with the pixel's distance from the brush center insures that the intensities remaining after the brush passes are the appropriate ones.

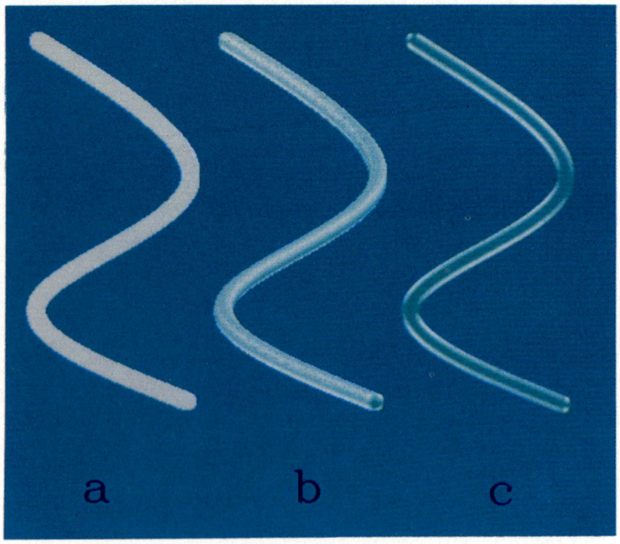

Figure 1. Drawing strokes with and without a z-buffer.

Anti-aliasing

All three strokes in figure 1 suffer from jagged edges caused by aliasing [6]. The naive (and often used) approach to solving this problem is produce the image at a resolution high enough to make the jaggies imperceptible. Most commercial systems for graphic arts feature resolutions in excess of 2048x2048 pixels. High resolution display devices are extremely expensive. Furthermore, the prevalence of 525 line monitors creates a need for high quality graphics at low resolution.

Alternatively, the image may be generated at high resolution and digitally filtered to eliminate the high frequencies that produce most of the aliases when the image is resampled at lower resolution. This method, called "super-sampling", has been employed with excellent results in spite of some serious shortcomings [8]. An obvious drawback of super-sampling is the need to create and store a high resolution copy of the image.

A more satisfactory approach is to perform the anti-aliasing computations as the low resolution image is being formed. Some very efficient line drawing methods [7,10,18] take advantage of the fact that a straight line is a special case to simplify the computation. Because the line intensity does not vary along the direction parallel to the line, the anti-aliasing filter kernel can be approximated by a one dimensional function of the perpendicular distance from a pixel to the line. These algorithms store the one dimensional function in a table and calculate the perpendicular distance as a line is being drawn. The ends of a line segment must be treated as special cases since the approximations fall apart there. These methods work only for straight lines of uniform shade, and they do not provide a way of gracefully handling the intersections of lines.

The skinny polygon algorithms [5, 2, 9] can properly handle crossing lines because they clip polygons against one another before filtering. They are more complicated to implement because they must store all polygons in main memory at one time. Although descriptions of these algorithms don't point it out, this general class of technique is fully capable of producing anti-aliased lines with a wide range of appearances including three dimensional effects.

For the brush dragging method of line drawing described in this paper, super-sampling is the only reasonable approach to anti-aliasing. The technique described in the next section is motivated by the desire to obtain the same result as super-sampling without paying the expected price of memory and processing.

Painting on a Virtual Canvas

The algorithm presented here uses a paint program that has a 4096x4096 (virtual) canvas. Anti-aliasing is performed through an adaptation of super-sampling. Lines are drawn at a resolution of 4096x4096, but displayed at 512x512 pixels.

The algorithm works as follows: Brushes are created at high resolution, and then filtered to bandlimit them to 1/16th the high resolution sampling frequency. The brush, or source, pixels are painted along a high resolution path, but only those brush pixels which exactly coincide with the lower resolution destination pixel locations (figure 2) are copied to the destination image (see [7] for a slightly different explanation of this same technique). Since the source pixel is copied or not copied depending on the relative depths of the source and destination pixels, and the source depth is a function of its distance from the center of the brush, the net effect is that the final intensity value of the destination pixel is a function of its perpendicular distance from the high resolution line path. This is exactly

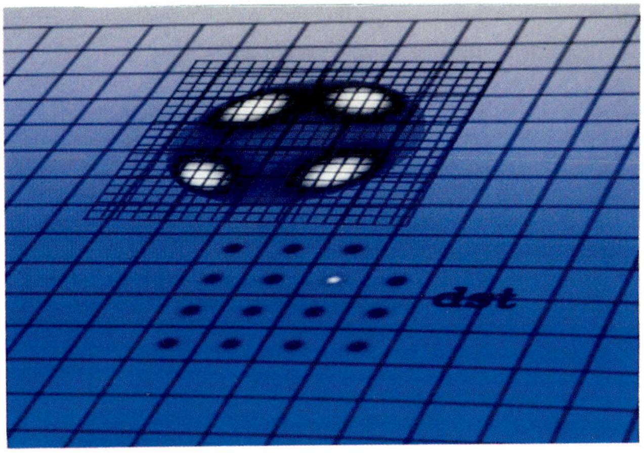

Figure 2. Only brush pixels which align exactly with low resolution destination pixels are copied.

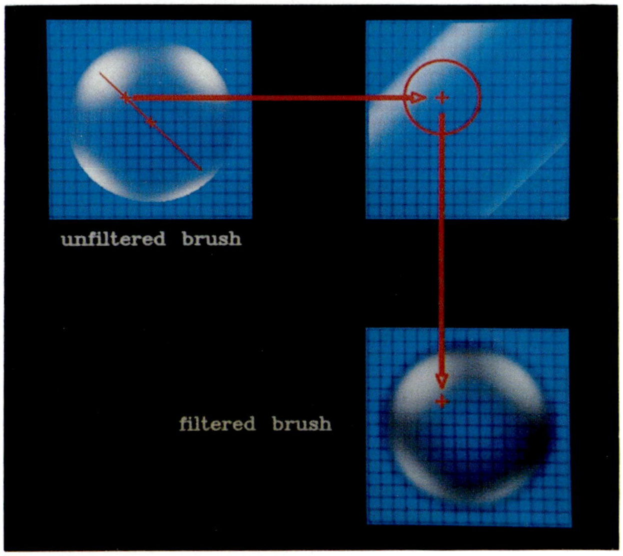

Figure 3. Filtering applied to brushes.

the mechanism employed in [10] and [18] except that in this case the perpendicular distance is never explicitly calculated..

The processing used in this technique includes only the copying operation with a modest enhancement of comparing depths and copying pixels conditionally. It does not create a high resolution image (other than the brush) as an intermediate step, and it does not require the filtering arithmetic normally associated with super-sampling. It is therefore a particularly simple algorithm. Its drawback is that it attempts to paint each pixel several times either with a value that will subsequently be overwritten or with a value whose depth is greater than what is already stored for the pixel. For a software implementation this is wasteful, but it lends itself to fast execution in simple hardware. The algorithm also requires that each line be drawn as an isolated image and merged with the background in a separate step. A later section shows a painless way to do this using a "pixel cache."

Filtering Brushes

The key to making this scheme work is to insure that the final intensity value of each low resolution pixel is the same as it would be if the unfiltered brush were painted into a real 4096x4096 pixel memory and then digitally filtered and resampled. It is not sufficient to simply apply a low pass filter to the brush.

Observe that for circular brushes the z-compare insures that the source pixel which will be visible at a particular destination lies on a line through the center of the brush which is perpendicular to the path of the brush. If all pixels which lie along the perpendicular radial line are extruded along the brush path, they will form the high resolution image that must be filtered to produce the desired filtered brush pixel as shown in figure 3. Whether the same argument holds for non-circular brushes depends on how one defines the extrusion process. For all of the brushes that we have created so far the z-function has been circular even when the brush's intensity function is not. In these cases the method of filtering remains accurate. Although the program that creates the filtered brush requires several seconds of computation, it is executed only once for each brush. A library of brushes is created and stored for later use.

The digital filter used to bandlimit the brush produces output samples as a weighted average of input samples. Near the edge of the brush some of the input samples are provided by the brush itself while those which lie outside the radius of the brush are provided by the background. Since there is no way of knowing what the background intensity will be until the brush is used to paint a line, some way of calculating the background's contribution to the output must be provided. The solution used here is to add all of the filter weights that are to be applied to the foreground to form a blending weight, *blend*. Then when a line is painted over a background, (1−*blend*) is multiplied by the background intensity to determine the background contribution to each pixel. Each output pixel is then a linear combination of a foreground and background component. This compositing operation is similar to ones used to merge separate overlays for cel animation into a final image [19]. It is not, however, a perfect way to create anti-aliased lines (see the Appendix).

Since the style of the line is purely a function of the brush shape and intensity, there are many possible line styles that this algorithm can produce. The brush filtering is not limited to symmetric brushes. However, for curved lines drawn with asymmetric brushes the filtered intensity is just an approximation, and for all lines the endpoints are a special case. Image quality suffers only slightly from ignoring these special cases. Each brush pixel contains 8 bits each of *red*, *green*, *blue*, and *blend* and 16 bits of z for a total of 48 bits. Figure 4 shows examples of brushes and their effect. Notice that the glossy brush is also transparent.

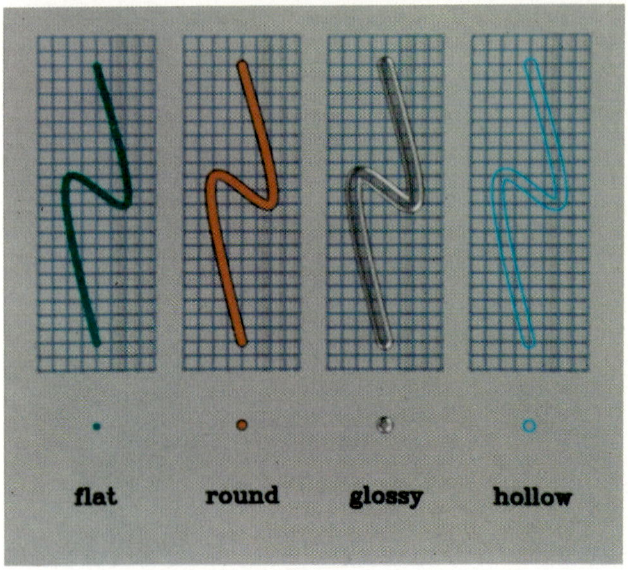

Figure 4. Brush style examples.

Implementation using a pixel cache

This algorithm plainly lies at the memory-intensive extreme of the memory -vs- processing tradeoff. Not only must each pixel have many additional bits in addition to the color components, but the memory must be frequently initialized. Furthermore, the need to draw each line in isolation appears to require a separate frame buffer. These problems are almost entirely eliminated by the use of a "pixel cache". The pixel cache is a memory that contains only a 32x32 array of pixels, but stores 48 bits per pixel. The destination frame buffer contains a 512x512 array of 24-bit pixels. The pixels in the cache correspond to a region in the frame buffer surrounding the current brush position. The cache address for screen location (x,y) is simply (x modulo 32, y modulo 32). Two additional 32 element look up tables, *xaddr* and *yaddr*, contain the actual x and y addresses corresponding to each column and row of the cache.

As the brush is moved, cache rows and columns through which the brush has already passed are flushed to the frame buffer and then reassigned to pixel locations along the advancing path of the brush. If a brush pixel is being copied to location (x,y) and

xaddr[x modulo 32] is not equal to x
or
yaddr[y modulo 32] is not equal to y

then a cache fault occurs and the offending row or column must be flushed. The cache flushing operation is an image compositing step in which the cache is a foreground image and the frame buffer is the background. As shown in eq. (1), cache flushing requires a multiply and two adds for each pixel being flushed. Once the cache data has been blended with the background pixel, all 48 bits of the cache pixel are reinitialized.

A 32x32 cache was chosen because it is just large enough to completely contain the largest brush that we use. For a hardware implementation, cache sizes of 16x16, 32x32, or 64x64 simplify the address logic considerably.

Anti-aliased Polygon Rendering

This algorithm becomes much more interesting when extended to handle polygons as well as lines. Some methods such as Turkowski's algorithm apply directly to polygons [18]. We have used this algorithm in conjunction with Smith's "tint fill" [16] to render anti-aliased polygons, but found that it was too slow. The algorithm used to make the filled polygons shown in the paper combines the "edge-flag" polygon fill method [1] with the soft flooding of tint fill.

Edge flag is basically a parity fill scheme which overcomes the failures of a simple parity fill. It yields the endpoints of each scan line segment within a filled region. Tint fill fills each of these scan line segments from the middle outward as long as *value* of the filled region is monotonically decreasing in the direction of fill. The modified edge flag algorithm fills each segment from left to right starting with the region on the left for which $1-blend$ is monotonically increasing and continuing to the right where $1-blend$ is monotonically decreasing.

It should be noted that this filling algorithm only works for polygons drawn as a list of edges, while tint fill works for scanned in polygons as well. Furthermore, the use of the *blend* value implies that the destination frame buffer must temporarily retain an extra 8 bits per pixel.

Performance

The astute reader will notice that the number of conditional copy operations, which cost an add as well as the associated memory access overhead, grows with the square of the brush diameter. This is unfortunate in view of the fact that the more interesting brush strokes are the larger ones. The $O(n^2)$ growth property would be discouraging enough to make us abandon the technique were it not so simple. In practice the number of pixel copying operations is reduced by programming tricks which take account of the orientation of the line segment being drawn. Because of its simplicity the algorithm is a natural candidate for hardware whose parallelism can compensate for its basic sluggishness.

The compositing operation, which contains a multiply and two adds, is no more expensive than any other properly implemented compositing operation. Thanks to the pixel cache, the algorithm's appetite for memory is not objectionable. Instead of needing a 512x512x48 bit frame memory, it needs only a 512x512x24 bit memory plus a 32x32x48 bit pixel cache.

The technique has been programmed in three forms: 1) all processing in a general purpose computer with an in core frame buffer, 2) all processing in a general purpose computer connected intimately to an external frame buffer, and 3) all processing in a bit-slice microprocessor contained within the display system. Even though the bit-slice processor is programmed in a higher level language [3], it runs about three times as fast as the other implementations.

Figure 5

Figure 6

Several front ends have been attached to the program including an interactive sketching program, a simple graphical language, and the existing languages PIC [13], EQN [12], and TROFF [15] which were originally designed for typesetter display. Figures 5 through 7 (as well as all other figures in the paper) were produced with the algorithm.

Acknowledgement

Lillian Schwartz, John Jarvis, Dave Weimer, Russ Andersson, and Bill Ninke provided help with this project. The micro-coded implementation of the algorithm was made possible through the use of the GIA microcode compiler provided by Gary Bishop of the University of North Carolina.

Figure 7

References

[1] Ackland, Bryan D., and Neil H.E. Weste, "The Edge Flag Algorithm - A Fill Method for Raster Scan Displays," *IEEE Transactions on Computers*, **C-30**, 1, January 1981, pp. 41-48.

[2] Barros, Jose, and Henry Fuchs, "Generating Smooth 2-D Monocolor Line Drawings on Video Displays," *Computer Graphics*, **13**, 2, August 1979, pp. 260-269.

[3] Bishop, Gary, "Gary's Ikonas Assembler," Department of Computer Science, University of North Carolina at Chapel Hill, 1982.

[4] Catmull, Edwin E., "A Subdivision Algorithm for Computer Display of Curved Surfaces," PhD thesis, Dept. of Computer Science, University of Utah, December 1974.

[5] Catmull, Edwin E., "A Hidden-Surface Algorithm with Anti-Aliasing," *Computer Graphics*, **12**, 3, August 1978, pp. 6-11.

[6] Crow, Franklin C., "The Aliasing Problem in Computer Synthesised Shaded Images," PhD thesis, Dept. of Computer Science, University of Utah, March 1976.

[7] Crow, Franklin C., "The Use of Grayscale for Improved Raster Display of Vectors and Characters," *Computer Graphics*, **12**, 3, August 1978, pp. 1-5.

[8] Crow, Franklin C., "A Comparison of Antialiasing Techniques," *IEEE Computer Graphics and Applications*, **1**, 1, January 1981, pp. 40-48.

[9] Feibush, Eliot A., Marc Levoy and Robert L. Cook, "Synthetic Texturing Using Digital Filters," *Computer Graphics*, **14**, 3, August 1980, pp. 294-301.

[10] Gupta, Satish, and Robert F. Sproull, "Filtering Edges for Gray-Scale Displays," *Computer Graphics*, **15**, 3, August 1981, pp. 1-5.

[11] Kajiya, James T., and M. Ullner, "Filtering High Quality Text for Display on Raster Scan Devices," *Computer Graphics*, **15**, 3, August 1981, pp. 7-15.

[12] Kernighan, Brian W., and Lorinda L. Cherry, "A System for Typesetting Mathematics," *Communications of the ACM*, **18**, 3, March 1975, pp. 151-157.

[13] Kernighan, Brian W., "PIC - A Graphics Language for Typesetting," *Software Practice and Experience*, January 1982.

[14] Newman, William M., and Robert F. Sproull, *Principles of Interactive Computer Graphics*, (McGraw-Hill, New York, ed. 2, 1979), p. 263.

[15] Ossana, Joseph F., "NROFF/TROFF User's Manual," Bell Laboratories Computing Science Technical Report #54, 1976.

[16] Smith, Alvy Ray, "Tint Fill," *Computer Graphics*, **13**, 2, August 1979, pp. 276-283.

[17] Smith, Alvy Ray, "Paint," in *Tutorial: Computer Graphics*, J.C. Beatty and K.S. Booth, eds., (IEEE Press, 1982), pp.501-515.

[18] Turkowski, Kenneth, "Anti-Aliasing through the Use of Coordinate Transformations," *ACM Transactions on Graphics*, **1**, 3, July 1982, pp. 215-234.

[19] Wallace, Bruce A., "Merging and Transformation of Raster Images for Cartoon Animation," *Computer Graphics*, **115**, 3, August 1981, pp. 253-262.

[20] Warnock, John, "The Display of Characters Using Gray Level Sample Arrays," *Computer Graphics*, **14**, 3, July 1980, pp. 302-307.

Appendix

Real pictures almost never contain isolated lines which do not cross each other, but many techniques for anti-aliasing seem to ignore this case. Notable exceptions are [5], [2], and [9]. A good reason for ignoring the case of crossing lines is that it tends to complicate the anti-aliasing algorithm. An analysis is presented here that should shed some light on how good or bad various approximations are for these cases.

Assume that the background is a signal of zero frequency, i.e. a constant intensity everywhere. If we simplify the analysis by expressing the continuous line $i(x,y)$ as the difference between its value and the background, we can conveniently ignore the background. For a pixel centered at screen coordinates (x,y), the intensity is given by the convolution integral

$$I(x,y) = \int_{u=-\infty}^{\infty} \int_{v=-\infty}^{\infty} i(u,v)\, h(x-u,y-v)\, du dv$$

where $h(,)$ is the filter kernel. Let I_1 and I_2 be the intensity of sample (x,y) for crossing lines $i_1(x,y)$ and $i_2(x,y)$ respectively when each is filtered in isolation. Furthermore, let A_1 be the area covered by i_1, A_2 the area covered by i_2, and A_{12} the area of overlap of i_1 and i_2. Then

$$\begin{aligned} I(x,y) &= \iint_{A_1} i_1(u,v)\, h(x-u,y-v)\, du dv \\ &+ \iint_{A_2} i_2(u,v)\, h(x-u,y-v)\, du dv \\ &- \iint_{A_{12}} i_2(u,v)\, h(x-u,y-v)\, du dv \\ &= I_1 + I_2 - f_{overlap}(i_2,A_{12})\ . \end{aligned} \qquad \text{(A1)}$$

There are four common ways of handling the case of crossing lines:

1) Do the entire convolution exactly. This implies that A_2 be clipped against A_1 as in [5], [9], and [2]. As stated earlier, the clipping is expensive. In the limit, as the sampling frequency nears infinity, supersampling [8] yields the same result.
2) Let $I(x,y)$ be the greater of I_2 or I_1. Eq. A1 shows that the error of this approximation is either $I_1 - f_{overlap}(i_2,A_{12})$ or $I_2 - f_{overlap}(i_2,A_{12})$. This approach is clearly inappropriate for the line styles described in this paper.
3) Let $I(x,y)$ be the sum of I_2 and I_1 [7]. The error is equal to $f_{overlap}(i_2,A_{12})$ unless arithmetic overflow occurs. This approach is intended for line drawing algorithms that emulate plotters.
4) Paint the lines in depth order, i.e. paint i_2 first. Line i_2's contribution to $I(x,y)$ can be expressed as a linear combination of an intensity derived from i_2 and the background (which is zero from a previous simplifying assumption). Then after painting i_2

$$I(x,y) = \alpha i_2 = I_2$$

where $(1-\alpha)$ is the background blending factor for the line i_2 at (x,y). Next, after drawing the line i_1,

$$\begin{aligned} I(x,y) &= \beta i_1 + (1-\beta)\alpha i_2\ . \\ &= \beta i_1 + \alpha i_2 - \alpha\beta i_2 \\ &= I_1 + I_2 - \alpha\beta i_2\ . \end{aligned}$$

where $(1-\beta)$ is the background blending factor for line i_1. Note that the form of this expression is the same as the exactly filtered intensity. The error of the approximation is the difference of the $f_{overlap}(i_2,A_{12})$ and $\alpha\beta i_2$ functions. This method is the merging operation described in the body of this paper as well as in [19].

Because method 4 avoids the computational expense of the method 1, it pays a penalty of somewhat lower image quality. The most visible artifact is the leakage of intensity from a line that should be completely obscured by a line draw over it. Although this algorithm is a adaptation of supersampling, it does not provide quite the same quality.

Edge Inference with Applications to Antialiasing

Jules Bloomenthal

Computer Graphics Laboratory
New York Institute of Technology
Old Westbury, New York

Abstract

An edge, when point-sampled for display by a raster device and not aligned with a display axis, appears as a staircase. This common aliasing artifact often occurs in computer images generated by two- and three-dimensional algorithms. The precise edge information often is no longer available but, from the set of vertical and horizontal segments which form the staircase, an approximation to the original edge with a precision beyond that of the raster may be inferred. This constitutes a smoothing of the staircase edge.

Among other applications, the inferred edges may be used to reshade the pixels they intersect, thereby antialiasing the inferred edges. The antialiased inferred edges prove a more attractive approximation to the real edges than their aliased counterparts.

Presented here are algorithms for the detection and smoothing of edges and the filtering of an image in accordance with the inferred edges.

General Terms: Algorithms.

Keywords and Phrases: Antialiasing, Edge Inference, Filtering.

CR Categories: I.3.7 [Computer Graphics]: Three-Dimensional Graphics and Realism--visible line/surface algorithms; I.4.1 [Image Processing]: Digitization--sampling; I.4.6 [Image Processing]: Segmentation--edge and feature detection.

1. Introduction

In 1961 Herbert Freeman published "Computer Processing of Line Drawings" in which he introduced the chain coding scheme for representing and processing edges [Freeman 1961; Freeman 1970]. Subsequent research with line representation has been applied widely to the problems of artificial intelligence [Duda 1973; Rosenfeld 1969] but the ability to construct edges from an image has rarely been applied to computer graphics.

One such application was presented in a 1978 dissertation by Garland Stern; as part of an animation system, outlines of animated figures were extracted from an image and then smoothed.

In 1974, Bruce Baumgart, in a seminal study of geometric modeling, extracted and smoothed line drawings from real world images of an object as an initial step in creating a computer model of the object [Baumgart 1974]. Eight years later, Scott Roth, using some of Freeman's techniques, extracted chain-encoded line structures from a rastered description of three-dimensional objects and, after processing the chain-codes, produced quite convincing line drawings of the objects [Roth 1982].

The extraction of edges may also be used to modify the original image. In 1977, Lance Williams demonstrated a technique ("dekink") for estimating edges of a two-dimensional region and then filtering the horizontal and vertical segments of the edges in two separate iterations [Williams].

It is not difficult to imagine other applications such as deriving closed contours from computer images in order to interpolate images or convert image data into a contour form (such as topographical maps).

Techniques for extracting edges from images are presented by Rosenfeld and Kak in their text Digital Picture Processing [Rosenfeld 1969]. Approaches for smoothing the edges are suggested as well.

2. Edge Inference and Antialiasing

Aliasing of objects (manifested by staircase edges, disappearing objects, or disconnected lines) has been minimized by a number of techniques including super-sampling [Crow 1981], adaptive super-sampling [Whitted 1980; Roth 1982], and analytical integration for certain kinds of objects [Catmull 1978]. There are also techniques which address aliasing in texture [Blinn 1976; Dungan 1978; Feibush 1980; Williams 1981], and highlighting [Whitted 1980; Roth 1982].

All of these techniques filter before sampling the image, but, with the exception of the computationally expensive super-sampling technique, none of the techniques works well with z-buffer based programs which render multiple types of objects (such as polygons, quadrics, and patches). Neither do they work well with "paint" programs or other programs which generate images in which edge information is not explicitly available.

Thus, the most intriguing use of edge inference may be to minimize the aliasing artifacts near object edges in the point-sampled computer generated images typically produced by z-buffer algorithms or paint programs. Filtering the image along inferred edges enjoys the advantages of post-processing flexibility and the concentration of processing along edges, where aliasing is usually most apparent.

The process of edge smoothing will be described below in two sections. The first describes a method for finding and tracking those rastered edges created by the point-sampling process. The second section discusses the smoothing of the rastered edges. Filtering an image along the smoothed edges is presented in a third section.

3. Edge Tracking

The tracking process is performed upon a frame of discrete, single-valued regions. It is usually a simple matter to create such a frame during the computer generation of an image. Alternatively, rastered images may be processed into a collection of regions of interest by various segmentation methods [Rosenfeld 1969].

A scan-line method similar to one developed by J. W. Butler [Butler 1963] was used to produce starting points for all the regions in a frame. A scan-line edge-detector could also be used [Agrawala 1977].

3.1. Tracking a Region

The "region" containing pixel (x,y) may be defined as the set of pixels connected to pixel (x,y) through a four-connected path of pixels, all the same value as pixel (x,y). A "four-connected path" is a connection or a series of connections from a pixel to any of its perpendicular neighbors.

In this discussion, "starting point" means a pixel located at a lower left corner of a region (see Figure 1). Given any point within a region, the determination of a starting point requires only a small amount of processing. Once the starting point is known, a region's boundary may be tracked, forming a closed circuit when the starting point is again reached. Rather than the chain coding representation of Freeman, the boundary is represented here as a sequence of corner locations in frame buffer coordinates (Figure 1). This has the advantage of readily accessible positional data for the boundary.

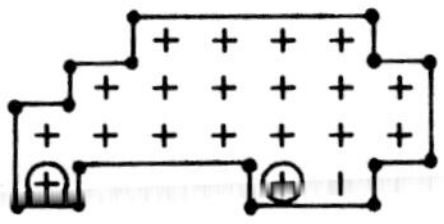

+ represents a pixel center
. represents a corner
o is a potential starting point

Figure 1: A 4-Connected Region

The tracking process is presented by the flowchart in Figure 3. The tracking proceeds in a clockwise direction about the region; the ability to determine the concavity or convexity of a corner is required (see Figure 2). The algorithm ensures that any two corner points share either their x or y coordinate and that no three corners are collinear. A detail of the flowchart is given in Figure 4.

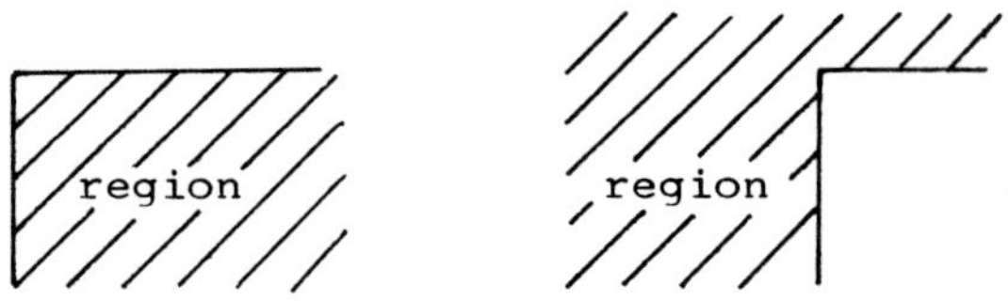

a convex corner a concave corner

Figure 2: Two Types of Corners

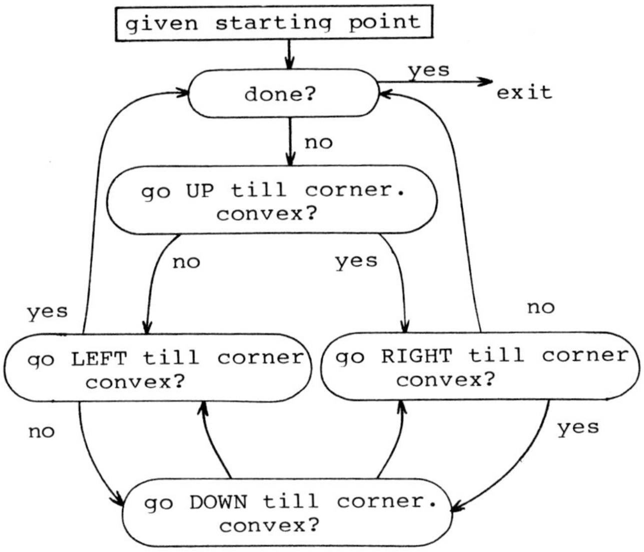

Figure 3: Flowchart for Edge Tracking

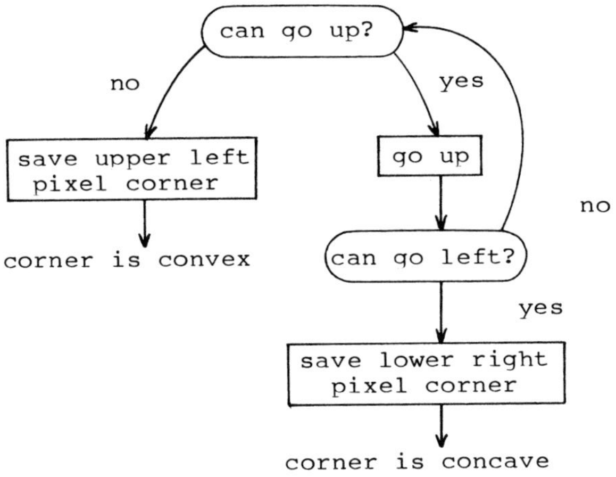

Figure 4: Detail for Figure 3

4. Edge Smoothing

Edges of surfaces in real space, when transformed to screen space, become aliased if the edge pixel values are not properly computed. This aliasing is manifested by "jaggies", sudden pixel-sized shifts in an otherwise straight line. Edge smoothing must disambiguate intended changes in direction from changes produced by jaggies.

A sudden pixel-sized shift, or "jag" is determined from four sequential corner points when the direction from point 1 to 2 is the same as from 3 to 4 and the distance from point 2 to 3 is one pixel unit. From a repeated jag pattern, Figure 5, left, a straight edge may be inferred with reasonable certainty. In Figure 5, right, the jag pattern changes midway and a change of slope is inferred.

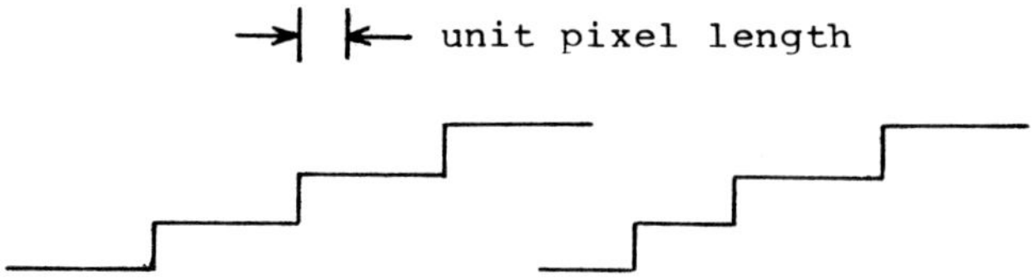

Figure 5: Jags

The edge inference algorithm cycles through each corner of a region. A first-in, first-out buffer of nine points is maintained which, for a given corner point, provides the positions of the four preceding and four following points, as well as the length and direction of the segments connecting the points. A series of tests is performed on this information to determine if and where a new endpoint should be created for the smoothed edge.

It is important to note that the inferred edge endpoints are given in floating point coordinates resolved beyond the raster. Further, the inferred edges are constrained to be within one pixel of the original, rastered edges.

5. Image Filtering

In this section "pixel" is used to mean the unit square surrounding the pixel center. Given the inferred boundary of a region, those pixels in the image which are intersected by the inferred edges are reshaded. In the present implementation, the percentage of the pixel covered by the region, as defined by the inferred edges, is first computed; it serves as a weighting coefficient for averaging the surrounding pixels. This is equivalent to a simple box filter; more complicated filters may be implemented as look-up tables with the table index a function of the distance from the inferred edge to the pixel center [Feibush 1980; Turkowski 1982].

Once the weighting coefficient is estimated, the pixel is reshaded as a linear combination of surrounding pixels averaged according to whether or not they belong to the region.

5.1. Computing the Estimate

Pitteway and Watkinson developed a method similar to Bresenham's line drawing algorithm which computes pixel area covered by an edge [Pitteway 1980].

Referring to Figure 6, one observes that the area covered in Pixel B is equal to that covered in Pixel A plus the shaded area. Thus, given an initial area, the areas of the remaining intersected pixels may each be computed with a single addition. At Pixel D, however, it is necessary to subtract the area of the black triangle from the new total. The area of the black triangle is then the initial area for Pixel E. This incremental technique is complicated by the need to accommodate endpoints not on a pixel boundary, or edges which re-enter a pixel.

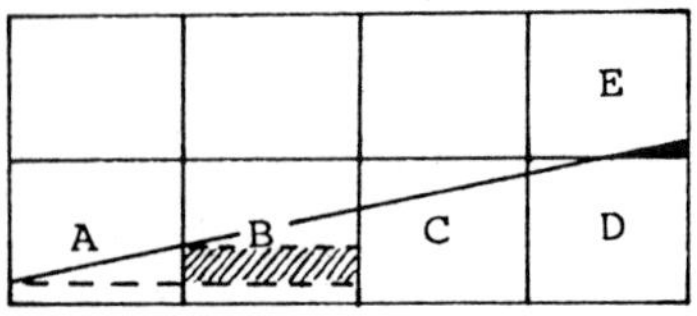

Figure 6: Computing Pixel Area

6. Conclusion

Proper antialiasing of computer generated pictures requires that the image be filtered before it is sampled for display on a raster device [Crow 1977]. Unfortunately, a high precision representation of the image is not always possible or practical with some hidden surface algorithms. Certain programs and input devices also produce aliased images.

Inferring, and then smoothing, an edge from an aliased image can produce convincing results, as shown in Figure 7. Figure 8 demonstrates one result of the post-process technique as well as a comparison with an image which exhibits no aliasing artifacts. Figure 9 presents magnified views of Figure 8. The post-process technique exhibits errors at some of the vertices as well as on the silhouette of the sphere. Further, the technique does not address other forms of aliasing such as small objects disappearing and thin, continuous lines breaking up.

It is worth noting that all the algorithms presented here operate in linear time with respect to the length of an edge. Figure 8, a 512 by 486 resolution image, was processed in 17 seconds with a VAX/780.

Some aspects of the technique are not limited to inferred edges. Filtering may occur along the true edges calculated by a hidden line eliminator program. This increases the accuracy of the edge position but usually limits the program to images generated using polygonal models. (Most hidden line eliminators work with polygonal surfaces only.) Conversely, antialiasing is not the only application for the inference of edges.

7. Acknowledgements

Lance Williams offered consistent support for this research, as well as many insightful concepts. Paul Heckbert provided critical reading of this paper as well as the model descriptions for Figure 8.

Figure 7: Test pattern before (top) and after (bottom) processing

Top: Antialiasing as a Post Process
Middle: Correctly Antialiased
Bottom: Without Antialiasing

Figure 8: Rendered Images, 512 Resolution

Figure 9: Rendered Images, Magnified

8. References

Agrawala, A. and Kulkarni, A., "A Sequential Approach to the Extraction of Shape Features", Computer Graphics and Image Processing, v.6, December 1977, pp. 538-557.

Baumgart, B.G., "Geometric Modeling for Computer Vision", Report STAN-CS-74-463, Stanford Artificial Intelligence Laboratory, Stanford University, 1974.

Butler, J.W., Butler M.K., and Stroud A., "Automatic Analysis of Chromosomes", Data Acquisition and Processing in Biology and Medicine, v.3, pp. 261-275, Pergamon, Oxford, 1963.

Catmull, E.E., "A Subdivision Algorithm for Computer Display of Curved Surfaces", Ph.D. Thesis, University of Utah, Computer Science Department, 1974.

Catmull, E.E., "A Hidden-Surface Algorithm with Antialiasing", Computer Graphics, v.12, August, 1978.

Crow, F.C., "The Aliasing Problem in Computer Generated Shaded Images", Communications of the ACM, v.20, November, 1977.

Crow, F.C., "A Comparison of Antialiasing Techniques", IEEE Computer Graphics and Applications, v.1, January, 1981.

Duda, R.O. and Hart, P.E., Pattern Classification and Scene Analysis, John Wiley and Sons, New York, 1973.

Dungan, W., Stenger, A., and Sutty, G., "Texture Tile Considerations for Raster Graphics", Computer Graphics, v.12, August, 1978.

Feibush, E.A., Levoy, M., and Cook, R.L., "Synthetic Texturing Using Digital Filters", Computer Graphics, v.14, July, 1980.

Freeman, H., "On the Encoding of Arbitrary Geometric Configurations", IRE Trans. EC-10, pp. 260 - 268, June, 1961. lp Freeman, H., "Boundary Encoding and Processing", Picture Processing and Psychopictorics, B. Lipkin and A. Rosenfeld, editors, Academic Press, Inc., NY, 1970.

Pitteway, M. and Watkinson, D., "Bresenham's Algorithm with Grey Scale," Communications of the ACM, v.23, November 1980, pp. 625-626.

Roth, S.D., "Ray Casting for Modeling Solids", Computer Graphics and Image Processing, v.18, February, 1982, p. 109-144.

Rosenfeld, A. and Kak, A.C., Digital Picture Processing, Academic Press, New York, 1969.

Stern, G., "A System for Computer-Aided Keyframe Animation", Ph.D. Thesis, University of Utah, Computer Science Department, 1978.

Turkowski, K., "Antialiasing Through the Use of Coordinate Transformations", Computer Graphics, v.16, July, 1982.

Whitted, T., "An Improved Illumination Model for Shaded Display", Communications of the ACM, v.23, June, 1980.

Williams, L.J., "Pyramidal Parametrics", Siggraph notes, Advanced Image Synthesis Seminar, August, 1981; see also Computer Graphics, v.17, July, 1983.

Williams, L.J., "Brute Force in Image Space", Ph.D. Thesis (unpublished), University of Utah, Computer Science Department.

PANEL

SOLID MODELING

CHAIR: Ronald N. Goldman, Control Data Corporation
PANELISTS: David Gossard, MIT
Richard Riesenfeld, University of Utah
Herbert Voelcker, University of Rochester
Tony Woo, University of Michigan

CHAIRMAN'S INTRODUCTION:

Many different techniques are now available for generating, storing, analyzing, and manipulating computer models of solid objects. These techniques include: constructive solid geometry and ray firing, boundary files and local operations, B-spline surfaces and subdivision techniques, and variational geometry and dimensioning schemes. In this panel discussion four leading academic experts representing four distinct and often divergent points of view, will discuss the pros and cons, the uses and abuses, the suitability and inappropriateness of these various techniques. To set the stage for the discussion, each panelist will give a formal ten to fifteen minute presentation on an aspect of solid modeling about which he feels most strongly. The panel chairman will then lead an informal discussion concentrating on specific areas of disagreement among the panelists.

Dave Gossard received his Bachelor's and Masters degrees in Mechanical Engineering from Purdue University in 1968 and 1970 respectively. He obtained his PhD from the Massachusetts Institute of Technology in 1975. He is currently an Associate Professor of Mechanical Engineering at M.I.T. where he is the Director of the Computer-Aided Design Laboratory.

Richard Riesenfeld received a Ph.D from the School of Computer and Information Science at Syracuse University, Syracuse, New York. He is professor and chairman of computer science and head of the Computer-Aided Geometric Design Group in Computer Science at the University of Utah, where he joined the faculty in 1972. Riesenfeld has published and consulted in the area of computer graphics and CAD/CAM/CAE and has gained an acquaintance both with the academic issues and with industrial applications and motivations in the field. The B-spline method of curve and surface design, which he proposed in his doctoral thesis, is used by many industries in many countries. His major research focus for the last year has been the design and implementation of a CAD system Alpha_1 which advances the state-of-the-art in both high quality computer graphics and freeform surface models. This system is designed to exploit the capabilities of the Oslo Algorithm, on which he collaborated.

Herbert Voelcker is Professor of Engineering at the University of Rochester and Director of the Production Automation Project. He holds B.S. and M.S. degrees in mechanical and electrical engineering from MIT and a PhD degree from the Imperial College of Science and Technology. Mr. Voelcker is a Fellow of IEEE and a member of ASME, ACM, SME, and NCS. He served in the U.S. Army for seven years, has worked for or consulted for various industrial and governmental organizations, and has won various research prizes, teaching prizes, and fellowships.

Tony Woo received his PhD in Electrical Engineering at the University of Illinois in 1975. After his graduation, he taught there in the Departments of Electrical Engineering and Mechanical and Industrial Engineering. Currently, he is Assistant Professor in Industrial and Operations Engineering and in the Program of Computer, Information and Control Engineering. Dr. Woo's research interests are in computer graphics, geometric modeling, and computational geometry with applications to manufacturing and design.

PANELISTS' ABSTRACTS:

D. C. Gossard, MIT

Boundary representations of solid objects are particularly well suited for interactive applications. This presentation will discuss the use of interactive methods for modifying boundary representations. Dimensions such as appear on a mechanical drawing are considered to impose constraints on the permissible locations of geometry to which they refer. These constraints may be described by a set of nonlinear algebraic equations. These constraint equations constitute a description of the entire family of parts which share a generic shape. This approach provides a powerful method for modification of models and a foundation for the automatic scaling of assemblies of components.

Light, R.A., "A Dimension Based 2-D Shape Editing Feature for Computer-Aided Drafting Systems", Bachelor's thesis, M.I.T. Cambridge, MA, June 1979.

Gossard, D.C., Light, R.A. and Lin, V., "A Computer Aided Design System for Design by Variation", Proceedings of the Fourth International Conference on Production Engineering, Tokyo, Japan, August, 1980.

Gossard, D.C., Light, R.A., Meyfarth, P.F., and Lin, V.C., "The Use of Symbolic Dimensioning in Computer-Aided Design", Annals of the CIRP, Vol. 29/2/1980.

Lin, V.C., "Three Dimensional Variational Geometry in Computer- Aided Design", Master's thesis, M.I.T., Cambridge, MA, May 1981

Gossard, D.C., Light, R.A., "Modification of Geometric Models through Variational Geometry", Computer Aided Design, Vol 14, No. 4, July 1982.

Richard Riesenfeld
University of Utah

The next generation of geometric modelling systems will probably provide a combination of sculptured surface capabilities and constructive solid geometry tools. Toward this goal, the Alpha_1 System is being developed at the University of Utah. In its evolution we have found the boundary representations are very useful in achieving this greater generality, for sculptured surfaces do not typically exhibit a simple intrinsic alternative manner of representation. On the other hand, the added complexity of using a spline surface representation may be offset to some extent by making the general intersection problem more tractable.

The experience of developing Alpha_1 has also brought us to investigate more relaxed object validity constraints than some which are currently in use. Overall, the advance to spline-based solid modelling will not be simply an incremental one but rather a larger one in which many existing concepts will have to be generalized.

Herbert B. Voelcker
University of Rochester

Solid modeling's raison d'etre is informational completeness, i.e., the notion that one can calculate automatically (at least in principle) any well defined geometrical property of a solid from a 'solid model'. Two sets of issues arise: how can one represent solids in an informationally complete manner, and then how can one use such representations to do useful work?

Quite alot was learned about representations in the 1970's, and today we have a new generation of CAD/CAM systems entering the market that is based on the best of the late 70's boundary- representation, constructive solid geometry (CSG), and approximation technologies. As yet these systems can't do very much in a free standing sense, because only a few applications (graphics, mass properties, static interference checking) are well understood in mathematical and algorithmic terms. Clearly a lot of work is needed to enable solid modellers to support a much broader range of applications. The character of this work is easy to specify: mathematization of each potential application, followed by algorithm development.

Results from the first stage -- mathematical problem formulation -- should apply to all solid modeling schemes, while second-stage results will be highly scheme-dependent. These latter should enable us to rank the effectiveness of the currently competing approaches to solid modeling and design yet another generation of systems that may embody elements form all of the current schemes.

A useful 81 entry bibliography that is only slightly obsolete may be found in "Solid Modeling: A Historical Summary and Contemporary Assessment", by A.A.G. Requicha and H. B. Voelcker, IEEE Computer Graphics & Applications, pp. 9-24, March 1982. The four other papers in that issue of CG & A provide additional material and reference lists.

Tony C. Woo,
University of Michigan

Set operations on boundary models of solids involve at least of the order of N^2 time to compute, where N is the number of surfaces of the solids. Because of the $O(N^2)$ nature, we can think of set operators as "global" operations. In this talk we examine a class of "local" operations that mimic set operations. The issue is how much do they cost?

We present a topological data structure that requires O(N) storage and gives constant expected time for retrieval. This performance is made possible by a surprising theorem: In an arbitrary 3D object with V Vertices, E edges, F faces and G holes, the average number of neighbours for any face (or vertex) is a constant C.

We next define locality $L = \log_c N$ as the number of subsequent topological neighbours an operation affects. If C is a small constant then a local operation has a global effect but gives a constant time performance.

A Device-Independent Network Graphics System

Deborah U. Cahn
Albert C. Yen

Computer Science and Mathematics Department
Lawrence Berkeley Laboratory
University of California
Berkeley, California 94720

Abstract

The design and implementation of a basic graphics system for a heterogeneous network environment is described. The design has been influenced by the SIGGRAPH Core System, GKS, and proposals being considered by the ANSI Technical Committee on Computer Graphics Programming Languages. It permits hierarchical object definition, direct and indirect attribute specification, screen window management and complex styles of interaction. Important parts of the implementation include a device-independent database for graphical objects, a workstation driver which produces device code, and a device kernel which manages the display list. Problems relating to device independence and network partitioning are discussed.

CR Categories and Subject Descriptors: I.3.2 **[Computer Graphics]:** Graphics Systems—*distributed/network graphics*; I.3.4 **[Computer Graphics]:** Graphics Utilities—*graphics packages*; I.3.6 **[Computer Graphics]:** Methodology and Techniques—*device independence, interaction techniques*

General Terms: Design, Standardization

Additional Key Words and Phrases: Core System, Graphical Kernel System, symbol system, workstation, attributes, graphics input

1. Introduction

This paper describes the development of a new graphics system called the *Network Graphics System* (*NGS*) [6] which is intended to support interactive, distributed applications. In its design we have drawn from our experience with other systems; for example, we participated in the George Washington University implementation [7, 20] of the SIGGRAPH Core System [9]. We have also been heavily involved with the work on Core-like systems of ANSI X3H3, the Technical Committee on Computer Graphics Programming Languages [1] and GKS, the ISO standard [10].

The computing environment which supports computer science research at Lawrence Berkeley Laboratory is characterized by diversity. It includes several different host computers, using different operating systems and utility software, connected in a local area network. Many types of graphics hardware are in use, including both calligraphic and raster devices, color and monochrome, storage tube and display-list, interactive and hardcopy, with or without local intelligence.

Two aspects of this environment have been particularly critical to the NGS project. First is the existence of the local area network and the possibility of distributed computing. A network graphics system should allow devices attached exclusively to a single host to be used by applications which run exclusively on other network nodes (due to database location, host configuration, software requirements, etc.).

A number of operating systems are found on the network, in particular UNIX, VMS and RSX-11M. Many software packages have different versions to run on different operating systems and host machines, but this graphics system potentially must deal with multiple operating systems in the context of a single distributed application. For example, a mapping application, using a large census database which resides on disks available only to a VAX-11/780 running VMS, may need to use a Megatek 7255 which is connected to a VAX-11/750 running UNIX. A network graphics system should use interprocess communications in such a way that it not only hides operating system differences, but also supports a flexible configuration of resources, including graphics devices, host processors and file servers, according to application requirements.

The second critical feature of our computing environment is that the graphics devices to be supported have a wide range of capabilities. Current developments in standards for user interfaces to computer graphics, such as the Core System, GKS, and the ANSI X3H3 work in progress, assume that general-purpose, medium to high-level graphics functions can be made available in a device-independent way. However, existing implementations of these standards have set some pragmatic limits, by allowing only a single workstation, or only homogeneous workstations, and by not dealing with a network environment. One aspect of this project is a deliberate attempt to test new ideas in device-independent graphics standards in a particularly diverse and challenging environment.

Applications anticipated for NGS include: display and analysis of scientific data, presentation and "business" graphics and picture editors [19, 4]. We explicitly did not consider applications such as CAD/CAM modeling and others in which application-specific hierarchical modeling or database systems are included in the non-graphics application.

2. The Design

The Core System and our previous Grafpac package [11] were the two starting points for the design of NGS. But we added major new functionality to meet the needs of evolving applications and changing computing environments. The following sections describe some significant aspects of this design.

2.1. Object Definition and Display

Graphical objects, in NGS, are called structures. *The body of a structure is a sequence of output primitives (lines, markers, polygons, text, and raster sequences), attribute selection functions, and references to other structures. A reference to another structure can have one of two forms, one macro-like, COPY, which interpolates a copy of the named structure into the calling structure, and the other subroutine-like, EXECUTE, which is a call by reference. Both COPY and EXECUTE can refer to structures which have not yet been defined (a null structure is referenced). A structure can be extended or deleted at any time.*

Since structures can contain other structures, NGS supports hierarchical picture definition. Hierarchical picture definition is needed to help users compose non-trivial pictures, especially for applications such as picture editors, chartmaking, and scientific data display which do not already include database systems for hierarchical models. Furthermore, dynamic picture modification is needed since the picture composition process is seen as a dynamic interaction between a user and a set of pictures displayed at workstations. These requirements meant that a simple method of picture definition, the one-dimensional segmentation model of Core-like systems, was inadequate. Hierarchy can be built on top of a Core-like system, but dynamics cannot.

NGS conceptually includes a database system, that is, it provides procedures to create, retrieve, modify and destroy structures. This kind of simple modeling facility is frequently called a *symbol system* [8]. It does not provide for inclusion of application data in the graphical database.

The two structure invocation facilities, COPY and EXECUTE, support different application needs. Copied structures lose their separate identity and are not affected by changes to the original; sometimes this is the desired effect. On the other hand, all instances of a structure called by EXECUTE immediately reflect changes to the original.

In addition to its body, a structure also has a header. *The header initializes the attribute state when the structure is traversed; it may hold a specific attribute value or specify that an attribute value is "inherited" from its caller. The current attribute state is saved when a structure is called and restored when it exits. The structure header (and only the header) may be dynamically edited at any time.*

The separate structure header allows structure content to be modified dynamically in a limited way. For the applications NGS is to support, we felt that a more elaborate modeling system which permitted generalized dynamic editing of structure elements was not necessary. Attributes in NGS include the modeling and viewing transformations, so that the geometry of an image, as well as its appearance, can be affected by the hierarchical relationships and dynamic interaction.

The process of picture definition is independent of picture display. A picture is displayed by explicitly posting *one or more structures to a workstation. This conceptually sends a copy of the named structures and all their hierarchical descendants to the workstation for display. As with the other structure invocations, a structure can be posted before it is defined.*

Orthogonality of object definition and picture display facilitates a very spontaneous interaction style in multi-workstation applications, since the creation of objects and the use of them to compose and display pictures on devices is completely independent. The application has completely flexible control over what image or combination of images is displayed on each display surface. Since structures can be referenced before definition, top-down or other structured approaches to hierarchical object definition are permitted; the picture can be displayed in real-time as created.

In NGS, storage of structures in a device-independent form is implicit and is performed above the workstation level. This differs from GKS, which stores device-independent segment definitions on a special kind of workstation. Both approaches contrast with that of the Core System, in which no device-independent information is retained and the association between segments and devices is determined by the state of the system at segment creation time.

Pictures can also include non-retained or unstructured *data. These are output primitives, attribute selections, and structure invocations which exist outside of any structure. Unstructured data is not kept in any device-independent display file, and may disappear from a workstation when a picture regeneration is performed.*

Unstructured data allows an application to bypass the complexity and overhead associated with storage in a device-independent database.

2.2. Attributes

NGS has a two tier attribute model, allowing an application both to select *(or set) attribute values and, when appropriate, to* define *the workstation-dependent meanings of those values. Each workstation maintains its own set of* attribute registers, *one register for each of the many attributes. The value in any register can be set globally, by an explicit function which applies to all workstations, or locally, using a stack discipline, during traversal of a structure.*

Most attributes can be specified either directly, by giving a particular value, or indirectly by giving an index into a table of values. Each workstation has its own table for each indexed attribute. The table entries, which can be workstation-dependent, are initialized by NGS and may be redefined by the application at any time.

Indirect specification of attributes allows the definition of an object to be device-independent, but permits its interpretation to vary on different devices so that the final visual effect can be the same (or different, when that is desired!). For example, the interpretation of color specifications could be workstation-dependent to compensate for differing hardware renditions of identical RGB coordinates. Polygons on one workstation could be filled with solid colors, while being filled with hatch patterns on another. Core-like systems only permit device-independent picture specification, not device-independent rendering. In addition, any interpretation, traversal, or binding of a structure to a device-specific image is conceptually postponed until the latest possible moment, when the device is actually displaying the picture. Thus an image can be modified by dynamic redefinition of the workstation attribute tables.

GKS and the work of ANSI X3H3 also use indirect specification through the use of index tables, but NGS combines this with direct specification. Direct specification presents a simpler user interface, especially when index tables can vary greatly in size between devices.

The mechanism of bundling *can be used to compose additional attributes from a set of independent* basis attributes. *Each workstation has a* bundle table *whose entries are selected by the attribute* bundle_index. *Each bundle specifies a selection of basis attributes and the values they are to assume, overriding their individual settings, when that bundle is selected.*

This bundling mechanism is similar to that included in GKS and proposed by ANSI X3H3. It could be used, for example, to compose an attribute called *density*, specifying how visually dense a primitive appears. This attribute would be "bundled" on each workstation as a workstation-dependent combination of the attributes linewidth and color. In NGS, the color attributes themselves are bundled, permitting a variety of color models at the user interface.

2.3. Workstations

The NGS application interfaces to physical devices through the abstract virtual workstation. Each workstation has at most one logical display surface for output and may have one or more logical input devices. A workstation may have one or more "hardcopy" devices slaved to it, such as a paper copier or a camera. Some workstations are permanently defined; each of these is associated with a particular device, and is the default mechanism by which an application would access that device. In addition, workstations can be created dynamically. Several of these can be assigned to a single terminal and each allocated a portion of its display surface or other resources.

The NGS workstation model is an enhanced version of the GKS workstation. "Virtual" workstations allow an output surface to be partitioned into different functional areas or screen windows, each controlled by an independent application or subprocess. Such a capability helps to support high-quality interactive systems [16].

2.4. Interaction

Graphical input is performed by interaction tasks. *An interaction task has an externally visible state consisting of its* value *and its* trigger. *The value is a variable which can be read by other interaction tasks, and the trigger is a signal which can be delivered to other tasks on request.*

Interaction tasks may exist at several levels. At the "terminal" or physical device level are the primitive interaction tasks which are abstractions of physical input devices. A terminal-level task may serve several workstations, one at a time or simultaneously. For example, a terminal equipped with a keyboard has an interaction task of type "keyboard". This task fires a trigger whenever a key is depressed, and its value is that of the key. Above the terminal level, interaction tasks are application-dependent; these could be at either the "workstation" or "application" levels.

Input devices are much more diverse than output devices. Earlier graphics systems have attempted to impose some order on this diversity by dividing input devices into logical classes, such as "pick", "valuator", "locator", etc. In these systems, detailed control of physical devices and simulation of absent ones is provided by the graphics system's input device driver, and is beyond the control of the application [18].

Although this model allows an application to be transported easily from one device to another, this device independence has a high price. Since the way in which a user perceives an interactive system depends primarily on its pragmatics or ergonomics [5], an application's user interface is frequently dependent on one particular input device or set of devices. Transporting an application substitutes a new set of devices. Because the application's designer has no control over the pragmatics of these new devices, the quality of its user interface may change dramatically.

Therefore, NGS provides a model in which an application can conceivably access physical input devices at a low level. Furthermore, simple abstract input devices can be combined into more complex ones in a hierarchical manner. This allows interaction styles to be individually tailored for each terminal, while isolating the device dependencies. The NGS design does not define any specific logical devices or interaction styles. Rather, it provides a framework on which may be built many different models of interaction, including the logical input classes of the Core or GKS.

Interaction tasks communicate through connections, *and a task may be connected to several client tasks simultaneously. Once a connection is established, it must be* enabled *in order for data to pass across it. Enabling a connection to a task starts its* measure process, *which is responsible for maintaining the task's value and trigger.*

NGS manages an application-level interaction task as a coroutine of the parent program. To define each such task, the application supplies seven functions, which are invoked, through NGS, to establish or break a connection, to enable or disable the task, to read the task's value, or to perform other task-specific actions. One function serves as the task's measure process. Control is transferred to a measure process, by NGS, when the main application calls the AWAIT INTERACTION function. Until the main program's request is satisfied, NGS switches control between active measure processes in response to AWAIT INTERACTION or FIRE TRIGGER calls. Though it runs synchronously with the main application, an application-level measure process has an independent flow of control.

The concept of interaction tasks is similar to ideas proposed by van den Bos [17] and Anson [2, 3]. While these authors each proposed special languages for defining input devices, we wanted NGS to work within the limits of existing languages and programming systems. Thus, rather than being definitional in nature, our model is procedural, involving explicit communications between independent tasks. Because an interaction task is a coroutine of the parent application, it may reference global program variables as well as call on any NGS function. Using coroutines allows the establishment of multiple threads of control within a single host operating system process.

In general, device-independent graphics systems find it very difficult to avoid placing limits on the use of devices so that the hardware appears more homogeneous to the device-independent software. Workstation level interaction tasks are one way of bypassing these limitations. They can be used to perform complex functions, including echoing, local image transformations, and modification of workstation attribute definitions. NGS also includes another mechanism, *escape functions*, which allow access, when needed, to the device-dependent capabilities of workstations. Reasons for their use include improved performance, more precise control over the appearance of the image, and use of the workstation for special purposes.

3. The Implementation

Internally, NGS is divided into several major components (Figure 1). As well as partitioning the work of implementation, the divisions represent cleavage points at which the code could be divided in a distributed system. These components include: user interface functions, device-independent structure database, workstation driver, and device kernel.

3.1. Device-Independent Structure Database

Structure data is kept in the Device-Independent Structure Database (DISDB). The interface to the DISDB is procedural, and is used by both the workstation-independent and workstation layers. The workstation-independent layer creates, modifies, and deletes information in the database, while the workstation-dependent layers read structure information in order to update their displays. The DISDB provides a means of hiding the detailed characteristics of the workstations from the workstation-independent layers. This makes it easier to implement new workstation types. Since the upper layers cannot anticipate the requirements of each workstation, transmission of data from the DISDB to a workstation is controlled from below by the workstation driver itself.

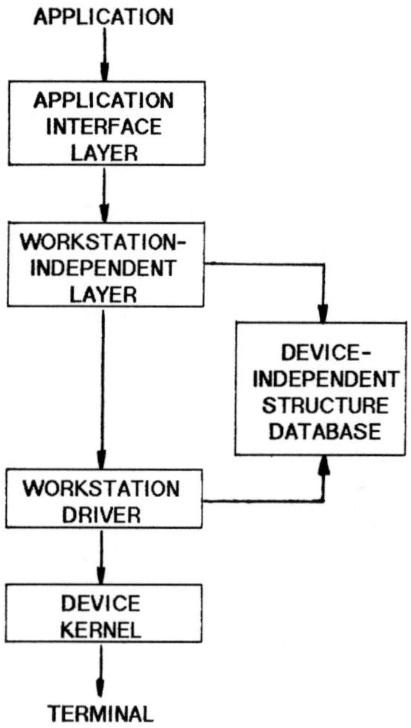

Figure 1. Flow of Control in NGS

A primitive locking mechanism is a part of the DISDB. The entire database is locked during a major restructuring (such as caused by the DELETE ALL STRUCTURES command), but ordinarily workstation drivers are allowed to read a structure body (for example if posted or otherwise needed at that workstation) concurrently as the workstation-independent layer is extending it. To simplify synchronization of writing and reading, the workstation-independent layer notifies the appropriate workstations when it sends a packet of data to the database.

A flexible approach to dynamic storage allocation has been taken, since NGS will be running in various environments. The manager of the DISDB accepts *data descriptors* rather than data itself. Storage is usually allocated or deallocated dynamically by the process which is controlling the generation of the data to fill the storage. This technique is less cumbersome than requiring the application to use fixed length blocks only, making multiple requests until all the information has been passed.

3.2. Workstation Driver

The workstation driver is responsible for converting device-independent structure definitions into device-specific graphics instructions. A major source of complexity at this level is the implementation of attributes.

At the user level, each attribute corresponds to a register in the workstation; the value in this register can be set in a structure header, structure body, or directly by the applications program. The attribute registers are saved when a structure is invoked and restored upon exit. This view is a generalization of the way real graphics devices work. However, different devices have widely differing sets of hardware registers while the graphics system is required to present to the user a uniform set of attributes.

If there is no hardware register corresponding to a specific abstract attribute, then it must be simulated. Usually this means that the value of the attribute must be bound within the body of a structure when it is translated into device code. For example, NGS defines separate color attributes for different contexts, "vector color", "text color", etc.; however, real devices commonly have only one register to control color. Therefore, it is necessary to incorporate code, which sets this register, into the body of a translated structure whenever a primitive in one context is followed by one belonging to another. Other attributes, such as linewidth or text precision, may cause the output code to contain different combinations of primitives depending on their values. Such artificial bindings must take place when a structure is translated, even though they are not contained in its device-independent structure definition.

The requirements for hierarchical picture definition and device-independent attribute specification complicate the design of the driver. A structure can be invoked by several callers and inherit a different set of attribute values from each. Therefore, for each structure, the driver maintains one or more *incarnations*, each of which binds a different set of attribute values in its body. An incarnation need not occupy real physical storage. For devices that are refreshed from the host machine's memory (non-display-list or "unbuffered" devices) each incarnation can be generated "on the fly". On the other hand, with display list devices, each incarnation must be computed and stored separately.

The driver processes a structure only when it is immediately going to be displayed, since at this point the attribute environment is fully known. This attribute environment is compared with those of the existing incarnations of the structure to find a match. If a new incarnation is required, it can be generated in one of two ways depending on the properties of the mismatched attributes.

An attribute may be controlled by a specific device register, but that register is shared by other attributes, e.g. vector color or text color if both are used in the same structure. In this case, the attribute is set by a specific device instruction. If there is an existing incarnation such that all mismatched attributes fall in this category, the workstation driver makes a new incarnation by replacing the required instructions in the existing one.

An attribute may be expressed by different combinations of primitives depending on its value, for example viewing, modeling, and depending on the device, polygon fill style. Such attributes must be bound during code generation. To change these attributes, the driver retrieves a device-independent copy of the structure and retranslates it.

The workstation driver operates in the context of a virtual workstation. However, it also performs the translation from device-independent virtual workstation functions to specific device instructions. This translation, whose parameters are obtained from the device kernel when the virtual workstation is opened, includes converting from virtual screen to physical screen coordinates, and changing references to virtual index tables into references to physical ones.

3.3. Device Kernel

The device kernel manages a single physical workstation, or terminal. This includes creating virtual workstations and allocating device resources among them; such resources include display screen space and hardware index tables.

Since it controls regeneration of the displayed picture, the kernel is responsible for managing display list memory for the workstation drivers. In this, it deals only with device-code translations of structures, which the drivers transmit. The driver stores these structures, controls their visibility, and also implements the structure invocations, COPY and EXECUTE.

3.4. Network Interface

NGS accesses the local area network with the set of user-level functions described in [12] and [13]. These are built on top of the ARPA TCP/IP [14, 15] communications protocols. The interface functions support network-wide address space, plus name services which can translate a logical resource name to a specific network address. A *server process* may be associated with a network address; then a client process can, by opening a connection to the designated address, *rendezvous* with the server.

When two processes rendezvous, a *virtual circuit* is established between them. This is a reliable bi-directional link which can handle an indefinite amount of data. A single server process can converse with many clients at once and can control the order in which clients' messages are received and processed.

Each graphics terminal is known on the network by a unique logical resource name. While a terminal can also be addressed by its specific network address, use of the resource name insulates user programs from changes in device configuration. Thus, to use the terminal as a graphics workstation, a user program opens a connection using the terminal's resource name, which activates a server process. This server always includes the device kernel, but since the network partitioning may depend on device type, it may also include higher levels of NGS.

When a user program wants to create a virtual workstation, the server process obtains a new network address and returns it to the client while associating itself as the server. The new workstation can then be used by any process which has obtained its address. In addition, the virtual workstation can be associated with a resource name, so that its specific network address need not be known. We have assumed that programs using virtual workstations will cooperate; thus, access control and other protection mechanisms are outside the scope of NGS.

4. Conclusions

NGS is a high-level device-independent graphics system which supports hierarchical object definition and dynamic picture changes. It also allows an application to sacrifice device-independence for close control of a specific device if so required. To implement these functions on a wide range of graphics devices requires a complex implementation, which is made easier by clearly separating the device-independent and device-dependent parts. Another division separates the functions of device code generation from display list management. The network interface allows a single device to host several virtual workstations, each controlled by a separate process.

At this time, NGS is in the implementation stage, with drivers initially planned for the Tektronix 4014 and Megatek 7255 graphics devices. We plan to instrument this implementation for performance analysis. With information on the amount of data passed to and from each module, we will be able to refine the interfaces between NGS subsystems in order to reduce the amount of network overhead.

5. Acknowledgements

The authors wish to acknowledge the contributions of the membership of ANSI X3H31 and the participants in the ACM-SIGGRAPH Workshop on Graphical Input Interaction Techniques. We would also like to thank Bill Johnston for many valuable discussions and general encouragement.

This work was supported by the Applied Mathematical Sciences Program of the Office of Energy Research, U.S. Department of Energy under Contract DE-AC03-76SF00098 and by the U.S. Defense Advanced Research Projects Agency under Order 4306.

References

1. ANSI X3H31. Functional specification of the Programmer's Hierarchical Interactive Graphics System. Working Document ANSI X3H31/82-45 (1982).

2. Anson, E. The semantics of graphical input. *Comput. Gr.* (Proc. Siggraph '79) *13*, 2 (Aug. 1979), 113-120.

3. Anson, E. The device model of interaction. *Comput. Gr.* (Proc. Siggraph '82) *16*, 3 (July 1982), 107-114.

4. Benson, W.H. and Kitous, B. Interactive analysis and display of tabular data. *Comput. Gr.* (Proc. Siggraph '77) *11*, 2 (1977), 48-53.

5. Buxton, W. Lexical and pragmatic considerations of input structures. *Comput. Gr. 17*, 1 (Jan. 1983), 31-37.

6. Cahn, D.U., Johnston, W.E., and Yen, A.C. Network Graphics System Design Document, Version 1.0. Technical Report LBID-644, Lawrence Berkeley Laboratory (Nov. 1982).

7. Foley, J.D. and Wenner, P.A. The George Washington University Core System implementation. *Comput. Gr.* (Proc. Siggraph '81) *15*, 3 (Aug. 1981), 123-132.

8. Foley, J.D. and van Dam, A. *Fundamentals of Interactive Computer Graphics*. Addison-Wesley (1982).

9. GSPC (SIGGRAPH-ACM). Status Report of the Graphics Standards Planning Committee. *Comput. Gr. 13*, 3 (Aug. 1979).

10. ISO. Graphical Kernel System (GKS): Functional Description. ISO TC97/SC5/WG2 N117 (Jan. 14, 1982).

11. Johnston, N.E., Cahn, D.U., and Johnston, W.E. Grafpac. LBL Report UCID-8094, Lawrence Berkeley Laboratory, Berkeley (Jan. 1979).

12. Joy, W. et. al. 4.2 BSD System Manual. Draft Report, Department of Electrical Engineering and Computer Science, University of California, Berkeley (Sept. 1982).

13. O'Dell, M.D. The CSS programmer's network semantic model. Internal Report, Lawrence Berkeley Laboratory (Nov. 1982).

14. Postel, J. DoD Standard Internet Protocol. RFC 760, IEN 128, USC Information Sciences Institute (Jan. 1980).

15. Postel, J. DoD Standard Transmission Control Protocol. RFC 761, IEN 128, USC Information Sciences Institute (Jan. 1980).

16. Rosenthal, D.S.H. Managing graphical resources. *Comput. Gr. 17*, 1 (Jan. 1983), 38-45.

17. van den Bos, J. Definition and use of higher-level graphics input tools. *Comput. Gr.* (Proc. Siggraph '78) *12*, 3 (Aug. 1978), 38-42.

18. Wallace, V.L. The semantics of graphics input devices. *Comput. Gr. 10*, 1 (Spring 1976).

19. Yen, A., Holmes, H., and Wood, P. Moving interactive thematic mapping from mainframe to mini: some design possibilities and development experience. *Proc. International Symposium on Computer-Assisted Cartography* (AUTO-CARTO IV), Vol. II (1979), 379-389.

20. Yen, A.C. DI/DD Interface Proposal. Internal Report, Lawrence Berkeley Laboratory (Nov. 1980).

A Core Graphics Environment for Teletext Simulations

Douglas F. Dixon

RCA Laboratories
Princeton, NJ 08540

ABSTRACT

The development of our graphics environment over the past year has been directed towards demonstrating the concept of broadcast teletext service, where pages of graphics and text are received in the home over existing television channels. We have developed a graphics editor, Radix, which uses an underlying Core graphics package to create teletext-compatible images. Radix is also used to display these images at arbitrary resolutions by scaling the graphics primitives, selecting the corresponding sizes of fonts and bitmaps, and then precisely adjusting the output video signal. The combination of powerful display hardware and a robust set of software tools has allowed us to rapidly prototype potential teletext features, and to provide these accurate simulations of teletext pages at any resolution. While this general graphics environment does impose some inefficiencies in running graphics applications, they are far outweighed by the ability to quickly respond to changing requirements.

CR Categories and Subject Descriptors: D.2.2 [**Software Engineering**]: Tools and Techniques; I.3 [**Computer Graphics**]: I.3.1 [**CG**] Hardware Architecture – *raster display devices*; I.3.4 [**CG**] Graphics Utilities – *graphics packages*, *picture description languages*, *software support*; I.3.6 [**CG**] Methodology and Techniques – *device independence*; I.7.2 [**Text Processing**] Document Preparation;

General Terms: Design, Experimentation, Standardization

Additional Key Words and Phrases: teletext, rapid prototyping, graphics editors, picture files, fonts, software tools, television compatibility, resolution independence

1. Introduction

Our involvement with teletext vividly demonstrates the need for a simulation system in developing and refining a new product concept. In our case, a VAX host computer, Ikonas graphics display hardware, and supporting software tools are all being used to simulate the features that soon could be built into home television sets. With this extremely flexible graphics environment, we have been able to quickly experiment with new features in response to technical questions, and to package demonstrations that have been used to promote the teletext concept to company management, standards organizations, other groups interested in the teletext market, and the press.

We have been able to exploit the speed and flexibility of our hardware environment by implementing new graphics commands in software on the VAX, and relying on the Ikonas microcode to draw them quickly. With this approach, we have been able to rapidly prototype new features such as proportional fonts and complex fill styles within a matter of days, instead of making the commitment to develop and maintain new microcode routines for each function.

Our graphics software environment begins with our Radix graphics editor, which allows the creation, editing, and display of pictures using teletext primitives, and also provides complete control over the characteristics of the resulting television image. Radix communicates with the Ikonas and other output devices through a Core graphics package from Brown University which not only provides the expected segmentation, input, and graphics translation functions, but also was explicitly designed to be re-configurable for experimentation.

This paper describes the technical issues and decisions that we have addressed in developing a graphics environment directed toward the simulation of proposed teletext features. It begins with a brief overview of the history and development of videotex and teletext. The following sections then provide a general overview of the capabilities of our hardware and software environment by discussing our approach in terms of specific problems raised by the teletext requirements. These issues include the display of arbitrary-resolution pages on a full television screen, supporting both Core and the teletext standard in our Radix editor, the selection and scaling of fonts and bitmaps for a desired resolution, and the rapid prototyping of new features in our system.

2. The Development of Videotex and Teletext

The development of videotex and teletext systems which transmit text and graphics to be viewed on home television sets has been a world-wide effort, with much work done in Europe, Canada, and Japan since the early 1970s, followed by more recent developments in the United States [14]. The idea of providing a video magazine to consumers stressing timely features such as news updates, weather reports, and consumer features is quite attractive to both broadcasters and advertizers. The user of such a system can browse at will, simply by calling up the index page, and then directly requesting a page containing an interesting news item, or stepping through consecutive pages of sports scores.

2.1. Videotex and Teletext

Videotex service provides for two-way communications, so that a user request is forwarded over a telephone line or cable system to the service provider, who then retrieves the information and transmits it back to the user. In contrast, one-way teletext service piggybacks on the existing television channels by transmitting digital information in the vertical blanking interval (the time between successive updates of the screen which is currently used in the United States to provide captioning for the deaf). Only a limited number of pages are therefore available, transmitted in a round-robin cycle. After requesting a page, the user must wait until it is next broadcast, so that it can be received, decoded, and displayed by the teletext decoder.

The method of transmitting pages, however, is independent of the standard used to describe and encode the image. The first systems developed by the English and French format a page simply as a fixed grid of rows and columns of characters, where only patterns of these alphamosaic characters are available for creating an image. While this approach requires only a simple decoder, the resulting images have a coarse and blocky appearance due to the low effective graphics resolution, as well as the additional limitation that only two colors can be used in each character cell. In Figure 1, the mosaic United States weather map clearly shows distinct horizontal and vertical edges at character boundaries, and also demonstrates the difficulties of creating small graphics symbols with these mosaic characters.

2.2. North American PLPS

The Canadians then developed a new display protocol in conjunction with a more complex decoder which can execute instructions to draw graphics primitives into a bitmap. Recently, both mosaic characters and graphics primitives have been incorporated into the Presentation Level Protocol Syntax (PLPS), which is now being standardized in North America [3]. The advantages of PLPS over mosaics include the improved quality of the graphics and bitmaps, as shown by the PLPS weather map in Figure 2, and also the promise of continued compatibility over a wide range of resolutions as graphics technology becomes less expensive.

RCA Laboratories has been involved with teletext in several areas. We have developed prototype decoders to experiment with the transmission and decoding of the PLPS. We also have been involved in refining the general PLPS standard and developing minimum requirements for teletext use [4]. However, a fixed product prototype and paper studies are not flexible enough to quickly answer technical questions, or to provide continued support for demonstrating a product concept under changing assumptions. The flexible design of our hardware and software graphics environment was the answer for meeting this continuing need.

3. Resolution Control Using The Ikonas Hardware

Our graphics hardware environment, as shown in Figure 3, is well suited to our requirements for rapid and accurate prototyping of teletext features. The DEC VAX 11/780 and the Ikonas RDS-3000 are both powerful machines, so that we are usually not limited by speed or space constraints. Although we do have to be sensitive to the needs of the other timesharing users on our host VAX, it does provide the large resources such as virtual memory and disk space necessary for processing graphics data, especially fonts and bitmaps.

The Ikonas display processor [9] has a general bus-oriented design, with software control over the configuration of each module, including the ability to define the precise characteristics of the output video signal. We therefore are able to draw an image into the bitmap at any resolution, and then adjust the image so that it fills the entire screen. We can then choose to view the image on an RGB monitor, or, since the signal is NTSC-compatible, view it on a baseband television monitor or antenna-attached television set.

We display pages at arbitrary resolutions by first instructing the Core package to scale the graphics into a viewport of the proper x and y pixel size in the bottom left corner of the Ikonas display memory. Then, we not only zoom the display to approximately the correct size, but we also adjust the Ikonas window and viewport registers so that only the desired pixels are displayed on the screen. Finally, we position the image on a particular monitor with the appropriate safe time (the active image time within each horizontal line) by adjusting the pixel clock to compress the image and add more black space on both sides. As a result, we can perform fair and accurate comparisons of the same page at different resolutions, with each image filling the entire area of the display screen. For example, the image in Figure 4 was created by displaying the weather map page at six different resolutions, capturing them in bitmap files, and then composing them into a single 512 x 512 bitmap. Notice the variations in aspect ratio and font sizes that are necessary to produce final images of the same size once the Ikonas is adjusted for these resolutions.

The result of this effort has been the ability to not only examine the effect of different resolutions on sample pages, but also to study the effect of resolution changes on proposed features of the teletext standard. For example, we have been able to make recommendations for minimum resolutions to be considered for an initial product, acceptable line and fill styles, and the size and length of text lines under various safe time constraints.

4. Core and PLPS Support in the Radix Editor

A graphics development environment requires not only a general graphics package, but also a format for defining pictures and a means for editing and displaying them. The user's view of our graphics system is focused on our Radix graphics editor, which provides all the high-level functions required for both editing and displaying pictures, using the underlying Core graphics model [8]. Figure 5 is a general block diagram of the major software components of our graphics environment, showing the data flow from using Radix to edit a picture file, through the Core package, and then to the display on the Ikonas system. Because of our software tool approach, most of our application programs do not call Core directly, but instead direct their output through Radix in order to use its higher-level capabilities. In fact, our most-used demonstrations are simply command files which prompt the terminal and then generate commands for Radix.

4.1. The SGP Core Graphics Package

Our graphics software is based on the SGP (Simple Graphics Package) Core graphics system from Brown University [13], which is described in Foley and van Dam's book [7]. Actually, SGP is simply the subroutine-call interface used by the applications programmer, while the major portion of the work is done by the COGS (Configurable Graphics System) back-end. COGS is the pipeline of Core graphics functions which clips primitives to the current window, maps them to the viewport on the output device, stores them in user-named segments, and finally displays them using device-specific drivers.

SGP / COGS, like most of our software, is written in the C language and runs under the Eunice implementation of Unix†, running with VMS on our VAX. While SGP is currently a relatively simple 2D Core package, it was designed from the start to be easily configurable and modifiable, and has never prevented us from implementing new primitives and definitions demanded by the PLPS.

4.2. The Radix Graphics Editor

The Radix graphics editor was developed at RCA Laboratories to create, modify, and display pictures composed of teletext graphics primitives and attributes. It uses a traditional menu-oriented user interface, along the lines of the picture layout system described in [6], with editing operations specified by using a stylus and data tablet to indicate data points and select entries from a tree-structured menu. However, Radix was designed from the start explicitly for designing teletext pages, so it provides the user with a complete set of PLPS-like instructions for page creation, and then translates them into calls to the SGP Core package. Figure 6 shows Radix being used to edit the weather map page, with the menu of PLPS primitives visible, and Figure 7 is a verification page, showing the range of PLPS primitives and attributes that Radix supports.

We have found little problem in mapping between PLPS concepts and Core instructions. Although Radix is designed as a vehicle for simulations, and not as a production teletext system like the AT&T Frame Creation Terminal [1], we also provide a separate translator from Radix format to PLPS binary instructions, which are formatted and optimized for broadcast transmission.

Radix also includes a display mode that turns off the menu and reformats the picture so that it exactly fills the entire screen. This allows a page to be edited with the menu at a standard resolution, and then previewed with the menu off at arbitrary resolutions and with precise control over the characteristics of the television image. All the images in this paper were displayed using Radix, either in editing mode with the menu on, or in display mode with the menu off.

† Unix is a trademark of Bell Laboratories.

4.3. Picture Files in Text Format

We have designed Radix to use an ASCII text format for picture files. Each primitive is entered as a text string, containing the command name as listed in the menus followed by its numeric or text parameters. For example, the picture file text for the verification page is shown in Figure 8. While this decision does impose some overhead in parsing and formatting picture files, it does have major benefits. The picture files are immediately accessible: they can be directly edited with a screen editor, and there is no need for a conversion program to print them out for debugging purposes. There are also many cases where a desirable but uncommon transformation can be easily applied to a picture file with a text editor or trivial program which parses and formats text. This kind of structural change to the components of an image is almost unthinkable with hand-editing of its visual representation.

In concert with the Unix software tools philosophy [11], this text format is also quite convenient for building individual tools to manipulate the picture files. For example, we have implemented the converter from Radix text format to PLPS binary, a text-processor front-end modelled on Nroff [12], an optimizer to remove redundant or unused definition statements, and tools to perform various graphics transformations on a picture, including perspective rotation in 3D [2].

Under Unix, we can also interactively pipeline the output from one program to the text input for Radix. For example, one demonstration runs a program to poll an infrared remote receiver and pipes its output to Radix. When a key on the wireless remote is pressed, the program outputs page display commands which then are passed directly to Radix and immediately executed.

In addition, we have converted the Dial animation language from Brown [5] to generate Radix commands from animation scripts. Again, although this imposes additional overhead when previewing the animation, it also allows us to use the full capabilities of Radix to specify and display the animated sequences, and also to convert the output directly into PLPS instructions. Since our Ikonas driver is capable of capturing the generated Ikonas binary instructions in a file, we can package and run official demonstrations with no visible delay, even on the timeshared VAX.

5. Variable-Resolution Font and Bitmap Support

In order to display an image at an arbitrary resolution, it is not enough just to scale the graphics primitives, but the text strings and bitmaps must be adjusted to the correct size as well. Text on teletext pages is typically laid out in a grid of twenty rows of forty characters each. When displaying pages at different resolutions, Radix is therefore capable of selecting the appropriate font size and correctly positioning the text in relation to the graphics primitives. Since the Ikonas hardware and microcode directly support character generation with user-defined fonts stored in the Ikonas memory, we have been able to build a catalog of fonts in the necessary sizes for the commonly-demonstrated teletext resolutions.

5.1. Scaling of Text and Bitmaps

Radix provides two levels of support for positioning text in relation to graphics primitives. First, it implements a text "gravity" mode which forces each character of each text string to the correct grid location for the current text format by generating individual draw instructions for each character. This is different from the more usual graphics gravity mode, which forces the points of each primitive (including the starting point of a text string) to the corners of a user-specified overlay grid.

Second, since text gravity still does not resolve the problem of scaling the text to the current resolution, Radix allows the user to either select a specific font by name, or to choose a generic font name and rely on Radix to select the closest available size of that font from our font data base to match the current text format and resolution. This produces a much more accurate result than attempting to algorithmically zoom and scale characters on the fly.

We also support bitmap drawings defined as large special characters in the teletext Dynamically Redefinable Character Set (DRCS). These are implemented as single-character Ikonas fonts and also are directly supported by Radix, which again selects the closest available DRCS font for the current resolution from the DRCS data base. Figures 9 and 10 show a sample sports page displayed at both a reasonable resolution for initial teletext service (256 x 210), and double that size to near NTSC television resolution (512 x 480). Radix not only has scaled the graphics primitives into the proper bitmap for each resolution, but also has chosen the closest available font size for both the lines of text and the two DRCS baseball team logos.

5.2. Font Files and Tools

Again following the software tools approach, we also use an ASCII text format for our font files, and have implemented several font tools to convert from existing sources of fonts to this text format, and then to the Ikonas binary format. This text representation, as shown in Figure 11, allows us to use the standard text editor to create and edit fonts, and to perform major changes like shifting all the characters in a font. We have also developed tools to algorithmically scale fonts so that new sizes can be created with a minimum of hand-editing. As a result, we have quickly developed a catalog of over a hundred fonts and DRCS characters.

Our philosophy of using software tools permitted us to add support for proportional fonts with only two days of work. First, the font conversion tools were changed to add width information for each character, and generate a variable-width binary file for the Ikonas driver containing offset and width information for each individual character. The VAX driver then was modified to use the existing Ikonas microcode for fixed-size characters to position each individual character of a text line into its correct place in the display. As a result, proportional fonts are now available directly from application programs simply by specifying the appropriate font name. For example, Figure 12 shows the sports page with the fixed-width font converted to variable-width, and Figure 13 shows the higher-resolution page with a different font designed explicitly for proportional spacing.

6. The Rapid Prototyping Approach

Well-defined graphics applications such as aircraft cockpit simulations typically require implementing special functions in microcode in order to achieve real-time performance. However, in our case, the speed and generality of our graphics environment gives us the freedom to experiment by implementing experimental features in the driver running on the VAX, without suffering a major degradation in the speed at which our pages are displayed.

The Ikonas Display Language (IDL) microcoded interpreter [10], gives us much more flexibility in implementing new features than would be provided by the instruction set of a more traditional graphics processor. For example, we have implemented an arbitrary-length delay by generating an IDL loop-repeat construct that contains a wait-for-next-frame instruction.

Using this approach, we have studied possible polygon fill patterns by implementing fill algorithms in the VAX driver. This not only allows rapid changes to the built-in fill styles, but also to the interaction of fill with the other polygon attributes. We therefore generate and download a long list of horizontal vector instructions for each filled polygon. In some cases, the Ikonas microcode still can process and draw these vector lists at a speed indistinguishable from the solid polygon fill microcode. Eventually, we will be able to define a general-purpose polygon fill microcode routine to satisfy all our needs, including arbitrary repeating fill patterns for filled, outlined, and highlighted polygons with different foreground, background, and highlight colors.

The usefulness of this host-based approach was again reinforced when we were asked to simulate the effects of viewing pages when they are generated at different drawing rates. First, we slowed down the Ikonas microcode by generating wait instructions between each graphics instruction. Then, for even more accuracy in simulating drawing speed, we inserted additional waits before the generation of each individual character and before each line of a complex polygon fill. This was possible because the driver already contained explicit code for these functions in order to support proportional fonts and fill patterns. The other alternative would have been to modify the actual Ikonas microcode routines to parameterize them with a slowdown feature.

While this approach does involve a performance penalty from generating extra instructions (which also fill up the output buffer sooner) and the longer drawing time (especially for complex fills), each of these new features was designed, implemented, and refined within a matter of days. As we become more certain of their importance, we can then consider migrating them into microcode.

7. Conclusion

Our continuing success in satisfying new demands to simulate possible teletext features is due to the power and flexibility of our hardware and software environment, and also to our decision to develop a robust set of integrated and modifiable graphics tools. The Radix editor uses a less efficient but much more accessible text format for its picture files, which allows us to routinely manipulate Radix commands from the text editor or pipelined programs for unanticipated but valuable purposes. By implementing new features in the VAX driver software we again lose efficiency in comparison to writing new Ikonas microcode, but gain the ability to design and implement major improvements with a turnaround of only a few days. Of course, for polished demonstrations we still can capture an entire sequence of sample pages in their generated Ikonas binary format, and replay them at a rate limited only by the drawing speed of the Ikonas microcode.

Our most visible result, however, is the ability to display the same picture file at widely varying resolutions, with no visible difference in the size of the image on the screen. This involves not only adjusting the parameters of the Ikonas hardware to produce a television-compatible video signal with the correct timing, but also scaling the graphics, fonts, and bitmaps in the image by selecting the closest available font size for the current text format and image resolution. While this ability to adjust resolution on demand will remain an important part of our capability, it is actually the general foundations of our design which will allow our graphics environment to continue to evolve towards new capabilities in the future.

Acknowledgements

Scott Marshall designed and developed the Radix editor, and, as our indispensable local expert in television and graphics hardware, made variable-resolution television-compatible images possible. Mike Keith developed the initial demonstration pages, and continues to be our major artistic influence. David Ripley developed the initial font tools, and helped to plan and guide this project.

References

1. AT&T Corp. Frame Creation Terminal. Product literature, 1982.

2. Dixon, D. F., Keith, M., Marshall, S. A., and Ripley, G. D. Graphics Programmer's Manual. RCA Laboratories, April 1983.

3. Draft Proposed American National Standard. Videotex/Teletext Presentation Level Protocol Syntax (North American PLPS). October 1982.

4. EIA Draft Proposal. A General Service Reference Model for Teletext. October 1982.

5. Feiner, S., Salesin, D., and Banchoff, T. Dial: A Diagrammatic Animation Language. *IEEE Computer Graphics and Applications 2*, 7 (September 1982), 43-54.

6. Feiner, S., Nagy, S., and van Dam, A. An experimental system for creating and presenting interactive graphical documents. *ACM Transactions on Graphics Systems 1*, 1 (January 1982), 59-77.

7. Foley, J. D., and van Dam, A. *Fundamentals of Interactive Computer Graphics*. Addison-Wesley, 1982.

8. GSPC. Status report of the Graphics Standards Planning Committee. *Computer Graphics 13*, 3 (August 1979).

9. Ikonas Graphics Systems. Ikonas RDS-3000 User's Guide. April 1982.

10. Ikonas Graphics Systems. IDL Reference Manual. May 1982.

11. Kernighan, B. W., and Plauger, P. J. *Software Tools*. Addison-Wesley, 1976.

12. Ossanna, J. F., Nroff/Troff User's Manual Computer Science Technical Report 54. Bell Laboratories, April 1977.

13. Pato, J. N., and Nanian, D. B. Simple Graphics Package Users Guide Version SGP2v1. Brown University, September 1982.

14. Truxal, C. Americanizing videotex. *IEEE Spectrum 19*, 11 (November 1982), 52-56.

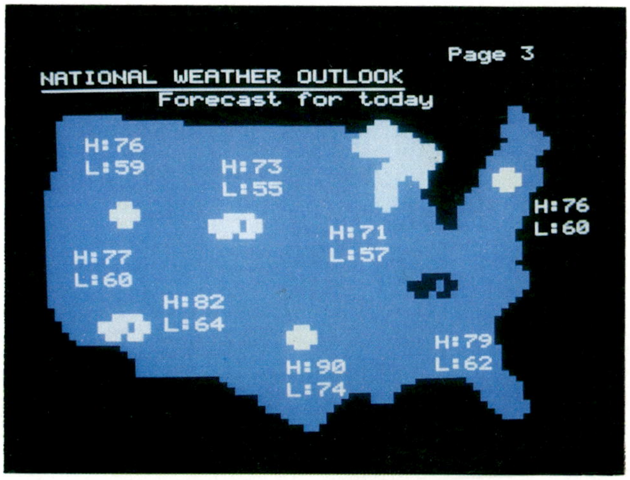

Fig. 1. Weather map page using mosaic characters at 240 x 240 resolution

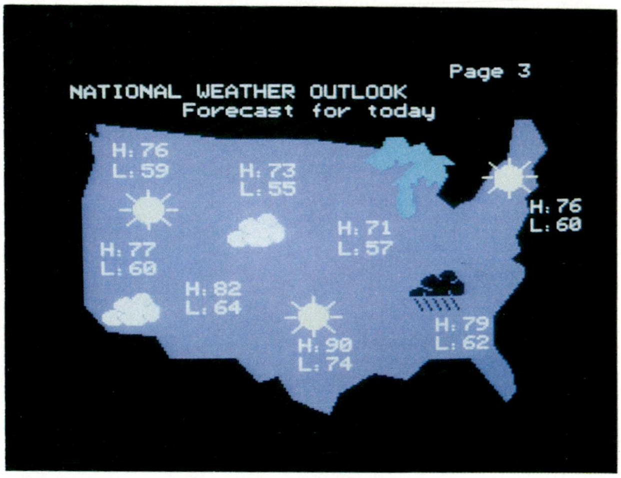

Fig. 2. Weather map page using PLPS geometrics at 240 x 210 resolution

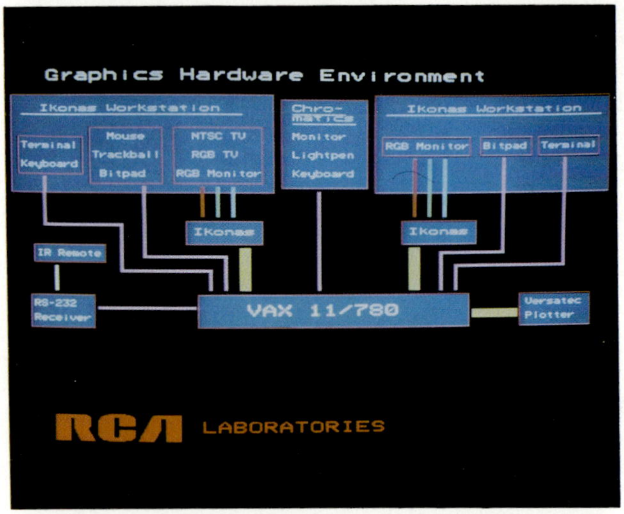

Fig. 3. Diagram of our graphics hardware environment

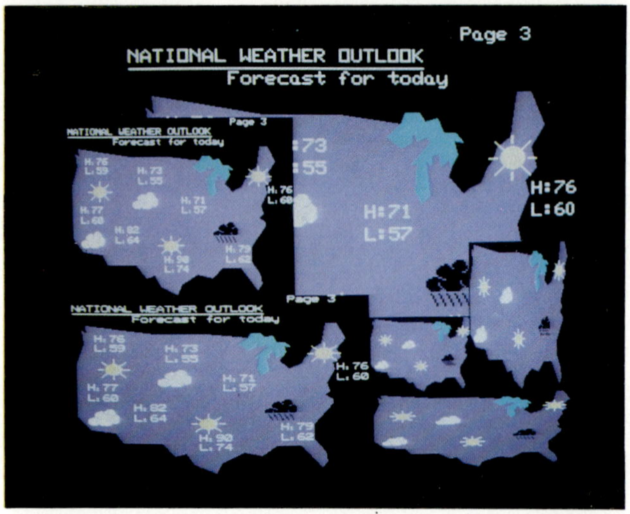

Fig. 4. Six resolutions of weather pages composed onto a 512 x 512 bitmap

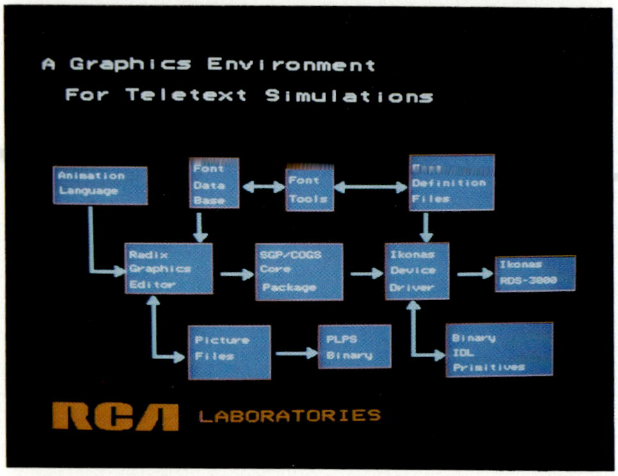

Fig. 5. Diagram of our graphics software environment

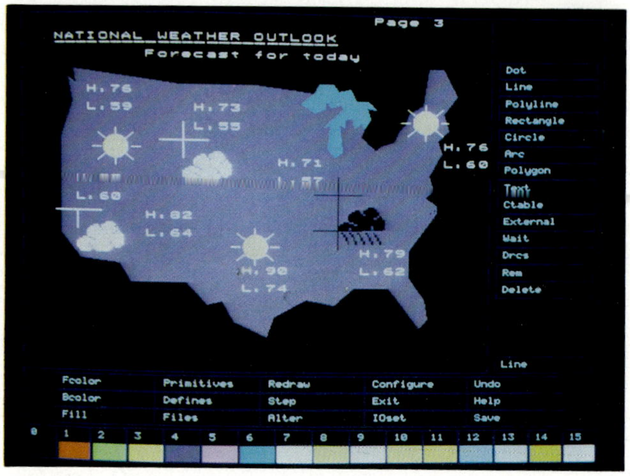

Fig. 6. Editing the weather map page using the Radix menu of PLPS primitives

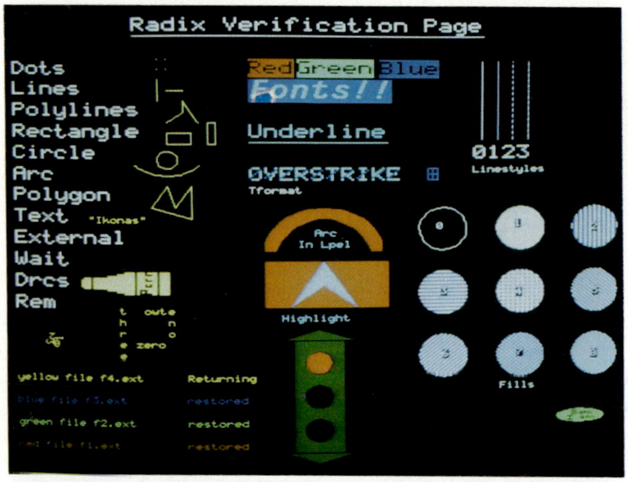

Fig. 7. The Radix verification page, showing PLPS primitives and attributes

```
Font H19
Underline 1
Text 0.250000 1.000000 "Radix Verification Page"
Underline 0
Text 0.000000 0.904762 "Dots"
Text 0.000000 0.857143 "Lines"
Text 0.000000 0.809524 "Polylines"
Text 0.000000 0.761905 "Rectangle"
Text 0.000000 0.714286 "Circle"
Text 0.000000 0.666667 "Arc"
Text 0.000000 0.619048 "Polygon"
Text 0.000000 0.571429 "Text"
Text 0.000000 0.523810 "External"
Text 0.000000 0.476190 "Wait"
Text 0.000000 0.428571 "Drcs"
Text 0.000000 0.380952 "Rem"
Fcolor 4
Dot 0.296875 0.904762
Dot 0.312500 0.904762
Dot 0.312500 0.880952
Dot 0.296875 0.880952
Line 0.296875 0.857143 0.296875 0.809524
Line 0.312500 0.833333 0.343750 0.833333
Polyline 0.312500 0.761905 0.343750 0.785714 0.343750 0.809524
0.375000 0.761905
Rectangle 0.312500 0.714286 0.359375 0.738095
Rectangle 0.390625 0.761905 0.406250 0.714286
Circle 0.296875 0.690476 0.328125 0.666667
Arc 0.250000 0.666667 0.312500 0.642857 0.375000 0.666667
Polygon 0.281250 0.571429 0.281250 0.571429 0.281250 0.571429
0.312500 0.619048 0.328125 0.571429 0.359375 0.619048 0.359375 0.547619
Tformat 80 40
Font H19
Text 0.155944 0.553653 """Ikonas"""
Tformat 40 21
External [sam.pic]f1.ext
Wait 1
Drcs 0.140625 0.428571 BOTTLE
Rem "this is a remark"
Tformat 80 40
Text 0.078125 0.275000 "0"
Charrot 1
Text 0.078125 0.275000 "1"
```

Fig. 8. The Radix picture file for the verification page

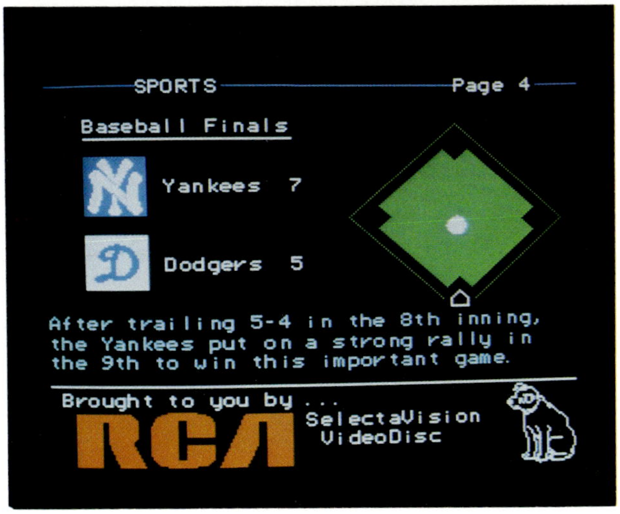

Fig. 9. Sports page at 256 x 210 resolution

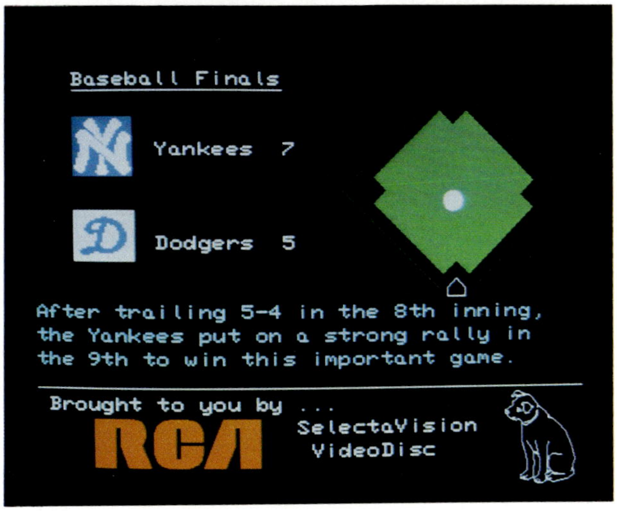

Fig. 10. Sports page at 512 x 480 resolution

```
.font ny  width 3Ø  height 32
.
.
.char ny  addr 1
.
         oo         oo
        oooo       oooo
       ooooo       ooooo
       oooooo     oooooo
        ooooo     ooooo
         ooooo   ooooo
     ooo  oooo   oooo
    ooooo  ooo   oooo    oo
   ooooooo  ooo oooo    oooo
   oooooooo ooo oooo    ooooo
    oooooooo oooooo    oooooo
    ooooooooo ooooo    oooooo
    oooooooooo ooo     ooooo
     oooooooooo oo     oooo
     oooo ooooooo     ooooo
     oooo  oooooo     ooooo
     oooo   oooooo    ooooo
     oooo    oooooo   ooooo
    ooooo      ooooo  ooooo
    ooooo     o oooooooooo
    ooooo     oo ooooooooo
   oooooo     oo  oooooooooo
   ooooo      oo  oooooooo
   ooooo      oo   oooooooo
   ooooo      oo    ooooooo
  ooooo      oooo     oooooo
  ooooo      oooo     ooooooo
   oooo      oooo      oooooo
    oo      oooooo      oooo
             oooo        oo
```

Fig. 11. Text format font file for a baseball logo

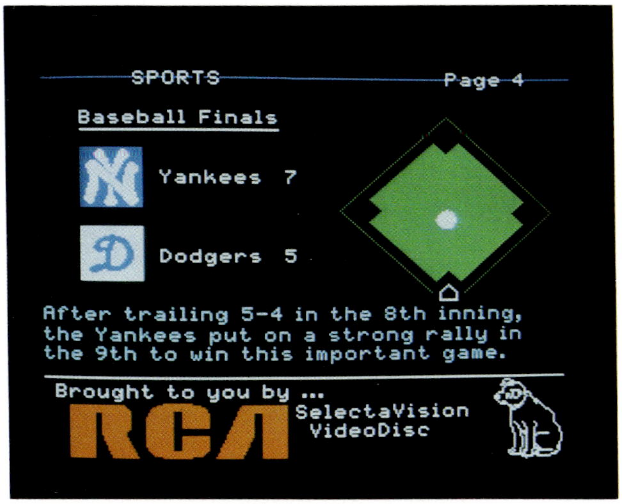

Fig. 12. Sports page with proportional font at 256 x 210 resolution

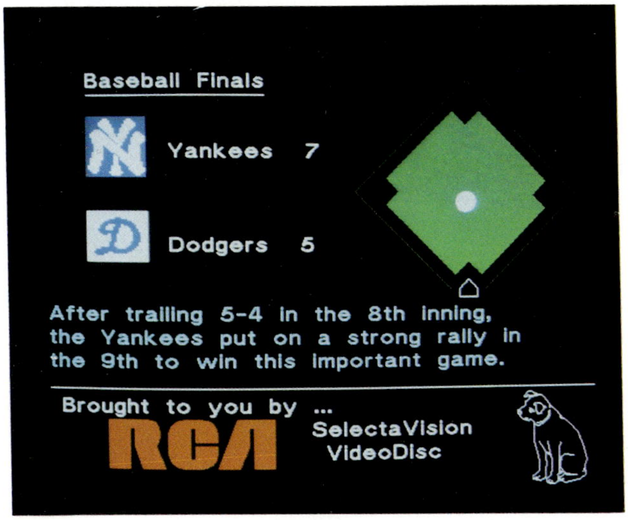

Fig. 13. Sports page with proportional font at 512 x 480 resolution

Minimal GKS

Randall W. Simons

Sandia National Laboratories
Albuquerque, New Mexico 87185

Abstract: Minimal GKS is a subset of the Draft International Standard Graphical Kernel System. Minimal GKS has been implemented at Sandia in the programming language C. This implementation confirms that Minimal GKS does indeed have the anticipated advantages of easy implementation and small size. Experience in using this implementation has also demonstrated that Minimal GKS is easy to learn and use, yet is powerful enough for non-trivial, real-world applications.

CR Categories and Subject Descriptors: I.3.4 [Computer Graphics]: Graphics Utilities - Graphics packages; I.3.6 [Computer Graphics]: Methodology and Techniques - Device Independence

General Terms: Design, Standardization

Additional Keywords and Phrases: Graphical Kernel System, Virtual Device Interface, ANSI X3H3

1. What Is Minimal GKS?

Early versions of GKS were developed in West Germany by DIN, the German National Standards body. The International Standards Organization working group on Computer Graphics (ISO/TC97/SC5/WG2) to which DIN, ANSI, and other national standards bodies send representatives, modified GKS to its present version [5], and made it a Draft International Standard. The Computer Graphics committee of the American National Standards Institute (ANSI X3H3) is considering making GKS an American National Standard. These two versions of GKS will hereafter be referred to as ISO GKS and ANSI GKS, respectively.

Among other changes, ANSI X3H3 is considering adding another output level to GKS before adopting it as an American National Standard. ISO GKS includes a level structure which defines three input levels and three output levels, such that one can choose any input level and any output level and combine the functions in each to define a valid level of GKS. The output level which ANSI X3H3 may add is a subset of what is currently the smallest level in ISO GKS.

This new lowest output level, when combined with input level "a" (which contains no functions), is what I will call Minimal GKS. The determination of which functions would be included in Minimal GKS is the result of the work of an ANSI X3H3 subcommittee called X3H35: Programmer's Minimal Interface to Graphics, or PMIG, plus inputs from the entire ANSI X3H3 committee. The goals for the set of functions developed by the PMIG subcommittee included easy implementation, learning, and use, implementation by small and efficient code, and sufficient power to support a wide range of 2-D passive graphics applications [1]. The functions selected are listed in appendix 1. Issues, alternatives, and arguments discussed by the PMIG subcommittee when selecting these functions and reviewed by the full ANSI X3H3 committee are recorded in [2].

2. The C Language Binding

GKS is defined independent of any particular programming language, so it is necessary to bind the abstract functions and data types of GKS to actual functions and data types in the language to be used for implementation. This was done for the programming language C by Rosenthal and ten Hagen [6].

C presents some problems for the language binder, primarily because there is no standard for C that defines precisely what is in and what is out of the language. Sandia's C compiler apparently differs from the one used by Rosenthal and ten Hagen in the following ways. It does not support the enumerated data type, which Rosenthal and ten Hagen used to bind some of the GKS abstract data types. It requires function names to be unique in the first six characters, but two of the names chosen by Rosenthal and ten Hagen (close_gks and close_ws) were not. Both of these problems were easy to fix. One can use integer data type instead of enumeration, and define constants with integer values so the GKS programmer can use the same nice names he would have had with an enumerated data type. This fix is even portable between the two systems, if you don't mind ignoring warnings about mismatched data types. A solution to the other problem is to change the names (clos_gks, clos_ws), but this unfortunately makes the programs not portable between the two implementations.

There is another problem with C in that it relies heavily on "standard" libraries and UNIX* system utilities for such functions as I/O, character string handling, math functions, and dynamic memory management. It is not always clear which of these capabilities one should expect to find in every C implementation, since they are not part of the compiler, but part of the compiler's operating environment. For example, the operating environment for Sandia's C compiler does not include dynamic memory management, yet this was a feature used by Rosenthal and ten Hagen. This can affect the C binding because one of the parameters to open gks is the size of a memory block given to GKS for use by its memory manager. This parameter, and more importantly, the memory it represents, are meaningless in a context without dynamic memory management. It was

*UNIX is a Trademark of Bell Laboratories.

decided for portability's sake to leave the parameter in and just ignore it. The absence of dynamic memory management is no problem for Minimal GKS, as we shall see later.

A final problem with the C binding did not surface until using Minimal GKS with a large application program. By defining data types for every parameter to every function in Minimal GKS, the C binding requires a calling program to use large amounts of symbol table space to store these defined data types. If the calling application program also requires large amounts of symbol table space for its own purposes, this can lead to symbol table overflow at compilation time. One solution is to not define all these data types in the calling program, but simply use the basic data types of C. In this case the lint processor will complain about mismatched data types, but the program will execute properly. This problem is of course entirely dependent on the symbol table space available to the compiler and the application program's use of that space, so in some environments the problem may never arise.

3. The Sandia Implementation

Sandia National Laboratories needed a graphics package to support real-time display of data. Since a Sperry Univac V77 minicomputer had already been designated as the host, memory space and speed of execution were serious considerations. It was anticipated that the graphics terminals used for display would be replaced in the near future, to take advantage of emerging technology, so device independence was required. A careful analysis of the data display requirements showed that Minimal GKS had all the functions required for this application.

A Digital Equipment Corporation PDP 11/44 running UNIX was used for developing this Minimal GKS implementation. Once development on UNIX was complete, the software was ported to the target Univac V77.

4. Size of Minimal GKS vs. Other Levels

The ISO GKS document is 285 pages long. We hoped that Minimal GKS would allow us to ignore the majority of those pages, and we were not disappointed. The entire sections on segment functions, input functions, metafile functions, and utility functions are not needed by Minimal GKS.

Full GKS, i.e., the highest input and output levels combined, includes 110 functions plus 75 inquiry functions. Even the lowest level of ISO GKS requires 52 functions plus 38 inquiry functions. Minimal GKS uses only 31 of these functions plus 17 inquiry functions (listed in appendix 1).

The data structures required by Minimal GKS are also significantly smaller than those defined for full GKS in the ISO GKS document. The segment state lists and input queue disappear completely. What Minimal GKS requires for a GKS state list, workstation state list, and workstation description table are given in appendix 2. The length of these lists is about 23%, 15%, and 14% respectively of the length of the corresponding lists in the ISO GKS document.

The list of errors that can be generated by Minimal GKS (appendix 3) is about 35% as long as that of full GKS.

5. Other Decisions Affecting Size

The number of simultaneously open workstations and the number of normalization transformations are constants that have to be chosen for each GKS implementation, regardless of level. Choosing the minimum in either case can result in a smaller, simpler implementation.

Supporting only one open workstation at a time can affect an implementation in many ways. The loops that check whether a specified workstation is open or active degenerate to a single if test. Likewise, the loops that send commands across the virtual device interface (see below) to each active workstation are no longer needed. Arrays or linked lists of open and active workstations become single variables. Device dependent code doesn't have to be made reentrant, and no mechanism is needed to switch this code from one physical device to another except at the time a workstation is opened.

Despite all these advantages of a single workstation implementation, the requirements of our application were the overriding factor. In this application, the same picture must often be presented simultaneously to several operators at different workstations. Therefore, the Sandia Minimal GKS implementation includes multiple simultaneous workstation capabilities. This is much more efficient than sequentially opening different workstations and redrawing the picture multiple times.

GKS requires a minimum of two normalization transformations, one of which is the unity transformation and can't be changed. By supporting only this minimum, only a single settable transformation needs to be saved. Explaining to the programmer becomes easier, too. He has the simple choice of using NDC coordinates (transformation 0), or setting up his own arbitrary world coordinates (transformation 1).

The Sandia Minimal GKS implementation allows the number of normalization transformations to be selected at compilation time. Currently, we have no need for more than transformations 0 and 1 mentioned above, but can easily add more later if that requirement should arise.

6. The Virtual Device Interface (VDI)

6.1 Functional Level of the VDI

Placing the virtual device interface is one of the most important decisions for any device independent graphics package. The VDI is the interface between device independent code and device dependent code. If the interface is placed too high, i.e., includes much powerful functionality, then device drivers for simple devices will be large and difficult to write (for example, see Figure 1). On the other hand, if the interface is placed too low, device drivers will not be able to take advantage of all the capabilities of more intelligent devices (for example, see Figure 2). This tradeoff must be resolved in the context of how the graphics package will be used and for what devices [3].

The following guidelines were considered desirable in Sandia's environment. First, all device dependencies must be below the VDI, i.e., code above the VDI should operate identically for all devices. This rules out GKS device independent code inquiring device capabilities and determining what to do from the answers it gets. Second, everything below the VDI should be capable of migrating naturally into a (hypothetical)

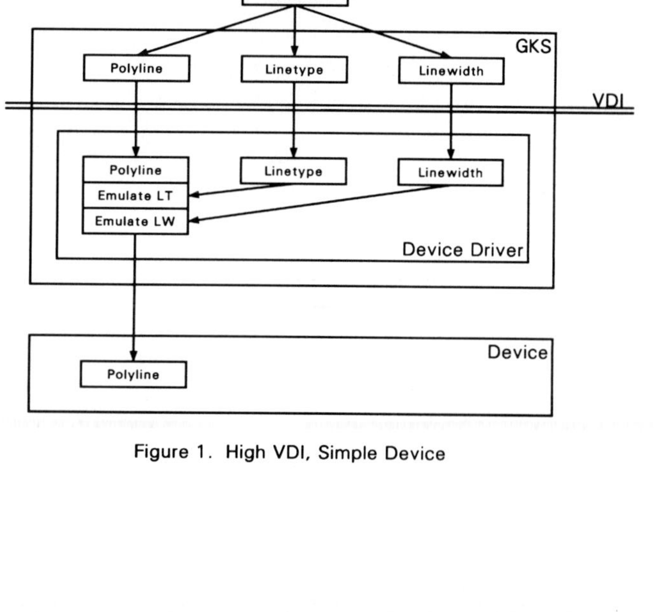

Figure 1. High VDI, Simple Device

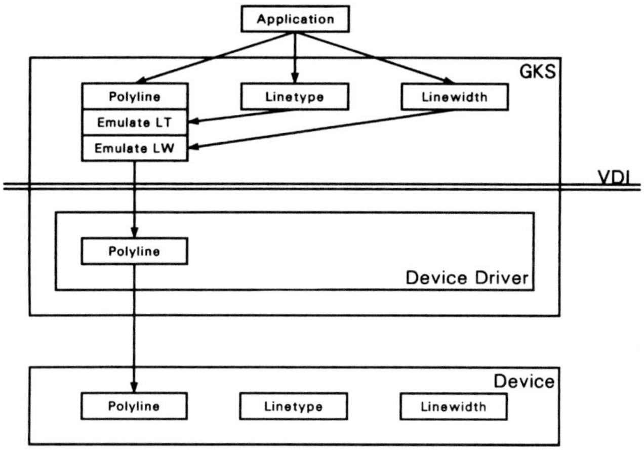

Figure 2. Low VDI, Intelligent Device

intelligent device. This means, for example, that you don't want to pass a workstation identifier across the VDI, because if there is a physical device immediately below that VDI, it certainly doesn't need to be told which workstation it is. Making the workstation identifier an external variable is preferable, so it will be available for code shared by different devices, but can be ignored by any physical device that takes VDI commands directly.

The structure of GKS suggests a natural place for the VDI, namely the workstation interface. Adopting this strategy, each device driver is responsible for maintaining its own workstation state table and performing all workstation dependent functions. The device independent portion of GKS above the VDI which is shared by all devices, performs all workstation independent functions, and passes on all workstation dependent functions through the VDI to the device drivers. These functions and their parameters are listed in appendix 4, using the C language type definitions from [6].

This approach has several advantages. It is not necessary to introduce a new concept into GKS to describe the VDI, since the VDI can simply be thought of as the interface to the workstations. By making each workstation responsible for its own workstation state table, we can treat each workstation as a data abstraction which hides the internal details of its data structures, and is accessible only through a well-defined set of operations — the VDI functions. The use of such data abstractions is a valuable technique for managing complex software while improving its reliability and maintainability [4].

This decision also impacts the method used for selecting the devices to which you output. Each workstation description table includes a list of pointers to VDI functions to be called to access the device corresponding to that workstation. Thus invoking a function in a particular device is done by referencing the workstation description table. This isolates the knowledge of device dependent function names to the workstation description table. Unlike some other schemes where the device independent code needs to know the appropriate function names for each of the devices it could output to, this method requires no changes to the device independent code to add a new device driver.

6.2 Subroutine Interface vs. Data Interface

There are two popular methods of implementing a VDI, as a subroutine interface or a data interface. In a subroutine interface, a separate subroutine is provided for each VDI function. These functions are invoked by calling the subroutine and passing the data required by the function as the subroutine parameters (Figure 3). A data interface, on the other hand, has only one subroutine as the entry point for VDI functions. Functions are invoked by encoding the function and its required data in a standard format and passing the whole package to the single subroutine which then decodes the package and performs the specified function (Figure 4).

The encoding and decoding overhead of the data interface are clearly worthwhile in certain cases. If the functions and data have to be encoded anyway to be stored in a segment, stored in a metafile, or sent to an intelligent device, then the same encoding might be used by the VDI. But Minimal GKS does not support segments or metafiles, and it's unlikely that all devices supported by an implementation would have sufficient intelligence to emulate the workstation interface. A subroutine interface implementation of the VDI seems preferable for use by Minimal GKS.

The ability to support multiple simultaneous workstations is sometimes cited as a benefit of a data interface. But a subroutine interface can also provide this capability, and do so elegantly if function pointers are available as in C. By using the function pointers in the workstation description table as discussed above, there is no problem routing control to the proper subroutines for each workstation.

7. Implementation Differences Between Minimal GKS and Full GKS

There are a number of implementation issues that may best be resolved differently for Minimal GKS and full GKS.

7.1 Dynamic Storage Allocation

In full GKS there are certain requirements for storage that can theoretically grow without bounds. Every time you open a new workstation, a new workstation state list is needed. Also, every new segment defined requires a segment state list and storage for the segment. If the environment in which GKS is running supports dynamic storage allocation, it works well to

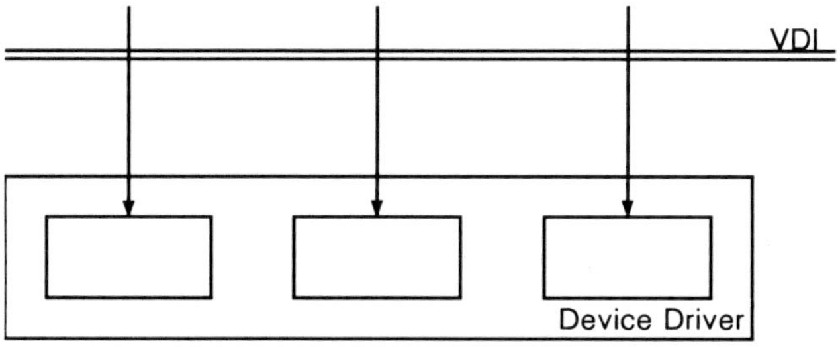

Figure 3. Subroutine Interface

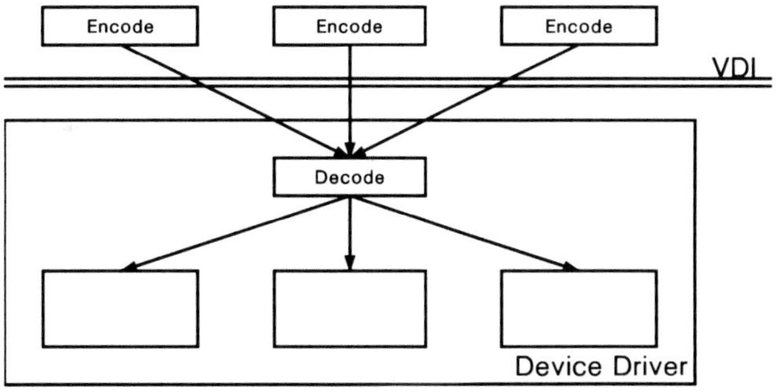

Figure 4. Data Interface

allocate and free these required storage areas as they are needed. But if no dynamic storage allocation is supported, all one can do is reserve a big block of memory at load time and write your own allocation utilities. This doesn't work so well because it ties up a lot of memory which in some cases won't be needed, and in other cases won't be enough.

These problems disappear when implementing Minimal GKS supporting only one workstation at a time. Only one workstation state list is needed, and since Minimal GKS doesn't support segments, no storage is required for them either.

7.2 Attribute Setting

ISO GKS states that geometric primitive attributes are expressed and stored (in the GKS state list) in world coordinates, and are subject to the same transformations as the primitives to which they are bound. A straightforward way of implementing this is to transform an attribute value each time it is actually used, i.e., when an output primitive affected by that attribute is invoked. However, many devices are capable of storing attribute values in device coordinates, so one might prefer to transform an attribute only once when it is first set, and let the device remember what its value is each time an output primitive uses it. In implementing this second solution, one must remember to transform attributes again whenever the normalization transformation or a workstation transformation changes, or a new workstation is activated. A variant of this second approach is to set a flag in each attribute, transformation, and activate workstation function, and check this flag in each output primitive function to determine if attributes need to be transformed again.

A number of interrelated factors affect this decision, including single vs. multiple simultaneous workstations, single vs. multiple settable normalization transformations, and device capabilities. But the most important consideration is application-dependent and requires that one know the relative frequencies of invocation of attribute, transformation, activate workstation, and output primitive functions. For the first solution, it is the output primitive functions that require the costly transformation, while in the second solution it is the attribute, transformation, and activate workstation functions that incur the cost.

Because Minimal GKS supports fewer attributes than full GKS, one might expect fewer attribute function invocations, so the second solution is relatively more attractive for Minimal GKS than full GKS.

7.3 Emulation of Unsupported Functions

In any device independent graphics package with a reasonably high-level VDI, it will be necessary to emulate certain functions for devices that don't support those functions directly. When emulation is required, at least two approaches are possible. The emulation can be done below the VDI by each device driver (see Figure 1). Alternatively, the device independent code can inquire whether the VDI supports a given function and if not, perform the emulation itself, above the VDI. In the first case, emulation code will be loaded for every workstation that needs it (unless it can be implemented as shared reentrant code), but not for workstations that don't need it. With the second solution, the emulation will be loaded only once, but it is loaded even when it is not needed. When you consider that one possible emulation might be software character generation, you realize the size of this code may be significant.

In a Minimal GKS implementation where only one workstation is allowed at a time, there is no need for sharing emulation code. Since one of the expected advantages of Minimal GKS is small load size, we should choose emulation below the VDI so that devices that don't need the emulation aren't forced to load it anyway.

7.4 Clipping and Transformations

GKS defines two clipping boundaries: the viewport of the normalization transformation, and the workstation window. Instead of actually clipping twice, it will usually be more efficient to compute the intersection of the areas enclosed by these two boundaries and clip only once. This has to be done below the VDI, since the second clipping boundary is workstation dependent. This behavior is practically required by ISO GKS, since clipping must be delayed until after primitives are extracted from segments and are to be displayed.

One might think efficiency could be gained in a similar way by combining the normalization transformation and the workstation transformation. But full GKS supports segments and segments require storage of primitives in NDCs. A full GKS implementation needs to keep the two transformations separate so it can still get at the NDC values for storage in segments. Not so with Minimal GKS, since there are no segments. This optimization is worth considering for Minimal GKS if speed is important, but it does effectively redefine the placement of the VDI. Coordinates passed to the VDI have been raised from the NDC level to the world coordinate level.

8. Performance Results

The Sandia implementation of Minimal GKS, including a Tektronix 4014* VDI driver, took less than three man-months of effort to design, code, test, and debug on the UNIX system. This effort borrowed from several available resources [3, 5, 6]. All of these are available to the public, and any would-be implementor starting the same task tomorrow could probably use them and this paper to generate the same product in the same amount of time.

Conversion from the UNIX system to the Univac V77 took about one man-month of debugging and learning how to rewrite code so it was portable between the two systems. The finished product was very satisfactory in that exactly the same source code is used for both the UNIX and V77 versions. Based on personal past experience with other VDI implementations, this portability seems to be a major advantage of C over FORTRAN.

The size of the implementation as measured in lines of code (excluding comments) and bytes of object code (stripped of symbol table) are given below for each class of GKS function:

Table 1 - Code Size

		lines	bytes
GKS	typedefs	62	-
	control	200	1730
	output	106	878
	attributes	166	1166
	transforms	150	1290
	inquiry	21	219
	errors	29	238
VDI	typedefs	243	-
	control	115	1534
	output	156	2004
	attributes	77	786
	transforms	60	688
	inquiry	52	458
	clipping	118	1158
TOTAL		1555	12148

*Tektronix is a registered trademark of Tektronix, Inc.

This implementation of Minimal GKS is small enough to fit in the limited memory available on the V77 minicomputer while leaving adequate room for the application programs which use Minimal GKS. We have not yet checked the speed of this implementation which must eventually run in a multiprogrammed environment and display data as it is received in real time. However, the small size and simplicity of the code encourage us to believe it will be fast.

Measuring the usefulness of the functionality of any package, including Minimal GKS, is not easy to do. The fact that Minimal GKS proved completely adequate for the data display requirements of this project proves that the functionality, small as it is, provides enough power for some real-world applications. We have built a simple plot package on top of Minimal GKS which provides single-call plot commands, linear and logarithmic axis commands, control over tick marks, tick mark labels, and axis labels, and plots data with or without markers and connecting lines. No omissions or errors in the functionality of Minimal GKS were uncovered while building this plot package.

So far, four people without any previous experience with GKS have learned to use Minimal GKS, each coding and debugging their first display in about four to eight hours, depending on display complexity. The biggest problem encountered in learning Minimal GKS was understanding when different coordinate systems applied. The fact that character height was specified in world coordinates and thus changed when the normalization transformation changed seemed counterintuitive in this plotting application.

The use of Minimal GKS has not influenced the nature of the displays produced, since the display formats were all defined long before Minimal GKS was chosen for this project. Since the new displays using Minimal GKS are replacing displays coded directly in Tektronix 4014 control codes, the biggest immediate effects are ease of programming and device independence. Expected long term effects include the easy conversion to more diverse, powerful, and modern graphics devices. While Minimal GKS contains all the functions currently needed, one of its advantages is the possibility of future expansion to higher levels to take advantage of more powerful devices.

Acknowledgments

The concept of a minimal graphics package and its functional design came out of the ANSI X3H35 subcommittee on the Programmer's Minimal Interface to Graphics. I would especially like to acknowledge the contributions of my fellow members of longest standing in that group, Tom Wright, David Straayer, Elaine Sonderegger, and Fred Canfield. I would also like to thank Tom Clarkson, Ted Reed, Hal Short, and Peter Watterberg for insightful discussions of Virtual Device Interfaces and implementation issues. Finally, my thanks to David Rosenthal and Paul ten Hagen for sharing with me their work on the C binding and a C implementation of full GKS.

References

1. ANSI. "Proposal for an ANSI X3 Standards Project for the Programmer's Minimal Interface to Graphics", ANSI Doc. X3H3/81-87 (December 1981).
2. ANSI. "X3H35 Issues", ANSI Doc. X3H3/83-11 (February 1983).
3. Erickson, K. M. and Simons, R. W. "Functional Specification of the Sandia Virtual Device Interface (SVDI)", SAND81-1900, Sandia National Laboratories, Albuquerque, NM (February 1982).
4. Isner, J. F. "A Fortran Programming Methodology Based on Data Abstraction", *Comm. Assoc. Comput. Mach.* Vol. 25(10), pp.686-697 (October 1982).
5. ISO. "Graphical Kernel System (GKS) - Functional Description", Draft International Standard ISO/DIS 7942 (November 1982).
6. Rosenthal, D. S. H., and ten Hagen, P. J. W. "GKS in C", *Proceedings of EUROGRAPHICS '82* pp.359-369 (September 1982).

Appendix 1 -- Minimal GKS Functions

ACTIVATE WORKSTATION
CLEAR WORKSTATION
CLOSE GKS
CLOSE WORKSTATION
DEACTIVATE WORKSTATION
ERROR HANDLING
ESCAPE
FILL AREA
INQUIRE CLIPPING INDICATOR
INQUIRE COLOUR FACILITIES
INQUIRE COLOUR REPRESENTATION
INQUIRE CURRENT INDIVIDUAL ATTRIBUTE VALUES
INQUIRE CURRENT NORMALIZATION TRANSFORMATION NUMBER
INQUIRE CURRENT PRIMITIVE ATTRIBUTES VALUES
INQUIRE FILL AREA FACILITIES
INQUIRE LEVEL OF GKS
INQUIRE LIST OF COLOUR INDICES
INQUIRE MAXIMUM DISPLAY SURFACE SIZE
INQUIRE NORMALIZATION TRANSFORMATION
INQUIRE POLYLINE FACILITIES
INQUIRE POLYMARKER FACILITIES
INQUIRE TEXT EXTENT
INQUIRE TEXT FACILITIES
INQUIRE WORKSTATION CONNECTION AND TYPE
INQUIRE WORKSTATION TRANSFORMATION
OPEN GKS
OPEN WORKSTATION
POLYLINE
POLYMARKER
SELECT NORMALIZATION TRANSFORMATION
SET CHARACTER HEIGHT
SET CHARACTER UP VECTOR
SET CLIPPING INDICATOR
SET COLOUR REPRESENTATION
SET FILL AREA COLOUR INDEX
SET FILL AREA INTERIOR STYLE
SET LINETYPE
SET MARKER TYPE
SET POLYLINE COLOUR INDEX
SET POLYMARKER COLOUR INDEX
SET TEXT ALIGNMENT
SET TEXT COLOUR INDEX
SET VIEWPORT
SET WINDOW
SET WORKSTATION VIEWPORT
SET WORKSTATION WINDOW
TEXT
UPDATE WORKSTATION

Appendix 2 -- Minimal GKS State Lists and Description Tables

GKS State List

set of open workstations
set of active workstations
current normalization transformation number
list of transformation numbers ordered by viewport input priority (0 highest initially)
list of windows (in above order)
list of viewports (in above order)

clipping indicator
current linetype
current polyline colour index
current marker type
current polymarker colour index
current text colour index
current character height
current character up vector
current text alignment (horizontal and vertical)
current fill area interior style
current fill area colour index

Workstation State List

workstation identifier
connection identifier
workstation type
number of colour table entries
table of colour representations containing:
  colour index
  colour (red/green/blue intensities)
implicit regeneration mode
workstation transformation update state
display surface empty
requested workstation window
current workstation window
requested workstation viewport
current workstation viewport
new frame action necessary at update

Workstation Description Table

workstation type
device coordinate units
maximum display surface (visible area of the display surface)
  in length units
  in device units
raster or vector display
  (VECTOR = vector display, RASTER = raster device,
  OTHER = other device, eg vector+raster)
number of available linetypes
list of available linetypes
number of available character heights (if the workstation supports continuous character heights, the number will be zero)
list of available character heights (if the workstation supports continuous character heights, the minimum and maximum will be listed)
number of colours (if workstation supports a continuous range of colours, the number will be zero)
colour available
maximum number of colour indices
number of predefined colour indices (representations)
table of predefined colour representations,
  for every entry
    colour (red/green/blue intensities)
default value for:
  implicit regeneration mode
  colour representation
  workstation transformation

Appendix 3 -- Minimal GKS Error Messages

States

1 GKS not in proper state: GKS must be in the state GKCL
2 GKS not in proper state: GKS must be in the state GKOP
3 GKS not in proper state: GKS must be in the state WSAC
5 GKS not in proper state: GKS must be either in the state WSAC or in the state SGOP
6 GKS not in proper state: GKS must be either in the state WSOP or in the state WSAC
7 GKS not in proper state: GKS must be in one of the states WSOP, WSAC, or SGOP
8 GKS not in proper state: GKS must be in one of the states GKOP, WSOP, WSAC or SGOP

Workstations

20 Specified workstation identifier is invalid
21 Specified connection identifier is invalid
22 Specified workstation type is invalid
23 Specified workstation type does not exist
24 Specified workstation is open
25 Specified workstation is not open
26 Specified workstation cannot be opened
29 Specified workstation is active
30 Specified workstation is not active

Transformations

50 Transformation number is invalid
51 Rectangle definition is invalid
52 Viewport is not within the Normalized Device Coordinate unit square
53 Workstation window is not within the Normalized Device Coordinate unit square
54 Workstation viewport is not within the display space

Output Attributes

62 Linetype is less than or equal to zero
63 Specified linetype is not supported on this workstation
66 Marker type is less than or equal to zero
67 Specified marker type is not supported on this workstation
73 Character height is less than or equal to zero
74 Length of character up vector is zero
77 Specified fill area interior style is not supported on this workstation
85 Colour index is less than zero
86 Colour index is invalid
87 A representation for the specified colour index has not been defined on this workstation
88 Colour is outside range [0, 1]

Output Primitives

100 Number of points is invalid
101 Invalid code in string

Escape

180 Specified function is not supported
181 Contents of escape data record are invalid

Implementation Dependent

300 Specified function is not supported in this level of GKS
301 Storage overflow has occurred in GKS
309 Arithmetic error has occurred

Appendix 4 -- VDI Functions

```
Wss *              /* Returns pointer to workstation
                   state list.*/
dt1ope(dev, wsd)   /* OPEN WORKSTATION */
File *dev;         /* File for workstation (must be
                   open).*/
Wsd *wsd;          /* Workstation description table.*/

dt1clo()           /* CLOSE WORKSTATION */

dt1cle(cf)         /* CLEAR WORKSTATION */
Clearf cf;         /* Control flag.*/
```

```
dtlupd(rf)          /* UPDATE WORKSTATION */
Regenf rf;          /* Regeneration flag.*/

dtlesc(ef, ed)      /* ESCAPE */
Es func ef;         /* Function.*/
Es data *ed;        /* Data.*/

dtlpln(n, p)        /* POLYLINE */
Size n;             /* Number of points.*/
Nc *p;              /* Coordinates of points.*/

dtlpmk(n, p)        /* POLYMARKER */
Size n;             /* Number of points.*/
Nc *p;              /* Coordinates of points.*/

dtltxt(p, s)        /* TEXT */
Nc *p;              /* Text position.*/
String s;           /* Character string.*/

dtlfar(n,p)         /* FILL AREA */
Size n;             /* Number of points.*/
Nc *p;              /* Coordinates of points.*/

dtlltp(lt)          /* SET POLYLINE LINE TYPE */
Ltype lt;           /* Linetype.*/

dtllco(ci)          /* SET POLYLINE COLOUR
                    INDEX */
Cindex ci;          /* Colour index.*/

dtlmtp(mt)          /* SET POLYMARKER MARKER
                    TYPE */
Mtype mt;           /* Marker type.*/

dtlmco(ci)          /* SET POLYMARKER COLOUR
                    INDEX */
Cindex ci;          /* Colour index.*/

dtltco(ci)          /* SET TEXT COLOUR INDEX */
Cindex ci;          /* Colour index.*/

dtlcht(ht)          /* SET CHARACTER HEIGHT */
Charhtn ht;         /* Character height.*/

dtlcal(ha, va)      /* SET CHARACTER
                    ALIGNMENT */
Horal ha;           /* Horizontal alignment.*/
Veral va;           /* Vertical alignment.*/

dtlfis(is)          /* SET FILL AREA INTERIOR
                    STYLE */
Istyle is;          /* Interior style.*/

dtlfco(ci)          /* SET FILL AREA COLOUR
                    INDEX */
Cindex ci;          /* Colour index.*/

dtlcol(ci, col)     /* SET COLOUR
                    REPRESENTATION */
Cindex ci;          /* Colour index.*/
Colour *col;        /* Colour.*/

dtlclp(cl)          /* SET CLIPPING RECTANGLE
                    (from normalization xform).*/
Nrect *cl;          /* Clipping rectangle.*/

dtlcli(in)          /* SET CLIPPING INDICATOR */
Bool in;            /* Clipping indicator.*/

dtlwin(nr)          /* SET WORKSTATION
                    WINDOW */
Nrect *nr;          /* Workstation window limits.*/

dtlvie(dr)          /* SET WORKSTATION
                    VIEWPORT */
Drect *dr;          /* Workstation viewport limits.*/

dtlite(p, s, cat, tr)  /* INQUIRE TEXT EXTENT */
Nc *p;              /* Text position.*/
String s;           /* Character string.*/
Nc *cat;            /* Concatenation position.*/
Nrect *tr;          /* Text rectangle.*/
```

PANEL

JAPANESE COMPUTER GRAPHICS: CHALLENGES AND OPPORTUNITIES

PART I: COMPUTER GRAPHICS IN THE WORLD OF JAPANESE COMMERCIAL PRODUCTION FOR ART, ENTERTAINMENT AND ADVERTISING

CHAIR: Laurin Herr, Pacific Interface
PANELISTS: Akira Amano, freelance writer
Madoka Katou, Dentsu Inc.
Yoichiro Kawaguchi, Nippon Electronics College
Kouichi Omura, Osaka University

CHAIRMAN'S INTRODUCTION

In a country as media-saturated as Japan, where the preservation of traditional social and aesthetic forms has been balanced over the past 120 years by a relentless quest for new ideas, fashions and techniques, computer graphics has found favor because of its novelty, expressive power and futuristic look. It fits nicely with the high-tech products and corporate images of many of Japan's largest advertisers. It is consistent with the national movement to enthusiastically embrace the "information age". And, it seems to offer significant productivity gains in several areas of commercial production. Finally, computer graphics has been the subject of extraordinary scrutiny simply because it is widely perceived in Japan to be the image-making system of the future. The past eighteen months have witnessed the beginning of a computer graphics boom within the world of Japanese commercial production and media. There have been many reports in books, magazines, newspapers and on television. Computer graphics conferences and events have been organized. The large advertising agencies have begun to show wide- ranging interest in the field. And several new computer graphics production companies have established facilities in Tokyo. This panel will introduce developments in the Japanese computer graphics world that could have impact on the international commercial production industry. The panelists were selected to represent a wide range of viewpoints: agency producer, industry observer, artist/educator and engineer. The audience will be encouraged to ask questions.

Laurin Herr graduated from Cornell University in 1972 with a B.A. degree in Government. He is currently the Director of Pacific Interface, a private New York-based firm founded in 1980 which specializes in computer graphics and Japanese/American interaction. His first trip to Japan was in 1973 and he has returned many times, both to continue his studies of the language and culture and to work as an interpreter/coordinator on a variety of international projects. Mr. Herr became involved in computer graphics in 1979 when he was international staff liaison for the production of the "Mind of the Universe Electro-Opera". He has authored a comprehensive report on "Siggraph'81 and trends in the Computer Graphics Industry" for a Japanese client, co-authored a six-part series of articles about computer graphics published in the Japanese magazine ASCII and produced the American segments of several lengthy Japanese television reports about the field. Most recently, he has served as the North American Coordinator for the Micrograph'82 Conference and as the Program Coordinator for the Intergraphics'83 Conference, both held in Tokyo. He currently resides in Tokyo where he serves as Siggraph's volunteer representative in Japan.

Madoka Katou will speak about common problems that often arise in Japanese/ American computer graphics productions, the possible uses of computer graphics at the 1985 Science and Technology Exposition planned for Tsukuba, and trends in Japanese commercial production. He will also show a short selection of Japanese commercial spots utilizing computer graphics and computer graphics look-alike techniques. Mr. Katou graduated from the Art Department of Nippon University in 1967 and entered the Dentsu advertising agency as a designer the same year. He became a commercial film planner/coordinator in 1970 and has worked on commercial production projects for many of the largest advertisers in Japan, including Hitachi, Matsushita Electric, Toyota, Coca Cola, Fujitsu and House Foods. His current interests are in the production of visuals for pavillions at the Tsukuba Expo'85 and other large-scale events.

Akira Amano will report on computer graphics production facilities in Japan, emphasizing current developments and future trends in the areas of hardware utilization, visual effect/software tools creation, and human resources. Mr. Amano graduated from the Art Department of Nippon University in 1966 with a major in Broadcasting. After working in television and publishing, he became a freelance writer in 1980 and currently commutes between Tokyo and New York. He frequently contributes articles about communications and high-technology to Japanese magazines and has served as the Editor-in-Chief of Business Video Magazine. In 1982, he wrote and edited The Leading Edge of Computer Graphics: CG'82 a large format four-color book.

Yoichiro Kawaguchi will explore the role of the artist in computer graphics and the education of computer graphics artists in Japan. He will also show new works utilizing his "Growth Algorithm" first introduced at Siggraph'82. Mr. Kawaguchi graduated from the Kyushu College of Industrial Design in 1976 with a major in Visual Design. He received his MFA from the Tokyo Education College (now Tsukuba University) in 1978 and is currently an Assistant Professor of Computer Graphics in the Department of Art of the privately-run Nippon Electronics College in Tokyo. He is a member of the Japan Graphics Designers Association (JAGDA) and has shown his computer graphics art work widely, both in Japan and overseas.

Kouichi Omura will report on the hardware architecture, software concepts and performance of the LINKS-1, a parallel pipelined multi-microcomputer system for image creation that he developed with a team of researchers at Osaka University. He will also discuss his theories of visual production, outline his involvement with parallel processing system for graphics applications and show sample output from the LINKS-1 system. Dr. Omura graduated from Osaka University in 1960 with a major in Electrical Engineering. He received his doctorate in 1968 for research in the field of Very High Speed Logic Circuit Elements and became an Associate Professor of Electrical Engineering in the Department of Engineering at Osaka University in 1973. His current interests include multi-computer applications and robotics.

Local Control of Bias and Tension in Beta-splines

BRIAN A. BARSKY
University of California, Berkeley
and
JOHN C. BEATTY
University of Waterloo, Canada

The Beta-spline introduced recently by Barsky is a generalization of the uniform cubic B-spline: parametric discontinuities are introduced in such a way as to preserve continuity of the unit tangent and curvature vectors at joints (*geometric continuity*) while providing bias and tension parameters, independent of the position of control vertices, by which the shape of a curve or surface can be manipulated. Using a restricted form of quintic Hermite interpolation, it is possible to allow distinct bias and tension parameters at each joint without destroying geometric continuity. This provides a new means of obtaining local control of bias and tension in piecewise polynomial curves and surfaces.

Categories and Subject Descriptors: I.3.5 [**Computer Graphics**]: Computational Geometry and Object Modeling—*Curve and surface representation*

General Terms: Algorithms

Additional Key Words and Phrases: Beta-splines, computer-aided design, geometric continuity, polynomial splines, tension

1. INTRODUCTION

Early work by Coons [13, 14] and Bézier [8, 9] introduced the use of nonlinear parametric polynomial representations for the *segments* and *patches* which are stitched together to form *piecewise* curves and surfaces, establishing their viability. More recently, Riesenfeld [17, 22] has advocated the use of B-splines to represent such polynomials on the grounds of greater flexibility and efficiency.

Parametric B-splines have many advantages. Among them is the ability to control the degree of continuity at the joints between adjacent curve segments, and at the borders between surface patches, independent of the order of the

This work was supported by funds from the U.S. National Science Foundation under grant ECS-82-04381, the Defense Advanced Research Projects Agency of the United States under contract N00039-82-C-0235, the Natural Sciences and Engineering Research Council of Canada under grants A3022 and G0651, and the National Research Council of Canada under contract 05SU.31155-1-3103.

Authors' addresses: B. A. Barsky, Berkeley Computer Graphics Laboratory, Computer Science Division, University of Calif., Berkeley, CA 94720; J. C. Beatty, Computer Graphics Laboratory, Department of Computer Science, University of Waterloo, Waterloo, Ontario, Canada N2L 3G1.

Reprinted From **acm Transactions On Graphics**—April 1983—Vol. 2, No. 2

segments or the number of control vertices. However, in [1] it is shown that the notion of parametric first- or second-degree continuity at joints does not always correspond to intuition or to a physically desired effect. For piecewise cubic curves and bicubic surfaces these parametric continuity constraints can be replaced by the more meaningful requirements of continuous unit tangent and curvature vectors. Doing so introduces certain constrained discontinuities in the first and second parametric derivatives. These are expressed in terms of *bias* and *tension* parameters, called $\beta 1$ and $\beta 2$ in [1], which give rise to *Beta-spline* curves and surfaces.

The application of tension to the cubic interpolatory spline was first analytically modeled in [23]. An alternative development was given in [12] and generalized in [21]. A detailed derivation of the generalized form based on a variational principle is given in [2]. The result of this approach is a spline curve which is no longer piecewise *polynomial*, but piecewise *exponential*; that is, each curve segment is expressed in terms of exponential functions.

From a computational standpoint, however, polynomial functions are much more desirable than exponentials. For this reason Nielson developed the Nu-spline, a polynomial alternative to the exponential spline under tension [19, 20]. It is derived in detail in [2] from the cubic Hermite basis functions, thereby emphasizing its relation to the conventional cubic interpolatory spline.

Unfortunately, neither of the above-mentioned interpolating spline curve representations provides *local control*, that is, the capability of modifying one portion of the curve without altering the remainder. Local control is inherent in the B-spline formulation [3, 22], suggesting that it is a natural representation from which to develop a means of applying tension locally. Lane experimented with this idea by adding knots to a nonuniform B-spline curve in the region of desired tension [18].

The Beta-spline is a new curve and surface representation having an inherent capability for modeling tension and containing the uniform cubic B-spline as a special case. This representation generalizes previous work on the mathematical modeling of tension insofar as it is based on the *shape parameters* $\beta 1$ and $\beta 2$.

The basic theory of Beta-splines is developed in [1] and [4]. This theory is expressed in terms of shape parameters which can be either uniform or varying throughout the curve or surface being defined. For the purposes of computer-aided geometric design, the ability to alter shape parameters is particularly useful because it provides an additional means of manipulating a curve or surface. In this paper we extend previous work on varying shape parameters.

We begin in Section 2 with a review of pertinent terminology, notation, and definitions. (A more leisurely presentation of this material may be found in [6].) In Section 3 we review the fundamental definition of a Beta-spline from [1] and [4]. This leads naturally to a discussion of how to vary the β parameters in a Beta-spline curve, and an analysis of the basic properties of the curves and surfaces which result.

2. PRELIMINARIES

The curves in which we are interested are *piecewise cubic polynomials* $\mathbf{Q}(u) = (X(u), Y(u))$ of the parameter $u \in [u_0, u_m]$. The values $u_0 < u_1 < \cdots < u_m$ of u

Reprinted From **acm Transactions On Graphics**—April 1983—Vol. 2, No. 2

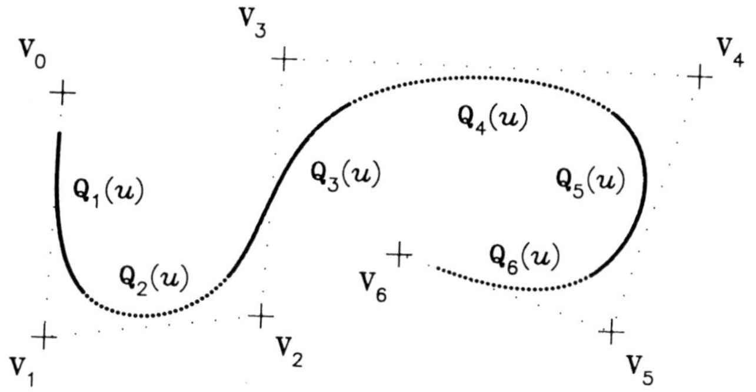

Fig. 1. An example of a curve defined by a sequence of *control vertices*, represented here by "+" signs, near which the curve passes. The lightly dotted line connecting the control vertices forms the *control polygon*, and indicates the order in which the control vertices are to be approximated. The solid and heavily dotted curves represent distinct curve *segments*. Each is a pure parametric cubic.

corresponding to the *joints* between successive polynomial *segments* are called *knots*. The segment generated as u runs from u_{i-1} to u_i is the ith segment $\mathbf{Q}_i(u)$. We will always assume that the knots are a consecutive sequence of integers, often with $u_i = i$; this is called a *uniform knot sequence*. Usually the piecewise polynomials $X(u)$ and $Y(u)$ are required to satisfy some continuity constraints at the joints between successive segments; if the 0th through dth derivatives $X(u)$, $X^{(1)}(u), \ldots, X^{(d)}(u)$ are everywhere continuous (in particular, at the joints), then X and Y are said to be C^d continuous. Also, it is usually simpler when formulating equations for the ith segment to write $X(u - u_{i-1})$ rather than $X(u)$, and we generally do so; the reparametrization is easily accomplished by substitution.

There are a variety of ways to actually define a specific curve. We are concerned with techniques in which the user provides a number of *control vertices*, near which the curve is to pass (see Figure 1). Moving the control vertices then alters the curve. Such curves can be constructed in the following way. Let us denote the control vertices by $\mathbf{V}_i = (x_i, y_i)$. Generically, one writes

$$X(u) = \sum_i x_i B_i(u) \qquad \text{and} \qquad Y(u) = \sum_i y_i B_i(u) \tag{1}$$

so that $Y(u)$, for example, is a weighted sum of the *basis functions* $B_i(u)$, as in Figure 2. In vector notation this becomes

$$\mathbf{Q}(u) = \sum_i \mathbf{V}_i B_i(u) = \sum_i (x_i B_i(u), y_i B_i(u)). \tag{2}$$

One chooses to work with some class of basis functions because of particular properties it possesses or imparts to the curves it can be used to define.

For example, when manipulating a curve it is often desirable that the position of each control vertex affect only a limited portion of the curve. Such *local control* makes it possible to change one part of a curve without altering other portions of the curve whose design is already satisfactory. To obtain local control,

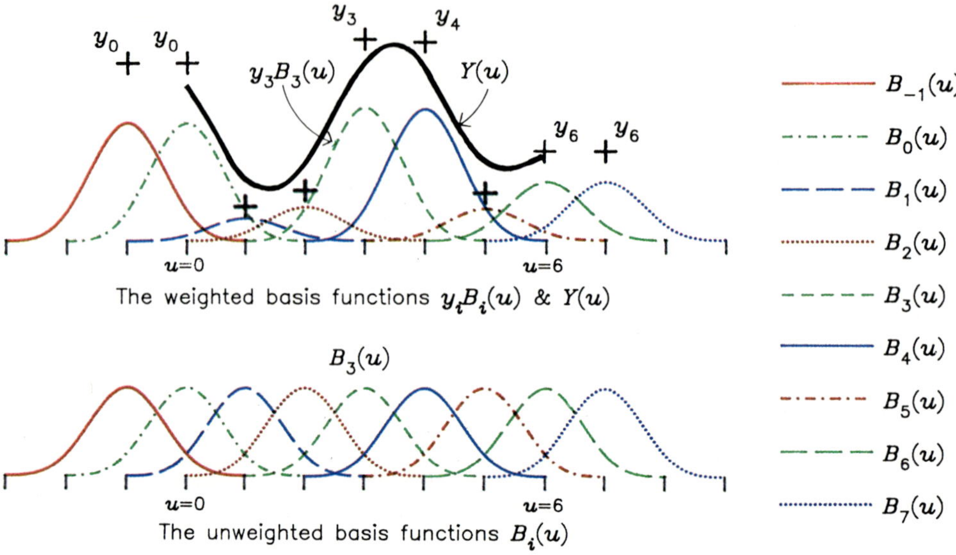

Fig. 2. The y component of the curve in Figure 1 as a weighted sum of basis functions. For reasons explained in Section 4.5, y_0 and y_6 appear twice.

it is sufficient if each $B_i(u)$ is nonzero only for a small range of u. This is the case for the basis functions appearing in Figure 2, which define the *uniform cubic B-spline curves.* These curves, of which the Beta-splines are a generalization, are assembled from cubic polynomials having positional, first-derivative, and second-derivative continuity at joints, so that they satisfy the equations

$$\mathbf{Q}_{i-1}(u_i) = \mathbf{Q}_i(u_i) \tag{3}$$

$$\mathbf{Q}_{i-1}^{(1)}(u_i) = \mathbf{Q}_i^{(1)}(u_i) \tag{4}$$

$$\mathbf{Q}_{i-1}^{(2)}(u_i) = \mathbf{Q}_i^{(2)}(u_i). \tag{5}$$

Using (1), $\mathbf{Q}(u)$ is defined as a weighted sum of identically shaped C^2 continuous piecewise cubic basis functions having knots at the u_i, since a weighted sum of such basis functions will also be a C^2 continuous piecewise cubic polynomial. Locality is obtained since each basis function is nonzero on only four successive intervals (see Figure 3). In particular, the *basis segments* $b_1(u)$, $b_0(u)$, $b_{-1}(u)$, and $b_{-2}(u)$ in Figure 3 are defined by

$$\begin{aligned} b_1(u) &= \tfrac{1}{6}u^3 \\ b_0(u) &= \tfrac{1}{6}(1 + 3u + 3u^2 - 3u^3) \\ b_{-1}(u) &= \tfrac{1}{6}(4 - 6u^2 + 3u^3) \\ b_{-2}(u) &= \tfrac{1}{6}(1 - 3u + 3u^2 - u^3) \end{aligned} \tag{6}$$

and the entire basis function is nonzero only over the four intervals adjacent to its center. For simplicity each of the basis segments is individually parametrized so that $u = 0$ corresponds to its left endpoint and $u = 1$ to its right endpoint.

Reprinted From **acm Transactions On Graphics**—April 1983—Vol. 2, No. 2

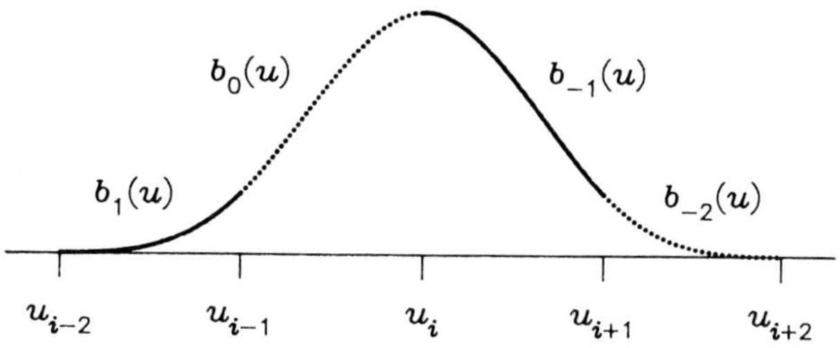

Fig. 3. The uniform cubic B-spline basis function $B_i(u)$ centered at u_i. It is zero for $u \le u_{i-2}$ and for $u \ge u_{i+2}$.

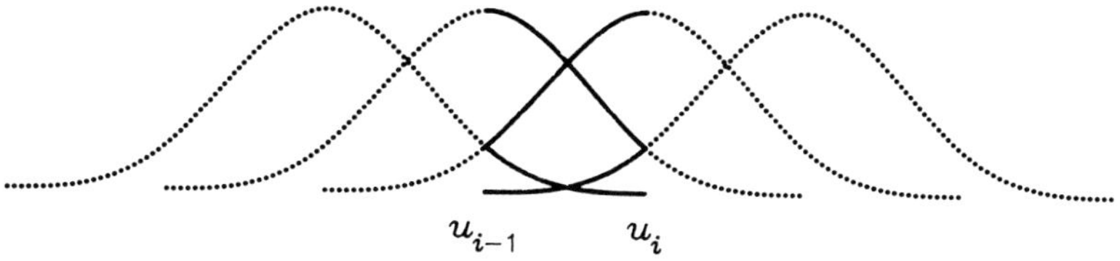

Fig. 4. The four uniform cubic B-spline basis functions which are nonzero on the interval $[u_{i-1}, u_i)$

All the B-spline basis functions are identical in shape; $B_i(u)$, however, is translated so as to be centered over u_i.[1] Because each $B_i(u)$ is nonzero on only four successive intervals (see Figure 4), if $u_{i-1} \le u < u_i$ then we may write (2) as

$$\begin{aligned} \mathbf{Q}_i(u) &= \sum_{r=-2}^{r=+1} \mathbf{V}_{i+r} B_{i+r}(u) \\ &= \mathbf{V}_{i-2} B_{i-2}(u) + \mathbf{V}_{i-1} B_{i-1}(u) + \mathbf{V}_i B_i(u) + \mathbf{V}_{i+1} B_{i+1}(u). \end{aligned} \tag{7}$$

If we replace each basis function $B_j(u)$ by the particular basis segment that pertains to the interval $[u_{i-1}, u_i)$, then (7) can be written as

$$\begin{aligned} \mathbf{Q}_i(u) &= \sum_{r=-2}^{r=+1} \mathbf{V}_{i+r} b_r(u) \\ &= \mathbf{V}_{i-2} b_{-2}(u) + \mathbf{V}_{i-1} b_{-1}(u) + \mathbf{V}_i b_0(u) + \mathbf{V}_{i+1} b_1(u). \end{aligned} \tag{8}$$

Notice that the segments of our basis function are numbered from right to left in Figure 3 because that is the order in which they appear when summed to form a curve; the leftmost control vertex weights the rightmost basis segment, and so on. Equation (8) also reflects the convenience of parametrizing each basis segment from $u = 0$ at its left end; since the basis functions are all translates of one another, this convention allows us to use the same formulas in defining and computing each curve segment.

[1] Authors like de Boor [11] who are concerned with B-splines of more than one order usually find it necessary (although it would be less natural for our purposes) to index each basis function from the left end of its support, so that in our case $B_i(u)$ would name the uniform cubic basis function centered at u_{i+2} rather than the basis function centered at u_i.

Reprinted From acm Transactions On Graphics—April 1983—Vol. 2, No. 2

3. UNIFORMLY SHAPED BETA-SPLINES

The details of what follows may be found in [1].

The *unit tangent vector* of a curve $\mathbf{Q}(u)$ is

$$\hat{\mathbf{T}}(u) = \frac{\mathbf{Q}^{(1)}(u)}{|\mathbf{Q}^{(1)}(u)|} \tag{9}$$

and the *curvature vector* is

$$\mathbf{K}(u) = \kappa(u)\hat{\mathbf{N}}(u) = \kappa(u)\frac{\hat{\mathbf{T}}^{(1)}(u)}{|\hat{\mathbf{T}}^{(1)}(u)|} \tag{10}$$

where $\kappa(u)$ is the curvature of $\mathbf{Q}$ at u and $\hat{\mathbf{N}}(u)$ is a unit vector pointing from $\mathbf{Q}(u)$ toward the center of the osculating circle at $\mathbf{Q}(u)$.[2] $\hat{\mathbf{T}}(u)$ and $\mathbf{K}(u)$ capture the physically meaningful notions of the direction of motion and curvature at a point on the curve. With some effort it is possible to show that

$$\mathbf{K}(u) = \frac{\mathbf{Q}^{(1)}(u) \times \mathbf{Q}^{(2)}(u) \times \mathbf{Q}^{(1)}(u)}{|\mathbf{Q}^{(1)}(u)|^4}. \tag{11}$$

(Equations (9) and (11) are (essentially) two of the Frenet-Serret formulas, written in terms of an arbitrary parametrization [16].) $\mathbf{Q}(u)$, $\hat{\mathbf{T}}(u)$, and $\mathbf{K}(u)$ are easily seen to be continuous away from the joints of a piecewise polynomial; from eqs. (9) and (11) it is possible to show that in order for $\mathbf{Q}(u)$, $\hat{\mathbf{T}}(u)$, and $\mathbf{K}(u)$ to be continuous also at the joints between consecutive curve segments of $\mathbf{Q}(u)$, which we call G^2 or *second-degree geometric continuity*, it is sufficient that

$$\mathbf{Q}_{i-1}(u_i) = \mathbf{Q}_i(u_i) \tag{12}$$

$$\beta 1 \mathbf{Q}_{i-1}^{(1)}(u_i) = \mathbf{Q}_i^{(1)}(u_i) \tag{13}$$

$$\beta 1^2 \mathbf{Q}_{i-1}^{(2)}(u_i) + \beta 2 \mathbf{Q}_{i-1}^{(1)}(u_i) = \mathbf{Q}_i^{(2)}(u_i) \tag{14}$$

at every knot u_i and for any $\beta 1$ and $\beta 2$ [1]. These equations are, by definition, less restrictive than simple continuity of position and parametric derivatives, which is the special case in which $\beta 1 = 1$ and $\beta 2 = 0$.

Equation (12) enforces positional continuity. Equation (13) requires that the first parametric derivative vectors from the left and right at a joint be collinear, but allows their magnitudes to differ. There is an instantaneous change in velocity at the joint, but not a change in direction.

The intuition behind eq. (14) is somewhat more subtle. A sufficient condition for curvature continuity is that $\mathbf{Q}_i^{(2)}(u_i) = \beta 1^2 \mathbf{Q}_{i-1}^{(2)}(u_i)$, the factor of $\beta 1^2$ arising from the assumption that eq. (13) holds (see [1], [4] and [6] for details.) However, $\mathbf{Q}_i^{(2)}(u_i)$ may have an additional component directed along the tangent $\mathbf{Q}_{i-1}^{(1)}(u_i)$, since acceleration along the tangent does not "deflect" a point traveling along the curve, and so does not affect the curvature there.

Let us consider a basis function composed of four cubic polynomial basis segments, like the uniform cubic B-splines, but ask that they satisfy the geometric

[2] The *osculating circle* at $\mathbf{Q}(u)$ is the circle whose first and second derivative vectors agree with those of $\mathbf{Q}$ at u. The curvature $\kappa(u)$ is then the reciprocal of the radius of this osculating circle.

Reprinted From **acm Transactions On Graphics**—April 1983—Vol. 2, No. 2

constraints (12)–(14) instead of the parametric constraints (3)–(5). If we parametrize each basis segment individually on [0, 1) as we did in (6), the equations which result are

$$\begin{aligned} 0 &= b_1(0) & 0 &= b_1^{(1)}(0) \\ b_1(1) &= b_0(0) & \beta 1\, b_1^{(1)}(1) &= b_0^{(1)}(0) \\ b_0(1) &= b_{-1}(0) & \beta 1\, b_0^{(1)}(1) &= b_{-1}^{(1)}(0) \\ b_{-1}(1) &= b_{-2}(0) & \beta 1\, b_{-1}^{(1)}(1) &= b_{-2}^{(1)}(0) \\ b_{-2}(1) &= 0 & \beta 1\, b_{-2}^{(1)}(1) &= 0 \end{aligned}$$

$$\begin{aligned} 0 &= b_1^{(2)}(0) \\ \beta 1^2\, b_1^{(2)}(1) + \beta 2\, b_1^{(1)}(1) &= b_0^{(2)}(0) \\ \beta 1^2\, b_0^{(2)}(1) + \beta 2\, b_0^{(1)}(1) &= b_{-1}^{(2)}(0) \\ \beta 1^2\, b_{-1}^{(2)}(1) + \beta 2\, b_{-1}^{(1)}(1) &= b_{-2}^{(2)}(0) \\ \beta 1^2\, b_{-2}^{(2)}(1) + \beta 2\, b_{-2}^{(1)}(1) &= 0. \end{aligned} \qquad (15)$$

In order that the identically shaped basis functions we obtain have the "convex hull property" discussed in Section 4.4, it is convenient to normalize their height by requiring that

$$\sum_{r=-2}^{r=+1} B_{i+r}(u_i) = b_1(0) + b_0(0) + b_{-1}(0) + b_{-2}(0) = 1,$$

yielding a total of 16 equations in 16 unknowns. For any particular values of $\beta 1$ and $\beta 2$ these equations can be solved numerically to obtain explicit formulas for the polynomials comprising the basis segments. This is not very practical, however, since we do not want to solve a new system every time we wish to alter one of the β parameters. Instead we can solve this system once and for all using a symbolic manipulation system such as Vaxima [10, 15], to obtain the following symbolic representation of the basis segments for all values of $\beta 1$ and $\beta 2$.

$$\begin{aligned} b_1(u) &= \frac{1}{\delta}[2u^3] \\ b_0(u) &= \frac{1}{\delta}[2 + (6(\beta 1)u + (3\,\beta 2 + 6\,\beta 1^2)u^2 \\ &\qquad - (2\,\beta 2 + 2\,\beta 1^2 + 2\,\beta 1 + 2)u^3] \\ b_{-1}(u) &= \frac{1}{\delta}[(\beta 2 + 4\,\beta 1^2 + 4\,\beta 1) + (6\,\beta 1^3 - 6\,\beta 1)u \\ &\qquad - (3\,\beta 2 + 6\,\beta 1^3 + 6\,\beta 1^2)u^2 \\ &\qquad + (2\,\beta 2 + 2\,\beta 1^3 + 2\,\beta 1^2 + 2\,\beta 1)u^3] \\ b_{-2}(u) &= \frac{1}{\delta}[(2\,\beta 1^3) - (6\,\beta 1^3)u + (6\,\beta 1^3)u^2 - (2\,\beta 1^3)u^3] \end{aligned} \qquad (16)$$

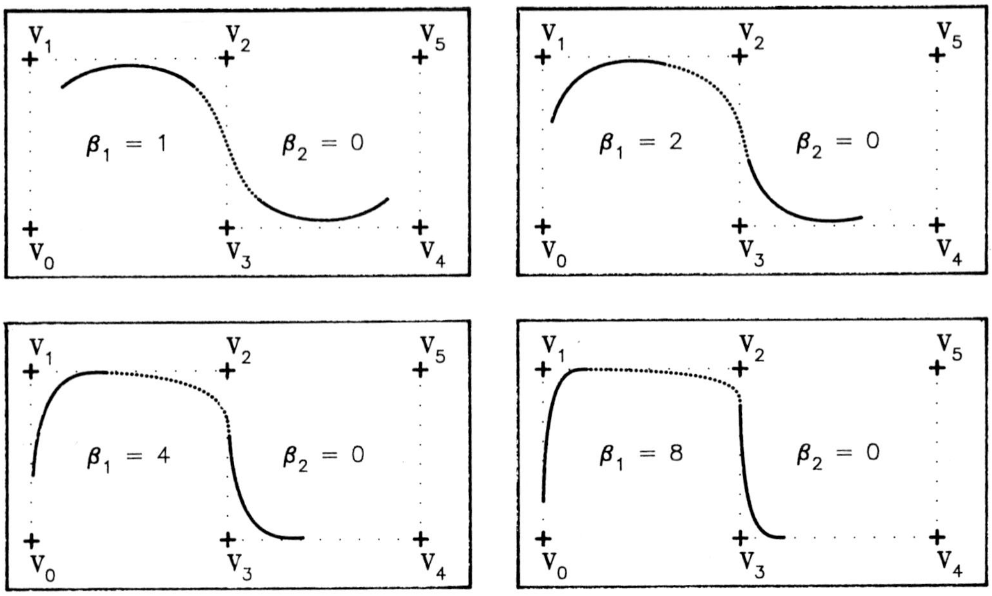

Fig. 5. This sequence of curves illustrates the effect of increasing $\beta 1$ on a uniformly shaped Beta-spline.

where

$$\delta = \beta 2 + 2\,\beta 1^3 + 4\,\beta 1^2 + 4\,\beta 1 + 2 \neq 0.$$

Notice that if we substitute $\beta 1 = 1$ and $\beta 2 = 0$ into the Beta-spline constraint equations (15) we obtain equations which define the uniform cubic B-splines, and that substituting these values into the Beta-spline basis segments (16) we obtain the B-spline basis segments (6). For other values of $\beta 1$ and $\beta 2$ the Beta-spline basis segments fail to be C^2 continuous at knots, although they do satisfy eqs. (15) and are therefore G^2 continuous.

Equations (16) can, of course, be evaluated more rapidly if they are factored. Since for any particular values of $\beta 1$ and $\beta 2$ they are cubic polynomials in u, forward differencing can also be used where appropriate. The efficient evaluation of these equations is discussed in [1] and [5].

We refer to a Beta-spline curve whose segments are defined by eqs. (7) and (16) as a *uniformly-shaped Beta-spline*, to distinguish it from the more general class of Beta-spline curves that are defined subsequently.

Increasing $\beta 1$ increases the "velocity" with which we traverse a curve (say from left to right) immediately to the right of a joint, with respect to the "velocity" just left of the joint, thus serving to *bias* the curve: values in excess of one cause the unit tangent vector at the joint (which is, of course, continuous) to have greater influence to the right than to the left, in that the curve will "continue in the direction of the tangent" longer in the rightmost segment (see Figure 5). Values of $\beta 1$ ranging from one down to zero have the reciprocal effect, causing the curve to lie close to the tangent longer to the left of a joint than to the right.

Because Beta-spline curves are weighted sums of basis functions, it is instruc-

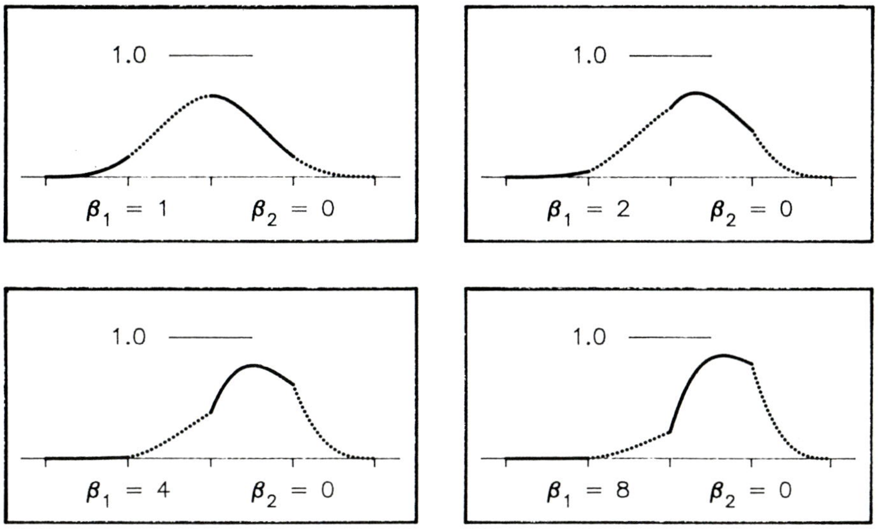

Fig. 6. These are the basis functions corresponding to the curves of Figure 5.

tive to examine the basis functions which define the curves of Figure 5. These are shown in Figure 6. Each is computed for a distinct value of $\beta 1$, which determines the relative magnitude of the slopes to the left and right of each joint. Notice that since the same basis function is used for each of $X(u)$ and $Y(u)$, any continuous basis function whose first derivative is continuous except for a jump of some arbitrary value ($\beta 1$) at the knots suffices to define a curve with unit tangent continuity.

The $\beta 2$ parameter serves to control *tension* in the curve: altering the value of $\beta 2$ moves the joint between $\mathbf{Q}_{i-1}(u)$ and $\mathbf{Q}_i(u)$ along a vector that passes through the ith control vertex, and this happens simultaneously for all the joints in a uniformly-shaped curve. For example, increasingly positive values move each joint toward its corresponding control vertex and flatten the curve against the control polygon (see Figure 7). The corresponding basis functions are shown in Figure 8. Notice that as $\beta 2$ increases, the peak of the basis function approaches one and the "tails" of the basis function, lying in the leftmost and rightmost intervals of its support, approach zero. This behavior is predictable from eqs. (16).

In some circumstances $\beta 1$ also functions as an "asymmetric tension parameter." If for any $\beta 2$ we allow $\beta 1$ to become arbitrarily large, then the ith curve segment converges to a straight line between $\mathbf{V}_{i-2}$ and $\mathbf{V}_{i-1}$. If $\beta 2$ is zero, then as $\beta 1$ goes to zero the ith curve segment converges to a straight line between $\mathbf{V}_i$ and $\mathbf{V}_{i+1}$. A more detailed discussion of this behavior may be found in [6] and [7].

$\beta 1$ and $\beta 2$ may be altered, independent of the control vertices, to change the shape of the curve. In the curves we have been discussing a single value of $\beta 1$ is used for the entire curve, and the same is true for $\beta 2$. We would prefer, if possible, to specify distinct values of $\beta 1$ and $\beta 2$ at each joint. Before discussing how this can be done, we indicate briefly how uniformly-shaped Beta-spline surfaces can be constructed from uniformly-shaped curves.

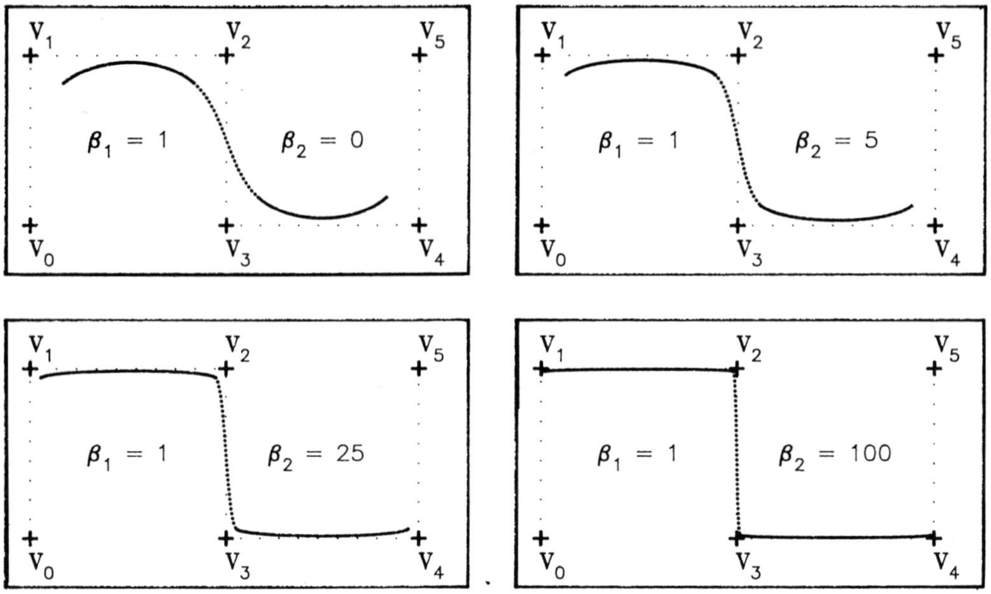

Fig. 7. This sequence of curves illustrates the effect of increasing $\beta 2$ on a uniformly shaped Beta-spline.

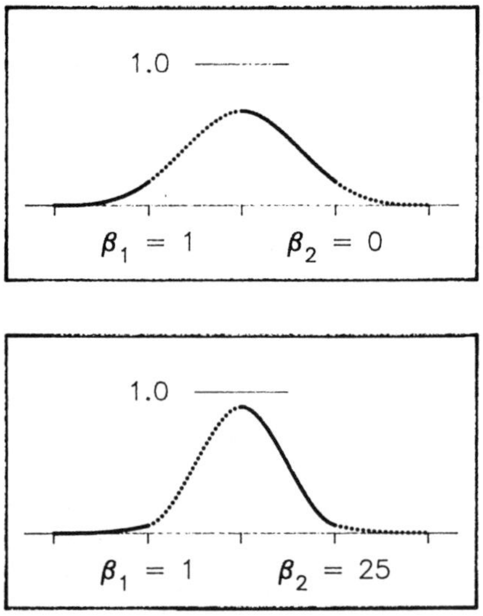

Fig. 8. These are the basis functions corresponding to the curves of Figure 7.

3.1. Surfaces

We want to form our surface as a weighted sum of basis functions, as in (2), but now X, Y, and Z must be functions of two independent variables:

$$\begin{aligned}\mathbf{Q}(u, v) &= \sum_{i,j} \mathbf{V}_{i,j} B_{i,j}(u, v) \\ &= \sum_{i,j} \left(x_{i,j} B_{i,j}(u, v),\ y_{i,j} B_{i,j}(u, v),\ z_{i,j} B_{i,j}(u, v) \right).\end{aligned} \tag{17}$$

Reprinted From **acm Transactions On Graphics**—April 1983—Vol. 2, No. 2

For weights we again use the x-, y-, and z-coordinates of what is now a two-dimensional array of control vertices called the *control mesh* or *control graph.* To obtain locality, we would like the new basis functions $B_{i,j}(u, v)$ to be nonzero only for a small range of u and v. An easy way to arrange this is to let $B_{i,j}(u, v) = B_i(u)B_j(v)$, where $B_i(u)$ and $B_j(v)$ are the univariate basis functions (16) which we developed for the Beta-spline curves. Since each is nonzero only over four successive intervals, if $u_{i-1} \le u < u_i$ and $v_{j-1} \le v < v_j$, we can rewrite (17) as

$$\mathbf{Q}(u, v) = \sum_{r=-2}^{r=+1} \sum_{s=-2}^{s=+1} \mathbf{V}_{i+r,j+s} B_{i+r}(u) B_{j+s}(v). \tag{18}$$

If we rewrite this in terms of basis segments instead of basis functions and adopt the convention that the portion of $\mathbf{Q}(u, v)$ defined by this set of values for u and v is denoted by $\mathbf{Q}_{i,j}(u, v)$, then we can write

$$\mathbf{Q}_{i,j}(u, v) = \sum_{r=-2}^{r=+1} \sum_{s=-2}^{s=+1} \mathbf{V}_{i+r,j+s} b_r(u) b_s(v), \tag{19}$$

so that $\mathbf{Q}_{i,j}(u, v)$, the i, jth *patch,* is completely determined by 16 control vertices. The separability of $B_{i,j}(u, v)$ into $B_i(u)$ and $B_j(v)$ can be useful. For example, we can expand (19) as

$$\begin{aligned}
\mathbf{Q}_{i,j}(u, v) \\
&= [\mathbf{V}_{i-2,j+1} b_{-2}(u) + \mathbf{V}_{i-1,j+1} b_{-1}(u) + \mathbf{V}_{i,j+1} b_0(u) + \mathbf{V}_{i+1,j+1} b_1(u)] b_1(v) \\
&+ [\mathbf{V}_{i-2,j} b_{-2}(u) + \mathbf{V}_{i-1,j} b_{-1}(u) + \mathbf{V}_{i,j} b_0(u) + \mathbf{V}_{i+1,j} b_1(u)] b_0(v) \\
&+ [\mathbf{V}_{i-2,j-1} b_{-2}(u) + \mathbf{V}_{i-1,j-1} b_{-1}(u) + \mathbf{V}_{i,j-1} b_0(u) + \mathbf{V}_{i+1,j-1} b_1(u)] b_{-1}(v) \\
&+ [\mathbf{V}_{i-2,j-2} b_{-2}(u) + \mathbf{V}_{i-1,j-2} b_{-1}(u) + \mathbf{V}_{i,j-2} b_0(u) + \mathbf{V}_{i+1,j-2} b_1(u)] b_{-2}(v).
\end{aligned} \tag{20}$$

From this it is clear that if we fix u at some arbitrary value between 0 and 1 then we can write (20) as

$$\mathbf{Q}_{i,j,u}(v) = \mathbf{W}_{-2} b_{-2}(v) + \mathbf{W}_{-1} b_{-1}(v) + \mathbf{W}_0 b_0(v) + \mathbf{W}_1 b_1(v)$$

where

$$\begin{aligned}
\mathbf{W}_1 &= \mathbf{V}_{i-2,j+1} b_{-2}(u) + \mathbf{V}_{i-1,j+1} b_{-1}(u) + \mathbf{V}_{i,j+1} b_0(u) + \mathbf{V}_{i+1,j+1} b_1(u) \\
\mathbf{W}_0 &= \mathbf{V}_{i-2,j} b_{-2}(u) + \mathbf{V}_{i-1,j} b_{-1}(u) + \mathbf{V}_{i,j} b_0(u) + \mathbf{V}_{i+1,j} b_1(u) \\
\mathbf{W}_{-1} &= \mathbf{V}_{i-2,j-1} b_{-2}(u) + \mathbf{V}_{i-1,j-1} b_{-1}(u) + \mathbf{V}_{i,j-1} b_0(u) + \mathbf{V}_{i+1,j-1} b_1(u) \\
\mathbf{W}_{-2} &= \mathbf{V}_{i-2,j-2} b_{-2}(u) + \mathbf{V}_{i-1,j-2} b_{-1}(u) + \mathbf{V}_{i,j-2} b_0(u) + \mathbf{V}_{i+1,j-2} b_1(u).
\end{aligned}$$

Thus $\mathbf{Q}_{i,j,u}(v)$ is simply the uniformly-shaped Beta-spline curve segment defined by the "control vertices" $\mathbf{W}_{-2}$, $\mathbf{W}_{-1}$, $\mathbf{W}_0$, and $\mathbf{W}_1$. It is not hard to see that $\mathbf{Q}_{i,j+1,u}(v)$, in the next patch "up," is given by

$$\mathbf{Q}_{i,j+1,u}(v) = \mathbf{W}_{-1} b_{-2}(v) + \mathbf{W}_0 b_{-1}(v) + \mathbf{W}_1 b_0(v) + \mathbf{W}_2 b_1(v)$$

where

$$\mathbf{W}_2 = \mathbf{V}_{i-2,j+2} b_{-2}(u) + \mathbf{V}_{i-1,j+2} b_{-1}(u) + \mathbf{V}_{i,j+2} b_0(u) + \mathbf{V}_{i+1,j+2} b_1(u).$$

This is simply the second segment in a uniformly-shaped Beta-spline curve defined by the "control vertices" $\mathbf{W}_{-2}$, $\mathbf{W}_{-1}$, $\mathbf{W}_0$, $\mathbf{W}_1$, and $\mathbf{W}_2$. It follows immediately that this curve is G^2 continuous. Since a completely analogous argument can be made with respect to u by factoring the $b_r(u)$ out of (19) instead of the $b_s(v)$, the uniformly shaped Beta-spline surface we have defined is G^2 continuous along lines of constant u and v.

4. INTERPOLATING DISTINCT β's

Let $\alpha 1_i$ and $\alpha 2_i$ be the values of $\beta 1$ and $\beta 2$ to be associated with the joint between $\mathbf{Q}_{i-1}(u)$ and $\mathbf{Q}_i(u)$. We would like to use the basis segments given by eqs. (16), making $\beta 1$ and $\beta 2$ functions of u in such a way as to interpolate between the $\alpha 1$'s and $\alpha 2$'s at each end of a segment while preserving G^2 continuity of the curve.

Let us consider the following derivative with respect to u of a representative term of (16).[3]

$$\frac{c[\beta(u)]^p u^q}{\delta(u)} \tag{21}$$

where c is a constant. Its first parametric derivative is

$$\frac{cq[\beta(u)]^p q^{q-1}}{\delta(u)} + \frac{cp[\beta(u)]^{p-1}\beta^{(1)}(u)u^q}{\delta(u)} - \frac{c[\beta(u)]^p\delta^{(1)}(u)u^q}{\delta(u)^2} \tag{22}$$

where

$$\begin{aligned}\delta(u) &= \beta 2(u) + 2[\beta 1(u)]^3 + 4[\beta 1(u)]^2 + 4\beta 1(u) + 2\\ \delta^{(1)}(u) &= \beta 2^{(1)}(u) + 6[\beta 1(u)]^2\beta 1^{(1)}(u)\\ &\quad + 8\beta 1(u)\beta 1^{(1)}(u) + 4\beta 1^{(1)}(u)\end{aligned} \tag{23}$$

Examination of (22) and (23) reveals that the second and third terms of (22) involve products with $\beta 1^{(1)}(u)$ or $\beta 2^{(1)}(u)$, while the first term of (22) would constitute the complete parametric derivative if $\beta 1$ and $\beta 2$ were not functions of u. If we were to compute $\beta 1(u)$ and $\beta 2(u)$ by interpolating between the $\alpha 1_i$'s and $\alpha 2_i$'s in such a way as to cause $\beta 1^{(1)}(u)$ and $\beta 2^{(1)}(u)$ to be zero at each joint, then eqs. (13) would hold and G^1 continuity would be preserved.

Similarly, the second parametric derivative of (21) is

$$\begin{aligned}&\frac{c(n-1)n[\beta(u)]^m u^{n-2}}{\delta(u)}\\ &- \frac{c[\beta(u)]^m\delta^{(2)}(u)u^n}{\delta(u)^2} + \frac{2c[\beta(u)]^m\delta^{(1)}(u)^2u^n}{\delta(u)^3}\\ &- \frac{2cm[\beta(u)]^{m-1}\beta^{(1)}(u)\delta^{(1)}(u)u^n}{\delta(u)^2} - \frac{2cn[\beta(u)]^m\delta^{(1)}(u)n^{n-1}}{\delta(u)^2}\\ &+ \frac{cm[\beta(u)]^{m-1}\beta^{(2)}(u)u^n}{\delta(u)} + \frac{c(m-1)m[\beta(u)]^{m-2}\beta^{(1)}(u)^2u^n}{\delta(u)}\\ &+ \frac{2cmn[\beta(u)]^{m-1}\beta^{(1)}(u)u^{n-1}}{\delta(u)}\end{aligned} \tag{24}$$

[3] We use $\beta(u)$ rather than $\beta 1(u)$ or $\beta 2(u)$ when the argument applies to both, but no confusion can occur because products of $\beta 1$ and $\beta 2$ do not arise. Similarly, α_i is used to represent both $\alpha 1_i$ and $\alpha 2_i$.

Reprinted From **acm Transactions On Graphics**—April 1983—Vol. 2, No. 2

where

$$\delta^{(2)}(u) = \beta 2^{(2)}(u) + 6[\beta 1(u)]^2 \beta 1^{(2)}(u) + 8\beta 1(u)\beta 1^{(2)}(u) + 4\beta 1^{(2)}(u) + 12\beta 1(u)[\beta 1^{(1)}(u)]^2 + 8\beta 1^{(1)}(u)^2.$$

Again, only the first term of (24) lacks a product with at least one of $\beta 1^{(1)}(u)$, $\beta 2^{(1)}(u)$, $\beta 1^{(2)}(u)$, or $\beta 2^{(2)}(u)$, and the first term would constitute the complete second parametric derivative if $\beta 1$ and $\beta 2$ were not functions of u. Thus arranging for all four derivatives to have the value zero at joints should be sufficient to preserve G^2 continuity of the curve. This is easily accomplished in the following manner.

Suppose that we use a polynomial $H(\alpha_{i-1}, \alpha_i; u)$ to interpolate between α_{i-1} and α_i. We have six constraints, since we would like

$$H(\alpha_{i-1}, \alpha_i; 0) = \alpha_{i-1}$$
$$H(\alpha_{i-1}, \alpha_i; 1) = \alpha_i$$
$$H^{(1)}(\alpha_{i-1}, \alpha_i; 0) = 0$$
$$H^{(1)}(\alpha_{i-1}, \alpha_i; 1) = 0$$
$$H^{(2)}(\alpha_{i-1}, \alpha_i; 0) = 0$$
$$H^{(2)}(\alpha_{i-1}, \alpha_i; 1) = 0.$$

This suggests the use of a fifth-degree polynomial. If

$$H(\alpha_{i-1}, \alpha_i; u) = a + bu + cu^2 + du^3 + eu^4 + fu^5,$$

then the above equations take the form

$$H(\alpha_{i-1}, \alpha_i; 0) = \alpha_{i-1} = a$$
$$H(\alpha_{i-1}, \alpha_i; 1) = \alpha_i = a + b + c + d + e + f$$
$$H^{(1)}(\alpha_{i-1}, \alpha_i; 0) = 0 = b$$
$$H^{(1)}(\alpha_{i-1}, \alpha_i; 1) = 0 = b + 2c + 3d + 4e + 5f$$
$$H^{(2)}(\alpha_{i-1}, \alpha_i; 0) = 0 = 2c$$
$$H^{(2)}(\alpha_{i-1}, \alpha_i; 1) = 0 = 2c + 6d + 12e + 20f.$$

It is straightforward to solve these for the polynomial

$$\begin{aligned}\beta_i(u) &= H(\alpha_{i-1}, \alpha_i; u)\\ &= \alpha_{i-1} + 10(\alpha_i - \alpha_{i-1})u^3 - 15(\alpha_i - \alpha_{i-1})u^4 + 6(\alpha_i - \alpha_{i-1})u^5\\ &= \alpha_{i-1} + (\alpha_i - \alpha_{i-1})[10u^3 - 15u^4 + 6u^5], \qquad (25)\end{aligned}$$

which is, in fact, a special case of quintic Hermite interpolation. (Figure 9 illustrates the use of this polynomial to interpolate between $\alpha 1_{i-1} = 0.5$ and $\alpha 1_i = 1.6$.) By the argument given above, the use of (25) to interpolate $\beta 1$ and $\beta 2$ in (16) preserves G^2 continuity of the curve.

It is, of course, possible that the derivative terms appearing in (22) and (24) might sum in such a way as to yield G^2 continuous curves even though the derivatives were nonzero; we have not ruled this out for all other interpolation

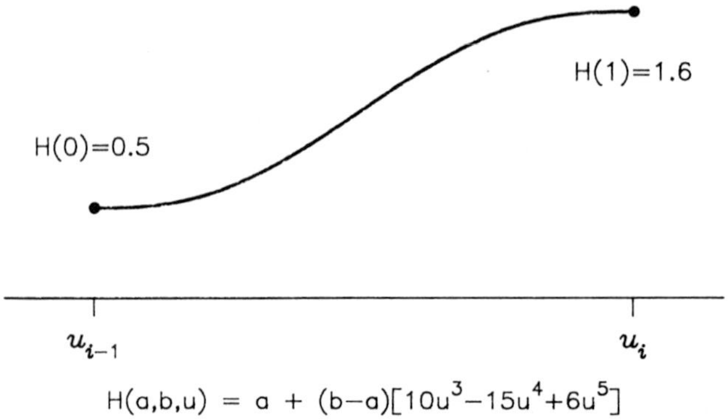

Fig. 9. An application of the formula for interpolating α values between joints.

schemes. However, using Vaxima [10, 15], it is not hard to produce examples which demonstrate that neither linear interpolation nor cubic Hermite interpolation work. Moreover, geometric continuity is not necessarily preserved by using general quintic Hermite interpolation, even if the same two nonzero values are used for the first and second derivatives of $\beta 1(u)$ at the joints (and similarly for $\beta 2(u)$). Thus C^2 continuity of $\beta 1(u)$ and $\beta 2(u)$ is not sufficient to ensure G^2 continuity. (See [7] for an example.)

We refer to the curves whose segments are defined by eqs. (7) and (16), where $\beta 1(u)$ and $\beta 2(u)$ are interpolated by eq. (25), as *continuously-shaped Beta-splines*.

4.1 Locality

As with the uniformly-shaped Beta-splines, each basis function is nonzero only over four successive intervals. Since each control vertex is used to weight a particular basis function, moving a control vertex will alter only the four corresponding curve segments. These are, of course, consecutive.

The effect of altering an α value is more localized still. The α value at a particular joint determines how the corresponding β parameter is interpolated over the segments which meet at that joint, so that only two curve segments are changed.

4.2 Bias

Figure 10 illustrates a few of the effects which can be obtained by altering $\alpha 1$'s. The extreme locality of the Beta-spline curves with respect to changes in the shape parameters can result in "kinks" if there are large differences in the α values at consecutive joints. A modest reduction in the size of the jumps (see Figure 11) can be used to ameliorate such effects, if that is desirable.

4.3 Tension

Since this scheme interpolates the $\alpha 1_i$ and $\alpha 2_i$, the discussion of tension in [1] and [4] is equally applicable here:

$$\mathbf{Q}_i(0) - \mathbf{V}_i = \mathbf{Q}_{i-1}(1) - \mathbf{V}_i = \frac{(\mathbf{C} - c\mathbf{V}_i)}{(c + \alpha 2_i)}$$

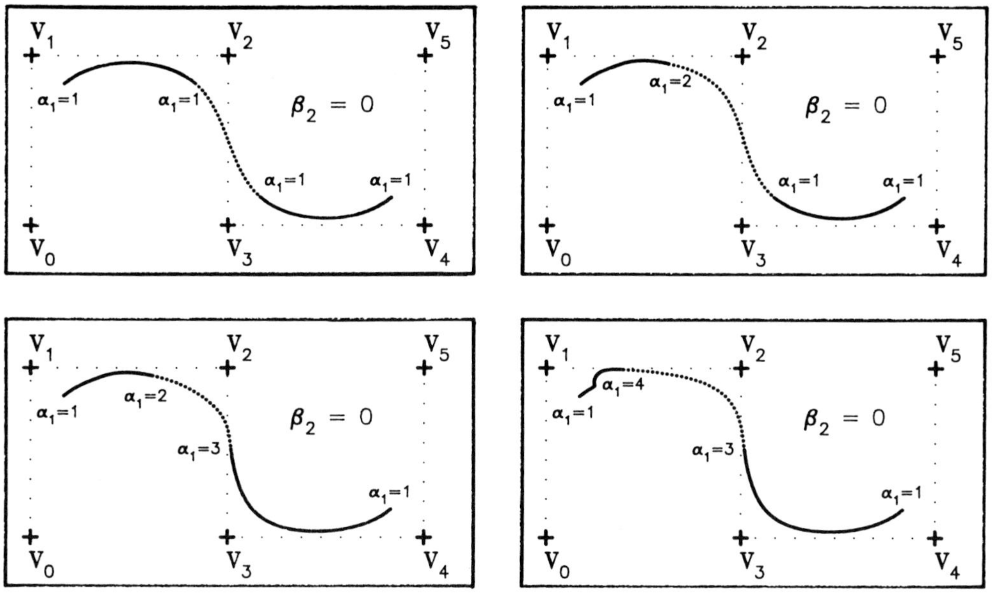

Fig. 10. For these curves $\beta 2$ is held constant at zero while $\beta 1$ interpolates the $\alpha 1$ values shown.

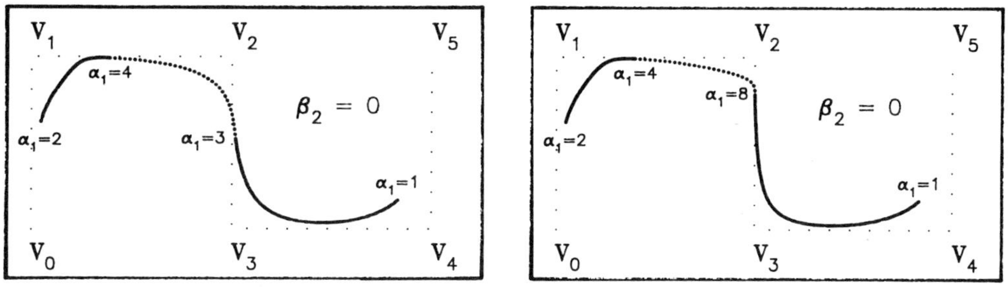

Fig. 11. Eliminating the kink in Figure 10.

is the vector from the ith control vertex to the joint between $\mathbf{Q}_{i-1}(u)$ and $\mathbf{Q}_i(u)$, where

$$C = 2\alpha 1_i^3 V_{i-1} + 4\alpha 1_i(\alpha 1_i + 1)\mathbf{V}_i + 2\mathbf{V}_{i+1}$$
$$c = 2\alpha 1_i^3 + 4\alpha 1_i^2 + 4\alpha 1_i + 2.$$

Altering $\alpha 2_i$ merely changes the length of this vector: values approaching $-c$ "push" the joint arbitrarily far away from $\mathbf{V}_i$, while large positive or negative values draw the joint arbitrarily close to $\mathbf{V}_i$ (see Figure 12). Hence $\alpha 2_i$ serves as a tension parameter, just as for uniformly-shaped Beta-spline curves. Again, wildly disparate values of $\beta 2$ for adjacent control vertices can be used to produce kinks. These can be removed (see Figure 13), if that is desirable, by smaller adjustments in neighboring $\beta 2$ values.

For comparison with earlier illustrations, Figure 14 gives some examples of continuously-shaped basis functions.

Reprinted From **acm Transactions On Graphics**—April 1983—Vol. 2, No. 2

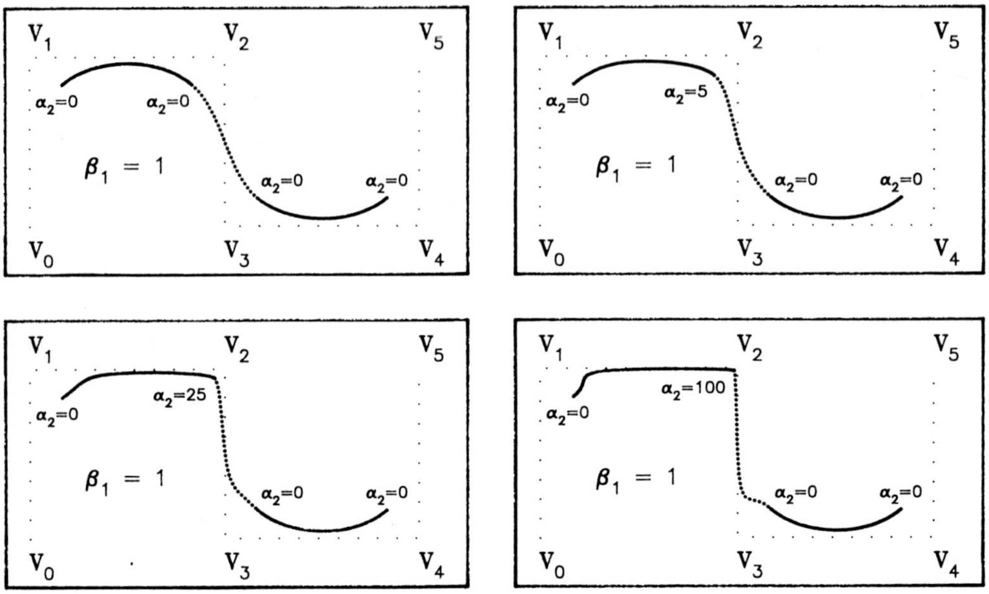

Fig. 12. The value of $\beta 2$ at the joint nearest to $\mathbf{V}_2$ is increased from 0 to 100 in three steps, pulling the joint toward $\mathbf{V}_2$. In the limit this joint converges to $\mathbf{V}_2$.

Fig. 13. Altering the value of $\beta 2$ at a joint affects only the two curve segments that meet there. Making one such $\alpha 2$ very large in comparison with its neighbors, as in Figure 12, causes these two segments to be abruptly pulled close to the control polygon. The value of $\beta 2$ at adjacent joints can be adjusted to smooth out the curve.

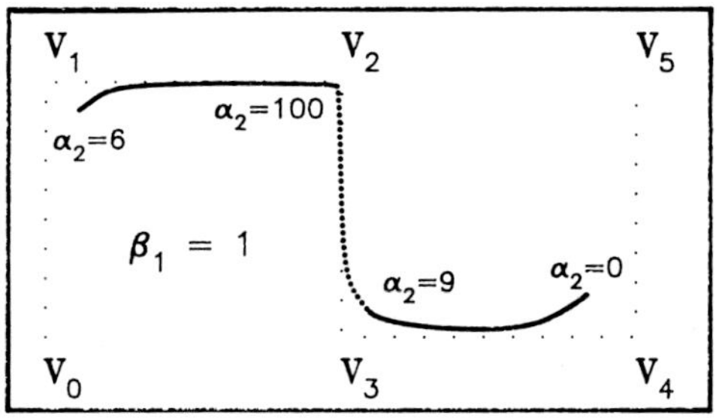

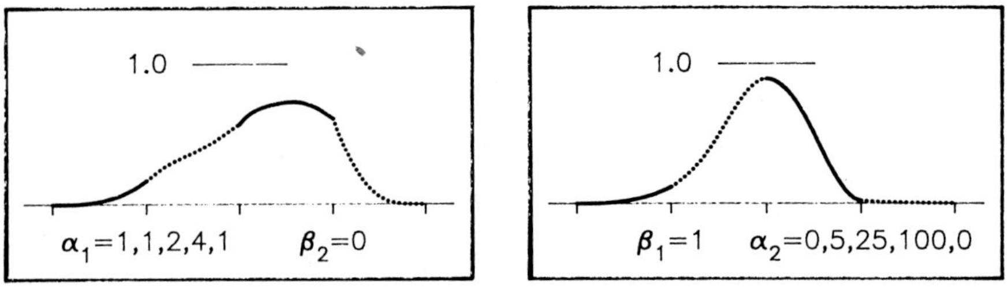

Fig. 14. Here we illustrate the effect of interpolating β values on the basis functions. On the left $\alpha 1$ changes value from joint to joint, while on the right $\alpha 2$ changes value.

4.4 Convex Hull

Intuitively, we obtain the *convex hull* of a set of vertices by "shrink wrapping" a rubber band in 2D or a balloon (in 3D) around them. A line segment joining any two points within such a convex hull is itself entirely within the convex hull. More

Reprinted From **acm Transactions On Graphics**—April 1983—Vol. 2, No. 2

generally, it is not hard to show (see [6] for a simple induction argument) that if we "weight" any set of $m + 1$ vertices $\mathbf{V}_0, \ldots, \mathbf{V}_m$ by nonnegative coefficients $c_0, \ldots, c_m$ which sum to one, then the point

$$\mathbf{P} = c_0\mathbf{V}_0 + c_1\mathbf{V}_1 + c_{m-1}\mathbf{V}_{m-1} + c_m\mathbf{V}_m$$

lies within the convex hull of the $\mathbf{V}_i$.

Like the uniformly-shaped Beta-splines, continuously-shaped Beta-spline curves posses a convex hull property in that the ith segment lies within the convex hull of control vertices $\mathbf{V}_{i-2}$, $\mathbf{V}_{i-1}$, $\mathbf{V}_i$, and $\mathbf{V}_{i+1}$, so long as $\beta 1$ and $\beta 2$ are nonnegative. The argument, as we shall see, is straightforward. Recall that each basis function is nonzero over four intervals, so that

$$\mathbf{Q}_i(u) = \mathbf{V}_{i-2}b_{-2}(u) + \mathbf{V}_{i-1}b_{-1}(u) + \mathbf{V}_i b_0(u) + \mathbf{V}_{i+1}b_1(u). \qquad (26)$$

Now for any given value of u, $\beta 1(u)$ and $\beta 2(u)$ yield some particular value of $\beta 1$ and $\beta 2$. By simply summing eqs. (16) we see that for every such $\beta 1$, $\beta 2$, and u

$$b_1(u) + b_0(u) + b_{-1}(u) + b_{-2}(u) = 1.$$

Next we must verify that these basis segments are nonnegative for all u in the interval [0, 1). If we rewrite eqs. (16) in the form

$$b_1(u) = \frac{1}{\delta}(2u^3)$$

$$b_0(u) = \frac{1}{\delta}[2\beta 1^2u^2(3 - u) + 2\beta 1u(3 - u^2) + \beta 2u^2(3 - 2u) + 2(1 - u^3)]$$

$$b_{-1}(u) = \frac{1}{\delta}[2\beta 1^3u((1 - u)(2 - u) + 1) + 2\beta 1^2(u^3 - 3u^2 + 2) + 2\beta 1(u^3 - 3u + 2) + \beta 2(2u^3 - 3u^2 + 1)]$$

$$b_{-2}(u) = \frac{1}{\delta}[2\beta 1^3(1 - u)^3]$$

where

$$\delta = \beta 2 + 2\beta 1^3 + 4\beta 1^2 + 4\beta 1 + 2$$

for $\beta 1 \geq 0$, $\beta 2 \geq 0$, and $u \in [0, 1)$, it is easy to see by inspection that $b_1(u)$, $b_0(u)$, and $b_{-2}(u)$ are nonnegative. For $b_{-1}(u)$, elementary consideration of the zeros of the derivatives $3u(u - 2)$, $3(u - 1)(u - 1)$, and $6u(u - 1)$ of $u^3 - 3u^2 + 2$, $u^3 - 3u + 2$, and $2u^3 - 3u^2 + 1$ yields the same conclusion. Since $\beta 1$ and $\beta 2$ are actually interpolated by (25), it is necessary to show that

$$\beta_i(u) = \alpha_{i-1} + (\alpha_i - \alpha_{i-1})[10u^3 - 15u^4 + 6u^5] \geq 0,$$

if $\alpha_{i-1} \geq 0$, $\alpha_i \geq 0$, and $u \in [0, 1]$. Consider

$$\beta_i^{(1)}(u) = 30(\alpha_i - \alpha_{i-1})u^2(1 - u)^2.$$

Clearly the slope changes sign only at $u = 0$ and $u = 1$. Since

$$\beta_i(0.5) = \frac{\alpha_{-i} + \alpha_i}{2} \geq 0 \quad \text{if} \quad \alpha_{i-1}, \alpha_i \geq 0,$$

$\beta_i(u)$ must be nonnegative on [0, 1) so long as the α_i are nonnegative.

Hence so long as the $\alpha 1_i \geq 0$ and $\alpha 2_i \geq 0$, each $\mathbf{Q}_i(u)$ lies within the convex hull of $\mathbf{V}_{i-2}$, $\mathbf{V}_{i-1}$, $\mathbf{V}_i$, and $\mathbf{V}_{i+1}$.

4.5 End Conditions

A properly defined curve segment is the sum of four weighted basis functions, as in eq. (26). Thus $m + 1$ control vertices $\mathbf{V}_0, \ldots, \mathbf{V}_m$ can be used to define $m - 2$ segments, which we index as $\mathbf{Q}_2(u), \ldots, \mathbf{Q}_{m-1}(u)$. The Beta-spline curve does not, in general, begin at a control vertex,[4] or even at a point along the line segment from $\mathbf{V}_0$ to $\mathbf{V}_1$. The most that we can say is that the initial point lies within the convex hull of $\mathbf{V}_0$, $\mathbf{V}_1$, and $\mathbf{V}_2$. To obtain better control of the endpoints, one therefore often treats them specially.

Let $\mathbf{Q}(u)$be a continuously-shaped Beta-spline with $\beta 1 = \alpha 1_i$ and $\beta 2 = \alpha 2_i$ at the joint between the ith and $(i + 1)$st segments. Let $\mathbf{R}(u)$ be a uniformly-shaped Beta-spline curve defined by the same control vertices, but with $\beta 1 = \alpha 1_i$ and $\beta 2 = \alpha 2_i$ throughout. By the definition of $\mathbf{Q}(u)$ we must have $\mathbf{Q}(u) = \mathbf{R}(u)$, $\mathbf{Q}^{(1)}(u) = \mathbf{R}^{(1)}(u)$, and $\mathbf{Q}^{(2)}(u) = \mathbf{R}^{(2)}(u)$ at the joint in question. Hence the analysis of end conditions in [1] applies immediately to the continuously-shaped Beta-splines. For convenience we summarize these results.

— *A Double First Vertex.* We define an additional segment at the beginning of the curve by

$$\mathbf{Q}_1(u) = \mathbf{V}_0[b_{-2}(u) + b_{-1}(u)] + \mathbf{V}_1 b_0(u) + \mathbf{V}_2 b_1(u).$$

$\mathbf{Q}_1(u)$ begins at a point lying along the line segment from $\mathbf{V}_0$ to $\mathbf{V}_1$, at which point it is tangent to that line and has zero curvature. (Figures 1 and 2 illustrate the use of double initial and final vertices.)

— *A Triple First Vertex.* We define two additional segments at the beginning of the curve by

$$\mathbf{Q}_0(u) = \mathbf{V}_0[b_{-2}(u) + b_{-1}(u) + b_0(u)] + \mathbf{V}_1 b_1(u)$$

$$\mathbf{Q}_1(u) = \mathbf{V}_0[b_{-2}(u) + b_{-1}(u)] + \mathbf{V}_1 b_0(u) + \mathbf{V}_2 b_1(u).$$

The curve then begins at $\mathbf{Q}_0(0) = \mathbf{V}_0$, and the first segment of the curve is a short straight line. The behavior of the second segment $\mathbf{Q}_1(u)$, which has a double first vertex, is described above.

The analysis of double and triple vertices is equally applicable on the interior of a curve. Triple interior vertices are particularly interesting since they result in a cusp, as in Figure 15. This cusp is not a violation of G^2 continuity because, or at least in the sense that, the first parametric derivative vector has the value $(0, 0)$ at the joint that coincides with the interpolated control vertex where the cusp occurs, so that the unit tangent vector is not defined. Multiple vertices give a tension-like effect, and it is instructive to compare the effect of repeating a vertex in Figure 15 with the effect of altering $\beta 2$ at the corresponding joint in Figure 16.

An alternative way of controlling the beginning of a curve is to automatically

[4] The terminal point of the curve is analyzed in an exactly analogous manner, and we therefore omit explicit treatment of it.

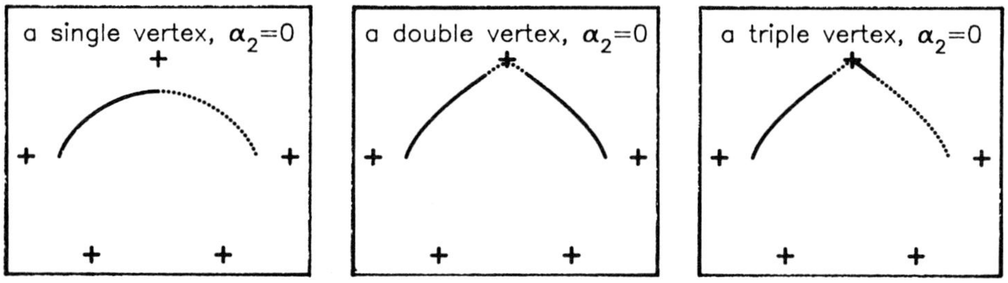

Fig. 15. $\alpha 1$ is one and $\alpha 2$ is zero at all joints; these are in fact simply uniform cubic B-splines, although a cusp results at a triple vertex for any values of $\alpha 1$ and $\alpha 2$ unless the control vertices immediately preceding and following the vertex are both collinear with it. The double control vertex is not interpolated, while the triple vertex is.

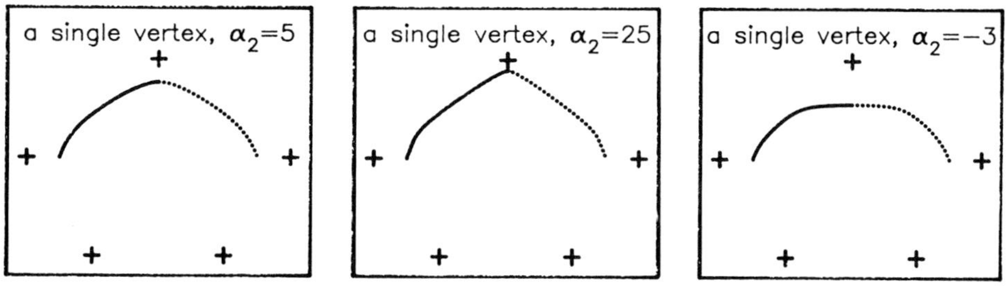

Fig. 16. Here $\alpha 1$ is one at all joints and $\alpha 2$ is zero except as indicated.

define a *phantom vertex* $\mathbf{V}_{-1}$ and a corresponding initial segment

$$\mathbf{Q}_1(u) = \mathbf{V}_{-1}b_{-2}(u) + \mathbf{V}_0 b_{-1}(u) + \mathbf{V}_1 b_0(u) + \mathbf{V}_2 b_1(u)$$

in such a way as to satisfy some requirement. We may ask that

— $\mathbf{Q}_1(0)$ interpolate some furnished point (usually with nonzero curvature),
— $\mathbf{Q}_1(0)$ interpolate $\mathbf{V}_0$ (at which point the curvature is then zero),
— $\mathbf{Q}_1^{(1)}(0)$ have a specified value (usually resulting in nonzero curvature),
— $\mathbf{Q}_1^{(2)}(0)$ have a specified value (usually resulting in nonzero curvature),
— $\mathbf{Q}_1^{(2)}(0)$ be zero, resulting in zero curvature at $\mathbf{Q}_1(0)$.

All of these techniques involve extending the curve by one or two segments at either end. This implies the existence of additional joints and associated α values. Hence the sequence of control vertices is extended in order to specify behavior at the ends of the curve, and additional $\alpha 1$ and $\alpha 2$ values must be specified as well. These may take any value without affecting the behavior described above. In practice it is probably easiest simply to replicate α values as well as vertices.

Again, the arguments establishing these results appear in [1] and the details are therefore omitted.

The curves we have discussed so far are *open* curves, which is to say that the two endpoints do not, in general, coincide. A G^2-continuous *closed* curve whose endpoints do meet and which is G^2-continuous there as well is obtained if the first three control vertices are identical to the last three and the same values of $\beta 1$ and $\beta 2$ are used at the joint between the beginning and ending of the curve.

4.6 Evaluation

If a single point on $\mathbf{Q}(u)$ is to be determined, eq. (25) can be evaluated in six multiplications and four additon/subtractions per coordinate if it is factored into the form

$$H(\alpha_{i-1}, \alpha_i; u) = \alpha_{i-1} + (\alpha_i - \alpha_{i-1})[10 + (6u - 15)u]u^3.$$

Since both $\beta 1(u)$ and $\beta 2(u)$ must be computed, both $H(\alpha 1_{i-1}, \alpha 1_i; u)$ and $H(\alpha 2_{i-1}, \alpha 2_i; u)$ must be evaluated. However, since $[10 + (6u - 15)u]u^3$ need only be evaluated once, the total cost of interpolation is seven multiplications and six addition/subtractions. If the uniformly-shaped Beta-spline basis functions are evaluated using the algorithms described in [1] and [5], then the cost of evaluating a continuously-shaped Beta-spline curve at one point is about 20 percent more than the cost of evaluating a uniformly-shaped Beta-spline.

More often we wish to evaluate a sequence of points along each segment in order to render a curve. If we compute these points by repeatedly evaluating the basis function as described above, then a continuously-shaped 2D Beta-spline segment can be evaluated at r values of u with about twice as much work as is required to evaluate a sequence of points on a uniformly-shaped segment. The difference results from the need to reevaluate the coefficients of the polynomials forming the basis segments, owing to the fact that $\beta 1$ and $\beta 2$ are no longer constant, as well as from the cost of actually performing the interpolation.

If instead we first sum the terms in eqs. (8) so as to compute the coefficients of $X(u)$ and $Y(u)$, and then use Horner's rule (nested multiplication), then the evaluation of a 2D continuously-shaped Beta-spline segment at r points requires approximately eight times as much work as does evaluation of the analogous uniformly-shaped segment.

A third alternative is to use forward differencing techniques. For large values of r the evaluation of a 2D uniformly-shaped curve in this way is almost a factor of 17 faster than the evaluation of a continuously-shaped curve using Horner's rule, although it is subject to cumulative roundoff error. While, in principle, forward differencing is applicable to the continuously-shaped Beta-splines as well, in fact it is impractical since each coordinate is the quotient of an 18th- and a 15th-degree polynomial. Where cost is a crucial factor, it may be desirable to fix $\beta 1$ at one and manipulate $\beta 2$ alone. Doing so significantly reduces the expense of evaluating eqs. (16) after interpolating $\beta 2$; each coordinate is then the quotient of an 8th- and a 5th-degree polynomial.

There are other possibilities. The basis functions of a uniformly-shaped Beta-spline are translates of one another and need only be evaluated for the first segment drawn if they are saved and reused. In the case of continuously-shaped Beta-splines, each joint is associated with distinct values of $\beta 1$ and $\beta 2$, so that in general each basis function has a different shape and must be individually evaluated.

Altering an existing curve can be done much more efficiently. If a control vertex is moved, then only four segments of the curve must be recomputed, since the basis function which the vertex weights is nonzero on only four successive intervals. Since the vertex is usually moved several times in succession, it is advantageous to save the basis segments as they are first evaluated to avoid recomputing them. Moreover, the portions of the computation for each segment which are actually dependent on the vertex which is being moved may be segregated from those portions of the computation which are not, and which therefore need not be recomputed.

Altering an α parameter necessitates recomputing only two intervals, although all the basis segments in each must be reevaluated.

4.7 Surfaces

Continuously-shaped Beta-spline curves can be elegantly generalized to define surfaces which preserve G^2 continuity at the boundaries between adjacent patches. The generalization we present allows the user to specify a bias and tension parameter at each corner of a patch; of course, patches which share a corner make use of the same α values at that corner. The technique is to generalize the univariate interpolation formula (25) to a bivariate formula in such a way that

—the α values at the four corners of a patch are interpolated,
—two patches that share an edge will have the same β values along that edge,
—the first and second partial derivatives of $\beta 1(u, v)$ and $\beta 2(u, v)$ across a patch boundary will be zero.

This last property will allow us to ignore (at boundaries) all but one of the terms which arise in computing the partial derivatives of a Beta-spline surface in which $\beta 1(u, v)$ and $\beta 2(u, v)$ are allowed to vary, so that the properties of a uniformly-shaped Beta-spline surface will be inherited by our continuously-shaped surface.

Thus our first consideration is to develop a bivariate interpolation formula. It is at least plausible that we would like lines of constant u or of constant v on a continuously-shaped surface to be continuously-shaped curves. Along such curves we would then expect $\beta 1$ and $\beta 2$ to vary as they do along continuously-shaped Beta-spline curves. For convenience let us write eq. (25) in two pieces as

$$s = 10u^3 - 15u^4 + 6u^5$$

$$H(\alpha_{i-1}, \alpha_i; u) = (1 - s)\alpha_{i-1} + s\alpha_i,$$

and along the top and bottom boundaries of the patch interpolate the α values

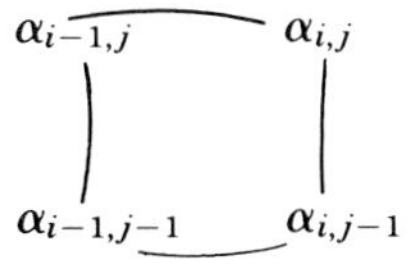

with our special quintic Hermite formula to obtain

$$\alpha_{\text{top}} = H(\alpha_{i-1,j}, \alpha_{i,j}; u) = (1 - s)\alpha_{i-1,j} + s\alpha_{i,j}$$

$$\alpha_{\text{bot}} = H(\alpha_{i-1,j-1}, \alpha_{i,j-1}; u) = (1 - s)\alpha_{i-1,j-1} + s\alpha_{i,j-1}.$$

This yields values of α at parametric distance u from the left edge along the top and bottom of the patch. To interpolate in the v direction across the interior of the patch it is natural to again use the formula

$$H(\alpha_{\text{bot}}, \alpha_{\text{top}}; v) = (1-t)\alpha_{\text{bot}} + t\alpha_{\text{top}}$$

with

$$t = 10v^3 - 15v^4 + 6v^5.$$

Substituting, we obtain the desired bivariate interpolation formula

$$\beta_{i,j}(u, v) = (1-s)(1-t)\alpha_{i-1,j-1} + s(1-t)\alpha_{i,j-1} + (1-s)t\,\alpha_{i-1,j} + st\,\alpha_{i,j} \tag{27}$$

with

$$s = 10u^3 - 15u^4 + 6u^5$$
$$t = 10v^3 - 15v^4 + 6v^5.$$

(We emphasize that s and t are used here for notational convenience.) $\beta_{i,j}(u, v)$ has some rather attractive properties:

— It interpolates $\alpha_{i-1,j-1}$, $\alpha_{i,j-1}$, $\alpha_{i-1,j}$, and $\alpha_{i,j}$.
— Along any of the four borders of a patch it reduces to the univariate interpolating formula (25).
— The first and second partial derivatives of $\beta_{i,j}(u, v)$ with respect to v for $v = 0$ and $v = 1$ (i.e., across a "horizontal" patch boundary) are zero, as are the first and second partial derivatives with respect to u for $u = 0$ and $u = 1$.

Now let us define a continuously-shaped Beta-spline surface patch $\mathbf{Q}_{i,j}$ by eq. (19) except that we let $\beta1$ and $\beta2$ be functions of u and v, using eq. (27) to interpolate between α values associated with the corners of each patch. To simplify the notation, we shall actually discuss $\mathbf{Q}_{2,2}$ and $\mathbf{Q}_{2,3}$, which are defined by the control vertex mesh

$$\begin{matrix} \mathbf{V}_{0,4} & \mathbf{V}_{1,4} & \mathbf{V}_{2,4} & \mathbf{V}_{3,4} \\ \mathbf{V}_{0,3} & \mathbf{V}_{1,3} & \mathbf{V}_{2,3} & \mathbf{V}_{3,3} \\ \mathbf{V}_{0,2} & \mathbf{V}_{1,2} & \mathbf{V}_{2,2} & \mathbf{V}_{3,2} \\ \mathbf{V}_{0,1} & \mathbf{V}_{1,1} & \mathbf{V}_{2,1} & \mathbf{V}_{3,1} \\ \mathbf{V}_{0,0} & \mathbf{V}_{1,0} & \mathbf{V}_{2,0} & \mathbf{V}_{3,0} \end{matrix}$$

(The generalization for arbitrary patches is straightforward.) Since the $b_r(u)$ and $b_s(v)$ are now functions of $\beta1(u, v)$ and $\beta2(u, v)$, we write eq. (20) for $\mathbf{Q}_{2,3}$ as

$$\begin{aligned} \mathbf{Q}_{2,3}(u, v) = {} & [V_{0,4}b_{-2}(\beta1, \beta2; u) + V_{1,4}b_{-1}(\beta1, \beta2; u) + V_{2,4}b_0(\beta1, \beta2; u) + V_{3,4}b_1(\beta1, \beta2; u)]\,b_1(\beta1, \beta2; v) \\ & + [V_{0,3}b_{-2}(\beta1, \beta2; u) + V_{1,3}b_{-1}(\beta1, \beta2; u) + V_{2,3}b_0(\beta1, \beta2; u) + V_{3,3}b_1(\beta1, \beta2; u)]\,b_0(\beta1, \beta2; v) \\ & + [V_{0,2}b_{-2}(\beta1, \beta2; u) + V_{1,2}b_{-1}(\beta1, \beta2; u) + V_{2,2}b_0(\beta1, \beta2; u) + V_{3,2}b_1(\beta1, \beta2; u)]\,b_{-1}(\beta1, \beta2; v) \\ & + [V_{0,1}b_{-2}(\beta1, \beta2; u) + V_{1,1}b_{-1}(\beta1, \beta2; u) + V_{2,1}b_0(\beta1, \beta2; u) + V_{3,1}b_1(\beta1, \beta2; u)]\,b_{-2}(\beta1, \beta2; v). \end{aligned} \tag{28}$$

$\mathbf{Q}_{2,2}$ is similarly defined by

$$\begin{aligned}\mathbf{Q}_{2,2}(u, v) \\ = & [V_{0,3}b_{-2}(\beta 1, \beta 2; u) + V_{1,3}b_{-1}(\beta 1, \beta 2; u) + V_{2,3}b_0(\beta 1, \beta 2; u) + V_{3,3}b_1(\beta 1, \beta 2; v)]b_1(\beta 1, \beta 2; v) \\ & + [V_{0,2}b_{-2}(\beta 1, \beta 2; u) + V_{1,2}b_{-1}(\beta 1, \beta 2; u) + V_{2,2}b_0(\beta 1, \beta 2; u) + V_{3,2}b_1(\beta 1, \beta 2; u)]b_0(\beta 1, \beta 2; v) \\ & + [V_{0,1}b_{-2}(\beta 1, \beta 2; u) + V_{1,1}b_{-1}(\beta 1, \beta 2; u) + V_{2,1}b_0(\beta 1, \beta 2; u) + V_{3,1}b_1(\beta 1, \beta 2; u)]b_{-1}(\beta 1, \beta 2; v) \\ & + [V_{0,0}b_{-2}(\beta 1, \beta 2; u) + V_{1,0}b_{-1}(\beta 1, \beta 2; u) + V_{2,0}b_0(\beta 1, \beta 2; u) + V_{3,0}b_1(\beta 1, \beta 2; u)]b_{-2}(\beta 1, \beta 2; v)\end{aligned} \tag{29}$$

We shall discuss the behavior of these patches at their common "horizontal" boundary, which is $\mathbf{Q}_{2,3}(u, 0)$ and $\mathbf{Q}_{2,2}(u, 1)$. (The argument for common "vertical" boundaries is analogous, and is therefore omitted.)

First, of course, we must verify that the curves $\mathbf{Q}_{2,3}(u, 0)$ and $\mathbf{Q}_{2,2}(u, 1)$ are actually identical. For any fixed u we may rewrite (28) and (29) as

$$\mathbf{Q}_{\text{bot}}(v) = \mathbf{W}_{-2}b_{-2}(v) + \mathbf{W}_{-1}b_{-1}(v) + \mathbf{W}_0 b_0(v) + \mathbf{W}_1 b_1(v) \tag{30}$$

and

$$\mathbf{Q}_{\text{top}}(v) = \mathbf{W}_{-1}\, b_{-2}(v) + \mathbf{W}_0 b_{-1}(v) + \mathbf{W}_1 b_0(v) + \mathbf{W}_2 b_1(v) \tag{31}$$

where

$$\begin{aligned}\mathbf{W}_2 &= \mathbf{V}_{0,4}b_{-2}(u) + \mathbf{V}_{1,4}b_{-1}(u) + \mathbf{V}_{2,4}b_0(u) + \mathbf{V}_{3,4}b_1(u) \\ \mathbf{W}_1 &= \mathbf{V}_{0,3}b_{-2}(u) + \mathbf{V}_{1,3}b_{-1}(u) + \mathbf{V}_{2,3}b_0(u) + \mathbf{V}_{3,3}b_1(u) \\ \mathbf{W}_0 &= \mathbf{V}_{0,2}b_{-2}(u) + \mathbf{V}_{1,2}b_{-1}(u) + \mathbf{V}_{2,2}b_0(u) + \mathbf{V}_{3,2}b_1(u) \\ \mathbf{W}_{-1} &= \mathbf{V}_{0,1}b_{-2}(u) + \mathbf{V}_{1,1}\, b_{-1}(u) + \mathbf{V}_{2,1}b_0(u) + \mathbf{V}_{3,1}b_1(u) \\ \mathbf{W}_{-2} &= \mathbf{V}_{0,0}b_{-2}(u) + \mathbf{V}_{1,0}b_{-1}(u) + \mathbf{V}_{2,0}b_0(u) + \mathbf{V}_{3,0}b_1(u).\end{aligned} \tag{32}$$

Along the common border $\beta_{2,3}(u, 0)$ and $\beta_{2,2}(u, 1)$ both reduce to $H(\alpha_{1,2}\ \alpha_{2,2}; u)$. Hence the $\beta 1$ and $\beta 2$ which appear in (28) and (29) are identical, so that (30) and (31) are simply two successive segments on a uniformly shaped Beta-spline curve. Hence $\mathbf{Q}_{\text{bot}}(1) = \mathbf{Q}_{\text{top}}(0)$. Hence, $\mathbf{Q}_{2,2}(u, 1) = \mathbf{Q}_{2,3}(u, 0)$, as desired.

Tangent and curvature continuity between patches follow similarly if we apply the argument used earlier. Recall that the partial derivatives of $\beta 1(u, v)$ and $\beta 2(u, v)$ with respect to v for $v = 0$ and $v = 1$ are zero. If we fully expand eq. (28) or (29), a typical term has the form

$$\frac{c[\beta 1(u, v)]^m[\beta 2(u, v)]^n u^p v^q}{[\beta 2(u, v)] + 2[\beta 1(u, v)]^3 + 4[\beta 1(u, v)]^2 + 4[\beta 1(u, v)] + 2}.$$

If we then compute the first partial derivative of this term with respect to v, we find, after repeated application of the product, quotient, and chain rules, that the only resulting term which does not contain a product with at least one of

$$\frac{\partial}{\partial v}\beta 1(u, v) \quad \text{and} \quad \frac{\partial}{\partial v}\beta 2(u, v),$$

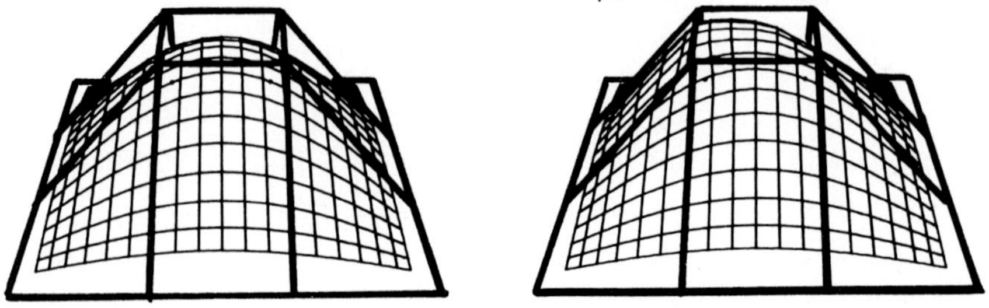

Fig. 17. On the left is a Beta-spline surface in which $\beta 1 = 1$ and $\beta 2 = 0$, a uniform bicubic B-spline surface. On the right the $\beta 2$ value at the joint corresponding to the indicated control vertex has been increased to 25. The 12 boundary vertices in the control graph have been "doubled" so as to define a total of 9 patches; otherwise the 16 control vertices shown would define only a single patch lying close to the 4 central control vertices.

both of which are zero, is

$$\frac{cq[\beta 1(u, v)]^m [\beta 2(u, v)]^n \; u^p \; v^{q-1}}{[\beta 2(u, v)] + 2[\beta 1(u, v)]^3 + 4[\beta 1(u, v)]^2 + 4[\beta 1(u, v)] + 2}.$$

This is exactly the derivative which would have been obtained if $\beta 1$ and $\beta 2$ had not been functions of v. Therefore the first partial derivative of (28) with respect to v, for any u and $v = 0$, is exactly

$$\mathbf{Q}^{(1)}_{\text{top}}(0) = \mathbf{W}_{-1} b^{(1)}_{-2}(0) + \mathbf{W}_0 b^{(1)}_{-1}(0) + \mathbf{W}_1 b^{(1)}_0(0) + \mathbf{W}_2 b^{(1)}_1(0),$$

and the first partial derivative of (29) with respect to v, for any u and $v = 1$, is exactly

$$\mathbf{Q}^{(1)}_{\text{bot}}(1) = \mathbf{W}_{-2} b^{(1)}_{-2}(1) + \mathbf{W}_{-1} b^{(1)}_{-1}(1) + \mathbf{W}_0 b^{(1)}_0(1) + \mathbf{W}_1 b^{(1)}_1(1).$$

These are simply the derivatives of two successive segments of a uniformly-shaped Beta-spline curve for particular values of $\beta 1$ and $\beta 2$, and we already know that such a curve has tangent continuity at its joints. Hence our surface has unit tangent vector continuity along its "horizontal" boundaries. The same argument works, *mutatis mutandis*, for the "vertical" boundaries as well, and generalizes to arbitrary patch boundaries, so that our surface is everywhere G^1 continuous.

An analogous argument suffices to establish curvature vector continuity. G^2 continuity can also be directly verified using Vaxima by evaluating the Beta-spline constraint equations if (27) is used to compute the values of $\beta 1$ and $\beta 2$.

Two continuously-shaped Beta-spline surfaces are shown in Figure 17. The 12 boundary vertices in the control graphs shown have been "doubled" so that the control array defining these surfaces is actually

$$\begin{matrix}
\mathbf{V}_{0,3} & \mathbf{V}_{0,3} & \mathbf{V}_{1,3} & \mathbf{V}_{2,3} & \mathbf{V}_{3,3} & \mathbf{V}_{3,3} \\
\mathbf{V}_{0,3} & \mathbf{V}_{0,3} & \mathbf{V}_{1,3} & \mathbf{V}_{2,3} & \mathbf{V}_{3,3} & \mathbf{V}_{3,3} \\
\mathbf{V}_{0,2} & \mathbf{V}_{0,2} & \mathbf{V}_{1,2} & \mathbf{V}_{2,2} & \mathbf{V}_{3,2} & \mathbf{V}_{3,2} \\
\mathbf{V}_{0,1} & \mathbf{V}_{0,1} & \mathbf{V}_{1,1} & \mathbf{V}_{2,1} & \mathbf{V}_{3,1} & \mathbf{V}_{3,1} \\
\mathbf{V}_{0,0} & \mathbf{V}_{0,0} & \mathbf{V}_{1,0} & \mathbf{V}_{2,0} & \mathbf{V}_{3,0} & \mathbf{V}_{3,0} \\
\mathbf{V}_{0,0} & \mathbf{V}_{0,0} & \mathbf{V}_{1,0} & \mathbf{V}_{2,0} & \mathbf{V}_{3,0} & \mathbf{V}_{3,0}
\end{matrix}$$

Thus each surface actually consists of 9 patches, each of which is rendered in Figure 17 by drawing 7 equally spaced lines of constant u and 7 equally spaced lines of constant v. Boundary conditions for Beta-spline surfaces are discussed further in [1], [4], and [6].

5. CONCLUSIONS

Though the continuously-shaped Beta-splines are more expensive to compute than their uniformly-shaped brethren, they provide the first means of locally controlling the bias and tension in a cubic polynomial spline. This is an important feature in computer-aided design applications. Although the continuously varying Beta-splines are, in principle, rather high-degree polynomials, they are naturally factored into tractable pieces. Indeed, they are interesting precisely because they provide a useful and convenient way of controlling higher than cubic piecewise polynomial curves.

REFERENCES

1. BARSKY, B.A. The Beta-spline: A local representation based on shape parameters and fundamental geometric measures. Ph.D. dissertation, Dept. of Computer Science, Univ. of Utah, Salt Lake City, Utah, Dec., 1981.
2. BARSKY, B.A. Exponential and polynomial methods for applying tension to an interpolating spline curve. *Computer Vision Graphic Image Processing* 1983, to appear.
3. BARSKY, B.A. A study of the parametric uniform B-spline curve and surface representations. Tech. Rep. CSD 83/118, Computer Science Div., Univ. of Calif., Berkeley, Calif., May 1983.
4. BARSKY, B.A. The Beta-spline: A curve and surface representation for computer graphics and computer aided geometric design. To be published.
5. BARSKY, B.A. Algorithms for the evaluation and perturbation of Beta-splines. To be published.
6. BARSKY, B.A., BARTELS, R.H., AND BEATTY, J.C. An introduction to the use of splines in computer graphics. CS-83-9, Dept. of Computer Science, Univ. of Waterloo, Waterloo, Ontario, Canada, 1983.
7. BARSKY, B.A., AND BEATTY, J.C. Varying the betas in Beta-splines. CS-82-49, Dept. of Computer Science, Univ. of Waterloo, Waterloo, Ontario, Canada, 1982. Also Tech. Rep. CSD 82/112, Computer Science Division, Univ. of Calif., Berkeley, Calif., Dec. 1982.
8. BÉZIER, P.E. *Emploi des Machines à Commande Numérique.* Masson et Cie., Paris, 1970. English ed., *Numerical Control—Mathematics and Applications,* A. R. Forrest and A. F. Pankhurst, Trans., Wiley, New York, 1972.
9. BÉZIER, P.E. Essai de définition numérique des courbes et des surfaces expérimentales. Ph.D. dissertation, Univ. Pierre et Marie Curie, Paris, Feb. 1977.
10. BOGEN, R., GOLDEN, J., GENESERETH, M., AND DOOHOVSKOY, A. *MACSYMA Reference Manual*, version 9., Massachussetts Institute of Technology, Cambridge, Mass., 1977.
11. DE BOOR, C. *A Practical Guide to Splines*, vol. 27, Applied Mathematical Sciences. Springer-Verlag, New York, 1978.
12. CLINE, A.K. Scalar- and planar-valued curve fitting using splines under tension. *Commun. ACM* 17, 4 (Apr. 1974), 218–220.
13. COONS, S.A. Surfaces for computer-aided design. Design Div., Mechanical Engineering Dept., Massachusetts Institute of Technology, Cambridge, Mass., 1964.
14. COONS, S.A. Surfaces for computer-aided design of space forms. MAC-TR-41, Project MAC, Massachusetts Institute of Technology, Cambridge, Mass., June 1967.
15. FATEMAN, R.J. Addendum to the *MACSYMA Reference Manual for the VAX.* Univ. of Calif., Berkeley, Calif., 1982.
16. FAUX, I.D., AND PRATT, M.J. *Computational Geometry for Design and Manufacture.* Wiley, New York, 1979.
17. GORDON, W.J., AND RIESENFELD, R.F. B-spline curves and surfaces. In *Computer Aided Geometric Design*, R. E. Barnhill and R. F. Riesenfeld, Eds. Academic Press, New York, 1974, pp. 95–126.

Reprinted From **acm Transactions On Graphics**—April 1983—Vol. 2, No. 2

18. LANE, J.M. Shape operators for computer aided geometric design. Ph.D. dissertation, Univ. of Utah, Salt Lake City, Utah, June 1977.
19. NIELSON, G.M. Some piecewise polynomial alternatives to splines under tension. In *Computer Aided Geometric Design*, R. E. Barnhill and R. F. Riesenfeld, Eds. Academic Press, New York, 1974, pp. 209–235.
20. NIELSON, G.M. Computation of Nu-splines. Dept. of Mathematics, Arizona State Univ., Tempe, Ariz., June 1974.
21. PILCHER, D.T. Smooth approximation of parametric curves and surfaces. Ph.D. dissertation, Univ. of Utah, Salt Lake City, Utah, Aug. 1973.
22. RIESENFELD, R.F. Applications of B-spline approximation to geometric problems of computer-aided design. Ph.D. dissertation, Dept. of Systems and Information Science, Syracuse Univ., New York, May 1973.
23. SCHWEIKERT, D.G. An interpolation curve using a spline in tension. *J. Math. Phys. 45* (1966), 312–317.

Received April 1983; accepted May 1983

TOPOLOGICALLY RELIABLE DISPLAY OF ALGEBRAIC CURVES

Dennis S. Arnon
Computer Science Department
Purdue University
West Lafayette, Indiana, USA 47907

ABSTRACT

An algebraic curve is a set of points in the plane satisfying an equation $F(x,y) = 0$, where $F(x,y)$ is a polynomial in x and y with rational number coefficients. The topological structure of an algebraic curve can be complicated. It may, for example, have multiple components, isolated points, or intricate self-crossings. In the field of Computer Algebra (Symbolic Mathematical Computation), algorithms for exact computations on polynomials with rational number coefficients have been developed. In particular, the cylindrical algebraic decomposition (cad) algorithm of Computer Algebra determines the topological structure of an algebraic curve, given $F(x,y)$ as input. We describe methods for algebraic curve display which, by making use of the cad algorithm, correctly portray the topological structure of the curve. The running times of our algorithms consist almost entirely of the time required for the cad algorithm, which varies from seconds to hours depending on the particular $F(x,y)$.

CR Categories and Subject Descriptors: I.3.3 [Computer Graphics]: Picture/Image Generation - Display algorithms; I.1.2 [Algebraic Manipulation]: Algorithms - Algebraic algorithms; I.3.5 [Computer Graphics]: Computational Geometry and Object Modeling; I.1.4 [Algebraic Manipulation]: Applications

General Terms: Algorithms

Additional Key Words and Phrases: Algebraic Curves

1. Introduction. An algebraic curve is a set of points in the plane satisfying an equation $F(x,y) = 0$, where $F(x,y)$ is a polynomial in x and y with rational number coefficients. The following are some examples:

Example 1.

$$F(x,y) = y^3 - 3xy + x^3.$$

Figure 1

Example 2.
$F(x,y) = y^2 + x^3 + x^2.$

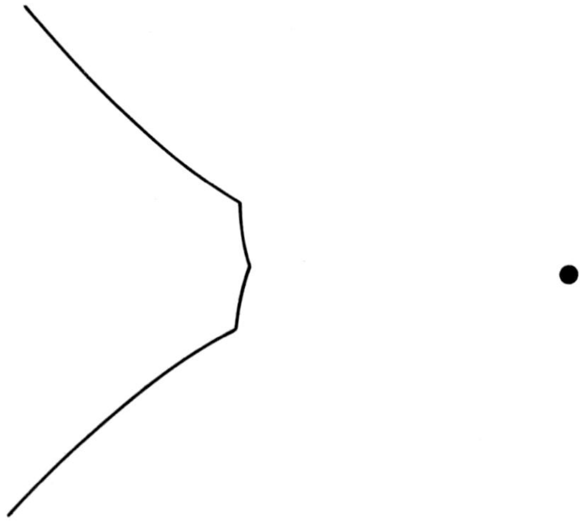

Figure 2.

Example 3.
$F(x,y) = 4y^4 + 17x^2y^2 - 20y^2 + 4x^4 - 20x^2 + 17.$

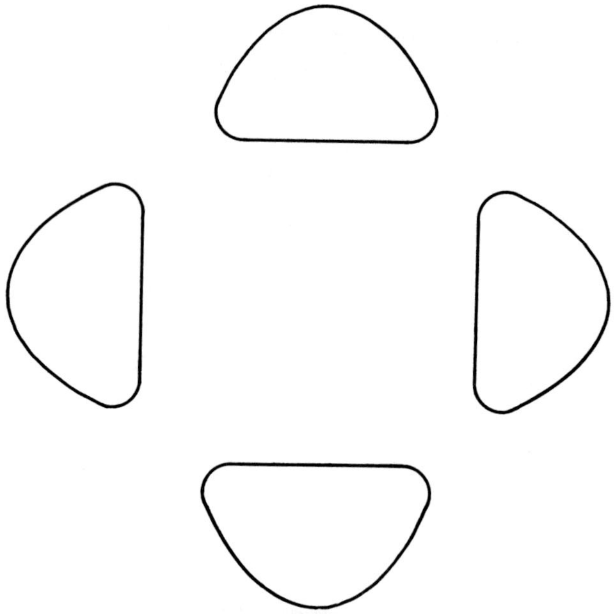

Figure 3

These examples indicate some of the diversity of structure found among algebraic curves. Example 1 crosses itself (at the origin). Example 2 has two connected components, one a curve and the other an isolated point (the origin). Example 3 has four components, each a closed curve.

By the term *topological structure* of a curve, we have in mind the properties of the curve which remain unchanged if the Cartesian plane in which the curve lies is, for example, rotated, bent, stretched, or compressed. Such transformations of the plane we will call *continuous deformations* of it. We may describe the topological structure of a curve in terms of finitely many vertices and edges, thought of as lying in the plane. Each edge either is incident with two vertices (which need not be distinct; the edge is then a loop) and hence is finite in extent, or is incident with exactly one vertex, and its other end is thought of as going to infinity. Edges may only meet at a vertex. The union of the vertices and edges must be a subset of the plane which, under some continuous deformation of the plane, can be transformed to the curve. The following is a collection of one vertex and three edges giving the topological structure of Example 1:

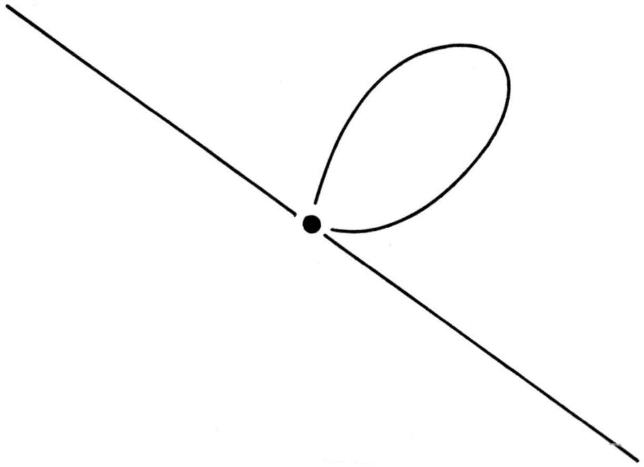

Figure 4

A description of the above sort is a kind of graph; we call it a *structure graph* for the curve, or *S-graph* for short. An S-graph for a curve is not unique; given one we can get another by subdividing any edge into a vertex and two edges. Also, the specific Cartesian coordinates of the vertices of an S-graph, and of the particular points on its edges, are not important. It is enough to say how many vertices and edges there are, and which vertices each edge is incident with. Thus the following is as good an S-graph for Example 1 as the previous figure:

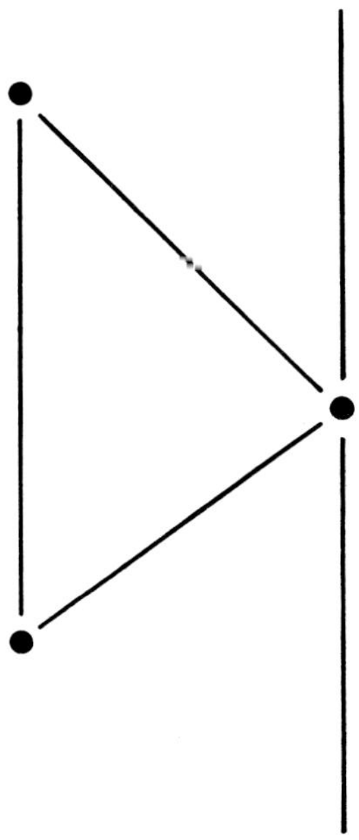

Figure 5

The diverse structures of Examples 1,2, and 3 are captured by their S-graphs. Any S-graph for Example 2 has a vertex with no incident edges. Any S-graph for Example 3 must have four components.

A standard definition of curve display is: "given a mathematical expression, identify the pixels that must be marked so that an image of the curve described by the expression is displayed" ([Pav82a], p. 215). A picture of a curve produced by an actual display device is necessarily only an approximation to the true curve. In looking at a picture of a curve, one consciously or unconsciously discerns some particular topological structure for the curve. Putting this another way, given a picture of a curve, one could get an S-graph from it, if asked to do so. For some algebraic curves, most any picture on most any display device is likely to be sufficient for the discernment of a correct S-graph for the curve. Lines, parabolas, and ellipses are examples of such curves. For more complex algebraic curves this may not be true. Even if we have somehow arranged for a display algorithm to deal with the specification of the curve in the implicit form $F(x,y) = 0$, we may wonder if all components (especially isolated points) are shown, and whether such potential behavior as:

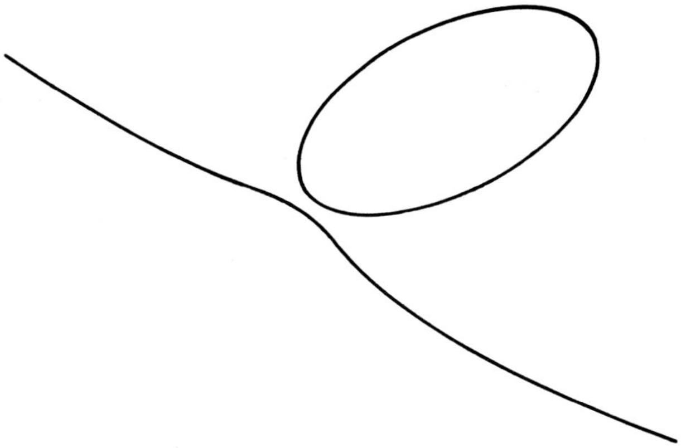

Figure 6

is correctly distinguished from:

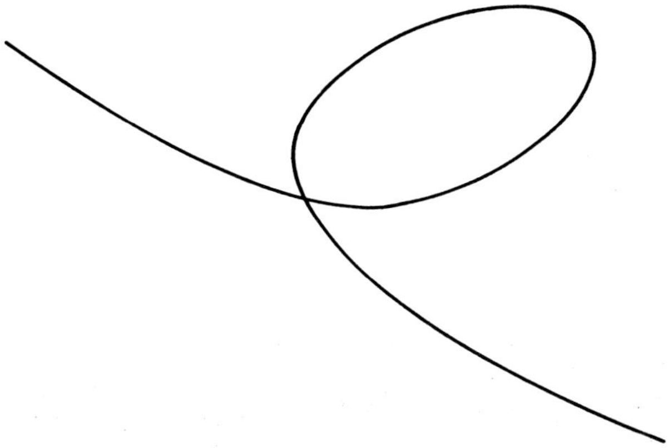

Figure 7

In the present paper we report on three display algorithms which take a polynomial $F(x,y)$ as input, and which are guaranteed to produce a topologically correct picture of the curve $F(x,y) = 0$. By a topologically correct picture we mean a picture in which one may readily discern a correct S-graph for the curve. In fact, the output of the first algorithm is just an S-graph. Our other two algorithms extend the first to produce increasingly accurate plots of the curve (in Cartesian coordinates), at corresponding increases in computing time.

To reliably determine the topological structure of a curve we use the cylindrical algebraic decomposition (cad) algorithm of Computer Algebra, as described in Sections 2 and 3 below. Section 4 describes S-graph display. Section 5 describes our general strategy for accurately plotting the shape of a curve. Section 6 presents our second display algorithm, which we call *numerical plotting*. This algorithm does a relatively fast plot using a standard numerical ODE solver (e.g. Runge-Kutta) applied to the differential equation:

$$y' = -\frac{F_x}{F_y}$$

where F_x and F_y denote the partial derivatives of $F(x,y)$. The use of the ODE routine is controlled by the (previously determined) S-graph for the curve, insuring that the final picture will correctly exhibit the S-graph. Our third display algorithm, which we call *algebraic plotting*, is slower, but is free from the effects of numerical instability. It uses Computer Algebra as much as possible, only converting to floating point numbers to pass the plotted points to a display device. Section 7 treats this algorithm, which has been previously abstracted in [Arn81a]. In Section 8 we discuss the performance of our algorithms, and mention the possibility of developing similar algorithms for surface display.

2. Computer Algebra. Computer Algebra is only one of the names currently in use for the field concerned with exact, symbolic, computations on mathematical expressions. Polynomials in several variables with rational number coefficients are a fundamental class of expressions considered. Other names used for the field are Symbolic Mathematical Computation, Algebraic Manipulation, and Formula Manipulation. Typical problems considered in the field are exact arithmetic of arbitrarily large integers, rational numbers, and symbolic matrices, polynomial factorization, symbolic integration, and simplification of mathematical expressions. Historically, there has been equal concern to develop new algorithms, and to implement existing algorithms in large, publicly available systems. Surveys of the field are [Pav81a] and [Sto80a].

Corresponding to the issues of roundoff and truncation error in numerical analysis, one has in Computer Algebra a persistent issue usually referred to as "intermediate expression swell". It is common for an algebraic computation whose input and output are brief to cause enormous intermediate expressions to be generated. In the worst cases the time and space required for subsidiary computations are so great as to make the desired computation impossible. Our curve display algorithms do not escape this problem. One can easily find curves which have simple topological structure, but which will cause intermediate expression swell sufficient to exhaust the available computing resources. A family of such curves is $x^{2n} + y^{2n} + 1 = 0$, for sufficiently large positive integers n. These curves are all empty, but for increasing n the cad algorithm (see Section 3) will carry out increasingly large intermediate computations.

3. Cylindrical algebraic decompositions. To determine the topological structure of an algebraic curve we utilize a major algorithm of Computer Algebra called the *cylindrical algebraic decomposition* algorithm [Col75a]. Given a bivariate polynomial $F(x,y)$ with rational number coefficients, the cad algorithm finds a decomposition of the plane into points, arcs, and "patches of white space" such that certain of the points and arcs constitute an S-graph for the curve defined by $F(x,y) = 0$. For example, if $F(x,y) = y^3 - 3xy + x^3$ as in Example 1, the cad algorithm would produce the following decomposition of the plane:

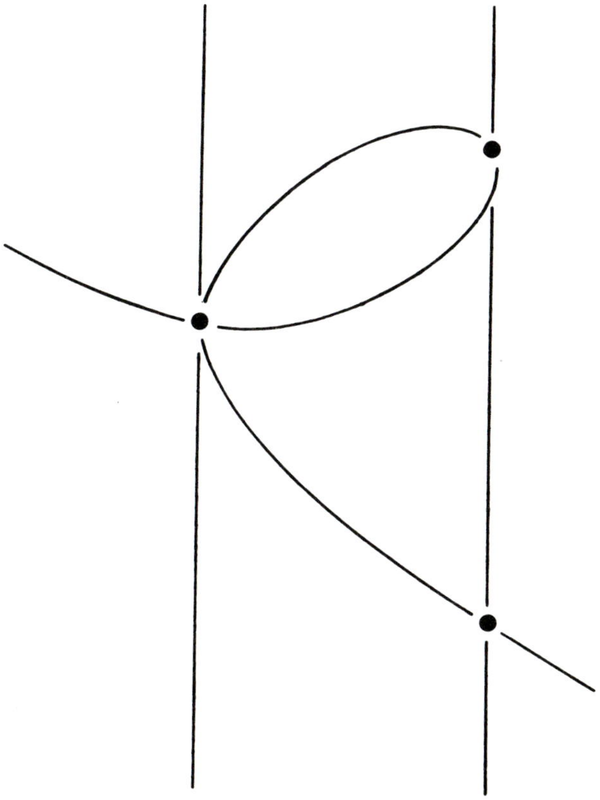

Figure 8

Clearly from this cad we may extract an S-graph for the curve consisting of three vertices and five edges.

The cad algorithm was first implemented in 1981, in the SAC-2 Computer Algebra system [Col80a, Arn81b]. It requires as subalgorithms a number of standard Computer Algebra algorithms which fall under the general heading "algebra of polynomials". The basic capability needed is exact arithmetic on arbitrary length integers, which is implemented with list processing. Building on this are algorithms for exact arithmetic on rational numbers of arbitrary size, followed by algorithms for exact arithmetic on multivariate polynomials with rational number coefficients, for polynomial greatest common divisors, and for polynomial factorization. These various algorithms are described in detail in [Col73a].

Because of the many elements and specialized theory of the cad algorithm, we do not attempt to further describe it here. We refer the reader to [Arn82a, Arn82b, Arn82c], and [Col75a] for further information. It is interesting to note that resultant calculation, apparently used for the first time in Computer Graphics in [Kaj82a], is an important part of the cad algorithm.

4. Structure graph display. Clearly a description of an S-graph can be simple indeed. One need only specify how many vertices and edges there are, and specify incidences in such terms as "edge #2 is incident with vertices #5 and #9".

It is convenient, however, for the cad algorithm to produce a slightly different description of the S-graph which has the advantage of giving one an idea of the actual shape of the curve. As suggested by Figure 8, the subsets of the plane which make up a cad (these subsets are called the *cells* of the cad) can be arranged into vertical strips. The cells which make up a particular strip are "stacked on top of each other". Thus to each cell we can assign an index consisting of two positive-integer components. We number the vertical strips from left to right, and define the first component of a cell's index to be the number of the vertical strip in which it lies. Within each vertical strip, we number the cells from bottom to top, and define the second component of a cell's index to be its number with respect to this ordering. Thus the indices of the cells in the cad of Figure 8 are (1,1), (1,2), (1,3), (2,1), (2,2), (2,3), (3,1), (3,2), (3,3), (3,4), (3,5), (3,6), (3,7), (4,1), (4,2), (4,3), (4,4), (4,5), (5,1), (5,2), and (5,3).

Our algorithm describes an S-graph as a collection of the following three kinds of statements: "edge (3,2) is incident with vertices (2,2) and (4,6)", "edge (1,2) is incident with vertex (2,2) only", and "vertex (4,4) is an isolated point". Thus from the cad of Figure 8, we get the following description of the S-graph for the curve $y^3 - 3xy + x^3 = 0$:

edge (1,2) is incident with vertex (2,2) only
edge (3,2) is incident with vertices (2,2) and (4,2)
edge (3,4) is incident with vertices (2,2) and (4,4)
edge (3,6) is incident with vertices (2,2) and (4,4)
edge (5,2) is incident with vertex (4,2) only

We can gain some knowledge of the shape of the curve by just diagramming this information:

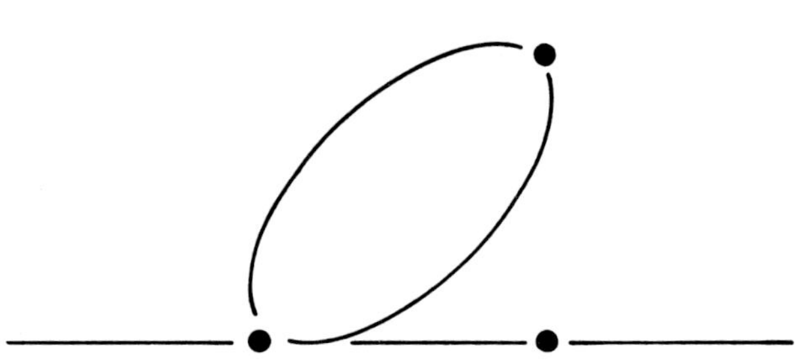

Figure 9

5. Accurate shape portrayal: general strategy. The output of our second and third display algorithms will be a collection of sequences of points in the plane. Each point in such a sequence will consist of a floating-point x-coordinate and y-coordinate; e.g. "-3.256 12.621" is such a point. The sequences of points will be fed to a display device which, for each sequence, will plot the points in the sequence and connect consecutive points with line segments. In our case, the sequences of points are passed to the "graph" command of the UNIX™ operating system running on a VAX™ 11/780 computer, driving a Versatec™ printer/plotter.

The output of the cad algorithm includes information (the so-called *sample points* for cells) which enables us to construct arbitrarily accurate floating-point approximations to the $x-$ and $y-$coordinates of each point that is to be a vertex of the S-graph (see [Arn82a] and [Col75a]). The cad output also enables us to construct arbitrarily accurate floating-point approximations to as many points as desired on each edge of the S-graph (using the so-called *defining formulas* for cells). The actual construction of such approximations is made possible by algebraic algorithms for approximating the real roots of a polynomial to any accuracy desired accuracy (see e.g [Arn81b]. We use the above properties of cad output in the following scheme for making up sequences of points.

For every edge of the S-graph, we make a preliminary sequence consisting of closely spaced, consecutive floating-point points, each of which lies close to an actual point on the edge. The user controls the horizontal spacing of the points. For edges incident with two vertices, the first point of the preliminary sequence lies close to one vertex, and the last point lies close to the other. For edges incident with only one vertex, the first point of the preliminary sequence lies close to that vertex, and the remaining points "go out towards infinity" along the edge for some distance specified by the user. With the algebraic plotting algorithm of Section 7 the user can specify a limit to the distance between each constructed point and a true edge point, hence with algebraic plotting the shape of the curve can be portrayed as accurately as desired. With the numerical plotting algorithm of Section 6 one cannot specify such a limit, but judicious use of the numerical differential equation solver can keep the approximation error small. Regardless of how large the approximation error becomes, the following precaution taken for both plotting methods suffices to insure that the final picture will show correct topological structure. We check each constructed point of each sequence to insure that the line segments joining the points of any one sequence will be disjoint from the line segments joining the points of every other sequence.

Having constructed a preliminary sequence for each edge of the S-graph, we use the ability to construct approximations to vertices, and the known incidences of the S-graph, to make final sequences. First, we construct floating-point approximations to each vertex. Next, whenever an edge is incident with a particular vertex, we make (the approximation to) that vertex the new initial or final point, whichever is appropriate, of the sequence for that edge. Finally, we make each vertex which is not incident with any edge into a sequence consisting of one point, and set a flag to have that point tagged with some easily visible character (we have arbitrarily selected asterisk) by the display device. In this way the viewer of the final picture will be unmistakably informed of isolated points.

6. Accurate shape portrayal with numerical edge plotting. Given a curve $F(x,y) = 0$, by the Implicit Function Theorem we have the ordinary differential equation

$$y' = -\frac{F_x}{F_y}$$

It is a property of cad's that if c is a cell of a cad which is an edge of an S-graph, then $F_y(x,y)$ is nonzero at every point (x,y) of c (see [Arn82a] or [Col75a]). Thus we can use a numerical ordinary differential equation solver (e.g. Runge-Kutta) to plot points of c "from left to right" and obtain one of the preliminary sequences defined in Section 5. We do this as follows. As mentioned in Section 5, we use the output of the cad algorithm to compute an (approximation to) a particular point of c "near the lefthand end" of c. The user specifies a stepsize, and we then run the ODE solver up to a point "near the righthand end" of c. Numerical effects can significantly distort the shape of the curve, as the following display of $y^3 - 3xy + x^3 = 0$ shows:

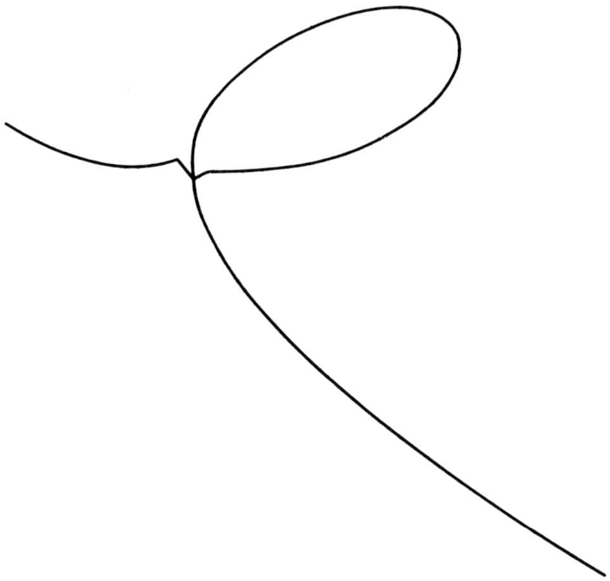

Figure 10

We remark that the SAC-2 Computer Algebra system is implemented in Fortran, so it is not difficult to mesh the algebraic and numerical algorithms.

7. Accurate shape portrayal with algebraic edge plotting. Algebraic edge plotting has the same general plan as the numerical plotting described in the last section, namely an edge c is plotted from left to right, using a stepsize specified by the user. But to do the plotting we use the defining formula for the cell constructed by the cad algorithm. This formula is a boolean combination of polynomial equations and inequalities which precisely defines the points in the plane belonging to the edge. For example, the defining formula for cell (3,2) in the cad of Figure 8 is:

$$\Psi(x,y) = (x > 0) \ \& \ (x^3 - 4 < 0) \ \& \ (x - 2 < 0) \ \& \ (y < 0)$$
$$\& \ (y^2 - x > 0) \ \& \ (y^3 - 3xy + x^3 = 0).$$

As in this example, the formula for a cell which is an edge in an S-graph always has the form $\psi(x,y) \ \& \ F(x,y) = 0$. Since the initial x-value is a rational number, and the step-size is a rational number, for every x-value a at which we wish to compute a point (a,b) of c, a is a rational number. Hence we can evaluate $\psi(a,y) = \phi(y)$ and $F(a,y)$ exactly (using Computer Algebra). We construct the exact real roots of $F(a,y)$ as algebraic numbers (see [Arn82a] or [Col75a]), and evaluate $\phi(y)$ at each. There will be exactly one root which satisfies ϕ, and thus we have found a point (a,b) on c, which we may approximate to any desired precision. Clearly a smaller step size and more accurate approximation in the above process will produce a more accurate rendering of the shape of c, but require more time.

The algorithm used in this section was used to produce Figures 1,2, and 3 (the actual plots shown are copies made by a draftsman).

8. Conclusions. The times for Examples 1,2, and 3 serve to illustrate the performance of our display algorithms. The total CPU time for Example 1 was about one and a half minutes (all times are on a VAX™ 11/780 computer running the UNIX™ operating system driving a Versatec™ printer/plotter). Example 2 took about four minutes, and Example 3 about eight minutes. Example 3 is a curve of degree four; it is not difficult to find degree four curves that will cause the cad algorithm to run for several hours. As mentioned in Section 2, curves of sufficiently high degree will cause the cad algorithm to exhaust available resources. Although it has been established that the computing time of the cad algorithm is polynomial in the degree of $F(x,y)$ [Col75a], its expected performance is still poorly understood.

The cad algorithm is applicable to polynomials in any number of variables. The cad-based approach we have used for curve display can be extended to surface display.

Acknowledgement We thank Professor J. Rice for alerting us to the equation $y' = -F_x / F_y$.

References

Arn81a.
DS Arnon, "Automatic analysis of real algebraic curves," *SIGSAM Bulletin (of the Association for Computing Machinery)* **15,** pp. 3-9 (1981).

Arn81b.
DS Arnon, "Algorithms for the geometry of semi-algebraic sets," Technical Report #436, Computer Science Dept., University of Wisconsin, Madison, Wisconsin(1981). (Ph.D. thesis)

Arn82b.
DS Arnon, GE Collins, and S McCallum, "Cylindrical algebraic decomposition II: an adjacency algorithm for the plane," Technical Report CSD TR-428, Computer Science Dept., Purdue University(December, 1982).

Arn82c.
DS Arnon and S McCallum, "Cylindrical algebraic decomposition by quantifier elimination," pp. 215-222 in *Proceedings of the European Computer Algebra Conference (EUROCAM '82),* ed. J Calmet ,Lecture Notes in Computer Science, 144, Springer-Verlag, Berlin(1982).

Arn82a.
DS Arnon, GE Collins, and S McCallum, "Cylindrical algebraic decomposition I: the basic algorithm," Technical Report CSD TR-427, Computer Science Dept., Purdue University(December, 1982).

Col73a.
GE Collins, "Computer algebra of polynomials and rational functions," *American Mathematical Monthly* **80,** pp. 725-755 (1973).

Col75a.
GE Collins, "Quantifier elimination for real closed fields by cylindrical algebraic decomposition," pp. 134-163 in *Proceedings of the Second GI Conference on Automata and Formal Languages,* Lecture notes in Computer Science, 33, Springer-Verlag, Berlin(1975).

Col80a.
GE Collins, "SAC-2 and ALDES now available,"

SIGSAM Bulletin (of the Association for Computing Machinery) **14,** p. 19 (1980).

Kaj82a.
JT Kajiya, "Ray tracing parametric patches," *Computer Graphics* **16,** pp. 245-254 (1982).

Pav81a.
R Pavelle, M Rothstein, and J Fitch, "Computer algebra," *Scientific American* **245,** pp. 136-152 (1981).

Pav82a.
T Pavlidis, *Algorithms for graphics and image processing,* Computer Science Press, Rockville, Maryland(1982).

Sto80a.
DR Stoutemyer and DYY Yun, "Symbolic mathematical computation," in *Encyclopedia of Computer Science and Technology*, ed. J Belzer, AG Holzman, A Kent ,Marcel Dekker(1980). (Supplement)

Curve-Fitting with Piecewise Parametric Cubics

Michael Plass and Maureen Stone
IMAGING SCIENCES LABORATORY
Xerox Palo Alto Research Center

Abstract: Parametric piecewise-cubic functions are used throughout the computer graphics industry to represent curved shapes. For many applications, it would be useful to be able to reliably derive this representation from a closely spaced set of points that approximate the desired curve, such as the input from a digitizing tablet or a scanner. This paper presents a solution to the problem of automatically generating efficient piecewise parametric cubic polynomial approximations to shapes from sampled data. We have developed an algorithm that takes a set of sample points, plus optional endpoint and tangent vector specifications, and iteratively derives a single parametric cubic polynomial that lies close to the data points as defined by an error metric based on least-squares. Combining this algorithm with dynamic programming techniques to determine the knot placement gives good results over a range of shapes and applications.

CR Categories and Subject Descriptors: G.1.2 [**Numerical Analysis**]: Approximation–Least squares approximation; Spline and piecewise polynomial approximation; G.1.5 [**Numerical Analysis**]: Roots of Nonlinear Equations–Iterative methods; I.2.8 [**Artificial Intelligence**]: Problem Solving, Control Methods and Search–Dynamic programming; I.3.3 [**Computer Graphics**]: Picture/Image Generation–Digitizing and scanning; I.3.5 [**Computer Graphics**]: Computational Geometry and Object Modeling–Curve, surface, solid, and object representations

General Terms: Algorithms

1. Introduction.

We are interested in the problems that arise when trying to use two-dimensional curved shapes in an interactive design environment. In particular, we are interested in finding the best ways for a designer to define such shapes. Our immediate focus is the production of publication-quality documents. The documents are designed using an interactive system with a raster display, then camera-ready copy is digitally produced at very high resolutions. Our design methodology is to represent all shapes analytically using piecewise parametric cubic polynomials [27]. There are many published methods for specifying such curves [2,12,15,23]. These methods all have in common the approach that the shape designer provides a small set of controlling points and parameters which act as handles to shape the curve. At Xerox PARC such algorithms, and similar ones for conics, have been used in design systems for making illustrations [4,3,16,26] and digital typefaces [5]. We conclude that it would be a powerful addition to the set of tools for specifying shapes to be able to reliably derive an efficient piecewise parametric cubic polynomial representation from a sequence of closely-spaced points that approximate the desired curve. The points could be produced in a variety of ways such as sketching with a digitizing pen, scanning and finding edges in an existing drawing, or writing a program to compute a set of data points. In this paper we will present a method deriving such an analytical representation from digitized data.

For the data in our curve-fitting work we have experimented with hand-tuned digital curves, optically-scanned images and simple hand-drawn sketches. We have found that the source of the digitized curve is relatively unimportant. The differences principally affect how tightly you want to follow the data; is it noisy, does it have pronounced rastering effects, are corners well defined? A scanned image will not have as sharp corners as a hand-tuned bitmap, for example. Also, the tolerance is a function of the image resolution. We feel our results are generally applicable to the problem of generating piecewise approximations to shapes from an ordered set of discrete data points.

The heart of our method is an algorithm that takes a set of sample points and derives a parametric cubic curve that lies close to the data points; this algorithm is presented in section 4. A more elaborate version of the algorithm, presented in section 5, allows the endpoints and/or the tangent directions at the endpoints of the piece to be specified.

A piecewise approximation to a shape consists of a number of single cubic pieces connected end-to-end. The location and smoothness of the joints or *knots* between the pieces is critical to getting a good representation of the shape. Sometimes we want a smooth connection between pieces, and sometimes we want to produce a sharp "corner." If we somehow knew in advance the position of the knots, and the tangent direction at each non-corner knot, we could simply apply the single-piece fitting algorithm to the points in each span, yielding a piecewise approximation. Finding the best knot positions and tangents, however, is no easy task. Our most promising results were obtained by setting tangents using fairly local information, and then using dynamic programming to search the space of potential knot positions.

The single-piece fitting routine is used in several places in the overall process. In the dynamic programming phase it is used as a way of measuring how well a span of sample points may be fit with a single cubic piece, and, after the knots have been found, it is used to find the piecewise approximation. The algorithm may also be used in the initial phase to compute tangent directions, by fitting a range of samples around the point of interest and finding the tangent of the resulting curve. This method works well for estimating tangent directions in noisy data.

In this paper we want to emphasize our parametric cubic curve-fitting algorithm and the use of dynamic programming to find the knots. While it is important to accurately find corners and tangents, we feel the choice of algorithms to do so is highly application dependent and we are not in a position to give a complete analysis here.

The next section of this paper is a general discussion of the problem of fitting shapes with piecewise functions. In section 3 we describe how we use dynamic programming to find the knot positions. Sections 4 and 5 will present in detail our algorithm for computing a single parametric cubic given a set of data points. We conclude with a summary and examples of our results.

2. Piecewise function approximation to shapes.

What do we mean by the best piecewise approximation to a shape such as Figure 1(a)? The curve must lie near the data points, of course, and the representation will be most efficient if we use as few pieces as possible. This presents an obvious trade-off between a tight fit and an efficient representation. Also, the desired tightness of the fit will vary with the amount of noise in the data. Usually the curve should be smooth, and the pieces of the curve should fit smoothly together. In some cases, however, we find that the shape will look better if we introduce sharp bends at locations that are perceived as "corners". There are other issues of perception as well. For example, if the samples lie on a straight line, most users will object if the approximating curve is slightly wavy even if it lies quite close to the sample points.

In this paper we will parameterize the problem as follows: The closeness of the fit is specified by a user-defined tolerance; it is the user's job to consider the resolution and accuracy of the input when specifying the tolerance. The fit is smooth if the direction of the tangent vector is continuous. Restricting only the direction of this vector to maintain smoothness gives us the maximum flexibility for two-dimensional curves. We use one of a number of algorithms to find the corners before finding any of the other knot locations. These methods all have the property that the user sets some parameters to tune the algorithm for a particular set of data. If a point is identified as a corner, we put a knot at that location and simply do not force tangent continuity there. While a parametric cubic is flexible enough to have a sharp cusp in it, the behavior of the curve near the cusp is quite constrained so we generally do not try to model corners with cusps.

Figure 1 is an example of the process we use to fit a shape. The original data, which in this case is derived from a high resolution bitmap, is shown in figure 1(a). We need to limit the choice of knot locations to a finite set so we can use a finite search technique like dynamic programming. This set is defined to be the set of sample points. For efficiency, we want to reduce the number of possible knot locations even further. In this example we restrict the potential knot locations to the vertices of a polygon fit to the sample points. Any vertex with an angle sharper than 135° is taken to be a corner. For this kind of data we usually filter the samples between corners to remove the more pronounced rastering effects. After filtering, the tangent vectors are set on each potential knot that is not a corner. Figure 1(b) shows the unfiltered samples, the potential knots, and the normal vectors to the tangents at each potential knot. If the potential knot is a corner, it has no tangent set and is marked with a cross. To calculate the tangents in this example we used the curve-fitting algorithm to fit a small number of points around each potential knot and determined the tangent to the resulting curve at the point nearest the potential knot. The computed curved shape is shown in figure 1(c). Figure 1(d) shows the result in more detail. The small dots are the samples, and the large dots are the knots that were actually chosen.

Further examples of shapes fit with our techniques are included in the conclusions.

3. Choosing the knots.

Before discussing methods for choosing knots, let us look first at the problem of predicting whether a set of samples can be closely fit by a single piece of the curve. A parametric cubic polynomial is quite flexible, but has some obvious limits. For example, it can contain at most one loop or, if it has no loop, at most two inflection points. It is tempting, therefore, to try to derive a set of algorithms that measure space-curve characteristics such as slope and curvature and use this information to set the knot positions. However, as you add constraints to guarantee continuity, the degrees of freedom available to fit the cubic to the samples are reduced. Furthermore, the fit is very vulnerable

(a): Original data, approximately 150 by 160 bits.

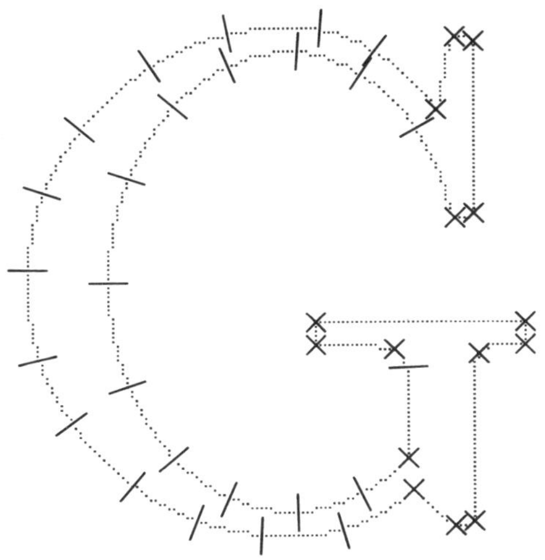

(b): Samples, potential knots and normal vectors.

(c): Result of curve fitting algorithm, 14 cubic pieces.

(d): Samples, curve and knots.

Figure 1. An example showing the steps involved in fitting a parametric cubic to a sampled shape. Figure (a) is the original data taken from a high resolution bitmap. Figure (b) shows the sample points, the potential knots and the corresponding normal vectors. Potential knots marked with a cross are corners. Figure (c) is the final shape. Figure (d) shows the curve, knots and samples in more detail.

to a poorly chosen continuity constraint such as a bad tangent vector. The only reliable way we have found to tell if a set of samples can be fit by a single cubic with constraints is to try it.

Given that we are going to pay the cost of trying out different cubic pieces, one simple method for defining the knots is to "grow" the pieces out until the fit for that piece exceeds some threshold. In other words, starting with the previous knot, keep adding data points until the piece is as long as possible. Each new piece must be constrained to maintain continuity. This works, in the sense that the resulting curve will fit everywhere within the specified tolerance, but is quite vulnerable to local phenomena such as noisy data or a badly defined tangent. We found this method works only moderately well in terms of the total number of knots in the final solution especially when trying to maintain tangent continuity. Subdivision is another obvious choice which has the same problem. These two techniques are also described by Reeves [20].

If we want to maintain continuity, the globally-best set of knots cannot be found by a method that only optimizes locally. For example, if the first and last sample points are constrained to lie on the curve, the error in fitting a parametric cubic piece is not a monotone function of the number of samples; it may be possible to get a better fit by using a longer run of samples with better endpoint locations. This is especially true if the data is noisy. In theory, to find the best solution we could try all possible arrangements of knots and then take the best fit. This solution is exponential in the number of data points, and is clearly out of the question for any useful cases. It is possible, however, to reduce the complexity to $O(n^3)$ by using dynamic programming.

Dynamic programming [1,6] is a method for efficiently searching a solution space where the problem can be recursively broken up into a set of subproblems. Since the same subproblems contribute to the solution of several larger subproblems, the total number of computations can be reduced by storing the results of each subproblem. We can apply this method to finding the knots as follows: Let e_{ij} be the error obtained when a single piece is fit to samples i through j. The exact definition of e_{ij} does not matter insofar as the dynamic programming algorithm is concerned, and we have obtained good results with several different ones. One reasonable choice for e_{ij} is simply the sum of the squares of the distances from the sample points to the curve, plus a constant $\tau > 0$. Increasing the value of τ will encourage fewer knots, at the expense of not fitting the samples as closely. The total error for a given arrangement of knots is just the sum of the errors for the individual pieces. Let E_{ij} be the least total error over all possible arrangements of knots for samples i thru j. This can be computed as

$$E_{ij} = \min(E_{ik} + e_{kj}), \quad i < k < j,$$

where we have already computed and tabulated the values for E_{ik} for $i < k < j-1$. We can compute all the values for e_{kj} by working backwards and fitting single pieces from samples j to k for all values of k in the range.

Even using dynamic programming it is very expensive to test all possible subranges for the best fit. We can do several things to prune the search space and improve the performance at the cost of no longer guaranteeing the optimum solution. For example, it is usually true that for each piece the shape of the curve distant from the area of interest will contribute little to the local best solution. Therefore, we limit how far back along the curve we search when computing E_{kj} above. As in the example of Figure 1, we generally use a subset of the sample points as potential knot positions to further reduce the cost.

The main contribution of dynamic programming to this algorithm is a way of searching in a more global manner for the best solution set of knots. However, one of the principal advantages of piecewise functions is that they are controlled mostly by local information. Said another way, for a particular subsection of the curve, the best locations for the knots is not going to be affected much by the shape of the curve far away. So it may be possible to construct a more efficient algorithm than ours that looks only in a small region of the curve for each knot location. What our experience indicates is that it is important to do some searching to give immunity from local aberrations.

The next two sections will describe our algorithm for fitting a parametric cubic polynomial to a set of data points.

4. Least-squares curve fitting with a parametric cubic polynomial.

For computer graphics applications, the common specification of a parametric cubic polynomial is $F(X(t), Y(t))$, where X and Y are cubic polynomials and t lies in the range 0 to 1. Such a curve can be thought of as a three-dimensional curve in the space X, Y, t. The curve is constrained such that the projections on the $X-t$ and $Y-t$ planes are cubic polynomials. What is usually displayed is the projection of this curve on the $X-Y$ plane. Our problem is: given a set of points on the $X-Y$ plane, find the 3-space curve whose $X-Y$ projection is such that the sum of the squares of the distances between the points and the projected curve is minimized. Note that there is not a unique solution to this problem. A simple example of this is that if X is a scalar multiple of Y, the resulting projected curve is a straight line, and many different (X, Y) pairs will yield the same line.

Let us look at this problem a bit differently. We are given a set of data points. If we knew the parametric curve that gave the best fit, we could find the points on the projected curve that were nearest each of the data points. If we assigned the corresponding value of t to the data point, we are in effect positioning the data points near the curve in X, Y, t space. The interesting thing about this representation is that if we consider the projection of the points and curve on, for example, the $X-t$ plane, we have the cubic polynomial that minimizes the sum of the squares of the distances to the points in X. This means if we only knew the correct t values for our data points, we could solve for our curve by performing simple least-squares fitting in X and Y independently. Our algorithm is an iterative technique that converges to this set of t values.

Our algorithm is simple to state: Assign an initial approximation to t for each data point. Solve $X(t)$ and $Y(t)$ independently using conventional least-squares techniques. Measure the result, and if necessary, adjust the t values for the data points and repeat. This is a fixed-point iteration that, if it converges, will converge to a local minimum for our non-linear system. For the class of curves we are using it usually does converge and gives a good solution.

We use an initial approximation based on the Euclidean distance between the data points in the $X-Y$ plane. That is, let

$$s_k = \sum_{i=1}^{k-1} \sqrt{(x_{i+1} - x_i)^2 + (y_{i+1} - y_i)^2}, \qquad (1)$$

be the total length of the polygonal segment connecting points 1 through k. We set the initial value of t_k be s_k/s_n.

To solve for $X(t)$ and $Y(t)$, simple least-squares curve-fitting [8] will be fine for this problem as stated. We will defer any further discussion of this part of the algorithm until section 5, where we will extend this technique so that it is possible to specify endpoint and tangent conditions for the final curve.

Given X and Y, we adjust the t_i values by finding for each data point the point on the curve closest to it. We then assign this new t value to the data point. In X, Y, t space, we are moving the data point closer to the current curve, changing only the value for t. We stop iterating when the values for t no longer change significantly, or when some other condition is satisfied; for example, if the maximum distance from the points to the curve falls below some threshold. We also set an upper bound on the number of iterations.

The square of the distance between a given point (x, y) and any point $(X(t), Y(t))$ that lies on the curve is

$$(X(t) - x)^2 + (Y(t) - y)^2 \qquad (2)$$

To find where this is minimum we differentiate and equate to zero, yielding

$$2(X(t) - x)X'(t) + 2(Y(t) - y)Y'(t) = 0 \qquad (3)$$

The left side of this equation is a fifth-degree polynomial in t. Since we have an approximation to the desired root, the previous value, we can use Newton-Raphson iteration to find the root. The formula for Newton-Raphson iteration for solving $f(t) = 0$ is

$$t \leftarrow t - \frac{f(t)}{f'(t)} \qquad (4)$$

so each iteration should decrease t by the amount

$$\frac{(X(t) - x)X'(t) + (Y(t) - y)Y'(t)}{X'(t)^2 + Y'(t)^2 + (X(t) - x)X''(t) + (Y(t) - y)Y''(t)} \qquad (5)$$

Because Newton-Raphson iteration converges quickly, only a few steps are needed to find a close approximation to the root. In fact, the algorithm performs well when only one iteration step is used to make the adjustment.

After all the t_i have been adjusted, it is important that they still lie in the range 0 to 1. Therefore, we linearly scale the values before each re-calculation of X and Y.

Figure 2 shows an example of the algorithm in operation. The small dots mark the sample points, and lines have been drawn from each data point (x_i, y_i) to the corresponding point $(X(t_i), Y(t_i))$ on the curve. When the algorithm has converged, it can be seen that the point $(X(t_i), Y(t_i))$ is the closest point on the curve to (x_i, y_i).

5. Handling continuity constraints.

The algorithm as stated in the previous section is not suitable for fitting smooth, continuous, piecewise functions because we cannot easily constrain the endpoints and tangents for each cubic piece. To understand how to extend this method, we must look at least-squares curve fitting in some more detail.

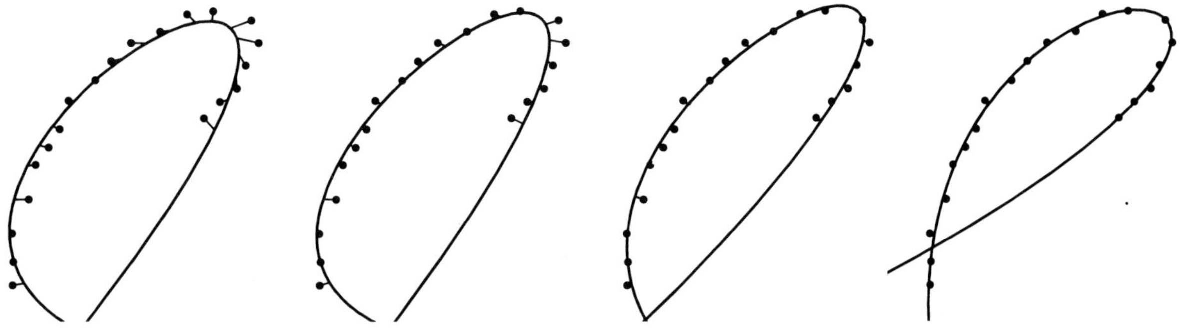

Initial fit. 1 iteration. 10 iterations. 100 iterations.

Figure 2. This figure shows several iterations of the curve-fitting algorithm. The sample points are shown as small dots, which are connected by straight lines to the points on the curve with the corresponding value of t. A portion of the curve outside the region $0 \leq t \leq 1$ is included give a better feel for the overall shape of the cubic.

Fitting a polynomial of one variable using least squares curve fitting means the following: given a set of data points $\{(x_i, y_i), 1 \le i \le n\}$, find the polynomial $p(x)$ that minimizes the sum

$$\sum_{i=1}^{n}(p(x_i) - y_i)^2 \tag{6}$$

This problem has a unique solution that can be derived as follows. Let the polynomial $p(x)$ be expressed as a linear combination of polynomial basis functions

$$\sum_{j=0}^{d} a_j \phi_j(x) \tag{7}$$

The problem at hand is to determine $A = \langle a_0, a_1, \ldots a_d\rangle$ such that the function

$$S = \sum_{i=1}^{n}\left(\sum_{j=0}^{d} a_j \phi_j(x_i) - y_i\right)^2 \tag{8}$$

is minimized. To do this we take the partial derivatives of S with respect to each value of A and set them to zero to obtain a set of $d+1$ linear equations.

The partial derivatives of S are given by

$$\frac{\partial S}{\partial a_k} = \sum_{i=1}^{n} 2\left(\sum_{j=0}^{d} a_j \phi_j(x_i) - y_i\right)\phi_k(x_i), \tag{9}$$

and by setting these to zero and rearranging, we obtain the linear system

$$\sum_{j=0}^{d} a_j \sum_{i=1}^{n} \phi_j(x_i)\phi_k(x_i) = \sum_{i=1}^{n} y_i \phi_k(x_i), \quad 0 \le k \le d. \tag{10}$$

This linear system may be easily solved, for example by using Gaussian elimination. Furthermore, for a small linear system like this, it is seldom necessary to worry about numerical instability problems.

The basis functions $\phi_j = x^j$, where $j = \langle 0, 1, 2, 3\rangle$ are typically used for cubic polynomials. However, the values of A multiplying these basis functions have no intuitive meaning with respect to the shape of the curve. Since any set of linearly independent polynomials would work as basis functions, consider what happens if we use instead the the Hermite polynomials $\langle s_0, s_1, s_2, s_3\rangle$ shown in Figure 3. These polynomials have the property that if you combine scalar multiples of them to produce a curve, the values of the position and tangent at each endpoint of the curve are each controlled by exactly one of the basis functions. The values of A are just scalar multiples for the basis functions, so this means that by setting an element of A to some fixed value, we can predefine the endpoint or tangent of the resulting curve.

Stated more formally: We may treat just a subset of $\{a_0, a_1, \ldots, a_d\}$ as variables, and the rest as constants. To simplify the notation, rename the basis functions as needed so that $\{a_0, a_1, \ldots, a_{m-1}\}$ are the free variables,

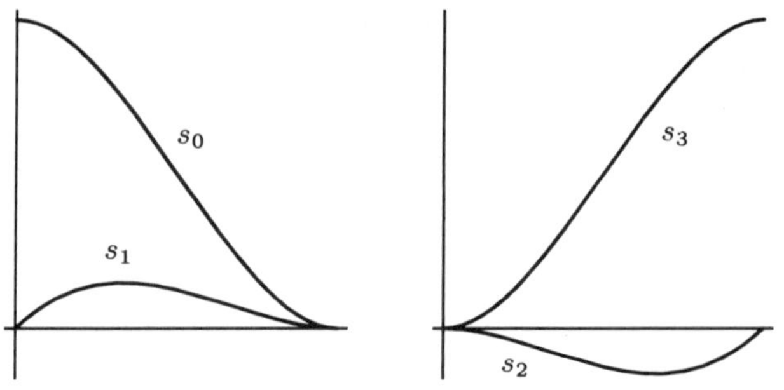

$s_0(t) = 2t^3 - 3t^2 + 1$ $\qquad$ $s_2(t) = t^3 - t^2$

$s_1(t) = t^3 - 2t^2 + t$ $\qquad$ $s_3(t) = -2t^3 + 3t^2$

Figure 3. The Hermite basis functions.

and $\{a_m, a_{m+1}, \ldots, a_d\}$ are the constants. Then equation 10 becomes, for $0 \le k < m$,

$$\sum_{j=0}^{m-1} a_j \sum_{i=1}^{n} \phi_j(x_i)\phi_k(x_i) = \sum_{i=1}^{n}\left(y_i - \sum_{j=m}^{d} a_j \phi_j(x_i)\right)\phi_k(x_i) \tag{11}$$

which specifies an $m \times m$ linear system.

This means that by using the Hermite basis in our least-squares fitting, we can preset the endpoints of the resulting cubic. The tangents in the above discussion, however, are the slopes of X or Y with respect to t. If we try to fix the slope of our curve by fixing those two values, the resulting curve is overconstrained for our purposes. The only value we need to fix is the slope of Y with respect to X; that is, the slope of the curve as projected on the X–Y plane. The length of this vector can be left free and used to improve the fit. We would like a representation where it is possible to have the length of this tangent be a variable in A.

As long as we are fitting the x and y components of the parametric curve independently, we cannot design our basis functions such that a single value of A controls the length of the tangent vector in the X–Y plane. The solution is to fit both x and y simultaneously by specifying the curve as a linear combination of basis functions that are vector-valued functions of the variable t. In other words, $\mathbf{F}(t_i) = (x, y)$. Formally, given a sequence of data points $\{\mathbf{z}_i \in \mathbb{R}^2 \,|\, 1 \le i \le n\}$, a corresponding sequence of parameters $\{t_i \in \mathbb{R} \,|\, 1 \le i \le n\}$, a set of linearly independent basis functions $\{\Phi_j : \mathbb{R} \to \mathbb{R}^2 \,|\, 0 \le j \le d\}$, and real numbers $\{a_m, a_{m+1}, \ldots, a_d\}$, we will find real numbers $\{a_0, a_1, \ldots, a_{m-1}\}$ that minimize the function

$$S = \sum_{i=1}^{n}\left(\sum_{j=0}^{d} a_j \Phi_j(t_i) - \mathbf{z}_i\right)^2 \tag{12}$$

The square denotes the dot product of the argument with itself.

For each point $\mathbf{z}_i$ we are computing the square of the magnitude of the vector between the point and the value of the curve at t_i. In other words, once $\mathbf{F}(t_i)$ is the closest point on the curve to $\mathbf{z}_i$, we are minimizing the projected distance between the data point and the curve, just as we wanted. As before, however, we don't know which values of t are the best to use in our minimization. If we think of each data point as a point in space at $(\mathbf{z}_x, \mathbf{z}_y, t)$, the inner term in equation 12 is just the square of the distance between the curve and the sample point computed in the plane $t = t_i$. Using this distance in our algorithm is equivalent to solving for X and Y independently. At each t_i, we are now computing $(\mathbf{F}_x(t_i) - \mathbf{z}_x)^2 + (\mathbf{F}_y(t_i) - \mathbf{z}_y)^2$. Before, we were computing for X the value $(X(t_i) - \mathbf{z}_x)^2$ and for Y similarly. Since

$$\sum_{i=1}^{n} (\mathbf{F}(t_i) - \mathbf{z}_i)^2 = \sum_{i=1}^{n} (X(t_i) - x_i)^2 + \sum_{i=1}^{n} (Y(t_i) - y_i)^2$$

if $X(t_i) = \mathbf{F}_x(t_i)$ and $Y(t_i) = \mathbf{F}_y(t_i)$ the results will be identical.

The derivation goes through as before, and the resulting linear system is

$$\sum_{j=0}^{m-1} a_j \sum_{i=1}^{n} \Phi_j(t_i) \cdot \Phi_k(t_i) = \sum_{i=1}^{n} \left(\mathbf{z}_i - \sum_{j=m}^{d} a_j \Phi_j(t_i) \right) \cdot \Phi_k(t_i) \tag{13}$$

for $0 \leq k < m$.

Once again we will use basis functions that are combinations of the Hermite polynomials. Each basis function will be of the form

$$\Phi(t) = (q(t), r(t))$$

where q and r are scalar multiples of Hermite polynomials. There are up to 8 basis functions, one for each degree of freedom in the curve. For example, if we choose the functions

$$\Phi_j(t) = (s_j(t), 0); \Phi_{j+3}(t) = (0, s_j(t)), \quad j = \langle 0, 1, 2, 3 \rangle$$

we get the same results as solving X and Y independently using the Hermite basis functions.

To pick a basis function such that direction of the tangent in the X–Y plane is constrained to a value, for example, (ξ, υ) at $t = 0$, we use a function of the form

$$\Phi(t) = (\xi s_1(t), \upsilon s_1(t))$$

where $s_1(t)$ is the Hermite polynomial that has a slope of 1 at $t = 0$. If we pick the rest of our basis functions such there is no other contribution to the slope at that point, the slope of the final curve is guaranteed to lie along the specified vector.

Let us give a complete example. Suppose we have the data points as shown in Figure 4(a), along with the desired position of the endpoints (x_0, y_0), (x_1, y_1) and the desired tangent direction (ξ, υ) at $t = 1$. The basis function that will control the tangent is $\Phi_0(t) = (\xi s_2(t), \upsilon s_2(t))$ and its associated free variable is a_0. To leave the other tangent free we need two basis functions: $\Phi_1(t) = (s_1(t), 0)$, $\Phi_2(t) = (0, s_1(t))$ and two free variables: a_1, a_2.

To fix the endpoint positions we use

$$\Phi_3(t) = (x_0 s_0(t), y_0 s_0(t)), \quad \Phi_4(t) = (x_1 s_3(t), y_1 s_3(t))$$

and preset the values of a_3 and a_4 to be 1. We now have 5 basis functions, 3 values of A that will vary and 2 fixed values of A that specify the solution for this example. There are 8 degrees of freedom in a parametric cubic piece, but since our goal is to restrict the shape of the curve that can result, we should not be surprised that we end up with fewer than 8 basis functions.

In this example, we have a 3×3 linear system to solve at each iteration of the general algorithm. The values of the t_i are still adjusted at each step, in accordance with equation 5. However, it is no longer necessary to rescale the t_i to lie between 0 and 1, because those extra degrees of freedom have already been specified by fixing the positions of the endpoints. When the algorithm is run, the result is the curve shown in Figure 4(b). To show that the tangent vector at (x_1, y_1) is really parallel to (ξ, υ), we can calculate this vector at $t = 1$ as

$$\sum_{j=0}^{d} a_j \Phi'_j(1) = a_0(\xi, \upsilon) \tag{14}$$

The value of $a_j \Phi'_j(1)$ is $(0, 0)$ for $j \neq 0$ because either the slope of the Hermite polynomial is 0 at $t = 1$, or the corresponding $a_j = 0$.

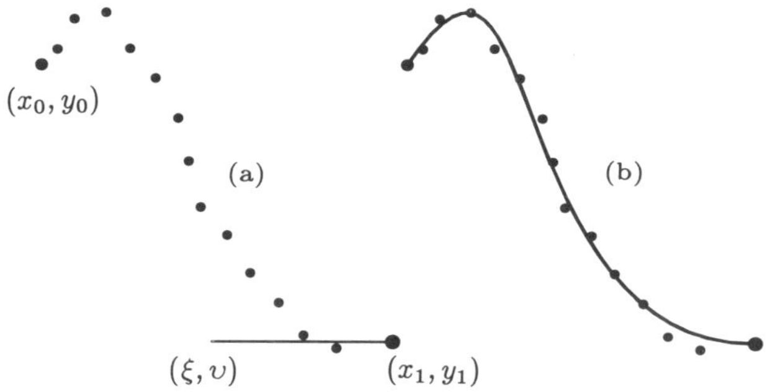

Figure 4. (a) Data points with both end positions and the tangent vector at $t = 1$ specified. The tangent direction is (ξ, υ). (b) The result of applying the fitting algorithm to (a).

Clearly this method of specifying parametric curves is not restricted to basis functions that are combinations of Hermite cubic polynomials—any set of linearly independent twice-differentiable functions will serve as well. If quadratic basis functions are substituted for the cubic ones, least-squares fitting of parabolas may be obtained. Circles or ellipses may be fit by using an appropriate set of trigonometric basis functions.

It is interesting to note how this representation for piecewise cubic polynomials relates to more common specifications, specifically Bézier curves and B-splines. In these representations, the variables are vector values (often called *control points*) which are multiplied by real-valued functions of t to fix the shape of the curve. Such a specification can be converted to a scheme of vector-valued basis function and real-valued coefficients as follows: let the control points be specified as $\mathbf{a}_j = a_{1j}\mathbf{b}_{1j} + a_{2j}\mathbf{b}_{2j}$, each control point having its own coordinate system with basis $\{\mathbf{b}_{1j}, \mathbf{b}_{2j}\}$. Furthermore, let the original basis functions be $\{\phi_j(t)\}$. Then the parametric curve is

$$\sum_j \mathbf{a}_j\phi_j(t) = \sum_j (a_{1j}\mathbf{b}_{1j} + a_{2j}\mathbf{b}_{2j})\phi_j(t) \\ = \sum_j (a_{1j}(\mathbf{b}_{1j}\phi_j(t)) + a_{2j}(\mathbf{b}_{2j}\phi_j(t))) \quad (15)$$

so the appropriate set of vector-valued basis functions is $\{\mathbf{b}_{ij}\phi_j(t) \mid i = 1, 2\}$. This means we can use this algorithm to solve for cubic polynomials with B-spline or Bernstein basis functions, and we can preset linear constraints on the control points for the resulting curve. Since each control point has been given its own coordinate system, by appropriate choice of the coordinate systems and the free coefficients, each control point can be constrained to be on a particular point or line, or to be free to move anywhere in the plane.

6. Relation to previous work.

There is a wealth of literature on piecewise polynomial functions or *splines*, and much of it is available in textbook form [10,21,24,25]. Spline functions are often used to approximate more complicated functions because they are computationally simpler. Much of the spline literature involves methods for smoothly interpolating a small set of data points. This is similar to the problem of designing with a small number of interpolating points. The applications that are relevant to our problem are those which try to fit a large set of data points with a small number of pieces. The first reference to this problem we can find is by Rice [21]. The paper by Cox [9] gives a nice description of the problem of curve fitting with splines using the least-squares error metric. He also mentions using dynamic programming as the method for finding knots, but does not extend it to spline functions with constraints. Some more recent publications that discuss curve fitting with splines are listed in the references [7,11,14,19,22].

There are two significant issues that separate the problem of fitting shapes from the problem of function approximation. First, shapes are usually represented as *parametric* functions to make the representation independent of the choice of axis. The usual technique in computer graphics applications is to use two functions, X and Y, each of which is a piecewise polynomial function of the parameter t. By assigning some value of t to each of the data points, it is possible to extend methods developed for spline functions to parametric spline functions by treating $X(t)$ and $Y(t)$ independently [11,20]. However, the shape of the curve can be dramatically influenced by the choice of parameterization (figure 5). The second issue is that the continuity constraints at the knots for shapes are quite relaxed by function fitting standards. A polynomial spline function of order k generally has $k - 1$ continuous derivatives at the knots. This is not necessary, or in most cases, even desirable for two-dimensional shapes. If we want the most efficient representation, clearly we must not constrain the curve unnecessarily. A more complete discussion of continuity conditions is available in the literature [17,18].

Flegal developed a method for fitting curves to hand-drawn sketches at Xerox PARC in 1974 [13]. In his thesis, Reeves [20] presents and compares several techniques, including Flegal's algorithm, for fitting piecewise parametric cubic polynomial curves to hand-drawn sketches. The focus is on algorithms that are computationally efficient enough to give real-time feedback in a sketching system, so in general the techniques tend to sacrifice output quality for speed. For many of our purposes, especially for deriving analytical representations for digital typefaces, we are willing to trade computational speed for better results.

There are two published algorithms which take a set of samples and produce the B-spline control points for the approximating curve for use in an interactive environment [28,29]. These algorithms create a representation that has the knots evenly spaced with respect to the parameter, which is not the most efficient representation for our purposes. Also, these techniques include a significant amount of user intervention to achieve the final shape. We want to minimize the amount of user interaction necessary.

7. Conclusions.

We have presented a method for fitting shapes defined by a discrete set of data points with a parametric piecewise cubic polynomial curve. Our goal is to give an efficient representation that "looks good" for graphics arts applications. The two new techniques we have introduced are dynamic programming for determining the knot positions, and an iterative method for fitting a parametric cubic with optional endpoint and tangent vector constraints to a set of data points.

Most of our work to date has been with letter-form shapes. One of the goals of our laboratory is to have a uniform, resolution-independent font representation for our digital printers. Many of the fonts we would like to use are currently defined only as a bitmaps. Therefore, we have been motivated to apply our system to convert fonts

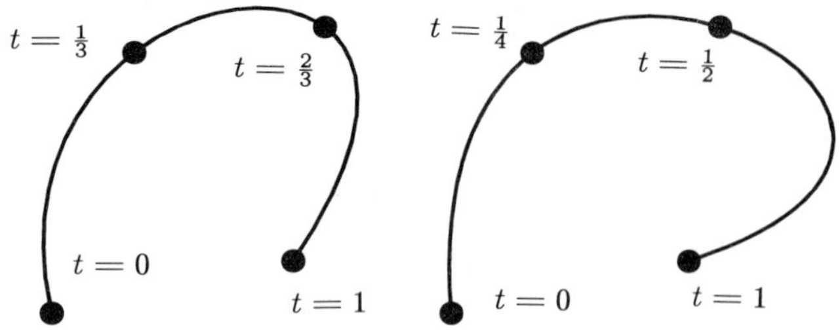

Figure 5. The curves are each defined by the same four data points. The only difference is the values of the parameter associated with the inner points. By comparing the two curves it is easy to see that the shape of the curve can be dramatically influenced by the choice of parameterization.

from bitmaps to curve outlines. Figure 1 and figure 6 are examples of data derived from such bitmaps.

Figure 7 shows an example of a more general graphics arts application. We have also used our methods on very simple hand-drawn sketches. The data points in figures 1 and 2 are hand-drawn, for example.

8. Future work.

There are several ways in which we would like to improve our method, a few of which are worth mentioning here.

We do not completely understand the convergence properties of our algorithm, especially why it sometimes

Figure 6. This font was converted from a bitmap (160 pixels per em) which was originally produced using Metafont[15]. Once the tolerance parameters were adjusted, no further user intervention was required to produce the cubic representation.

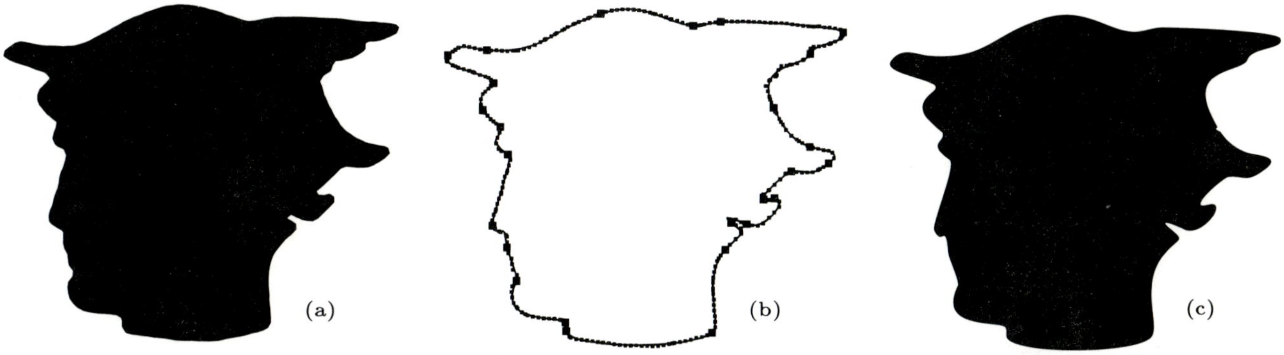

Figure 7. The data for this sample comes scanning a 3/4 inch high original with a 95 line/inch scanner. Some detail was lost in this process, especially with respect to corners. The image was fit using a loose tolerance to achieve further smoothing. (a) The original image, approximately 72 by 72. (b) The sample points and the result of the curve-fitting process. (c) Final curve in more detail, showing the curve, the knots and the samples.

does not converge at all. While our system can easily reject these cases as part of the fitting process (because they are simply instances of a very bad fit), we would like to avoid them. The type of iteration method we use is suitable for convergence acceleration techniques. However, we observe that these methods decrease the stability of the algorithm even further. Further understanding of these properties, especially with respect to the initial approximation for the parameter values, should lead to a more efficient and stable algorithm.

We have chosen a method for fitting piecewise functions that separates somewhat the problems of finding the knots and fitting the curve for each piece. This is not the only way to solve this problem. It is possible to set up a global system that does a least-squares fit for an entire spline [9,11,22]. Then, on each iteration we can adjust the values for t or adjust the knot locations or both. It is easiest to think of solving X and Y separately in this case, although it is also possible to extend the idea of vector basis functions to spline curves. The problem with this approach is that it requires the solution of a large linear system, proportional to the number of pieces, during each iteration. Our experience has been that this quickly becomes too expensive to be practical. Also, it is not clear what is the best way to adjust the number and location of the knots each time. However, a good algorithm of this sort might converge to a globally better solution.

Both the iteration technique and the dynamic programming application presented in this paper can be computationally expensive, and some applications do not need the full power of these algorithms to get acceptable results. We have developed a system for experimenting with methods for fitting shapes. In the future, we would like to get a better understanding of how to parameterize the application-dependent aspects of this problem.

9. Acknowledgements.

We would like to thank John Warnock, Robin Forrest and Lyle Ramshaw for their contributions to this project and for their many helpful comments on this paper.

10. References.

1. Aho, A. V., Hopcroft, J. E. and Ullman, J. D., *The Design and Analysis of Computer Algorithms*, Addison-Wesley, Reading, Massachusetts, 1974.

2. Barnhill, R. E. and Riesenfeld, R. F., eds., *Computer Aided Geometric Design*, Academic Press, New York, 1974.

3. Baudelaire, P. and Stone, M., "Techniques for Interactive Raster Graphics." *Computer Graphics 14,* 3 (1980), 302-307.

4. Baudelaire, P., *The Draw User's Manual*, internal report. Xerox Palo Alto Research Center, Palo Alto, CA, 1978.

5. Baudelaire, P., *The Fred User's Manual*, internal report. Xerox Palo Alto Research Center, Palo Alto, CA, 1976.

6. Bellman, R., *Dynamic Programming*, University Press, Princeton, N. J., 1957.

7. Chung, W. L., "Automatic Curve Fitting Using and Adaptive Local Algorithm." *ACM Transactions on Mathematical Software 6,* 1 (1980), 45-57.

8. Conte, S. D., and de Boor, C., *Elementary Numerical Analysis: An Algorithmic Approach*, second edition, McGraw-Hill, New York, 1972.

9. Cox, M. G., "Curve Fitting with Piecewise Polynomials." *J. Inst. Maths Applications 8,* (1971), 36-52.

10. de Boor, C., *A Practical Guide to Splines*, Springer-Verlag, 1978.

11. Dierckx, P., "Algorithms for Smoothing Data with Periodic and Parametric Splines." *Computer Graphics and Image Processing 20,* (1982), 171-184.

12. Faux, I. D., and Pratt, M. J., *Computational Geometry for Design and Manufacture*, Ellis Horwood, 1979.

13. Flegal, R., private communication. Xerox Palo Alto Research Center, Palo Alto, CA, 1978.

14. Ichida, K and Yoshimoto, F., "Curve Fitting by a One-Pass Method with a Piecewise Cubic Polynomial." *ACM Transactions on Mathematical Software 3,* 2 (1977), 164-174.

15. Knuth, D. E., *TEX and Metafont: New Directions in Typesetting*, Digital Press and American Mathematical Society, 1979.

16. Lipkie, D. E., Evans, S. R., Newlin, J. K., and Weissman, R. L., "Star Graphics: An Object-Oriented Implementation." *Computer Graphics 16,* 3 (1982), 115-124.

17. Manning, J. R., "Continuity Conditions for Spline Curves." *Computer Journal 17,* (1974), 181-186.

18. Nielson, G. M. "Some Piecewise Polynomial Alternatives to Splines in Tension" in *Computer Aided Geometric Design*, Barnhill, R. E. and Riesenfeld, R. F., eds., Academic Press, New York, 1974.

19. Pavlidis, T., *Algorithms for Graphics and Image Processing*, Computer Science Press, 1982.

20. Reeves, W. T., "Quantitative Representation of Complex Dynamic Shapes for Motion Analysis." PhD Thesis, Department of Computer Science, University of Toronto, 1980.

21. Rice, J. R., *The Approximation Of Functions*, vols. 1 and 2, Addison-Wesley, Reading, Mass., 1964.

22. Rice, J. R., Algorithm 525. ADAPT, adaptive smooth curve fitting, *ACM Transactions on Mathematical Software 4,* 1 (1978) 82-94.

23. Rogers, D. F., and Adams, J. A., *Mathematical Elements for Computer Graphics*, McGraw-Hill, New York, 1976.

24. Schultz, M., *Spline Analysis*, Prentice-Hall, Englewood Cliffs, N. J., 1973.

25. Schumaker, Larry L., *Spline Functions: Basic Theory*, John Wiley & Sons, New York, 1981.

26. Stone, M., *The Griffin User's Manual*, internal report. Xerox Palo Alto Research Center, Palo Alto, CA, 1979.

27. Warnock, J. and Wyatt, D., "A Device Independent Graphics Imaging Model for use with Raster Devices." *Computer Graphics 16,* 3 (1982), 313-320.

28. Wu, S., Abel, J.F., and Greenburg, D.P., "An Interactive Computer Graphics Approach to Surface Representation." *CACM 20,* 10 (1977), 703-712.

29. Yamaguchi, F., "A New Curve Fitting Method Using a CRT Computer Display." *Computer Graphics and Image Processing, 7* (1978), 425-437.

PANEL

JAPANESE COMPUTER GRAPHICS: CHALLENGES AND OPPORTUNITIES

PART II: INDUSTRIAL STRATEGIES OF JAPANESE COMPUTER MANUFACTURERS

CHAIR: Toshiyasu Kunii, University of Tokyo
PANEL COORDINATOR: Laurin Herr, Pacific Interface

PANELISTS: Tsuneo Ikedo, Seillac Company Ltd.
Kazukiyo Ishimura, Yamaha Research Institute
Kansei Iwata, Graphica Computer Corp.
Kazuo Naito, Daini Seikosha
Shohei Saimi, Japan Radio Corp.

PANEL COORDINATOR'S INTRODUCTORY REMARKS

Japanese interest in computer graphics in the past has been led by users whose needs have been satisfied primarily by U. S. sources. However, as the Japanese market has grown, domestic players have emerged, especially commercial production companies and venture-type hardware manufacturers. In the world of commercial production, this trend has been spurred by the cross-cultural difficulties and expenses of trans-Pacific projects, as well as the new accessibility of computer graphics production technology. In the hardware field, this tendency has been fed by rapid Japanese advances in semiconductor memories and color monitors.

Growing Japanese strength in computer graphics is important to the international community for several reasons. First, it confirms the viability and sales potential of the domestic Japanese market. Second, it increases competition within Japan. Third, it will probably increase competition outside of Japan as well. Fourth, this competition should stimulate development of superior products at a lower cost, yielding considerable benefit to users. Fifth, there will be many new opportunities for internationally- minded distributors, systems builders, software suppliers and R & D groups. Finally, if approached correctly, Japan can be a source of fresh aesthetic and technical input.

During the past few years, many Japanese have made extensive efforts to learn everything they can about computer graphics. Numerous foreign experts have been invited to Japan to lecture at conferences. The Japanese themselves have criss-crossed America visiting major computer graphics installations. At Siggraph'82 238 Japanese registered for tutorials and technical sessions and many more attended the hardware exposition. Japanese press coverage was aggressive. This panel is an attempt to balance the information flow by offering Siggraph attendees an opportunity to educate themselves about Japanese computer graphics.

CHAIRMAN'S INTRODUCTION:

While the Japanese electronics industry in general has been dominated by a few large firms, the computer graphics industry in Japan has been led by a number of small, venture-type companies offering original technology and close customer support. They are self- sustaining and not part of so-called "Japan Inc". Currently, there are quite a number of these firms with a relatively high level of hardware and software expertise. This knowledge base has been developing for some time. For example, in association with some of the earlier companies, the Tokyo Raster Computer Graphics (TRCG) Project was begun in 1968 to develop a raster system capable of displying 4096 colors concurrently. The partial results the TRCG research were reported at the first Siggraph Conference held in Boulder, Colorado in 1974. This panel will examine progress since that time. The panelists were selected to fairly represent the people behind the development of Japanese computer graphics companies who significantly influence industrial strategies. Each panelist will briefly describe his involvement in computer graphics, views of the world market, and areas of current interest in terms of future product development. General discussion of differences and commonalities among the panelists will follow the presentations. Questions from the audience will be encouraged.

Toshiyasu L. Kunii received the B.Sc. and M.Sc. and B.Sc. degrees in chemistry from the University of Tokyo in 1962, 1964 and 1967, respectively. He is currently Professor of Information and Computer Science in the Department of Information Science of the Faculty of Science at the University of Tokyo. His research interests include computer graphics, database systems and software engineering. He has authored and edited more than 70 refereed academic/technical papers in computer science and application areas. He was the principal researcher in the Tokyo Raster Graphics Project. He is currently President of the Japan Computer Graphics Association, an editor of IEEE Computer Graphics and Applications, and the Chairman of the IBM, Japan Computer Science Symposium Organizing Committee. He is on the IFIP Database Working Group and the IFIP Systems Modeling Working Group. From 1976 to 1981, Dr. Kunii organized and chaired the Technical Committee on Software Engineering of the Information Processing Society of Japan. Most recently, he served on the Organizing Committee of the Micrograph'82 Conference and was Program Chairman of the Intergraphics'83 conference, both held in Tokyo.

Tsuneo Ikedo graduated from Tokyo Metropolitan University in 1971 with a major in Electrical Engineering. He is the Founder and President of Seillac Co. Ltd., a manufacturer of high performance computer graphics display systems. He is dedicated to the pursuit of the state of the art in computer graphics technology, and is particularly interested at this time in specialized processors such as homogeneous and spline processors (either micro-coded or hard-coded).

Kazukiyo Ishimura graduated from Maseda University in 1960 with a major in Electronics. He is General Manager of Research and Development for Nippon Gakki Co. Ltd. (Yamaha). His current area of interest is the development of interactive color graphics terminals for home entertainment centers which would also include digital electric organs and other digital audio components.

Kansei Iwata graduated from Tohoku University in 1964 with a major in Electrical Engineering. He founded Graphica Computer Co. Ltd. in the early 1970's and now serves as the President of this pioneering firm. His interest has been in the development of fast, multi-colored raster graphics systems with very deep bit-maps and/or flexible pipeline architecture for easy integration into customized computer graphics or image processing systems.

Kazuo Naito graduated from Yamanashi University in 1945 with a major in Industrial Engineering. He has been a key figure in the development of SEIKO's computer graphics technology and now serves as General Manager of the Industrial Electronics Division and Senior Managing Director of Dainiseikosha Co. Ltd. His current area of interest is in the creation of a broad family of mass- produceable, highly reliable raster graphics products characterized by a relatively modest number of concurrently displayable colors.

Shohei Saimi graduated from the University of Osaka in 1954 with a major in Physics. He is currently the manager of the Systems Engineering Department of the Japan Radio Corporation (JRC). At JRC he has emphasized the development of high and multi-color graphics with reliable, well-tested hardware/software components.

SOLID MODEL INPUT THROUGH ORTHOGRAPHIC VIEWS

Hiroshi Sakurai
Research Engineer
Nissan Motor Company

David C. Gossard
Associate Professor
Computer Aided Design Laboratory
Department of Mechanical Engineering
Massachusetts Institute of Technology

Abstract: This paper describes the results of basic studies on procedures for creating solid models of component geometry from two-dimensional orthographic projections. An interactive graphic program was developed to allow the input of three orthographic views of a component geometry by digitizing from a drawing. The views may contain straight lines and circular arcs, solid or dashed. No restrictions are placed on the order or direction of lines and arcs in any view. Using an extension of the Wesley-Markowski procedure, the program constructs a three-dimensional solid model of the object. When the projections are ambiguous, multiple solid models are produced. The solid model may contain planar, cylindrical, conical, spherical and toroidal surfaces. Topological information of the solid model is stored in a winged edge structure. Geometric information is stored as vertex coordinates and surface equations.

The procedure for 2D-3D conversion provides a powerful new method for manual input of solid models, a common interface to all turnkey graphics systems, and, properly integrated with existing technology for scanning of drawings, a powerful new method for acquisition of CAD/CAM data bases from existing drawings.

The procedure is described, examples of typical input and output are shown, and possible extensions are discussed.

1. INTRODUCTION

Many research efforts are being conducted to realize complete geometric models of mechanical components for use in design and manufacturing. One method used to create a complete model of the shape of a mechanical part has been called constructive solid geometry. In this method, set operators are applied to a collection of primitive solids (e.g. cube, cylinder, sphere, cone, ...) to construct a solid model. Though this approach has its advantages, it cannot convert white-frame models constructed by wire-frame CAD/CAM systems into solid models. Because solid modeling systems will coexist with wire-frame systems for some years to come, an interface between the two is desireable. Also, systems based on constructive solid geometry cannot utilize a variety of graphic input techniques used in wire-frame CAD/CAM systems.

This research effort was aimed at interfacing wire-frame and solid modeling CAD/CAM systems as well as at providing designers with more natural ways of constructing solid models. A program was developed in which a set of orthographic views, a very natural way for designers to express geometry which can be created easily with wire-frame systems, is processed into a solid model. Though currently only lines and arcs are accepted in orthographic views, many mechanical parts can be expressed by these two geometric entities. Hidden lines and hidden arcs must be identified as in conventional engineering drawings. No restrictions are placed on the order and direction of lines and arcs in each view. Planar, cylindrical, conical, spherical and toroidal surfaces are allowed in the solid model generated.

A graphics program was also developed to allow the input of orthographic views by digitizing and to allow visual verification of a generated solid model.

Much work has been done to generate polyhedral objects from their projections.

Sutherland's work in three dimensional input [1] was focused on hardware and software for digitizing. He introduced a tablet with multiple pens so that a 3D vertex could be generated by digitizing vertices in two views. He also discussed how to treat digitized data from perspective views. Thornton's work [2] concerned interactive techniques for three dimensional input from 2D views. Neither Sutherland nor Thornton investigated algorithms for construction of solid models from projections.

The first effort to construct solid models from projections was initiated by Idesawa [3], [4]. His approach was as follows.

1. Generate 3D vertices from 2D vertices.
2. Generate 3D edges from 3D vertices.

3. Generate 3D faces from 3D edges
4. Assemble faces into an object.

With this approach, false elements can be generated.

Idesawa identified some criteria to remove these false elements. For example, a 3D vertex belonging to only one face is false. Lafue [5] added a heuristic procedure for removing false elements and finding true elements. This approach has two drawbacks. First, the method cannot remove all the possible false elements and can remove some true elements in multiple solution cases. Second, they require input data to conform to a prescribed format. For example, Lafue required that 2D lines be input in such a way that a sequence of lines bounds a face.

Preiss [6] freed input from a prescribed format. He generated visible surfaces from polygons in orthographic views. He claims that he generated invisible faces using a scene analysis technique, but does not show the method. His approach also does not work for multiple solution cases.

G. Markowsky and M.A. Wesley [7], [8] treated the construction problem in a mathematically formal way so that even pathological cases, (not allowed in former work) can be accepted. An example pathological case is an edge shared by more than two faces. Their most important achievement is their method of assembling faces. Faces are connected into closures which divide infinite space into subspaces. The combinations of subspaces which give the input projections are solutions. In this way, their approach can remove all false elements and ensure that all the solutions are obtained.

All the above work concerns planar polyhedral geometries whose projections contain only lines. The work described here extends the approach of Wesley and Markowsky to create geometries which include planar, cylindrical, spherical, conical, and toroidal surfaces.

2. OBJECT AND ORTHOGRAPHIC VIEWS

In this section, orthographic views as the input to the solid model generation procedure and the object as its output are discussed briefly.

2.1 Object

An object is a finite segment of three-dimensional space and is expressed with the following elements.

Face: A face is a finite segment of a surface which is a part of the boundary separating an object from the rest of the three dimensional space.

Edge: An edge is a finite segment of a three dimensional line or curve which is a part of the boundary between a face and the remainder of the surface. An edge is shared by at least two faces.

Vertex: A vertex is one of the two points which separate an edge from the remainder of the line or curve. A vertex is shared by at least three edges.

2.2 Orthographic Views

Among many conventions in engineering drawing, the following are important in this work.

1. Three Orthographic Views: Basically, engineers express objects (mechanical parts) by a number of projected views of which three orthographic or principal views are the most important: top view, front view and side view. This work deals with the case of three orthographic views.

2. Identification of Hidden Edges: In engineering drawings, hidden edges are identified by dashed lines.

3. Silhouette Lines and Arcs: Another basic convention is to draw silhouette lines and arcs of curved faces in orthographic views. An artificial edge corresponding to a silhouette line or arc is called a silhouette edge hereafter. It lies on only one surface and appears in only one of the three views.

4. Tangency edge: In objects with planar and curved faces, two faces can be tangent to each other along a shared edge. This edge is called a tangency edge hereafter. A tangency edge does not appear in any views.

2.3 Geometric Elements

Lines and arcs are accepted in the input orthographic views.

On the output object, the following types of surfaces and edges are allowed.

1. Surfaces: Planar, cylindrical, conical, toroidal and spherical surfaces. The axes of cylindrical, conical, and toroidal surfaces must be parallel to one of the axes of the body coordinate system.

2. Edges: Three dimensional lines and circular arcs. The axes of circular arcs must be parallel to one of the axes of the body coordinate system.

Though these restrictions seem to be severe, most mechanical parts can be expressed by this set of surfaces and edges.

3. PROCEDURE

The object generation procedure has six steps. In each step, all the possible elements are generated. In some steps, generated elements are tested with various criteria, which do not eliminate all false elements but significantly reduce the effort in later steps. The final test is performed by comparing the input orthographic views with the three orthographic views regenerated from the generated object. If they match each other, the object is one of the objects or the only object expressed by the input views.

3.1 Generate P-Vertices

A p-vertex is a 2D point in a view and is a projection of a vertex. Because of the existence of silhouette edges and tangency edges, all the p-vertices cannot be obtained by just calculating intersections in input views. In addition to intersections (p-vertices with the attribute of standard), 2D points where lines are tangent to arcs (p-vertices with the attribute of tangency) and 2D points where lines parallel to coordinate axes are tangent to arcs (p-vertices with the attribute of silhouette) are calculated. Then using the coordinate values of thes points, lines in other views are cut to obtain candidate p-vertices on silhouette edges and tangency edges (candidate p-vertices with the attribute of tangency-generated and silhouette-generated). A p-vertex can have more than one attribute.

3.2 Generate Candidate Vertices

In this step, candidate vertices (c-vertices) are generated from candidate p-vertices. Then vertices whose projections were not recovered in the preceding step are generated.

1. Generate candidate vertices from candidate p-vertices: A 3D point is generated from a pair of candidate p-vertices which belong to different views and have the same coordinate value for the shared coordinate. Then a projection of the 3D point onto the third view is searched. If it is found in the third view, the 3D point is a c-vertex. Although there are five types of candidate p-vertices, only four combinations of them are allowed.

- A c-vertex with standard attribute is generated from three candidate p-vertices, all with standard attribute.

- A c-vertex with tangency attribute is generated from three candidate p-vertices, one with tangency attribute and the other two with tangency-generated attribute.

- A c-vertex with silhouette attribute is generated from three candidate p-vertices, one with silhouette attribute, one with standard attribute and one with silhouette-generated attribute.

- A c-vertex with double-silhouette attribute is generated from two candidate p-vertices, both with silhouette attribute.

All the vertices, except ones on both of silhouette edges and tangency edges, are recovered.

2. Generate c-vertices directly from the three views: A toroidal surface is assumed when the following facts are found in the three views.

- Two arcs in different views have the same radius.

- The center points of the two arcs have the same coordinate value for the shared coordinate.

- The distances from the center points to the center point of an arc in the third view are equal.

A spherical surface is assumed when the following fact is found in the three views.

- A 3D point generated from arc centers in two views has its corresponding arc center in the third view.

Once a torus is assumed from arcs, then c-vertices on that surface can be generated. Those c-vertices are given torus attribute. A c-vertice can have more than one attibute. Figure 3 shows c-vertices generated.

3.3 Generate Candidate Edges

Candidate edges (c-edges) are generated from c-vertices generated in the previous step. C-edges have three types, standard, silhouette, and tangency.

Standard c-edge: Two c-vertices are checked if their projections lie on the same line or arc in each view. If they do, the two vertices are connected by a 3D line or arc to form a standard c-edge.

Silhouette c-edge: Two c-vertices with silhouette attribute are checked if their projections lie on the same line or arc in a view. If they do, the two c-vertices are connected by a 3D line or arc to form a silhouette c-edge.

Tangency c-edge: A line-tangency c-edge is generated from two c-vertices with tangency attributes whose candidate p-vertices lie on the same arc or the coaxial arcs at the same angle. Arc-tangency c-edges are generated as follows. Two arc c-edges, each of which has at least one c-vertex with tangency attribute, torus attribute, or sphere attribute, are tested if they lie on the same torus or sphere. If they do, an arc-tangency c-edge is generated by connecting the two vertices of each arc c-edge.

In practice, more detailed c-edge types are required to avoid as many false edges as possible.

Once c-edges are generated, all the c-vertices are tested whether they lie on more than or equal to three edges, otherwise, the c-vertex is deleted and c-edges are generated again from a new set of c-vertices. Figure 4 shows c-edges generated.

3.4 Generate Candidate Faces

This step is divided into four parts. First, surfaces are generated from c-edges. A planar surface is generated from an arc c-edge or two line c-edges sharing a c-vertex. A cylindrical or a conical surface is generated from two arc c-edges connected by at least one line c-edge. A toroidal or a spherical surface has already been generated in the c-vertex generation step. For each surface, all the c-edges lying on the surface are collected. (Figure 5 (a)).

Second, a set of c-edge loops which divides the surface into the smallest subsurfaces is searched. C-edge loops, which bound their left side of a surface, are found by traversing c-edges with turn-to-the-leftmost rule. The procedure used by Markowsky and Wesley [7] to find out loops on a plane can be applied to curved surfaces with small modification of the criterion differentiating between in-loop and out-loop. [9] In-loop bounds its inside and out-loop bounds its outside (Figure 5(b)).

Third, a hierarchical tree of c-edge loops is generated for each surface and candidate faces (c-faces) are derived from the tree. The tree shows the relationships between c-edge loops, i.e., which loop includes which loop. From the tree, c-faces are found as follows. The out-loop which is not contained in any in-loop is discarded. In-loops at the root of the tree bound c-faces. An in-loop with its subordinate out-loops also bounds a face. (Figure 5(c)).

Fourth, the following conditions are tested for all the c-faces generated. Any standard c-edge and tangency-edge should lie on at least two different surfaces, otherwise, the c-edge is deleted. A c-face should be tangent to another c-face at its tangency c-edge, otherwise, the c-face is deleted. A c-edge related to a dashed entity in a view should have at least one c-face which hides the c-edge when it is projected onto that view, otherwise, the c-edge is deleted. If any of the c-edges are deleted, the process has to be carried out again from the beginning of this step (Figure 5(d)).

3.5 Generate Candidate Objects

C-faces are connected to form c-face loops which divide the three dimensional space into subspaces in the analogical way as c-edges are connected to c-edge loops. [9] Two c-faces sharing an edge are connected to each other. When more than two c-faces share a c-edge, a c-face which gives the smallest face connection angle is chosen.

Each c-face loop forms a candidate object (c-object). One of the c-object generated is an infinite subspace and is discarded.

3.6 Generate Objects

C-objects can be categorized into certain c-objects, and uncertain c-objects. If a 2D edge, a straight line or a circular arc in any projected view, is related to only one c-object, then that c-object is a necessary part of the object and is called a certain c-object. If a c-object has no 2D edge which is related uniquely to the c-object, that object is an uncertain c-object.

All the certain c-objects are assembled and tested. Then each of the possible combinations of uncertain c-object is added to the assembly of the certain c-objects and tested.

The test is made as follows. The assembly is checked if it can give all the 2D edges in the input views, if so, the orthographic view is generated for each view and compared with the output views otherwise the assembly is discarded.

If the projection of the assembly matches the input view for every view, the assembly is one of the objects or the only object expressed by the input views.

4. IMPLEMENTATION

Based on the algorithm described above, a solid model generation program was developed on VAX 11/750. The program is comprised of six parts which correspond to the six steps of the algorithm. It generates solid models expressed in a winged edge data structure from the data of three orthographic views.

Though the focus of this research is the generation of solid models, a graphic program was also developed, using MEGATEK 7200 connected to the VAX 11/750, to allow the interactive input of existing drawings via a digitizer and to allow the visual verification and the selection of the generated solid models. As the solid model generation program was incorporated into this graphic program, all the work from the input of drawings to the selection of the results can be done interactively.

Solid models composed of planar, cylindrical, conical, toroidal and spherical bounding surfaces have been generated from the data describing their three orthographic views containing both lines and circular arcs.

Figures 9, 10 and 11 show some examples. Twenty to thirty seconds of VAX 11/750 CPU time were required to generate each object.

5. CONCLUSION

The method described here is more practical and useful than existing methods for the following reasons.

1. Circular arcs in input views: Most drawings of mechanical parts contain circular arcs. The method described here is the only one which allows circular arcs in input views.

2. Minimum input requirement: This method imposes less requirement on input than existing methods. For example, there is no requirement on the order of input or the labeling of the output.

The system based on the algorithm discussed here can serve as an interface between wire-frame CAD system and solid model CAD system. The system can be also used directly for the purpose of the input of solid models.

To make the system more practical, a number ofproblems have to be solved. In engineering drawings, there can be more or less than three projections for an object, partial projections rather than full projections may appear in some views, auxiliary views and/or sectional views may be given. It is believed that the algorithm described here can be extended to take care of the problems above, and the extension is under study.

ACKNOWLEDGEMENT

The authors gratefully acknowledge the financial support of the Control Data Corporation and the Nissan Motor Company.

REFERENCES

[1] I.E. Sutherland, "Three-Dimensional Data Input by Tablet", Proc. IEEE, Special Issue on Computer Graphics, Vol. 62, No. 4, 1974.

[2] R.W. Thornton, "Interactive Modelling in Three Dimensions through Two-Dimensional Windows", Third International Conference and Exhibition on Computer in Engineering and Building Design, 1978.

[3] M. Idesawa, "A System to Generate a Solid Figure from a Three View", Bull. JSME 16, pp. 216-225, February 1973.

[4] M. Idesawa, et al, "Automatic Input of Line Drawing and Generation of Solid Figure from Three-View Data", Proceedings of the International Joint Computer Symposium, pp. 304-311, 1975.

[5] G. Lafue, "Recognition of Three Dimensional Objects from Orthographic Views", Computer Graphics, Vol. 10, No. 2, 1976.

[6] K. Preiss, "Constructing the 3-D Representation of a Plane-Faced Object from a Digitized Engineering Drawings", Fifth International Conference and Exhibition on Computer in Engineering and Building Design, 1980.

[7] G. Markowsky and M.A. Wesley, "Fleshing Out Wire Frames", IBM J. Res. Develop. 24, pp. 582-587, September 1980.

[8] G. Markowsky and M.A. Wesley, "Fleshing Out Projections", IBM J. Res. Develop. 25, pp. 934-954, November 1981.

[9] H. Sakurai, "Solid Model Input Through Orthographic Views", M.S. Thesis, Massachusetts Institute of Technology, Cambridge, Massachusetts, 1982.

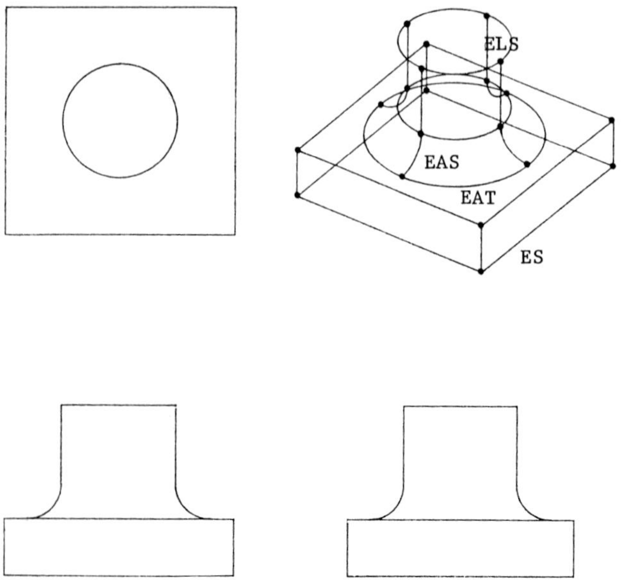

ES Standard edge
ELS, EAS Silhouette edge
EAT Tangency edge

FIGURE 1 SILHOUETTE AND TANGENCY EDGES

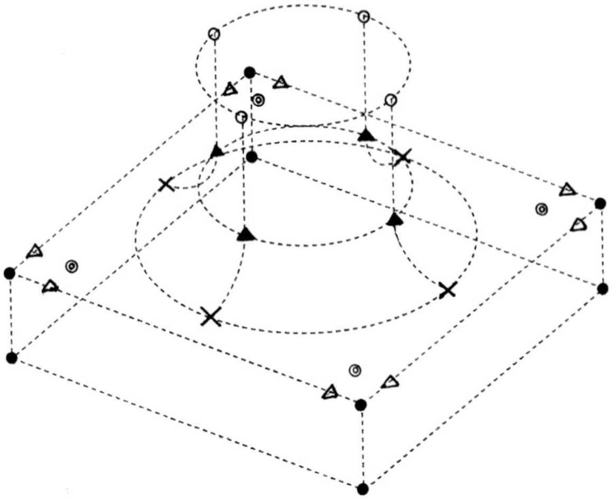

C-vertices with the attribute of

- · Standard
- o Silhouette
- ◉ Double-silhouette
- Δ Silhouette and tangency
- ▲ Double-silhouette and tangency
- x Torus-silhouette and tangency

FIGURE 3 C-VERTICES

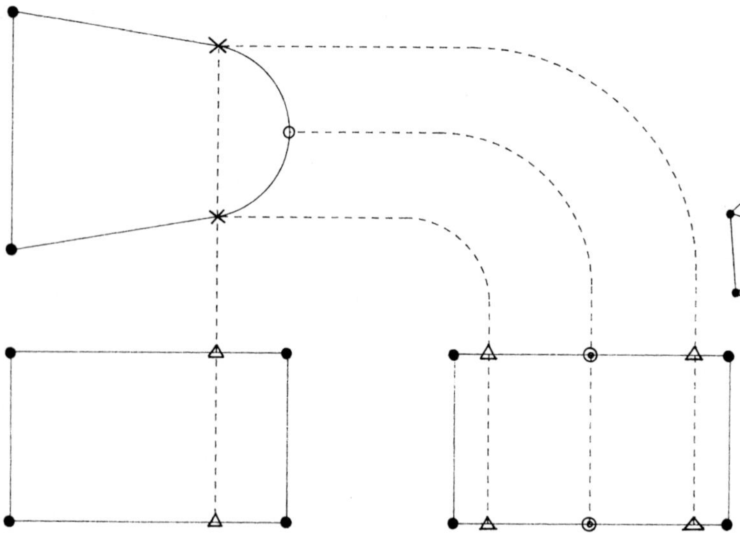

Candidate p-vertices with the attribute of

- · Standard
- x Tangency
- o Silhouette
- Δ Tangency-generated
- ◉ Silhouette-generated

FIGURE 2 EXAMPLES OF CANDIDATE P-VERTICES

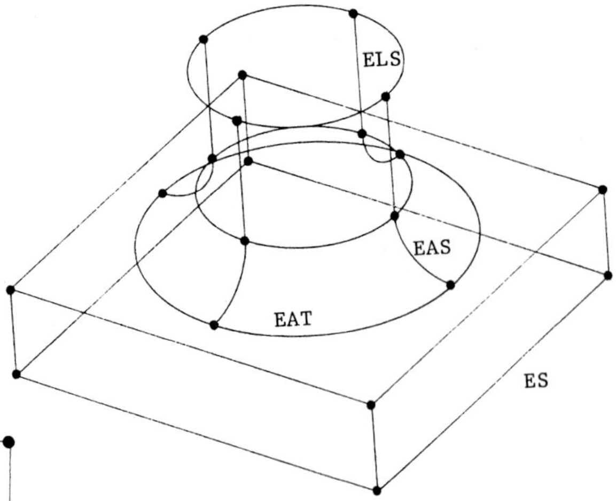

ES Standard c-edge
ELS Line-silhouette c-edge
EAS Arc-silhouette c-edge
EAT Arc-tangency c-edge

FIGURE 4 C-EDGES

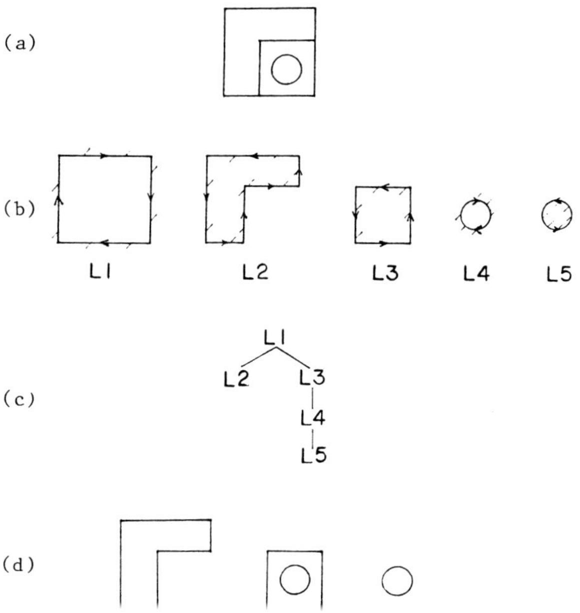

FIGURE 5 C-EDGE GENERATION: (a) c-edges on a plane; (b) c-edge loops; (c) hierarchical tree of c-edge loops; (d) c-faces generated

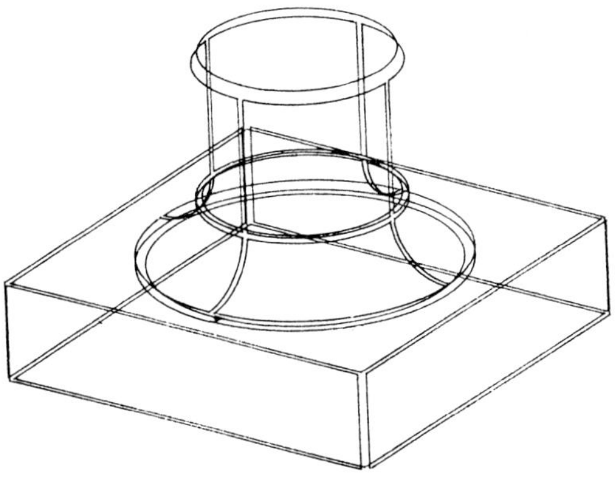

FIGURE 6 C-FACES

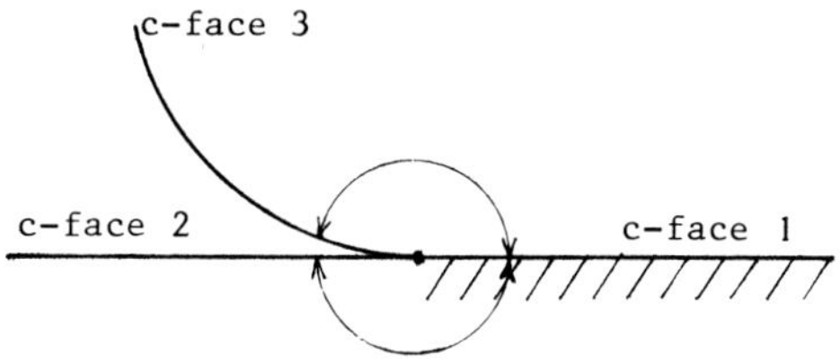

face connection angle

When c-face 1 encloses the hatched side, c-face 2 is connected, otherwise c-face 3 is connected.

FIGURE 7 C-FACE CONNECTION

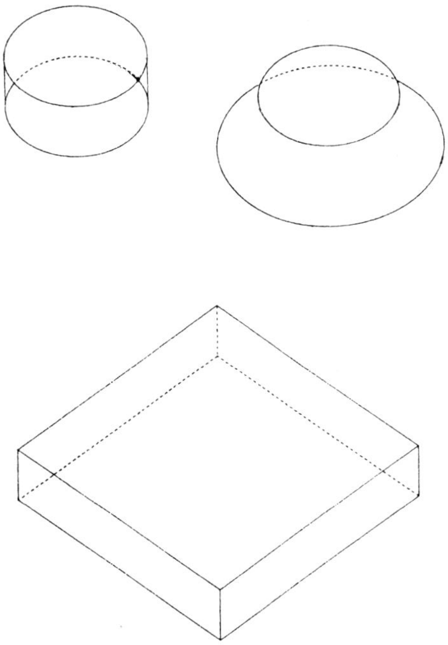

FIGURE 8 C-FACE CONNECTION

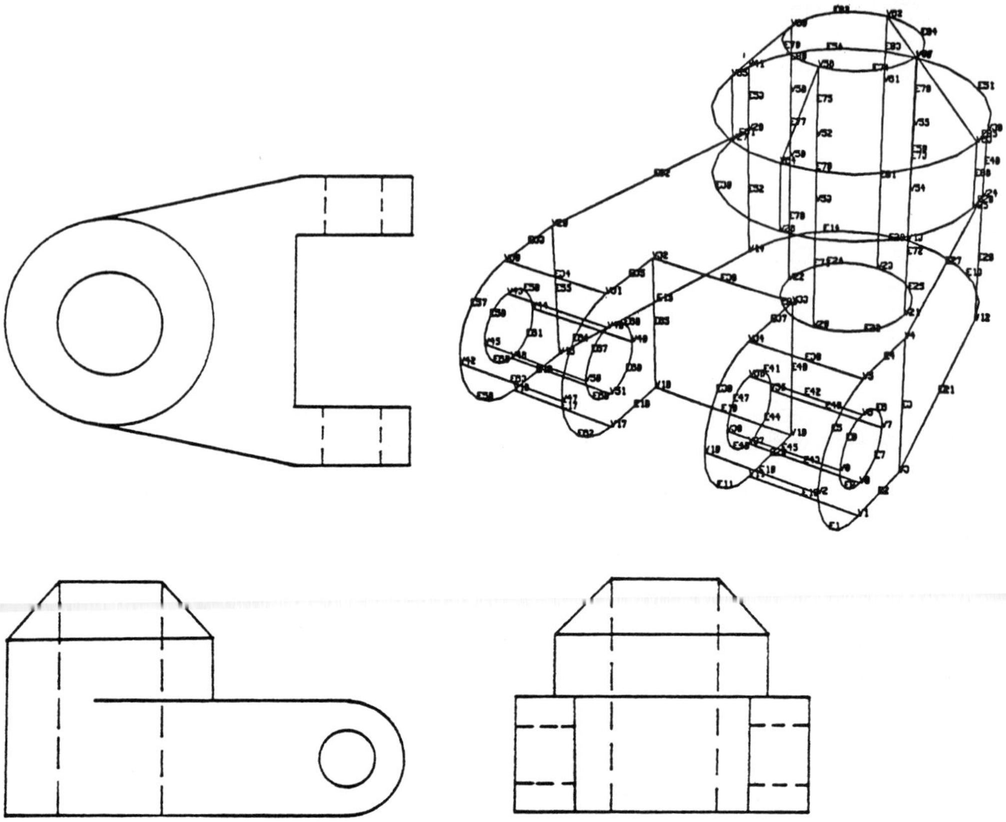

FIGURE 9 EXAMPLE 1

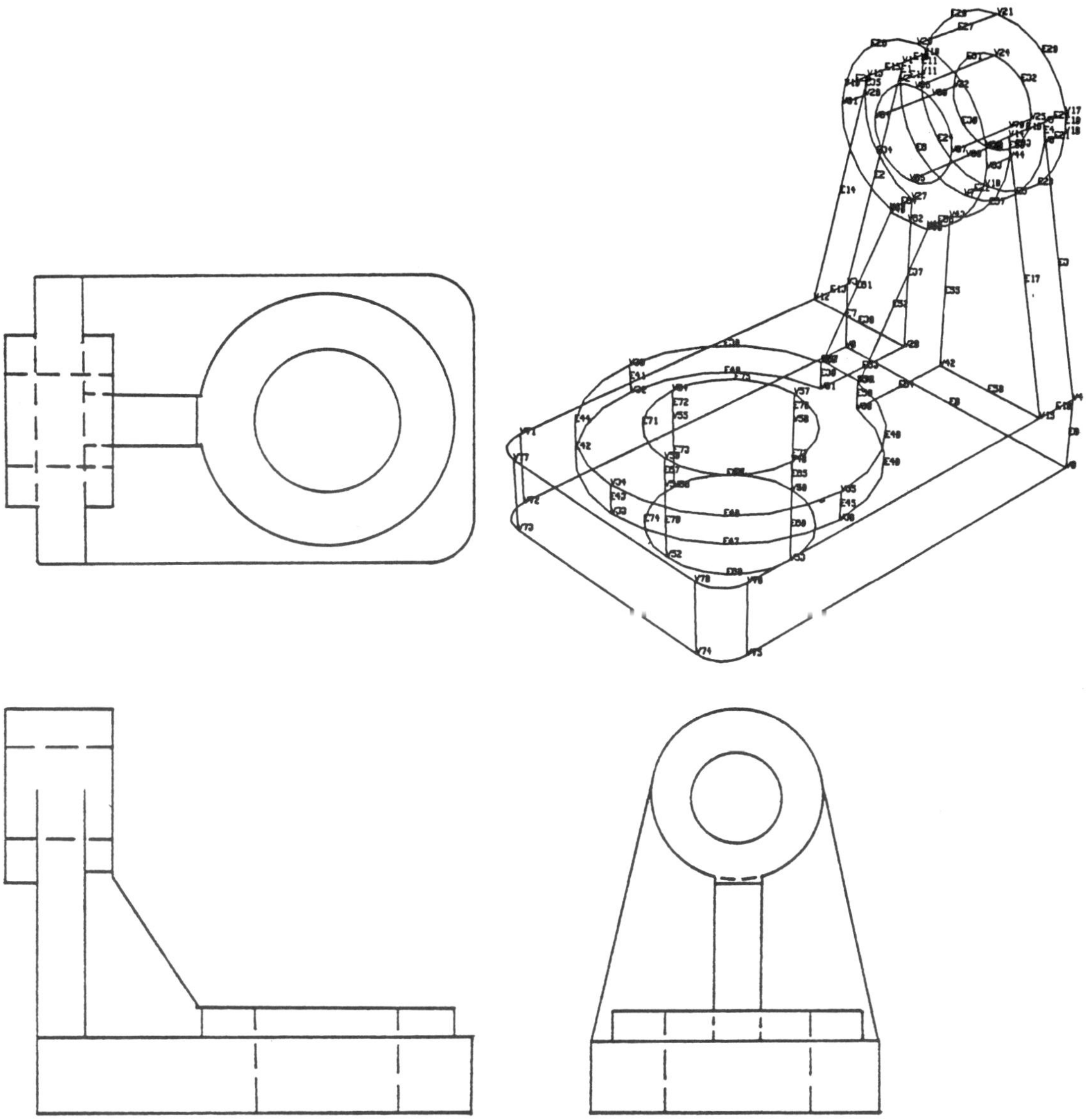

FIGURE 10 EXAMPLE 2

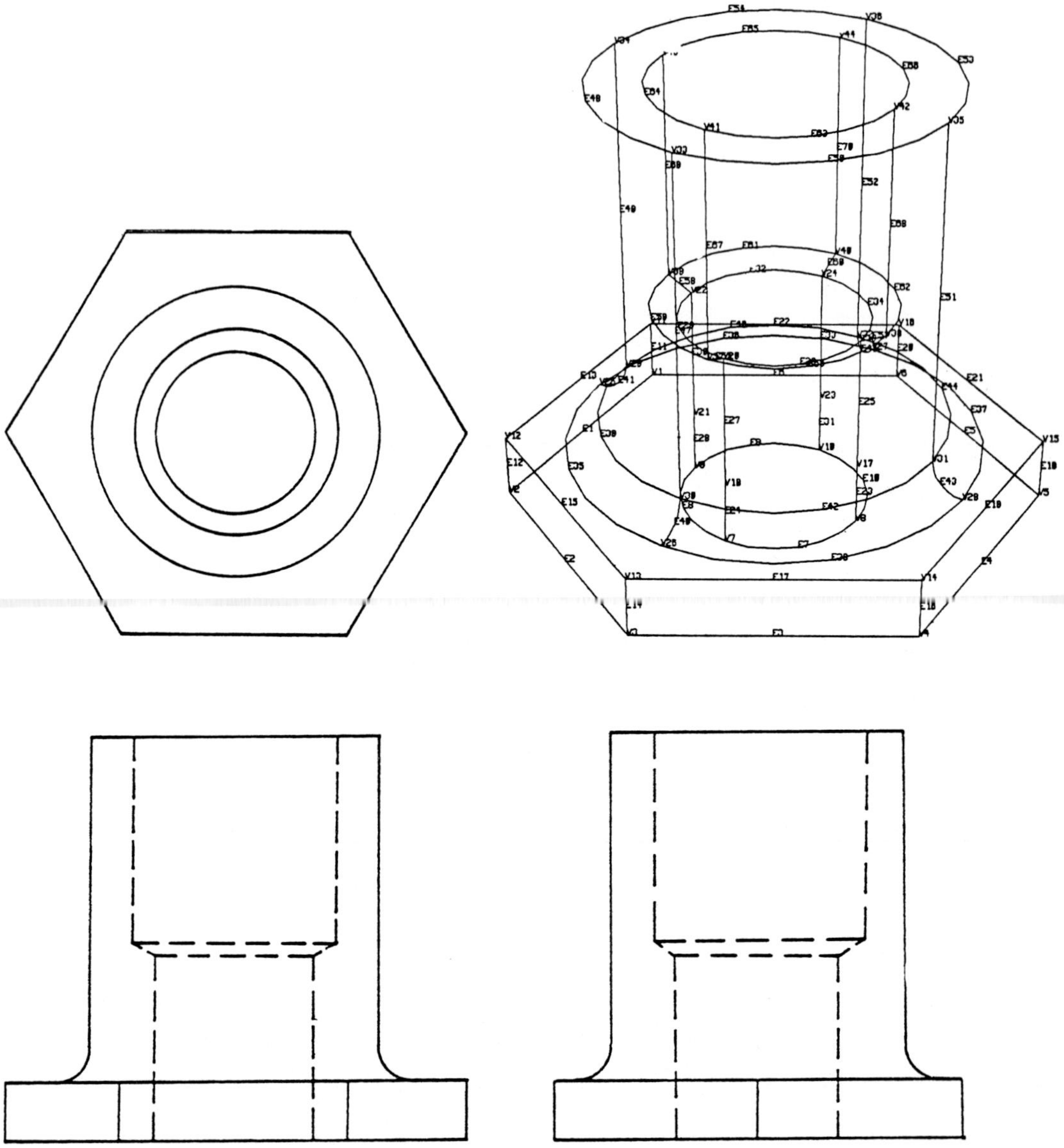

FIGURE 11 EXAMPLE 3

SPATIAL INPUT/DISPLAY CORRESPONDENCE IN A STEREOSCOPIC COMPUTER GRAPHIC WORK STATION

Christopher Schmandt

Architecture Machine Group
Massachusetts Institute of Technology

ABSTRACT

An interactive stereoscopic computer graphic workspace is described. A conventional frame store is used for three-dimensional display, with left/right eye views interlaced in video and viewed through PLZT shutter glasses. The video monitor is seen reflected from a half silvered mirror which projects the graphics into a workspace, into which one can reach and manipulate the image directly with a "magic wand". The wand uses a magnetic six degree-of-freedom digitizer. In an alternative configuration, a graphics tablet was placed within the workspace for input intensive tasks.

CR catagories: I.3.2 [Computer Graphics]: Graphics Systems; I.3.6 [Computer Graphics]: Methodology and Techniques; I.4.8 [Image Processing]: Scene Analysis-Stereo.

Key Words: Stereoscopic display, half silvered mirror, three-dimensional digitization.

INTRODUCTION

The last decade has seen a resurgence of interest in three-dimensional imaging, such as holography, commercial 3-D movies, experimental anaglyphic television broadcasts, and lenticular 35mm cameras. Some of this enthusiasm has overflowed into computer graphic applications, most noteably computer aided design, medical imaging, and seismic exploration, but widespread appreciation of the utility of stereoscopic displays has yet to happen. This may be in part due to the lack of convincing interactive capabilities of such displays.

The fields with the most interest in three-dimensional display are those with a need to analyze complex spatially structured real world data, gathered by or part of a process requiring expensive data acquisition hardware (hence the willingness to experiment with relatively expensive displays). Although a variety of techniques exist for stereoscopic display, there has been little work done in interacting with 3-D data by 3-D modes: using motion parallax to look around objects [Fisher, Littlefield], peeling away interfering data layers, or constructing additional data types in image space itself.

Figure 1. A cutaway view of the work station, showing the view through the half silvered mirror of the video monitor and user's hand.

In short, the blossoming of conventional two-dimensional interactive computer graphics has yet to penetrate the three-dimensional world. Such graphic interactivity requires three components: display technology (e.g., digital frame store), input technology (e.g., tablet, mouse) and algorithms or techniques linking the two.

This paper will briefly survey existing three-dimensional display and input technologies. It will then focus on a style of interaction characterized by spatial correspondence between the display and input devices; we desire to build a stereoscopic workspace which will allow a user to reach into the midst of a three-dimensional image and interact with it at exactly that point in space which he is touching.

The workstation display is a conventional color frame buffer using television interlace and special opto-electric shutter glasses for stereoscopic viewing. The monitor is viewed through a half-silvered mirror, which projects its image into an illuminated workspace (figure 1). The user views his hand and the graphics, mixed by the mirror, overlapping in three-dimensional space. Input technology has included a six degree-of-freedom magnetic digitizer and a conventional magnetostrictive tablet.

A series of experiments will be discussed. Early experiments exercised the work station, using the magnetic digitizer, in various applications; despite early optimism, numerous limitations on interaction were noticed. After discussing these, we will explore alternative applications, with more clearly defined interaction goals, as well as a second workstation configuration which uses two-dimensional tablet input to build 2½-D databases.

DISPLAY TECHNOLOGY

Stereopsis is the perception of depth from the binocular fusion of the slightly offset views of our left and right eyes. Stereo display systems must somehow correctly generate left and right eye views, and present them separately, avoiding crosstalk, to the respective eyes. As this paper focuses on real-time interactive computer generated display of information, we will limit this section to various forms of computer controllable video display [Okoshi].

A number of techniques for display of three-dimensional video have been developed. Points may be displayed on a CRT in synchronization with a vibrating mirror, which generates a true three-dimensional image under ordinary viewing conditions [Stover, Fuchs]. Two CRTs may be used in a head mounted display, using optics to deliver each image to the respective eye [Sutherland, Callahan]. Two CRTs may be viewed through orthogonal pairs of polarizers, as is commonly done in movie theater projection, although crosstalk may be a problem and the viewer must keep his head fairly erect. Two images may be mixed on a single CRT as a color anaglyph and viewed through red and green/blue filter glasses. Finally, two images may be time-multiplexed on the CRT and viewed through electrically controlled glasses [Roese].

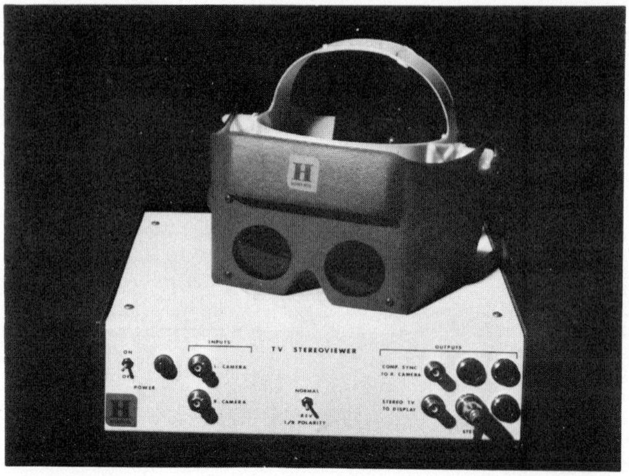

Figure 3. The PLZT glasses and electronic controller box.

The latter technique was used in our work. Conventional interlaced video actually displays two fields sequentially; one field consists of the even scan lines, the other of the odd lines. Using an ordinary frame buffer, the right eye view is drawn on even lines, with the left eye view on odd lines (figure 2). This mixed image is viewed through wafers of a lead lanthanum zirconate titanium (PLZT) ceramic, a very fast electrically triggered shutter (figure 3). Electronics detect the video vertical interval, alternately opening and closing each eye's shutter while the corresponding field is being displayed. Our controller and PLZT glasses were obtained from Honeywell, with additional glasses from Matsushita.

In terms of the computer graphics algorithms, the depth of an object is a function of the distance between the even and odd line portions of the image (figure 4). Zero disparity makes the graphic appear on the surface of the screen, as we are accustomed to viewing. When the horizontal position of left and right eye portions of the object are different, eye convergence will make the object appear behind or in front of the screen. This relationship can be expressed as:

$$dx = IO \left(\frac{d}{Ds+d} \right)$$

where dx is image disparity, d the apparent distance of the object from the screen, Ds the viewer's distance from the screen, and IO the interocular distance (about 65mm).

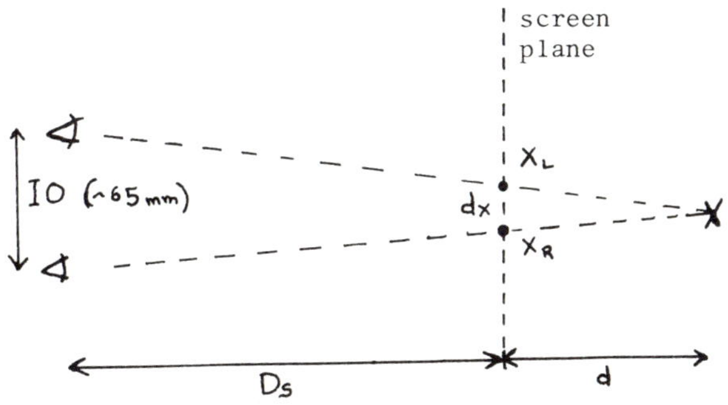

Figure 4. Ocular convergence and depth perception. The left eye sees an object at Xl on the screen, the right eye sees it at Xr, with disparity dx. The object will be perceived to lie at distance d behind the screen. Note that if dx were negative the object would appear in front of the screen.

INPUT TECHNOLOGY

Digitizing three dimensional data points for system input has been a more difficult problem than stereo display. One approach uses various forms of mechanical linkages (such as fishing line) connected to measuring devices [Roberts, Clark]. Although high accuracy may be obtained, these linkages limit freedom of movement and are somewhat awkward.

Other techniques use infrared light sources, worn on the body, as transmitters and light sensing hardware as recievers to track multiple points in three space [Burton, Woltring]. Although the commercial product (Selspot) is quite expensive, recent work indicates lower cost tracking may be possible in simplified configurations [Ginsberg]. The main problem with light transmission is obscuration by the user's body.

We chose a magnetic six degree-of-freedom digitizer developed by Polhemus Navigational Sciences [Polhemus, Rabb]; while still fairly expensive, it avoids most problems of previous technologies and is very accurate under ordinary circumstances. This digitizer returns the position (x,y, and z) and attitude (azimuth, elevation, and roll) of a small sensor relative to a larger radiator 40 times per second. Radiator and sensor electronics are connected to a Nova 1200 minicompuer which is interfaced to our laboratory's machines (Perkin-Elmer 3230's).

Three mutually orthogonal dipole coils in the radiator generate a rotating magnetic field, which induces currents in the sensor, a plastic cube about 1.5 cm on edge which also contains a similar array of receiver coils (figure 5). The sensor is small and light, connected to nearby preamplifiers by a thin, flexible cable. As position is sensed magnetically, there are no awkward linkages, and a user's body does not interfere with the device (although, as will be discussed below, color monitors do).

For the purposes of this work station, a sensor has been mounted at the end of a small wooden "magic wand" which also has a momentary contact bush button switch placed within the handle. The wand, switch, and cable are black, while a white spot on the sensor aids visibility and indicates the "active" portion of the wand. The radiator is mounted out of sight behind the work area. In later versions of the workspace, a conventional magnetostrictive graphics tablet, also painted black with a white spot on the puck, was used for input.

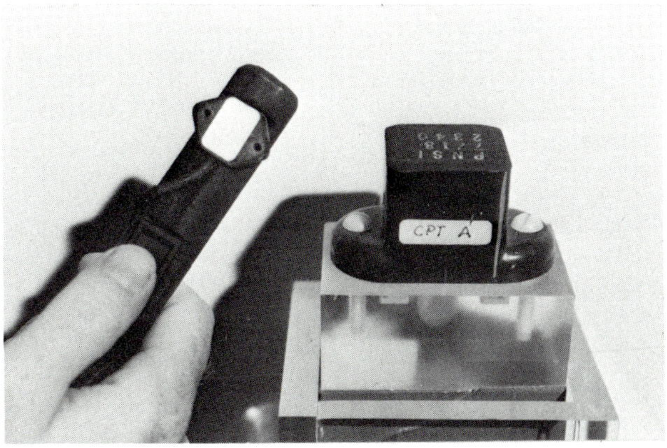

Figure 5. The Polhemus radiator and wand, with the sensor mounted near its end.

THE WORKSPACE

The goal in workspace design was to allow a style of interaction in which spatial correspondence between the particular input and output devices could be maintained. We wished to be able to project the stereoscopic image into an unobscured space which would allow one to reach into the projection with the wand and modify the graphic by touching where it appeared to be. Proper illumination would be essential to maintain the optical mix of the projected image and the user's hand.

Prior work, both at MIT and elsewhere, used half-silvered mirrors to mix computer graphics with reality. The various head mounted displays attempted to place graphics in known positions in the environment with mirrors mounted immediately in front of the viewer's eyes [Vickers, Callahan]. Larger mirrors had been used to overlay graphics onto keyboards and tablets [Knowlton, Lippman]. Our task was to extend this concept into three-space.

A 19 inch color CRT is mounted at a 45 degree angle above and in front of the operator's head, and viewed through the half-silvered mirror parallel to the floor (figure 6). Thus the reflected graphics appear to lie in the space in front of the operator and below the mirror. This space below the mirror is painted black and illuminated, so he can see his hand in the midst of the image. In some configurations this lighting was dimmed under computer control.

The following sections will describe several early applications for which this workspace was used, with the wand as input. Despite the optimism of our early reports [Schmandt], various limitations interfered with fully satisfactory interaction. After discussing these flaws, and our attempts to remedy them, we will present a second generation of applications which matched the capability of this configuration more closely. More recent work has explored alternative input schemes, using a graphics tablet.

IMAGE CREATION

3-D Paint

Early work was aimed at developing spatial correspondence algorithms in the context of a 3-D paint program. Menu buttons at the front edge of the work station allowed color selection; when the user pressed the button in the wand, colored paint would appear in space, at the location of the white spot on the end of the wand (figure 7), dribbling out as the wand was moved. If the positions of the graphic and wand were well correlated, no cursor would be necessary, as the white spot on the wand is itself a real world "cursor".

Several calculations determine the position of the paint. First, the digitizer's location, in its own coordinate system, must be rotated, translated, and scaled into the screen coordinate system (actually, that of the projected image of the screen). This transformation matrix is a function of the user's point of view, so it was derived from a calibration step at the beginning of a session. Next, the line of sight from the eye to the digitizer is extended to intersect the projected screen. This gives an (x,y) coordinate in screen space (that of the frame buffer, except that x is mirrored). The z coordinate is used to determine the left/right disparity with which to draw the graphic at that point.

In practice, this correspondence works excellently most of the time and the paint actually appears to flow from the end of the wand, provided it is not moved quickly (see below). One can draw lines, spirals, knots, etc.; nearer objects obscure more distant ones, but in turn draw behind still closer lines.

Depth perception adjuncts

Early in this stage we discovered that only an experienced viewer could reliably and comfortably see the proper depth in the PLZT video image. Purely binocular convergence is missing many strong depth cues such as shadows, textures, perspective, and motion parallax. Of course, hidden surface obscuration provides an obvious depth perception aid, but further cues ease perception greatly.

In all demonstrations, hidden surface removal is done in real time during image generation using false color and arithmetic frame buffer write operations. Associated with each of the 64 discrete depth levels are several slots in the color table, one for each of the eight displayable colors. Distance is encoded in the high order bits of color, increasing farther away from the viewer; while the low order bits determine which particular color is displayed. Graphics are added to the screen by writing the appropriate value (a function of color and distance) into the frame buffer under a minimum function; the lesser (i.e., closer) of the new value and current value gets written into the display.

When additional depth cues are provided, depth perception is significantly facilitated. The brightness and size of lines decrease as they are drawn farther away, as exaggerated perspective and lighting effects. We noted that although stereoscopic depth perception was improved with these adjuncts, they did not work well enough in isolation to render the convergence cues redundant; rather convergence, obscuration, luminance and size all worked together to give a strong three-dimensional sense.

VLSI design station

These results were encouraging enough to move toward a more practical demonstration, using the wand to input vertices of a 2½ dimensional polygon database. Such databases were later used to generate animation on a write-once optical videodisc, for viewpoint dependent image work [Fisher]. For a practical application, we chose to work with the graphic component of a VLSI integrated circuit design station.

Integrated circuits consist of approximately rectilinear components ordered spatially in a laminar manner, with much information contained in how such layers overlap spatially. This content lends itself well to the 2-½ D environment that is suited to real-time frame buffer work. As we were concerned with only the graphic component, VLSI designs of varying complexity were selected from textbooks, and entered by several students using the workspace and wand.

INTERACTION LIMITATIONS

After initial enthusiasm over the ability to accurately track the wand graphically in three space wore off, we were confronted with several aspects of the workspace which detracted from performance in the chosen applications

Magnetic interference

The most disturbing aspect of this hardware configuration is magnetic interference with the Polhemus digitizer caused by the color CRT. Magnetic fields from the monitor disturb the digitizer in two ways: the normally Cartesian digitizer coordinate space is badly warped, and noise is introduced.

As the magnetic space warping is temporally constant, it was sufficient to derive a single mapping from the warped to a Cartesian three space. This was done by hand mapping magnetic contour lines in the workspace, and approximating them by circular sections. Such an approach works reasonably well except at extremes of the active graphical volume. The unwarped coordinates are then transformed, in software, by a transformation matrix that is generated before each session by having the user touch a succession of displayed dots.

Digitizer noise is induced by strong magnetic field components at the 15.75 kHz horizontal video frequency. Despite the addition of a hardware notch filter to attenuate this frequency in the preamplifier, noise remains excessive with the close proximity of monitor and radiator in the workspace. We placed an ordinary aluminum window screen across the face of the monitor (it can be seen in some of the photographs), which reduces noise to a level such that software filtering could generate useful data.

This additional filtering has the unfortunate effect of introducing a lag, or lack of responsiveness, into the system, with the obvious loss of interactivity. We partially compensated for this with an adaptive filter, which uses a larger sample window when the sensor is nearer the CRT, and hence more noise prone, but remain disappointed with response time.

Depth judgement

As already mentioned, exaggerated drop off in brightness and premature foreshortening were early additions to aid depth perception, an indication that purely binocular depth cues may be insufficient. Although this enhances perception of the relative distance of pieces of the image, it remains very demanding to properly determine the distance of one's hand relative to the image. Accurate distance judgement is crucial in an input task in which discrete objects may be logically required to lie on coincident planes, or when relative depth between planes conveys needed information.

A partial explanation of this difficulty is that although image components may obscure each other, they are always visable through the user's hand. We attempted, not particularly successfully, to alleviate this problem by allowing computer control of the workspace lighting. When the wand was moved farther away, the lights were dimmed to allow nearer, and hence brighter, components of the image to obscure the hand; unfortunately, the light dimmer response time was poor and the overall effect novel but unconvincing.

Drawing difficulties

Most users of the VLSI design station complained of the difficulty experienced in trying to draw planar objects floating in space because of the lack of arm support and limited hand stability. It was nearly impossible to repeatably draw rectilinear objects with proper right angled corners, and required great care to insure that all vertices of a polygon lay on the same z plane, aggravated by the depth perception difficulty.

Several improvements were tried. An invisible grid of variable resolution is used to force input points to land on lower resolution (x,y) coordinates, making input of orthogonal line segments easier. Subsequent vertices were automatically forced to lie in the plane of the initial vertex, a usefual aid only if the first vertex is indeed at the proper depth. Although these additions are in fact helpful, most users find complex input tasks difficult and tedious.

NEW DIRECTIONS

From the work with VLSI design graphics, several new directions emerged due to recognition of the above constraints. User response had indicated that although the spatial correspondence between graphics and the wand was a simple and intuitive mapping, the arrangment was unsuitable for tasks highly oriented toward the input of data.

One follow on approach explored the usefulness of the same work station configuration for tasks more oriented toward interaction with or manipulation of previously input or generated data. The other path focused on overcoming input limitations using a graphics tablet instead of the 3-D digitizer. Both approaches retained the stereoscopic video display viewed through the half-silvered mirror.

Data manipulation

Efficient graphical input requires a stable and responsive digitizing technology; these requirements were mutually exclusive in the workspace, with the wand so close to the monitor. Accuracy could be traded off for speed by modifying the software filter, suggesting use of the wand as a target selection, rather than positioning, device.

In the case of complex 3-D data, one may well need to manipulate or highlight the data in order to understand it; interactive graphics should assist this. One of the obvious complexities with a three-dimensional database is the variety of ways objects can obscure each other. Tools are needed to take scenes apart, rearrange them, or accent local volumes for more detailed analysis or separation.

A fairly ambitious implementation of these concepts was attempted in a "Model Kit" project [Nisselson], which allows the rearrangement of 3-D scenes composed of pieces of small, digitized pictures of architectural landmarks, medical images, or microscopy slides as primitives (figure 9). Using the wand in the same work station, the user can move or remove objects, call up new primitives from the photographic database, add text, and save periodic "snapshots" of work in progress.

Many prior limitations of the wand as an input device are avoided by this approach. As it is used much more often to "acquire" one target from many in the scene, highly accurate positioning is less crucial, and response is quickened by tolerating more noise with less filtering.

Tablet input

An alternative input technology was needed for such tasks as building the polygonal components of VLSI design. We mounted a conventional graphics tablet, painted black to avoid image crosstalk, inside the workstation at a 45 degree angle to the floor, such that the image of the CRT screen coincided with the plane of the tablet (figure 10). We desired to retain as much spatial correspondence as possible, with an intuitive 3-D interaction.

The tablet is used to input data only on the plane defined by its surface. Access to the complete visual volume is provided by moving the entire image towards or away from the viewer, under control of a soft "slider" selection graphic, until the appropriate image slice corresonds to the tablet plane. The whole image moves in and out such that one is always working on a level currently displayed with zero disparity (figure 11).

Moving the entire image in the Z direction is done by shifting the horizontal position of the odd scan line graphics with respect to the even lines. This is done by two methods. The odd scan lines can be read out of the frame buffer, then written back with the appropriate new x offset. A coherence table indicating the left and rightmost extent of each line is maintained to minimize the pixel data transfer necessary.

A faster method utilizes two complete frame buffers, one for the left eye view and the other for the right eye view. The two images are mixed into one signal in the video domain by the same electronics that detect interlace to control the glasses; the vertical interval detector selects alternate fields from two video sources. With this configuration, the image can be moved very quickly simply by a horizontal pan by one of the frame buffers.

In addition to greatly increasing the speed with which the image can be shifted in and out, this technique can allow faster image generation and manipulation. Instead of breaking the graphics into an even and odd line portion, preventing use of conventional internal frame buffer primitives (such as "line", "rectangle", etc.), each frame buffer maintains a separate complete image. Left and right eye views can be generated in parallel using the processors in the frame stores.

Tablet input has been used in a variety of styles. The original VLSI design task lends itself quite well to this method, allowing easy input of rectilinear graphic components while retaining needed stereoscopic viewing. Other work will use the tablet to input vertices of 3-D solids, built and edited as wire frame models. Once the final design is satisfactory, slower shaded surface algorithms generate solid model views of these objects for animations. The higher speed, high resolution, and noise immune tablet data is much more suited to these graphically detailed tasks than the wand.

CONCLUSIONS

A stereoscopic video display lends itself well to interactive computer graphics, literally opening up a new dimension of graphical control. Elegant input techniques require careful thought to provide the tools of real use, however.

All work described in this paper exploits the spatial mapping of the graphic display into or over the work area, an arrangement which was found to provide intuitive access to the third dimension. This was without a doubt the most exciting element of the project. Our work certainly suggests that the input configuration and support software will need to be developed around requirements of each individual application, and indeed a task area may require several configurations, some for input and others for image manipulation.

ACKNOWLEDGEMENTS

As with many projects at the Architecture Machine Group, many people participated in various aspects of this work. Topping the list are Jim Zamiska, who wrote the most difficult early software, and Scott Fisher for the optics and convergence algorithm. Without their work this project would have never been more than an idea. Eric Hulteen built the workstation. Additional programming was done by David Mellinger, Jane Nisselson, Charles Simmons, and Carol Yao. Photos are by Scott Fisher and Barry Arons; Carol Boemer drew the first illustration. Kathy Coppola assisted with production. Orlen Rice of Honeywell graciously loaned the Laboratory our first pair of PLZT glasses, where it all began.

This project was funded by Atari, Inc. and the Defense Advanced Research Projects Agency, Cybernetics Technology Division, under contract MDA 903-81-C-0097.

REFERENCES

Burton, R.P. and Sutherland, I.E. Twinkle box: a three-dimensional computer input device. NCC 1974, pp. 513-520.

Callahan, M.A. A 3-D display head set for personalized computer, M.S. Thesis, Dept. of Arch., MIT 1983.

Clark, J.H. Designing surfaces in 3-D. Comm. ACM 19,8 (Aug. 1976) pp. 454-460.

Fisher, S.S. Viewpoint dependent imaging: an interactive stereoscopic display, M.S. Thesis, Dept. of Arch., MIT 1981

Fuchs, H., Pizer, S.M., Tsai, L.C., Bloomberg, S.H., and Heinz, E. R., Adding a true 3-D display to a raster graphics system. IEEE Computer Graphics and Applications, Sept. 1982. pp. 73-78.

Ginsberg, C.M. and Maxwell, D. Graphical marionette. Proceedings, SIGGRAPH/SIGART interdisciplinary workshop, ACM. April, 1983 pp. 172-179.

Knowlton, K.C., Computer displays optically superimposed on input devices. Bell Syst. Tech. J. 56:3 (1977).

Lippman, A. And seeing through your hand. Proceedings of the SID, 22:2 (1981) pp. 103-107.

Littlefield, R.J., Stereo and motion in the display of 3-D scattergrams. Proc., Engineering Society of Detroit Computer Graphics Conference, 1982.

Okoshi, T. <u>Three Dimensional Imaging Techniques</u>. Academic Press, N.Y. 1976.

Nisselson, J. A model kit: a system for constructing three-dimensional interactive graphic models. M.S. thesis, Dept. of Arch., MIT 1983.

Polhemus Navigational Sciences, Inc. P.O. Box A, Essex Junction, VT.

Rabb, F.H., Blood, E.B., Steiner, T.O., and Jones, H.R. Magnetic position and orientation tracking system. IEEE Trans. on Aerospace and Electronic Systems Sept. 1979. pp 709-718.

Roberts, L.G. The Lincoln wand. MIT Lincoln Laboratories Report, Lexington, MA. 1966.

Roese, J.A. and McCleary, L.E., Stereoscopic computer graphics for simulation and modeling, Proc. SIGGRAPH 13:2 (1979). pp. 41-47.

Schmandt, C.M., Interactive three-dimensional computer space, Proc., SPIE conference on processing and display of three-dimensional data, Aug. 1982 (in publication).

Vickers, D.L. Sorcerer's apprentice: headmounted display and wand. Ph.D. thesis University of Utah, Dept. Elec. Eng., 1974

Woltring, H.J. and Marsolais, E.B. Opto-electric (Selspot) gait measurement in two- and three- dimensional space, a preliminary report. Bulletin of Prosthetics Research 17:2 (fall, 1980). pp. 46-52

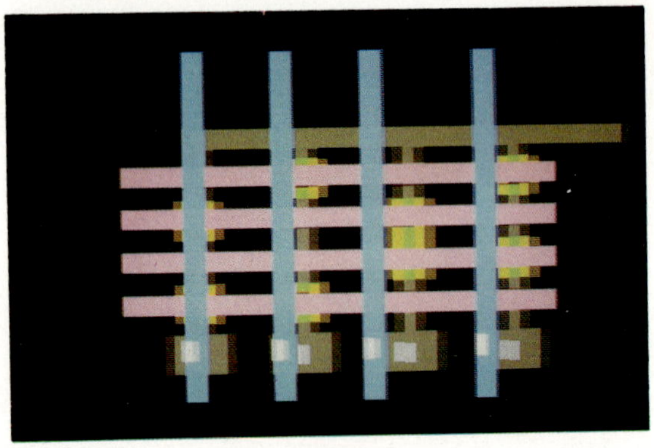

Figure 2. A VLSI design. Note the use of interlace to convey disparity along edges of vertical components.

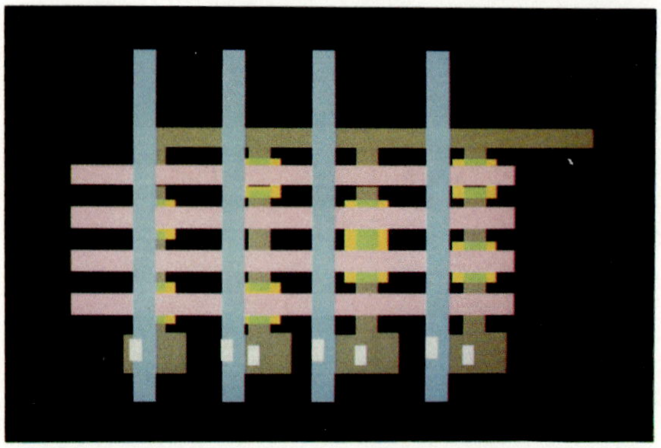

Figure 8. One of the single eye views of the adjacent VLSI component.

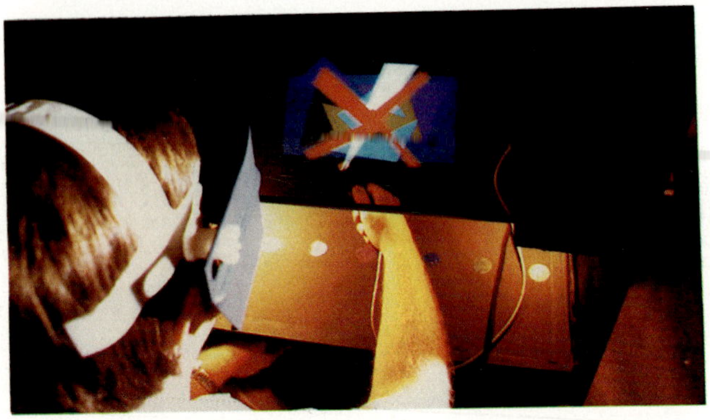

Figure 6. The work station. The graphics are reflected from a monitor at the same height as the user's head.

Figure 9. Moving architectural icons with the "Model Kit".

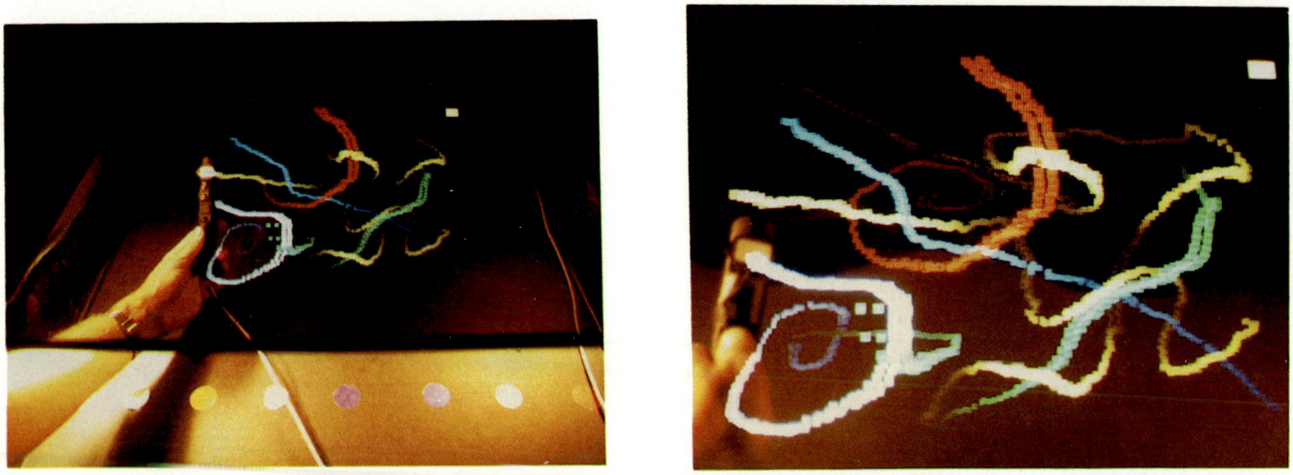

Figure 7. Two views through the mirror, showing the overlap of graphics and the hand/wand. Lines that appear double show the disparity between the left/right eye views (presented on alternate video scan lines).

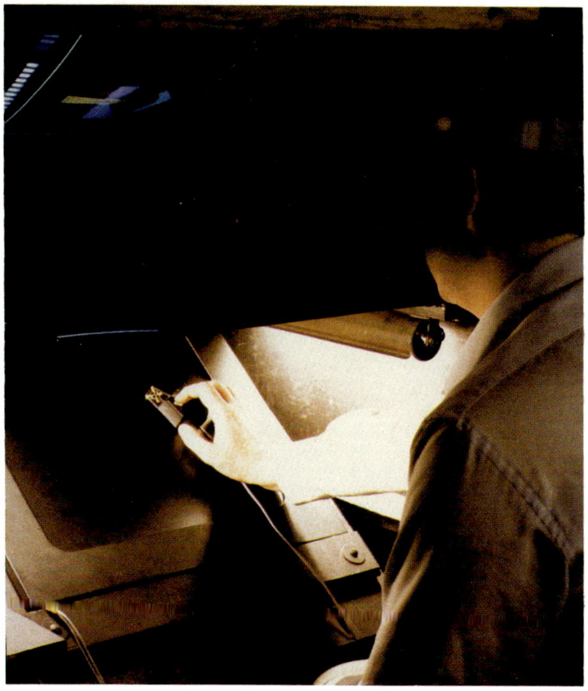

Figure 10. (Left and above) The tablet workspace configuration.

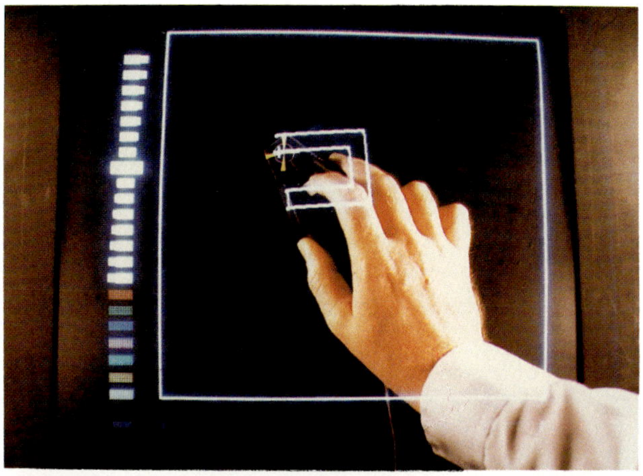

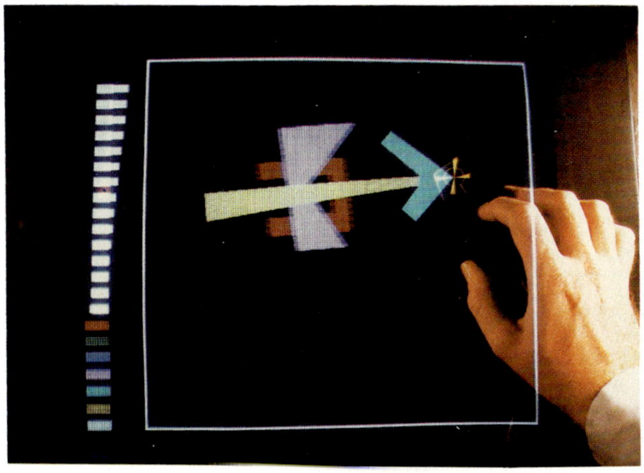

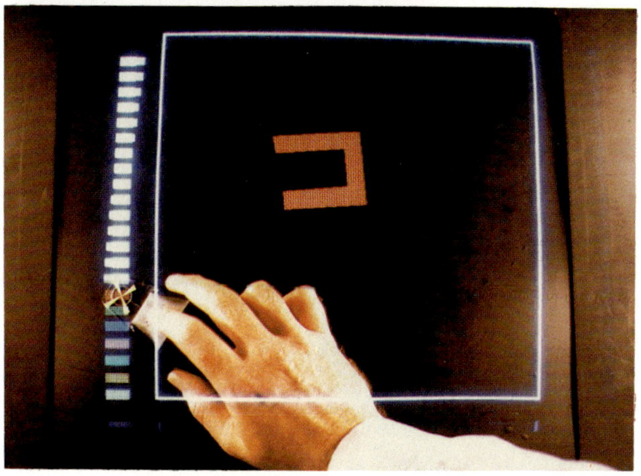

Figure 11. (Above, and to the left). Use of the tablet to input data. Rubber band outlines are drawn, and the polygon is filled when a color is selected. The white rectangles to the left, above the color menu, select the Z plane on which to work.

THREE DIMENSIONAL COMPUTER GRAPHICS FOR CRANIOFACIAL SURGICAL PLANNING AND EVALUATION

Michael W. Vannier, M.D.[1]
Jeffrey L. Marsh, M.D.[2]
James O. Warren, B.S.A.E.[3]

[1]Mallinckrodt Institute of Radiology, Washington University School of Medicine, 510 South Kingshighway Boulevard, St. Louis, Missouri 63110.

[2]Cleft Palate and Craniofacial Deformities Institute, St. Louis Children's Hospital, Washington University School of Medicine, St. Louis, Missouri 63110.

[3]McDonnell Douglas Aircraft Company, P.O. Box 516, St. Louis, Missouri 63166.

Abstract

The understanding of complex craniofacial deformities has been aided by high resolution computed tomography. Nonetheless, the planar format limits spatial comprehension. Reconstruction of fully three-dimensional bony and soft tissue surfaces from high resolution CT scans has been accomplished by a level slicing edge detector coupled to a hidden surface processor without perspective depth transformation. This method has clarified aberrant anatomy, facilitated surgical planning and improved quantitative postoperative evaluation in more than 200 clinical cases. Advanced computer aided design techniques, originally developed for the manufacture of military aircraft, have been applied to the planning and evaluation of craniofacial procedures as well. This allows the application of interactive digital graphic technology to surgical patient management.

CR Categories and Subject Descriptors: I.3.0. (Computer Graphics): General; J.6 (Computer Aided Engineering) - computer aided design (CAD); J.3 (Life and Medical Sciences) - Biology; Health.

General Terms: Computer aided design, computer graphics, craniofacial surgery, CT scan.

INTRODUCTION

Craniofacial surgery has developed over the past 15 years as a discipline capable of habilitating individuals with major deformities of the head (1). This discipline is based on the premise that surgical correction of aberrant skeletal anatomy must precede attempts at soft tissue reconstruction for normalization of craniofacial features and functions. Thus, the planning and evaluation of such operations is dependent on radiological imaging for defining the underlying bony structures and their relationship to overlying soft tissue contours. Traditionally this planning has been accomplished using acetate tracings of cephalometric skull radiographs in the AP and lateral projections (Fig. 1).

Recently, the availability of high resolution CT scanners has altered our approach to the study of complex craniofacial anomalies. We now routinely obtain, pre- and postoperatively, a set of equi-spaced, nonoverlapping, high resolution CT scans of the face with narrow collimation. This set of scans is augmented by reformatting sagittal, coronal and oblique planar reconstructions to demonstrate aberrant anatomy and facilitate surgical planning and evaluation.

Unfortunately, the complex structural anomalies the surgeon encounters are not completely explained by planar reconstructions. These malformations are 3-dimensional and no purely 2-dimensional reconstruction will suffice. To date, the surgeon has had to imagine the 3-dimensional projection, based on a sequence of 2-dimensional images (CT axial scans and reformatted planar views) supplied by the radiologist.

Some preliminary experiments in 3-dimensional reconstructions from CT scans have been performed by others (2,3). In general, these methods are quite complex, time consuming and require computer equipment that is not available in most x-ray departments. These methods may involve three-dimensional edge detection (2) or encoding and display from a 3-dimensional geometrical model derived from the original scans (3). These steps imply a computational burden that is orders of magnitude greater than desired and storage requirements that exceed reasonable limits for 3-dimensional reconstructions with acceptable resolution.

We have developed a new computer method which reconstructs three dimensional bone and soft tissue surfaces given a series of high resolution CT scans of the face. This method, implemented as a series of computer programs, is efficient in both computation time and storage requirements and can be added with modest effort to virtually any CT scanner. We have applied these programs to sets of scans from more than 200 patients with congenital and acquired craniofacial abnormalities. The surface reconstructions of bone and soft tissue contours has been helpful for understanding and interpretation of the abnormalities under study.

MATERIALS AND METHODS

CT Scans

High resolution CT scans of facial structures were obtained using an unmodified commercially available instrument (Siemens Somatom 2). Each study consisted of between 30 and 64 non-overlapping sections obtained at 2mm intervals with 2mm collimation (Fig.2). A

256X256 reconstruction matrix was used. To better delineate the facial structures, only the frontal half of the subject's skull was included in the original transverse transaxial CT images. Young subjects were sedated during scanning to minimize motion and improve the registration of the scan sequence.

The reconstructed scans were recorded on double-density floppy diskettes and transferred to an independent CT scan viewing console (Siemens Evaluscope RC, Fig. 8). The image data was copied to a large capacity (28 Mbyte) cartridge disk (Digital Equipment Corp., Maynard, Mass., Model RK07) integrated in the viewing console. Routine planar reconstructions in the sagittal, coronal and oblique orientations were obtained.

Computer Programs

A set of computer programs was specifically developed for 3-dimensional surface reconstruction from sequences of high resolution CT scans. These programs were written in the Fortran IV language to operate on a minicomputer (Digital Equipment Corp., Maynard, Mass., Model PDP-11/34, Figure 8) incorporated in the CT viewing console. These programs will operate without modification on the CT scanner (Siemens Somatom 2) as well. The programs accept the sequence of transaxial high resolution CT scans as input and produce a set of 3-dimensional surface reconstruction images as output.

Algorithm

The surface reconstruction computer program reads each of the original high resolution CT scans (Fig.3A) in sequence from the cartridge disk and loads the image into the 256X256 display memory of the evaluation console (or CT scanner). Since the scans are obtained with the patient supine, in passing from the top of each image to the bottom, we encounter air, skin, facial bones and finally intracranial contents.

Each column of the image is read in sequence from left to right. The soft tissue contour (Fig. 3B) is extracted by comparing each value of CT density in the column from top to bottom of the image with a preset threshold. (This threshold represents the CT attenuation that distinguishes air from soft tissue (nominally -100 CT units for our scanner). The column index where an air to soft tissue transition occurs is used to form the soft tissue contour for each CT scan slice. This index value is scaled and output to the cartridge disk as a line in the reconstructed soft tissue 3-dimensional surface image.

In a similar manner, each column of the CT scan slice is examined from top to bottom and compared with a bone threshold (+150 CT units nominally). The set of scaled indices of soft tissue to bone density transitions detected in this manner is the bone contour (Fig. 3C). The bone contour is written to a separate file on the cartridge disk. During the contour extraction process, the detected frontal contours are written on the evaluation console display as a quality control measure (Fig. 3D).

In order to complete the surface reconstructions, each succeeding CT scan is loaded into display memory, bone and soft tissue contours extracted, and results (Fig.4A-D) written to the cartridge disk.

In order to facilitate the display and handling of surface reconstruction files, these 3-dimensional images were written on the cartridge disk in the same format as the original CT scans. These 3-dimensional reconstructions can be viewed and manipulated in the same manner as any CT scan. The relationship between pairs of soft tissue and bone reconstructed surfaces is maintained and comparisons of soft tissue thicknesses may be directly computed as their difference, for example. The gray scale values in the surface reconstructions represent actual distances, and within the geometrical resolution of the CT scanner, can be used for rectilinear measurements.

Smoothing and Interpolation

In order to obtain an accurate surface image, the extracted contours are replicated several times in the output file so the vertical sample interval is equal to the horizontal interval. For example, when the pixel size in the raw CT scans is 0.5mm square, four lines must be replicated for each contour extracted to produce correct vertical spacing given 2mm non-overlapping slice thickness. Using a 256X256 matrix, this means that up to 64 sequential CT slices may be included in each surface reconstruction. The replication of contours produces undesirable effects with a coarse "digital" appearance that is particularly pronounced at obliquely oriented edges, such as the lateral orbital margins (Fig. 4A,B). Smoothing programs have been developed to reduce this effect based on local averaging or median filtering. The median filter (4,5,8) is especially useful since significant edges are preserved while artifacts are reduced (Fig. 4C,D).

There is no information on the behavior of the extracted surfaces between the contours, and we may also expect the presence of some motion and partial volume effects in the original set of CT scans. The appearance of the surface reconstructions may be improved by interpolating between the extracted contours using a bilinear interpolator or smooth surface fitting based on local procedures (6). Both of these methods have been implemented.

Efficiency

The computational efficiency of the entire contour extraction and surface reconstruction process is excellent since minimal computer operations are needed. The speed of the reconstruction process is mostly determined by the input/output operations to and from the cartridge disk. Typically, the reconstruction process for a sequence of 40 scans requires approximately 10 minutes. This process results in a complete set of soft tissue and bone contours.

Contour extraction at other than soft tissue-air or soft tissue-bone interfaces requires an image segmentation (7) scheme that is more sophisticated than the simple thresholding or level slicing we have employed. This sophistication would be reflected in increased computational and storage requirements.

Display Considerations

The surface reconstruction algorithm produces very accurate and detailed information regarding craniofacial morphology. However, these surfaces have considerably greater dynamic range and resolution than can be displayed on a typical monochrome (black and white) CT scanner or evaluation console display using a simple linear gray scale window. We have employed histogram modification and contrast enhancement techniques to improve the information transfer from the surface display to the observer. Color display may allow even greater detail and contrast and true color renditions including flesh tones, hair and eye color may become available.

Results

The programs developed for high resolution CT

scan surface reconstruction are available for routine use at the Mallinckrodt Institute of Radiology (9-14). These programs were developed to study craniofacial deformities and several representative cases are described.

Case No.1

GJ is an 18 year old white male with polyostotic fibrous dysplasia involving the skull, especially the facial bones on the right side. Surface 3-dimensional facial reconstructions were helpful (Fig. 4) in the planning and evaluation of an extensive debulking procedure. The marked facial asymmetry due to bony overgrowth on the affected right side is evident.

Case No. 2

LD is an 11 year 11 month old white female with Crouzon's disease. A tracheostomy, in infancy, was the only surgical intervention made prior to our initial evaluation.

Photographs in the frontal, chin up and bird's eye projections were made (Fig. 5 A-C). These photographs demonstrate the stigmata of craniofacial dysostosis including maxillary retrusion, exorbitism and moderate oxycephaly.

Computer reconstruction of frontal bony and soft tissue surfaces was performed using a set of 40 high resolution CT scans. The same set of soft tissue contours used to reconstruct the 3-dimensional soft tissue surface (Fig. 5F) was used to generate worm's eye (Fig. 5B) and bird's eye contour plots (Fig. 5D).

Case No. 3

JH is a 12 year old black male with Tessier type 4-10 craniofacial clefts (5). The left globe is deviated laterally and inferiorly in comparison with the normal right side. Surgical cranioplasty was performed on two occasions in early childhood with placement of a methylmethacrylate plate and tantalum mesh over the left frontal encephalocele defect. The upper and lower lid colobomata were repaired as well, but the asymmetric hypertelorism was not.

In the preoperative surface reconstructions, the soft tissue protruberance (Fig. 6C) over the large frontal cleft (Fig. 6B) is seen. The postoperative reconstructions (Fig. 6D,E) show mesial and superior movement of the bony orbit to restore facial symmetry.

Interactive Computer Aided Design

The design of advanced military aircraft is dependent on the availability of computer aided technology to permit examination of alternative solutions. The three dimensional analysis of an aircraft fuselage surface is analogous to the bony and soft tissue surface of the face. Using a sophisticated computer aided design system (15) (CADD for Computer Aided Design and Drafting system by McDonnell Douglas Automation Company, St. Louis, Mo.) operating on an advanced three dimensional display console (Evans and Sutherland Picture System 2, Salt Lake City, Utah), we have developed methodology for the planning and evaluation of craniofacial surgical procedures.

After extracting frontal soft tissue and bone contours using the level slicing method described above, the corresponding point data (Fig. 7A) was curve-fitted using cubic splines (Fig. 7B).

For patient number 3, the three dimensional surface geometry of frontal bony contours was encoded in fewer than 2500 coordinates using 40 CT scans as input (Fig. 7D). Soft tissue contours were separately entered in the system using the same technique. Using the interactive capablities of this system, these contours were rotated to show the plan or top view (Fig. 7D). The inferolateral displacement of the left orbit is seen on the near frontal view. The left frontal bone cleft is clearly demonstrated.

In both the frontal (Fig. 7C) and plan (Fig. 7D) views, the right handed three dimensional coordinate system is shown in the left corner. By convention, we consider the X-Y plane to be parallel to the transaxial CT plane of section. This is nearly parallel to the base of the skull in CT examinations conducted without gantry tilt. We have assigned the Z-axis to the longitudinal body axis.

The major advantages of the CADD system approach to craniofacial surgical planning and evaluation include interactive display, quantitation of linear, surface and volumetric measurements, and ability to move image components independently. The soft tissue and bony contours may be overlaid to study their relationship with the face by displaying them simultaneously (Fig. 7E).

A most effective means of planning an orbital translocation procedure is demonstrated in this example of asymmetric hypertelorism. The right orbit and its contents are normal while the left orbit is displaced inferiorly, anteriorly and laterally. By measuring these displacements in three dimensions, the surgeon can execute the orbital translocation with improved precision.

The computer aided measurements were obtained with CADD in the planning of orbital translocation by choosing a plane of symmetry in the mid-sagittal region. An arbitrary point of reference was selected above the nasion in the midfrontal region. The normal right orbit was converted from a solid to dashed line type for ease of display. The delineation of the normal orbit was then reflected about the mid-sagittal plane of symmetry (Fig. 7F). Measurements of the X,Y and Z displacements were made with references to this arbitrary fixed point. The dimensions are given in inches on the images in the frontal (Fig. 7F) and plan views (Fig. 7G). (Advanced American-made military aircraft are presently built to English measures, although metric conversion is underway). The most useful measurements are the X,Y and Z differences between the normal transposed and abnormal dislocated orbit. These measurements serve to define the required translocation procedure to realign the left orbit to normalcy. The required superior, medial and posterior displacements (Fig. 7F-G) are shown to be 0.231 inches (0.59cm), 0.408 inches (1.04cm) and 0.266 inches (0.68cm) respectively.

Discussion

Craniofacial surgical procedures have traditionally been planned and evaluated radiographically using cephalometric AP and lateral skull x-rays. With the availability of high resolution CT scanners, reformatted (sagittal, coronal and oblique) images obtained from contiguous sections through the facial structures have found application.

Both methods are subject to the limitations imposed by 2-dimensional imaging applied to the analysis of 3-dimensional aberrant anatomy. CT scans and reformatted planar images contain significant information regarding anatomic abnormalities. The form of CT data presentation, however, may create difficulties in interpretation for the radiologist and problems when the scan results must be communicated to the surgeon.

Consider the difficulty in mentally reconstructing a patient's facial appearance from a sequence of CT scans (Fig. 2). If we cannot visualize the exact nature of abnormal facial appearance by inspecting a set of CT scans, do we truly understand the nature of the bony defects that created the problem? The radiologist or surgeon can better plan and evaluate the complex procedures needed to correct 3-dimensional bony anomalies with a means to fully characterize facial anatomy. This tool, realized by computer processing of a sequence of CT scans, is 3-dimensional surface reconstruction of bony and soft tissue structures.

We have developed such a tool and recognize several additional practical benefits. There is no geometric error due to magnification effects (inherent in cehpalometric skull x-rays) in these surface images. The true character of bilaterally asymmetric malformations may be appreciated (Fig.6). The surface images allow the surgeon to precisely visualize the abnormality to be corrected at operation. Life size surface images may be produced to permit accurate dimensional measurement required for surgical planning. Finally, using interactive digital graphic systems, the surface images can be altered to simulate surgery. These images are helpful for instructing physicians and even patients themselves in pathologic anatomy and craniofacial surgical procedures.

Conclusion

A new method for reconstruction of a 3-dimensional surface from a sequence of high resolution CT scans has been developed. This algorithm, realized as a set of computer programs that can operate on a CT scanner or evaluation console, is both efficient and easy to implement. No operator intervention is required.

The CT data has also been used to generate surface images on an industrial computer aided design system. This allows the generation of industrial blueprint diagrams for application to craniofacial surgery (Fig. 7F-G).

These methods have been utilized to assist management of over 200 patients with congenital or acquired craniofacial deformities by extracting important anatomic details from a sequence of high resolution CT scans. These surface reconstructions have aided the surgeon's comprehension of the primary deformity, facilitated surgical planning and clarified postoperative results.

Acknowledgements

The generous assistance of McDonnell Douglas Automation and Aircraft Company (St. Louis, Missouri) and especially Mr. A. Doelling, Mr. F. Phillips, and Mr. J. Sullivan is appreciated. Technical consultaton and the use of facilities at the Evans and Sutherland Computer Corporation (Salt Lake City, Utah) with the assistance of Mr. T. Naanes, Mr. J. Callen and Mr. S. Artick is acknowledged.

REFERENCES

1. Kawamoto H. The kaleidoscope world of rare craniofacial clefts: Tessier classification. Clinics in Plastic Surgery 1976; 3:529-572.
2. Artzy E, Frieder G, and Herman GT. The theory, design, implementation and evaluation of a three-dimensional surface detection algorithm. Comput Graph & Image Proc 1981; 15:1-24.
3. Herman GT Image reconstruction from projections. New York: Academic Press, 1980:260-176.
4. Nagao M, Matsuyama T. Edge preservation smoothing. Proc International Joint Conference Pattern Recognition, Kyoto, Japan, 1978;IV:518-520.
5. Rabiner LR, Sambur MR, Schmidt CE. Applications of a nonlinear smoothing algorithm to speech processing. IEEE Trans. Acoust. Speech and Signal Proc. 1975; 23:552-557.
6. Akima H. A new method of interpolation and smooth surface fitting based on local procedures. JACM 1970; 17:589-602.
7. Fu KS, Mui JK. A survey on image segmentation. Pattern Recog 1981; 13:65-77.
8. Huang TS, ed. Two-dimensional digital signal processing II. Transforms and median filters. Springer Verlag, Berlin, 1981, 3-7 and 161-218.
9. Vannier M, Marsh JL, Warren JO and Barbier J. Craniofacial disorders. Diagnostic Imaging, (5)3, 36-43.
10. Marsh JL and Vannier MW. The third dimension in craniofacial surgery. Plast and Reconstr Surg 71:June, 1983.
11. Vannier MW, Gado MH and Marsh JL. Three dimensional display of intracranial soft tissue structures, American Journal of Neuroradiology, May, 1983.
12. Merz B. Computer guides facial reconstruction. Journal AMA, 18 March 83, (249) 11, 1409-15.
13. Clayton D. Craniofacial CT. Computers in Medicine, (12), Feb. 1983, 3-4.
14. Vannier MW, Marsh JL, Warren JO and Barbier J. Three dimensional CAD for craniofacial surgery. Electronic Imaging, in press.
15. Doelling AE. CAD/CAM Computer Aided Technology, Engineering Communications Report, McDonnell Douglas Aircraft Co., 26pp.

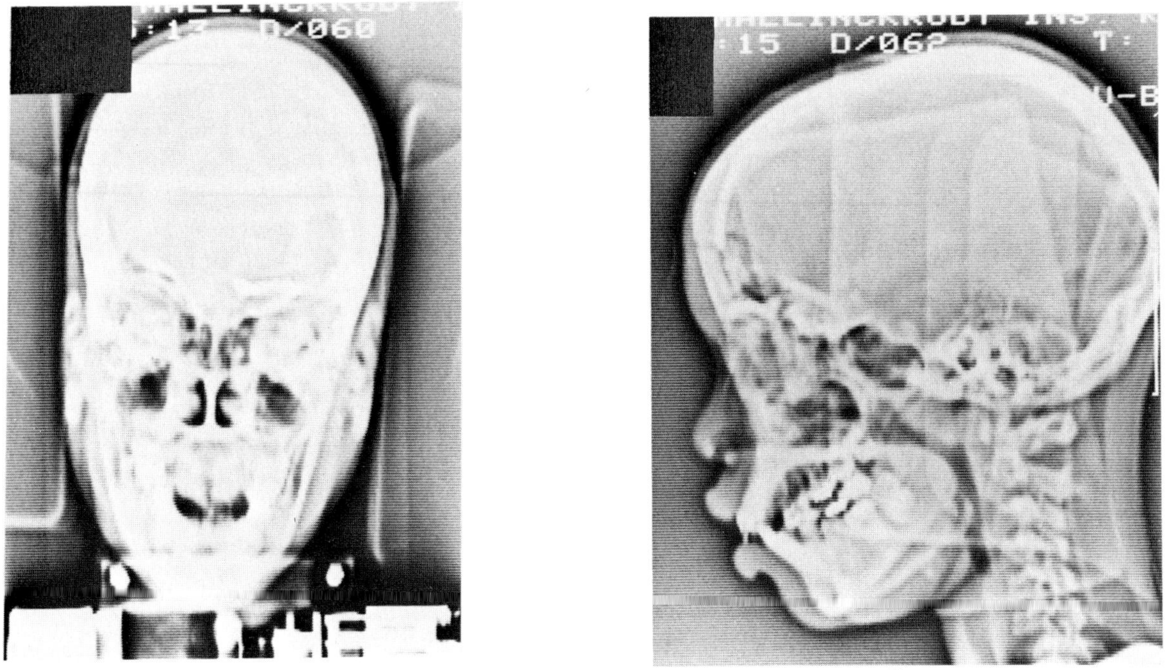

A. B.

Figure 1. Digital skull radiographs representing the routine cephalometric projections in a patient with major facial cleft malformations (Case No. 3). A. AP view. B. Lateral view.

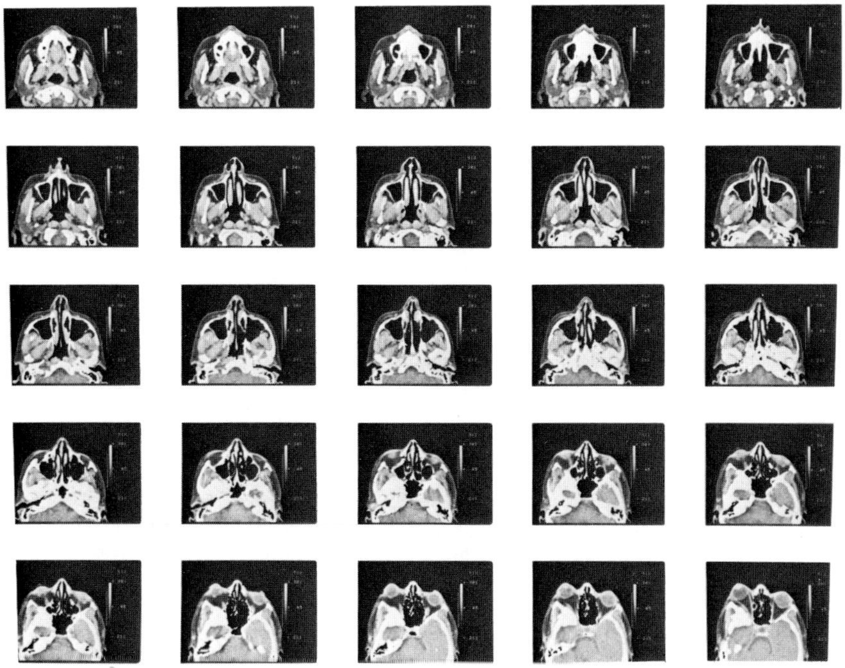

Figure 2. An example of input data for the surface reconstruction program. Sequence of 25 CT scans from a high resolution study (total: 50 scans) of the face. These scans were obtained at 2mm intervals with 2mm collimation. The scans begin at the maxillary alveolus in the upper left and extend to the orbits in the final scan at the lower right.

A. Original CT scan

B. Soft tissue-air interface

C. Soft tissue -bone interfac

D. Contour points extracted on this scan

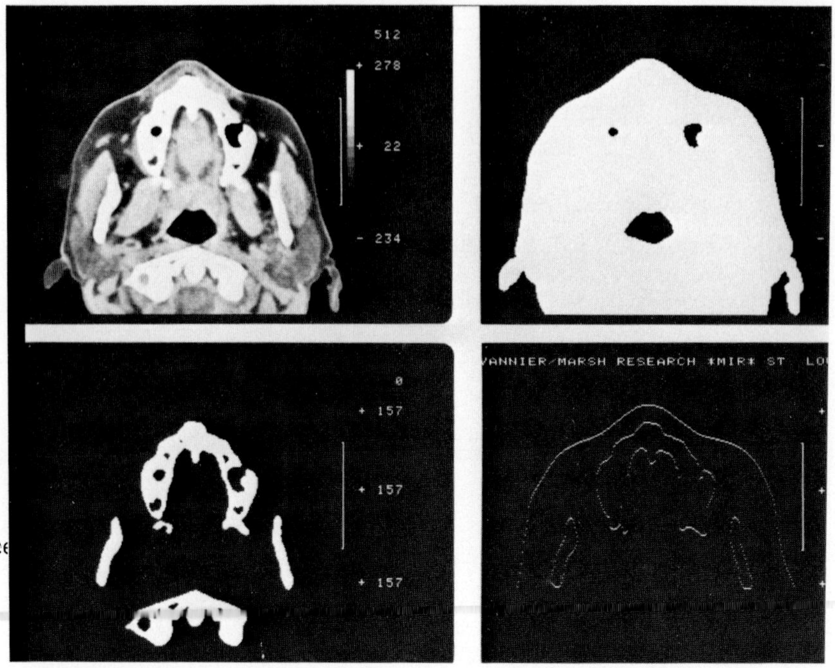

Figure 3. Contour extraction process (e.g. level slicing).

A. Original soft tissue surface reconstruction

B. Original bone surface reconstruction

C. Median filtered bone surface

C. Median filtered soft tissue surface

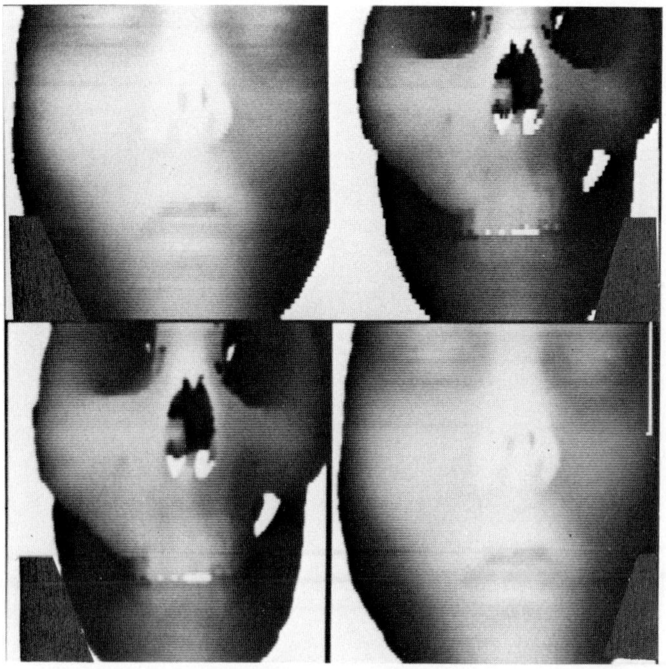

Figure 4. Case No. 1. Polyostotic fibrous dysplasia, frontal view.

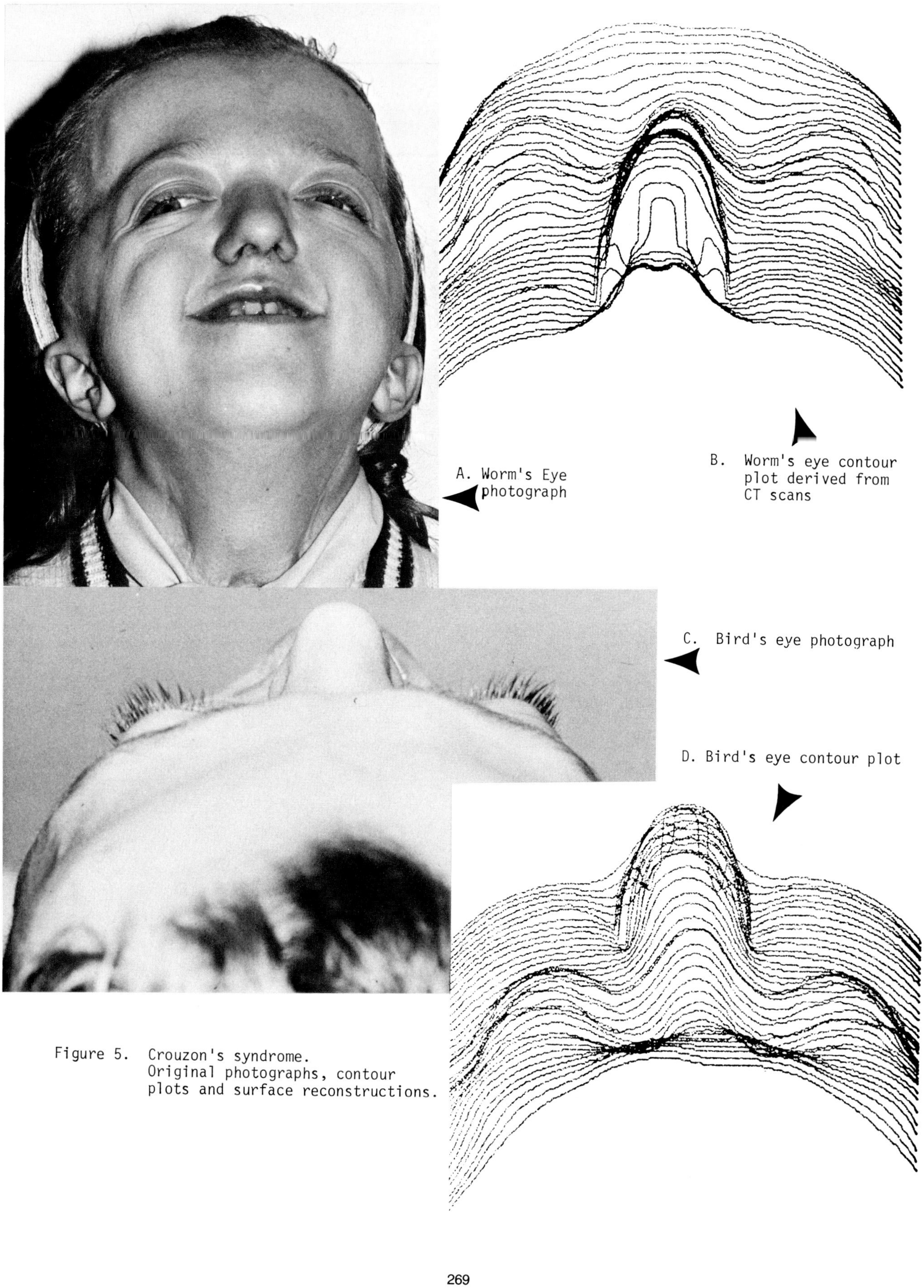

Figure 5. Crouzon's syndrome.
Original photographs, contour plots and surface reconstructions.

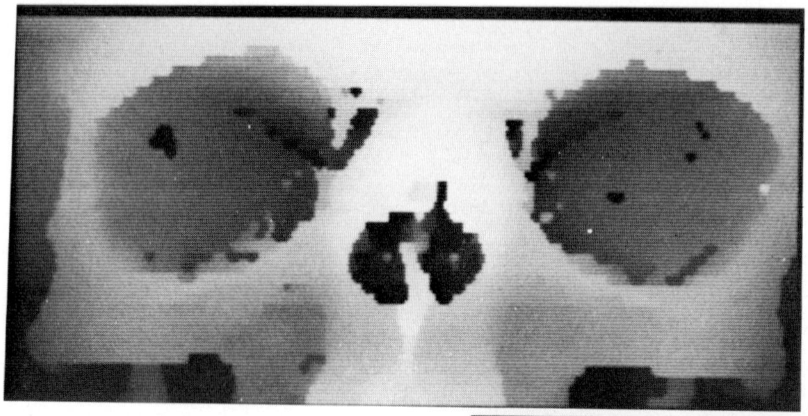

Figure 5E. Bone surface reconstruction from CT scans (frontal view).

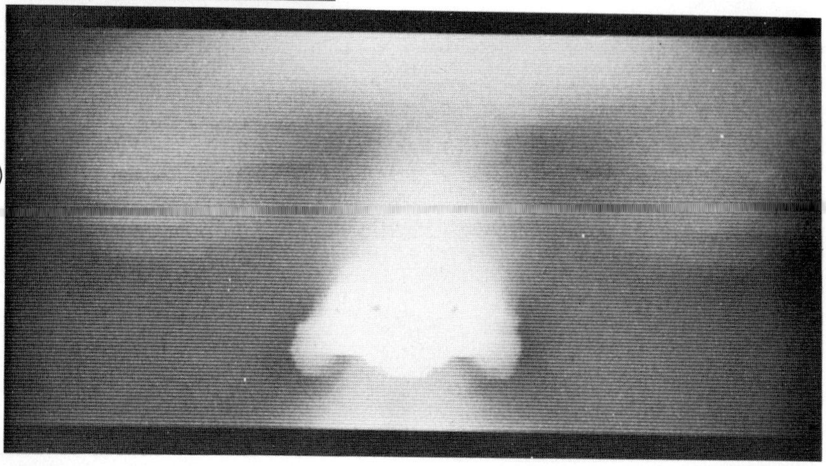

Figure 5F. Soft tissue surface reconstruction from CT scans (frontal view)

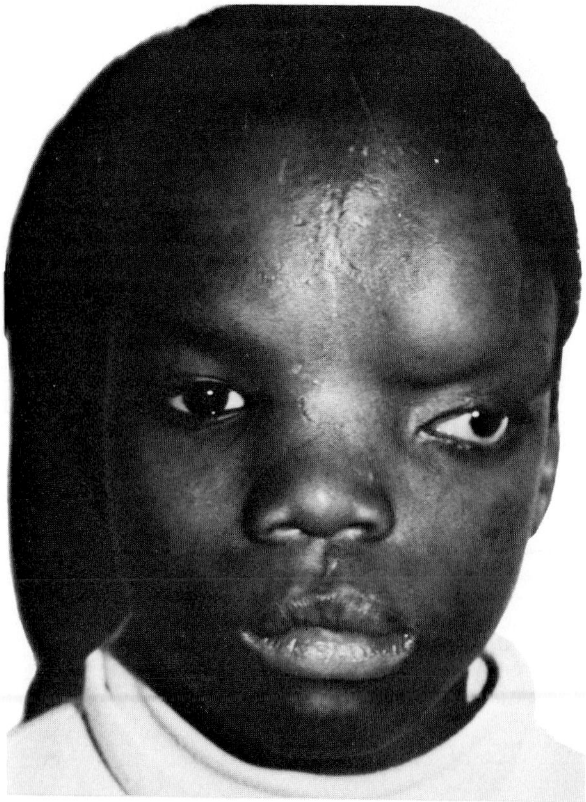

Figure 6. Case No. 3, asymmetric hypertelorism and facial cleft with an associated frontal encephalocoele.

A. Photograph of patient.

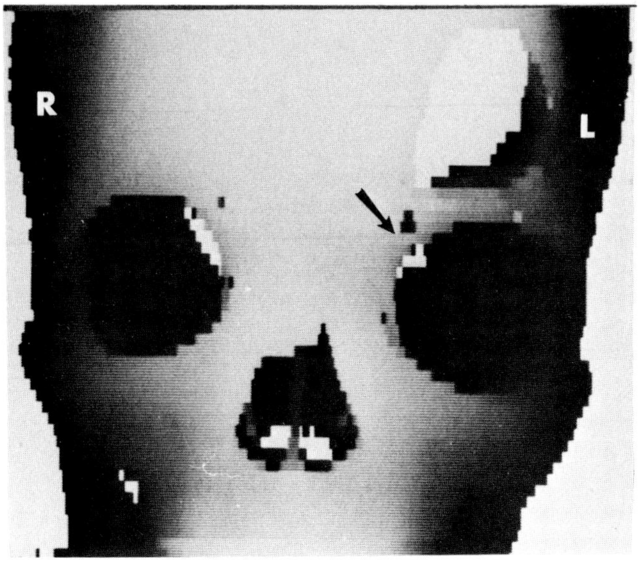

Figure 6B. Preoperative bone surface reconstruction. The left orbit is displaced infero-laterally (arrow)

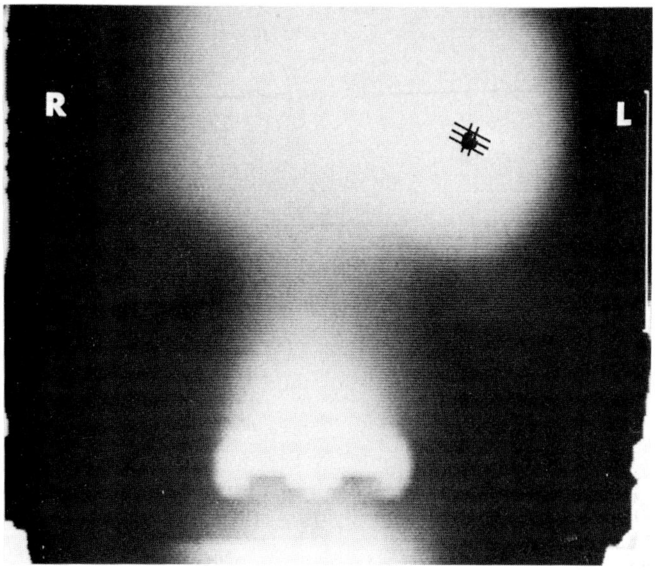

Figure 6C. Preoperative soft tissue surface reconstruction. The left forehead bulge is due to a frontal encephalocoele (star).

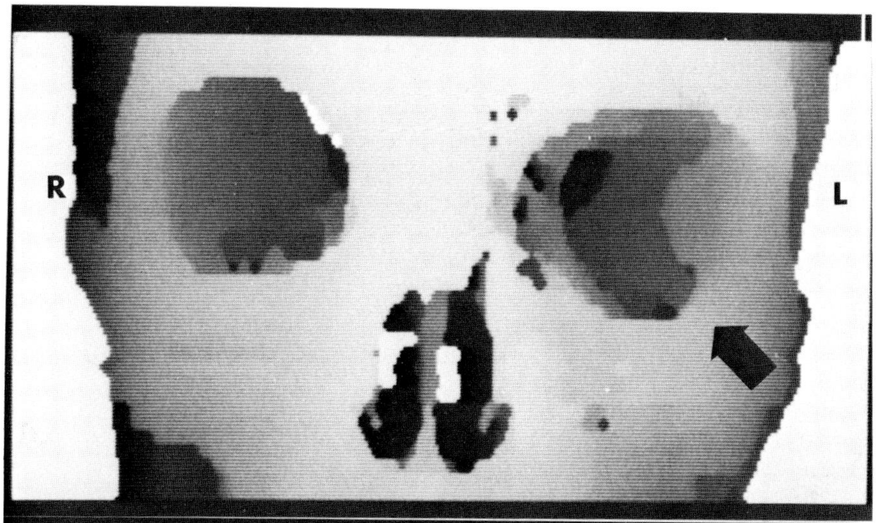

Figure 6D. Postoperative bone tissue surface reconstruction.

The left orbit has been relocated and grafted (arrow).

Figure 6E. Postoperative soft tissue surface reconstruction.

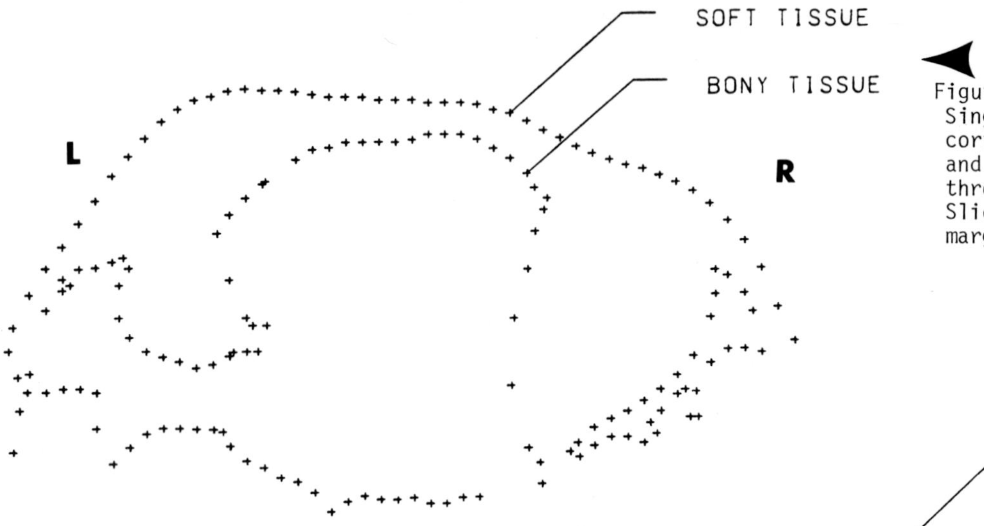

Figure 7A.
Single CT slice, points corresponding to soft tissue and bone contours obtained by threshold edge detector. Slice was taken at superior margin of bony orbits.

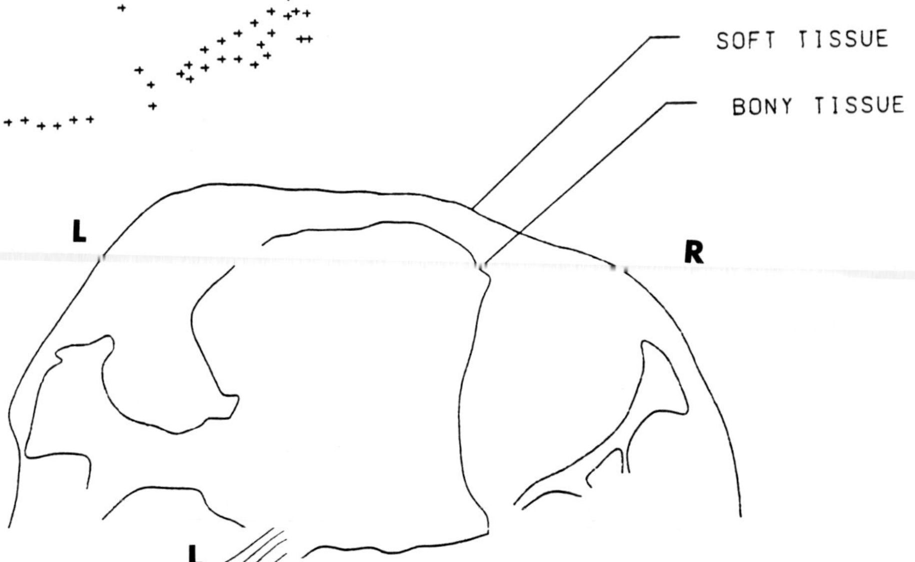

Figure 7B.
Same as Fig. 7A, except the contours have been curve fit using cubic splines.

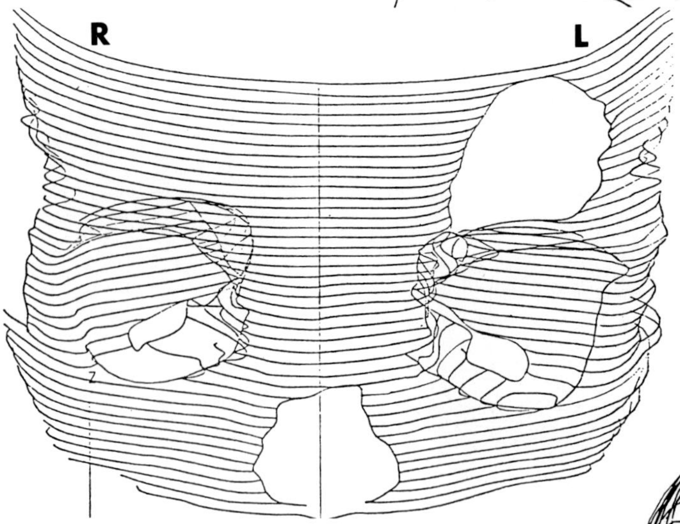

Figure 7C.
Frontal view of bony contours obtained from a sequence of 40 high resolution CT scans.

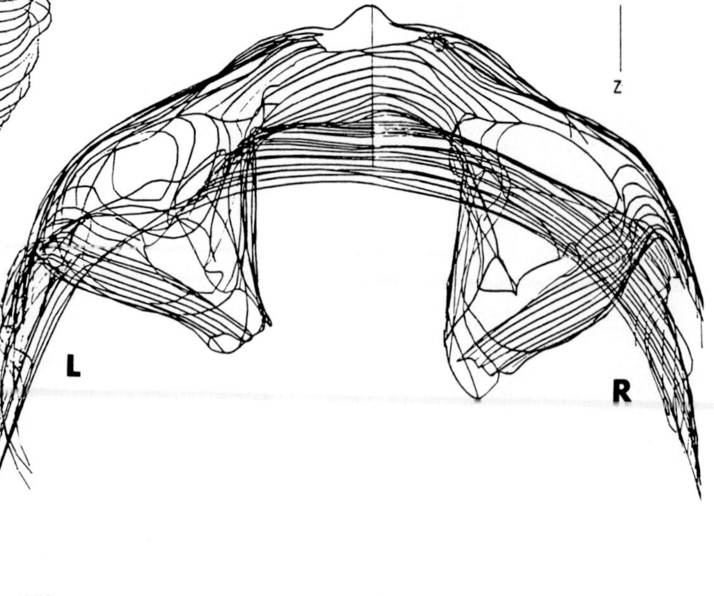

Figure 7D.
Top or plan view of bony contours obtained from the same 40 scans show the abnormal left and normal right orbits.

Figure 7. Case No. 3, CADD Analysis.

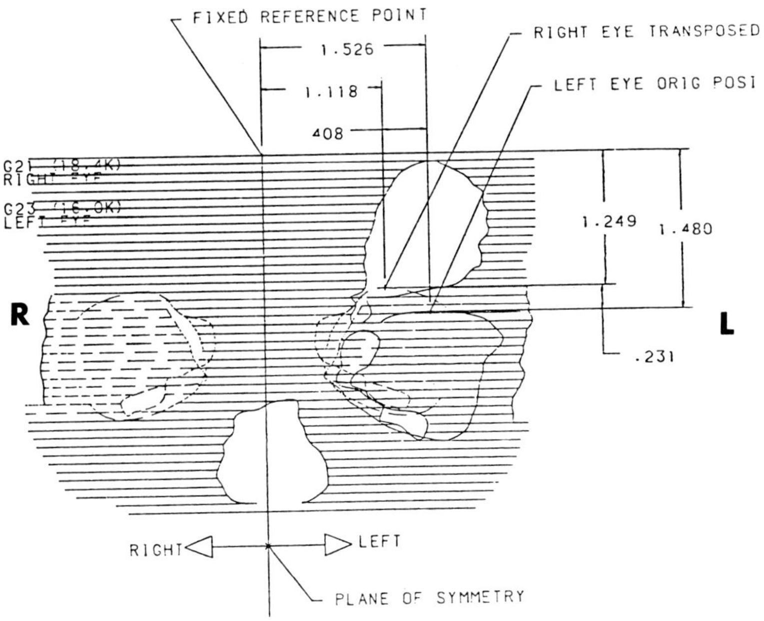

Figure 7F.
Frontal view with measurements of orbital displacement in the X-Z plane.

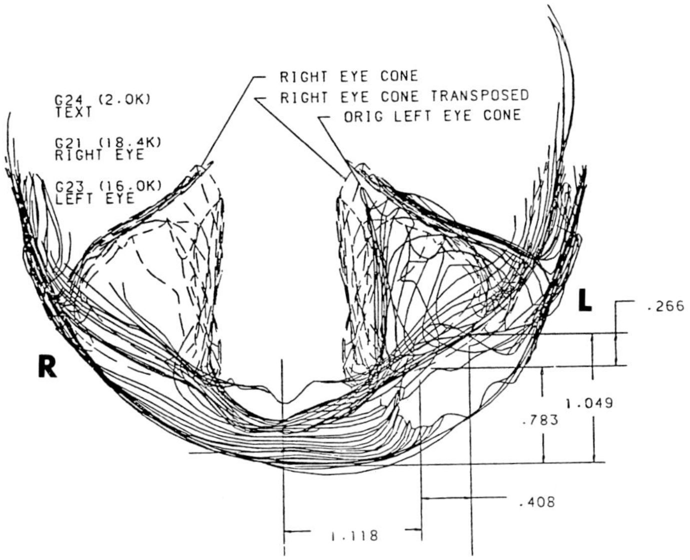

Figure 7G.
Plan view with measurements of orbital displacement in the X-Y plane.

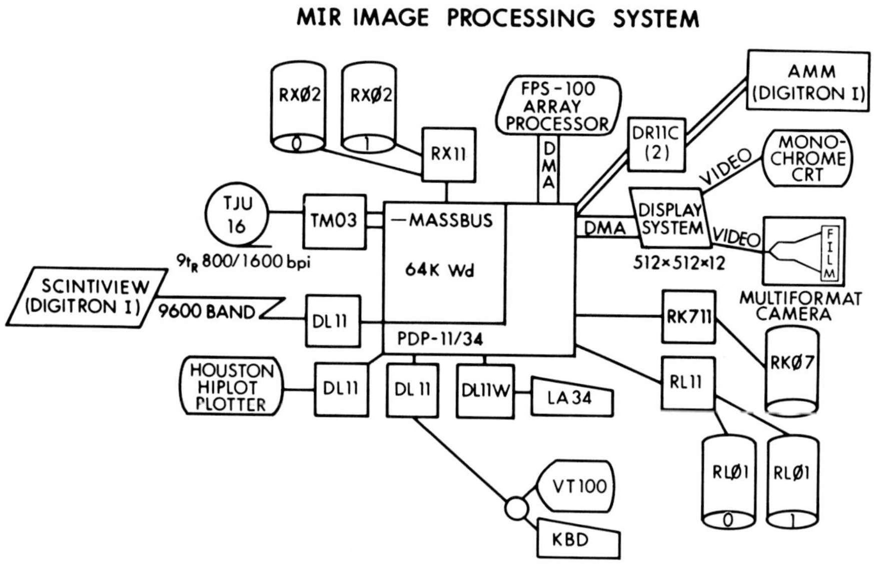

Figure 8.
Hardware configuration block diagram for the digital image processing system used to generate surface images.

PANEL

COMPUTER GRAPHICS AND VISUAL DESIGNERS

CHAIR: Aaron Marcus, Aaron Marcus and Associates
PANELISTS: Del Coates, design consultant
William Mitchell, CAD Design Group

CHAIRMAN'S INTRODUCTION

Within the last three years, the computer graphics field has become increasingly attentive to design issues in the research, development, and production of terminals, hard copy devices, workstations, and networks. Characteristic of these changes have been the enhancement of symbol processing and visual database management functions, increased visual resolution and speed of display, and the elaboration of "friendly" iconic interfaces. Many of these changes have resulted from interactions with graphic designers and industrial designers who have influenced strategic planning and practical marketing decisions among business graphics, CAD/CAM, games, video production systems, etc. Recently the design professions themselves have come to the attention of the computer graphics industry as a potential market for graphics editing work stations. A number of new start-up companies are currently at work on designer-oriented work stations, and some larger manufacturers have focused efforts in this direction.

Changes in computer graphics technology have evoked changes in attitude among the visual design professionals such as graphic designers, industrial designers, and architectural designers. The professional design community is rapidly becoming aware of what computer graphics can and can not accomplish. These professionals and their managers are investigating the retooling of their work environments to accommodate the potential of electronic telecommunication and sophisticated mass communication/production systems. Because of these changes it is appropriate that Siggraph offer design professionals an opportunity to clarify their needs and desires. Designers have continuously grumbled about the lack of specific functions suited to their natural working methods and the poor quality of the graphic display media in terms of typography, color, line weight, solid modeling, symbol libraries, etc.

In this panel session we shall explore the nature of the designer's cognitive approach, task structure, and the capabilities for computer graphics to enhance the working environment. Representatives from graphic design, industrial design, and architectural design will present relevant examples of computer graphics output, discuss the shortcomings of current systems, and suggest what computer graphics should be developing for the design professional in the next five years of computer graphics. The lessons to be learned can be generalized to all users of computer graphics systems in the sense that computer graphics permits and encourages every user to become a visual designer.

Aaron Marcus is the head of Aaron Marcus and Associates, a graphic design research and development firm specializing in computer graphics. They develop specifications for unique or generic displays of text documents, forms, charts, maps, and diagrams in a wide range of applications, from educational games to financial graphics. They also design the screens and paper documentation of the human-computer interface for interactive systems in the CAD/CAM, automated office, and personal computer fields. They are currently engaged in a two-year research effort to determine the ideal graphic design format for computer programs in a project sponsored by the US Department of Defense. Although educated as a graphic designer at Yale University, Mr. Marcus learned computer graphics programming on his own and was a consultant in computer graphics to Bell Telephone Labs in the early 1970's while he taught at Princeton University. He was recently a staff scientist in the Computer Science and Mathematics Department of Lawrence Berkeley Laboratory. He is a member of the American Institute of Graphic Arts, is on the advisory board of the Design Arts Program of the National Endowment for the Arts, and is the co-author of The Computer Image, published by Addison-Wesley.

Del Coates has BS and MA degrees in industrial design from the University of Michigan, where he also studied computer graphics. He was an industrial designer with General Electric, Herman Miller Research Corp. and Ford Motor Company. For 16 years he was professor and chairman, Department of Industrial Design, at the Center for Creative Studies, College of Art and Design in Detroit. As a consultant he has done product planning, design, and human factors for automotive and product manufacturers, and advised industrial design offices in matter of computer-aided design (CAD). He writes a regular column on CAD for Industrial Design magazine and has conducted CAD workshops for the Industrial Designers Society of America. He does research on quantification of aesthetic design variables.

William J. Mitchell is Professor of Architecture and head of the Architecture/Urban Design Program at the Graduate School of Architecture and Urban Planning, UCLA. He has also taught at Berkeley, Carnegie Mellon, Sydney, Yale and Cambridge. His research focuses on the logic of design processes, and computer methods in architecture. He is the author of numerous technical papers in these areas, and of the text Computer-aided Architectural Design. He is also principal of the Computer-Aided Design Group, a Santa Monica, California software and development firm.

PANELISTS' ABSTRACTS:

Aaron Marcus, Aaron Marcus and Associates

Graphic designers use typography, symbolism, color, spatial organization, and temporal sequencing to communicate facts, concepts, and emotions through texts, forms, charts, maps, diagrams and illustrations in a wide and every changing array of mass communication media. They develop ideas through sketching, critique and refine their graphics visually, present visual prototypes to clients, and oversee the final production of visual communication. Computer graphics systems must emulate and enhance the traditional means for accomplishing these tasks. Currently computer graphics systems specialize in elaborate image development for slide, film and video production, a limited set of chart-making operations, or else sophisticated typesetting for printed documents. Few systems enjoy extensive applications development, database management or networking capabilities. Among other features that general purpose graphic design workstations must account for are multi-media orientation that combines illustration, typesetting, and database management capabilities. Non-verbal visually oriented interfaces requiring a minimum of keyboard activity also seem desirable. Finally, elaborate online help and symbol libraries together with network access to visual mail would seem to be useful. In combining and focusing specialized features of current and state-of-the-art computer graphics systems, effective work stations for graphic designers can emerge.

Marcus, Aaron, "Color: A Tool for Communication", in Greenberg, Donald, Aaron Marcus et al, The Computer Image, Addison-Wesley, Reading, 1982

Marcus, Aaron and Ronald Baecker, "On the Graphic Design of Program Text", Proc. Graphics Interface '82, 1982 pp. 303-311

Marcus, Aaron, "Designing the Face of an Interface", Proc. Second National Computer Graphics Assoc. Conference 1981, pp. 207-219, and Tech. Memo. No. LBL-12733, Lawrence Berkeley Laboratory, Berkeley, 1981.

Marcus, Aaron, "Graphic Design and Computer Design: Know Business is Show Business, Centerline, Center for Design, San Francisco, July 1981, pp. 6-7, and Industrial Design, January-February 1982.

Marcus, Aaron, "Computer-Assisted Chart Making from the Graphic Designer's Perspective", Lawrence Berkeley Laboratory, Tech. Report LBL-10239 April 1980.

Marcus, Aaron, "A Prototypical Computerized Page Design System" Visible Language, Vol.5, No. 3, summer 1971, pp. 196-220.

Marcus, Aaron, The Designer, the Computer and Two-Way Communication, Print Magazine, Vol.25 No.4, July/August 1971, pp.34-39.

Del Coates, Del Coates Associates

Like mechanical engineers, industrial designers define and develop product concepts. They are concerned with mechanical feasibility, performance, efficiency, reliability, manufacturability, and cost. Like human factors engineers, they are concerned with aesthetic determinants of consumer preference. Using the skills of visual artists, they visualize imaginary concepts and communicate them to others as realistically as possible. The ideal computer system for industrial designers would incorporate the most advanced capabilities of both 3-dimensional CAD and animation systems: solid-modeling for complete physical and functional descriptions; and ability to depict all material and surface qualities with photographic fidelity. It would stress easy interactive capabilities like quick response to user input, comprehensive communication and "transparent" analog input and output devices. It would have a high-resolution color display capable of depicting both diffuse and specular reflection. Beyond that, progress will parallel development of artificial intelligence and "expert systems" that will lead eventually to automatic analysis and adjustment of aesthetic variables to optimize the visual appeal of products.

Coates, Del. "The Computer-Aided Designer", in each issue of Industrial Design since November/December 1981

Coates, Del. "Industrial Design and the CAD/CAM Revolution" in The 1981 IDSA Papers, published by the Industrial Designers Society of America, 1981, pp. 17-20.

Coates, Del. "Understanding aesthetics: from old shoes to a teacup" Industrial Design, September/October 1979, pp 32-35.

Foley, J.D., & A. van Dam, Fundamentals of Interactive Computer Graphics, Addison-Wesley, Reading, MA, 1982.

Newman, William M. & Sproull, Robert F. "Principles of Interactive Computer Graphics", 2nd Ed., McGraw-Hill, New York, 1979

Whitney, John. Digital Harmony, Byte Books/McGraw-Hill, Peterborough, N.H. 1980.

William J. Mitchell, Computer-Aided Design Group

The design of a building is normally a top down process, taking place over an extended period: weeks, months, or even years. It begins with the rapid exploration of schematic design concepts, through the medium of quick, rough sketches, at a high level of abstraction, and proceeds by a process of recursive elaboration and refinement through successively more precise and detailed representations of the proposed building to terminate with the production of very extensive and detailed working drawings and specifications. During this process, frequent use is made of catalogue and reference databases of various kinds: previous projects, standard details, building product catalogues, master specifications, etc. In addition to the architect, various specialized consultants (structural engineers, mechanical engineers, interior specialists, etc.), work on the design as it evolves, and must have access to current and accurate descriptions of it.

An effective computer-aided architectural design system must integrate the flow of graphic data, both vertically through stages of a project, and horizontally across different design disciplines. This requires sophisticated database capabilities and great flexibility in the graphics interface. Exploration of schematic design alternatives is very different from the drafting of final working drawings, and a mechanical engineer's view of a building is very different from that of an architect. The design process must be supported by extensive and conveniently accessible libraries of architectural symbols, details, etc. This has implications for the design of menus and commands. In order to achieve useful productivity, high level design operations, incorporating knowledge of architectural techniques and conventions must be available; low level general drafting operations will not suffice. Display technology and interfaces must be capable of dealing with drawings that are both very large and very dense in detail. Integration of non-graphic functions with the graphics system must be supported to the maximum feasible extent. All this must be accomplished at relatively low cost, since most architectural firms are small and do not have a high and steady workflow.

Mitchell, William J, Computer Aided Architectural Design, Van Nostrand Reinhold, New York 1977

Eastman, Charles, Ed., Spatial Synthesis in Computer Aided Design, Applied Science London, 1975

John F. Gero, Ed., Computer Applications in Architecture, Applied Science, London 1977.

LOCALIZED SET OPERATIONS FOR SOLID MODELING

Martti Mäntylä
Markku Tamminen
Helsinki University of Technology
Laboratory of Information Processing Science
02150, Espoo 15, Finland

ABSTRACT

Set operation algorithms form an important component of solid modeling systems. Their efficiency can be enhanced by localizing the search for geometric intersections to the region of overlap using a spatial directory. We present an algorithm that employs a three-dimensional extendible cell (EXCELL) directory to the set operation problem, and demonstrate by practical experiments the efficiency and the local nature of the algorithm.

CR Categories and Subject Descriptors: H.2.2 Database Management : Access methods; I.3.5 Computer Graphics : Geometric algorithms, languages, and systems

General Terms: algorithms, data structures, performance

Additional Key Words and Phrases: set operations, geometric directories, spatial search

1. Introduction

A solid modeler is the part of a computer-aided design system responsible for creating, manipulating, storing, and transmitting spatially complete data on the geometric form of three-dimensional solid objects (Requicha 1980, Requicha and Voelcker 1982). So called **set operations** form an especially important class of manipulations. With them, the user (a human being or an algorithm) may easily add, subtract, or intersect solids with each other to generate new models of unlimited complexity.

It is customary to divide solid modelers into two families with regard to the role of set operations. So-called **Constructive Solid Geometry** modelers (Voelcker and Requicha 1977) view set operations as the primary means of definition. They represent a solid by a tree of set operations and rigid motions. In contrast, **Boundary Representation** modelers (Braid 1979, Eastman and Weiler 1979) define a solid by a collection of faces, edges and vertices and their neighborhood relationships. A third, radically different approach is the octree solid modeling scheme (Meagher 1982), which records the regions of space occupied by a solid at a fixed maximal resolution.

A set operation algorithm depends completely on the underlying solid representation. CSG modelers calculate set operations by so-called Boundary Evaluation (Requicha and Voelcker 1977), ordinarily based on a "divide-and-conquer" algorithm reflecting the structure of the CSG tree. Boundary modelers operate directly on faces, edges, and vertices.

The basic computational task of a set operation algorithm is to find the intersection of the boundaries of two solids. Since any algorithm must with certainty detect each intersection between faces, and since for objects of sizes n and m there may be O(nm) intersections, the worst-case computational complexity must be at least O(nm).

In practical cases the effect of a set operation is often "small" compared to the total amount of data (Tilove 1981). In Figure 1-1 nm = 2,5000,000, but only 40 true intersections between faces exist.

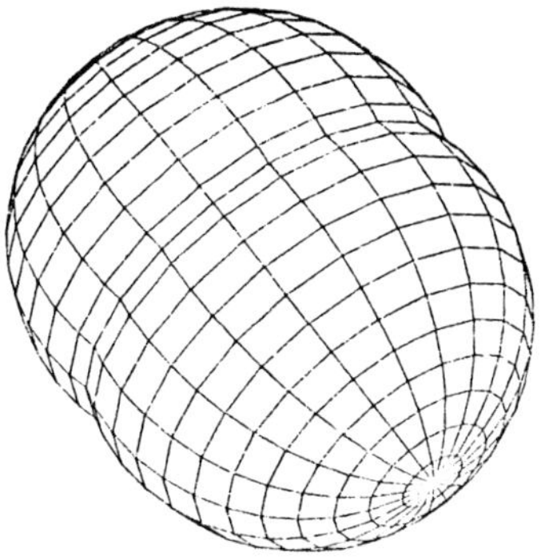

Figure 1-1
Test Case A(1600) of Section 6

The expected, "practical" complexity of a good set operation algorithm should be much smaller than O(nm). Denote the number of pairwise intersections between faces by s. Assuming that we have to generate the two solid data structures, the lower limit for the complexity of set operations can be rewritten as O(n + m + s) because each intersection gives raise to a new edge that must be formed. While s may be O(nm), in practical situations it is typically O(m), m being the size of the "smaller" argument. Thus the aim of algorithm design would be to achieve a complexity of just O(n + m).

Going a step further, set operations are often used repetitively on solid models generated by previous operations. An example is the "drilling" of a sequence of small holes into a large model (Figure 5–2). In this dynamic situation, a complexity of O(m + s), where m and s denote the size of the small argument and the number of intersections, respectively, should be achievable for each operation. If s = O(m), this amounts to mere O(m).

In this paper, we aim to derive set operation algorithms achieving the above limits. This is possible only if we can **localize** the computations to the region where intersections may occur, thus avoiding the explicit complete geometric search. Our solution to this is a separate **geometric directory** (in the data base terminology) to the relevant parts of the underlying data structures. The directory is organized by a variant of the EXCELL principle (Tamminen and Sulonen 1982) making it very adaptable while allowing especially efficient geometric search by location.

The practical framework of our research is the Geometric Workbench (Mäntylä and Sulonen 1982), an experimental solid modeler constructed at the Helsinki University of Technology. GWB is based on a pervasive use of Euler operators (Baumgart 1974, Eastman and Weiler 1979, Braid 1979) for all manipulations of the underlying data structures. This is also a characteristic of our set operation algorithm. However, the EXCELL directory is in no way limited to this approach.

To make this exposition self contained we first give a "bird's–eye–view" of set operation algorithms in Section 2. Section 3 describes the geometric directory, and Section 4 applies it to the set operation problem. We verify the performance claims by experimental results in Section 5. By series of synthetic test cases we show that the processing is truly local in the sense defined above; the computational cost of a series of "small" set operations depends only on the amount of "geometric interaction" between the solids. Section 6 discusses briefly related approaches.

2. Set Operation Algorithms

Set operation algorithms are complicated programs, necessitating a clear design rationale. This section provides an overview of the algorithm used as the basis of our work.

The complexity of the problem is mainly a result of the combinatorial richness of situations arising in three dimensions. To present the algorithms in a concise manner, we here rule out the special cases where the two solids just "touch" each other along co–planar faces. With this restriction, if two solids intersect at all, they do so along one or more closed (non–planar) **intersection polygons.**

For instance, the intersection polygon of two intersecting blocks is depicted in Figure 2–1. Any set operation can be performed by creating the intersection polygons and "summing" the relevant parts of boundaries along them.

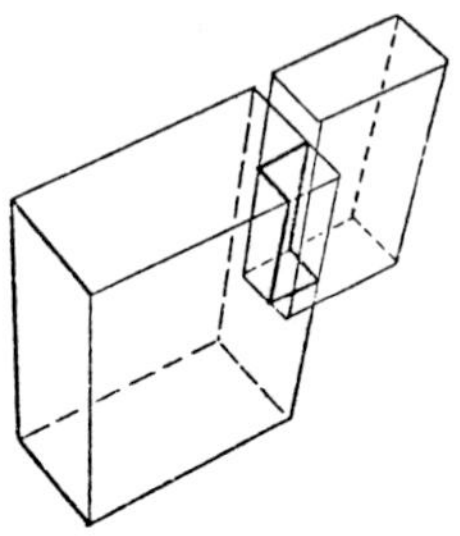

Figure 2–1
Intersection Polygon of Two Blocks

Generally set operation algorithms first locate the individual intersections between faces of the two argument solids. Next, intersection polygons are formed by inserting new edges and vertices into both solids. Finally, resulting faces are classified according to whether they must be included into the final result. The result is then calculated by removing irrelevant parts.

An unusual feature of our algorithm is the separation of the steps of intersection location and intersection polygon formation. As the algorithm of Steinberg (1982) also ours works by comparing edges of one solid against faces of the other. To locate all intersections, this process is performed twice, once for edges of solid A and faces of solid B, and once vice versa. After all intersections of an edge are found, they are analyzed treating separately the various special cases (such as edge–edge intersections) and the underlying data structure is updated by Euler operators. In a second step, the individual intersections are joined (using Euler operators) to construct the intersection polygons. See (Mäntylä and Sulonen 1982) for a more detailed description of similar operations.

After constructing the intersection polygon the boundaries of the solids can immediately be classified with respect to each other. The faces of solid A, for instance, are divided into sets AinB, AoutB of faces inside or outside the other solid, B. The concept of classification and the notation for its results stems from Tilove (1980). An overview of the set operation algorithm is given by Figure 2–2.

The main problems in any complex geometric algorithm are the integrity of data structures, numerical robustness, and computational efficiency. We approach the problem of integrity by performing all modifications by Euler operators. Thus the data structures are always topologically consistent. Problems of numerical robustness are lessened by the separation of the detection of intersections from their analysis.

```
procedure set_op(A, B:solid, op:opcode)
begin
     for each edge E of A do
     begin
          /* locate intersections */
          for each face F of B do
               if E and F intersect then
                    store_intersection;

          /* analyze intersections and store */
          /* them in both solids */
          sort intersections along E;
          analyze_and_process_intersections();
     end;

     /* repeat for edges of B and faces of A */
     for each edge E of B do
     begin
          for each face F of A do
               if E and F intersect then
                    store_intersection;
          sort intersections along E;
          analyze_and_process_intersections();
     end;

     /* join intersections in both solids */
     connect();

     /* divide solids along intersection polygons */
     divide(A, AinB, AoutB);
     divide(B, BinA, BoutA);

     /* form result */
     case op of
     "union":  result = glue(AoutB, BoutA);
     "minus":  result = glue(AoutB, BinA);
     "inter":  result = glue(AinB, BinA);
     endcase
end;
```

Figure 2–2
The Basic Set Operation Algorithm

Computational efficiency remains a problem, however. In a naive implementation for tasks of moderate size, over 90 percent of time is typically spent in locating intersecting faces and edges. This can be viewed as a "geometric query" against the two data structures: Given an edge E, list all faces that (may) intersect it. The straightforward implementation ("compare E against all faces") leads to a quadratic asymptotic growth rate. For the rest of this paper we concentrate on a specific approach to enhancing the efficiency of geometric search.

3. The EXCELL Geometric Directory

3.1. Geometric Queries and Directories

The basic task of Algorithm 2–2 typifies the more general problem of providing access by location in geometric algorithms. Other examples are listed below.

(1) **Box Query:** which geometric entities intersect a parallelepiped with faces parallel to the coordinate axes ("box")?

(2) **Edge Query:** which entities intersect a given edge?

(3) **Neighbor Query:** which entities are close to a given point?

We call these and similar tasks **geometric queries.** A **geometric directory** is a data structure that enhances the efficiency of geometric queries. These terms are chosen in analogy to the corresponding data base management concepts.

Ordinary access methods (B–trees, hashing, and so forth) are not directly applicable to geometric directories, because coordinate values may seldom be utilized as exact keys in access by location. While access to points is similar to range queries in a general data base (Bentley and Friedman 1979), entities with geometric extent pose more difficult problems.

The simplest useful geometric directory for set operations is a 2–level hierarchy consisting of a box enclosing each solid and each face. This is the **reference method** in our comparisons. More complicated **hierarchic box directories** will be discussed in Section 6.

3.2. EXCELL: an Extendible Cell Structure

Grid directories form a specific family of geometric directories. A grid directory consists of a collection of nonoverlapping cells that can be efficiently accessed. Each cell points to all geometric entities (usually faces) that potentially intersect it.

Regular grids form the simplest case of grid directories. If the individual cells may vary in size according to the amount of data we obtain an **extendible cell structure.** Such a structure is analogous to the spatial partitions used in the Warnock hidden surface method (Sutherland et al. 1974) and the octree and quadtree approaches (Meagher 1982).

The geometric directory used in our work, **EXCELL** (Tamminen and Sulonen 1982), is an extendible cell structure. It is an application of order preserving extendible hashing (Fagin et al. 1979) to multidimensional problems.

An EXCELL structure consists of two parts: a data part and a directory. The cells of the data part are formed by recursively halving the space of interest until some criterion of well–formedness (usually bucket size) is met. The directory is an array providing maximally efficient access by location to data cells. Figure 3–1 shows EXCELL applied to point files. Here the halving is controlled by the bucket size b, i.e. the maximal number of points in a data cell.

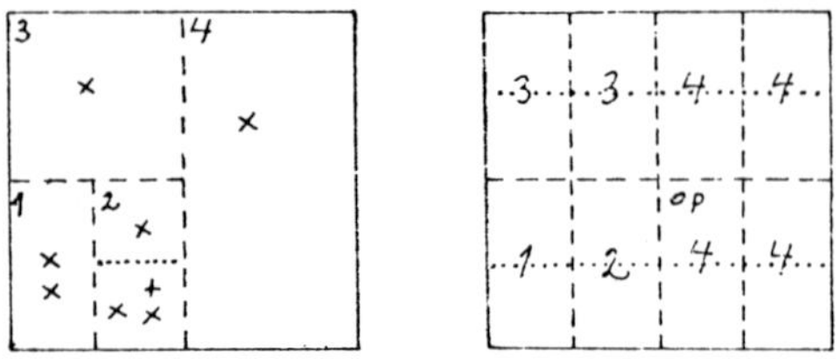

data part
x: points
o: cursor
------: cell borders

directory

Figure 3–1. An example of point–EXCELL concepts. The two–dimensional space of interest is divided into four data cells (rectangles), none of which contains more than three (bucket size) points. The directory is an array of elements each corresponding to a rectangle of minimal size and indicating the data cell containing it. The cell of a cursor point p is retrieved by first calculating the directory array index. The insertion of the new point (+) would here require the cell halving and directory doubling operation as indicated by short dashes.

3.3. EXCELL for Three–Dimensional Boxes

When applied to structured geometric objects, EXCELL data cells contain a reference to all entities (potentially) intersecting it. Now the halving process is controlled by the maximal number of references allowed per cell.

The result of applying the above approach in two dimensions is depicted by Figure 3–2. This structure may be used for any kinds of geometric entities by using their enclosing boxes to construct it.

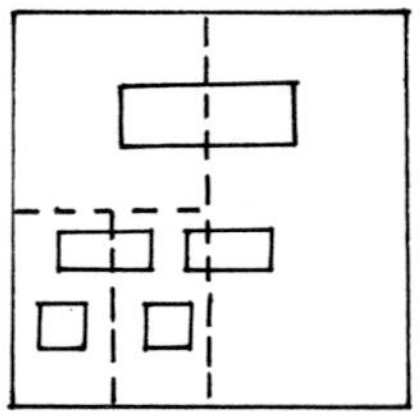

Figure 3–2
Two–Dimensional Box–Excell, Data Part, b = 3

A naive generalization of the above to three dimensions suffers from not being able to handle a situation where more than b boxes intersect each other. Also the directory becomes prohibitively large when the spatial density of data is very variable.

As demonstrated in (Tamminen 1982) for point files, these problems can be overcome by including hierarchic directories and overflow into the basic method. We call the result **hierarchic box–EXCELL with overflow,** or box–EXCELL for short. As a concept it is rather similar to the digital B–tree (Lomet 1981). A two–level hierarchy seems sufficient and even optimal in external storage.

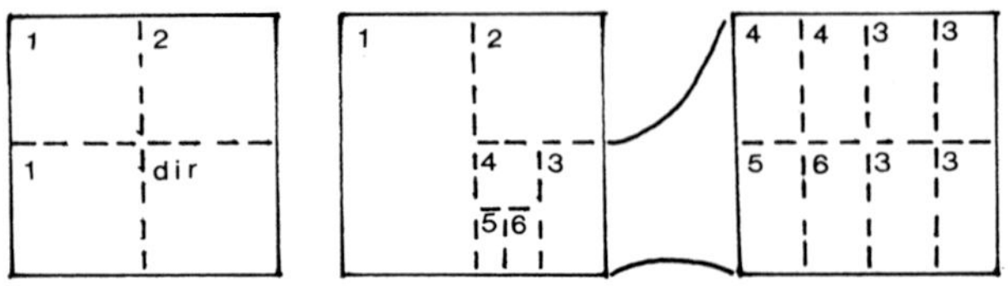

1st level directory

data part

2nd level directory

Figure 3–3
Hierarchic EXCELL with D = 4

In box–EXCELL the directory size may not exceed some threshold D. Should this happen, we (instead of the ordinary halving) form a second level directory to correspond to this data cell. The growth of second level directories is controlled by allowing overflow in certain cases. The parameter controlling overflow is R, the maximal allowed ratio of the number of elements in the directory to the number of its data cells. Should a data cell division cause this ratio to exceed R, we let the cell overflow, i.e. intersect more than b boxes.

Figure 3–4 depicts a solid we have used in tests (a sphere approximated with 400 faces) together with a hidden surface view of a corresponding EXCELL structure with parameters b = 22 and R = 5.

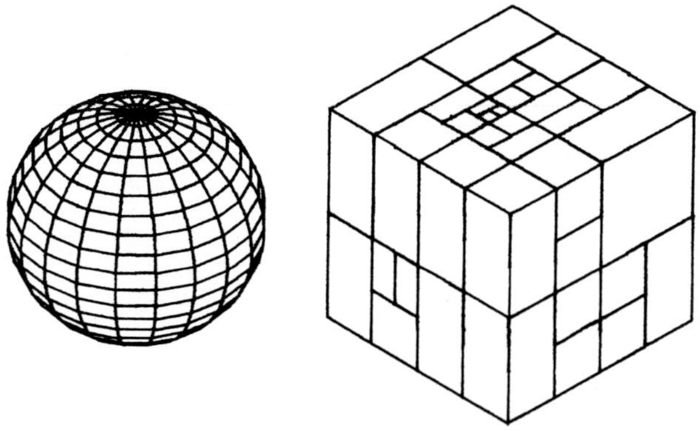

Figure 3–4
Three–Dimensional Box–EXCELL for Faces of a Solid

Figure 3–5 gives an EXCELL algorithm for the edge query defined in section 3.1. We have used a similar algorithm for a point–in–volume "ray"–test.

Box insertion is effected by first performing a box query for all cells intersecting the new box. It is then inserted into each of these cells. If a cell is full it must first be divided and then a similar insertion applied recursively (Figure 3–6). Box deletion is implemented similarly but without recursion.

```
var sb : set of box;

procedure open_equery(var E : edge)
begin
/* open query for edge E */
sb = empty set;
while E not null do
        begin c = get_cell(start_point_of(E));
              /* cell containing start of E */
              for each box b in c do
                      sb = sb + b; /* set addition */
              E = portion of E outside of c
        end
end;

function next_query() : box
begin
/* get next box potentially satisfying query */
if sb = empty set then next_query = NIL
else begin choose a box b of sb;
           sb = sb - b;
           next_query = b
     end
end;
```

Figure 3–5
Edge Query Algorithm

```
procedure insert_gdir(box: B,B1)
begin
/* B: box to be inserted; B1: for recursion */
/* the original call is: insert_gdir(B,B); */
    sc = set of all cells intersected by B1;
    for each cell c of sc do
        if not full(c) then insert_into_cell(c,B);
        else begin divide_cell(c);
                   insert_gdir(B,intersection_of(B,c))
             end
end;
```

Figure 3–6
Insertion of a Box into EXCELL

4. Set Operations With EXCELL

Two enhanced versions of the Algorithm 2–2 were implemented using box–EXCELL. The first one has directories for both argument solids. Each directory is created by inserting the boxes of all the faces intersecting the global box of the other solid.

Exhaustive search is now replaced by an edge query that gives the set of boxes intersecting a given edge. The modularity of the basic algorithm has the nice consequence that no other changes need to be made. The relevant new steps are given in Figure 4–1.

In Algorithm 4–1 two directories are generated in each set operation. If a model is repeatedly used as an argument it would be more efficient to construct the directory once, updating it as needed. This is implemented in our "toolbench" algorithm. In it a distinct initialization step creates a directory for a solid, the "workpiece". After this, a sequence of other solids, "tools", can be operated against it. The toolbench algorithm typifies the very common situation where the result of a set operation is used as input to the next one in a long chain.

```
procedure set_op_A(A, B: solid, op: opcode)
begin
     /* initialize */
     boxa = global box of A;
     boxb = global box of B;

     /* phase 1 */
     create_gdir();
     for each face F of B do
          if F intersects boxa then
               insert_gdir(box of F);
     /* geometric step */
     for each edge E of A do
     if E intersects boxb then
     begin
         /* open edge-query by E in directory of b */
          open_equery(E);
          for each box = next_query() do
          begin
               if E and face of box intersect then
                    store_intersection
          end;
          /* analyze */
          sort intersections along E;
          analyze_and_process_intersections();
     end;
     /* phase 2 as above, other steps as in Fig. 2-2 */
end;
```

Figure 4–1
Set Operation With Two Directories

The first pass of edge–face comparisons (i.e. edges of tool against faces of workpiece) is similar to that of Figure 4–1. To perform the second pass, "relevant" edges of the workpiece (i.e. those that may intersect faces of tool) are generated by a box query with the global box of the tool. The second pass (i.e. comparison between edges of workpiece and faces of tool) is then performed by comparing each relevant edge against all tool faces.

The toolbench algorithm (Figure 4–2) must update the geometric directory of the workpiece. The availability of the total fourfold classification of faces makes the update operation straightforward. For instance, in a "minus" operation workpiece faces within the tool are removed, tool faces within the workpiece are added, and workpiece faces intersected are updated.

5. Analysis and Experiences

5.1. Methods and Test Series

To analyze empirically the efficiency of the enhanced set operations, Algorithms 4–1 and 4–2 were implemented in C under UNIX on a VAX 11/750 without floating point accelerator. Their asymptotic (within computational resources) behaviour was compared to that of the reference method described in section 4. As the topological manipulations in all these algorithms were the same, we made measurements only of the geometric steps.

```
/* the global box and directory of workpiece
are created in a separate initialization step */

procedure set_op_B(Workpiece, Tool: solid, op: opcode)
begin
      Toolbox = global box of Tool;

      /* phase 1 */
      for each edge E of Tool do
      if E intersects Workbox then
      begin
            /* perform edge query as in Figure 4-1 */
            ...
      end;

      /* perform a box query */
      Rel_edges = empty set;
      open_bquery(Toolbox);
      for each box = next_query() do
            add edges of this face to Rel_edges;

      /* phase 2 */
      for each edge E of Rel_edges do
      begin
            for each face F of Tool do
                  if E and F intersect
                        store_intersection;
            ...
      end;

      /* construct intersection polygons */
      connect();

      /* divide boundaries */
      divide(Work, Work_in_Tool, Work_out_Tool);
      divide(Tool, Tool_in_Work, Tool_out_Work);

      /* update geometric directory */
      case op of
      "union":
      begin
            for each face F of Work_in_Tool do
                  remove_gdir(F);
            for each face F of Tool_out_Work do
                  insert_gdir(F);
            for each face F of Work_out_Tool
            adjacent to intersection polygons do
            begin
                  remove_gdir(box of F);
                  recalculate box of F;
                  insert_gdir(box of F);
            end
      end
      ...
      /* other cases similar */
      endcase;

      /* form results as in Figure 2-2 */
      ...
end;
```

Figure 4-2
The Toolbench Algorithm

Extrapolation from theoretical work on other variants of EXCELL (Tamminen and Sulonen 1982) makes us expect that for homogeneous geometric models of "size" n the expected cost of establishing an EXCELL structure is O(n), and that the expected cost of a geometric query is O(R), where R is the amount of data retrieved.

Here these statements must be considered only informal objectives. We have no analytical means of studying box-EXCELL or characterizing homogeneity precisely. Intuitively, we expect that as the number of parts in a model grows these parts and typical geometric queries get relatively "smaller".

As there are no well established series of test cases or synthetic models such as those utilized in (Sutherland et al. 1974) we have been obliged to construct artificial series of tasks. Despite their simplistic nature, we believe that they allow extrapolations because they correspond to what Tilove (1981) considers typical of practical applications. They also allow easier comparisons with other methods than "real" problems.

All our test objects are planar approximations of solids with curved faces: cylinders, spheres and tori. Test series A constructs the union of two spheres, approximated with n faces (Figure 1-1). Test series B consists of two non-intersecting tori, each approximated with n faces. In these series Algorithm 4-1 was used.

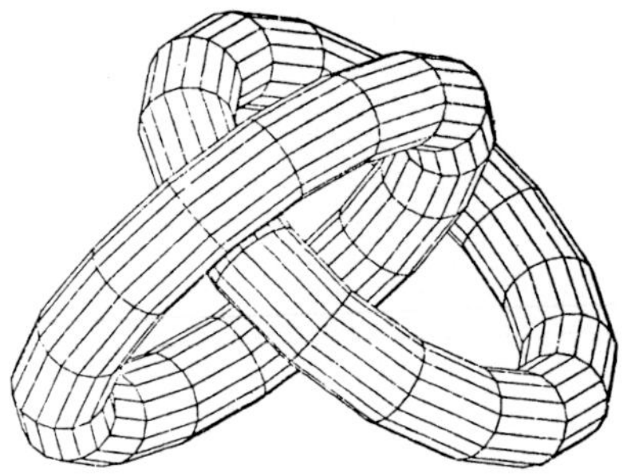

Figure 5-1
Test Case B(256)

Test series C is somewhat more complicated and utilizes the "toolbench" Algorithm 4-2. This series "drills" holes into a sphere, modeled with a varying number n of faces. The numbers of side faces (10) approximating each hole and the number of holes (20) remain constant. As n grows we make the holes proportionally smaller so as to maintain the number of faces intersected by each hole approximately constant throughout the series.

All our test runs were performed in central storage. However, box-EXCELL is implemented on top of a buffered paged memory manager Blk (Tikkanen 1981) to permit the transparent use of external storage. Cells were represented by a linked list of fixed-length pages (arrays). A list with more than one page is needed only in case of overflow. The resource utilization of Blk is included in our results. Direct implementation on top of the operating system would make the system somewhat more efficient.

Experiments with page size led to the choice of 128 bytes, sufficient for a maximum of b = 22 page references. As the size of the first directory level we have chosen D = 512 = 2**(3*3) and as the overflow parameter R = 5.

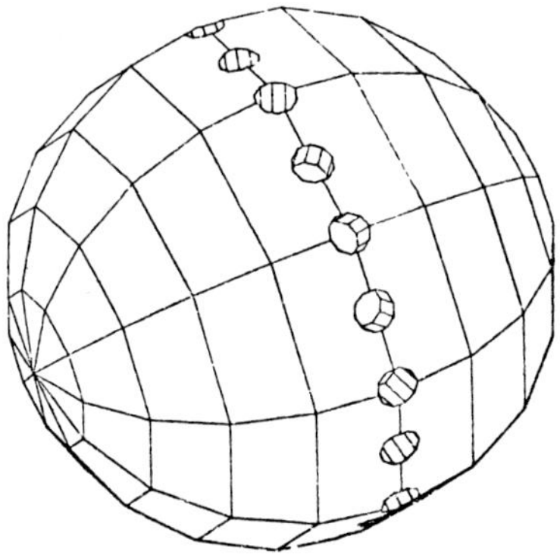

Figure 5–2
Test Case C(100)

5.2. Results

The tables and figures of this section each highlight a specific aspect of EXCELL on the basis of a single test series. However, extrapolation to the other series is possible because they all behaved similarly. Table 2 describes the hypotheses of our tests.

Series	Asymptotic behaviour of EXCELL	Reference
A	O(n)	$O(n^2)$
B	O(n)	$O(n^2)$
C	EXCELL formation O(n)	in total O(n*t)
	geometric queries O(t)	

Table 2. Expected behaviour of tests. Parameter n is the number of faces in an approximation. In series C parameter t is the number of tooling operations performed. In the actual tests t is held constant as 20.

We first demonstrate the function of box tests and a geometric directory in Table 3.

Box tests reference	Box tests EXCELL	Faces passing box tests	Face–edge intersections
	Test case A(1600)		
6,800,000	79,000	848	80

Table 3. Pruning power of box tests

In test series A and B the total number of box tests is expected to be $O(n^2)$ in the reference method and O(n) for EXCELL. Our hypotheses for series A and B were largely validated. Table 4 demonstrates this for series B. The surprisingly sublinear performance of EXCELL is explained by the tori not intersecting each other. The geometric queries are often performed against empty cells. Actually, in task B(1024) **all** queries touch only empty cells.

	Size of task 64	256	1024
EXCELL	1024	3280	4096
reference	3328	25600	344064

Table 4. Number of box tests in test series B

Run time differences between EXCELL and the reference method are smaller than in the number of box tests. However, for large tasks (as in Table 3), box tests account for most of the cost of the geometric step even for EXCELL. Figure 5–3 demonstrates the different behaviour of the run time of EXCELL (O(n)) compared to the reference method ($O(n^2)$). In all the figures x-axis is the number of faces in an approximation. Y is in CPU seconds (time) or pages of 128 bytes (storage).

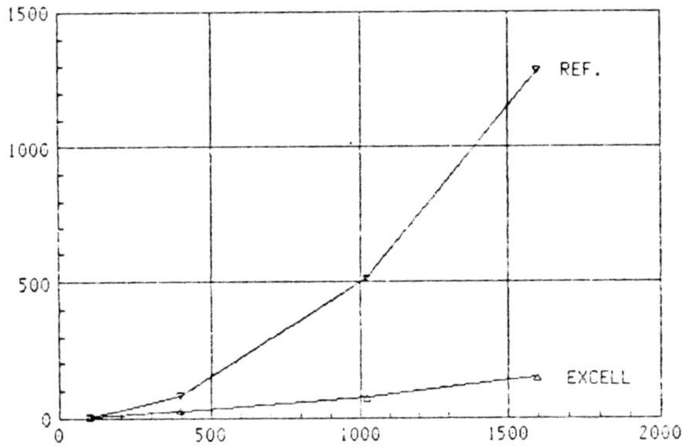

Figure 5–3
Run Time of Geometric Step for Series A

We studied also some variants of the A series. If the two spheres overlap only slightly the global box test of Algorithm 4–1 does most of the work and EXCELL hardly differs in performance from the reference method, as expected. With more overlap our results are accentuated.

In the toolbench algorithm, the cost of establishing the EXCELL structure for the workpiece must be separated from the cost proportional to the number of set operations here fixed as 20. Figure 5–4 shows these components (approximately) verifying the hypotheses of Table 2. We have found no good explanation for the cycle or jump at the end of the query cost curve. Cyclic variation is typical of EXCELL type data structures (Fagin et al. 1979). To some extent the phenomenon is also explained by that the lengths of the hole-cylinders do not vary with n. As the EXCELL structure grows each cylinder intersects more cells.

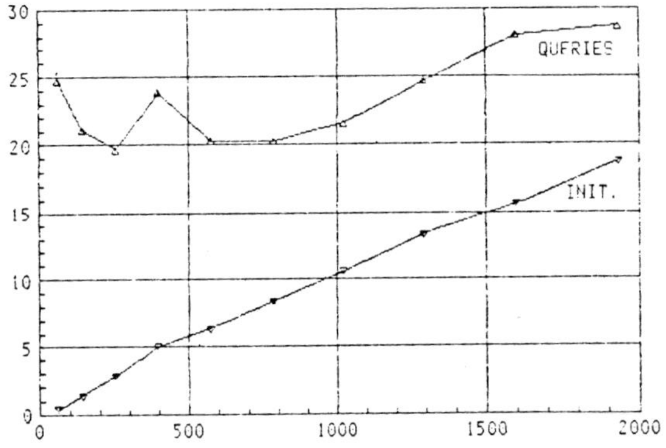

Figure 5–4
EXCELL Time Components in Series C

Figure 5–5 compares the total run times of the geometric step of EXCELL to those of the reference method for test series C.

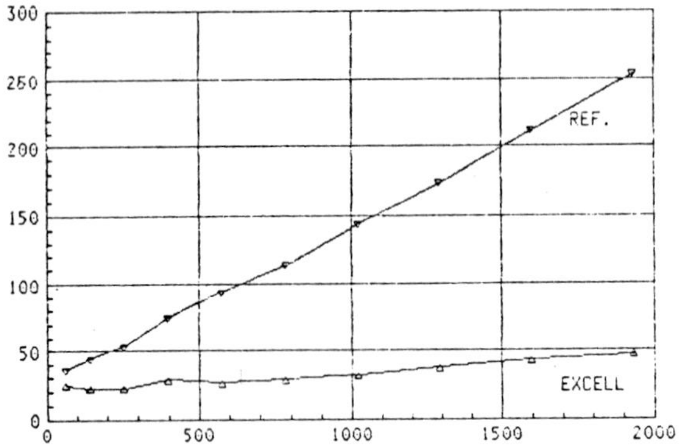

Figure 5–5
Run Times for Geometric Step of Series C

We have not optimized our data structures with respect to size or for use in central memory. However, Figure 5–6 shows that the size of an EXCELL structure responds well to the growth of a model. The figure depicts the end state of EXCELL after all the updating brought about by the set operations in series C.

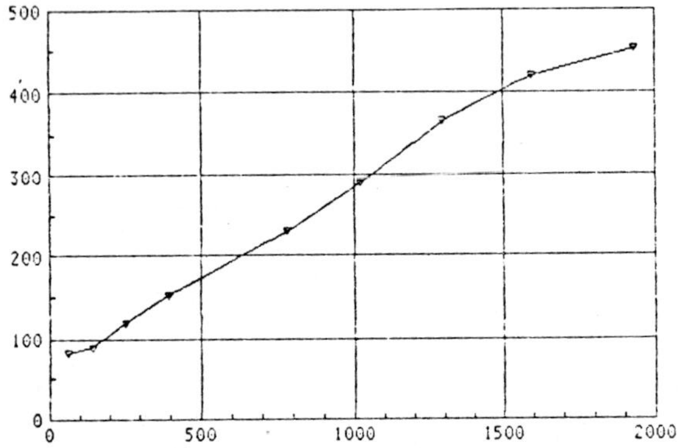

Figure 5–6
Storage Usage of EXCELL, Series C

In two dimensions certain important statistics of EXCELL depend only on the page size and not on the size of the task (Tamminen and Sulonen 1982). An interesting finding of the present work is that similar results hold also in the homogeneous three-dimensional case. The most important statistics for storage and processing performance are the average numbers of cells intersected by a box and of cells intersected by query edges. Table 5 shows the relative invariance of these measures in our tests. Specifically, the table shows that most queries touch only one cell.

	Test case		
	A(400)	A(1600)	B(1024)
cells/box	2.2	2.0	2.3
cells/query	1.4	1.3	1.2

Table 5. Main relative performance statistics.

In our experience, the size of an EXCELL structure seldom exceeds the amount of data required to define the boxes. It appears that our choice of page size (22 references) is good: for smaller pages both indicators above grow rapidly, while for larger ones they decrease quite slowly.

Both hierarchy and overflow are necessary: to store a sphere with 40x40 faces, we must be able to store the 40 boxes intersecting at the poles. Our largest directory, in task C(1936), reaches a depth of 15 corresponding to a one level directory of 32000 elements. The hierarchic version utilizes only 956 elements, however.

6. Related Work

Every serious solid modeler must use performance enhancing techniques to speed up geometric search. Hierarchic structures form an important class of these techniques. For instance, BUILD 2 (Braid 1979) uses a hierarchic "bubble environment" formed explicitly during the generation of the model. A similar method is used by Roth (1982). Both structures mirror the way solids are constructed.

In the above approaches, the directory is intricately embedded in the underlying data structure and its generation algorithms. In our opinion, it is better to have them logically separate as in data base management systems thus making programs simpler and more adaptable to new geometric search strategies. This has been one our aims.

Grid directories have been widely used in geometric problems, such as hidden line and surface removal (Griffiths 1979, Franklin 1980). TIPS (Okino et al. 1977) gives an early example of their use in solid modeling. Hierarchic grid structures have been suggested by Tilove (1981). He also has compared so called primitive disjointness tables to uniform grids. Quinlan and Woodwark (1982) marry the octree idea with the CSG approach while Kedem (1982) presents a two-dimensional "box-directory" based on quad trees. It is somewhat more complicated than box-EXCELL.

In our opinion, box-EXCELL is more robust against non-uniform spatial distribution of data than simpler fixed or variable grid methods. In three dimensions regular grids tend to grow especially large. Binary division of space is also more efficient than the 8-ary octree approach in the number of data cells formed. At the same time the directory provides for maximally efficient access. The advantages of EXCELL are most evident if secondary storage must be used.

If worst case efficiency is essential geometric intersection problems (Shamos 1978) should be approached in other ways, for instance by plane sweep algorithms (Nievergelt and Preparata 1982) that organize all processing in a spatially sorted manner. See also (Six and Wood 1982) for an O(nlogn)–space tree structure for reporting intersections of three dimensional boxes. However, it is not clear how "small" operations can be processed locally using such global methods.

7. Extensions

The EXCELL directory is especially suited for geometric data residing in external storage in that it provides very good **locality of access** and a data base type programming environment. Table 3 is indicative of the dramatic difference between EXCELL and the reference method if operated in external storage. However, some of this effect is lost if also other parts of the data structure are not suitably localized.

In a separate project we are developing GWB/DMS, a system that includes both geometric directories and tools to control locality of access.

8. Conclusions

The problem of localizing geometric computations seems most relevant now as solid modelers are striving for practical recognition. Although the general problem (geometric search) that we pose has been extensively studied under the heading of computational geometry, not many practical experiences have been reported. Many algorithms are "primarily theoretical devices (being very difficult to code)" as confessed in (Bentley and Wood 1980). In contrast the EXCELL directory presented here is very simple to implement.

As shown in more detail elsewhere (Tamminen and Sulonen 1982) the efficiency of EXCELL in localized geometric search can be characterized as similar to that of external hashing schemes for exact match search.

We have shown that EXCELL never brings about large extra costs and – for moderate to large tasks – greatly enhances the efficiency of the geometric step of a set operation. While our limited resources enabled us to demonstrate this only for a rather simple reference method, we believe that similar but more complicated alternatives would merely change the break–even point.

Our hypotheses on the asymptotic behaviour of EXCELL were roughly validated. The toolbench algorithm 4–2 demonstrates that dynamic maintenance of the directory is possible without loss of efficiency, with the consequence that good locality may be achieved in set operations. We have not been able to construct realistic tasks that would have been difficult for EXCELL, even though this is possible in theory.

Acknowledgements

This work has been supported by the Academy of Finland. We thank Matti Mitjonen for his help and the anonymous referees for their detailed comments.

References

1. Baumgart, B.G., Geometric modeling for computer vision. Report No. AIM–249, STAN–CS–74–463, Stanford AI Lab., Stanford University, Oct. 1974

2. Bentley, J.L. and Friedman, J.H., A survey of algorithms and data structures for range searching. ACM Comp. Surv. **11**(1979)4, p. 397–409.

3. Bentley, J.L. and Wood, D., An optimal worst case algorithm for reporting intersections of rectangles. IEEE Trans. Comp. **C–29**(1980)7, p. 571–577.

4. Braid, I.C., Notes on a Geometric Modeller. CAD Group Document No. 101, Computer Laboratory, University of Cambridge, Cambridge, England, June, 1979

5. Eastman, C.M. and Weiler, K., Geometric Modeling Using the Euler Operators. Proc. First Ann. Conf. on Computer Graphics in CAD/CAM Systems, MIT, Apr. 1979, p. 248–254

6. Fagin, R., Nievergelt, J., Pippenger, N. and Strong H.R., Extendible hashing, a fast access method for dynamic files. ACM TODS **4**(1979)3, p. 315–344.

7. Franklin, W.R., A linear exact hidden surface algorithm. ACM Computer Graphics **14**(1980)3, p. 117–123.

8. Griffiths, J.G., Eliminating hidden edges in line drawings. Comput. Aided Des. **11**(1979)2, p. 71–78.

9. Kedem, G., The quad–CIF tree data structure for hierarchical on–line algorithms, Proc. ACM Nineteenth Design Automation Conference, 1982, Las Vegas.

10. Lomet, D.B., Digital B–trees. Proc. 7th Int. Conf. on Very Large Data Bases, Cannes, 1981, p. 333–344.

11. Meagher, D., Geometric modeling using octree encoding. Computer Graphics and Image Processing **19**(1982), p. 129–147.

12. Mäntylä, M. and Sulonen, R., GWB – A Solid Modeler With Euler Operators. IEEE Computer Graphics & Applications **2**(1982)7, p. 17–31

13. Nievergelt, J. and Preparata, F.P., Plane–sweep algorithms for intersecting geometric figures. Comm. ACM **25**(1982)10, p. 739–747.

14. Okino, N. et al., TIPS–1 '77 Version. Hokkaido University, 1977.

15. Quinlan, K.M. and Woodwark, J.R., A spatially–segmented solids datamase – justification and design, Proc. CAD 82 Conference, Brighton, England, 1982.

16. Requicha, A.A.G., Representations of rigid solids: theory, methods and systems. ACM Comp. Surv. **12**(1980), p. 437–464.

17. Requicha, A.A.G. and Voelcker, H.B., Constructive Solid Geometry. Tech. Memo. No 25, Production Automation Project, University of Rochester, Rochester, N.Y., 1977.

18. Requicha, A.A.G. and Voelcker, H.B., Solid modeling: a historical summary and contemporary assessment. IEEE Computer Graphics and Applications **2**(1982)6, p. 9–24.

19. Roth, S.D., Ray Casting for Modeling Solids. Computer Graphics and Image Processing **18**(1982)2, p. 109–144

20. Shamos, M.I., Computational Geometry. PhD thesis, Yale University, 1978.

21. Six, H.W. and Wood, D., Counting and reporting intersections of d–ranges. IEEE trans. Comp. **C–31**(1982)3, p. 181–187.

22. Steinberg, H.A., Overlap and separation calculations using the SynthaVision three dimensional solid modeling system. Proc. Conf. on CAD/CAM Technology in Mechanical Engineering, Cambridge, Mass., March 24–26, 1982, p. 13–19.

23. Sutherland, I.E., Sproull, R.F. and Schumacher, R.A., A characterization of ten hidden–surface algorithms. ACM Comp. Surv. **6**(1974)1, p. 1–55.

24. Tamminen, M., A note on extendible hashing with overflow. Info. Proc. Lett. **15**(1982)5, p. 227–232.

25. Tamminen, M. and Sulonen, R., The EXCELL method for efficient geometric access to data. Proc. ACM Nineteenth Design Automation Conference, 1982, Las Vegas, p. 345–351.

26. Tikkanen, M., User's manual of Blk. Rep. HTKK–TKO–B36, CAD–Project, Laboratory of Information Processing Science, Helsinki University of Technology, Espoo, 1981

27. Tilove, R.B., Set membership classification: a unified approach to geometric intersection problems. IEEE Trans. Computers, **C–29**(1980)10, p. 874–883.

28. Tilove, R.B., Exploiting spatial and structural locality in geometric modeling. Tech. Memo. No 38, Production Automation Project, University of Rochester, 1981.

29. Voelcker, H.B. and Requicha, A.A.G., Geometric Modeling of Mechanical Parts and Processes. IEEE Computer **10**(1977)2, p. 48–57

DESIGN OF SOLIDS WITH FREE-FORM SURFACES

Hiroaki Chiyokura & Fumihiko Kimura

Dept. of Precision Machinery Engineering
University of Tokyo
Hongo, Bunkyo-ku, Tokyo, JAPAN

Abstract

We propose a unified method of generating a wide range of three dimensional objects from polyhedra to solids with free-form surfaces. Modeling systems for polyhedra and systems for free-form surfaces have been developed independently in the past because of the difference in their underlying theory and practices. However, this is not desirable for a designer. So in this paper, we have shown a method in which a wide range of shapes are generated in one system by using local modifications. Local modifications are procedures used to change the shape of solids locally. The construction and the modification of three dimensional shapes by these procedures are natural and easy for a designer in many cases. The implementation of these procedures in a computer is easy and their execution does not require much time.

Our method to construct a solid with free-form surfaces consists of following three phases. 1) A solid which serves as a basis of free-form shape design is generated by local modifications. Edges of this solid are straight lines but its faces are not necessarily flat planes. 2) From this model, a curve model which adequately represents the characteristics of a free-form shape is generated. 3) Surface equations interpolating over the curve model are generated.

We have made a geometric modeling system MODIF. Using this system, a complicated solid with free-form surfaces can be designed easily. MODIF can generate color shaded pictures and cutter path data for making a real object model by NC machining tool.

CR Categories and Subject Descriptors: I.3.5 [Computer Graphics]: Computational Geometry and Object Modeling - Curve, Surface, Solid and Object Modeling; J.5 [Computer Applications]: Computer Aided Engineering - Computer Aided Design (CAD)

1. Introduction

In computer aided design and manufacturing, models representing the shapes of three dimensional objects play an important role. By using geometric information in the models, a computer can do various engineering applications such as drafting and planning for NC machining. Therefore, how these objects are modeled in a computer is an important problem. However, practical engineering objects have a wide range of shapes from polyhedra to free-form shapes, that is, solids with free-form surfaces. So we have devised a unified method for modeling a wide range of shapes with more ease and developed a geometric modeling system MODIF.

Broadly speaking, there are two fields in computer aided geometric design, that is, sculptured surface modeling and solid modeling. The systems in each field have been developed independently in the past because of the difference in their underlying theory and practices [10]. Sculptured surface modeling is a study for representing curved surfaces which are involved in such shapes as the bodies of a car or an airplane. Various mathematical expressions for surface shape design have been proposed by Coons [5] , Bezier [3] and Riesenfeld [15]. They have been used in many fields of practical applications. There are already many methods for representing sculptured surfaces by these patches, and many systems have developed. But there still remain many problems for practical shape design.

In solid modeling, three dimensional objects are represented as rigid solids. The usefulness of a solid model has been discussed by many people and solid modeling systems have been implemented in several places [12,14]. In these systems, complicated shapes are usually constructed from some primitive elements such as cubes and cylinders by set operations (sometimes called Boolean operations). The set operation has many advantages for constructing shapes and detecting interference between objects. But primitive solids are normally polyhedra or simple curved surface objects such as cylinders and cones. If simple free-form shapes are added as primitive solids, it become difficult to develop the set operations for these.

In shape design process, it is desirable to represent a wide range of shapes from polyhedra to free-form shapes in one system. We therefore propose a unified method, in which a wide range of shapes can be constructed by local modification procedures. Using local modifications, geometrical and topological information representing the shape of a solid can be changed locally by producing, deleting and moving local elements of a solid such as faces, edges and vertices. Our method to construct a free-form shape model consists of the following process. First, a polyhedral model which serves as a basis of free-form shape design is generated by local modifications. Next, a curve model for a free-form shape is generated from this polyhedral model. Finally, surface equations interpolating over the curve model are generated. The construction of the shapes by using local modifications can naturally be understood for a designer in many cases. From an implementer's point of view, local modifications and our surface interpolation method are easy and their execution in a computer does not require much time. So our method is feasible for interactive shape design.

The Euler operation which is a basis of local modifications was developed by Baumgart [2]. By this operation, faces, edges and vertices are added or deleted according to the Euler equation for solid objects. Later, Braid et. al [4] developed Stepwise Construction method as an extended Baumgart's method. While these operations have been used in order to construct polyhedra and solids with simple curved surfaces, we devised a rounding modification as one of local modifications to round off edges and corners of solids locally, and use local modifications to construct complex free-form shapes.

The methods for rounding off corners and edges of polyhedra have been proposed by Doo et. al [6,7]. In Doo's method, extroudinary points are represented by many subdivided patches and globally rounded surfaces are generated directly from polyhedra. By such means, it is difficult to round off a solid locally or generate sharp edge curves on which two different surfaces meet. Not only smoothness of surfaces but also characteristic curves are important for a designer. So we have devised a new rounding method which solves these problems. Since our method is divided into a phase for producing polyhedral models and a phase for producing curve models distinctly, rough modifications can be done to polyhedral models and precise modifications can be done to curve models. It is therefore possible to realize subtle features of free-form shapes which a designer wishes.

Section 2 of this paper shows the total process of our free-form shape design and section 3 discusses the modifications of polyhedra, which are the bases for our new method. Section 4 describes a rounding modification for modeling free-form shapes. In section 5, a new method for interpolating curve models by surface patches is shown.

2. Free-Form Shape Design Process

Our free-form shape design process consists of the following three phases.

1) A solid which serves as a basis of a free-form shape design is generated by local modifications. Edges of this solid are straight lines, but faces need not be flat surfaces. This solid will be referred to as a basis solid in this paper. A solid model in MODIF has the topological information, how faces, edges and vertices are connected, represented by winged-edge structure [2]. But since this model does not store surfaces equations, it is allowable to generate a solid with twisted faces.

2) Three dimensional curve models are generated from basis solids by rounding modification, and then precise curve modifications are done. For rounding modifications, a designer adds the information for rounding off corners and edges to all the edges in the model. If he wishes that an edge should be rounded off, the information "0" is added. If he does not wish so, the information "1" is added. According to this information, new curved or straight edges are made instead of edges and vertices in the original solid, and a curve model for a free-form shape are built from these edges. Fig.1 shows an example of rounding modifications. The edges of the curve models consist of cubic Bezier curves and straight lines. The curve model has the topological information similar to a basis solid.

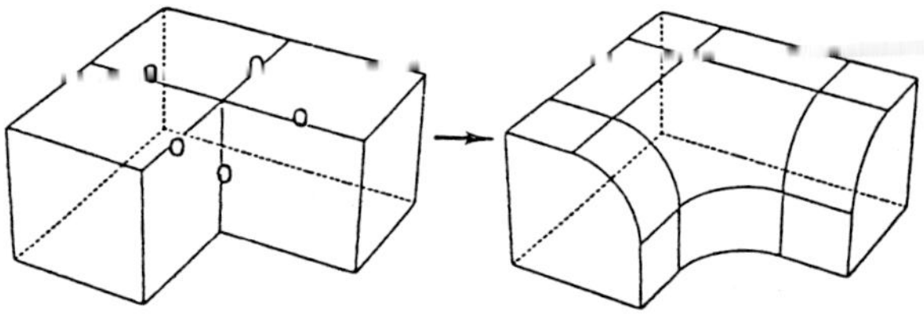

(a) (b)

Fig.1. An example of a rounding modification

3) Smooth surface patches interpolating over faces of the curve model are generated automatically and the model is represented as a closed space in a computer. Because surface patches are defined only by the boundary curves with ease, the model in MODIF does not store surface patch expression. Only specified faces are interpolated when surface equations are necessary, for example, when cutter path data and color shaded pictures are generated. Our method can interpolate over not only four-sided faces but also faces having three, five or more edges.

In the third phase, a designer does not modify the shape but check the smoothness of surface patches defined by the boundary curves. For this purpose, MODIF can draw cross sections and generate color shaded pictures and cutter path data for making real object models by NC machining tool. When a designer want to change the shape, he should return to basis solid or curve model design phase and modify these models. In our method, the important task of a designer is to produce curve models which adequately represent the characteristics of free-form shapes. And then, the smooth surface patches are automatically generated over the given curve model. So the final curve model must not have curved faces whose interpolation is difficult. For example, these are faces whose boundary shapes are extremely concave. If the curve model has these faces, a designer must subdivide these faces by adding edges in the second phase or return the first phase and modify basis solids in order not to produce these faces by rounding modification.

3. Local Modifications for Polyhedra

Set operations have been used as primary procedures for solid construction in many geometric modeling systems. However, when the shape of a solid is complicated, set operations are not necessarily reliable, and require much computational time. So in MODIF, local modifications are used to construct and modify solids. They are easy and natural for a designer. Fig.2 shows a summary of the functions of local modifications procedures. Lifting is an operation to add a solid generated by

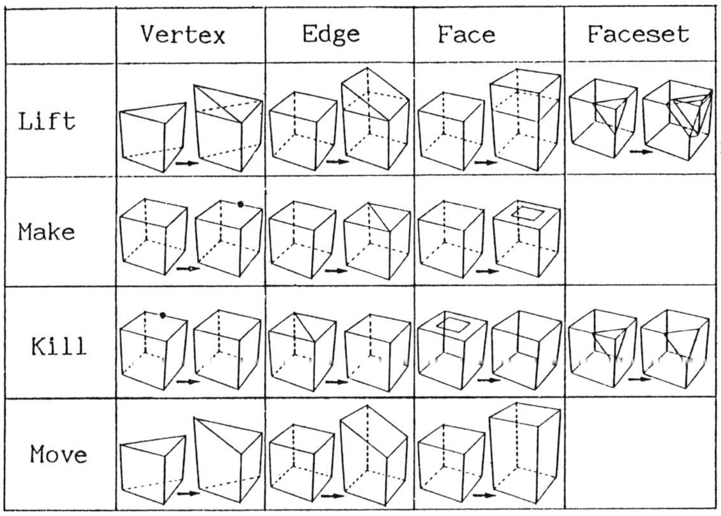

Fig.2. Local modification procedures for a polyhedron

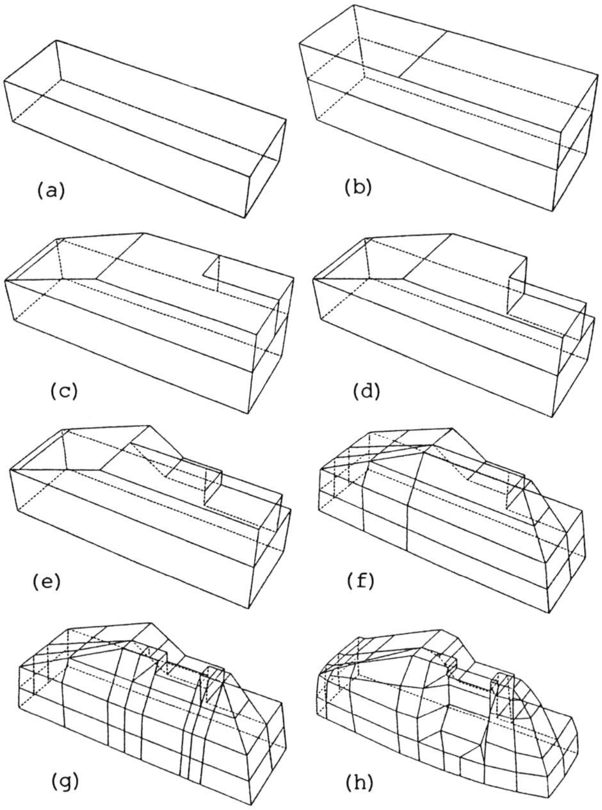

Fig.3. Process of basis solid generation

sweeping local elements to the original solid. Making and killing change the topology of solids. These topological operations are often used as preparations for lifting and a rounding modification. Also they are used to implement the rounding modification. This is described in the next section in detail. Moving is an operation to translate local elements. It is difficult to change shapes by moving, if the condition that solids must be polyhedra is imposed. But this is a useful operation to construct basis solids. Fig.3 shows the process that a basis solid for a telephone is ganerated by local modifications.

When a designer uses local modifications in MODIF, local elements such as faces and edges are usually specified by a graphic cursor and movements vectors inputted by keyboad. In local modifications, the topological consistency of an object is kept automatically, but its geometric consistency is not always kept. So if the designer makes mistakes in the selection of local elements and a distance of a movement for lifting and moving, a model of an object intersecting itself is sometimes constructed. By drawing the model on a graphic display after this modification, a designer can usually find these errors. However, the program for checking the correctness of the model will be required. This still remains as our next study.

4. Rounding Modification for Free-Form Shape Design

4.1 The rule of new edges generation

This section shows how new curved or straight edges of a free-form shape are generated according to edges and vertíces of a basis solid with rounding information when rounding modifications are done. This rule of new edge generation is for a designer to understand how to specify rounding information 'Ø' and '1' of edges. When we produced the rule, we considered that solids with dangling edges must not be generated even if rounding information is given arbitrarily. But this rule was produced in an experiential point of view and does not have theoretical bases. So various modifications and extensions of this rule for a designer's wish will be possible.

First we show how new edges are made according to the edges of basis solids. Fig.4 shows that edge E_0 belongs to two faces F_1 and F_2 and runs between vertices V_1 and V_2. E_1, E_2, E_3 and E_4 are edges touching E_0, F_1 and F_2. Points P_0, G_1 and G_2 are the centers of edge E_0 and faces F_1 and F_2. Here, we define that the centers of an edge and a face are the average of coordinates of vertices belonging to them. When the information for rounding off edge E_0 is "Ø", a curve segment is made, as shown in

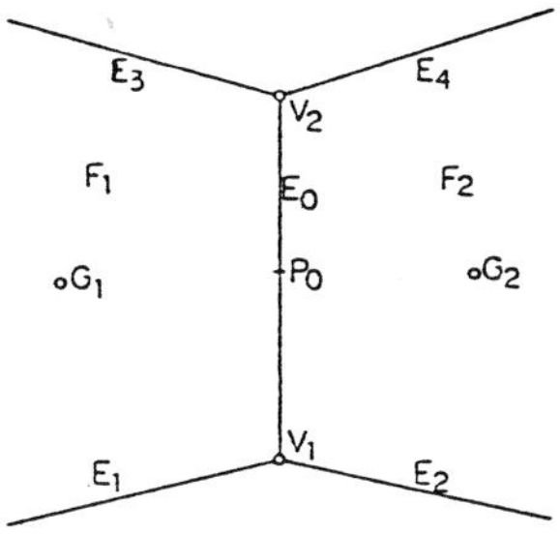

Fig.4. Edge of a basis solid

Fig.5(a). The end points of the curve are G_1 and G_2 and tangents at G_1 and G_2 are line $G_1P_\emptyset$ and $P_\emptyset G_2$. Then, when the information is "1", two line segments $G_1P_\emptyset$ and $P_\emptyset G_2$ are produced, as shown in Fig.5(b). But if new edges are produced only by this rule, the model will have some unnecessary edges for the representation of the shape. So when the information of all edges around a face in a basis solid is "1", a new edge is not made on the face, as shown in Fig.5(c). Also, when edges E_1, E_2, E_3 and E_4 have the information "1", the rounding information of edge $E_\emptyset$ are ignored and a new edge will not be not made, as shown in Fig.5(d).

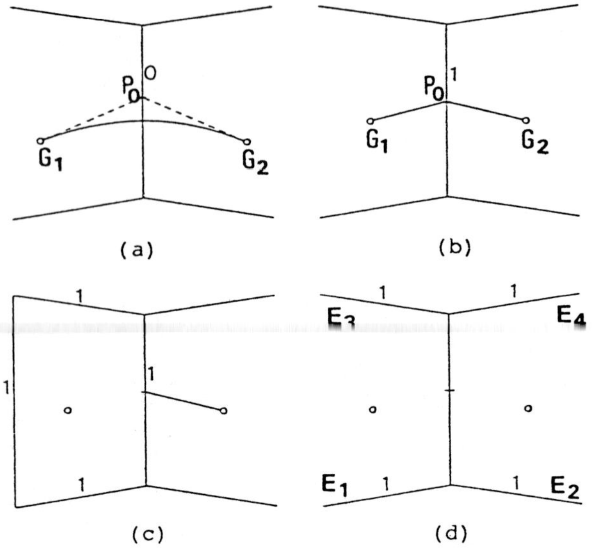

Fig.5. New edges generated on an edge of a basis solid

When new curved edges are produced according to edges belonging to a face whose boundary shape is concave, a self-intersected solid is sometimes generated, because new vertices are produced on the outside of the faces. In order to avoid this problem, a designer must subdivide the faces having edges with rounding information "Ø" into some convex faces by adding appropriate edges. There is no problem about the faces whose edges all have the rounding information "1". Such subdivision is not troublesome but it will be necessary to devise a rule for rounding over edges touching concave faces.

Next, we show the rule of making new edges for a free-form shape according to vertices of a basis solid. Fig.6 shows that vertex $V_\emptyset$ is connected to edges E_i (i=1..n). Points P_i (i=1..n) are the centers of these edges. Vertex $V_\emptyset$ is rounded off according to the rounding information of edges E_i. When there

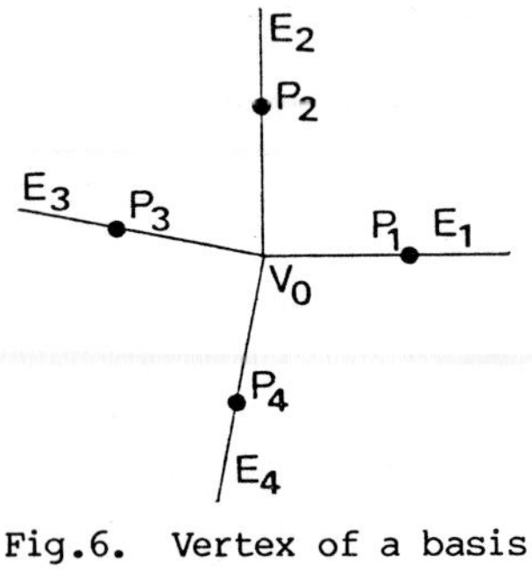

Fig.6. Vertex of a basis solid

is no edge or one edge which has the information "1", no edge is made since vertex $V_\emptyset$ is rounded off, as shown in Fig.7(a) and (b). When only two edges E_k and E_m ($1 \le k,m \le n$) have the information "1", a curve is made as an edge, as shown in Fig.7(c). The end points of the curve are P_k and P_m, and the tangents at P_k and P_m are lines $P_kV_\emptyset$ and $V_\emptyset P_m$. When there are more than two edges which have the information "1", line segments are made from the centers of these edges to vertex $V_\emptyset$, as shown in Fig.7(d).

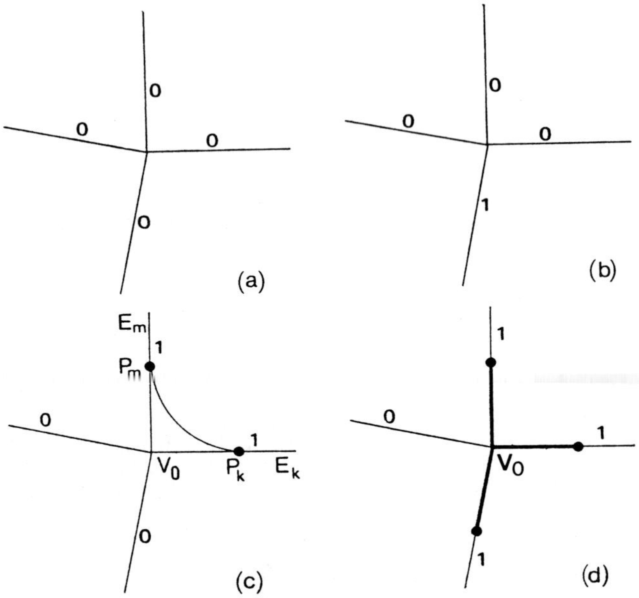

Fig.7. New edges generated on vertices of a solid

When a curve is generated in the rounding modification, three points $P_\emptyset$, P_1 and P_2 are always given, as shown in Fig.8. $P_\emptyset$ and P_1 are end points of the curve generated. Line $P_\emptyset P_1$ is a tangent at $P_\emptyset$ and line P_1P_2 is a tangent at P_2. This condition can be satisfied by a quadratic Bezier curve whose control points three points $P_\emptyset$, P_1 and P_2. However, a quadratic curve is not necessarily fair. When the length of line $P_\emptyset P_1$ is the same as the length of line P_1P_2, it is desirable that a curve approximating a arc is generated. So in the rounding modification, the method are used which can satisfy this requirement by using a cubic Bezier curve.

Designers will wish to control the shape of curves when curve models are generated. So we show one simple method. The shape of an curved edge in a free-form shape is determined by the position of the centers of a face or an edge in an original solid.

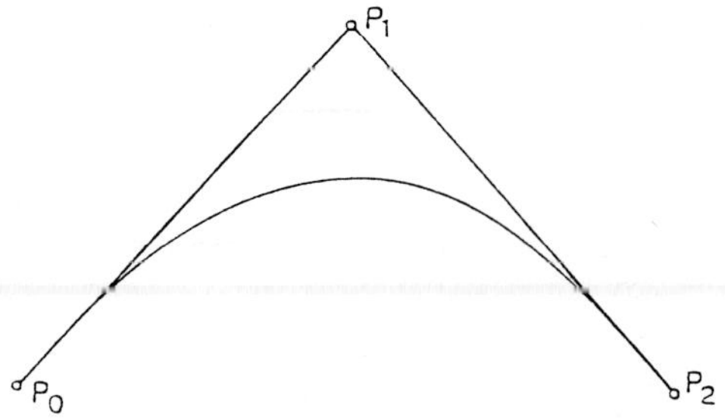

Fig.8. Condition of a curve generation

So, if appropriate weights are given to vertices, the centers of faces and edges are moved toward vertices with large weights. By using this property, we can control the shape of the curves with ease. Fig.9 shows examples done by this method. The shape shown in Fig.9(b) is made from the polyhedron shown in Fig.9(a), whose edges E_1, E_2 and E_3 are given the rounding information 'Ø' and weights of all vertices are 1. The shape shown in Fig.9(c) is made by changing the weights of vertices $V_Ø$, V_1, V_2 and V_3 to 9, 3, 3 and 3 respectively.

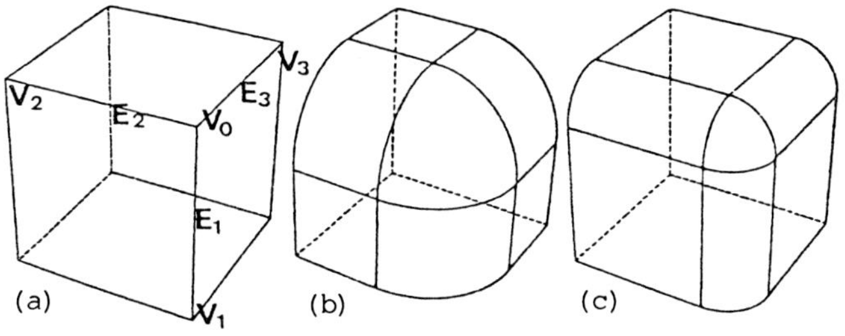

Fig.9. Rounding control by adding weights to vertices

4.2 Implementation of a Rounding Modification

This section shows how to implement rounding modifications. The rule described in the previous section explains only how to make curves and lines. This is not for the implementation. It is difficult to make models having the topological information from many curves and lines. So in the implementation, necessary edges added to the solid and then unnecessary edges are deleted according the rule, so that the model can keep the topological information. Fig.1Ø shows how this procedure is done in a computer. The solid shown in Fig.1Ø(a) is a cube, whose three edges have the information 'Ø' and all other edges have the information '1'. First, new edges from the center of faces to the center of edges are made and faces are subdivided as shown in Fig.1Ø(b). Here, if all edges of a face are '1', the face will not be subdivided. According to the rule of generating new edges around vertices of the original solid, unnecessary edges are deleted and curved edges will be made from two straight edges, as shown in Fig.1Ø(c). Similarly, around the vertices made on the center of all original edges, edges are deleted or curved edges are made, as shown in Fig.1Ø(d). These procedures can be composed by local modifications for polyhedra described in the previous section.

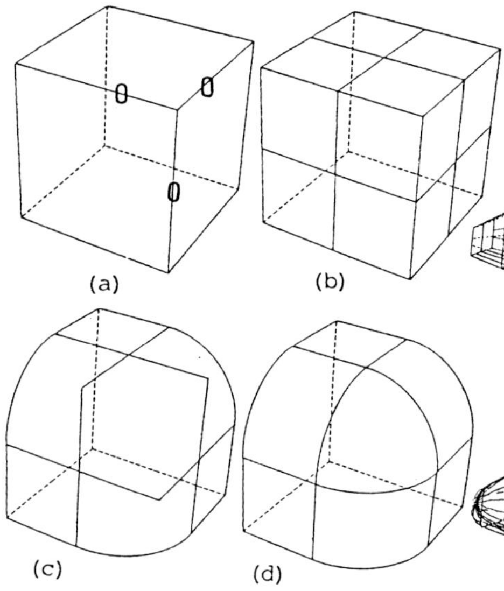

Fig.1Ø. Implementation process of the rounding modification

4.3 Examples of Rounding Modifications

Some examples of the models shown in Fig.11 and Fig.12 are produced by MODIF. Fig.11(a) and Fig.12(a) are basis solid models which are produced by local modifications described in section 3. Fig.11(b) and Fig.12(b) are curve models for free-form shapes which are produced from the basis solids by rounding modification.

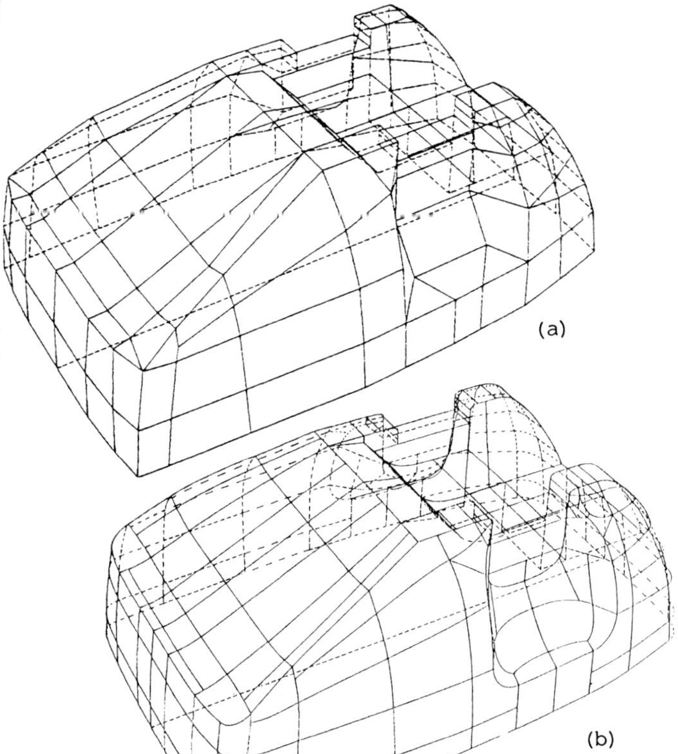

Fig.11. Telephone

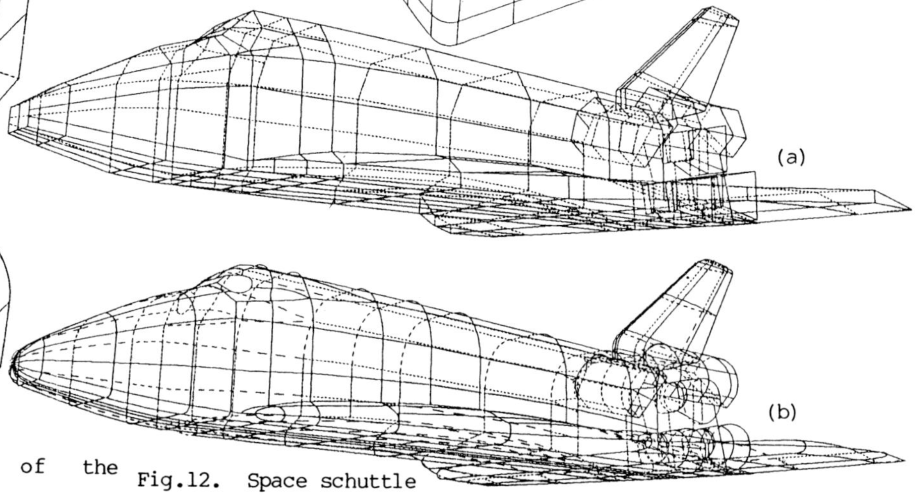

Fig.12. Space schuttle

5. Interpolation over Faces

The curve models produced by rounding modification usually include non-rectangular faces and vertices connected to three, five or more edges. In this section, an interpolation method of such irregular curve model is shown.

Bicubic Coons patches and Bezier patches have been used to interpolate over curve models. However, these are generally patches for interpolating only over regular curve models shown in Fig.13 under the condition that the directions of the surface normal are continuous across the boundary. Faces of these models always have four curves, and its vertices are defined as cross points of two curves. Also, the cross-boundary tangent magnitude ratio k must be constant along the common boundary [8]. For example, k_1, k_2 and k_3 in Fig.13 should have the same value. This restriction is very severe for representing free-form shapes by curves. We therefore devised a method of generating surfaces whose normal directions are continuous over curve models having irregular regions shown in Fig.14. Fig.14(a) shows the regular curve model whose cross-boundary tangent magnitude ratio is not constant. Fig.14(b) shows one example that three or more than four patches meet at one corner. In addition, Fig.14(c) shows a non-rectangular face.

In this paper, we assume that designers should produce a curve model which represents the characteristics of a free-form shape adequately. So when one face is interpolated in our method, patches are defined only by edges attached to the interpolated face. For example, if a face has four sides, a patch is defined only by four edges. Because this method is simple, the implementation is easy and its execution does not require much time. This means that the internal model of solids in a computer need not have the control points of the patches if a modeling system has our interpolation procedure. So MODIF does not store patch data. Generally speaking, large memory area is used in order to store patch data. Therefore, it is possible to represent complicated free-form shapes by relatively small area in MODIF.

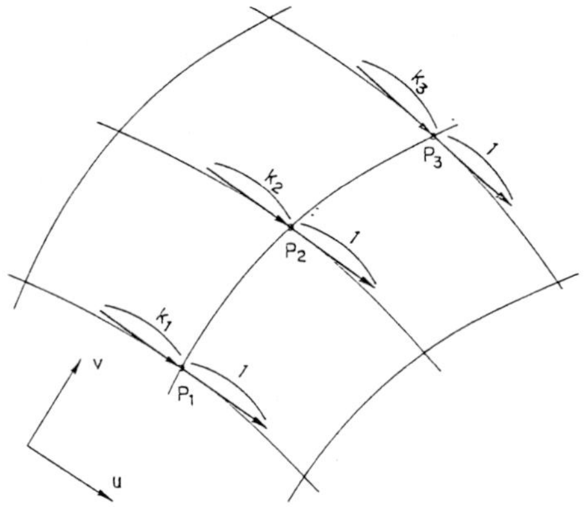

Fig.13. Regular curve model

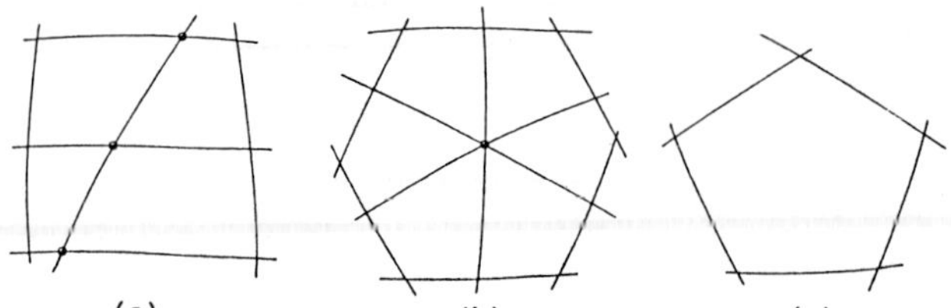

Fig.14. Irregular curve regions

5.1 Gregory Patch

This section describes about a patch used in our interpolation method. The bicubically blended Coons patch S(u,w) [9] can interpolate four boundary curves and normal derivatives along boundary curves, as shown in Fig.15. However, these normal derivatives can not be specified independently. We must specify these, satisfying the following equation on four corners of a patch.

$$\partial^2 S(u,w)/\partial u \partial w = \partial^2 S(u,w)/\partial w \partial u \qquad (1)$$

This is called a "compatibility condition" [1]. When various surfaces are interpolated by this patch, this condition becomes constraint. So Gregory [11] has modified an equation of this patch and devised a new patch whose four normal derivatives can be specified with no constraint. In this paper, we modify a bicubic Bezier patch [13] similarly which has good properties for shape design, and propose an interpolation method using this patch. We call this new patch a "Gregory patch". As shown in Fig.16, this patch S(u,w) is defined by twenty control points and the equations are as follows.

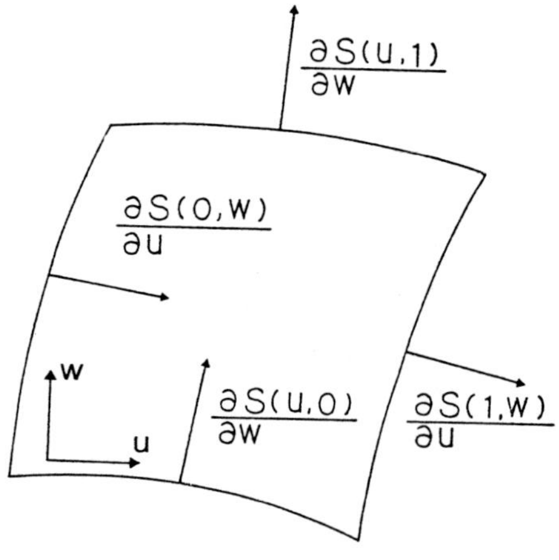

Fig.15. Normal derivatives of a patch

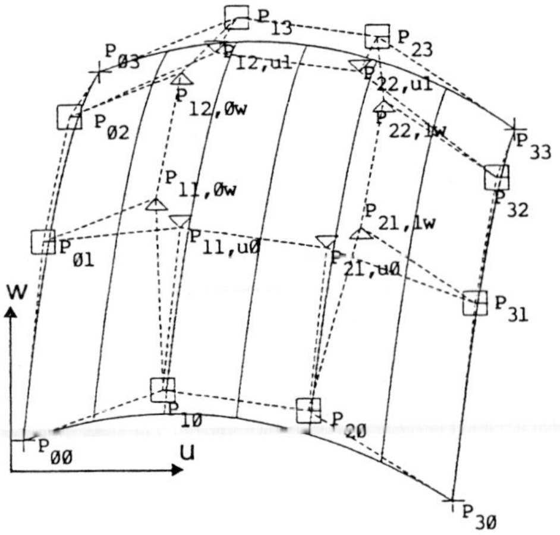

Fig.16. Gregory patch

$$S(u,w) = (1-u+uE)^3 \, (1-w+wF)^3 \, P_{00}(u,w) \qquad (2)$$

$$0 \le u, w \le 1$$

$$P_{11}(u,w) = \frac{wP_{11,u0} + uP_{11,0w}}{u + w}$$

$$P_{12}(u,w) = \frac{wP_{12,u1} + (1-u)P_{12,0w}}{(1-u) + w}$$

$$P_{21}(u,w) = \frac{(1-w)P_{21,u0} + uP_{21,1w}}{u + (1-w)}$$

$$P_{22}(u,w) = \frac{(1-w)P_{22,u1} + (1-u)P_{22,1w}}{(1-u) + (1-w)}$$

The shift operators E and F have the property that $EP_{ij} = P_{i+1j}$ and $FP_{ij} = P_{ij+1}$. These equations (2) mean that the position of a point on this patch is represented as an addition of sixteen points to which various weights are given. Point P_{11} moves on straight line segments between two control points $P_{11,u0}$ and $P_{11,0w}$ according to parameter u and w. Similarly, points P_{12}, P_{21} and P_{22} move on straight line segments between corresponding two control points. Twelve other points which define boundary curves are fixed points. This patch has the convex hull property like a Bezier patch that an arbitrary point on the patch exists in the convex hull defined by all control points. This property is advantageous for rough interference check.

5.2 Connection of Patches

In order to represent smooth free-form surfaces by patches, it is necessary that the surface normal directions are continuous across the boundary curves. In this section, we discuss the connection of two Gregory patches in preparation for explaining our interpolation method. Fig.17 shows connected patches $S_a(u,w)$ and $S_b(u,w)$. In Fig.17, a_i, $b_i(i=0..3)$ and $c_i(i=0..2)$ are vectors between the control points and are defined as follows.

$$a_0 = P^a_{30} - P^a_{20}, \; a_1 = P^a_{31} - P^a_{21,1w}$$
$$a_2 = P^a_{32} - P^a_{22,1w}, \; a_3 = P^a_{33} - P^a_{23}$$
$$b_0 = P^b_{10} - P^b_{00}, \; b_1 = P^b_{11,0w} - P^b_{01} \qquad (3)$$

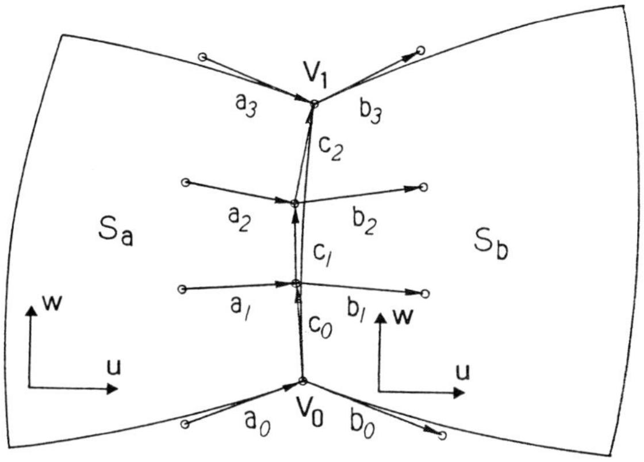

Fig.17. Connection of two patches

$$b_2 = P^b_{12,0w} - P^b_{02}, \; b_3 = P^b_{13} - P^b_{03}$$
$$c_0 = P^a_{31} - P^a_{30}, \; c_1 = P^a_{32} - P^a_{31}, \; c_2 = P^a_{33} - P^a_{32}$$

P^a and P^b are control points of patches S_a and S_b respectively. The derivatives of parameters u and w along the boundary curves of the patches are defined by a_i, b_i and c_i. The derivatives are represented by the following Bezier expressions.

$$\partial S_a(1,w)/\partial u = 3\,(1-w+wE)^3 a_0$$
$$\partial S_b(0,w)/\partial u = 3\,(1-w+wE)^3 b_0 \qquad (4)$$
$$\partial S_a(1,w)/\partial w = 3\,(1-w+wE)^2 c_0$$

Under the condition of normal direction continuity, three derivatives of a point on the boundary curve always exist in the same plane. This is represented as follows.

$$\frac{\partial S_b(0,w)}{\partial u} = k(w)\frac{\partial S_a(1,w)}{\partial u} + h(w)\frac{\partial S_a(1,w)}{\partial w} \qquad (5)$$

k(w) and h(w) are scalar functions. At the patch corner V_0 and V_1 in Fig.17, three vectors must satisfy the following equations in order to generate connected patches.

$$b_0 = k_0 a_0 + h_0 c_0$$
$$b_3 = k_1 a_3 + h_1 c_2 \qquad (6)$$

k_0, k_1, h_0 and h_1 are scalar constants and can be obtained easily because curved edges are already represented by Bezier curves. To satisfy equations (5) and simplify the computation, we assume that k(w) and h(w) are linear functions as follows.

$$k(w) = (1-w)k_0 + wk_1$$
$$h(w) = (1-w)h_0 + wh_1 \qquad (7)$$

We also require that the normal derivative of a patch S_a is quadratic to satisfy equation (5). This is represented as follows.

$$a_0 - 3a_1 + 3a_2 - a_3 = 0 \qquad (8)$$

The following equations, the relation of a_i, b_i and c_i, are given from equations (4), (5) and (7).

$$b_1 = (k_1-k_0)a_0/3 + k_0 a_1 + 2h_0 c_1/3 + h_1 c_0/3$$
$$b_2 = k_1 a_2 - (k_1-k_0)a_3/3 + h_0 c_2/3 + 2h_1 c_1/3 \qquad (9)$$

When the control points of two patches satisfy equations (8) and (9), normal directions of two patches become continuous.

5.3 Interpolation of four sided faces

This section shows an integrated interpolation method of various four sided faces shown in Fig.11 and Fig.12(a)(b). We showed equations (9) for connecting patches in the previous section. But by equations (9) alone, the control points of patches can not be determined. The normal derivative of patch $S_a(u,w)$ must be specified under the condition that the function is quadratic. However, since the relation of the normal derivative and the shape of the patch is not obvious, it is difficult for a designer to specify the derivative. There also remains another serious problem. If normal derivatives are determined by equations (9) alone, the normal derivative of patch S_a will be quadratic but the derivative of patch S_b will become cubic. This means that asymmetric surfaces are generated when symmetric curved edges are given. These problems will be solved by the usage of a "basis patch".

As shown in Fig.18, we consider the connection of real patch S_b and virtual basis patch S'_a in order to determine the control points of S_b. The normal derivative of S'_a is defined by the boundary curves of patch S_b. Vector a'_0 in S'_a is a unit vector which is normal to c_0 and exists on a plane defined by b_0 and c_0. Similarly, a'_3 is defined by b_3 and c_2 and is normal to c_2. When the curve model represents the characteristics of the shape adequately, the normal derivatives along the boundary curves changes smoothly. So we assume that the derivatives are linear and determine a'_1 and a'_2. From equations (9), b_1 and b_2 are given. This procedure for earning b_1 and b_2 is done on four edges of the interpolated face. Then one patch is generated. When the boundary curves of faces satisfy equations (6), two normal derivatives of respective basis patches defined by the boundary of patch S_b and patch S_a become the same. Accordingly, two patches are connected smoothly and problems described above are solved. The shape edge curves where two different surfaces meet does not satisfy equation (6). In such case, patches whose normal directions are not continuous are generated. In our method, the boundary curves determine if normal directions of patches are continuous or not.

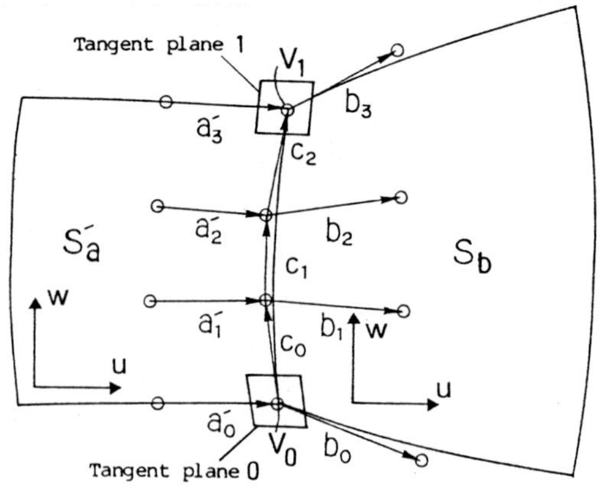

Fig.18. Connection of a basis patch and a real patch

5.4 Interpolation of non-rectangular faces

When non-rectangular faces are interpolated, the normal derivatives across the boundary curves are determined by using the basis patch, as shown in Fig.19(a). Then, internal curves satisfying these derivatives are generated, and faces are subdivided by some rectangular faces, as shown in Fig.19(b). Finally, Gregory patches are generated over these rectangular faces under the condition that all patches satisfy equation (1) at the patch corner P where internal curves meet. These procedures are done automatically. The methods using subdivisions have been already proposed. Because conventional bicubic patches are used in these method, the connections of patches on the internal curves and the boundary curves are difficult. But our method using Gregory patches can avoid this difficulty. The detail of our interpolation method for non-rectangular faces will be appeared in the other report. Fig.20 shows examples of interpolated non-rectangular faces. Fig.20 (a)(c)(e) show edges and cross sections of solids. In addition, Fig.20 (b)(d)(f) show control points of patches. Because faces in which control points are not drown are planes, patches are not generated.

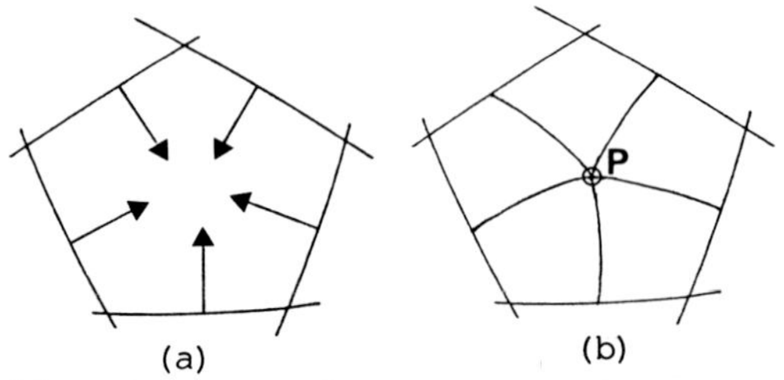

Fig.19. Process of non-rectangular face interpolation

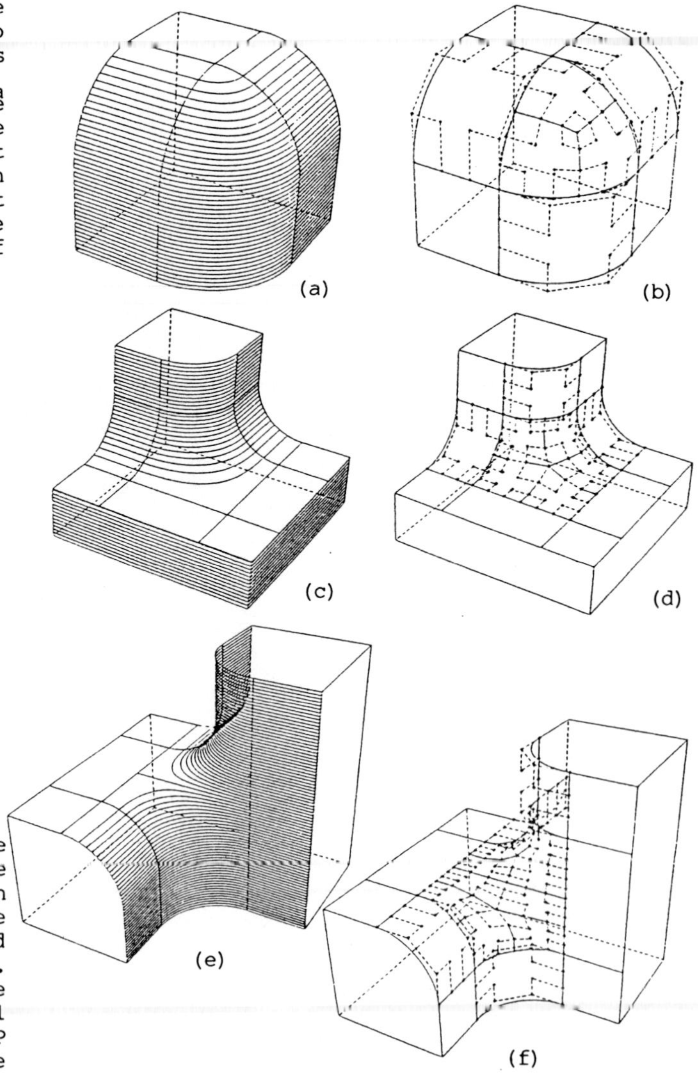

Fig.20. Non-rectangular faces interpolated by Gregory patches

6. Display

Fig.21 shows a curve model of a telephone and cross sections of patches generated over faces are drawn. Wire drawing pictures like Fig.21 have been used to display a model of a free-form shape. However, they are not sufficient for a designer to understand the shape represented in a computer. We therefore have developed two types of displays in MODIF, namely a real object model and a color shaded picture. As shown in Fig.22, MODIF can generate cutter path data to produce a real object model by NC machining tool. Fig.23 shows a real object model produced by these data. Fig.24 shows a color shaded picture of a telephone. We have used the ray tracing algorithm as a method of display. In this program, curved surface patches are neither subdivided nor approximated by planes. Intersection points between patches and rays and their normal vectors for shaded levels at pixels are calculated correctly so that a designer can check smoothness of curved surfaces by shaded pictures. When a man designs a free-form shape by MODIF, these displays will become his good tools.

Our system MODIF has been developed on VAX 11/780 running VMS. This system was written in FORTRAN. As graphic devices, the Tektronix 4014 for wire drawing pictures and the JRC 235 for color shaded pictures have been used.

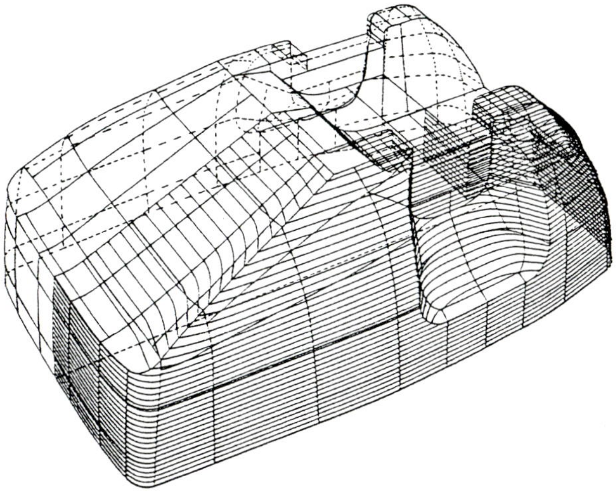

Fig.21. Telephone

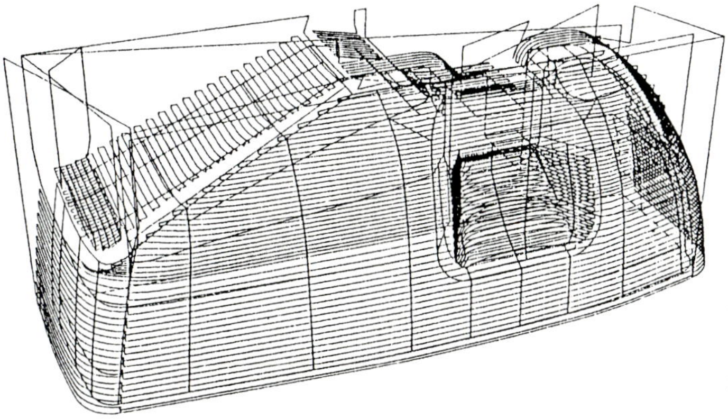

Fig.22. Cutter path data

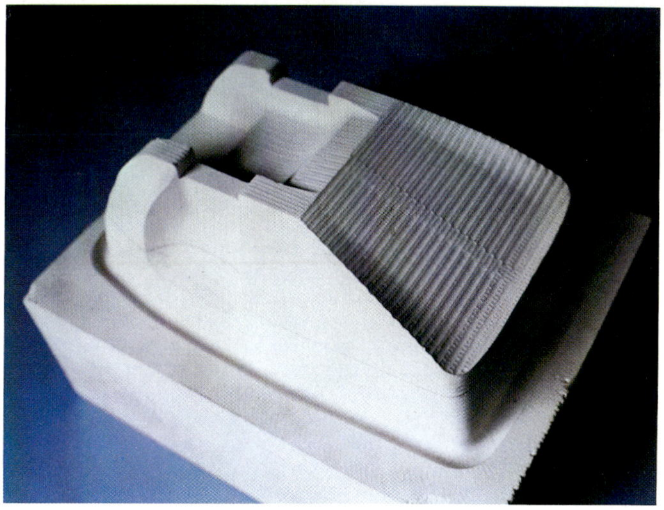

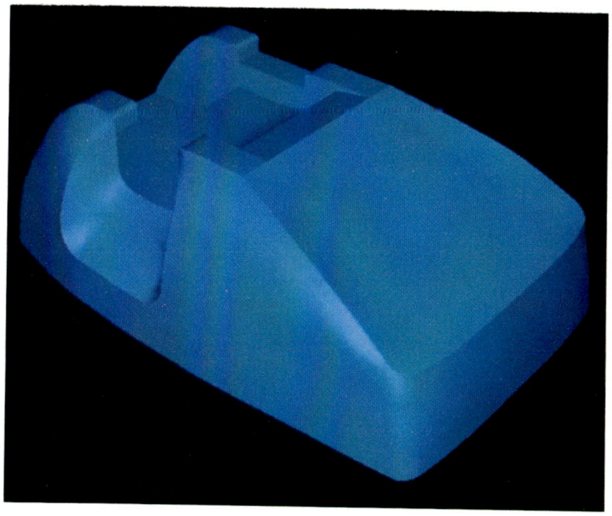

Fig.24. Color shaded picture

7. Conclusion

We have proposed a unified method for generating a wide range of shapes in one modeling system by using local modifications. In our method, a designer produces a curve model which adequately represents the characteristics of a free-form shape by local modifications. Then surface equations interpolating over the curve model are generated by computer. The construction of the shapes by using local modifications can naturally be understood for a designer. The local modifications and our surface interpolation method are easy to be implemented and their execution in a computer does not require much time.

Recently, many solid modeling systems have been developed and are used in the fields of practical engineering because solid models are far more desirable for various applications than surface models and wire-frame models. However, solids which these systems can generate are usually polyhedra with simple surfaces. So it is a very important problem how free-form surface modeling facilities are added to these systems. The method described in this paper is one solution to this problem. If solid modeling systems use boundary representations, it is possible to add this method to the systems. And if systems have Euler operators (making edges, killing vertices and so on), it will become more easy to add the method.

In this paper, we have shown a basic principle of modeling free-form shapes. The important matters in modeling free-form shapes are not only producing fine and precise models quickly but also flexible representations of the shape for various modifications and useful techniques of changing the shapes. Conventional curve and surface models can represent the shapes but are not necessarily feasible representations for various modifications. When the objects designed are polyhedra, it is not difficult to change the shape. However, when the object has free-form surfaces, designer's wish for the shape becomes complex. Accordingly, the flexible representation and useful modifications will be necessary. In our method, the basis solid with rounding information is one flexible representation. Using the basis solid, it is possible to control curved surfaces and sharp curved edges where two different curved surfaces meet. But our rounding modifications and local modifications alone are not sufficient for free-form shape design. Extension of the rounding modification's rule and developing new modification's techniques are our future work.

Acknowledgments

We wish to thank Prof. M.Hosaka and Prof. T.Sata for helpful suggestions. We also wish to thank M.Fujimoto and N.Okada for technical help in using the NC machine tool, and A.Hayashi and S.Uno for their assistance in implementing the color shading program. In addition, we thank K.Matsushima and Y.Ohno for variable comments on ealier version of this paper.

References

[1] Barnhill,R.E., Brown,J.H. and Klucewicz,I.M. : A New Twist in Computer Aided Geometric Design, Computer Graphics and Image Processing 8, pp.78-91, 1978.

[2] Baumgart,B.G. : GEOMED-A GEOMETRIC EDITOR, Stanford Artificial Intelligence Laboratory Memo AIM-232, Computer Science Department Report no. cs-414, May 1974.

[3] Bezier,P.E. : Numerical Control - Mathematics and Applications, John Wiley and Sons, London, 1972.

[4] Braid,I.C., Hillyard,R.C. and Stroud,I.A. : Stepwise Construction of Polyhedra in Geometric Modelling, Mathematical Methods in Computer Graphics and Design (Ed. by K.W.Brodlie) Academic Press, pp.123-141, 1980.

[5] Coons,S.A. : Surfaces for Computer Aided Design of Space Forms, MIT Project MAC TR-41, June 1967.

[6] Catmull,E. and Clark,J. : Recursively Generated B-spline Surfaces on Arbitrary Topological Meshes, Computer Aided Design, pp.350-355, vol.10, no.6, November, 1978.

[7] Doo,D. : A Subdivision Algorithm for Smoothing Down Irregular Shaped Polyhedrons, Proc. Conf. Interactive Technique in CAD, pp.157-165, IEEE Computer Society 78CH1289-8C, 1978.

[8] Faux,I.D. and Pratt,M.J. : Computational Geometry for Design and Manufacture, Chapter 7, ELLIS HORWOOD LIMITED, 1979.

[9] Forrest,A.R. : On Coons and Other Methods for the Representation of Curved Surfaces, Computer Graphics and Image Processing 1, pp.341-359, 1972.

[10] Forrest,A.R. : A Unified Approach to Geometric Modelling, SIGGRAPH 78 Proceedings, pp.264-269, 1978.

[11] Gregory,J.A. : Smooth Interpolation Without Twist Constraints, in Computer Aided Geometric Design (R. E. Barnhill and R. F. Riesenfeld, Eds.), pp.71-87, Academic Press, New York, 1974.

[12] Hosaka,M. and Kimura,F. : An Interactive Geometrical Design System with Handwriting Input, Information Processing 77, pp.167-172, North-Holland, Amsterdam, 1977.

[13] Hosaka,M. and Kimura,F. : Synthesis Methods of Curves and Surfaces in Interactive CAD, Proc. Conf. Interactive Technique in CAD, pp.151-156, IEEE Computer Society 78CH1289-8C, 1978.

[14] Requicha,A.G. : Representation for Rigid Solids : Theory, Method and Systems, Computing Surveys, vol.12, no.4, pp.437-464, December 1980.

[15] Riesenfeld,R.F. : Applications of B-spline Approximation to Geometric Problems of Computer Aided Design, Ph.D. thesis, Syracuse University, May 1973.

GEOMETRIC MODELLING AND DISPLAY PRIMITIVES TOWARDS SPECIALISED HARDWARE

Dr. A.L. Thomas
Department of Mathematical Sciences
Durham University
Durham
ENGLAND

Abstract

Work over the last ten years developing a simple geometric modelling scheme has led to the design of a high speed display processor capable of generating real time moving displays directly from a three dimensional model. The geometric model consists of a graph-matrix boundary representation linked to a boolean expression volume overlap representation. The architecture of the display processor is particularly suitable for implementation as a pipeline of VLSI components, and current work is exploring this possibility. A divide and conquer, quad tree algorithm applied to the boolean expression model allows the system to make use of scene coherence, and used with the hardware will make it possible to handle scenes of high complexity.

CR Categories and Subject Descriptors

I.3.1 [Computer Graphics] Hardware Architecture - Raster Display Devices; I.3.5 [Computer Graphics] Computational Geometry and Object Modelling; I.3.7 [Computer Graphics] Three Dimensional Graphics and Realism - Visible Line/Surface Elimination; B.7.1 [Integrated Circuits] Algorithms Implemented in Hardware, VLSI; C.1.2 [Processor Architectures] Multiple Data Stream Architectures - Pipeline Processors.

Introduction

The current project arose from a longer term, more broadly based study which was started in 1970. The aim was to improve information processing techniques which depended on the use of drawings in the design work of architects and engineers by applying computer based methods. It became clear almost as soon as the study was started that for most engineering applications, products which were traditionally modelled as a set of two dimensional drawings would in the new environment be far more usefully modelled as three dimensional entities.(1) Since then most of the work has been concentrated on building three dimensional models of objects, and finding ways of using and displaying the results.

The first objective was to find a way of describing three dimensional objects in a convenient formal language, which was versatile enough to allow a variety of computer models to be constructed for different applications. These object descriptions had to satisfy demands made on them at two levels. Firstly they had to be self consistent, non ambiguous and in a form which could act as an interface to higher level systems which might want to automatically create or manipulate object descriptions. Secondly they had to make man machine interaction simple and convenient to manage.

The second main objective also arose from this need to improve the man machine interface and consisted of finding better ways of generating graphic displays directly from three dimensional models.

Geometric Models

Geometric models are multi-level data structures where the lowest level consists of primitive geometric components such as points, lines, planes, spheres, cylinders and even sculptured surface patches; and the upper levels consist of structures which compose these basic elements together in a way which defines the required shape. For example, a general form for one type of object model often consists of a set of surface patches, linked to a boundary network which ties them together as a closed surface. If the surface patches in such a model are restricted to being planes, then the model will be restricted to representing polyhedra. By 1972 two interrelated data stuctures had been defined which allowed polyhedra to be constructed in a moderately controlled way.(10,11) These two structures were a) graph-matrix volume models and derived from them b) boolean expression volume models.

Graph-Matrix Models

The starting point in developing these models was the set of polygon-boundary lists used in contemporary systems to define the surface facets of a polyhedron(1). Following this, the dual naming of edges, as used in the GIMMS(18) cartographic system was introduced to link together adjacent facet boundaries and cut down search time in volume editing operations. The edges of facets were usually defined by pairs of vertex labels, for example 5/4 in Figure 1; but it was also possible in a network to name edges by using the labels of the zones separated by each edge. In the example, 5/4 is C/B and the complete dual name for the edge becomes 5/4:C/B.(7)

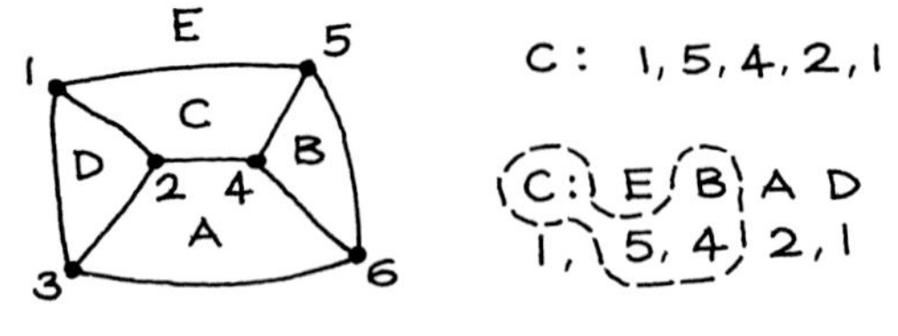

Figure 1

The consequence of using dual naming was that the polygon boundary lists were tied together in a single structure which was more complex to manipulate. This in itself was not a problem so long as the programmer could avoid having to work at the level of the linked lists all the time. One way to avoid this low level programming was to work through a limited set of well understood higher level procedures such as Euler Operators, which were more closely related to the geometric and topological properties of the complete model.(4,5) A related way was to convert the lists into a more readily comprehended intermediate data structure. This is the approach adopted below, and the structure used is the graph matrix.

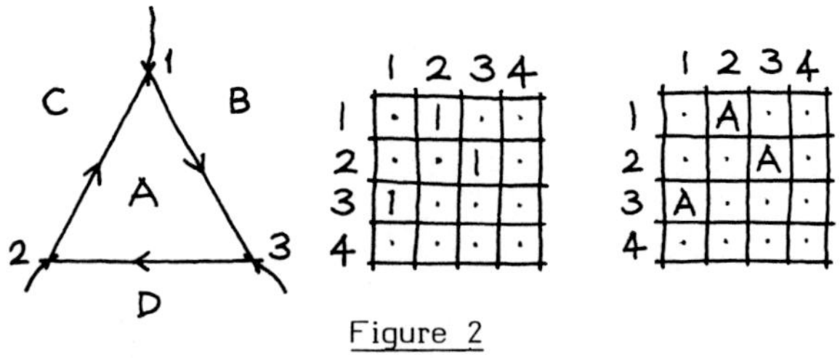

Figure 2

Figure 2 shows the way to code up a graph-matrix. If the edges of each facet are treated as a directed graph but instead of the boolean 0 or 1 the name of the facet is entered into the matrix, the result for a single facet will be that shown in Figure 2, and the result for a tetrahedron that shown in Figure 3.

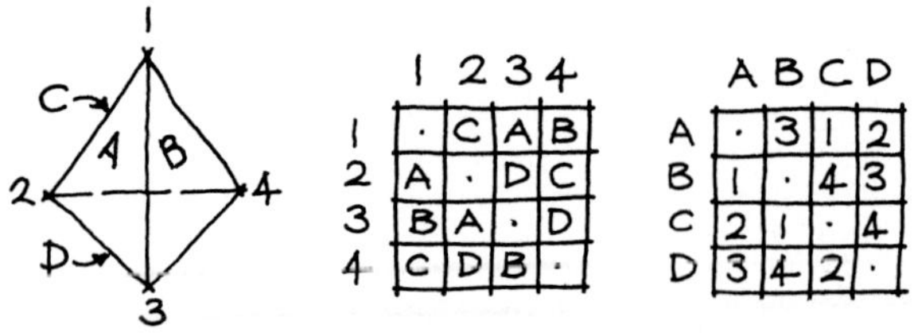

Figure 3

The dual naming of edges results in two forms for these matrices: the vertex facet form and the facet vertex form, both shown in Figure 3. The order in which vertex labels are taken round a polygon boundary has to be consistent, for example if a clockwise order is used to reference the inside of the polygon, then an anti-clockwise order will reference its outside.

Figure 4

Consequently, the inside outside relationship for a polygon can be reversed by reversing the order of coordinates in the polygon boundary list. A similar operation applies to the volume matrices. Given a set of vertices and a matrix defining a solid, then the transpose matrix will model a void: in much the same way that the island is converted into a lake in Figure 4.

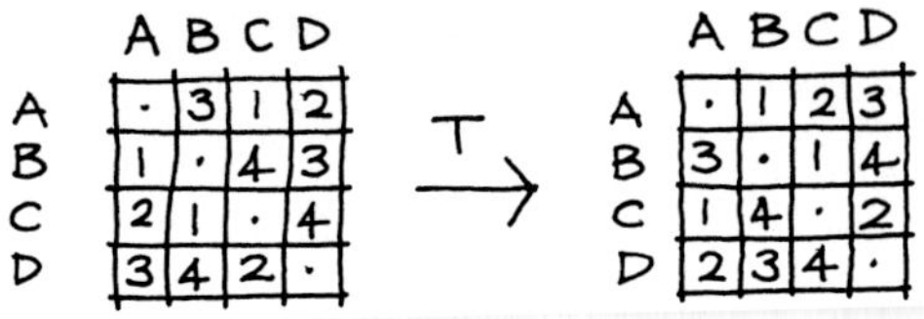

Figure 5

Under certain conditions it is possible to add and multiply these matrices together. Addition is a simple operation once it is remembered that rows and columns are labelled and it is only the contents of cells indexed by the same names which can be added together. A geometrical interpretation for this addition is defining the union of the volumes which the matrices represent. Matrix multiplication based on a scalar operation which is a form of label comparison (A.A = A, A.0 = 0, A.B = 0, A+B = A+B) provides a way of recovering the order of facet boundary lists. Circuits, either round named facets or named vertices, can be obtained by following the changing column positions of a given name in a particular row, through a series of matrix multiplications.(13) However there is a simpler way to obtain the same result.

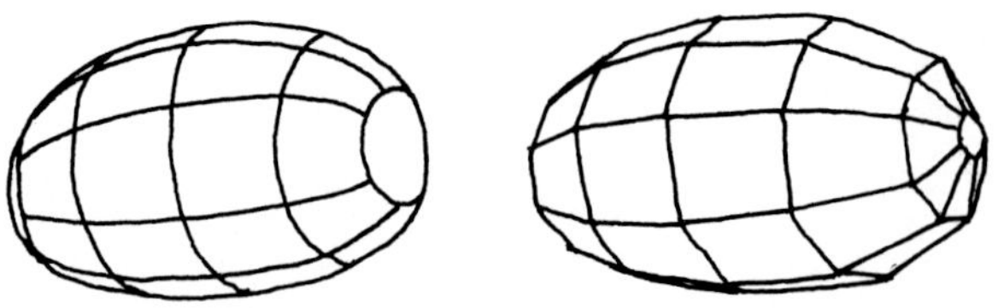

Figure 6

These graph-matrices do not in themselves restrict the model to plane faceted objects; however if such a restriction is made, some very useful simplifications result: the immediate one being that all geometrical operations can be carried out on the volume's set of edges.

Joining and Editing

Building more complex volumes can be approached in two ways. The direct way is the one illustrated in Figure 7. A collection of vertices are linked together as a set of adjacent tetrahedra which are then joined together. The outcome of this operation will be a fully triangulated surface network, and final editing to any required shape can be achieved by locally transforming vertex coordinates.

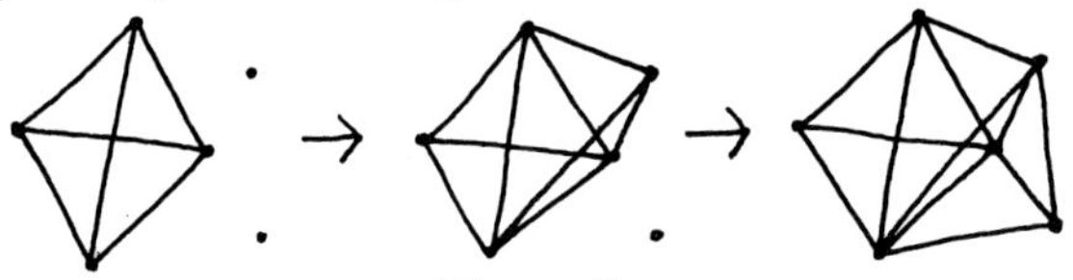

Figure 7

The topological operation of joining two tetrahedra is demonstrated in Figures 8 and 9. The first step is to add the two component matrices together to give a single common matrix as shown in Figure 8.

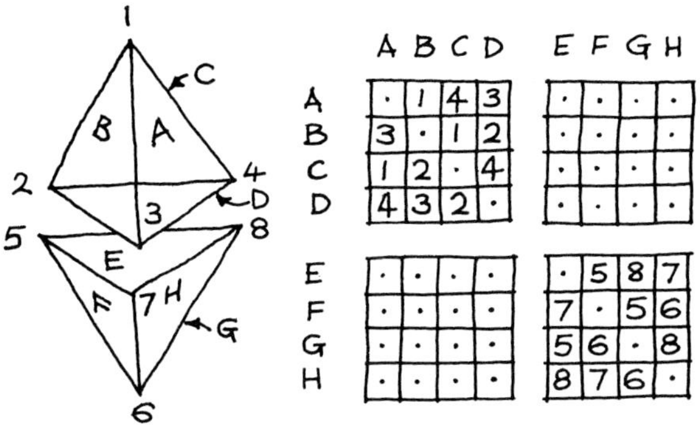

Figure 8

If the two separate volumes are merged at faces E and D so that the vertex pairs 2,5; 3,7 and 4,8 are made to coincide, then these two facets will vanish from the final volume. In Figure 9 vertex labels 5,7,8 are replaced by 2,3,4 respectively, and rows and columns labelled D and E are removed. However it is an important property of these matrices that the set of labels in any column has to be the same as the set of labels in the corresponding row. Deleting the rows and columns labelled D and E will violate this property. It is a simple matter, however, to correct the matrix structure by locating the rows and columns which are missing the same label and entering it where they cross. This bookkeeping operation is shown in Figure 9.

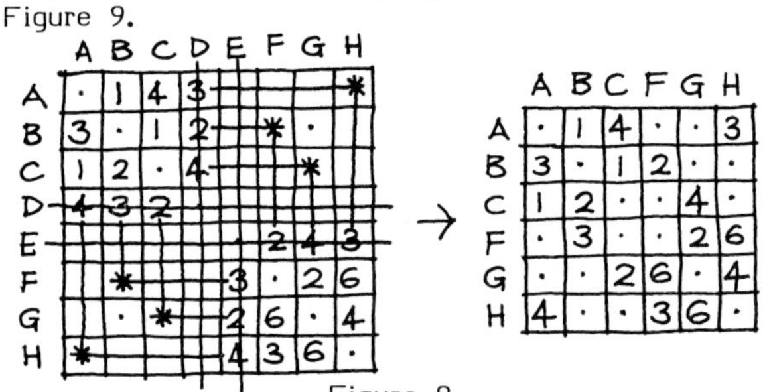

Figure 9

Obtaining a specified object this way requires the number of edges, vertices and facets to be known. An intermediate triangulated volume has to be constructed and then edited to conform to the specification. This approach like the use of Euler operators, ensures a correct and complete volume model. An example of the editing operation used in this process consists of removing an edge to merge two facets into one: shown in Figure 10 for B/F.

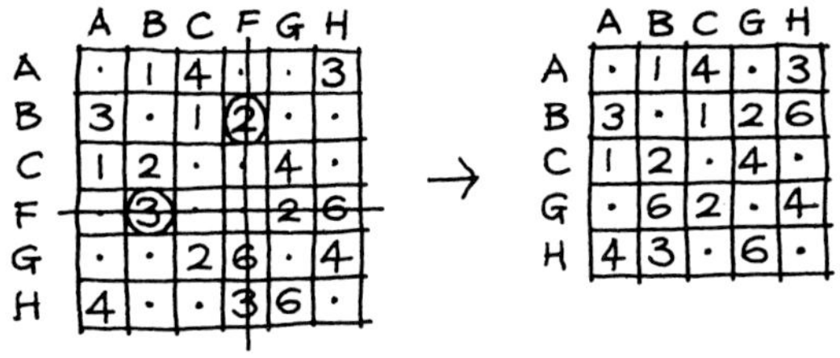

Figure 10

This topological editing, however, can raise geometrical problems, if, for example, facets are to be maintained as plane surfaces.

Overlap and Selection

An alternative way of generating volume models where non triangular plane facets are required can be achieved by overlapping existing volumes and then selecting the new volume from the result.

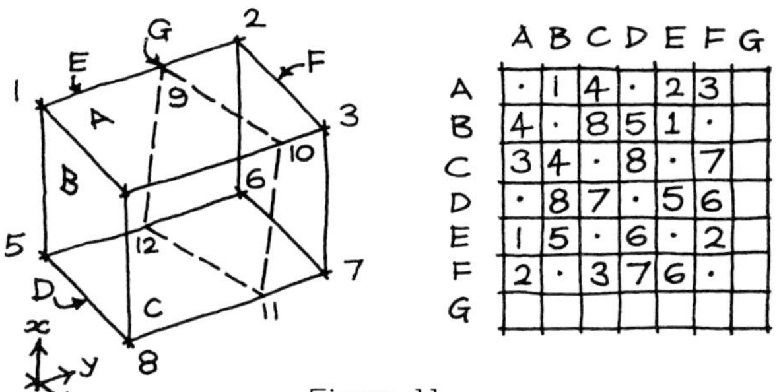

Figure 11

It is a simple task to set up an accurate universe box whose facets are parallel to the axes planes of the coordinate system being used. Facets from a new convex volume can then be created by taking the plane of each of its facets in turn and using it as a cutting plane to cut off a portion of the initial box(19). The principal geometrical operation employed in this task is illustrated in Figure 12 and is the familiar line clipping function which uses the dot product of the coefficients of the cutting plane equation, and the coordinates of the end points of each edge being clipped.

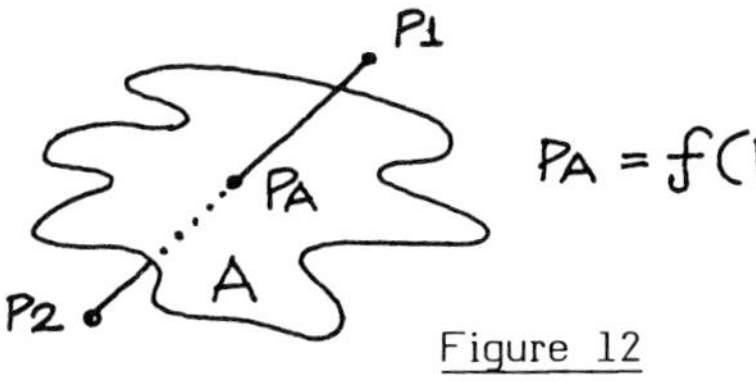

Figure 12

The simplest application of the cutting plane process produces the convex volume which is the intersection of the inside regions of the half spaces defined by the cutting planes. A cutting plane G is illustrated in Figure 11. The first step using G is to test on which side of it each vertex in the universe volume lies. All edges with both vertices inside the cutting plane can be retained, and all edges with both vertices outside the cutting plane can be discarded. Edges crossing the cutting plane must be clipped and the new end points entered into the matrix to replace the ones left out. Once this is done, the entries in the matrix can be completed by using the bookkeeping operation shown in Figure 13.

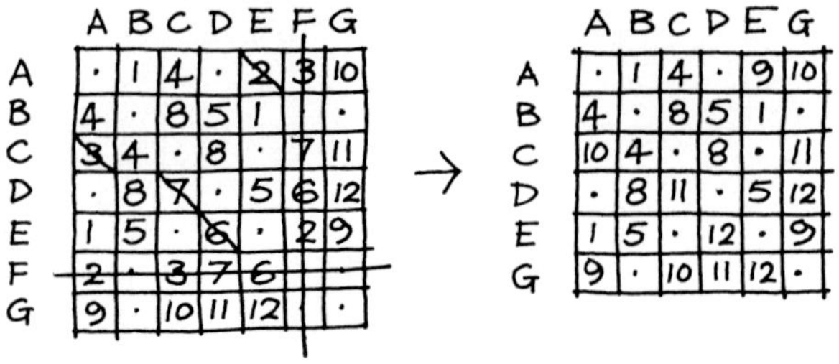

Figure 13

The simplest way of extending this process to create objects with concave surfaces is by overlapping convex volumes, and then creating their volume of union. Figure 14 illustrates the union of two tetrahedra giving the labelling in the exploded view to the right.

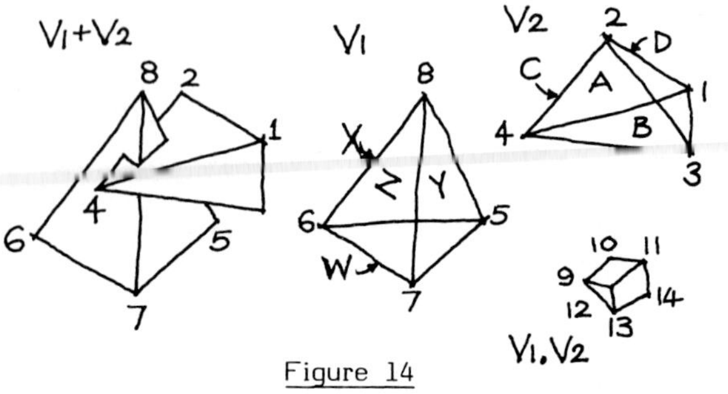

Figure 14

Figure 15 shows the volume matrix representing the figure V1+V2 shown in Figure 14. It also shows a problem if these matrices are implemented using conventional arrays. The assumption that each edge only generates two facet names and two vertex labels is not necessarily true. For example, edge A/C is made up from two line segments 2/10 and 9/4, which if they are to be entered into the matrix means that more than one label must be entered in each matrix cell.

	A	B	C	D	W	X	Y	Z
A	·	1	4+10	2	·	11	12	9
B	4	·	3	1	·	·	·	·
C	2+9	4	·	3	·	10	14	13
D	1	3	2	·	·	·	·	·
W	·	·	·	·	·	5	7	6
X	10	·	14	·	6	·	5+11	8
Y	11	·	13	·	5	8+14	·	7+12
Z	12	·	9	·	7	6	8+13	

Figure 15

Matrix Partitioning

In some cases it is possible to systematically restructure the matrix to remove this naming problem. If each pair of facets referencing multiple edge segments is duplicated, creating new facet names, and the vertex labels redistributed to maintain the correct matrix structure, then the result is a partitioned matrix of the form shown in Figure 16. The duplicated facets in Figure 16 have been given the new names A:I, C:J, X:K, Y:L, Z:M.

		A	B	C	D	W	X	Y	Z	I	J	K	L	M
V1	A	·	1	4	2	·	·	·	·	·	·	·	·	·
	B	4	·	3	1	·	·	·	·	·	·	·	·	·
	C	2	4	·	3	·	·	·	·	·	·	·	·	·
	D	1	3	2	·	·	·	·	·	·	·	·	·	·
V2	W	·	·	·	·	·	5	7	6	·	·	·	·	·
	X	·	·	·	·	6	·	5	8	·	·	·	·	·
	Y	·	·	·	·	5	8	·	7	·	·	·	·	·
	Z	·	·	·	·	7	6	8	·	·	·	·	·	·
	I	·	·	·	·	·	·	·	·	·	10	11	12	9
	J	·	·	·	·	·	·	·	·	9	·	10	14	13
$\overline{V1.V2}$	K	·	·	·	·	·	·	·	·	10	14	·	11	·
	L	·	·	·	·	·	·	·	·	11	13	14	·	12
	M	·	·	·	·	·	·	·	·	12	9	·	13	·

Figure 16

The partitioning of the matrix corresponds to the volume being divided into sub-volumes. An interesting aspect of the example given is the way these sub-volumes are related to the original tetrahedra V1 and V2. The partition regenerates V1 and V2 and also a new volume which is modelled by the transpose of the matrix which would represent the intersection volumes of V1 and V2. If we were to use the two original matrices to represent the union of V1 and V2, simply by adding them together, then intuitively it can be seen that any zone of overlap would be counted twice, and such a model could not therefore be used to calculate the volume of the final figure, or its surface area using conventional methods. This double counting is removed in Figure 16 by including a form of negative volume which represents the zone of overlap.

Implementations of Graph Matrices

These graph matrices can be implemented as standard arrays for small simple volumes. However, if we consider Euler's relationship between the number of edges, facets and vertices of a polyhedron:

$$\underline{n} - \underline{m} + \underline{r} = 2$$

where $\underline{n}$: number of facets, $\underline{m}$: number of edges, and $\underline{r}$: number of vertices; then if the rows and columns of a particular matrix are labelled by the facet names then the array will be $\underline{n} \times \underline{n}$. If we assume that $\underline{n} = \underline{r}$ then $\underline{m} = 2\underline{n} - 2$, and the approximate number of empty cells in the array will be $\underline{n}^2 - 4\underline{n} + 4$. If $\underline{n} = 16$ there will be at least 196 empty cells in the 16 by 16 array. Clearly, implementation as an array becomes grossly inefficient for larger volumes.

An obvious alternative is to implement the matrices as sparse arrays, when the volume in question gets beyond a critical size. If these are implemented as linked lists and a few extra links are included in each cell-record, to make them easier to use, such as two way pointers between diagonally symmetrical cells, then an implementation reminiscent of a winged edge data structure starts to emerge.(3)

A slightly less obvious alternative arises from the way the matrices are used. Consider the union operation. In Figure 14 the first stage is to process all the edges stored as sets of 4 tuples A/B:1/2 using geometrical tests to see whether they need to be modified. The second stage then consists of using the matrix structure to carry out the bookkeeping tasks necessary to complete the new volume description. If only the edges which need to be modified are collected together and their incident facet labels are used to create a workspace array, then in most cases this will be much smaller than the full volume array, but will still be adequate to allow the bookkeeping tasks to be completed. Accessing the new array can be achieved by indirect indexing as shown in Figure 17.

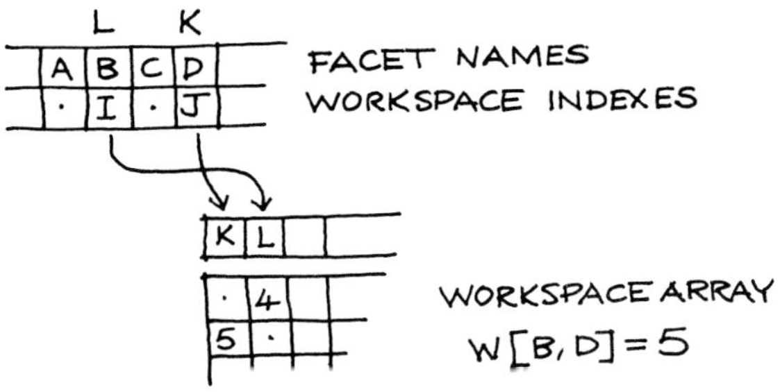

Figure 17

This workspace array could be more efficiently implemented as a list using associative memory, if the host computer provided such a facility. Contents addressable memory would appear to provide the best hardware primitives on which the use of these matrices could be developed.

Boolean Expression Models

In this project, the use of boolean expressions as a geometric modelling structure evolved from the use of graph matrix models.(6) They were used initially as a way of specifying the volume required from overlapping simpler volumes. The extension of the system to allow the cutting plane to be used in the boolean expressions led to their use as an independent model: initially as a powerful language form for entering volume descriptions and later as a way of defining displays. The basic syntax to enter a polyhedron as a boolean expression model will be of the form:

```
<statement> ::=
    NAME, '=',<right name>.
<right name> ::=
    <plane definition>|<boolean expression>.
<plane definition> ::=
    '(', NUMBER, NUMBER, NUMBER, NUMBER, ')'.
<boolean expression> ::=
    <phrase>,'+',<boolean expression>|<phrase>.
<phrase> ::=
    <factor>,'.',<phrase>|<factor>.
<factor> ::=
    <operand>|'!',<operand>.
<operand> ::=
    NAME|'(',<boolean expression>,')'.
```

Applying this boolean expression syntax creates a tree data structure for a particular volume. Although the parse tree generated by syntax analysis is not the ideal form for this tree, it is a fairly simple task to convert the parse tree into a Knuth tree where alternating levels represent boolean product and the boolean summation strings in turn. To achieve this result it is necessary to apply De Morgan's Theorem in the conversion, to change subexpressions of the form !(A+B) into !A.!B, so the expression !(A+B+!C).D + F creates one of the trees in Figure 18.

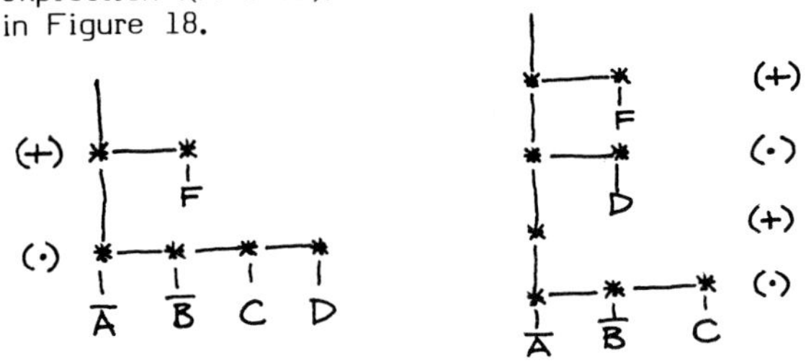

Figure 18

Once this boolean expression data structure has been created, it can be used in a variety of ways. It can, as already suggested, be used to control the creation of graph-matrices. However, to do this it is necessary to define an operation on the boolean expression model, which is made up from overlapping subvolumes, that will generate a new model which is a boundary model more closely related to the graph matrix structure. Consider the triangles shown in Figure 19; if we create a boundary operator β then the edges of the two triangles can be given by the two expressions given below, with their expansions.

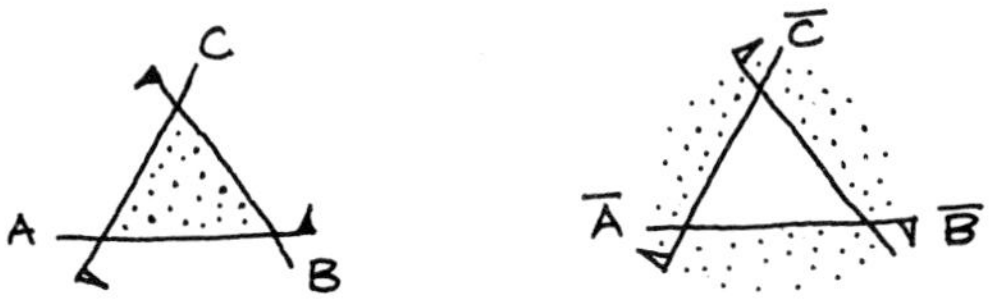

$$\beta(A.B.C) = \beta A.B.C + \beta B.A.C + \beta C.A.B$$
$$\beta(\bar{A}+\bar{B}+\bar{C}) = \beta A.B.C + \beta B.A.C + \beta C.A.B$$

Figure 19

What these expansions do is to take each half space in turn, convert it into a surface and then clip it into a facet by selecting the part which lies within the appropriate boolean function of the remaining half spaces. The same process can be applied to more complex boolean expressions. It is possible to create a graph-matrix representation of the boundary of a convex solid or void using the cutting plane process already outlined. The graph matrix for any volume can be generated using the boundary operator expansion in the way illustrated in Figure 20 for the union of two tetrahedra.

$$\beta(V1 + V2)$$
$$\beta V1 \, . \, \overline{V2} \; + \; \beta V2 \, . \, \overline{V1}$$
$$\begin{bmatrix} A & & & \\ & B & & \\ & & C & \\ & & & D \end{bmatrix} . \overline{W.X.Y.Z} + \begin{bmatrix} W & & & \\ & X & & \\ & & Y & \\ & & & Z \end{bmatrix} . \overline{A.B.C.D}$$

Figure 20

In this case the basic unit for the expansion of the expression is the convex volume made up in the form A.B.C.D or A+B+C+D where A,B,C,D represent plane half spaces. The boundaries of these volumes are created using the cutting plane process, and then the boundary expansion is used to determine which parts of these convex surfaces will be retained in the final volume matrix. The semantic stage of the boolean expression analysis, required to create these matrices, must collect together at each level in the expression tree all the plane half spaces and group then together to give the convex subvolumes used in the cutting plane process in the way shown in Figure 21.

$$A.B.(C+D.G+H).K+L+M$$

$$(\underbrace{L,M}_{W}\,(\underbrace{A,B,K}_{X}\,(\underbrace{C,H}_{Y}\,(\underbrace{D,G}_{Z}))))$$

$$\beta W.[\overline{X.(Y+Z)}]$$
$$\beta X.[\overline{W}.(Y+Z)]$$
$$\beta Y.[\overline{W}.X.\overline{Z}]$$
$$\beta Z.[\overline{W}.\overline{Y}.X]$$

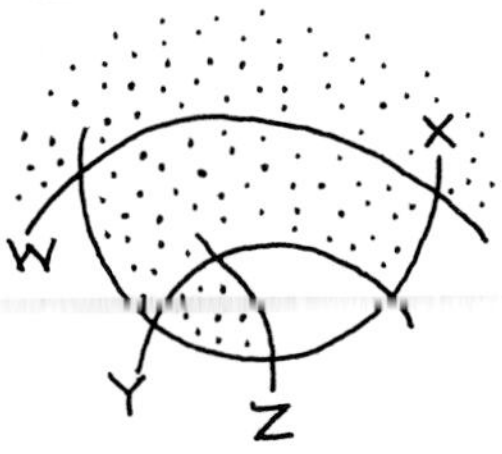

Figure 21

The convex volumes relabelled W,X,Y,Z in Figure 21 can each be converted into a graph-matrix directly, by using cutting planes. The set of edges created in this way can then be clipped using the boundary phrases generated by the boundary-operator expansion; and finally these edges can be entered into a new volume matrix: missing edge segments being filled in by the appropriate bookkeeping operation.

Generating Displays for Interactive Use

Both these forms of model provided a reasonably tractable way of building volume descriptions. However, in both cases when complex volumes were encountered, or when fine editing adjustments needed to be made, it became necessary to provide a display so that the process could be carried out interactively. In the early work this could only be done easily for the edge based models. This was because hidden line or hidden area removal algorithms at the time all seemed to use edge based models.(8,16,17) This restriction biased the initial explorations of volume construction methods towards the approach summarised in Figure 7, since this approach worked directly with edges and vertices and only required one process to create a display. The overlap approach, on the other hand, required two consecutive processes to create a display both computationally intensive.

Edge Based Hidden Line Removal

The hidden line removal problem for edge based models is illustrated in its general form in Figure 22, where the object is constructed from a collection of curved patches.(12)

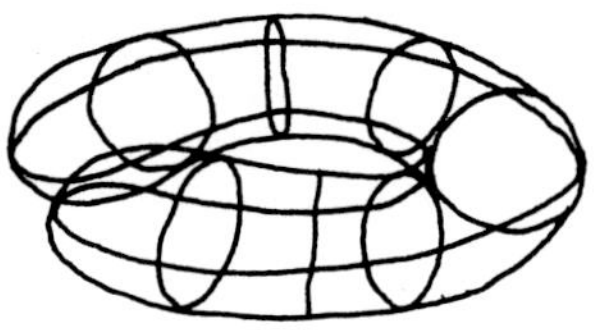

Figure 22

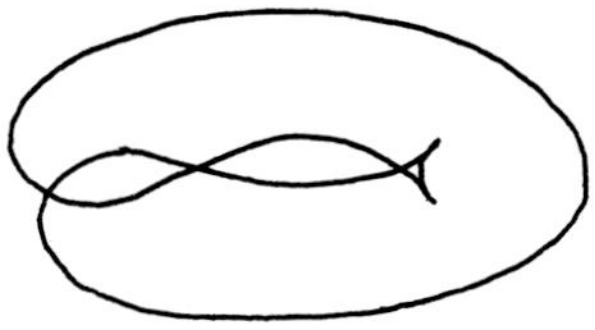

Figure 23

In this diagram the silhouette edges of the object do not exist explicitly as edges in the model of the volume. They have to be derived from the view point position viewing direction and the geometry of the surface patches defining the volume. These new edges can be generated in two stages. First of all the boundary line between front facing surfaces and back facing surfaces can be generated as illustrated in Figure 23 for the object in Figure 22.

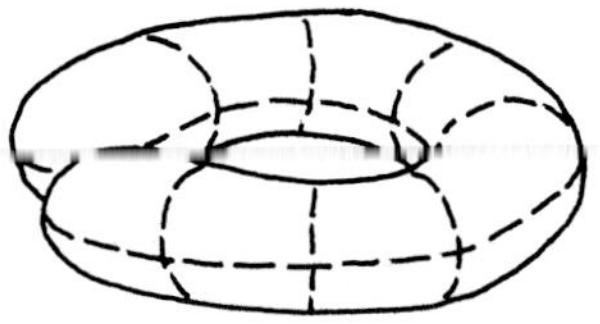

Figure 24

Secondly, once this contour is defined, it can be converted into the boundary of the visible front facing surfaces by simple line crossing overlap test, and the lines which lie on this section of the volume's surface can then be drawn in as shown in Figure 24.

How this general problem is tackled clearly depends on the way that the surface patches are represented. If we restrict the patches to plane facets, then we obtain important simplifications.(9) The silhouette edges of an object can in this case be obtained as a subset of the facet edges which are used to model the volume itself. Processing these edges with other visible edges becomes a problem very similar to a polygon overlay analysis.(13) Unfortunately the best worst-case behaviour of this kind of algorithm is $O(n^2)$ where $\underline{n}$ edges are being processed in an arrangement like that shown in Figure 25.

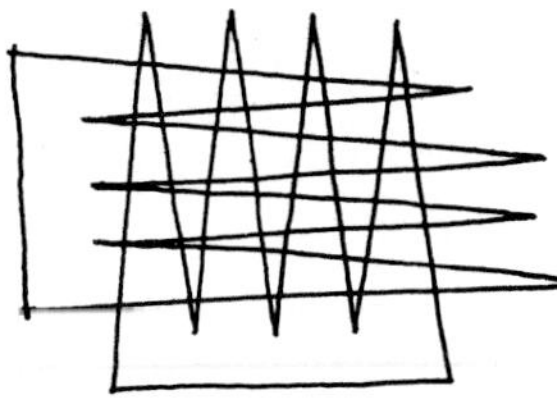

Figure 25

Fortunately, most scenes are built up in a simpler way than this example, and the problem in reality is how to produce an algorithm which will take advantage of the coherent structure of a scene to improve on this worst case behaviour. There seem to be two main, general approaches to carrying out this task. The first is based on a form of binary subdivision, either of the object space or of the display space, and results in a divide and conquer algorithm.(16) The second is based on sorting objects into spatial order, and this generally results in the object or display space being divided into strips.(17) Both these methods were applied successfully to the graph-matrix models, but none of the existing implementations seemed applicable to a boolean expression model based on half spaces.

Ray Casting Algorithms

Once the formal language advantages of the boolean expression models were realised, ways were sought to simplify the display generation process associated with them. Feedback was needed to check input, and it did not have to be very sophisticated to be useful. A model based on surface definitions as the only explicit geometric data needed a different approach, and this approach was provided by ray casting. Ray casting is one of the main geometric constructions of the perspectivist; however, in this context it can be said to emerge from work on display space algorithms. In the display space there is little point in taking the analysis of hidden areas beyond the accuracy that can be displayed by the resolution of the screen. In simple terms this means that it is adequate to follow a single viewing ray from the eye through each pixel position in the display surface and selecting the first surface facet encountered as the visible surface for that pixel position. This approach avoids the need to explicitly define silhouette edges for the general curved patch models, and it also allows illumination effects to be modelled in a direct way.

The ray casting algorithm designed for use with the boolean expression model was a little more complex than selecting the first surface encountered, since the surfaces were infinite in extent, unlike the edge bound facets of the matrix models. Figure 26 illustrates one way in which the front and back surface of a convex object, defined by the intersection of half-spaces can be determined.

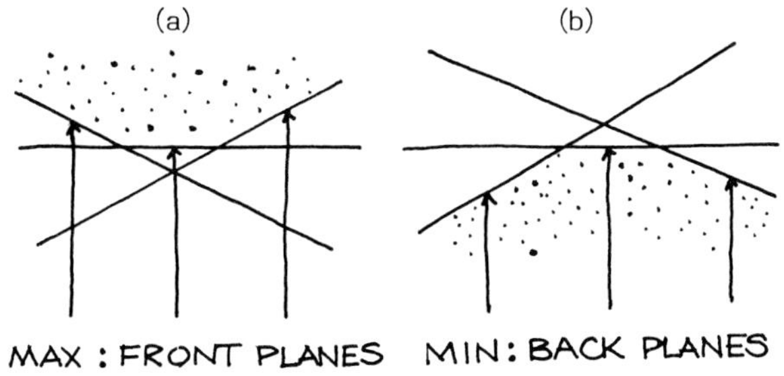

Figure 26

The front surface of the convex object will be defined by taking the front plane which intersects the viewing ray at the greatest distance from the eye, as shown in Figure 26a, while the back surface will be defined by taking the back plane which intersects the viewing ray at the least distance from the eye, as shown in Figure 26b. Clearly these results are conditional on the back surface being behind the front surface, as shown in Figure 27a. In other words, F must be less than B for the object to be defined. If more than one convex object is found along a given viewing ray, then the nearest to the eye will be the visible one, as shown in Figure 27b.

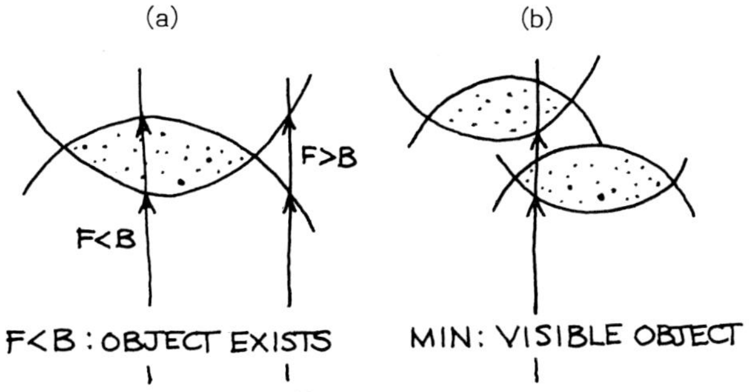

Figure 27

The distance from a plane surface to a display point R along a viewing ray can be calculated in the following way. In Figure 28:

$$\frac{MR}{ME} = \frac{CR}{PE}$$

$$MR.PE = CR.(MR + RE)$$

$$MR = \frac{RE.CR}{(PE-CR)}$$

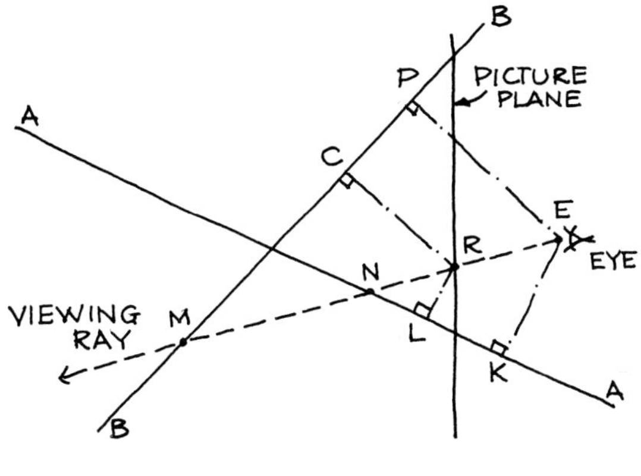

Figure 28

Since for a particular pixel position RE will be a constant for all planes, the distance to plane A can be expressed as the ratio:

$$\frac{L1A}{(L2A-L1A)}$$

where L1A represents the dot product of the coefficients of the plane equation of A and the coordinate of the point R, and L2A represents the corresponding product for the point E. In fact, the display algorithm given above does not require the exact distances to planes, merely the order in which they intersect the viewing ray to be provided. Consequently we can convert the relationship:

$$\frac{L1A}{(L2A-L1A)} < \frac{L1B}{(L2B-L1B)} < \frac{L1C}{(L2C-L1C)}$$

to $$\frac{L1A}{L2A} < \frac{L1B}{L2B} < \frac{L1C}{L2C}$$

which is an important simplification because the value of this ratio lies between 0 and 1. If

$$\frac{L1}{L2} = \frac{A.X1 + B.Y1 + C.Z1 + D}{A.X2 + B.Y2 + C.Z2 + D} = Z \qquad [1]$$

is used to define the display space shown in Figure 29, then we can express the relationship between the object space and the display space by re-arranging [1] to give

$$[A,B,C,D] \cdot \begin{bmatrix} 1, & 0, & -X2, & 0 \\ 0, & 1, & -Y2, & 0 \\ 0, & 0, & -Z2, & Z1 \\ 0, & 0, & -1. & 1 \end{bmatrix} \cdot \begin{bmatrix} X1 \\ Y1 \\ Z \\ 1 \end{bmatrix} = 0$$

where the matrix defines the perspective transformation. Once in this form it is simple to see how this matrix can be concatenated with rotation and translation matrices in the standard way, allowing us to work with a new plane in the display space given by:

$$[A,B,C,D] \quad \begin{bmatrix} E & F & G & H \\ I & J & K & L \\ M & N & O & P \\ Q & R & S & T \end{bmatrix} \rightarrow [A',B',C',D']$$

If the eye is assumed to be at the origin looking along the Z axis in the object space, then distance Z to this transformed plane at X=0 and Y=0 will be -D'/C'. If the display screen is placed parallel to the XY plane with raster lines parallel to the X axis, then if the spacing between pixels is u in the X direction and v in the Y direction, the increments to the value of Z moving from pixel to pixel along a row will be A'.u/C' and along a column B'.v/C'.

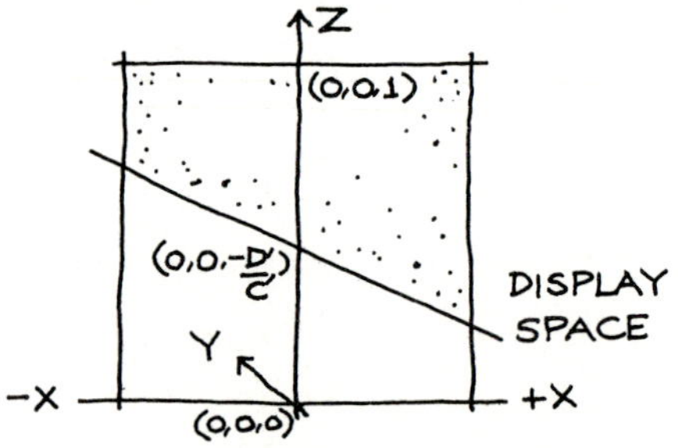

Figure 29

This approach allows us to obtain the distances from any given pixel to all the planes in a scene at a reasonable computational cost. The initial depth values can be calculated at some reference point, say the top left hand corner of the display screen. The depth values for the remaining pixels can then be generated by stepping from one pixel to the next, adding or subtracting the appropriate increment at each step. The only difficulty with this scheme occurs when a plane is perpendicular to the picture plane. In practice it is possible to limit all such planes to a slope represented byan incre ment of 1 in Z moving from one pixel to the next, since steeper slopes could not be displayed. This means all planes can be represented in the same way and the algorithm to process them can be correspondingly simple.

The display file for the reference pixel position consists of a list of the form A.B.C*.D*+E.F* where the names stand for the initial depth values. The list is ordered so that in each product phrase back planes, marked by an asterisk, come after front planes. The boolean operators are associated directly with each following plane to control the display algorithm. At the beginning of the expression list, the first depth value is entered into a temporary storage space. It is then compared with subsequent depth values in the first product phrase. If the depth value of any front plane is greater than it, then they are swapped. If the depth value of any back plane is less than it, then the result is ignored and the process moves on to the next product phrase. When the end of the first product phrase is reached the first temporary depth value is copied to a second temporary storage location. At the end of subsequent product phrases, their first stage depth values will be copied to the second storage space only if they are smaller than the existing stored value. When the end of expression is reached the output from this second storage location will provide the visible surface for that pixel position. Once a plane has been processed in this way its depth value in the list can be incremented to define the surface at the next pixel position, ready for the whole process to be repeated.

Display Hardware

The display algorithm outlined above divides into two stages. The first generates the depth values for planes the second compares and selects the depth values along with associated property data, under the control of the boolean expression structure which defines the scene:

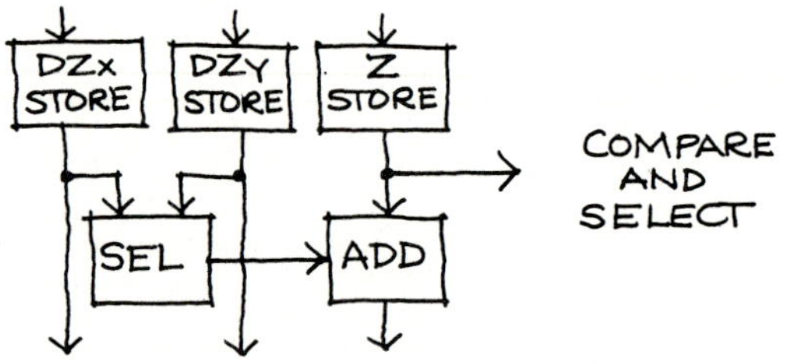

Figure 30

Although this algorithm is computationally intensive, it is extremely simple, and can be implemented directly in low level hardware. More significantly it can be implemented as parallel hardware.

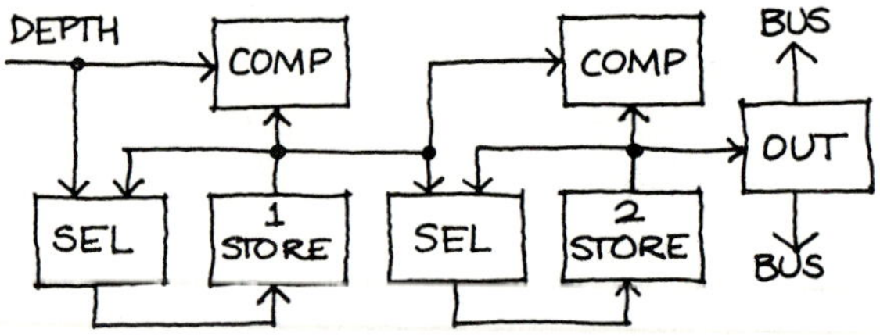

Figure 31

Figures 30, 31 and 32 illustrate the components of a processing unit designed to implement the algorithm. The incrementing unit shown in Figure 30 receives the depth values for the current pixel position and depending on the next pixel position adds to or subtracts from them either the appropriate X

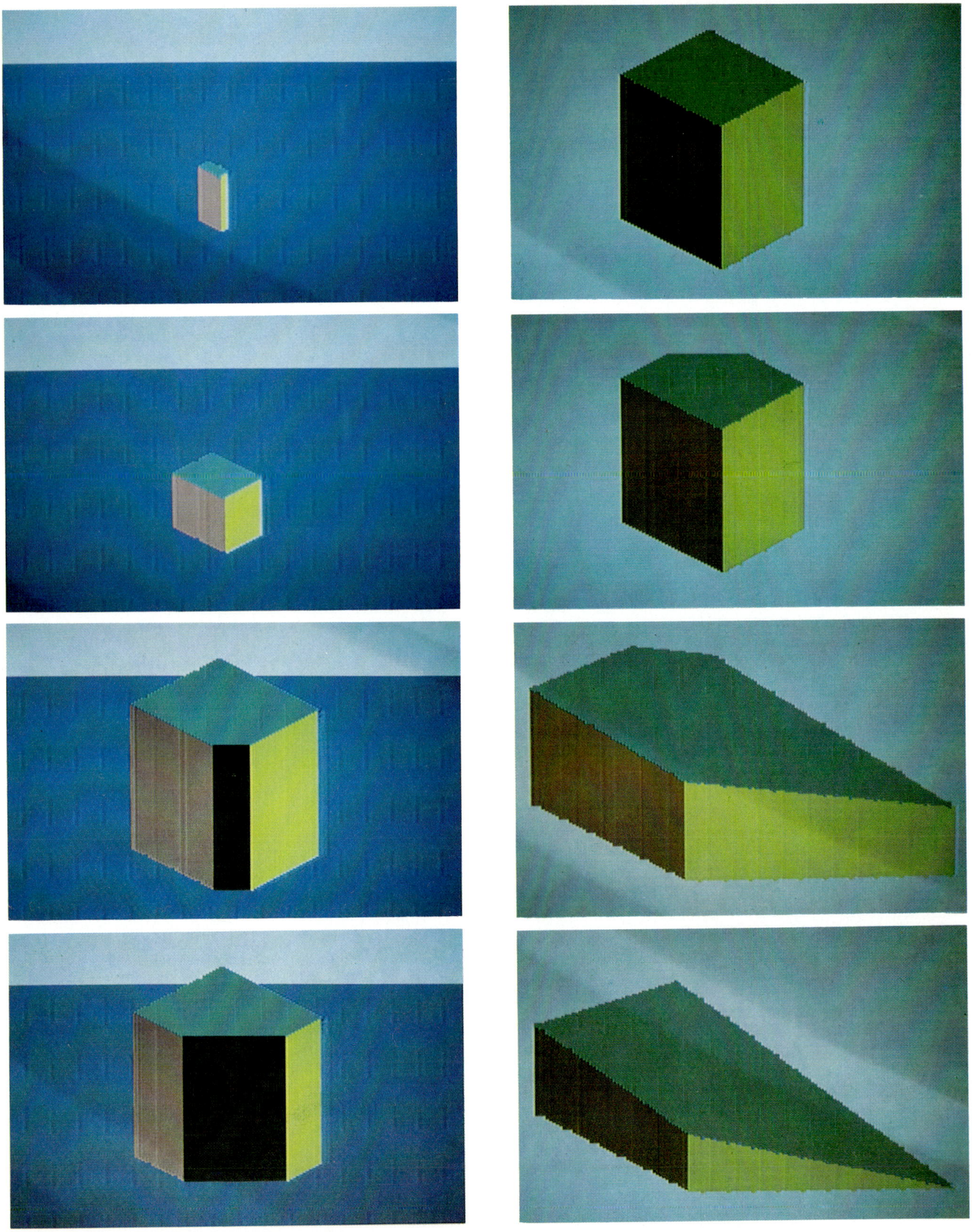

Editing Sequences: Display Surface used as a Cutting Plane, and Surface Rotations and Translations

increments or Y increments. The depth values for the current pixel are passed to the comparison and selection unit shown in Figure 31. This consists of two similar units in sequence. The first extracts product-phrase results; in other words determines whether convex intersection volumes exist at the current pixel position, the second stage selects the nearest convex volume, and in doing so generates a display of the union of product-phrase volumes.

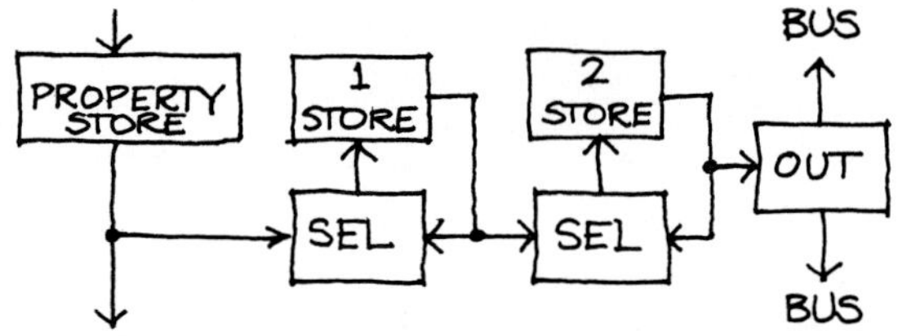

Figure 32

The property data unit in Figure 32 acts as a slave unit that merely selects the property data of the planes selected in the main unit shown in Figure 31. These units are used in parallel to give the pipeline processor shown in Figure 33.

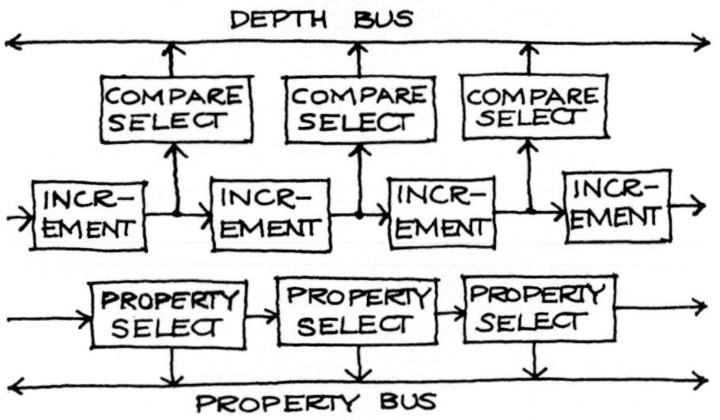

Figure 33

This represents only one of four possible ways in which the basic processing units can be combined in parallel(14), but it is the design with the smallest number of inter processor links and can, in fact, be implemented as an integrated circuit, within the current limits of 64 to 80 pins per IC package.(15) By directing all output onto a bus, the actual number of processors placed on a single IC is not affected by the pin count, so this approach is well set to take advantage of the improvements in the scale of integration promised for the next decade.

The basic display process can successfully create displays from boolean expressions of the form:

$$A.B.C.D + E.F.G.H + \ldots .$$

at video rates, as can be seen from the colour plates, where output is given from an editing sequence using a prototype pipeline processor built in 1977. Displays are generated directly without using a frame buffer.

More complex boolean expression models have to be converted into this form to use the algorithm. In early experiments using a software system, complex object descriptions were created and then automatic algebraic manipulation was employed, similar to that used in the design of combinatorial circuits to give the appropriate form for the display file. The difficulty which emerged from this work was the explosive expansion of the expression which defined volumes with concave surfaces. Consider the objects shown in Figure 34, containing three spheres. Initially the two examples can be modelled by equal-lengthed boolean expressions. If each sphere is the intersection volume of 200 plane facets, then for the second example we will have an expression of the form:

$$(A1.A2.A3\ldots A200).\overline{(B1.B2\ldots B200)}.\overline{(C1\ldots C200)}$$

However, this will multiply out to give:

$$A1.A2\ldots A200.\overline{B1}.\overline{C1} + A1.A2\ldots A200.\overline{B1}.\overline{C2} + \ldots \quad A1.A2\ldots A200.\overline{B200}.\overline{C200}$$

The original string length will be 600 names long, but the expansion will be 8,080,000 names long! This is clearly unacceptable.

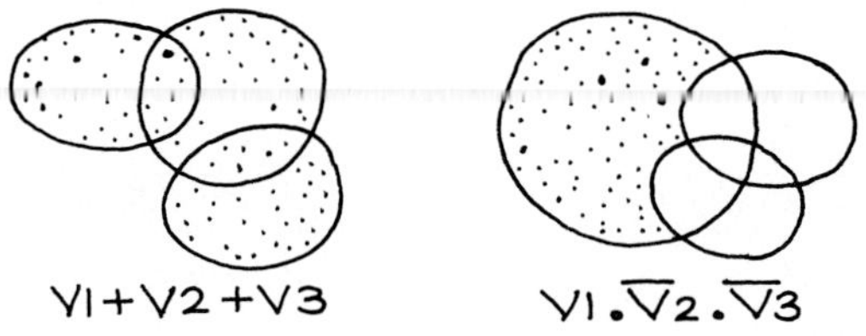

Figure 34

There are three ways in which this problem can be effectively tackled.

1. Build models in ways which specifically avoid a combinatorial explosion.
2. Employ the boundary expansion to obtain single level expressions.
3. Develop a divide and conquer strategy to make use of scene coherence.

A simple way of using the first approach is to start with an edge based model, and convert each facet polygon into a pyramid using some convenient internal point as the apex. This will convert the object into a set of convex volumes which can be used directly with the simple display algorithm described above. The second approach achieves a similar result by manipulating the boolean expression model. In the example in Figure 35 the boundary expansion starts with the convex surfaces A,B,C and D, and then clips them to give the boundary segments B1, B2, B3 and B4. The expanded display string becoming:

$$\beta A.[(\overline{C}+B).\overline{D}] + \beta C.[A.\overline{D}] + \beta B.[A.\overline{D}] + \beta D.[A.(\overline{C}+B)]$$

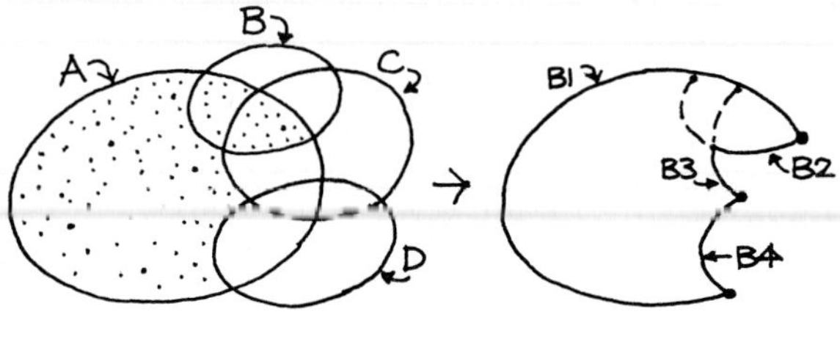

Figure 35

This string can still be processed by the circuit outlined in Figure 31. The boundary surface, for example βA is handled in the same way as a simple convex volume. If it exists at a particular pixel position, then its depth value will be held in the first stage store in Figure 31. This depth value can then be tested against the clipping expression in the square brackets. The clipping expression can be viewed as a set of convex volumes related together in a boolean expression. The depth value will lie inside one of these convex volumes if it is less than the back surface depth value and greater than the front surface depth value of the convex volume. This is a boolean result: inside or outside, which can be combined with other results from the clipping expression for other component convex volumes. If the boundary lies inside the clipping volume, its depth value can be passed to the second stage selection process as before, otherwise it must be discarded. In the example shown in Figure 35, simple expansion gives a string length of 16,080,000 names, but boundary expansion gives a string length of 2,800 names from an original expression of 800 names. This is a major improvement and is achieved without making use of scene coherence.

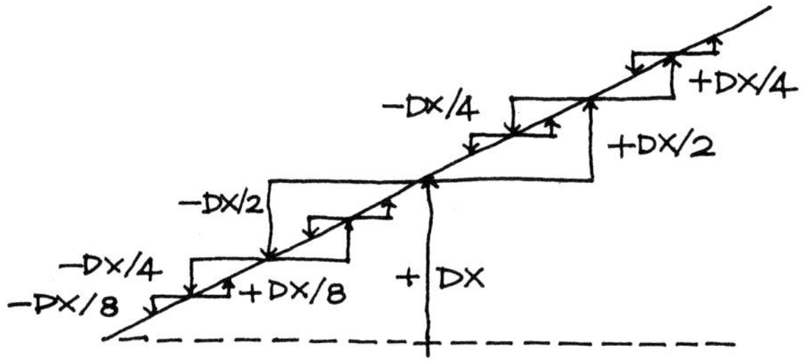

Figure 36

Scene Coherence

The third approach adopts a recursive subdivision of the display screen for the surface based boolean expression model, an approach first employed by Warnock(16) for edge based models. In Figure 36, a recursive incrementing procedure is illustrated for generating plane surfaces. This permits the visibility of a scene to be evaluated at the nodes of a quad-tree in the way shown in Figure 37.

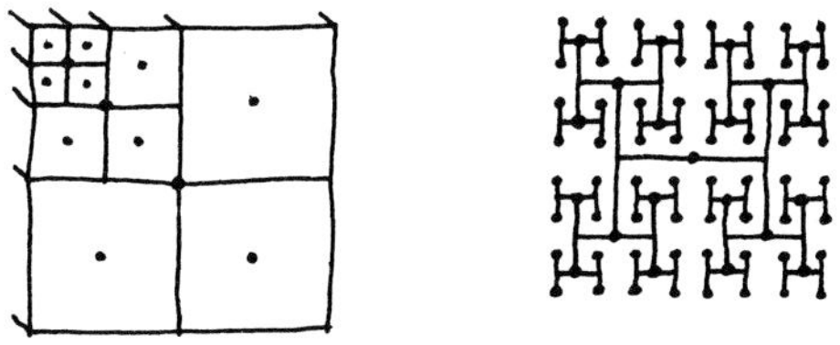

Figure 37

The first step is to establish the visibility of each convex volume in the model. This is done before the expression is expanded because it will be possible to carry out sub-expression pruning; for example, if A were not to be visible in Figure 35, then B, C and D would be irrelevant and could be ignored.(20) The next step is to extend the result obtained for the centre point of a quad to the whole area of the quad. This can be done by geometrically expanding each convex volume in the way illustrated in Figure 38.

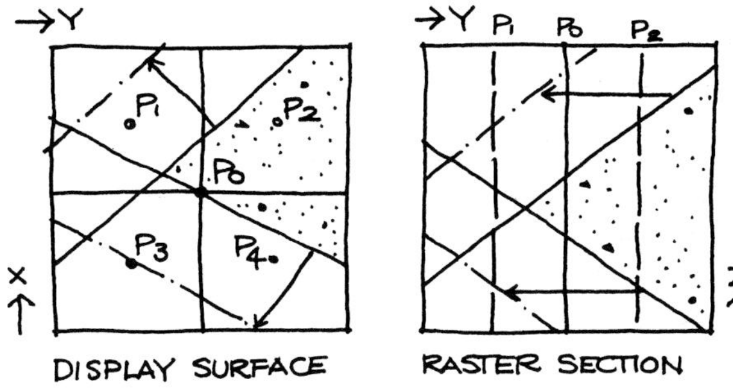

Figure 38

If a volume is expanded by the appropriate function of the quad size, then a point test at the centre of the quad can be used to determine whether the volume exists anywhere else in the quad. The simplest way to implement this volume expansion is to move each plane sideways the appropriate amount. This can be done by an operation on the depth values:

$$Z_E = Z - |dZ_X| - |dZ_Y| \quad \text{front faces}$$
$$Z_E = Z + |dZ_X| + |dZ_Y| \quad \text{back faces}$$

Where the object is round as shown in Figure 39a, this is an adequate approach; where an object has a feathered edge as in Figure 39b, then it may expand too far in a particular direction for efficiency. In such a case the solution is to include vertical and horizontal planes boxing the object, before expansion. This gives a similar result to convolving the object with the quad as shown in Figure 40, which is mathematically the ideal form of expansion.

(a) (b)

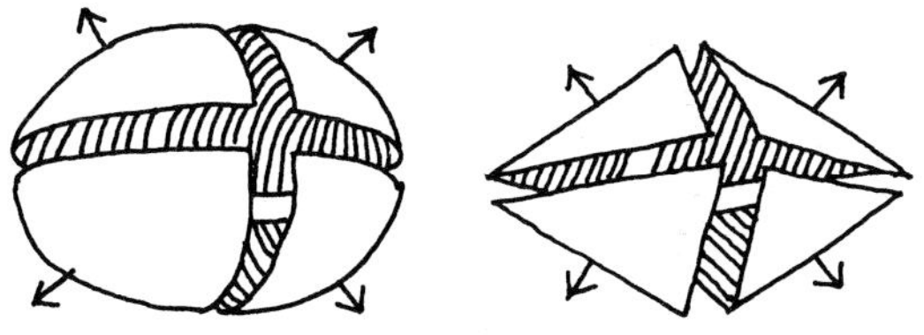

Figure 39

Once an object is found to be invisible, or not to exist in a quad, then its description can be removed from the scene description used for generating the display for that quad. This provides the basic mechanism for the divide and conquer algorithm. The display space is divided into four and the scene display list is reduced into four lists of quarter the original length.

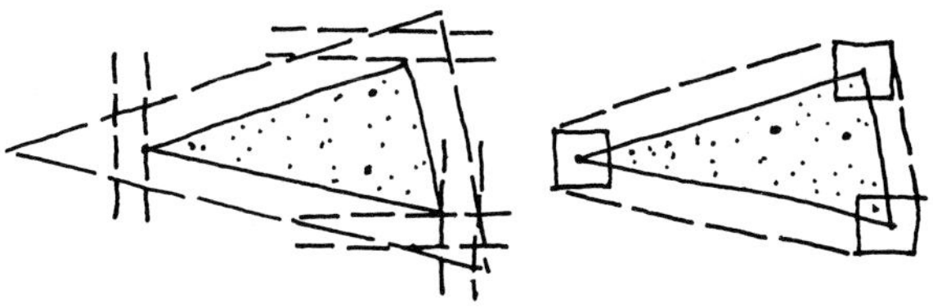

Figure 40

This algorithm can be improved in a variety of ways still under investigation. It is possible to geometrically contract volumes which prove to be visible before expansion. If they remain visible, then the conclusion is that they cover the quad in question, and this can be used to remove objects with greater depth values from the display list for that quad. The most important overall aspect of this approach is its simplicity, and the way it allows display lists to be subdivided to the point where the number of planes in a list is less than or equal to the number of processors in a pipeline of the form shown in Figure 33. This means real-time display of scenes of high complexity will be possible using processors of the layout shown in Figure 41.

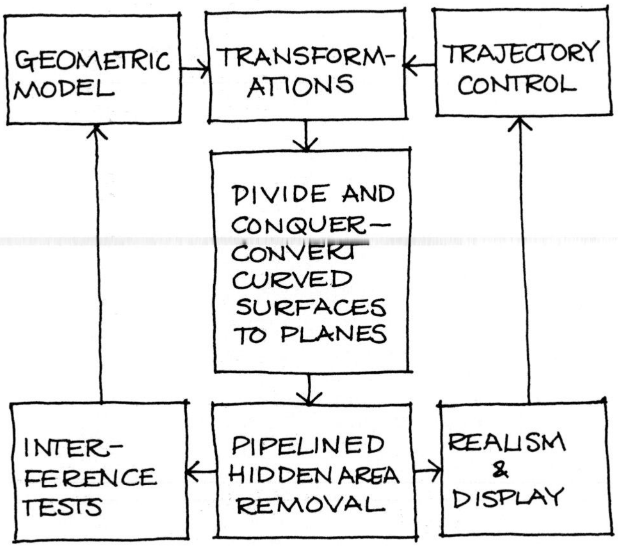

Figure 41

Conclusions

The two main objectives for CAD systems appear to have been achieved. Current work is exploring the way that the boolean expression and matrix based models can be implemented as an extension to an existing high level language, as a specialised data type for geometric modelling and display purposes. If this work is successful it will allow higher level geometric modelling systems to be based on these new language primitives. The hardware developments should lead to small real-time display systems, and because they are based on overlap testing could also find application in future robot systems. This would allow the language extensions to be used in writing control systems which employ spatial information.

Acknowledgements

Discussion with Dr. M. Sabin, Dr. J. Woodwark and Dr. P. Willis on divide and conquer algorithms.
Dr. M.J. Morant, Mr. D. Dwyer, VLSI Development; High Speed Display Processor Research Group, Durham University.
Science Research Council grant number B/RG/90495 to Heriot Watt University Department of Electrical and Electronic Engineering.

References

1. APPELL, A. 'Modelling in Three Dimensions', Interactive Graphics in Data Processing IBM Systems J. 7 No. 3,4 (1968).
2. APPELL, A. 'The Notion of Quantitative Invisibility, and the Machine Rendering of Solids', Proceedings ACM National Conference (1967).
3. BAUMGART, B.G. 'Winged Edge Polyhedron Representation', Stanford University Computer Science Department, Stanford-320 (1972).
4. BAUMGART, B.G. Ph.D. Thesis 1974 Stanford University.
5. BRAID, I.C., HILLYARD, R.C. & STROUD, I.A. 'Stepwise Construction of Polyhedra in Geometric Modelling'. (Ed) Brodlie, K.W. Mathematical Methods in Computer Graphics and Design, Academic Press (1980).
6. COMBA, P.G. 'A Language for Three Dimensional Geometry', Interactive Graphics in Data Processing, IBM Systems J. 7 No. 3,4 (1968).
7. COOK, B.G. 'A Computer Representation of Plane Regional Boundaries', Australian Computer J. (1967).
8. JONES, C. 'A New Approach to the Hidden Line Problem', Computer J. 14, part 3 (August 1971).
9. SUTHERLAND, I.E., SPROULL, R.F. & SHUMACKER, R.A. 'A Characterisation of Ten Hidden Surface Algorithms', Computing Surveys 6, No.1 (March 1974).
10. THOMAS, A.L. The Application of Computer Graphics to Planning. British Council/Latin American Planners Seminar, Dept. of Urban Design and Regional Planning, University of Edinburgh, August 1972.
11. THOMAS, A.L. Two Models for Spatial Information Processing and Display. NATO Advanced Study Institute on Display and Analysis of Spatial Data, University of Nottingham, 1973.
12 THOMAS, A.L. 'Spatial Models in Computer Based Information Systems', Ph.D. Thesis, University of Edinburgh (April 1976).
13. THOMAS, A.L. 'Data Structures for Modelling Polygonal and Polyhedral Objects', First International Advanced Study Symposium on Topological Data Structures for Geographic Information Systems (1977. (Ed.) G. Dutton (Addison Wesley, 1979).
14. THOMAS, A.L. 'Hardware Display Processor, Displays Magazine (IPC Business Press Ltd., October 1979).
15. THOMAS, A.L. 'Micro Display-Processor Components', CAD 80 Conference Proceedings (IPC Science and Technology Press, March 1980).
16. WARNOCK, J.E. 'A Hidden-Surface Algorithm for Computer Generated Pictures', University of Utah, Computer Science Department Report TR4 - 15 (1969).
17. WATKINS, G.S. 'A Real Time Visible Surface Algorithm', Thesis, Computer Science Department, University of Utah. UTECH-CSc-70-101 (June 1970).
18. WAUGH, T.C. & THOMAS, A.L. Geographic Information Management and Mapping System. System Manual, Leyland Systems, Boston, June 1970.
19. WEHRLI, R., SMITH, M.J. & SMITH, E.F. 'The Architect's Computer Graphics AID', Thesis, Computer Science Department, University of Utah. UTECH-Csc-70-102 (June 1970).
20. WOODWARK, J.R. & QUINLAN, K.M. 'The Derivation of Graphics from Volume Models by Recursive Subdivision of the Object Space', Proceedings, Computer Graphics '80 Conference.

PANEL

ARTISTS INTERFACING WITH TECHNOLOGY: BASIC CONCEPTS OF DIGITAL CREATION

CHAIR: Frank Dietrich, West Coast University
PANELISTS: Larry Cuba, independent artist
Darcy Gerbarg, New York University
Andrew Lippman, MIT
Dan Sandin, University of Illinois - Chicago

CHAIRMAN'S INTRODUCTION

Computer art has in its short two decade history undergone significant changes. Initially, only a few scientists started using the expensive machines in their research labs to generate visuals; now computers have become an affordable household item, and accessible to children. The advent of graphic peripherals and programming languages specially designed for artists established the computer as a medium well suited for the creation of visual artwork.

More than just a mechanical device, the computer challenges the technological artist to discover unknown visual territory by finding appropriate concepts of digital creation. The computer is a general purpose machine capable of accomplishing a variety of different tasks. The creative concepts chosen by the artist to define a particular aesthetic strategy remain the most important artistic ingredient, even though the specific configuration of the computer used determines to a certain degree the final visual result.

VISUALIZATION OF ABSTRACT STRUCTURES: Programming is an essential way of controlling digital machines. The artist structures the elements of the visual output in a logical fashion by breaking down the entire process of creation into finite steps. The result is a visualization of the abstract logic involved or a simulation of a geometrically conceived world. The strict determinism of the machine to execute prescribed rules offers the chance to systematically explore the complete set of possible combinations. Chance can be evoked by introduction of automatic randomness or by spontaneous artist-machine interaction.

CONNECTING THE COMPUTER TO REALITY: The possibility of feeding visuals into the machine with an electronic pen or a video camera brought computer technology significantly closer to existing artistic activities. Painters and video artists don't have to give up their traditional expressive forms of creativity in order to gain the additional power of image processing methods unique to the computer. The real world becomes connected to the machine by sensing the brush stroke of the artist or by collecting the video data gathered by the camera.

INTERACTIVE ENVIRONMENTS: Finally, the artist can set up a complex human-machine communication environment inviting the participation of an audience. The work becomes a process of ongoing collective creativity. The artist initially facilitates the communication environment with the computer as an information processor and display device at its core. But the installation only starts generating communication and meaning if activated by the audience.

Further artistic experiments in digital creation will contribute to a higher level of computer literacy and visual communciation within our computerized society.

COMPUTER GRAPHICS AND ART, ed. Grace Hertlein, 5 Vols. 1976-1981

Cuba, Larry. The Rules of the Game, Computer Graphics World, Vol 2 #8, 1979, pp.52-55

Davis, Douglas, Art and the Future, New York: Praeger 1973

Dietrich, Frank/ Molnar, Zsuzsa. Pictures by Funny Numbers, Creative Computing, Vol 7, #6, 1981 pp.102-107

Franke, Herbert W. Computer Graphics - Computer Art. New York: Phaidon 1973

Gerbarg, Darcy. Art Gallery. Computer Graphics World, Vol 4, #7, 1981

Kawaguchi, Yoichiro, Digital Image. Tokyo: ASCII Publishers. 1982

Kranz, Stewart. Science & Technology in the Arts. New York: Van Nostrand - Reinhold, 1974

Leavitt, Ruth, ed. Artist and Computer. New York: Harmony 1976

Lippman, Andrew. Movie-Maps: An Application of the Optical Videodisc to Computer Graphics. Proceedings: SIGGRAPH 80, Seattle, 1980, pp.32-42

______________, Backer, D. Future Interactive Graphics: Personal Video. Proceedings NCGA Conference, Baltimore 1981

Malina, Frank, ed, Visual Art, Mathematics & Computers, Oxford: Pergamon Press 1979

Palyka, Duane. Artistic Reflections on Man-Machine Interfaces. Proceedings: Graphics Interface, Toronto, 1982, pp.291-293.

Reichardt, Jasia. Ed. Cybernetic Serendipity: The Computer and the Arts. New York: Studio International, 1968

Sandin, Dan. Videotape by de Lignieres, Christine/Morton, Phil. Video Data Bank, School of the Art Institute of Chicago, 1981

Small Computers in the Arts: Proceedings: 1st and 2nd Symposium, IEEE, Philadelphia 1981 and 1982

Whitney, John. Digital Harmony. Peterborough: BYTE Books 1980

Wilson, Stephen. Computer Art: Artificial Intelligence and the Arts. Leonardo Vo. 16 #1, 1983, pp.15-20

Youngblood, Gene. Expanded Cinema. New York: Dutton 1970

PANELISTS' ABSTRACTS:

Larry Cuba, Independent Artist

Paralleling the development of the commercial film industry, there is a history of individual artists working within the discipline of the fine arts, creating an alternative film art guided by the aesthetics of music and painting rather than drama. Even before film technology was developed, the founders of abstract art, Kandinsky in particular, invoked musical analogies to describe their artistic goals. Many saw film as a new technology that would make a new art possible, an art that would combine abstract painting and music.

Artists involved in the movements of Futurism in Italy and Cubism in France began making abstract films as early as 1910. Throughout the history of abstract film, artists continually used musical analogies in the titles and descriptions of their work: "Chromatic Music", Colored Rhythm", "Rhythmus 21", and "Diagonal Symphony". They also encountered the many production problems associated with animation. Most returned to painting or turned to live action filmmaking. Some realized that film by itself was not the musical/ visual art technology they had hoped it would be, and that another was needed to produce the countless drawings required. In 1921, Van Doesburg wrote, "...the need for these rigorously precise drawings demand that...these drawings be mechanically produced... When one realizes that 300 drawings are needed for a film "score", one can understand that abstract filmmaking is an area where mechanical means of drawing can render important services."

It has been said that these film artists are like aviation's early pioneers who tried to fly with wings of feather and wax. The graphics computer may be (at last) the flying machine of musical/ visual art, but we have yet to learn how to fly.

Darcy Gerbarg, New York University

My background is painting. I've used many mediums including acrylic, watercolor, gouache, silkscreen, lithography, etching, paper, ceramics, etc. The computer is my favorite. It is closest to my sensibilities. It allows me to create images in an endless variety of ways and constantly challenges me to try new ideas. In a way, making the image on the computer is the easy part. I use highly interactive, user friendly computer graphic paint systems. Because of this, the transition from pigment (paint) to computers is not as great as one might imagine. Instead of mixing a pallet of paint before beginning to paint, I mix light to create a colormap. Colormaps and pallets are very similar. Each contains a specific set of colors. When working with pigment, I would choose brushes to paint with of varying sizes according to my needs. On the computer I create brushes I wish to use; thick ones, thin ones, multicolor ones. There is virtually no delay between the act of creating a picture on a computer and seeing it created. The picture happens in "real" time. If I choose to change a color or remove a line, I can do it easily on a computer. I can work and rework a picture until it is exactly what I want and then have the computer give me a full color slide of that image. The image can also be stored in the computer's memory, manipulated or transformed. The hard part is taking the image off the system and turning it into an art object, i.e., physical reality. Until I have finished art work in some physical medium the image exists only in the memory of the computer or the CRT (TV screen). Many artists are interested in moving pictures, film and video, but I am not. I want my images to hold up over time as all great works of art have from the past. The challenge for me is to develop ways of creating images on computers and then take them and fabricate finished works that can hang on walls, cover floors or ceilings. To date, I have done editions of prints, cibachromes, ceramic tiles, printed fabric, and murals on canvas using my computer images. Each physical medium has its strengths and limitations. Part of the difficulty is determining what medium will enhance a specific image. Finding new ways to take information from the computer system so that the information is in a useable form is another area that requires alot of research. Each time I create a piece it is the culmination of experimentation with many parameters. Of course I remain an artist and keep aesthetic concerns in mind as I work. I am a formalist painter; I paint directly with light, colored light.

Andrew Lippman, MIT

An interesting and perhaps unavoidable corollary of technical innovations is that they are often misunderstood and parochially developed until compelling applications emerge and become directive forces. As an example, electricity was used first to further research in the physical sciences and later as a carrier of power and information. Digital computing is as revolutionary, and only now is it developing in the context of applications; its history is as an arithmetic processor but its future is intertwined with artificial intelligence and signal processing as well. In social terms, it is possible that the impact of the arithmetic revolution may be past, but the impact of the communicative revolution caused by computing is only beginning.

This presentation will concentrate on the emergence of personal computing as a creative and cognitive aid, a communications medium in its own right. In contrast to what is commonly associated with personal computing, the interface rather than the processing power is the critical element. As a personal aid, the communciation with the owner is as critical as the electrical communications. Further, the technical means are available to vastly improve the interface past the simple goal of "user friendliness". This will be illustrated by several examples. Each is an attempt to explore an application from the point of view that the introduction of computing to it can result both in the standard improvements associated with "electronification" and more fundamental change: an electronic map can display cartography on television screens, but it can as well serve as an experimental familiarization tool. More important, however, the examples are indications of a more general system approach to the merger of computing with traditional communications media. They generate directive guidelines for interface and interactive systems design that can, with proper test, be more generally useful.

Illustrations will include the following:

-- The Movie Manual: A personalized electronic book. Optical storage contains the data and images that describe maintenance procedures presented as dynamic "pages" that are generated on-the-fly as needed, and are explorable as part of the reading process.

-- The Electronic Newspaper: An analysis interface to rapidly changing data. The paper analogy is a newsmagazine, personally published, and read associatively, in combination with a growing library from past issues.

-- Scripting by enactment: Full body involvement in the direction of instructions for graphical actors.

Dan Sandin, University of Illinois

What Digital Software/Hardware Designers Can Learn From Analog Sound and Video Instrument Designs

There are two common paradigms used in computer graphic systems: writing programs in a general purpose computer language and menu- driven paint programs. Traditions in analog music and video synthesizer design use different paradigms from analog computation and musical instruments.

Videotapes of analog audio and video synthesizers and the Graphic Symbiosis System will be shown to demonstrate these control structures.

In addition, these paradigms will be applied to a new digital image processing system which is presently under development.

AN INEXPENSIVE SCHEME FOR CALIBRATION OF A COLOUR MONITOR IN TERMS OF CIE STANDARD COORDINATES

William B. Cowan

Optics Section
Division of Physics
National Research Council of Canada
Ottawa, Ontario, Canada.

ABSTRACT

The Commission Internationale d'Eclairage system of colorimetry is a method of measuring colours that has been standardized, and is widely used by industries involved with colour. Knowing the CIE coordinates of a colour allows it to be reproduced easily and exactly in many different media. For this reason graphics installations which utilize colour extensively ought to have the capability of knowing the CIE coordinates of displayed colours, and of displaying colours of given CIE coordinates. Such a capability requires a function which transforms video monitor gun voltages (RGB colour space) into CIE coordinates (XYZ colour space), and vice versa. The function incorporates certain monitor parameters. The purpose of this paper is to demonstrate the form that such a function takes, and to show how the necessary monitor parameters can be measured using little more than a simple light meter. Because space is limited, and because each user is likely to implement the calibration differently, few technical details are given, but principles and methods are discussed in sufficient depth to allow the full use of the system. In addition, several visual checks which can be used for quick verification of the integrity of the calibration are described.

The paper begins with an overview of the CIE system of colorimetry. It continues with a general discussion of transformations from RGB colour space to XYZ colour space, after which a detailed step-by-step procedure for monitor calibration is presented.

KEYWORDS: computer graphics, colour science, colorimetry, colour calibration.

1. Introduction.

Colour graphics applications generally use raster CRT technology for colour generation. Voltages, which are applied to each of the three guns of a colour video monitor, produce distinct levels of excitation in the three phosphors of the monitor, and the consequent light, when it reaches the eye, produces a sensation of colour. The voltages are controlled by digital to analogue converters whose inputs come from application software. Users of the software generally select colours by trial and error. That is, a peripheral device alters the inputs to the D/A and the user alters the colour (using a set of valuators or a pick) while observing the result on the monitor. When he sees the colour he wants he accepts it, and uses it. Now, suppose the same colour is to be retrieved on another occasion.

1. The user may wish to produce exactly the same colour on the same monitor at a later time.
2. He may wish to produce the same colour on another monitor, or an another graphics system.
3. He may wish to produce the same colour in a different medium, e.g. paint, dye, ink.

Each of these proposals raises a different set of problems.

1. It is easy to reproduce the voltages that were applied to the monitor when the colour was initially generated. But, is the colour the same? This amounts to asking how stable the monitor is, and there is no immediate set of units for measuring the stability, and no obvious way to tell how much instability is objectionable.
2. It is easy to reproduce the voltages, and apply them to the second monitor, but not very likely that the colour is the same. How should the voltages be changed to produce the same colour?
3. For colours produced in different media there is no reference to voltages at all.

What is wanted in each case is a visual match. In other words, it should be the case that a "normal" observer, looking at the two colours under appropriate viewing conditions, should see them to be the same. This does not necessarily mean that two sources of photons should have the same spectral distributions; that objective is impossible for most cross monitor and cross medium transfers. Rather, it means that two impressions of colour must be made the same, which involves quantifying the human response to light.

Problems similar to the ones mentioned above have been addressed for many years in industries that utilize colour. They have been solved by devising a method for deciding when two coloured samples will be seen to be the same. This method, which has been standardized by the Commission Internationale d'Eclairage (CIE), is an interface for users of colour. Thus, each particular industry need know only how to measure the CIE coordinates of colours it produces, and how to generate colours of given CIE coordinates. These abilities are used on a day-to-day basis for the standardization, reproduction, and transfer of colours. Clearly, a CIE interface for video display technology solves the three problems mentioned above, and a great many more like them. It also provides a link to colour research and to the many industries that use CIE coordinates. The purpose of this paper is to address these issues by describing the principles whereby a video monitor may be calibrated in terms of CIE coordinates, so that the transfer of colours among monitors and other media may be performed.

2. The CIE System

The basic CIE system has been set up to allow a determination of whether or not two colour samples will be seen to be the same colour. Extensions to it address peripheral problems, e.g. colour differences, brightness of lights differing in hue, etc, which are not of concern to the subject of this paper.

It is based on two concepts: metamerism and additive colour mixture. Metamerism expresses the empirical fact that lights of different spectral composition can be seen to be the same colour. For example, white can be produced by light which has roughly equal numbers of photons at each wavelength, such as sunlight, or by a mixture of relatively narrow-band red green and blue components, such as occurs in a colour monitor. Lights of differing spectral composition that are the same colour are said to be metamerism. We can say that the set of all possible spectral compositions is divided by colour matching into subsets such that all members of any subset are metameric to all other members. Then, the problem of transferring colour across systems amounts to finding on the target system colours that are metameric to those of the source system. Thus, we cannot reproduce the spectral composition of sunlight on a colour monitor, but we can produce its colour by appropriate values of the red green and blue components.

Metamerism is closely linked to additive colour mixture. Additive mixture occurs when two lights coincide spatially and temporally so as to be seen as a single colour. Specifically, the photons from each source add together in stimulating a single area of the visual field. Such mixture occurs in theatre lighting and offset printing. Yellow on a colour video monitor is an example of additive mixture, since red and green phosphors are active in such close proximity that they are mixed additively into a yellow colour. Metamerism is preserved under additive mixture, which means that when additive mixture is performed the resulting colour is independent of whichever of the metameric possibilities are used for the component colours.

Taking metamerism and additive mixture together it is clear that there is a minimal set of primary colours from which any colour can be produced by additive mixture. Furthermore, the method of production, for a given minimal set, is unique. Trichromacy, which is almost certainly related to the existence of three types of photoreceptor, is the statement that the minimal set has exactly three members for observers with normal colour vision. Thus, for a given set of three primaries there is a unique way to specify each colour, which is the same for all spectral distributions that match the colour, and is different for all that do not. The CIE is responsible for specifying a standard set of primaries, which allows common use of the system. The ones in most common use are the (XYZ) set of primaries, standardized in 1931. Using them, a colour is specified by a triplet of positive numbers, known as tristimulus values, which are defined in terms of the spectral power, $P(\lambda)$.

$$X = \int P(\lambda)\bar{x}_\lambda d\lambda$$

$$Y = \int P(\lambda)\bar{y}_\lambda d\lambda$$

$$Z = \int P(\lambda)\bar{z}_\lambda d\lambda$$

The functions x_λ, y_λ, and z_λ are the colour matching functions. They are defined in terms of empirical data, and tabulated, among other places, in [8], where a much fuller account of these matters is presented. For our present purposes, however, all we must know is how to determine X, Y, and Z for colours on a colour video monitor, and how, given X, Y, and Z, to display the colour they signify.

The colour systems in common use in colour graphics are easily related to XYZ space. All utilize the same metamerism relations as XYZ. Some are linear, as is the XYZ space. (Linearity means that when two lights are mixed additively their sum is at the colour space point which is the vector sum of points corresponding to the two component lights.) Three examples are RGB, YIQ, and $CIELuv$. Others are non-linear, such as Munsell, HSV, and $CIELab$. [6] shows how to convert HSV and YIQ to RGB; [8] how to convert $CIELuv$, Munsell, $CIELab$, and many other systems to XYZ; sections 4 to 9, below, will show how to interconvert RGB and XYZ.

3. Calibration Generalities

A video monitor is calibrated if we know the functions

$$X = f_X(v_R, v_G, v_B)$$

$$Y = f_Y(v_R, v_G, v_B)$$

$$Z = f_Z(v_R, v_G, v_B)$$

which give the tristimulus values X, Y, and Z of the colour produced in terms of the voltages v_R, v_G, and v_B applied to the three guns of the monitor. (We depart somewhat from common usage, using v_R, v_G, v_B for the gun voltages; E_R, E_G, E_B (below) for the excitation of the phosphors. R, G, B

are sometimes used to represent the voltages; more often they are the excitations. The latter sense is used in defining the *RGB* colour system, as in [6] or [5]. The present notation is used to remove any ambiguity.) These functions, and their inverses, can be implemented in software to transform voltages to tristimulus values, and vice versa. Such an implementation calibrates the monitor.

There is a brute force solution to this problem, using a spectrophotometer to measure the spectral power of the emitted light. It is straight-forward to sample exhaustively the voltage space, calculating X, Y, and Z for each sample. The results can be used as a calibration, either in parametrized functional form, or as an interpolated table. This approach is unsatisfactory for several reasons:

1. Spectrophotometers adequate for this task are quite expensive.
2. Because many phosphors have narrow spectral lines, $P(\lambda)$ must be measured at 1-2 nanometer intervals, so that the spectral scan is very time-consuming.
3. The main reason for using this method would be its potential accuracy (better than 1%), but our experience suggests that colour monitors are insufficiently stable to warrant this precision, especially when the time needed to make a complete calibration (many hours) is considered. It is not likely, on the basis of monitors we have examined, that the monitor has the same calibration function (to the degree of precision of which spectrophotometry is capable) at the end of the calibration as it did while the calibration was in progress.

An approach which is probably better than the brute force method for most cases breaks determination of the calibration functions into several stages. Most of the stages can be done without needing spectrophotometry (i.e. inexpensively), and those that do need it often have the necessary spectrophotometric data available from the monitor manufacturer or some other source. These features (phosphor chromaticities) are among the most stable of monitor properties, so that there is likely to be no need for spectrophotometry. Furthermore, the calibration stages admit of quick visual checks, which can be programmed into the system that drives the monitor. Through them the calibration can be checked each time the monitor is used, giving confidence that the calibration is accurate, and minimizing the need for recalibration.

4. Preliminaries

Before a monitor is calibrated it should be set up exactly as it will be when in use. This includes:

1. Its position in the laboratory, since moving or rotating a monitor can change its calibration.
2. Purity and convergence adjustment.
3. Adjustment of picture size, brightness, contrast, relative gains of the three guns, etc. These quantities can be adjusted in a way that minimizes the measurement needed for calibration. It seems preferable, however, to adjust them so that the picture is best for the application, then to calibrate that setting of the monitor.

This paper assumes that the monitor is set up to suit the application and then calibrated, since the measurements needed for the general case are only slightly more complicated than for any particular case.

5. Phosphor Chromaticities

When phosphor a ($a = R, G, or\ B$) of a colour monitor is excited it emits light of relative spectral power $p_a(\lambda)$, which is independent of the level of excitation. Thus, if $E_a(v_R,v_G,v_B)$ is a variable representing the degree of excitation of phosphor a, which can, in general, depend on all three voltages, the light output from the monitor is

$$P(\lambda) = \sum_a E_a(v_R,v_G,v_B)p_a(\lambda).$$

To find out the colour of this light calculate its tristimulus values

$$X = \sum_a E_a(v_R,v_G,v_B)\int \bar{x}_\lambda p_a(\lambda)d\lambda$$

$$= \sum_a x_a E_a(v_R,v_G,v_B)$$

$$Y = \sum_a y_a E_a(v_R,v_G,v_B)$$

$$Z = \sum_a z_a E_a(v_R,v_G,v_B)$$

The quantities

$$x_a = \int \bar{x}_\lambda p_a(\lambda)d\lambda$$

$$y_a = \int \bar{y}_\lambda p_a(\lambda)d\lambda$$

$$z_a = \int \bar{z}_\lambda p_a(\lambda)d\lambda$$

are known as the chromaticity coordinates of phosphor a. They are normalized so that

$$x_a + y_a + z_a = 1$$

with any normalizing factor absorbed into $E_a(v_R,v_G,v_B)$. (The above equations are a generalization of equation (3) of [5].)

Thus, it is necessary to find the chromaticities of the three phosphors. There are several methods, listed here from worst to best.

1. Do **not** use the standard P22 chromaticities, since many monitors have phosphors that do not match the P22 chromaticities.
2. Measure the phosphors with a tristimulus colorimeter. Such an instrument uses a filter/photodector combination that mimics the spectral response of the colour matching functions: x_λ, y_λ, and z_λ. Although the meter does not precisely reproduce the desired functions, the error is not serious for measuring broad band spectral distributions, such as occur in natural objects, pigments, etc. It is more of a problem when measuring samples with narrow spectral bands, such as monitor phosphors. If this method is used, it should agree with some other one, probably 3.
3. Use chromaticities supplied by the manufacturer. These are presumably the result of a spectropho-

tometric measurement, though not of the exact tube to be calibrated. There is not much variation from tube to tube, but one must be confident that convergence and purity are good to use this method. Be sure that the manufacturer is not specifying "nominal" chromaticities.

4. Have a friend who has done method 5. on a monitor with the same tube.
5. Make a spectrophotometric measurement of the phosphors. This method is best, catching narrow spectral lines, misconvergence, and lack of purity. It should be done at 1-2 nanometer intervals, and checked against 3. or 4. for best results.

As long as the purity and convergence remain well adjusted, it is not necessary to redetermine phosphor chromaticities when the preliminary adjustments of section 4 are redone.

6. Phosphor Excitations

In general, the excitation of phosphor a depends on the voltages of all three guns. Thus, we have written $E_a(v_R,v_G,v_B)$. It is possible, but unduly complicated, to calibrate such a monitor using only a simple light meter. (The details may be found in [4].) The purpose, however, of convergence and purity adjustments is to make phosphor a excited only by gun a, and we can assume that this condition, which is called gun-independence, is fulfilled for all well-adjusted monitors. When gun- independence, which is expressed as

$$E_a(v_R,v_G,v_B) \equiv E_a(v_a)$$

is true, the relationship of phosphor excitation to gun voltage is known as gamma correction. We must remember, however, that it holds only for a range of gun voltages, albeit a wide one. The range varies from monitor to monitor, and must be determined empirically. Outside it the calibration is not valid.

7. Gamma Correction

Gamma correction can be done using any light meter whose output is linear with the number of input photons. The meter's spectral sensitivity need not be known. A photodiode, or a hand-held luminance meter is ideal for this measurement. To make it, split the phosphor excitation function into two factors

$$E_a(v_a) = N_a e_a(v_a)$$

where $e_a(v_a)$, the relative excitation function, gives the voltage dependence, and N_a, the phosphor-gun normalizing factor, is determined by how the three guns have been balanced. Normalize $e_a(v_a)$ so that

$$e_a(v_{amax}) = 1$$

with v_{amax} at the top of the gun independent range.

Now, when gun a only is turned on to voltage v_a the meter reads

$$R(v_a) = N_a e_a(v_a) \int F(\lambda) p_a(\lambda) d\lambda$$

where $F(\lambda)$ is its unknown spectral sensitivity. From the readings we get the three excitation functions

$$e_a(v_a) = \frac{R(v_a)}{R(v_{amax})}$$

These functions can be stored for table look-up [3], or maintained in parametrized form.

Gun-independence should be confirmed by measuring these functions with the other guns having various values within the gun-independent range. For such measurements

$$R(v_a) = N_a e_a(v_a) \int F(\lambda) p_a(\lambda) d\lambda + \sum_{a \neq b} N_b e_b(v_b) \int F(\lambda) p_b(\lambda) d\lambda$$

and

$$e_a(v_a) = \frac{R(v_a) - R(0)}{R(v_{amax}) - R(0)}$$

If gun-independence holds the same function will appear in each case. These functions should be checked fairly frequently.

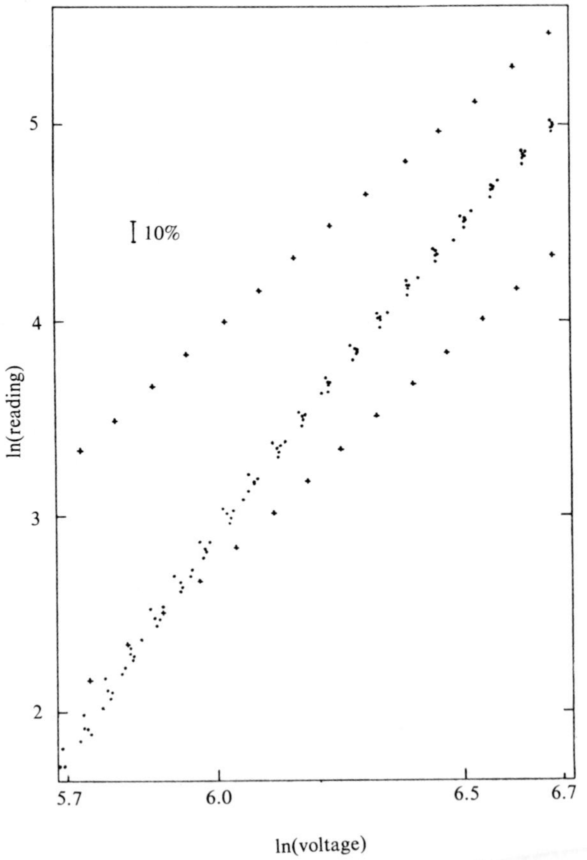

Figure 1. Natural logarithm of meter reading, plotted as a function of the natural logarithm of driving voltage for the red gun. The main curve (•) has various field rates, various blue and green gun voltages, and was measured on various days. The other curves (✦) were produced at two settings of the contrast, with brightness set to make the curve a straight line.

Regarding parametrized forms, let us examine some measurements performed on one of our video monitors, a 13", high-resolution (512 x 720), in-line gun unit. Figure 1 shows the light-meter output as the voltage delivered to the red gun is varied. In figure 1, the main curve represents the results of many runs, made on several days. Brightness and contrast settings of the monitor were held constant at randomly chosen values for all these runs. Observe the following:

1. The monitor has day-to-day drift the order of a few percent. To that accuracy a calibration can be made and used for several days (until some visual test, such as those described below, shows it to be varying). It is hopeless to try to calibrate it to better accuracy.
2. The field rate and the green and blue voltages varied from run to run, but the curve didn't shift. The guns are indeed independent, and, within the range tested, the calibration did not depend on field rate.
3. The points do not lie on a straight line, so that the frequently-quoted parametric expression

$$e_a(v_a) = (v_a / v_{amax})^{\gamma_a}$$

(see, for example, [5]) does not fit them well. In fact, such an expression, depending on the part of the curve from which γ_a is derived, makes errors up to 100%, which can, for example, change unsaturated red to unsaturated blue.

4. $e_a(v_a)$ is well fit by the two parameter expression

$$ln(e_a(v_a)) = A_a ln(v_a / v_{amax}) + B_a (ln(v_a / v_{amax}))^2$$

5. The slope (γ) of the fit ranges between 2.75 at the highest values of gun voltage and 4.0 at the lowest values. This range is well above the often-quoted value of 2.5.

The two other sets of points are produced by altering the brightness control to a point where the $ln - ln$ plot is a straight line and taking two different settings for contrast. At this setting gamma correction is appropriate, with γ at 2.33. However, when we examine all three guns at this brightness setting (figure 2) we see that the blue gun requires a two parameter fit, and the green gun's γ ranges between 2.33 and 2.44. This suggests that using the simple exponent law is not reasonable, even in this case. We think that the best strategy is to find brightness and contrast settings which suit the application, then to use a light meter to find an appropriate parametrized form and to set the parameters. In most cases the two parameter form (above) will work adequately.

It is important to check periodically whether the calibration parameters continue to be correct. This can be done by eye, without needing a meter. Display two patterns in such a way that they are additively mixed, either by temporal succession (e.g. the two patterns alternate so fast that they are fused into one) or by spatial contiguity (e.g. the two patterns are mixed together spatially - dithered - so that any discriminable visual area contains elements of both patterns). Then the meter reading at any point will be

$$R(v_{1a}, v_{2a}) = N_a [e_a(v_{1a}) + e_a(v_{2a})] \times \int F(\lambda) p_a(\lambda) d\lambda$$

where v_{1a} (v_{2a}) is the voltage applied at that point in pattern 1 (2). Different areas of the patterns will sum to the same reading only if those areas have the same sums $e_a(v_{1a}) + e_a(v_{2a})$. Thus, we can set up two patterns, each comprising many areas, such that the sum of the two patterns is the same in every area if the relative excitation function is right. Such a pattern is, of course, visually homogeneous, so that by displaying it on the monitor we have a quick **visual** check that this part of the calibration is correct. Only when inhomogeneities can be seen need a meter be used to recalculate the parameters. Such a visual check, which requires only a minute or two, should be performed frequently for each gun, and with more than one gun turned on to ensure gun independence.

Visual parameter setting can also be done, using patterns like those described above, and adjusting parameters until the disply is homogeneous. It is not as precise, however, as using a meter, and it is **very** important to use a meter at least once to to establish the right parametric form for a particular monitor.

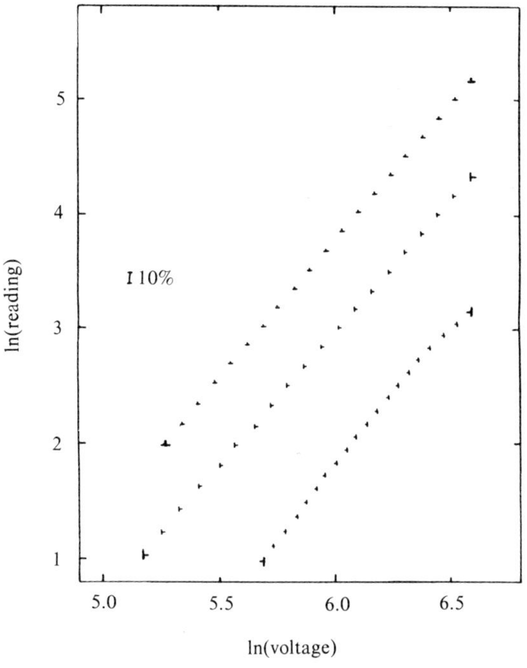

Figure 2. Natural logarithm of meter reading, plotted as a function of the natural logarithm of driving voltage for all three guns. Brightness is set to make the red gun curve (⊢) a straight line, but green (⊥) and blue (⊣) gun curves are not.

8. Gun Normalization

To complete the calibration we must find the phosphor-gun normalizing factors. If a colour sample with known tristimulus values is available, this process is straightforward. Adjust the gun voltages until the screen matches the sample. Then

$$X = \sum_a N_a x_a e_a(v_a)$$

$$Y = \sum_a N_a y_a e_a(v_a)$$

$$Z = \sum_a N_a z_a e_a(v_a)$$

and the three normalizing factors can be found directly. This might be done using a standard TV colour comparator. Alternatively, if a spectrophotometer is available, measure the tristimulus values corresponding to a set of gun voltages and solve the above equations. It is essential to match or measure several different values to test the consistency of the calibration.

The above procedure, if it can be performed, completes the calibration; the remainder of this section is not necessary. Otherwise, separate the phosphor-gun normalizing factors into relative normalizing factors, n_a, and a single overall normalizing factor, N. That is

$$N_a = N n_a$$

and arbitrarily set $\sum n_a = 1$. Now, if we have a colour sample of known chromaticity, (x,y), we can adjust the gun voltages until the screen matches it. Then

$$x = \frac{\sum_a n_a x_a e_a(v_a)}{\sum_a n_a e_a(v_a)}$$

$$y = \frac{\sum_a n_a y_a e_a(v_a)}{\sum_a n_a e_a(v_a)}$$

from which the values of n_a can be calculated.

Alternatively, we can use a technique whereby two different colours are made equal on a single tristimulus value. Suppose the value to be Y. Adjust the red gun voltage, v_R, in one area and the green gun voltage, v_G, in another until the two areas have equal Y values. For these voltages

$$n_R y_R e_R(v_R) = n_G y_G e_G(v_G)$$

which determines the ratio n_R/n_G. Repeat this process using the blue gun and the ensuing ratios, together with the condition $\sum n_a = 1$, give the relative normalizing factors.

There are visual techniques for making two colours equal on the Y tristimulus value. One is heterochromatic flicker [8]. If two colours are alternated temporally at about 20 Hz (25 msec of one followed by 25 msec of the other) there is a visual impression of flicker. As the overall level of one is varied there is a point at which the impression of flicker is a minimum. There the two colours have the same Y value. A similar technique is called minimally distinct border [7]. When two colours adjoin one another there is a border (edge) produced by the difference between them. If the level of one is adjusted until the border is minimally distinct, the two colours have the same Y value. Other techniques (e.g. [1]) exist as well.

Non-visual techniques also exist. Spectrophotometry is a possibility, or a luminance meter may be used. Unfortunately, the former is too expensive, and the latter too imprecise. They can be combined in a useful way by using the spectrophometer to calibrate the luminance meter when spectrophotometry is being done. Remember that any calibration is specific to a particular set of phosphors.

To sum up, the non-visual techniques for gun normalization, matching or using a meter, are best. Visual techniques are less accurate. However, because they are easy to set up, and quick to do, they are ideal as a check to ensure that a monitor has not drifted seriously out of calibration.

9. Overall Normalization

If a chromaticity match or a visual match is used for the phosphor-gun normalizing factor, there is an overall normalizing factor, N, which remains undetermined. Accurate determination of this factor is, in fact, not too important, since error in its determination changes only the overall luminance of all colours in the scene. The eye is not very sensitive to such changes, so that errors of 50% or so are quite tolerable. By contrast, errors in the determination of relative normalization factors are quite noticeable, since they alter hue and saturation.

Because high precision is not important here, it is quite adequate to set up a white colour and measure it with an inexpensive luminance meter, or to match a not very well known white luminance by varying voltages to the screen. Either method determines N to a precision adequate for practical purposes.

10. Discussion

Sections 4 to 9 suffice to completely calibrate a monitor in terms of CIE coordinates. Thus, if the voltages producing a colour are known, its CIE tristimulus values are

$$X = N\sum_a n_a x_a e_a(v_a)$$

$$Y = N\sum_a n_a y_a e_a(v_a)$$

$$Z = N\sum_a n_a z_a e_a(v_a)$$

with

$$ln(e_a(v_a)) = A_a ln(v_a/v_{amax}) + B_a(ln(v_a/v_{amax}))^2$$

The inverse transformation, which determines the voltages needed to produce given tristimulus values, requires the inverse of matrix M.

$$M = \begin{pmatrix} x_R & x_G & x_B \\ y_R & y_G & y_B \\ z_R & z_G & z_B \end{pmatrix}$$

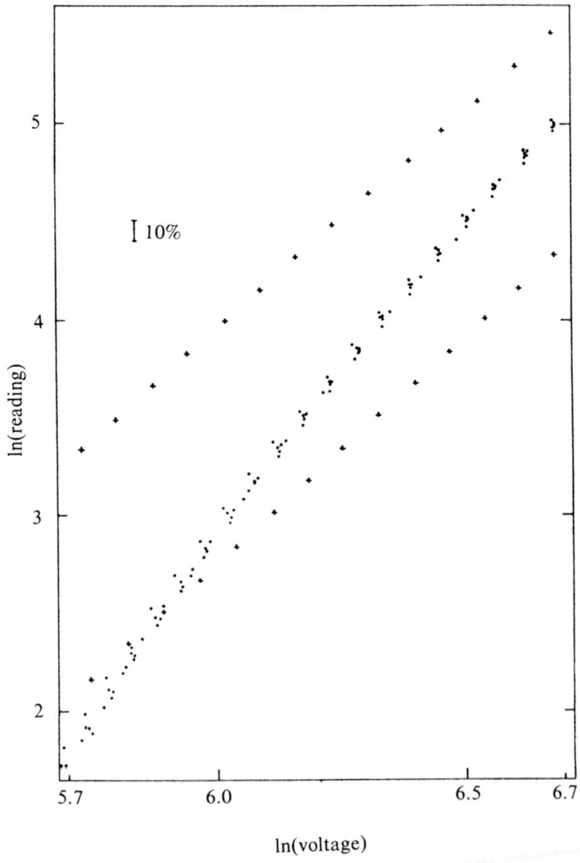

Using the inverse of M,

$$\begin{pmatrix} n_R e_R \\ n_G e_G \\ n_B e_B \end{pmatrix} = \frac{1}{N}(M^{-1})\begin{pmatrix} X \\ Y \\ Z \end{pmatrix}$$

and the voltages are given by

$$v_a = v_{amax} exp[ln(e_a)/(A_a + B_a ln(e_a)/ (A_a + B_a ln(e_a)/(A_a + ...)))]$$

The continued fraction form for the solution of a quadratic equation is most convenient computationally.

In the preceding we have not discussed the consequences of calibration error. Clearly, some types of mis-calibration are more objectionable than others, but the subject of how observers respond to overall distortions of colour space is very complicated. Although a large literature exists (see [2] for references), little is understood. One rule of thumb is probably worth remembering. Miscalculating the gamma correction function on a single gun means that, although chromaticities are true at the gun voltage where the gun balance is done, they vary, with respect to the true chromaticity, as the gun voltage varies. Such discrepancies are, in most cases, more objectionable than an error of similar size in the gun balance, for such an error produces a shift of chromaticities which doesn't vary with level. Least objectionable of all, as mentioned above, is an error which gets chromaticities right but shifts the overall level.

In this connection, let us consider the usual method of balancing a broadcast monitor. Briefly, the electronics of the monitor are tuned so that white is produced whenever all three guns are driven equally. This procedure produces the same gamma correction for each gun, and then uses adjustment by eye to generate a natural range of colours around white. It works well for realistic scenes, which have a wide and predictable range of chromaticities. In these cases the viewer's colour intuition works well, and there is an adequate variety of colour for his eye to sample. Similar methods, used to balance the colour in printing or photography, produce reproductions which, although they may not be close colour matches to the original monitor colours, seem to catch the important colour relations. Unfortunately, the conditions that make these intuitive procedures possible are often not met in computer-generated images. Thus, it is necessary to go through a calibration procedure like the one described in this paper.

Length constraints have prohibited much discussion of the practical details of calibration: actual instrumentation, exact procedures for visual tests, actual monitor properties, etc. These matters are discussed in a National Research Council of Canada technical report [4] which will be available from the author.

11. Acknowledgements

The author wishes to thank Peter Tanner for his encouragement, and for helping to find references, G. Wyszecki for general advice on calibration, and the anonymous reviewers, whose comments materially improved the paper. He also wishes to thank the Computer Graphics Lab at the University of Waterloo, which made production facilities available when the NRC secretarial staff was unable to produce this paper.

12. References

1. Anstis, S. and Cavanaugh, P., "An Apparent Motion Technique for Judging Equiluminance of Colours in a Television Display", Proceedings of Colour Vision, an International Conference, Cambridge, 1982 (in press).
2. Bartleson, C.J., "Changes in Color Appearance with Variations in Chromatic Adaptation", Color Research and Application, **4** 119-138, 1979; "Predicting Corresponding Colors with Changes in Adaptation", Color Research and Application, **4** 143-155, 1979.
3. Catmull, E., "A Tutorial on Compensation Tables", Computer Graphics, **13** 1-7, 1979.
4. Cowan, W.B., "CIE Calibration of Video Monitors", National Research Council of Canada Technical Report, 1983.
5. Meyers, G.W. and Greenberg, D.P., "Perceptual Color Spaces for Computer Graphics", Computer Graphics, **14** 254-261, 1980.
6. Smith, A.R., "Color Gamut Transform Pairs", Computer Graphics, **12** 12-19, 1978.
7. Tansley, B.R. and Boynton, R.M., "A Line, not a Space, Represents Visual Distinctness of Borders formed by Different Colors", Science, **191** 954-957, 1976.
8. Wyszecki, G. and Stiles, W.S., "Color Science", second edition, New York: Wiley, 1982.

INTERACTIVE IMAGE QUERY SYSTEM USING PROGRESSIVE TRANSMISSION

by

F.S.Hill,Jr
University of Massachusetts
Amherst, Mass.

Sheldon Walker,Jr.
University of Maine
Orono, Maine

Fuwen Gao
Beijing Normal University
Beijing,China

ABSTRACT

There is a growing need for people to browse through files of images such as satellite or medical photos, to determine which ones warrant further examination. Users located at some distance from the image archive often must use slow transmission links such as telephone lines. If an image is scanned out line-by-line, top-to-bottom, the user must often wait too long to determine whether the image is of any use. Using the Progressive Transmission Method, however, images are encoded so that during transmission the entire display shows a rough version of the image in 'fat pixels'. If the user wishes to see more detail, additional data is sent and used to refine these pixels, until the exact original image is seen. We report here on extensions of this method to the rich color imagery found in remote-sensing applications. A significant advance is the elimination of unworkably large look-up tables by using a single simple algorithm for performing the required encoding and decoding operations. The method is conceptualized in a 'transmission cone' context which assists a user in interacting with the system. The user can roam over large images, zoom to various levels of resolution, and cause specified subregions of interest in the image to fill in to full resolution, at a tremendous saving in time.

I). INTRODUCTION:

Our goal is to provide a system of users with rapid and flexible access to images. As shown in Fig.1, we envision a central 'image repository' consisting of a host computer and a large archive of many images, along with transmission links to a network of interactive remotely situated users. The users can browse through a file of images, obtain copies of their favorites at various levels of resolution, and possibly collaborate with other users in processing and analyzing them. The ability to browse is particularly important when using satellite images, since one wants to look over the most recently acquired file, yet some images may suffer from excessive cloud cover. A user wants to detect this situation quickly and abort further transmission of faulty or uninteresting images, in order to browse through others. The remote stations must be reasonably priced and user-friendly, and the browse capability provided must be responsive enough so that user's attention does not waiver excessively. Central to the system envisioned is the need for transmitting images over possibly slow communication links, yet with time delays which are acceptable to interactive users.

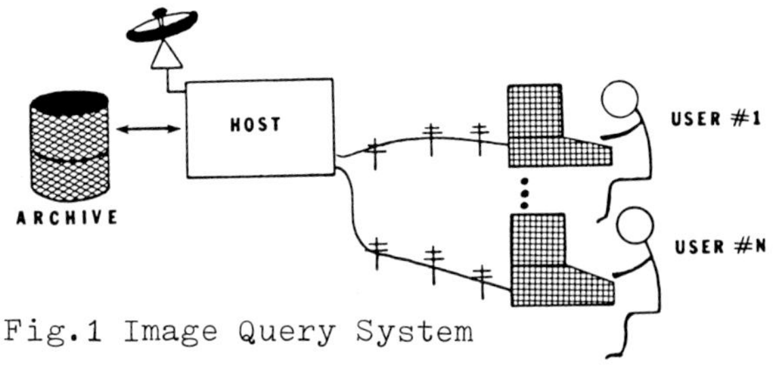

Fig.1 Image Query System

We focus on remote-sensing images here, but one can foresee a much broader set of potential users, in such fields as medicine, law, intelligence, and the graphic arts. We emphasize images such as LANDSAT and GOES photos here, anticipating a potentially large base of image users in the Northeastern United States, for such uses as weather, intelligence, land use planning, and agriculture, who may wish to link into the proposed satellite tracking ground-station to be located at the University of Massachusetts.

With standard transmission techniques, an image is sent to a terminal so that it is scanned out as in a tv raster: line-by-line from top-to-bottom. Normally at least half of the image must be received before the user can make a judgement as to its use-fulness. If standard telephone lines are used, it can take a pro-hibitively long time to send a small fraction of an image in this manner.

We envision images with r rows, c columns, and b bits/pixel, hence r*c*b bits in all. Usually c and r will be the same power of 2. For concreteness we hereafter refer to the 'typical image' as having 512 rows, 512 columns, and 24 bits/pixel, giving r.c.b = 6.3 megabits. We also take as 'typical' a transmission rate of 4800 bits/second, so that the 'typical image' would require 21.8 minutes to be received. The transmission time is the major bottleneck here, far outweighing any local processing time we envision.

IA). SCENARIO:

Our approach to dealing effectively with long image transmission times is illustrated in the following user interaction sequence.

For each image requested, data is sent so that the entire image emerges progressively, from low to higher resolution, until the user can decide whether the image is potentially of interest. (Examples below indicate that this point may occur after only 2% of the image data has been received!) If it is of no further interest, the user signals that a new image is to be sent, and no precious time is wasted in sending useless data. If it appears useful, on the other hand, the user has several options. Frequently he wishes to closely examine only a portion of the image, and so he specifies a window into that portion of the low-resolution version, whereupon it fills into full resolution. This 'selective fill-in' occurs rapidly since only the data relevant to pixels in the windowed area need be transmitted. In this fashion the user can 'roam' over the image, obtaining full resolution versions of all interesting parts. Local processing of course allows any portion to be enlarged to fill the display screen.

IB). PREVIOUS APPROACHES AND LIMITATIONS.

The problem of excessive transmission time has been addressed through the use of progressive refinement of images using quadtrees <1>, as well as extensions to binary trees using Progressive Transmission (hereafter PT) <2>. Both approaches send 'coarse information first' to inform the user early in the reception phase about the general nature of the image. The quadtree method usually forms 'fat pixels' by computing numerical averages of four neighboring small pixels. This approach can suffer from round-off error unless additional bits are used to represent the average values <3>. By contrast, with the PT method there is no loss of precision as the encoding progresses: exactly the same number of bits is needed to represent the image at each stage. The method is simple and efficient, and is completely reversible, as discussed below.

With the PT method, the original r*c*b bits of the image are first ENCODED into a new set of r*c*b bits at the archive site, and stored in encoded format. Supposing this has been done, we focus first on the image reception phase, which involves DECODING. When an image is requested by a remote user, bits are sent so that the received image fills in. During reception, the image is successively bisected (alternately in the horizontal and vertical directions) by sending b bit quantities which Knowlton called DIFFERENTIATORS (hereafter "diff's"). Figure 2 shows the progression. Each diff combines with a displayed COMPOSITE ("comp") value to produce two new comp's for the new smaller pixels.

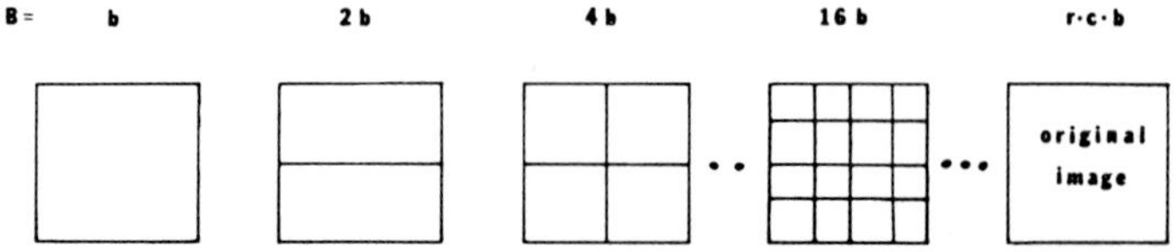

Fig.2 Image Seen after Receipt of B bits.

The decoding process begins upon receipt of b bits for the comp of the single fat pixel, and each splitting requires b bits more. Hence after M*b bits have been received the displayed image consists of M 'fat pixels'. In order that the low resolution versions faithfully imitate the true image, the b bit color/intensity in each fat pixel must approximate the average value of all the small pixels contained within the fat pixel. An important advantage in Knowlton's PT method is that all quantities are b bit integers, and the usual numerical roundoff errors which would accumulate in finding the averages are avoided. Instead of calculating averages, look-up tables (of size 2**b of a side) are used to map a comp and diff pair into two new comp's. One may view this process as a decoding transformation D which maps pairs of b bit values into similar pairs, denoted:

$$D(comp,diff) = (comp1,comp2). \quad (1)$$

The possible comp & diff values are used as indices, and the resulting pair of decoded comp's is found in the table. (This is consistent with Knowlton's approach, although couched in somewhat different terms.) Fig.3a shows such a table for the simple case b=2. For example, (2,3), (i.e. the element in row 2 and column 3), maps into (3,0), so a fat pixel with comp value of 2 will be split by a diff of value 3 into 2 new comp's with values 3 and 0.

a.) Look-up Table

	0	1	2	3
3	23	33	32	31
2	13	22	21	30
1	03	12	11	20
0	02	01	00	10

b.) Error Distribution

	0	1	2	3
3	$\frac{1}{2}$	1	$\frac{1}{2}$	0
2	0	$\frac{1}{2}$	0	$\frac{1}{2}$
1	$\frac{1}{2}$	0	$\frac{1}{2}$	0
0	0	$\frac{1}{2}$	1	$\frac{1}{2}$

Fig.3 An Example Look-Up Table.

In concert with the decoding process performed at the user's terminal, the ENCODING process maps original pixel pairs into (comp,diff) pairs. Adjacent image pixels are combined in pairs, the two comp values producing a single fat pixel comp and a new diff according to an encoding transformation E(comp1,comp2) = (comp,diff). This encoding is done at the image archive site, after which the image is stored in PT format, as one comp and r*c-1 diff's. Knowlton again used look-up tables for this mapping E. An essential requirement is that the mappings D and E be inverses of each other: D(E(.,.)) = (.,.), so that the recovered pixels are always identical to the originals. In this sense the method is information lossless and reversible, while the numerical averaging approach is reversible only if averages are computed and retained exactly.

Returning to the decoding stage, the table defining mapping D is arranged so that each comp splits into two new comp's whose average is as close as possible to the original comp. Inspection of the table in Fig.3a shows an error distribution (error = true average - original comp) as in Fig.3b. For instance, along the i=j diagonal the error can be made 0 by using i as the comp. In general,the error values are bounded by 2**(b-2). Due to reversibiity, however, these errors do not accumulate: if the decoding is allowed to proceed to its conclusion, there will be NO error in the final recovered pixel values.

It is useful to view PT in the context of a 'transmission cone' as shown in Fig.4, analogous to the familiar 'processing cones' and 'quadtree pyramids' <3,4>. Although in fact images are bisected at each stage,allowing a gradual increase in resolution, we think of combining two stages together, bisecting the image in both directions (thus quadrupling the number of fat pixels), and denote different LEVEL's of resolution. Thus an image of level L contains 4**L pixels, and the 'typical image' has a maximum display level of 9. The encoding process progresses down the cone until the single fat pixel at level 0 is reached, while decoding with the stream of diff's progresses up the cone to the level desired.

To obtain a level L+1 image from one at level L requires the transmission of an additional 3*(4**L) diff's, and so takes four times as long to receive the data for each successive level. For this reason it is particularly advantageous for a

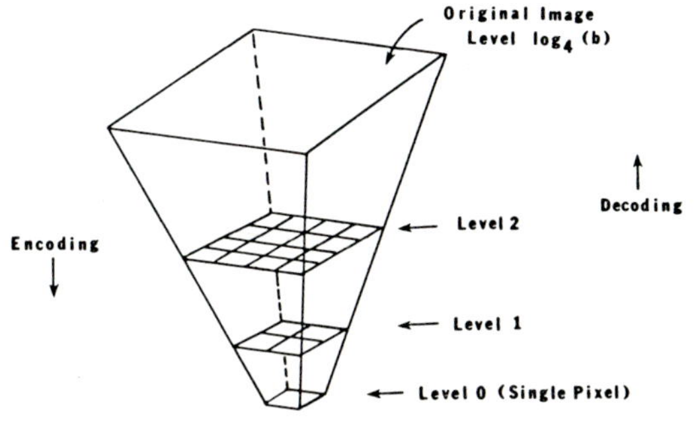

Fig.4 The Transmission Cone.

user to be able to decide at a low level whether or not an image is interesting. For instance, if Time(L) is the time required to transmit an image at level L then Time(6)/Time(9)= 1/64, and the user acquires a level 6 version in 1/64 the time needed for the level 9 image.

A significant limitation in the original PT scheme is the requirement for the two look-up tables. In Knowlton's examples each pixel was represented by only four bits, hence the tables were only 16 by 16. However, the much richer images associated with remotely sensed data may contain 24 bits/pixel, requiring a user to construct two unmanageable 8.5 gigabyte tables to use PT.

We present below an extension of Knowlton's method to allow its application to the very demanding area of full-color images with any number of bits/pixel. The look-up tables are replaced with a SINGLE simple procedure that works for BOTH encoding and decoding. Its space complexity is independent of the number of bits/pixel. We discuss the tables and algorithms in the context of more general transformations. We also present several results with color images. We describe an efficient and unifom storage scheme which facilitates the various query modes, and describe ways to save even futher time by reducing the color resolution during 'browsing' under the user's control.

II. EXTENDING PROGRESSIVE TRANSMISSION TO RICH IMAGERY.

IIA). Elimination of the Look-up Tables.

We focus on the nature of the transformations D and E above which map ordered pairs of b-bit numbers into other ordered pairs. Knowlton reported one such mapping for 4-bit values, in which he distributed values in a clever ad hoc way to build the desired tables: those having small errors in their error distributions (see Fig.3b). Because the table was constructed in this way, it is not clear whether a simple and compact algorithm exists that COMPUTES D(comp,diff) rather than looks up its values. We also need ways to extend the method to higher values of b.

We first develop a simple geometric view of D which allows one to build a look-up table for any b. The tables agree exactly with Knowlton's reported cases. Using this structure we then construct a simple algorithm which replaces the table, at a tremendous space saving.

IIB). The Ring Neighbor Algorithm:

An image using b bits/pixel requires the equivalent of an M by M table, where M=2**b. Call by N the set of possible pixel values:

N = (0,1,...,M-1). (2)

Elements of the table are ordered pairs with components taken from set N. The table may be viewed as a mapping from the Cartesian product N X N onto itself: the pair of indices (i,j) maps into the pair D(i,j). The table must be one-to-one and onto (i.e. must be a permutation) for the inverse transformation E to exist: otherwise encoding and decoding would not be inverse operations, and PT would not be information lossless.

There are many possible such tables, (Knowlton reported a particularly good one for b=4), but only a few will yield good error distributions. For instance, the IDENTITY mapping D(i,j) = (i,j) is indeed a permutation, but does not produce comp's with the desired average value. In fact, one can see that the use of PT with the identity mapping is a simple sampling operation: each fat pixel at level L equals the Northwest pixel in its group of four at level L+1.

Figure 5 shows a table template for the case b=3 which reveals the structure of PT tables, and leads to a general algorithm. View the table as consisting of concentric rings. The innermost ring is composed of the central four elements, while the r-th ring has 4*(2r-1) elements. We find the 'ring neighbor' of any cell in the r-th ring by traversing the ring r elements in a clockwise direction, as shown in Figure 5. To build the table we use for each cell the INDICES of its ring neighbor. That is, for the cell at indices (i,j):

a). Determine which ring this cell lies within.
b). Find the indices of its ring neighbor.
c). Interchange the indices.
d). Write them into cell (i,j) as the required ordered pair.

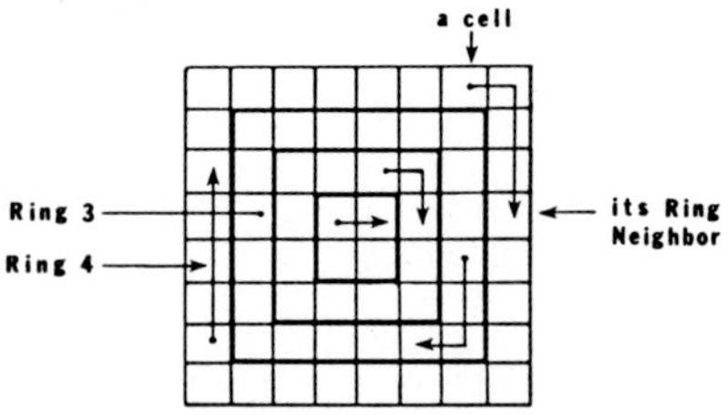

Fig.5 Defining Ring Neighbors.

For example, in Fig. 3a, cell (2,3) lies in ring 2, and has as ring neighbor the cell at (0,3), so place (3,0) in the cell at (2,3). Note that a table built using this method will be identical to Knowlton's, except for a reflection about the i=j axis (a transposition), an operation which has no effect on the average error distribution of the PT method. (Also note that the table displaying the first element in each cell is a simple quarter-turn rotation of the table displaying the second element.)

A remarkable property of the tables which are generated by this approach is that they are INVOLUTIONS: Applying the mapping twice recovers the original index pair: D(D(i,j))=(i,j). This means that D is its own inverse, and that E and D are the SAME! Hence only ONE transformation must be constructed, and can be used for both encoding and decoding, a welcome simplification. Involutions are easy to construct: In general a table is an involution whenever the elements of N X N are taken in pairs, and each is placed at the other's index position. What is interesting here is that Knowlton's table (after a reflection) is automatically an involution. The ring neighbor approach demonstrates this involution property: For any cell find its ring neighbor, then reflect about the i=j axis, to locate the cell whose position is the image of the original cell. Now start at this point, again find the ring neighbor and reflect. You always return to the original cell.

In the Appendix we list procedure CODE which computes D(i,j) for any (i,j). It is based on the ring neighbor algorithm, capitalizing on certain symmetries in order to reduce computation time. It operates on integers and has a trivial space complexity independent of b. Each encode or decode operation requires at most 4 integer compares and 7 integer adds,(3 compares and 4 adds on the average).

IIC) ON THE TRANSMISSION CONE

The transmission cone's pyramid structure helps the user visualize the various processing steps, and simplifies queries, while organizing the data for efficient image management. Although our transmission cone is quite similar to processing cones and quadtrees, several significant differences are worth noting:

a). Two passes over the image are required to move from one level to the next. Each pass requires only very simple algorithms, however, compared with the corresponding quadtree operations. Whereas the resulting intermediate stage is not normally available with the quadtree structure, with PT the user can display this intermediate stage if desired, and thus attain a smoother increase in resolution for a given volume of data.

b). The ring neighbor encoding algorithm is used in lieu of numerical averaging. Hence moving between levels is an exactly reversible operation.

c). If it is important to save memory at the user's terminal, only one level of the image need be stored at a time. Once the data for a certain level image has been received, the user can migrate to lower levels by converting some comp's back to diff's, reusing the same memory locations. If he wishes to do some local processing, however, such as lowpass filtering the image in order to reduce the 'jaggies', or some early segmentation of the image, the diff's would have to be stored in auxiliary memory.

III). SOME USER INTERACTION.

Many current image transmission systems send data with little regard for the user. In the highly interactive but low data rate environment we envision it is important that each remote user be able to make the most of the data received at any point, and to zoom, pan, and change resolution freely in various ways.

Since we are envisioning relatively inexpensive user terminals in this system, the amount of memory available will be limited. One approach would be to place the decoded image directly into the frame buffer. As the initial diff's arrive they are decoded to form the lower level images. It will take only a few seconds to receive an image to level 4 or 5, and rather than display such rapidly changing (and not very informative) images, the user's display will most likely be blanked until an image of level 5 or so is available. At this point the user will begin to interact with the received data, either requesting more detail for that image, or issuing a command to send a different image. Figures 6 and 7 illustrate the dramatic increase in intelligibility as an image progresses from level 5 to level 6. In Fig.7 each of the 64 by 64 fat pixels consists of an 8 by 8 pixel block, since the original data is 512 by 512. In this green-only version there are 8 bits/pixel of intensity resolution.

As an example interactive scenario, suppose the user with a 512 by 512 (level 9) display asks to receive LANDSAT image #423 to level 5, using a command such as LAND423/LEV5. Based on this rough view, the user might discard this image (e.g. if there is too much cloud cover). Or he may issue "UP-A-LEVEL" to move up the transmission cone. The archival host would then send new diff's, and the image would fill in to the next level,as each prior fat pixel subdivides into four thinner ones. Fig. 8 shows an example, taken from a Landsat photo of the Quabbin Reservoir region of Western Massachusetts.

The user may now be able to recognize certain key regions in the image, and may want to see only PORTIONS at fuller resolution. He then uses a suitable input device to specify a window on the display, and types in "FILL/LEV9", whereupon only the relevant diff's are sent for the SUBCONE which represents the windowed region. Accessing the proper diff's to accomplish this is discussed below. Fig.s 9 and 10 show example level 6 images with several regions filled in to full resolution in this manner. If a subregion being filled consists of only a fraction of the 64*64 fat pixels at level 6, then only that fraction of the number of diff's must be sent,providing a tremendous saving in transmission time. Fig. 11 shows how the user would view the transmission cone for this 'selective fill-in' mode. We see below how this view mirrors the actual storage of data in the terminal.

Fig.6 Example Image at Level 5.

Fig.7 Example Image at Level 6.

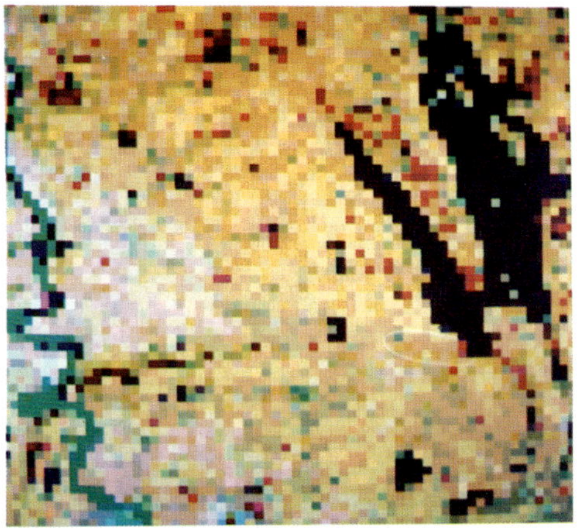

Fig.8 Part of LANDSAT Image at Level 6.

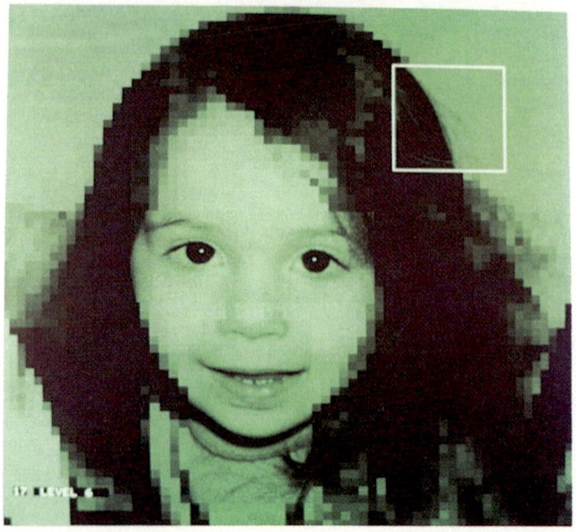

Fig.9 Selective Fill-in to Level 9, (3 regions filled;one encircled.)

Fig.10 Selective Fill-in To Level 9.

Fig.12 Roaming with Selective Fill-in.

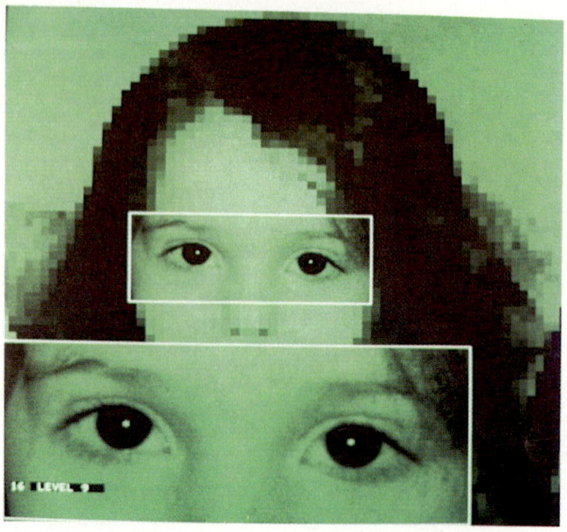

Fig.13 Fill-in with Zoom.

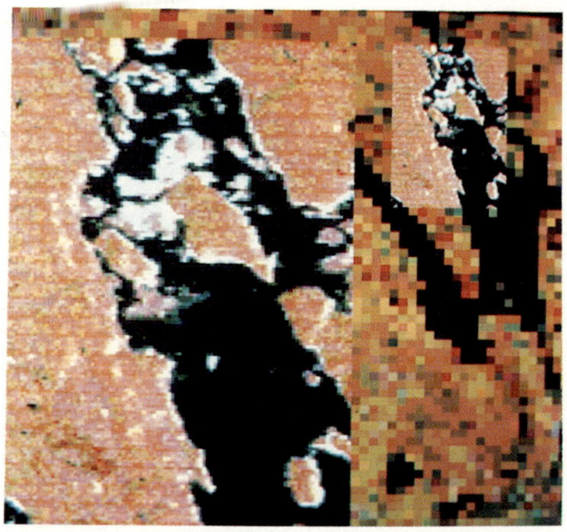

Fig.14 Fill-in with Zoom.

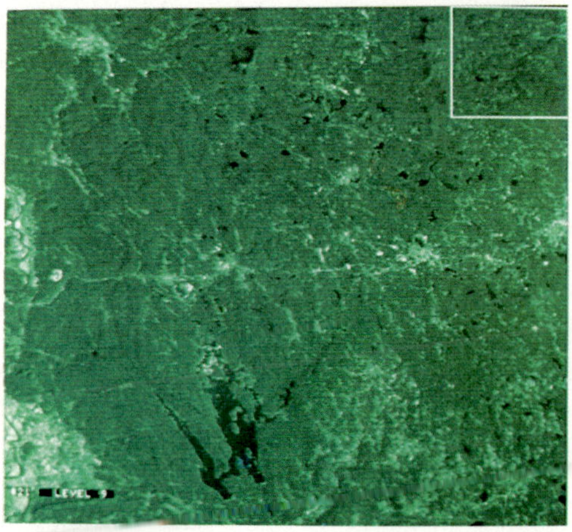

Fig.15 Level 10 Data Shown at Level 9.

To roam one simply does a sequence of window specifications, followed by fill's. Figure 12 shows some examples, where the user has filled in various regions of interest, tracing along rivers and mountains, until his curiosity was satisfied. The user's productivity is greatly increased using this mode, not only because each region fills in so quickly, but also because he ADAPTIVELY chooses the next region to fill in based on viewing earlier regions. The user can also zoom in on a region if desired, by pixel replication, (Fig.s 13 & 14).

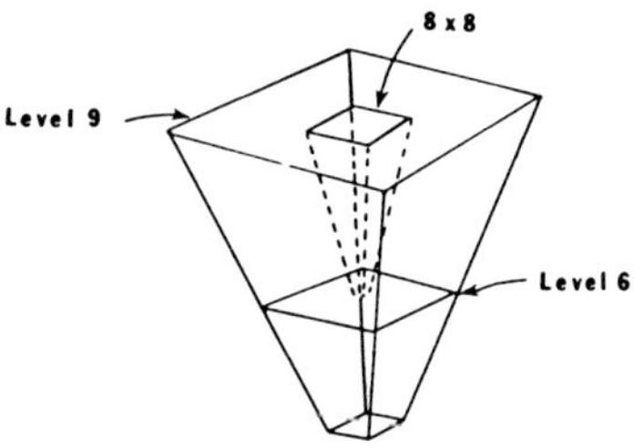

Fig.11 Cone with Fill-in Operation.

There would be additional utilities stored in the user terminal to do processing on images at whatever level had been received. Besides routines to change between levels, some operations would manipulate image data at the same level, performing such things as edge detection or geometric corrections. Software and protocols would also be available to allow the user's terminal to receive and store images in an unattended mode, say overnight.

Some images such as GOES weather photos (r=1800,c=3822,b=8, two taken each hour) are so large they cannot be displayed at full resolution on a typical (level 9) terminal. If they are encoded into PT format at the archive, however, the user can display one or any portion of one up to level 9. Each displayed pixel is then actually an average of many original pixels. In Fig. 15 a 1024 X 1024 (level 10) LANDSAT image is shown on a level 9 display, providing the user with a more global view of the area.

IIIA). Image Memory Organization.

In order to carry out the various tasks, it is important to store image data at both the archive site and the user's terminal in a manner that permits easy access and modification, yet is not wasteful of memory. For instance, when the user wishes to fill-in only a portion of the image, how are the new requested diff's accessed and folded into the existing image memory?

Fig. 16 suggests one scheme for storing a completely encoded image at the archive site. A single comp c0 will reside in the upper left corner of archive memory, and all other locations will contain diff's, ready for transmission. For concreteness view 'typical' archive memory as a 512 by 512 array of cells. User refresh memory may be similarly configured, or may be reorganized so

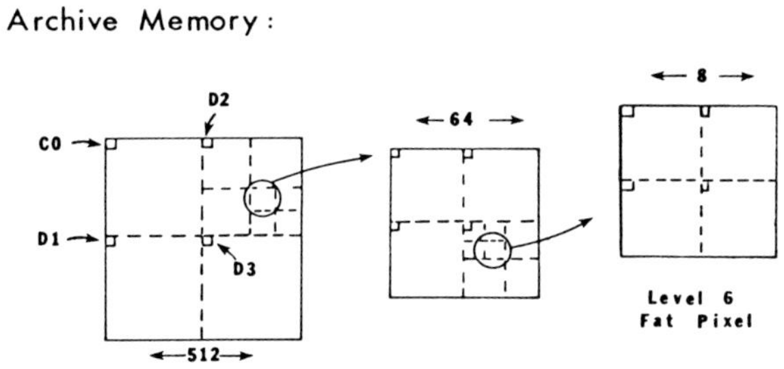

Fig.16 Storage Scheme for Encoded Image.

that for low-level images the refresh buffer can use a flood-fill approach to paint fat pixels without disturbing stored diff's.

To transmit an image, the diff's are sent in the order d1, d2,d3,... As d1 is decoded it combines with the previously received c0 to form two new comp's, say c1 and c2. These are stored in the user terminal, and are are displayed by flood-filling the upper and lower half of the screen respectively. Similarly, d2 will combine with c1, and split the upper half into two square regions, etc. The important feature is that the relevant diff at each splitting stage resides in archive memory at the upper left corner of a certain region, and this position corresponds to the new subregion in user refresh memory that is being formed in the split. This hierarchical imbedding process continues to all levels, as suggested in the figure.

One can see by working this process backwards that during the encoding phase of comp's to diff's no extra memory is required: as each pair of comp's is mapped into a new comp and a diff, the new values are put right back into memory in the spaces originally occupied by the two comp's. This both saves extra memory and facilitates addressing.

Now suppose the user displays a level 6 image, indicates a window to be filled in, and describes the window to the archive. The chosen window will contain several fat pixels, each one corresponding in archive memory to 64 cells, containing one comp and 63 diff's. These are precisely the diff's needed to fill in that fat pixel. The proper diff's for the fat pixels are thus easily identified at the archive and sent to the user.

IIIB). Color Quantization:

In browse mode the user will not usually need to see the fat pixels in their true colors. In order to save transmission time, the first set of comp's and diff's can be sent with fewer than b bits. For instance, the two most significant bits for each of the three colors could be sent, thus giving the fat pixels 64 possible colors. Alternatively, the user could request to see only say, the green portion of the image, and perhaps only its first 2 or 3 bits. Later, if the user desires to let the image fill in to its full quality, the remaining bits for each pixel could be sent (perhaps between interactive sessions in a form of batch mode), and the final image constructed. There are many possible ways to precode, transmit, and recombine the color information, and suitable studies will be done on how much color information a user needs in order to make reasonable judgements about the content of an image based on viewing pixels at reduced resolution in both the spatial and color domains. This is currently a topic of ongoing research.

IV).CONCLUSION:

An image query system is described wherein an image archive host sends image data to remote users upon request over possibly slow transmission links. Progressive transmission is used to provide the user with a quick-look capability at reduced resolution, so that he can abort further transmission if the image is not needed. We have extended the PT scheme to the area of rich full color imagery, circumventing the barrier of impossibly large look-up tables by fashioning a simple algorithm to perform the required intensity mappings. Some more fundamental properties of this mapping are noted as well. We also describe different user query modes in the context of a 'transmission cone' metaphor, which is used to allow the user to fill in selected subregions of an image to full resolution, and to roam incrementally over images.

Acknowledgement:

This work was supported in part by the Remote Sensing Center at the University of Massachusetts, through the ASTECH Corp. The Visions Group at the University graciously donated use of their facilities. Thanks also go to Ken Ward for his help in coding various experiments.

REFERENCES:

(1) K. R. Sloan & S. L. Tanimoto, "Progressive Refinement of Raster Images", IEEE Trans. on Computers, C-28, No. 11, Nov. 1979, pp.871-874.

(2) Ken Knowlton, "Progressive Transmission of Grey-Scale and Binary Pictures by Simple, Efficient, and Loss-less Encoding Schemes" Proc. of IEEE, Vol. 68, No. 7, 1980, pp.885-896.

(3) Theo Pavlidis, GRAPHICS AND IMAGE PROCESSING, Computer Science Press, Rockville, MD 1982.

(4) A. Hanson & E. Riseman, "Segmentation of Natural Scenes" in COMPUTER VISION SYSTEMS (A. Hanson & E. Riseman, eds.) Academic Press, New York, 1978.

(5) S. E. Walker, Jr & F. S. Hill, Jr., "Progressive Transmission of Remotely Sensed Images" 4-th Symposium on Automation in Engineering Data Handling, Naval Postgraduate School, Monterrey, CA, Nov. 3, 1982.

APPENDIX :

A listing of procedure CODE follows, showing how to map two pixel values P1 and P2 into a comp and a diff. The same routine may be used for the inverse mapping. M=2**b, where b is the number of bits/pixel.

```
Procedure Code (M,P1,P2:integer; Var
               comp,diff:integer);
  Var MM: integer;
    begin
      MM : = M div 2;
      if (P1+1)<= MM then
         if P2<=P1 then begin
              comp:=P2;
              diff:= P1+MM -P2
            end
         else begin
            comp:=P1+P2-MM;
            if comp<=P1 then comp:=P1;
            diff:=P1+MM - P2;
            if MM < P2 then
                 if P2 < (M- P1) then diff := P1
                 else diff := M - P2 - 1
            end

    else if (P2+1) <= MM then begin
            comp:= P1+P2+1-MM;
            diff:= P1;

         if diff <= (M-P2-1) then diff:= M -
                                   P2-1
           end

     else begin
           comp:=P2;
           if comp <= P1 then comp:=P1;
           diff:= P1+MM -1 -P2
         end

  end (*proc CODE*);
```

Graphics in Overlapping Bitmap Layers

ROB PIKE
Bell Laboratories

One of the common uses of bitmap terminals is storing multiple programming contexts in multiple, possibly overlapping, areas of the screen called windows. Windows traditionally store the visible state of a programming environment, such as an editor or debugger, while the user works with some other program. This model of interaction is attractive for one-process systems, but to make full use of a multiprogramming environment, windows must be asynchronously updated, even when partially or wholly obscured by other windows. For example, a long compilation may run in one window, displaying messages as appropriate, while the user edits a file in another window.

This paper describes a set of low-level graphics primitives to manipulate overlapping asynchronous windows, called *layers*, on a bitmap display terminal. Unlike previous window software, these primitives extend the domain of the general bitmap operator *bitblt* to include bitmaps that are partially or wholly obscured.

CR Categories and Subject Descriptors: I.3.3 [**Computer Graphics**]: Picture/Image Generation; I.3.4 [**Computer Graphics**]: Graphics Utilities.

General Terms: Algorithms

Additional Key Words and Phrases: Raster image, bitmaps, bitblt instruction, windows.

1. INTRODUCTION

Bitmap displays are in vogue. Despite their drawbacks, they are sufficiently inexpensive to be personal equipment rather than shared computer center resources. Unfortunately, although their use has become widespread, most bitmap displays are controlled by primitive software.

Bitmap screens are commonly divided into a set of rectangular areas called *windows*, each of which maintains the input and output context for a particular program or graphics application. A bitmap display can become several screens at once—different windows can be emulating standard terminals, graphics terminals, drafting tables, or even arcade games. The screen areas need not be disjoint—the display areas of two programs may overlap, with one area fully visible and the other partially or wholly obscured. This paper describes software to manipulate these overlapping windows, or *layers*, on a single display. A program drawing in a layer is fully isolated from other programs drawing on the same screen, even if one layer overlaps, and thereby obscures part of, the other. By extending the

Author's address: Rob Pike, Bell Laboratories, Murray Hill, NJ 07974.

Reprinted From **acm Transactions On Graphics**—April 1983—Vol. 2, No. 2

basic bitmap operators to work with layers, which may be regarded as possibly obscured, subdivided bitmaps, each program manipulates its layer just as it would manipulate the full screen or any other bitmap in a more conventional environment. Each program is removed from considerations regarding, for example, which layers obscure which, and two programs may simultaneously draw in their respective layers, even though some of the drawn objects are currently obscured from view.

2. COMPARISONS WITH PREVIOUS WORK

A number of window systems have been implemented by others [4, 5, 7, 8], but the software presented here has some distinguishing characteristics, dictated largely by the environment in which it is run. The environment is a bitmap display connected to a multiprogrammed timesharing system, with a limited but useful amount of offscreen memory (about a screenful) for storing bitmaps. Because the system is multiprogrammed, any program may want to update its window at any time, regardless of whether it is bound to the keyboard and mouse or even whether it is fully visible. It is also important that the user program be removed from concerns about window update: changes in the window configuration should be invisible to the program. This precludes the simple "repaint" mechanism, wherein a program is instructed to redraw its window whenever its visibility changes, because repainting forces the user program to deal with issues better left to lower level software. Like the file system, which makes a user file look like a continuously addressable stream of bytes even though it might be scattered across the disk, the window system should provide a simple programming interface so a program can always draw in its window as though it were a contiguous bitmap, regardless of its position or visibility on the screen.

There are two basic approaches to providing this transparency. The first, exemplified by the BRUWIN system [5], is to maintain a display list that is reevaluated when the window configuration changes. Although this method typically uses a relatively small amount of memory to hold the display list, and makes it easy to rearrange the layout of the windows on the display, it presents a few problems. One problem is that the time it takes to redraw a freshly uncovered portion of a window is substantial if the window's display list is long. More important, it is only possible to draw what the display list can encode. BRUWIN, for example, only supports characters, contradicting the generality of the bitmap data structure. Even adding bitmap primitives to the display list is not entirely satisfactory, however. Consider using a bitmap paint program for creating a realistic scene: the bitmap containing the scene is probably smaller than the display list that describes it, and certainly takes much less time to draw on the screen. Display lists introduce an unnecessary level of indirection.

The second method, used on the LISP Machine [8], is to keep the window image in a contiguous off-screen bitmap and copy data from there to the visible portions of the on-screen window. This simple method has the advantage of supporting any bitmap operation, but takes a constant large amount of auxiliary memory and can be inefficient—it may be necessary to execute each bitmap operation twice: once off-screen and once on-screen.

The layers software is in some sense an optimization of this "shadow bitmap" method. By dividing the windows into visible and obscured parts, and only keeping obscured parts off-screen, it uses the minimum memory possible (assuming no display lists) by letting the screen memory itself hold the visible parts. The basic idea is to extend the domain of the general bitmap operator *bitblt* [2] to include windows that are wholly or partially obscured. Layer drawing operations, therefore, touch the same number of pixels regardless of visibility, although the number of bitblt operations may be larger if there are on-screen and off-screen components. The data structures and software are designed to make drawing in a layer as fast as possible, at the expense of slower creation and deletion operators (although creation and deletion are still fast). The most common layer shuffling operator (making a layer fully visible) is also efficient because it touches only those pixels that need to be updated. There are disadvantages, of course: the data structures become unwieldy with more than about a dozen overlapping layers, and translating a layer across the screen is clumsy, but the software has been implemented and works comfortably in our time-sharing environment, where the number of layers is fairly small and their average lifetime long.

3. DEFINITIONS

The programs described herein, written in a pseudo-C dialect, use several simple defined types and primitive bitmap operations. This section describes the basic concepts for bitmap operations, but does not attempt to be complete. The next section defines bitmaps precisely.

A Point is an ordered pair

```
typedef struct{
        int x, y;
}Point;
```

that defines a location in a bitmap such as the screen.

This paper uses some typographical conventions to clarify the distinctions between abstract objects and their software analogs. Abstract data types are in roman font, with their first letters capitalized (e.g., Point). Following C notation, functions and procedures are written in Helvetica typeface, with a (usually empty) parenthesis set after them (e.g., bitblt( )). The generalizations of bitmap operators for layers are named by the bitmap operator prefixed by an "l" (e.g., bibtlt( ), as opposed to Lbitblt( )). Finally, entry point subroutines are in lowercase, while subservient routines called by layerop( ) (see Section 6) have their first letters capitalized (e.g., lblt( ), as opposed to Lblt( )).

A Rectangle is defined by a pair of Points spanning a diagonal:

```
typedef struct{
        Point origin;   /* min x,y */
        Point corner;   /* max x,y */
}Rectangle;
```

Reprinted From acm Transactions On Graphics—April 1983—Vol. 2, No. 2

By definition, corner.x ≥ origin.x and corner.y ≥ origin.y. Rectangles are half-open: a Rectangle contains the horizontal and vertical lines through origin, and abuts, but does not contain, the lines through corner. Two abutting Rectangles r_0 and r_1, with r_1.origin = (r_0.corner.x, r_0.origin.y), therefore have no point in common. The same applies to lines in any direction: a line segment drawn from (x_0, y_0) to (x_1, y_1) does not contain (x_1, y_1). These curious definitions simplify drawing objects in pieces, which is essential to the layer primitives.

The routine rectf(b, r, f) performs a function specified by an integer code f, in a Rectangular r, in a bitmap b. The function code is one of

CLR:	clear Rectangle to zeros
OR:	set Rectangle to ones
XOR:	invert bits in Rectangle

The routine bitblt(sb, r, db, p, f) (bit block transfer) copies a source Rectangle r in a bitmap sb to a corresponding Rectangle with origin p in a destination bitmap db. bitblt( ) is therefore a form of Rectangle assignment operator, and the function code f specifies the nature of the assignment;

STORE:	dest = source
OR:	dest |= source
CLR:	dest &= ~source
XOR:	dest ^= source

For example, OR specifies that the destination Rectangle is formed from the bitwise OR of the source and destination Rectangles before the bitblt( ). Here, |, &,^, and ~ are C's bitwise OR, AND, exclusive-OR, and NOT operators, and the notation x *= y is equivalent to x = x * y, but is notationally and semantically closer to the machine.

Often, bitblt( ) is defined to copy through a two-dimensional mask, to permit stippling and related operations. Our original bitblt( ) had implementation problems (which have since been resolved) that forced us not to incorporate a mask into the primitive; for compatibility, our current bitblt( ) also does not have a mask. However, whether a mask is present has no bearing on the ideas presented here.

bitblt( ) is a fundemental bitmap operation. It is used to draw characters, save screen rectangles, and present menus. Defined with a bit mask, it includes rectf( ). For a thorough description, see [2] or [3]. bitblt( ) can be a very expensive operation, however. Generally, the data from the source Rectangle must be shifted or rotated and masked before being written to the destination Rectangle, and the amount of data processed in a single bitblt( ) can be surprisingly large.

4. BITMAPS

A bitmap is a dot-matrix representation of a rectangular image. The details of the representation depend on the display hardware, or, more specifically, on the arrangement of memory in the display. For bitmaps to mesh well with the software in a display, the screen must appear to the program as a bitmap with no special properties other than its visibility. Because images (bitmaps) are stored off-screen, off-screen memory should have the same format as the screen itself, so that copying images to and from the screen is not a special case in the software.

Reprinted From acm Transactions On Graphics—April 1983—Vol. 2, No. 2

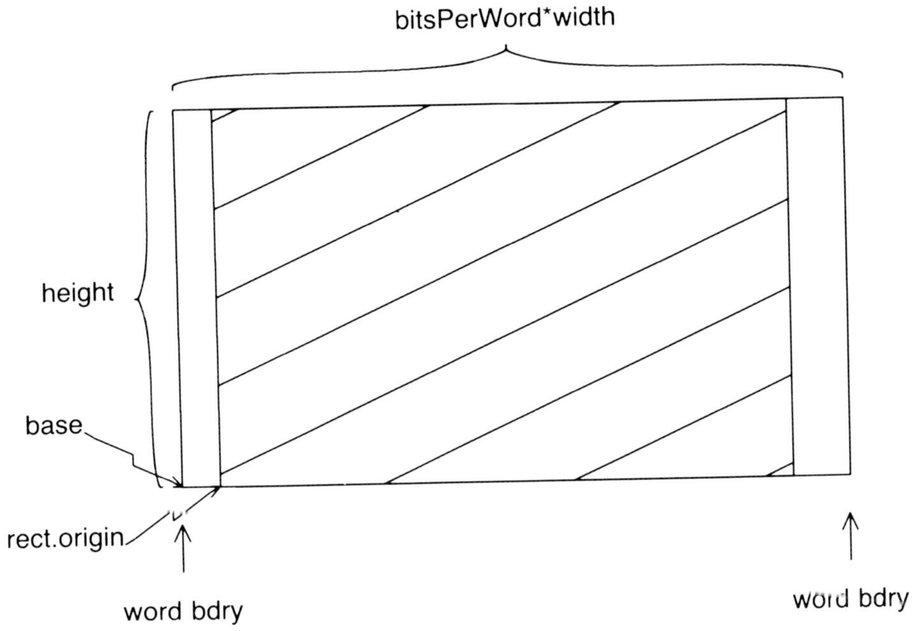

Fig. 1. Layout of a bitmap. The storage begins and ends on word boundaries, with the last word of one scan line followed immediately by the first word of the next scan line. The hatched area, Bitmap. rect, stores the image.

The simplest way to achieve this generality is to make the screen a contiguous array of memory, with the last word in a scan line followed immediately by the first word of the next scan line. Under this scheme, bitmaps become something familiar to the programmer: a two-dimensional array.

Given a two-dimensional array in which to store the actual image, some auxiliary information is required for its interpretation. Figure 1 illustrates how a bitmap is interpreted. The hatched region is the location of the image. When a bitmap is allocated, the allocation routine, balloc( ), assumes the bitmap data will correspond to a screen Rectangle, for example, a part of one layer obscured by another. balloc( ) creates the left and right margins of the bitmap to word-align the bitmap with the screen, so that word boundaries in the bitmap will be in the same relative positions as in the screen. This technique can make a significant performance difference for the common operation of saving and restoring screen rectangles.

balloc( ) takes one argument, the on-screen rectangle that corresponds to the bitmap image, and returns a pointer to a data structure of type Bitmap. Bitmap is defined thus:

```
typedef struct{
        Word *base;             /* start of data */
        unsigned width;         /* width in words */
        Rectangle rect;         /* image rectangle */
}Bitmap;
```

The declaration Word *base states that base points to an object of type Word,

Reprinted From acm Transactions On Graphics—April 1983—Vol. 2, No. 2

or rather that *base is a Word pointed to by base. (Pointers in C can point to objects not allocated dynamically; the layers software depends on this.) The elements of the structure are illustrated in Figure 1. width is in Words, which are some convenient unit of storage. rect is the argument to balloc( ) and defines the coordinate system inside the Bitmap (the next section, which deals with the Layer data structure, explains why this is done). The storage in the Bitmap outside rect—the unhatched portion in Figure 1—is unused, as described above.

Typically, width is the number of Words that fit horizontally within the Bitmap, between the arrows in Figure 1. A Bitmap may be contained in another Bitmap, however, if its width is the same as that of the outer Bitmap, and base points as usual to the first Word in the Bitmap—the Word containing the pixel at the origin of the Bitmap. Although such Bitmaps are not created by balloc( ), they have utility—they can represent the portion of the screen occupied by a layer, for instance.

balloc( ) and its obvious counterpart bfree( ) hide all issues of storage management for bitmaps. Because the sizes of bitmaps are widely variable, balloc( ) does garbage compaction, moving all allocated bitmaps to one end of the arena when space runs low, thereby ensuring that memory does not fragment.

The Bitmap structure is used throughout the layer software. Graphics primitives operate on points, lines, and rectangles within all Bitmaps, not just those on the screen. The screen itself is simply a globally accessible Bitmap structure, called display, and is unknown within the graphics primitives.

5. LAYERS

A layer is a rectangular portion of the screen and its associated image. It may be thought of as a virtual display screen. Layers may overlap (although they need not), but the image in the obscured portion of a layer is always kept current. Typically, an asynchronous process, such as a terminal program or circuit design system, draws pictures and text in a layer, just as it might draw in any bitmap (such as the full screen if it were the only process on the display). Because processes are asynchronous, drawing actions can take place at any time in an obscured layer, and a graphical object such as a line may be partially visible on the screen and partially in the obscured portion of the layer. The layer software isolates a program drawing in a layer on the screen from other such programs in other layers, and guarantees that the image on- and off-screen is always correct, regardless of the configuration of the layers on the screen.

Layers must be differentiated from the common notion of windows.[1] Windows are used to *save* a programming or working environment, such as a text editing session; to process "interrupts," such as looking at a file or sending mail; or to keep several *static* contexts, such as file contents, on the screen. Layers are intended to *maintain* an environment, even though it may change because the associated programs are still running. For example, a programmer could be editing the program source in one layer while watching for diagnostic messages from a long compilation taking place in another, and waiting for intruders into

[1] The term "window" in common usage is a misnomer (see, e.g., [6]). The meaning is actually closer to that of the older term "viewport."

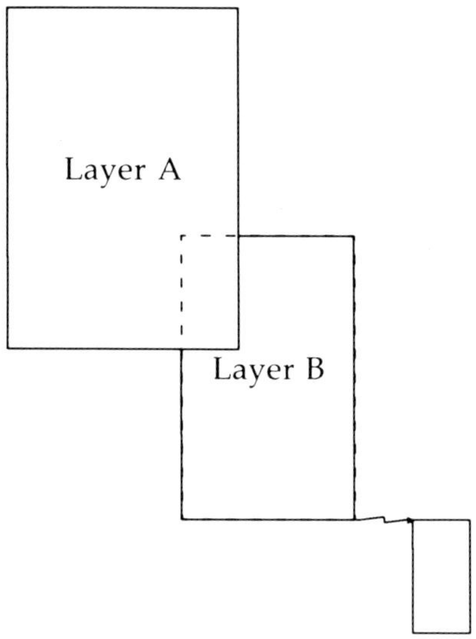

Fig. 2. Obscured portions of a layer are stored off-screen and linked to the obscured layer.

his corner of the labyrinth in a real-time game in a third. There is, of course, nothing profound in the distinction between layers and windows; the term "layer" was coined to avoid the more cumbersome phrase "asynchronous window." Nonetheless, the difference between layers and windows is significant. Multiple active contexts are natural to use and powerful to exploit.

Truly asynchronous graphics operations are difficult to support, because the state of a layer may change while a graphics operation is underway. The obvious simple solution is to perform graphical operations atomically by inhibiting process switches during calls to the layer software.

The data structures for layers are illustrated in Figures 2 and 3. A partially obscured layer has an *obscured list*: a list of disjoint rectangles *in that layer* obscured by another layer or layers. In Figure 2, layer A obscures layer B. Layer B's obscured list has a single entry, which is marked "obscured by A." If more than one layer obscures a rectangle, the rectangle is marked as obscured by the *frontmost* (unobscured) layer intersecting the rectangle. This is illustrated by rectangle 4 in Figure 3. Rectangle 4 is an obscured part of both layer B and C, so these layers store their obscured pieces off-screen and mark them blocked by layer A.

Rectangles 3 and 4 in layer B (Figure 3) may be stored as a single rectangle, as they are in Figure 2. They are stored as two because if layer C is later moved to the front of the screen (i.e., to the top of the pile of layers), it will obscure portions of both layers A and B. Rectangle 4 in layer B would be obscured by C, but rectangle 3 would still be obscured by A. To simplify the algorithms for rearranging layers, the layer creation routine does all necessary subdivision when the layer is first made, so when layer C is created[2], the obscured rectangle in B is split in two along the edge of the new layer.

[2] Despite Figure 3, layer C is actually created at the *front*, but the argument is nonetheless true.

Reprinted From **acm Transactions On Graphics**—April 1983—Vol. 2, No. 2

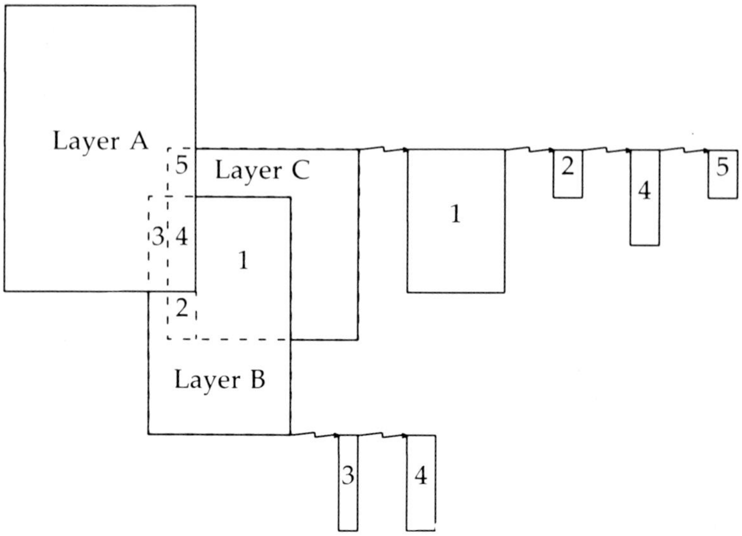

Fig. 3. Rectangle 4 is obscured in layers B and C, and is maintained off-screen by both. The addition of layer C divides the obscured part of layer B into two rectangles, 3 and 4.

The Layer structure is

```
typedef struct{
        Word *base;             /* start of data */
        unsigned width;         /* width in words */
        Rectangle rect;         /* image rectangle */
        Obscured *obs;          /* linked list of obscured rectangles */
        Layer *front;           /* adjacent layer in front */
        Layer *back;            /* adjacent layer behind */
} Layer;
typedef struct{
        Layer *lobs;            /* frontmost obscuring Layer */
        Bitmap *bmap;           /* where the obscured data resides */
        Obscured *next;         /* chaining */
        Obscured *prev;
} Obscured;
```

The first part of the Layer structure is identical to that of a Bitmap. Actually, the Bitmap structure has an extra item to it: a NULL obs pointer, so that a Bitmap may be passed to a graphics routine expecting a Layer as argument. The next section explains why a Bitmap with a NULL obs pointer looks like a Layer.

The individual Layers are chained together as a doubly linked list, in order from "front" to "back" on the screen. (When they do not overlap, the order is irrelevant.) Besides the link pointers, a Layer structure contains a pointer to the list of obscured rectangles and the bounding rectangle on the screen. The obscured lists are also doubly linked, but in no particular order. Each element in the

Reprinted From acm Transactions On Graphics—April 1983—Vol 2, No. 2

obscured list contains a Bitmap for storing the off-screen image, and a pointer to the frontmost Layer that obscures it. As we shall see later, an Obscured element need only record which Layer is visible on the screen "in front" of it, not any other obscured Layers that also share that portion of the screen. The screen coordinates of the obscured Rectangle are held in the rect field of the Bitmap structure pointed to by the Obscured list entry, Obscured.bmap-> rect. All coordinates in the layer manipulations are screen coordinates.

Note that a Bitmap holding an obscured rectangle of a Layer has in its rect field a definition of the screen space it would occupy were it visible. This is an appealing model: as a Layer's contents are subdivided into visible and obscured portions, so is its coordinate system. More generally, since a Layer structure must contain a rectangle defining the portion of the screen it occupies, so must a Bitmap, because Layers are simply a generalization of Bitmaps.

6. LAYEROP

layerop( ) is the main interface between layers and the bitmap graphics primitives. Given a Layer, a Rectangle within the Layer, and a bitmap operator, it recursively subdivides the Rectangle into Rectangles contained in single Bitmaps, and invokes the operator on the Rectangle/Bitmap pairs. To simplify the operators, layerop( ) also passes along to the bitmap generator a pointer to a set of parameters. For example, to clear a rectangle in a layer, layerop( ) is called with the target Layer, the rectangle within the layer in screen coordinates, and a procedure (the bitmap operator), to invoke rectf( ). layerop( ) divides the rectangle into its components in obscured and visible portions of the layer, and calls the procedure to clear the component rectangles. A complete example is worked through at the end of this section. layerop( ) itself does no graphical operation; it merely *controls* graphical operations done by the bitmap operator handed to it. It is a functional that turns a bitmap operator into a layer operator.

layerop( ) first clips the target Rectangle to the Layer, then calls the recursive routine Rlayerop( ) to do the subdivision:

```
/*
 * Clip to outer rectangle of layer, then call Rlayerop()
 */
layerop(lp, fn, r, otherargs)
        Layer *lp;
        procedure (*fn)();        /* Pointer to bitmap operator */
        Rectangle r;
        misc otherargs;           /* Other arguments used by (*fn)() */
{
        r = intersection of r and lp->rect;
        if(r not null)
                Rlayerop(lp, fn, r, otherargs, lp->obs);
}
```

The argument (*fn)( ) is the pointer to the bitmap-level procedure. Rlayerop( ) recursively chains along the obscured list of the Layer, performing the operation on the intersection of the argument Rectangle and the obscured Bitmap, and passing nonintersecting portions on to be intersected with other Bitmaps on the obscured list. When the obscured list is empty, the rectangle must be drawn on the screen.

The code to test if two rectangles overlap is simple, but not well known:

```
rectXrect(r, s)   /* Do r and s intersect? */
        Rectangle r, s;
{
        return( r.origin.x < s.corner.x &&
                s.origin.x < r.corner.x &&
                r.origin.y < s.corner.y &&
                s.origin.y < r.corner.y   );
}
```

The && operator in C is a logical AND that does not evaluate the right operand if the left operand is false. Similarly, the == operator used below is the equality operator.

Here is Rlayerop( ):

```
/*
 * Rlayerop -- recursively subdivide and intersect
 *              rectangles with obscured bitmaps in layer
 */
Rlayerop(lp, fn, r, otherargs, op)
        Layer *lp;
        procedure (*fn)();
        Rectangle r;
        misc otherargs;
        Obscured *op;  /* Element of obscured list with which
                                to intersect r */
{
        if(op == NULL)                  /* This rectangle not obscured */
                (*fn)(lp, r, display, otherargs, op);       /* Draw on screen */
        else if(rectXrect(r, op->bmap->rect) == FALSE)        /* They miss */
                Rlayerop(lp, fn, r, otherargs, op->next); /* Chain */
        else{           /* They must intersect */
                if(r.origin.x < op->bmap->rect.origin.x){
                        Rectangle temp = piece of r left of op->bmap->rect;
                        Rlayerop(lp, fn, temp, otherargs, op->next);
                        r->origin.x = op->bmap->rect.origin.x;
                }
                /* etc. for other three sides of rectangle */
                /* What's left goes in this obscured bitmap */
                (*fn)(lp, r, op->bmap, otherargs, op);
        }
}
```

The Layer pointer and Obscured pointer are passed to the bitmap operator (*fn)( ) because, although they are clearly not needed for graphical operations, layerop( )'s subdivision is useful enough to be exploited by some of the software to maintain the layers themselves; we see an example of such usage later on. Note that if layerop( ) is handed a Layer with a NULL obs pointer, or a Bitmap, its effect is simply to clip the rectangle and call the bitmap operator.

So far, otherargs has been referred to in a deliberately vague manner. In practice, layerop( ) works something like the standard C formatted output routine printf( ): after the arguments required by layerop( ) (the Layer, bitmap operator, and Rectangle), the calling function passes the further arguments needed by the Bitmap operator. layerop( ) passes the address of the first of these arguments through the operator, which therefore sees a pointer to a structure containing the necessary arguments.

The following example illustrates the action of layerop( ). Although we will see several examples later, this is the simplest and most common use. lblt( ) uses layerop( ) and bitblt( ) to copy an off-screen Bitmap to a Rectangle within a Layer. The Bitmap may contain, for example, a character. The general case of copying a Rectangle from one Layer to another is discussed later.

```
Lblt(l, r, db, fp, o)
        Layer *l;
        Rectangle r;
        Bitmap *db;             /* Destination Bitmap */
        struct{
                Bitmap *sb;     /* Source Bitmap */
                int f;          /* Function code */
        } *fp;
        Obscured *o;
{
        bitblt(fp->sb, r, db, r.origin, fp->f);
}

lblt(l, sb, r, f)
        Layer *l;
        Bitmap *sb;
        Rectangle r;
{
        layerop(l, Lblt, r, sb, f);
}
```

Notice that the bulk of the code is declarations. This code assumes that the source Bitmap is in screen coordinates; if it were not, extra arguments to lblt( ) woule be passed to the operation routine Lblt( ) to describe the necessary coordinate transformation. The "extra" arguments to layerop, sb and f, are seen by Lblt as elements of a structure pointed to by fp.

As an example, consider drawing a character (the hashed rectangle) in Layer B in Figure 4. The first call to Rlayerop( ) has op set to the obscured, off-screen element of layer B. op is not NULL, nor is the overlap of r and rp- > rect, so we fall into the last block of the large if-else: part of the rectangle must be drawn in this obscured bitmap. The test

```
if(r.origin.x < op-> bmap-> rect.origin.x)
```

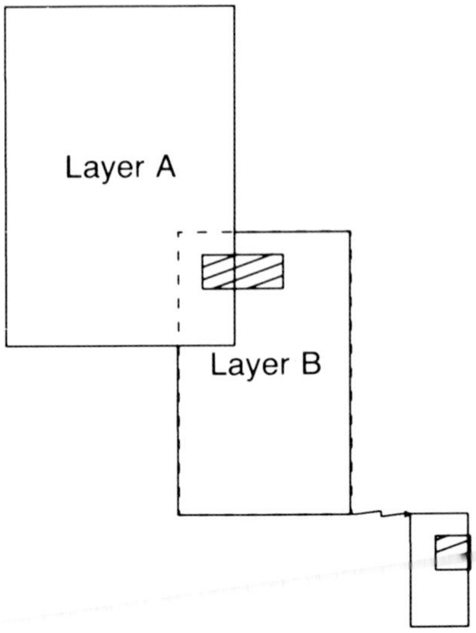

Fig. 4. Drawing a rectangle (for example a character) in a layer. Some of the rectangle is drawn on the screen, some in the obscured parts of the layer. The portion of the rectangle overlapping layer A is drawn in the obscured bitmap, not on the screen.

succeeds, so the right portion of the rectangle (to the right of Layer A) is cut off and passed on to a second invocation of Rlayerop( ). Here, the first if statement succeeds, the visible portion of the rectangle is drawn on the screen, and Rlayerop( ) returns to its first invocation. No further clipping is required, so the left portion of the rectangle is drawn in the obscured bitmap and the job is complete.

Although it is a complicated operation, layerop( ) is fast compared to the expensive graphics operations it invokes. When layerop( ) is called, its overhead is usually unimportant. This is because the data structures to manipulate layers were explicitly designed to make *drawing* as rapid as possible, since that is the most common operation. The less common interlayer manipulations such as creating and deleting layers are slower, but their price is still reasonable, considering how relatively infrequently they are invoked.

7. UPFRONT

There are three basic transformations that can in principle be applied to layers: changing the dimensions of a layer (scaling), changing the position of a layer on the screen (translation), and changing the front-to-back positions of overlapping layers (stacking).

The issues of scaling—changing a layer's size, as distinct from changing the scale of the coordinate systems inside the layer—and translation are not handled at all by the layer software, primarily because the subdivided nature of the data structures makes them difficult to implement. This is not to say that scaling and translation are not important transformations. Translation services, in particular, must be provided, perhaps by creating a new layer at the destination position, using lbitblt( ) (the generalized bitblt( ) operator, discussed later) to copy the data to the new position, and deleting the old layer. Note that the *data* in the layer can be dragged dynamically across the screen, using an auxiliary bitmap to hold the data obscured by the dragged rectangle, or even just dragging a rectangle outline, without dynamically and incrementally modifying the layer data structure. Given the relative complexity of the subdivided layer structure, this approach is more reasonable, and certainly adequate (it is the way our higher level software does translation). The notion of copying the data rather than signaling the application program to recreate it is consistent with the layer model: the application program is freed from the responsibility of maintaining its layer during rearrangement of the layers on the screen.

Scaling, however, does not fit as well into the software. Because there is no display list, the data in the different-sized layer cannot be recreated perfectly by the lower level software—at best, an intersection of the source and destination layers can be maintained. We have no solution to this problem, but do not regard it as critical; the importance of the extended bitmap idea is powerful enough for us to prefer to give up low-level support for scaling rather than to revert display lists. Also, it is unclear whether a layer should be regarded as a window or as a viewport. Does a different sized layer show the same thing at a different scale or a different-sized portion of the same thing? For example, if a large layer contains a picture composed of incompressible bitmaps, such as a page of characters in a text editor, what would happen to the image if the layer were shrunk to half its size? In particular, should the same configuration of smaller characters be drawn, or fewer characters of the same size? Either option might be correct under some conditions, and rather than make a decision we chose to ignore the issue.

Any stacking transformation can be defined as a sequential set of one-layer rearrangement operations, moving a single layer to another position (e.g., the front or back of the stack of layers). For example, the stack can be inverted by an action similar to counting through a deck of cards. upfront( ) is an operator that moves a layer to the front of the stack, making it completely visible. It is the only stacking operator in the layer software, because in the one place (deleting a layer) where a different operation is required, the desired effect can be achieved with acceptable efficiency by calls to upfront( ). The action of pulling a layer to the front was chosen because it is the most natural. When something interesting happens in a partially obscured layer, the instinctive reaction is to pull the layer to the front where it can be studied. upfront( ) also turns out be a useful operation during the creation and deletion of layers.

upfront( ) has a simple structure. Most of the code is concerned with maintaining the linked lists. The basic algorithm exchanges the obscured rectangles in the layer with those of the layer obscuring them, swapping the contents of the obscured bitmap for those on the screen (Figure 5). Since the obscured rectangle has the same dimensions before and after the swap, the exchange can be done in place, and it is not necessary to allocate a new bitmap; we need merely link it into the new obscured layer. Obscured rectangles are marked with the *frontmost* obscuring layer for upfront( )'s benefit: the frontmost layer is the layer that occupies the portion of the screen the rectangle would occupy were it at the front.

```
/*
 * upfront -- pull layer to the front of the screen
 */
upfront(lp)
        Layer *lp;
```

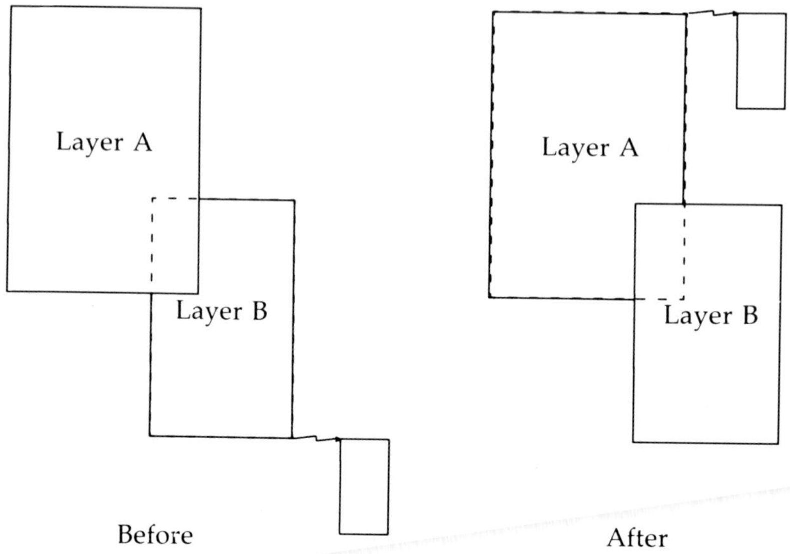

Fig. 5. Moving a layer to the front requires interchanging its off-screen bitmaps with screen rectangles.

```
{
        Layer *fr;          /* a layer in front of lp */
        Layer *beh;         /* a layer behind lp */
        Obscured *op;

        for(fr = each layer in front of lp){
                for(op = each obscured portion of lp){
                        if(op->lobs == fr){      /* fr obscures op */
                                screenswap(op->bitmap, op->rect);
                                unlink op from lp;
                                link op into fr;
                        }
                }
        }
        move lp to front of layer list;
        for(beh = all other Layers from back to front)
                for(op = each obscured portion of beh)
                        if(lp->rect overlaps op->bmap->rect)
                                op->lobs = lp;   /* mark op obscured by lp */
}
```

screenswap( ) interchanges the data in the bitmap with the contents of the rectangle on the screen, in place. It is easily implemented, without auxiliary storage, using three calls to bitblt( ) with function code XOR. Note that because of the fragmentation of the obscured portions done when a new Layer is created, it

Reprinted From acm Transactions On Graphics—April 1983—Vol. 2, No. 2

lp–>rect and op–>bmap–>rect intersect, the Layer must *completely* obscure it. Note also that it is upfront( ) that enforces the rule that the frontmost Layer obscuring a portion of a second Layer is the Layer marked as obscuring it. Only if these two Layers are interchanged is the screen updated.

The last loop is required; it is not sufficient to mark obscured rectangles only in the main loop, because rectangles initially behind lp may also need to be marked.

8. DELLAYER

It is simpler to delete a Layer than to create one, so we discuss deletion first. The algorithm is easy:

(1) Pull the layer to the front. It now has no obscured pieces, and is a contiguous rectangle on the screen.
(2) Color the screen rectangle the background color.
(3) Push the layer to the back. All storage needed for the obscured portions of the layer is now bound to the layer, since it obscures no other layer.
(4) Free all storage associated with the layer.
(5) Unlink the layer from the layer list.

A special routine, the opposite of upfront( ), could be written to push the layer to the back, but upfront( ) can be used for the task:

```
/*
 * dellayer -- delete a layer
 */
dellayer(lp)
        Layer *lp;
{
        Obscured *op;

        upfront(lp);
        background(lp->rect);
        /* Push to back using upfront */
        while(lp not rearmost layer)
                upfront(rearmost layer);
        /* Free the storage */
        for(op = each obscured part of lp){
                bfree(op->bmap);
                free(op);
        }
        unlink lp from Layer list;
}
```

Using successive calls to upfront( ) to push a layer to the back gives the screen a curious appearance during the deletion. dellayer( ) is so simple, though, that it seems unnecessary to give it extra support by providing a more efficient "downback( )" routine. upfront( ) does *not* join disconnected obscured bitmaps that could be joined because of the deletion, although it could. The difficulty of recognizing which bitmaps can be joined is too great to justify the usually small storage compaction and execution efficiency that would be gained thereby. Joining would be facilitated if the obscured lists of the layers contained information about which layer caused which edge to be cut during creation (e.g., see Rectangle 2 in Figure 3). In retrospect, it would probably have been better to use some form of tree structure for the obscured lists, with an indication at each node of the layer "responsible" for creating the obscured element or dividing the underlying structure into two or more elements.

9. NEWLAYER

Making a new layer is the most difficult layer operation, for it may require modifying obscured lists of other layers. If the new layer creates any new overlaps, the obscured list of the overlapped layer must be restructured so that upfront( ) need not subdivide any rectangles to pull the obscured layer to the front. The creation routine, newlayer( ), pays the price for the simplicity of upfront( ) and layerop( ).

The basic structure of newlayer( ) is to build the layer at the back, constructing the obscured list by intersecting the layer's rectangle with the obscured rectangles and visible portions of the current layers. After allocating storage for the obscured bitmaps, the layer is pulled to the front, making it completely visible on the screen and forcing the rectangles obscured by the new layer to occupy the new storage required by the addition of the new layer. Finally, the screen rectangle occupied by the new layer is cleared to complete the operation.

Several ancillary routines are used by newlayer( ). addrect( ) adds rectangles to the obscured list, obs, of the new layer. Since the new layer is built at the "back" of the screen, any obscured rectangle of the new layer will be obscured by a layer already on the screen. addrect( ) builds the list of unique obscured rectangles, marked by whichever layer is currently occupying the screen in each rectangle. To be sure that a rectangle is unique, it is sufficient to check only the origin point of that rectangle. The rectangles passed to addrect( ) are ordered so that the first layer associated with a particular rectangle occupies the screen in that rectangle.

```
/*
 * addrect -- add (unique) rectangle to
 *              obscured list of new layer
 */
Obscured *obs; /* Pointer to obscured list for new layer */
addrect(r, lp)
        Rectangle r;
        Layer *lp;        /* Layer currently occupying r on screen */
{
        Obscured *op, *newop;

        for(op = each element of obs)
                if(op->rect.origin == r.origin)
                        return;  /* Not unique */
```

```
                newop = new Obscured;
                newop->rect = r;
                newop->lobs = lp;
                link newop into obs list;
        }
```

Because it is called once for each rectangle, addrect( ) takes time proportional to the square of the number of obscured rectangles in the new layer. But since newlayer( ) will ultimately perform a series of expensive bitblt( )s, the time taken by the list operations is insignificant.

addobs( ) does recursive subdivision of the obscured rectangles that intersect the new layer, calling addrect( ) when an overlap is established. It is similar to layerop( ) except that it does not chain along the obscured list, and no special action (i.e., storage allocation) is required if the rectangles match exactly. As subdivided pieces are added to the obscured list of a current layer, the original rectangle must remain in the list until all the subdivided pieces are also in the list, whereupon it is deleted. New pieces must therefore be added *after* the original piece. When the topmost call to addobs( ) returns, the subdivision (if any) is complete, and the return value is whether the argument rectangle was subdivided. newlayer( ) then removes the original rectangle from the list if addobs( ) returns TRUE.

```
/*
 * addobs -- add obscured rectangle to list, subdividing obscured
 *              portions of layers as necessary
 */
boolean
addobs(op, argr, newr, lp)
        Obscured *op;
        Rectangle argr;         /* Obscured rectangle */
        Rectangle newr;         /* Complete rectangle of new layer */
        Layer *lp;              /* Layer op belongs to */
{
        Obscured *newop;
        Rectangle r;
        Bitmap *bp;

        r = argr;    /* argr will be unchanged through addobs() */
        if(rectXrect(r, newr)){
                /* This is much like layerop() */
                if(r.origin.x < newr.origin.x){
                        Rectangle temp = piece of r left of newr;
                        addobs(op, temp, newr, lp);
                        r.origin.x = newr.origin.x;
                }
                /* etc. for other three sides */
                /* r is now contained in rectangle of new layer */
```

```
            if(r == argr){   /* no clip, just bookkeeping */
                    addrect(r, lp);
                    return FALSE;  /* No subdivision */
            }
            addrect(r, lp);
        }
        bp = balloc(r);
        newop = new Obscured;
        /* Copy the subdivided portion of the image */
        bitblt(op->bmap, r, bp, bp->rect.origin, STORE);
        newop->bmap = bp;
        newop->rect = r;
        newop->lobs = lp;       /* Layer lp obscures this part of the new layer */
        link op into lp->obs;
        return TRUE;  /* Subdivision */
}
```

newlayer( ) is long but straightforward:

```
Obscured obs;  /* obscured list of new layer when at back */
/*
 * newlayer -- make a new layer in rectangle r of bitmap *bp
 */
Layer *
newlayer(bp, r)
        Bitmap *bp;
        Rectangle r;
{
        Layer *lp, *newlp;
        Obscured *op;

        /* First build, in obs, a list of all obscured rectangles that
         * will be obscured by the new layer, doing subdivision with
         * addobs()
         */
        obs = NULL;
        for(lp = each layer from front to back){
                for(op = each obscured portion of lp){
                        if(rectXrect(r, op->rect) &&
                          addobs(op, op->rect, r, lp)){
                                unlink op from lp->obs;
                                bfree(op->bmap);
                                free(op);
                        }
                }
        }
        /* Now add the rectangles not currently obscured, but that will
         * be obscured by new layer, by building layer & calling layerop()
         */
```

```
		newlp = new Layer;
		Bitmap part of newlp = *bp;
		newlp->obs = obs;	/* currently obscured ... */
		for(lp = each layer from front to back)
			layerop(lp, addpiece, lp->rect);
		newlp->obs = obs;	/* ... and soon to be */
		for(op = each element of obs)
			op->bmap = balloc(op->rect);
		link newlp into back of layer list;
		upfront(newlp);
		rectf(newlp->rect, CLR);		/* Clear the screen rectangle */
		return newlp;
	}
```

newlayer( ) takes an argument Bitmap, which is typically the screen Bitmap display, but may be any other. It is a simple (untried) generalization from Layers within Bitmaps to Layers within Layers, and a true hierarchy.

addpiece( ) is a trivial routine to add to the obscured list the rectangles that are currently unobscured (i.e. that have only one layer), but that will be obscured by the new layer.

```
addpiece(lp, r, bp, otherargs, op)
	Layer *lp;
	Rectangle r;
	Bitmap *bp;
	char *otherargs;/* Unused */
	Obscured *op;
{
	if(op == NULL)		/* This piece occupied by one layer only */
		addrect(r, lp);
	/* Otherwise it's already in obs list */
}
```

10. SCROLLING AND THE GENERAL BITBLT OPERATOR

So far, we have only discussed *support* for graphics, not graphical actions themselves. This section, on scrolling, and the next, on line drawing, illustrate how difficult graphics can be on a bitmap display, and how layerop( ) can help.

For simplicity of exposition, this section uses as an example the case of scrolling a layer; although the subdivision of rectangles can get complicated in sophisticated examples, the issues are all addressed by a simple case. Since the general case is not significantly harder to implement, this section presents a general lbitblt( ) operator that extends the bitmap-level bitblt( ) functionality to layers.

Scrolling a layer—moving a layer full of text up one line—is a special case of a bitblt operation. Scrolling a screen rectangle r is a single bitblt:

```
#define NLSZ 16 /* height of a text line */
bitblt(display, Rect(r.origin, Pt(r.corner.x, r.corner.y-NLSZ)),
		display, Pt(r.origin.x, r.origin.y+NLSZ), STORE);
```

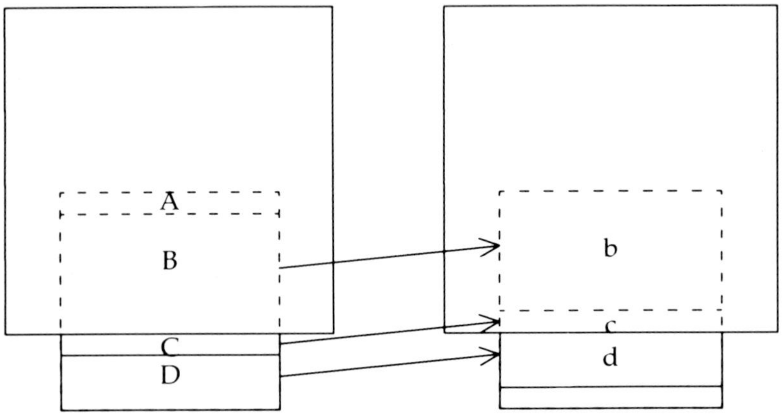

Fig. 6. To scroll the rear layer, the source rectangles B through D are copied to the destination rectangles b through d.

This bitblt copies all but the first line of text up one line. Rect( ) and Pt( ) create Rectangles and Points from their arguments. Scrolling a layer requires a series of bitblts, which must also be done in a certain order. Figure 6 illustrates a simple sample of scrolling a partially obscured layer. The scroll is broken into three bitblts, so that the source and destination rectangles each lie within a single bitmap.

The routine lbitblt( ) has semantics identical to bitblt( ), but accepts Layer arguments as well as Bitmaps, does the necessary subdivision of obscured rectangles, and executes the atomic bitblt( ) calls in the correct order. There are two basic methods for organizing lbitblt( ). The first method calls layerop( ) to create a list of source rectangles by dividing the original rectangle ((B + C + D) in Figure 6, with (A + B) off-screen and (C + D) visible) into a set of rectangles contained within single bitmaps. layerop( ) is then called for each source rectangle to subdivide it so the destination rectangles will also be contained in single bitmaps (separating C and D in Figure 6 because c is in a different bitmap from d). This has the disadvantage that it calls layerop( ) once for each source rectangle, even though simpler, faster code can accomplish the task.

The second method, and the one we use, calls layerop( ) twice: once to subdivide the source rectangles and once to subdivide the destination rectangles. The loop to intersect the source and destination rectangles is then trivial.

lbitblt( ) uses the defined type ListElement to couple the bitmaps to the rectangles:

```
typedef struct{
        Rectangle rect;
        Bitmap *bp;
} ListElement;
```

The type List chains together ListElements. Two calls to layerop( ), one in the coordinate system of the source Layer and one in the coordinates of the destination, generate the lists of rectangles in sorted order. A simple loop then executes the component bitblt( ) calls:

```
Point delta;      /* difference between source and dest. origin */
List SrcList;     /* list of source rect/bitmap pairs */
List DestList;    /* list of destination rect/bitmap pairs */

lbitblt(sl, rect, dl, pt, f)
        Layer *sl, *dl;
        Rectangle rect;
        Point pt;
        Code f;
{
        ListElement *s, *d;
        Rectangle r;

        delta = pt - rect.origin;
        layerop(sl, Pass, rect, SrcList);
        layerop(dl, Pass, raddp(rect, delta), DestList);
        for(s = each element of SrcList)
                for(d = each element of DestList) {
                        r = intersection of d->rect
                                and raddp(s->rect, delta);
                        if(r not null)
                                bitblt(s->bp, rsubp(r, delta),
                                        d->bp, r.origin, f);
                }
```

raddp( ) adds its second argument, a Point, to the origin and corner of its first argument, a Rectangle; rsubp( ) is the corresponding subtraction operator. Pass( ) is a trivial routine for creating the lists. The rectangles in the lists are sorted according to an ordering operator lessthan( ).

```
Pass(lp, r, sb, ap, op)
        /* the usual declarations */
        struct {
                List l;
        } *fp;
{
        ListElement *e;

        for(e = each element of fp->l)
                if(not lessthan(r, e->rect)) {
                        insert the ListElement {sb, r} into fp->l
                                before e;
                        return;
                }
        append {sb, r} to fp->l
}
```

```
boolean
lessthan(a, b)
        Rectangle a, b;
{
        if((a->origin.y < b->corner.y) && (b->origin.y < a->corner.y))
                return ((a->origin.x - b->origin.x)*delta.x) >= 0;
        else
                return ((a->origin.y - b->origin.y)*delta.y) >= 0;
}
```

The first test sees if the two rectangles overlap in y, and if so checks the x ordering; otherwise the y ordering is sufficient. The ordering of the lists simplifies doing the bitblts in the correct sequence. For the scrolling example, delta.y is positive, and lessthan( ) orders the rectangles so they are copied in decreasing y order (see Figure 6).

There are a few efficiency issues. If the source and destination bitmaps are distinct in the uppermost call, (e.g., in drawing a character in a layer), the rectangles need not be sorted, but lbitblt( ) sorts them anyway. Also, if one or both of the layers has an empty obscured list, lbitblt( ) could recognize these degenerate cases and call bitblt( ) directly if neither layer has obscured components, or lblt( ) if only one does.

More seriously, the implementation of lbitblt( ) presented here contains some code with quadratic complexity—specifically, the inner loops of Pass( ) and bitblt( ). (The first method described above only executes n times, but calls layerop( ) to (recursively) run down the destination lists, so the complexity is the same.) In our application the obscured lists are typically short, so this complexity is dwarfed by the expense of the underlying bitblt( ) calls. If this were not true, it would be straightforward to rewrite both Pass( ) and lbitblt( ) to use $n \log n$ search algorithms. The structure of the code would be the same, however, and the use of layerop( ) to organize the clipping would be unaffected.

11. LINES

Drawing lines on a dot-matrix display is an old problem (see, e.g., [6]). Drawing lines in layers is more difficult because the sequence of dots approximating a line must be independent of the structure of the layer. To draw a line efficiently in a partially obscured layer, the line-drawing algorithm must draw the line as a set of line segments in bitmaps, but the endpoints of the segments (which must be in integer coordinates) might not be points on the actual line being approximated. A line from (0, 0) to (300, 100) is not approximated by the same points as two lines, one from (0, 0) to (100, 33) and one from (100, 33) to (300, 100). Of course, if efficiency is not an issue, lines may be drawn by generating the set of dots for the approximation and deciding for each dot in which bitmap it will be drawn. Here we assume that a line segment may be drawn efficiently in a bitmap (which is true on any reasonable display), and that the problem is one of dividing up the original line.

Most line-drawing algorithms simulate a digital differential analyzer (DDA) to reduce the strength of the rational arithmetic in

$$y = \frac{\Delta y}{\Delta x} x + y_0$$

to increments and decrements. Different DDAs approximate a given line by different sets of points. Bresenham's algorithm [1] has no multiplications or divisions, and uses only integer arithmetic:

```
int e, Δx, Δy;
e=2Δy-Δx;
for(i=1; i<Δx; i++){
        drawpoint(x, y);
        if(e>0){
                y++;
                e+=2Δy-2Δx;
        }else
                e+=2Δy;
        x++;
}
```

(As mentioned earlier, this algorithm is usually implemented efficiently; drawpoint( ) is not a subroutine call, and the constants come out of the loop.) Here, e is an offset and scaled error term that represents the vertical distance between the actual line and the approximating points. Each time the algorithm draws a point, e is adjusted to track the local deviation from the actual line. When e is positive, the actual line is too far above the dots, and the dots are therefore moved up one unit in y.

The line algorithm can be restarted as it passes from obscured bitmap to bitmap in the layer by carrying the value of e across the boundary. But since layerop( ) calls the bitmap-level operators in a nondeterministic order, a simpler solution is to evaluate e at the (x, y) location where the line intersects the bitmap, and reset the line algorithm in each component bitmap. We are assuming $0 < \Delta y/\Delta x \leq 1$, a shallow line of positive slope. If we further assume that the real line passes through (0, 0), we can analytically specify points generated by Bresenham's algorithm. The equation of the actual line is

$$y\Delta x - x\Delta y = 0,$$

so at a generated point

$$y\Delta x - x\Delta y = r,$$

where r is the residual, that is, the deviation from the actual line, measured parallel to the y axis. For computational efficiency, e is offset and scaled from r:

$$\mathrm{e} = -2r + 2\Delta y - \Delta x. \tag{1}$$

To minimize r, we round to calculate y:

$$y = \left\lfloor \frac{x2\Delta y + \Delta x}{2\Delta x} \right\rfloor, \tag{2}$$

implying, as above,

$$r = y\Delta x - x\Delta y.$$

Substituting,

$$\mathrm{e} = (2x + 2)\Delta y - (2y + 1)\Delta x. \tag{3}$$

Note that if $(x, y) = (0, 0)$, $e = 2\Delta y - \Delta x$, as in the original algorithm. Equation (3) can also be derived directly from the algorithm (and vice versa). Given eqs. (2) and (3), we can break a line into a set of segments in bitmaps independently of the layer's configuration by resetting the DDA for each segment. This method generates a unique approximation because the state of the DDA is a strict function of x.

One problem remains. The clipping routine (see [6]) that divides the line into segments individually within bitmaps may clip to a horizontal or a vertical edge of a bitmap. If the edge is horizontal, several possible x values may be chosen (see Figure 7). Because lines are half-open, the desired value is the least x such that (x, y) is a point on the approximated line, as defined by eq. (1). It can be shown that the desired value is

$$x = \left\lceil \frac{2y\Delta x - \Delta x}{2\Delta y} \right\rceil \tag{4}$$

Turning these equations into working code involves a few obvious transformations to cover all possible cases. The transformations must be done carefully, to preserve the half-open property of lines. Given a routine clipline( ), which clips a line segment to a bitmap and draws it, using a line drawer which loads the DDA on the basis of the initial x value, layerop( ) can control drawing a line in a layer:

```
Lline(lp, r, db, fp, op)
        Layer *lp;
        Rectangle r;
        Bitmap *db;
        struct{
                Point p0, p1;   /* Endpoints of complete line */
                int mode;       /* Function code */
        }*fp;
        Obscured *op;
{
        clipline(db, r, fp->p0, fp->p1, fp->mode);
}
lline(lp, p, q, f)
        Layer *lp;
        Point p, q;
        int f;
{
        setline(p, q);    /* Initialize global parameters for line() */
        layerop(lp, Lline, lp->rect, p, q, f);
}
```

setline( ) initializes the global variables for the line, in particular Δx and Δy, and canonicalizes the line by coordinate transformations so that $0 < \Delta y/\Delta x \leq 1$. This line algorithm has advantages over an unadorned DDA, even for nonoverlapping bitmaps: the sequence of dots generated is independent of the direction in which the line is drawn, and portions of a line may be "undrawn." Both of these

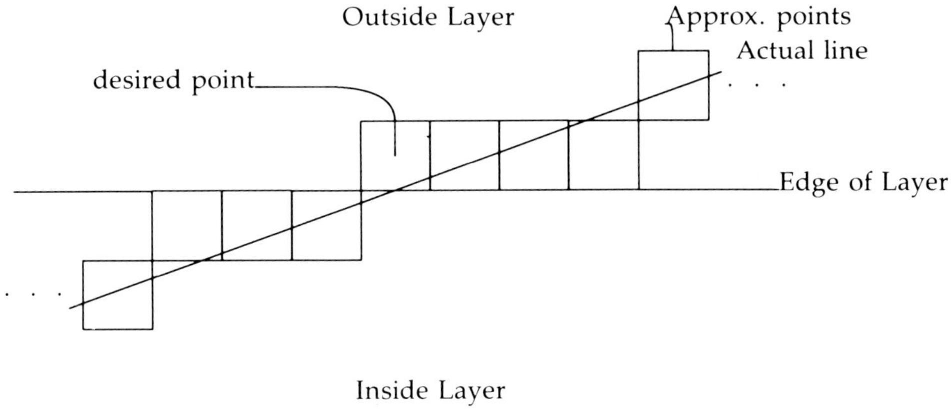

Fig. 7. Lines must be clipped to the first point outside a layer or bitmap.

advantages stem from the DDA being a strict function of x, instead of the distance from the starting point of the line.

The point of this section is not that lines can be drawn in layers, but how layerop( ) helps draw them. Given an object to be drawn—a line, a circle, an ellipse, a polygon, a spline, etc.—and an operator that can draw the object in a bitmap, layerop( ) will invoke the operator with the clipped rectangle/bitmap pairs that draw the complete object in a layer. The implementation of the bitmap operators can be tuned for performance. In our application, we build lines out of line segments with a restartable DDA for maximum speed, but draw arcs and circles as sequences of points because we do not draw them nearly as often. If circles were important to an application, the same sort of DDA restarting could be applied, using layerop( ) to define the clipping rectangles for each component of the circle.

12. CONCLUSIONS

The software described here is in day-to-day use on hundreds of "Blit" terminals throughout Bell Labs, providing an asynchronous window interface to the multiprogrammed Unix[3] system. Unlike previous window systems, the layers software does not keep display lists [5], force "repainting" during window operations [7], or restrict graphical operations in any way. Instead, it supports general bitblt-style raster graphics by extending the notion of a bitmap to encompass rectangular regions that are subdivided into visible and invisible portions, and provides an elegant interface between the simple, traditional bitmap operations and the more general ones. The role of the traditional "window manager" is reduced to providing a user interface. In [5] appears the sentence, "Research needs to be done to develop a way in which to conveniently store and manipulate graphics data in the context of a window manager." layerop( ) and its associated primitives meet this challenge.

[3] Unix is a trademark of Bell Laboratories.

ACKNOWLEDGMENTS

Many people helped develop the algorithms discussed herein. The data structures grew out of discussions with Ken Thompson; Doug McIlroy guided me through the mazes of integer geometry; Peter Weinberger got my line-drawing theorems straight; Andrew Koenig simplified the Bitmap data structure; Andrew Hume spent a difficult week getting the details of lbitblt( ) right; John Reiser wrote an astonishing and indispensable implementation of bitblt( ); and Brian Kernighan, Dave MacQueen, and Chris van Wyk made helpful constructive criticism on an early manuscript, which led me to rethink and rewrite large portions of the software as well as of the paper. I thank them all. I am most deeply indebted, however, to Bart Locanthi, who wrote the first bitblt( ), greatly improved the interface to layerop( ), and, most important, designed and built a bitmap terminal and placed it on my desk, thereby challenging me to tame the bitmap world.

REFERENCES

1. BRESENHAM, J. E. Algorithm for computer control of a digital plotter. *IBM Syst. J. 4*, 1 (1965), 25–30.
2. GUIBAS, L. J., AND STOLFI, J. A language for bitmap manipulation. *ACM Trans. Gr. 1*, 3 (July 1982), 191–214.
3. INGALLS, D. H. H. The Smalltalk graphics kernel. *Byte 6*, 8 (Aug. 1981), 168–194.
4. LANTZ, K. A. AND RASHID, R. F. Virtual terminal management in a multiple process environment. In *Proc. 7th Symp. Operating Systems Principles* (Pacific Grove, Calif., Dec. 10–12), ACM, New York, 1979, pp. 86-97.
5. MEYROWITZ, N., AND MOSER, M. BRUWIN: An adaptable design strategy for window manager/ virtual terminal systems. In *Proc. 8th Symp. Operating Systems Principles 15*, 5 (Pacific Grove, Calif., Dec. 14–16), ACM, New York, 1981, pp. 180–189.
6. NEWMAN, W. M., AND SPROULL, R. F. *Principles of Interactive Computer Graphics*, 2nd ed. McGraw-Hill, New York, 1979
7. TESLER, L. The Smalltalk environment. *Byte 6*, 8 (Aug. 1981), 90–147.
8. WEINREB, D., AND MOON, D. *Introduction to using the window system.* Symbolics, Inc., 1981.

Received February 1983; revised April 1983; accepted April 1983

Reprinted From **acm Transactions On Graphics**—April 1983—Vol. 2, No. 2

PANEL

SOLID MODELING: A USER PERSPECTIVE

CHAIR: Frank W. Bliss, Ford Motor Company
PANELISTS: Carl Machover, Machover Associates
Carl Vogel, General Motors Corporation
Donald R. Witte, Bendix Kansas City

CHAIRMAN'S INTRODUCTION:

In the past few years there has been a lot of interest and excitement generated by solid modeling. Numerous papers have been presented on the value and benefits of this technology. Many talented individuals have contributed to the state of the art. Solid modeling has played a larger role at SIGGRAPH in the past three years, with tutorials, panel discussions and technical papers. All this material has been presented for the most part by academics, researchers and developers of solid modeling systems.

The users of solid modeling systems have yet to be heard from. The reason is that there have been very few of them out there in the past. However, that situation is slowly changing. Now that several CAD/CAM vendors are marketing solid modeling systems, a small cadre of users does exist.

This panel will be composed primarily of users of solid modeling systems. They will discuss topics of interest to potential users (and also developers) of solid modelers. Questions to be addressed include:

What is the status of solid modeling systems from a user standpoint?

Can the present solid modelers be used in a production environment today?

Should a solid modeling system replace the present wire frame and surface systems or be integrated with them?

What are the problems associated with using a solid modeling system?

How good is the user interface?

Does the necessary application software exist?

The primary intent of this Panel discussion is to give the potential user some idea as to whether the available solid modeling systems are useful for his applications.

It is beginning to look like the next generation CAD/CAM system for mechanical design will be a solid modeler. The big question is "when will this occur?"

Frank W. Bliss of Ford Motor Company is in charge of the Solid Modeling Project at the Scientific Research Lab. Work has been done in the area of Mass Properties and the generation of very realistic color shaded pictures of automotive components. In addition, several commercial solid modeling systems have been evaluated. The results of this effort will be discussed.

Carl Machover, President of Machover Associates, is a well known CAD/CAM industry consultant. He has over 25 years experience in graphics and has consulted with a number of companies concerning solid modeling. He is particularly interested in the problems associated with using solid modeling systems.

Carl Vogel is a senior designer at the Chevrolet Division of General Motors. GM is using its in-house developed solid modeling system GMSOLID. Vogel will discuss the use of this system in the Powertrain and Chassis component design areas.

Donald R. Witte is a Staff Engineer at Bendix Kansas City Division. He is using Control Data's Synthavision system to generate color shaded pictures of castings. Bendix has effected cost savings on supplier-built prototype parts by including color pictures with the detail drawing of parts. Witte will discuss this work.

Particle Systems—A Technique for Modeling a Class of Fuzzy Objects

WILLIAM T. REEVES
Lucasfilm Ltd

This paper introduces particle systems—a method for modeling fuzzy objects such as fire, clouds, and water. Particle systems model an object as a cloud of primitive particles that define its volume. Over a period of time, particles are generated into the system, move and change form within the system, and die from the system. The resulting model is able to represent motion, changes of form, and dynamics that are not possible with classical surface-based representations. The particles can easily be motion blurred, and therefore do not exhibit temporal aliasing or strobing. Stochastic processes are used to generate and control the many particles within a particle system. The application of particle systems to the wall of fire element from the Genesis Demo sequence of the film *Star Trek II: The Wrath of Khan* [10] is presented.

Categories and Subject Descriptors: I.3.3 [**Computer Graphics**]: Picture/Image Generation; I.3.5 [**Computer Graphics**]: Computational Geometry and Object Modeling; I.3.7 [**Computer Graphics**]: Three-Dimensional Graphics and Realism

General Terms: Algorithms, Design

Additional Key Words and Phrases: Motion blur, stochastic modeling, temporal aliasing, dynamic objects

1. INTRODUCTION

Modeling phenomena such as clouds, smoke, water, and fire has proved difficult with the existing techniques of computer image synthesis. These "fuzzy" objects do not have smooth, well-defined, and shiny surfaces; instead their surfaces are irregular, complex, and ill defined. We are interested in their dynamic and fluid changes in shape and appearance. They are not rigid objects nor can their motions be described by the simple affine transformations that are common in computer graphics.

This paper presents a method for the modeling of fuzzy objects that we call particle systems. The representation of particle systems differs in three basic ways from representations normally used in image synthesis. First, an object is represented not by a set of primitive surface elements, such as polygons or patches, that define its boundary, but as clouds of primitive particles that define its volume. Second, a particle system is not a static entity. Its particles change form and move with the passage of time. New particles are "born" and old

Author's address: William T. Reeves, Lucasfilm Ltd, P.O. Box 2009, San Rafael, CA 94912.

Reprinted From **acm Transactions On Graphics**—April 1983—Vol. 2, No. 2

particles "die." Third, an object represented by a particle system is not deterministic, since its shape and form are not completely specified. Instead, stochastic processes are used to create and change an object's shape and appearance.

In modeling fuzzy objects, the particle system approach has several important advantages over classical surface-oriented techniques. First, a particle (for now, think of a particle as a point in three-dimensional space) is a much simpler primitive than a polygon, the simplest of the surface representations. Therefore, in the same amount of computation time one can process more of the basic primitives and produce a more complex image. Because a particle is simple, it is also easy to motion-blur. Motion-blurring of fast-moving objects for the removal of temporal aliasing effects has been largely ignored in computer image synthesis to date. A second advantage is that the model definition is procedural and is controlled by random numbers. Therefore, obtaining a highly detailed model does not necessarily require a great deal of human design time as is often the case with existing surface-based systems. Because it is procedural, a particle system can adjust its level of detail to suit a specific set of viewing parameters. As with fractal surfaces [5], zooming in on a particle system can reveal more and more detail. Third, particle systems model objects that are "alive," that is, they change form over a period of time. It is difficult to represent complex dynamics of this form with surface-based modeling techniques.

Modeling objects as collections of particles is not a new idea. Fifteen years ago, the earliest computer video games depicted exploding spaceships with many little glowing dots that filled the screen. Point sources have been used as a graphics data type in many three-dimensional modeling systems (e.g., the early Evans and Sutherland flight simulators), although there are few real references to them in the literature. Roger Wilson at Ohio State [4] used particles to model smoke emerging from a smokestack. There were neither stochastic controls nor dynamics in his model. Alvy Ray Smith and Jim Blinn used particles to model star creation and death in galaxies for the Cosmos series [11]. Alan Norton [9] used particles to generate and display three-dimensional fractal shapes. Jim Blinn [3] discussed light reflection functions for simulating light passing through and being reflected by layers of particles. His technique was used to produce images of the rings of Saturn. Blinn did not address the fuzzy object modeling problem which is the topic of this paper. Volumetric representations have also been proposed as viable alternatives to surface representations. Solid modeling [13] is a form of volumetric representation, as is the work of Norm Badler and Joe O'Rourke on "bubbleman" [2]. The use of stochastic modeling relates our work to the recent advances in fractal modeling [5].

Section 2 decribes the basic framework of particle systems in more detail. Section 3 examines how particle systems were used to produce the fire element in the Genesis Demo sequence from the movie *Star Trek II: The Wrath of Khan* [10]. Section 4 presents several other applications of particle systems, and Section 5 discusses ongoing and future research in this area.

2. BASIC MODEL OF PARTICLE SYSTEMS

A particle system is a collection of many minute particles that together represent a fuzzy object. Over a period of time, particles are generated into a system, move and change from within the system, and die from the system.

Reprinted From **acm Transactions On Graphics**—April 1983—Vol. 2, No. 2

To compute each frame in a motion sequence, the following sequence of steps is performed: (1) new particles are generated into the system, (2) each new particle is assigned its individual attributes, (3) any particles that have existed within the system past their prescribed lifetime are extinguished, (4) the remaining particles are moved and transformed according to their dynamic attributes, and finally (5) an image of the living particles is rendered in a frame buffer. The particle system can be programmed to execute any set of instructions at each step. Because it is procedural, this approach can incorporate any computational model that describes the appearance or dynamics of the object. For example, the motions and transformations of particles could be tied to the solution of a system of partial differential equations, or particle attributes could be assigned on the basis of statistical mechanics. We can, therefore, take advantage of models which have been developed in other scientific or engineering disciplines.

In the research presented here, we use simple stochastic processes as the procedural elements of each step in the generation of a frame. To control the shape, appearance, and dynamics of the particles within a particle system, the model designer has access to a set of parameters. Stochastic processes that randomly select each particle's appearance and movement are constrained by these parameters. In general, each parameter specifies a range in which a particle's value must lie. Normally, a range is specified by providing its mean value and its maximum variance.

The following subsections describe in more detail the basic model for particle systems, and how they are controlled and specified within the software we have written.

2.1 Particle Generation

Particles are generated into a particle system by means of controlled stochastic processes. One process determines the number of particles entering the system during each interval of time, that is, at a given frame. The number of particles generated is important because it strongly influences the density of the fuzzy object.

The model designer can choose to control the number of new particles in one of two ways. In the first method, the designer controls the mean number of particles generated at a frame and its variance. The actual number of particles generated at frame f is

$$NParts_f = MeanParts_f + Rand(\,) \times VarParts_f,$$

where $Rand$ is a procedure returning a uniformly distributed random number between -1.0 and $+1.0$, $MeanParts_f$ the mean number of particles, and $VarParts_f$ its variance.

In the second method, the number of new particles depends on the screen size of the object. The model designer controls the mean number of particles generated per unit of screen area and its variance. The procedural particle system can determine the view parameters at a particular frame, calculate the approximate screen area that it covers, and set the number of new particles accordingly. The corresponding equation is

$$NParts_f = (MeanParts_{sa_f} + Rand(\,) \times VarParts_{sa_f}) \times ScreenArea,$$

Reprinted From **acm Transactions On Graphics**—April 1983—Vol. 2, No. 2

where $MeanParts_{sa}$ is the mean per screen area, $VarParts_{sa_f}$ its variance, and *ScreenArea* the particle system's screen area. This method controls the level of detail of the particle system and, therefore, the time required to render its image. For example, there is no need to generate 100,000 particles in an object that covers 4 pixels on the screen.

To enable a particle system to grow or shrink in intensity, the designer is able to vary over time the mean number of particles generated per frame (i.e., $MeanParts_f$ and $MeanParts_{sa_f}$ are, as used above, functions of frame number). Currently, we use a simple linear function

$$MeanParts_f = InitialMeanParts + DeltaMeanParts \times (f - f_0)$$

or

$$MeanParts_{sa_f} = InitialMeanParts_{sa} + DeltaMeanParts_{sa} \times (f - f_0),$$

where f is the current frame, f_0 the first frame during which the particle system is alive, *InitialMeanParts* the mean number of particles at this first frame, and *DeltaMeanParts* its rate of change. The variance controls, $VarParts_f$ and $VarParts_{sa_f}$, are currently constant over all frames. More sophisticated quadratic, cubic, or perhaps even stochastic variations in both the mean and variance parameters would be easy to add.

To control the particle generation of a particle system, therefore, the designer specifies f_0 and either the parameters *InitialMeanParts*, *DeltaMeanParts*, and *VarParts*, or the parameters $InitialMeanParts_{sa}$, $DeltaMeanParts_{sa}$, and $VarParts_{sa}$.

2.2 Particle Attributes

For each new particle generated, the particle system must determine values for the following attributes:

(1) initial position,
(2) initial velocity (both speed and direction),
(3) initial size,
(4) initial color,
(5) initial transparency,
(6) shape,
(7) lifetime.

Several parameters of a particle system control the initial position of its particles. A particle system has a position in three-dimensional space that defines its origin. Two angles of rotation about a coordinate system through this origin give it an orientation. A particle system also has a *generation shape* which defines a region about its origin into which newly born particles are randomly placed. Among the generation shapes we have implemented are: a sphere of radius r, a circle of radius r in the x–y plane of its coordinate system, and a rectangle of length l and width w in the x–y plane of its coordinate system. Figure 1 shows a typical particle system with a spherical generation shape. More complicated generation shapes based on the laws of nature or on chaotic attractors [1] have been envisioned but not yet implemented.

Reprinted From **acm Transactions On Graphics**—April 1983—Vol. 2, No. 2

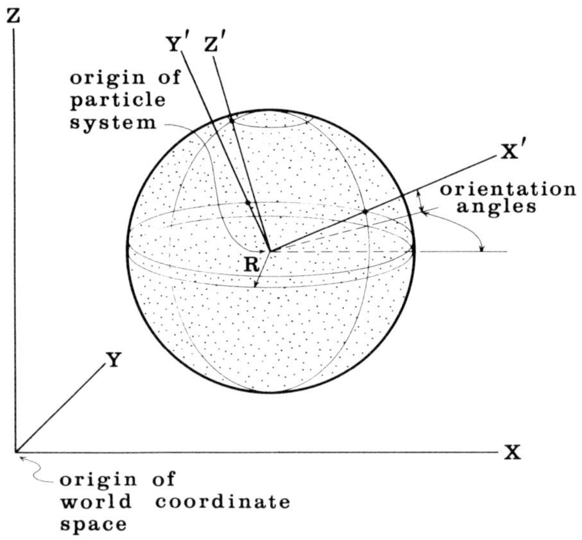

Fig. 1. Typical particle system with spherical generation shape.

The generation shape of a particle system also describes the initial direction in which new particles move. In a spherical generation shape, particles move outward away from the origin of the particle system. In a circular or rectangular shape, particles move upward from the x–y plane, but are allowed to vary from the vertical according to an "ejection" angle, which is another parameter (see Figure 3). The initial speed of a particle is determined by

$$InitialSpeed = MeanSpeed + Rand(\,) \times VarSpeed,$$

where *MeanSpeed* and *VarSpeed* are two other parameters of the particle system, the mean speed and its variance.

To determine a particle's initial color, a particle system is given an average color,[1] and the maximum deviation from that color. Particle transparency and particle size are also determined by mean values and maximum variations. The equations are similar to the one given above for initial speed.

A particle system has a parameter that specifies the shape of each of the particles it generates. The particle shapes implemented so far are spherical, rectangular, and streaked spherical. The latter is used to motion-blur particles—a very important feature when modeling fast-moving objects. We discuss streaking particles in more detail in Sections 2.5 and 3.

The number of possible attribute control parameters and their variants is endless. We are presenting those that we have found to be most useful and interesting.

2.3 Particle Dynamics

Individual particles within a particle system move in three-dimensional space and also change over time in color, transparency, and size.

[1] In more detail, average red, green, and blue values are specified.

To move a particle from one frame to the next is a simple matter of adding its velocity vector to its position vector. To add more complexity, a particle system also uses an acceleration factor to modify the velocity of its particles from frame to frame. With this parameter the model designer can simulate gravity and cause particles to move in parabolic arcs rather than in straight lines.

A particle's color changes over time as prescribed by the rate-of-color-change parameter. The transparency and size of particles are controlled in exactly the same way. In our implementation, these rates of change are global for all particles in a particle system, but one can easily imagine making this parameter stochastic too.

2.4 Particle Extinction

When it is generated, a particle is given a lifetime measured in frames. As each frame is computed, this lifetime is decremented. A particle is killed when its lifetime reaches zero.

Other mechanisms, if enabled, arrange for particles to be killed because they can contribute nothing to the image. If the intensity of a particle, calculated from its color and transparency, drops below a specified threshold, the particle is killed. A particle that moves more than a given distance in a given direction from the origin of its parent particle system may also be killed. This mechanism can be used to clip away particles that stray outside a region of interest.[2]

2.5 Particle Rendering

Once the position and appearance parameters of all particles have been calculated for a frame, the rendering algorithm makes a picture. The general particle-rendering problem is as complicated as the rendering of objects composed of the more common graphical primitives, such as polygons and curved surfaces. Particles can obscure other particles that are behind them in screen depth. They can be transparent and can cast shadows on other particles. Furthermore, particles can coexist in a scene with objects modeled by surface-based primitives, and these objects can intersect with the particles.

In our existing system, two assumptions allow us to simplify the rendering algorithm. First, we assume that particle systems do not intersect with other surface-based modeling primitives, and hence our rendering algorithm need only handle particles. Objects modeled using other techniques are composited together with particle system objects in a postrendering compositing stage. In order for a particle system to intersect or be behind other objects, the rendering system will split the image of a particle system into subimages based on clipping planes defined in the model coordinate space. These subimages are then combined with other images in the compositing stage.

The other simplifying assumption made in our current rendering system is that each particle can be displayed as a point light source.[3] With this assumption,

[2] Note that this clipping is performed in modeling space—to a given plane for example. Clipping to the viewing frustum occurs later in the rendering stage and is discussed below.

[3] Explosions and fire, the two fuzzy objects we have worked with the most, are modeled well with this assumption. Other fuzzy objects, such as clouds and water, are not. Section 5 discusses rendering algorithms for these objects.

Reprinted From **acm Transactions On Graphics**—April 1983—Vol. 2, No. 2

determining hidden surfaces is no longer a problem. Each particle adds a bit of light to the pixels that it covers. A particle behind another particle is not obscured but rather adds more light to the pixels covered. The amount of light added, and its color depend on the particle's transparency and color. Currently, the amount of light added does not depend on the distance between the particle and the viewing position, but that would be an easy extension. The viewing transformation, the particle's size, and its shape determine which pixels are covered. All particle shapes are drawn antialiased in order to prevent temporal aliasing and strobing. Light may be added to a pixel by many particles, so the rendering algorithm clamps the individual red, green, and blue intensities at the maximum intensity value of the frame buffer instead of letting them wrap around.

With this algorithm and assumptions, no sorting of the particles is needed. They are rendered into the frame buffer in whatever order they are generated. Shadows are no longer a problem, since particles do not reflect but emit light.

2.6 Particle Hierarchy

Our system has a mechanism that supports the formation and control of particle system hierarchies. The model designer creates a particle system in which the particles are themselves particle systems. When the parent particle system is transformed, so are all of its descendant particle systems and their particles. The parent particle system's mean color and its variance are used to select the mean color and variance of the offspring particle systems using the same equations presented earlier. The number of new particle systems generated at a frame is based on the parent's particle generation rate. The other parameters of the parent similarly affect those of its children. The data structure used to represent the hierarchy is a tree.

A hierarchy can be used to exert global control on a complicated fuzzy object that is composed of many particle systems. For example, a cloud might be composed of many particle systems, each representing a billowing region of water particles. A parent particle system could group these all together and control the cloud's global movement and appearance as influenced by the wind and terrain.

3. USING PARTICLE SYSTEMS TO MODEL A WALL OF FIRE AND EXPLOSIONS

The Genesis Demo sequence [14] from the movie *Star Trek II: The Wrath of Khan* [10] was generated by the Computer Graphics project of Lucasfilm Ltd. The sequence depicts the transformation of a dead, moonlike planet into a warm, earthlike planet by an experimental device called the Genesis bomb. In a computer-simulated demonstration, the bomb hits the planet's surface and an expanding wall of fire spreads out from the point of impact to eventually "cleanse" the entire planet. The planet's surface begins to buckle, mountains grow, and oceans, vegetation, and an atmosphere form to produce an earthlike environment.

The wall-of-fire element in the Genesis Demo was generated using a two-level hierarchy of particle systems. The top-level system was centered at the impact point of the genesis bomb. It generated particles which were themselves particle systems. Figure 2 illustrates the positions of these second-level particle systems and how they formed expanding concentric rings on the surface of the planet.

Reprinted From **acm Transactions On Graphics**—April 1983—Vol. 2, No. 2

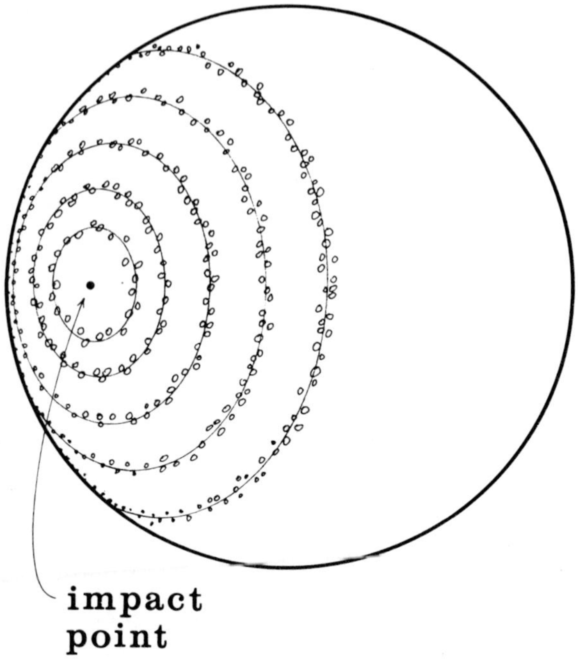

Fig. 2. Distribution of particle systems on the planet's surface.

The number of new particle systems generated in each ring was based on the circumference of the ring and a controlling density parameter. New particle systems were spaced randomly around the ring. Particle systems overlapping others in the same or adjacent rings gave the ring a solid, continuous look.

The second-level particle systems began generating particles at varying times on the basis of their distance from the point of impact. By varying the starting times of the particle systems, the effect of an expanding wall of fire was produced.

The second-level particle systems were modeled to look like explosions. Figure 3 shows an example. The generation shape was a circle on the surface of the planet. Each particle system was oriented so that particles, generated at random positions within the circle, flew upward away from the planet's surface. The initial direction of the particles' movement was constrained by the system's ejection angle to fall within the region bounded by the inverted cone shown in Figure 3. As particles flew upward, the gravity parameter pulled them back down to the planet's surface, giving them a parabolic motion path. The number of particles generated per frame was based on the amount of screen area covered by the particle system.

The individual particle systems were not identical. Their average color and the rates at which the colors changed were inherited from the parent particle system, but varied stochastically. The initial mean velocity, generation circle radius, ejection angle, mean particle size, mean lifetime, mean particle generation rate, and mean particle transparency parameters were also based on their parent's

Reprinted From **acm Transactions On Graphics**—April 1983—Vol. 2, No. 2

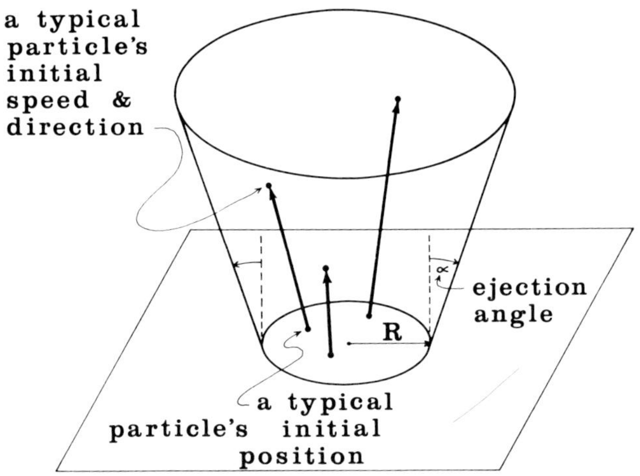

Fig. 3. Form of an explosion-like particle system.

parameters, but varied stochastically. Varying the mean velocity parameter caused the explosions to be of different heights.

All particles generated by the second-level particle systems were predominately red in color with a touch of green. Recall from Section 2.5 that particles are treated as point light sources and that colors are added, not matted, into a pixel. When many particles covered a pixel, as was the case near the center and base of each explosion, the red component was quickly clamped at full intensity and the green component increased to a point where the resulting color was orange and even yellow. Thus, the heart of the explosion had a hot yellow-orange glow which faded off to shades of red elsewhere. Actually, a small blue component caused pixels covered by very many particles to appear white. The rate at which a particle's color changed simulated the cooling of a glowing piece of some hypothetical material. The green and blue components dropped off quickly, and the red followed at a slower rate. Particles were killed when their lifetime expired, when their intensity fell below the minimum intensity parameter, or if they happened to fall below the surface of the planet.

A quickly moving object leaves a blurred image on the retina of the human eye. When a motion picture camera is used to film live action at 24 frames per second, the camera shutter typically remains open for 1/50 of a second. The image captured on a frame is actually an integration of approximately half the motion that occurred between successive frames. An object moving quickly appears blurred in the individual still frames. Computer animation has traditionally imaged scenes as individual instants in time and has ignored motion blur. The resulting motion often exhibits temporal aliasing and strobing effects that are disconcerting to the human eye. Motion blur is a complex topic that is beginning to appear in the literature [7, 12].

The particles in our wall-of-fire element are motion-blurred. Three-dimensional positions are calculated for a particle at the beginning of a frame and about halfway through the frame, and an antialiased straight line is drawn between the corresponding screen coordinate positions in the frame buffer.[4] Antialiased lines are used to prevent staircasing (moving jaggies) and strobing (popping on and off) effects. To be perfectly correct, screen motion due to movement of the camera should be considered when calculating where to blur a particle. One can also argue that simulating the imperfect temporal sampling of a movie camera is not ideal and that motion blur should really simulate what happens in the human eye. This is a good area for future research.

In the finished sequence, the wall of fire spread over the surface of the planet both in front of and behind the planet's limb (outer edge). The rendering algorithm generated two images per frame—one for all particles between the camera's position and the silhouette plane of the planet, and one for all particles on the other side of this clipping plane. These two elements were composited with the barren moonlike planet element and the stars element in back-to-front order—stars, background fires, planet, and foreground fires.

Because the wall of fire was modeled using many small light-emitting particles, light from the fire should have reflected off the planet's surface. Our current implementation of particle systems does not handle light reflection on surface-based objects. To achieve this effect, Lucasfilm team member Tom Duff added an additional strong local light source above the center of the rings of fire when he rendered the planet's surface. This produced the glow that circles the ring of fire on the planet's surface. (This glow is visible in Figure 5.)

Figure 4 is a frame showing the initial impact of the Genesis bomb. It was generated from one very large particle system and about 20 smaller ones about its base. About 25,000 particles exist in this image. Figure 5 occurs partway through the first half of the sequence. It contains about 200 particle systems and 75,000 particles. Figure 6 shows the ring of fire extending over and beyond the limb of the planet. It is formed from about 200 explosions and 85,000 particles. Figure 7 shows the wall of fire just before it engulfs the camera; in Figure 8 the camera is completely engulfed. Both employ about 400 particle systems and contain over 750,000 particles. The textures in Figure 8 are completely synthetic and yet have a "natural" and highly detailed appearance that is uncommon in most computer graphics images. These images are interesting statically, but they only really come alive on the movie screen. It is interesting to note that this is also the case for many of the best traditional (i.e., non-computer-generated) special effects shots where motion blur is an important factor.

A few points concerning random numbers are of interest from a production point of view. The random number routine we use is based on [6], and generates numbers uniformly in the range [0.0, 1.0]. It is an incremental algorithm based on updating a table of seed values. To checkpoint a production, all that need be saved is this random number table—we do not save all the parameters of 750,000 particles. To restart a computation at frame n, the closest preceding frame p is found that cannot contribute particles to frame n (this is determined from the lifetime parameters of all the active particle systems). Frame $p + 1$'s random number table is then read, and particle generation can begin from there. No

[4] A particle's trajectory is actually parabolic, but the straight-line approximation has so far proved sufficient.

Reprinted From **acm Transactions On Graphics**—April 1983—Vol. 2, No. 2

Fig. 4. Initial explosion.

Fig. 5. Expanding wall of fire.

Reprinted From acm Transactions On Graphics—April 1983—Vol. 2, No. 2

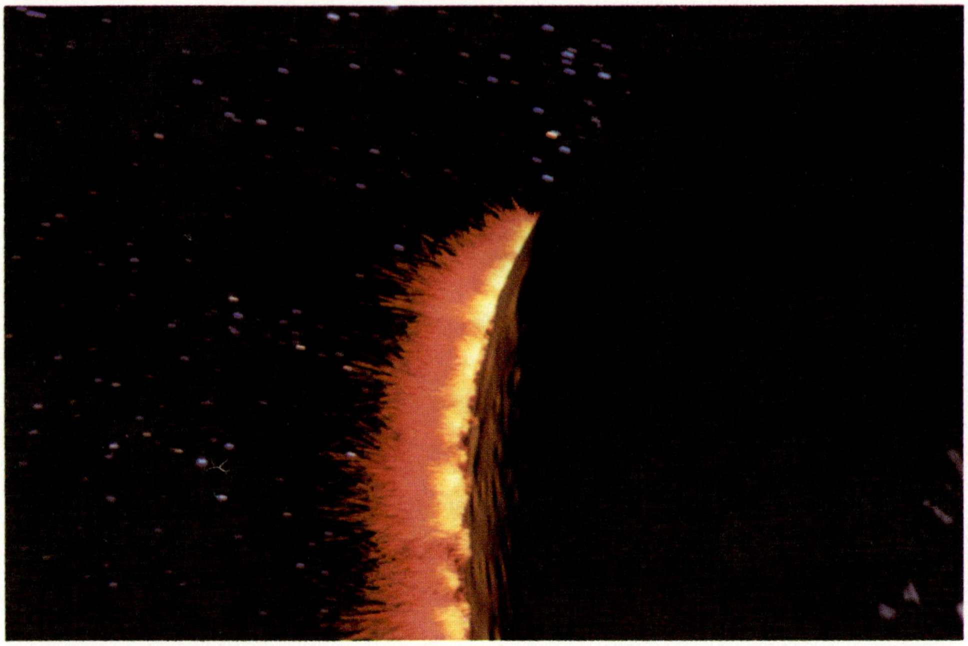

Fig. 6. Wall of fire over limb of planet.

Fig. 7. Wall of fire about to engulf camera.

Reprinted From **acm Transactions On Graphics**—April 1983—Vol. 2, No. 2

Fig. 8. Wall of fire completely engulfing camera.

particles are drawn until the simulation reaches frame *n*, so this backing up and restarting usually takes only a few minutes.

Particles moving off screen or being extinguished for any reason do not affect the randomness of other particles. This is because all stochastic decisions concerning a particle are performed when it is generated. After that, its motion is deterministic. If stochastic elements were to be used to perturbate the dynamics of a particle (e.g., to simulate turbulence), more care would have to be taken when checkpointing a frame and killing particles. In that case, it would probably be better to use a more deterministic and reproducible random number generator.

4. OTHER APPLICATIONS OF PARTICLE SYSTEMS

4.1 Fireworks

We are currently using particle systems to model fireworks. The fireworks differ from the Genesis Demo in that the control parameters of the particle systems vary more widely, and streaking is more predominate. Figure 9 shows two red explosions superimposed. One explosion is tall, thin, and near the end of its lifetime, and the other is short, fat, and building up to full steam. Figure 10 shows several green explosions dying off and blue spherical explosion starting up. Figure 11 contains overlapping, multicolored explosions formed with different generation shapes and ejection angles. Again, these images only really come alive when projected at 24 frames per second.

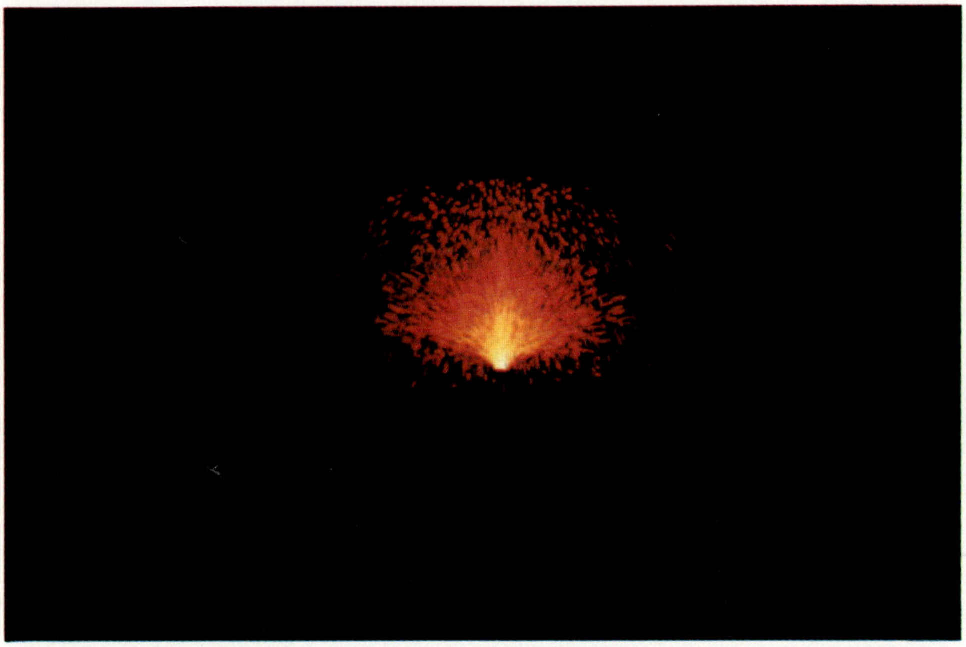

Fig. 9. Two red fireworks.

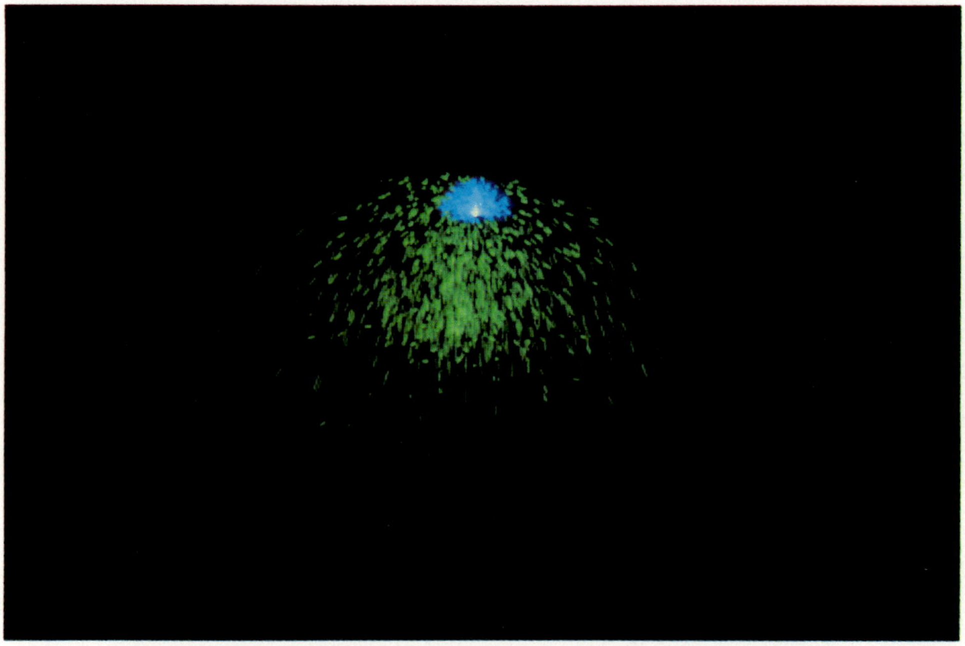

Fig. 10. Green and blue fireworks.

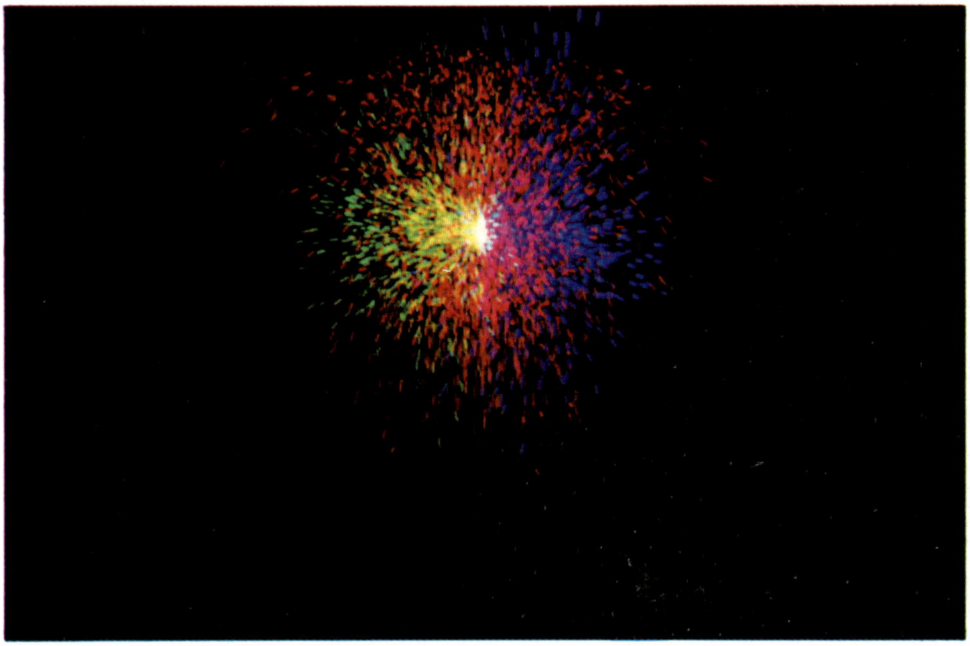

Fig. 11. Multicolored fireworks.

4.2 Line Drawing Explosions

Particle systems are being used to model exploding objects in a computer-simulated tactical display for a scene from the movie *Return of the Jedi* [8]. In this case, the particle systems are implemented on a line-drawing display. In order to simulate motion blur, the particles are drawn as very small straight lines instead of as points. The texturing effects that are evident in the previous examples are lost on a line-drawing display, and yet the motion still looks real and the sequence gives the viewer the impression that something is exploding. This is because the model is dynamic—it moves well.

4.3 Grass

To model grass, we use an explosive type of particle system, similar to that used in the Genesis Effect. Instead of drawing particles as little streaks, the parabolic trajectory of each particle over its entire lifetime is drawn. Thus, the time-domain motion of the particle is used to make a static shape. Grasslike green and dark green colors are assigned to the particles which are shaded on the basis of the scene's light sources. Each particle becomes a simple representation of a blade of grass and the particle system as a whole becomes a clump of grass. Particle systems randomly placed on a surface and overlapping one another are used to model a bed or patch of grass.

Figure 12 is a picture entitled *white.sand* by Alvy Ray Smith of Lucasfilm. The grass elements of this image were generated as described above. The plant

Fig. 12. *white.sand.*

elements were generated using a partially stochastic technique similar to particle systems.

5. ONGOING RESEARCH IN PARTICLE SYSTEMS

A logical extension of this research will be to use particle systems to model fuzzy objects in which the individual particles can not be rendered as point light sources, but must be rendered as individual light-reflecting objects.

To this end, we have begun to investigate the modeling of clouds. Clouds are difficult for several reasons. First, the shape and form of clouds are complex, depending on many factors such as wind direction, temperature, terrain, and humidity. The atmospheric literature abounds with cloud models that are simple in concept but computationally difficult, since most are based on partial differential equations. Second, clouds are difficult because they can throw shadows on themselves. This property is very important in making a cloud look like a cloud. Third, the number of particles needed to model a cloud will be very large. This will require an efficient rendering algorithm.

8. CONCLUSIONS

We have presented particle systems, a method for the modeling of a class of fuzzy objects, and have shown how they were used in making the fire element of the Genesis Demo sequence for the movie *Star Trek II*: *The Wrath of Khan.* Particle systems have been used as a modeling tool for other effects and appear promising for the modeling of phenomena like clouds and smoke.

Reprinted From **acm Transactions On Graphics**—April 1983—Vol. 2, No. 2

Particles, especially when modeled as point light sources or as streaks of light, have proved efficient to render—they are merely antialiased lines. Because they are so simple, they lend themselves to a hardware or firmware implementation. With a hardware antialiased line-drawing routine, the computation of our wall-of-fire element would have been two to three times faster.

Particle systems are procedural stochastic representations controlled by several global parameters. Stochastic representations are capable of producing minute detail without requiring substantial user design time. The textures in the fire sequence could not have been modeled with other existing methods. Fire images, scanned in from a photograph or painted, could have been texture mapped, but they would still have been static. Another advantage of a procedural representation is its ability to adapt to several different viewing environments. For example, procedural representations can generate only as much detail as is needed in a frame, potentially saving significant amounts of computation time.

Having finally come to grips with spatial aliasing, it is now time for computer image synthesis to being to investigate and solve temporal aliasing problems. The Genesis Demo is the first "big screen" computer-synthesized sequence to include three-dimensional dynamic motion blur. The particles in a particle system can easily be motion-blurred because they are so simple. A great deal of work remains to be done in this area—blurring particles is much easier than blurring curved surface patches.

Particle systems can model objects that explode, flow, splatter, puff up, and billow. These kinds of dynamics have not been produced with surface-based representations. The most important aspect of particle systems is that they move: good dynamics are quite often the key to making objects look real.

7. ACKNOWLEDGMENTS

The author gratefully acknowledges the suggestions and encouragement of all members of the graphics project at Lucasfilm Ltd, especially those who worked on the Genesis Demo sequence: Loren Carpenter, Ed Catmull, Pat Cole, Rob Cook, David DiFrancesco, Tom Duff, Rob Poor, Tom Porter, and Alvy Ray Smith. The crusade for motion blur and antialiasing in computer image synthesis is a goal of the entire graphics project and Lucasfilm as a whole. One of the referees deserves credit for pointing out several extensions and improvements to the motion blurring discussion. Finally, thanks to Ricki Blau for editorial and photographic assistance.

REFERENCES

1. ABRAHAM, R., AND SHAW, C. *DYNAMICS—The Geometry of Behavior*. City on the Hill Press, Santa Cruz, Calif., 1981.
2. BADLER, N. I., O'ROURKE, J., AND TOLTZIS, H. A spherical human body model for visualizing movement. *Proc. IEEE 67*, 10 (Oct. 1979).
3. BLINN, J. F. Light reflection functions for simulation of clouds and dusty surfaces. Proc. SIGGRAPH '82. In *Comput. Gr. 16, 3*, (July 1982), 21–29.
4. CSURI, C., HACKATHORN, R., PARENT, R., CARLSON, W., AND HOWARD, M. Towards an interactive high visual complexity animation system. Proc. SIGGRAPH 79. In *Comput. Gr. 13*, 2 (Aug. 1979), 289–299.
5. FOURNIER, A., FUSSEL, D., AND CARPENTER, L. Computer rendering of stochastic models. *Commun. ACM 25*, 6, (June 1982), 371–384.

6. Knuth, D. E. *The Art of Computer Programming*, vol. 2. Addison-Wesley, Reading, Mass., (1969), p. 464.
7. Korein, J., and Badler, N. I. Temporal anti-aliasing in computer generated animation. To appear in Proc. SIGGRAPH '83 (July 1983).
8. Lucasfilm. *Return of the Jedi* (film), May 1983.
9. Norton, A. Generation and display of geometric fractals in 3-D. Proc. SIGGRAPH '82. In *Comput. Gr. 16*, 3 (July 1982), 61–67.
10. Paramount. *Star Trek II: The Wrath of Khan* (film), June 1982.
11. PBS. *Carl Sagan's Cosmos Series.* (television series), Public Broadcasting System, 1980.
12. Potmesil, M., and Chakravarty, I. Modeling motion blur in computer-generated images. To appear in Proc. SIGGRAPH '83 (July 1983).
13. Requicha, A. A. G., and Voelcker, H. B. Solid modelling: A historical summary and contemporary assessment. *IEEE Comput. Gr. Appl.* (March 1982).
14. Smith, A. R., Carpenter, L., Catmull, E., Cole, P., Cook, R., Poor, T., Porter, T. and Reeves, W. *Genesis Demo Documentary* (film), June 1982, Lucasfilm Ltd.

Received February 1983; revised April 1983; accepted April 1983

Reprinted From **acm Transactions On Graphics**—April 1983—Vol. 2, No. 2

Temporal Anti-Aliasing in Computer Generated Animation

Jonathan Korein
Norman Badler

Department of Computer and Information Science
Moore School D2
University of Pennsylvania
Philadelphia, Pennsylvania 19104

Abstract

The desirability of incorporating temporal anti-aliasing, or motion blur, into computer generated animation is discussed and two algorithms for achieving this effect are described. The first approximates continuous object movement and determines intervals during which each object covers each pixel. Hidden surface removal is then performed, allowing the calculation of visible object intensity functions and subsequent filtering. The second form of algorithm detailed involves supersampling the moving image and then filtering the resulting intensity function to "multiply-expose" each output picture. The effects of filter types and the relationship of the algorithms to forms of spatial anti-aliasing are discussed.

CR Categories and Subject Descriptors: I.3.3 [Computer Graphics]: Picture/Image Generation - display algorithms; I.3.7 [Computer Graphics]: Three-Dimensional Graphics and Realism - animation, visible line/surface algorithms.

1. Introduction

In computer generated animation, a frame is typically generated by sampling an application model at an instant of time. The image created is then used, on output, to represent a small interval of time in the full animated sequence. While this form of sampling is satisfactory with scenes of low and moderate action, it has unpleasant effects when rapidly moving objects are present. At high speeds, movement begins to have a stilted, jerky appearance. An ax swung into a log may seem to simply appear in the wood without descending towards it. Rain is perceived as flashing dots, rather than streaks, and wagon wheels may start spinning slowly backward.

An analogy with a movie camera taking pictures of live action is appropriate. If the camera shutter speed is set extremely high little real world motion will be directly represented within each individual frame. The situation is typically the same in computer generated animation: the image is sampled at an instant of time. A movie camera normally opens its shutter for a short interval of time, and movement is represented as a slight blur of the image of the moving object. It is this slight blur which ameliorates the effects of sampling on the final film: the jerkiness is smoothed out, and quickly moving objects are displayed as streaks.

Traditional animators have confronted the problem in various ways. In cel animation speed lines, illustrated in figure 1, are drawn to suggest the blur of the movement. Repeated instances of a rapidly moving object often trail in its path, as shown in figure 1b. Broken spokes may be added to wheels to force the viewer to make the desired correspondences [17,19]. Williams [21] reports that Industrial Light and Magic has made efforts to alleviate the jerkiness typically accompanying stop-motion model animation through the use of motion blur.

Methods for achieving similar motion effects within a single frame are needed in computer generated animation. While the graphics literature is rich in papers on spatial anti-aliasing (eg. [5,6,9]), little research has been done investigating temporal anti-aliasing. Williams [20,21] gives short but enlightening discussions on the subject, and some of his unpublished notes contributed to the ideas in this paper. Szabo [16] also briefly surveys common temporal anomalies. Lipscomb [10] investigated the temporal aliasing occuring from differing update and display rates, a form which creates particularly irksome visual effects in real time refresh vector systems. Norton, Rockwood and Skolmoski [12] extend their efficient spatial anti-aliasing algorithm for surface textures to the temporal dimension. Two new papers not yet available to the present authors also attempt to simulate motion blur and should be published in tandem with the current research[1]. Potmesil and Chakravarty have evidently expanded their sophisticated camera model [13] to include motion blur as a special effect [14], and Reeves [15] has implemented a method of streaking dots representing stars and fire for use in the second Star Trek movie.

The goal of the current paper is to examine methods of temporal anti-aliasing which respect and augment the visible surface problem. It is necessary to determine not only which objects project onto a given pixel, but when they do so. A high resolution temporal intensity function may then be derived on the basis of visible object attributes; this function is in turn convolved with an appropriate averaging filter. Two methods for determining this high resolution intensity function are discussed. The first approximates object movement with continuous functions and, within the limits of this approximation, determines the precise intervals during which each pixel center is covered by an unoccluded object. The resulting intensity function is then derived using continuous approximations of the object attributes required by the shading routines. The second method uses a standard rendering algorithm to repeatedly 'supersample' the moving scene and determine a discrete approximation of the needed pixel intensity function. In the camera analogy the continuous algorithm may be compared to lengthening the interval during which the shutter is open while supersampling is similar to taking multiple instantaneous exposures. It should be noted that neither method attempts to integrate temporal and spatial anti-aliasing; this important topic is discussed in a subsequent section.

1. Peter Tanner, personal communication.

(a)

(b)

Figure 1

2. Continuous Algorithms

This class of algorithms is distinguished by its attempt to represent object movement, and object attribute changes in general, as continuous functions. The pixel intensity function (which is not continuous) is determined on the basis of these object change functions. This may be contrasted to a strict supersampling approach, in which a standard rendering algorithm uses static object attributes to determine the pixel intensity function at discrete points in time.

The goal of the procedure is to accurately represent the motion blur one would expect in a photograph of moving objects, though different filters may be used to achieve different effects. The algorithm will be presented in a highly parallel, pixel oriented form, primarily to simplify the exposition. The actual implementation is scan line based and uses some simple forms of coherence to increase efficiency. The outline below describes the creation of a single image. The 'filtered interval' refers to the temporal interval which the output frame will represent (ie. the interval over which the filter is non-zero), and the terms 'cover' and 'project onto' are used interchangeably.

For each object:

1. Determine a temporal transformation function for each dynamic object attribute.

2. Determine the areas which the moving object covers during the filtered interval.

For each pixel:

1. Determine which objects cover that pixel at some time in the filtered interval.

2. Determine the subinterval(s) during which each of these objects projects onto that pixel.

3. Perform hidden surface removal by eliminating subintervals associated with occluded objects.

4. Determine the pixel intensity function on the basis of the remaining subintervals and the corresponding object attribute functions.

5. Filter the resulting pixel intensity function.

In determining the feasibility of this type of solution, we limited the implementation to images made from objects composed of spheres which are projected as disks [1,11]. A similar algorithm for temporally anti-aliasing polygons, polyhedra, and curved surfaces approximated by polyhedra is described in the appendix.

2.1 Determining Continuous Movement Functions

In any animation system, it must be possible to determine the values of object attributes (eg. color, polygon vertices, circle center and radius) at various points in time. Ideally, the functions used to determine these values could be used as the temporal attribute functions directly. But while these functions may sometimes be explicitly represented, they are more often buried implicitly in the structure of the animating procedures. Even in the case of explicit representation, the form of the functions used and parameters modified are often too complex for efficient analysis. Thus these more exact functions must generally be substituted with interpolations between sampled values of the functions.

The animating program is expected to maintain correspondences between objects so that the anti-aliasing program can tell which object in one frame is 'the same' object in a previous frame. Interpolation functions are then computed to define each dynamic attribute value continuously, and these functions are used to create a blur representing this approximation of an object's transformation between sampled points. In the general case, the filtered interval need not correspond to the interval between successive scene samples, and neither of these need correspond to the interval between two output frames. The following description, however, will make these assumptions for the sake of clarity; relaxing them does not significantly complicate the algorithm.

Two important decisions must be made: what attributes should be interpolated, and with what form of function? The former question not only requires a separation of dynamic from static attributes, but also determines the level in the output pipeline at which temporal anti-aliasing becomes involved. In the simple case of spheres projected as disks it is possible to work with image space attributes. For shaded polygons, some object space calculations are necessary and more complex objects may require an algorithm based completely in object space. Care must also be taken to understand the geometric significance of the interpolated attributes. Interpolating the coefficients of each term of an expanded polynomial has very different results than the interpolation of the disk center and radius. In general, interpolation of geometrically meaningful parameters leads to more intuitive and predictable, though less general, results.

The forms of the interpolation functions are dictated by the usual trade-offs between accuracy and efficiency. The implementation described uses only linear interpolation functions: simplicity and speed were emphasized. The major sacrifice made is that the path each disk travels on the image plane is straight. This approximation of curved movement by piecewise linear blurs is satisfactory only if rapidly arcing motions are sampled frequently. Higher order interpolation functions could alleviate this effect (William's notes suggest B-splines), but would substantially increase the cost of subsequent processing.

For disks, the attributes for which interpolation functions are formed are specifically:

- the x coordinate of the disk center;
- the y coordinate of the disk center;
- the depth of the disk from the view plane;
- the disk radius;
- the disk intensity.

Each of these attributes will now be considered piecewise linear functions of time.

2.2 Determining the Covering Intervals

In the current algorithm a pixel is considered as a point on the image plane (alternatives will be discussed later). Accurately determining the pixel intensity function requires finding the subintervals of the filtered interval during which a given object covers the pixel. This in turn requires the determination of the times when an object boundary crosses over that pixel. Because this is a relatively expensive operation, it must only be performed when necessary. Both bounding boxes and exact boundaries of object paths are used to reduce the number of such calculations in the current implementation.

When linear attribute interpolations are used, finding these areas is quite simple. The bounding box of the movement path between a pair of disks is simply the bounding box of the pair of disks. The scan line algorithm implemented maintains sorted active scan line and active pixel lists so that only object paths whose bounding box covers a pixel are ever considered in subsequent processing.

Determining the moving disk boundary exactly is almost equally simple. Disk movement on the image plane is completely determined by the radius interpolation function, which controls scaling, and the x and y disk center interpolation functions, which control translation. If the radial scaling is greater than the center translation, as shown in figure 2a, then the boundary of the moving disk over the interval is simply the circle surrounding the larger of the two sampled disks. Testing for inclusion in the boundary is done by testing for inclusion in this circle.

If the center translation component of the movement is greater than the radial scaling, a boundary of the shape shown in figure 2b will arise. This shape is always bounded by arcs from the sampled circles and line segments from the outer pair of lines tangent to both of these circles. Testing for a pixel's inclusion in this boundary is simply a matter of testing for its inclusion in either of the sampled circles or in the isosceles trapezoid connecting the four tangent points defined by these lines.

When the points at which the disk attributes are sampled are more closely spaced than the endpoints of the interval to be filtered, testing for inclusion in the path of the disk requires testing for inclusion in numerous boundaries of the type just discussed. A filtered interval may also truncate a sampled interval. In this case the circles defined by the interpolation functions at that time, rather than at the time actually sampled, are used in the inclusion tests and in deriving the trapezoid.

While the boundary serves to define which pixels are, at some time in the filtered interval, covered by a disk, it does not derive the subinterval during which they are actually covered by the disk. When the filtered interval corresponds to the interval between attribute

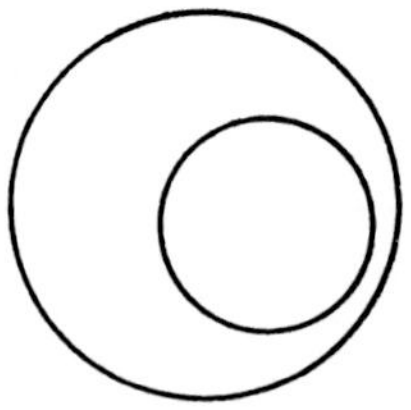

Figure 2a. When scaling dominates image motion, the larger of the two circles bounds the movement path.

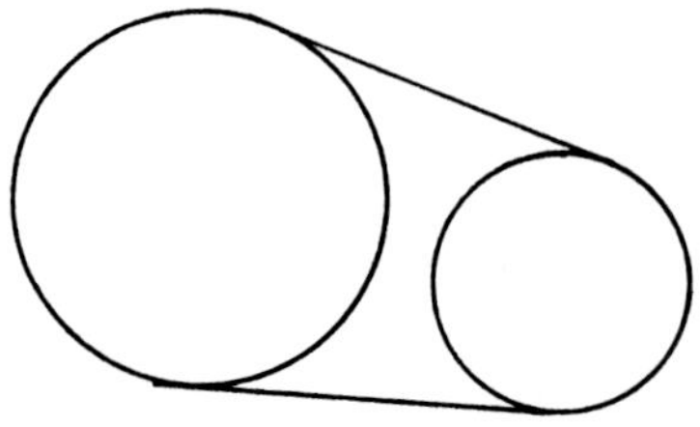

Figure 2b. When translation dominates image motion, parts of each circle and the two outer lines tangent to each circle bound the movement path.

samples, determining this subinterval is especially simple. If a pixel is within the disk at the start and/or end of the interval, the subinterval starts and/or stops there as well. Otherwise, the subinterval endpoint(s) can be determined by intersecting the circle surrounding the moving disk with the pixel location. The following terms will be used in describing this equation, which must be solved for time t:

px, py : the pixel location;

ax * t + bx : the interpolation function for the x coordinate of the disk center;

ay * t + by : the interpolation function for the y coordinate of the disk center;

ar * t + br : the interpolation function for the disk radius.

The actual equation follows, with the general equation for a circle listed below it to indicate its derivation.

$$(px - (ax * t + bx))^2 + (py - (ay * t + by))^2 = (ar * t + br)^2$$

$$(x - h)^2 + (y - k)^2 = r^2$$

If the filtered interval is greater than the sampling interval, this quadratic may have to be evaluated more than once. It should also be noted that the use of image space coordinates does not account for perspective foreshortening, and thus the time intervals derived will only be an approximation of three-dimensional linear movement is most situations.

It is possible to label each disk as moving or non-moving on the basis of some movement threshold, and only blur those disks which exceed that threshold. This occasionally gives an unpleasant all-or-nothing effect, as objects just under the threshold will appear as still disks and those just above the threshold appear as blurs. Nonetheless, it is a useful efficiency measure. The supersampling method turns out to be more conducive to tailoring the amount of anti-aliasing to be done to the amount of movement present.

2.3 Eliminating Occluded Intervals

For a given pixel, we now have the intervals during which every object projects onto it. These intervals, however, do not account for occlusion by other objects also projecting onto that pixel. To determine the intervals in which each object is actually visible, temporal depth functions must be derived[1].

---

1. There is a similar problem in area-sampling for visible surfaces [5].

For disks, the depth interpolation function may be used directly. The intervals so far derived can be pared down to reflect only intervals during which a specific disk projects to the pixel unoccluded: only 'visible disk intervals' will remain. Figure 3a shows the depth functions of three disks (a,b and c) over the subintervals during which they are determined to project onto a specific pixel. It can be seen that in interval $[a_s, a_e]$, disk a occludes disk b. Furthurmore, in interval $[c_s, i]$, disk c covers disk b, while afterwords disk b covers disk c. After taking depth into account, the new intervals, shown in figure 3b, represent only the times that a disk is actually projecting onto a pixel unimpeded.

The problem of removing the occluded intervals is quite similar to determining the continuous visiblity of polygons on a single scan line [3,18]. Time replaces the scan line, the subinterval endpoints replace the intersection of the scan line with polygon edges, and the depth interpolation function replaces the depth of the polygon for that scan line. The current implementation starts with the earliest, shallowest interval and determines the end of its visible portion by finding intersections (if any) with other intervals, after which the process is iterated with the new shallowest interval. It is important to note that methods utilizing coherence between scan lines in spatial hidden surface algorithms apply between adjacent pixels in the temporal case.

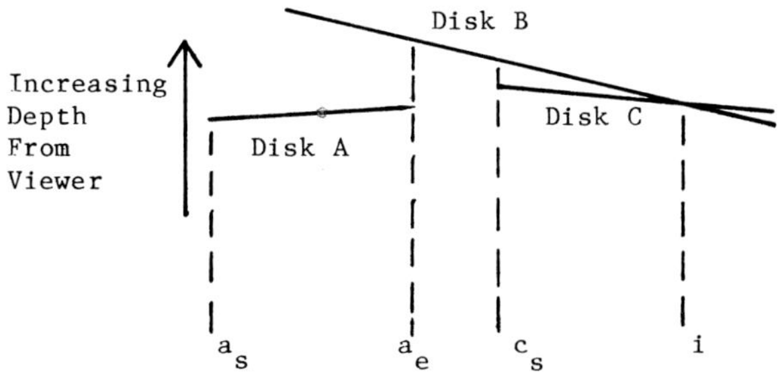

Figure 3a. The intervals associated with disks A,B and C before hidden surface removal.

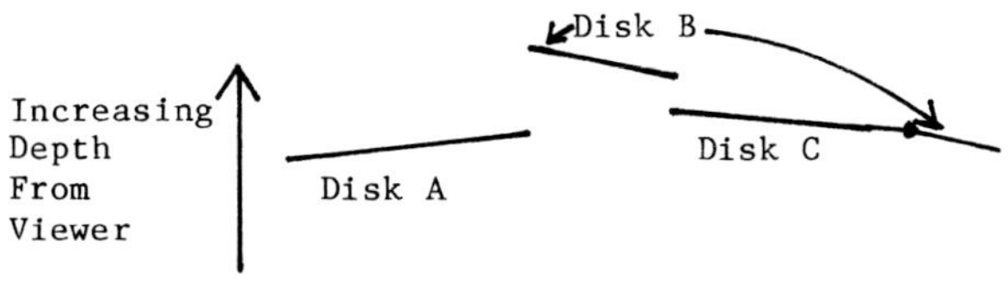

Figure 3b. The intervals after hidden surface removal.

2.4 Determining the Pixel Intensity Function

At this point a set of time intervals, each specifying a single visible object, have been determined. An intensity function must then be derived for each of these intervals using the attribute functions defined for the corresponding objects. The complexity of these calculations is directly related to the complexity of the shading algorithm used; for disks, we may simply use the intensity interpolation function already calculated. Using these functions, a piecewise linear pixel intensity function is easily derived. The appendix illustrates the more sophisticated techniques necessary when dealing with shaded polygons.

The intensity function may now be filtered and the final pixel intensity calculated. The effects of various filter types are discussed later: the results shown in figures 4a through 4f and in figure 4h were achieved with a simple rectangular filter. Figure 4a shows a single disk expanding and moving diagonally. In figure 4b two moving disks are piercing two still disks. The two disks in figure 4c are both moving from their left to right, and thus the shallower yellow disk almost always occludes the purple disk. This may be contrasted to the opposing movements occurring in figure 4d: the deeper disk is now visible for a much greater period of time towards the ends of the motion. In figure 4e eight disks are expanding and moving from the center of the screen in different directions. The yellow disks begin motion deeper than the pink disks but soon become more shallow. A still disk covering an expanding disk gives figure 4f the semblance of an eclipse. Figure 4g displays unblurred photos of bubbleman throwing a ball to compare with the various anti-aliased sequences shown. Figure 4h was created with the standard box filter, while the filter used to generate figure 4i emphasized later movement.

3. Supersampling Algorithms

In spatial anti-aliasing, determining an approximation of the image intensity function is often accomplished by simply sampling the image at a greater resolution than that of the output display [7]. Thus for each pixel the intensity might be determined in four or more different locations, rather than just one. A filter may then be applied to derive the actual intensity of the output pixel.

The same technique can be applied in temporal anti-aliasing. The animation system generates not one, but multiple intensity buffers for a single output frame, each corresponding to a slightly different point in time. The intensities of each pixel in the sequence of buffers form a pixel intensity function which has been digitized at a greater resolution than the output frame rate, and this function may then be filtered to create the actual output image. This approach is simple to implement and has the major advantage of being adaptable to any form of image; it is irrelevant what object representations or rendering techniques are being used. It is hard to overestimate the

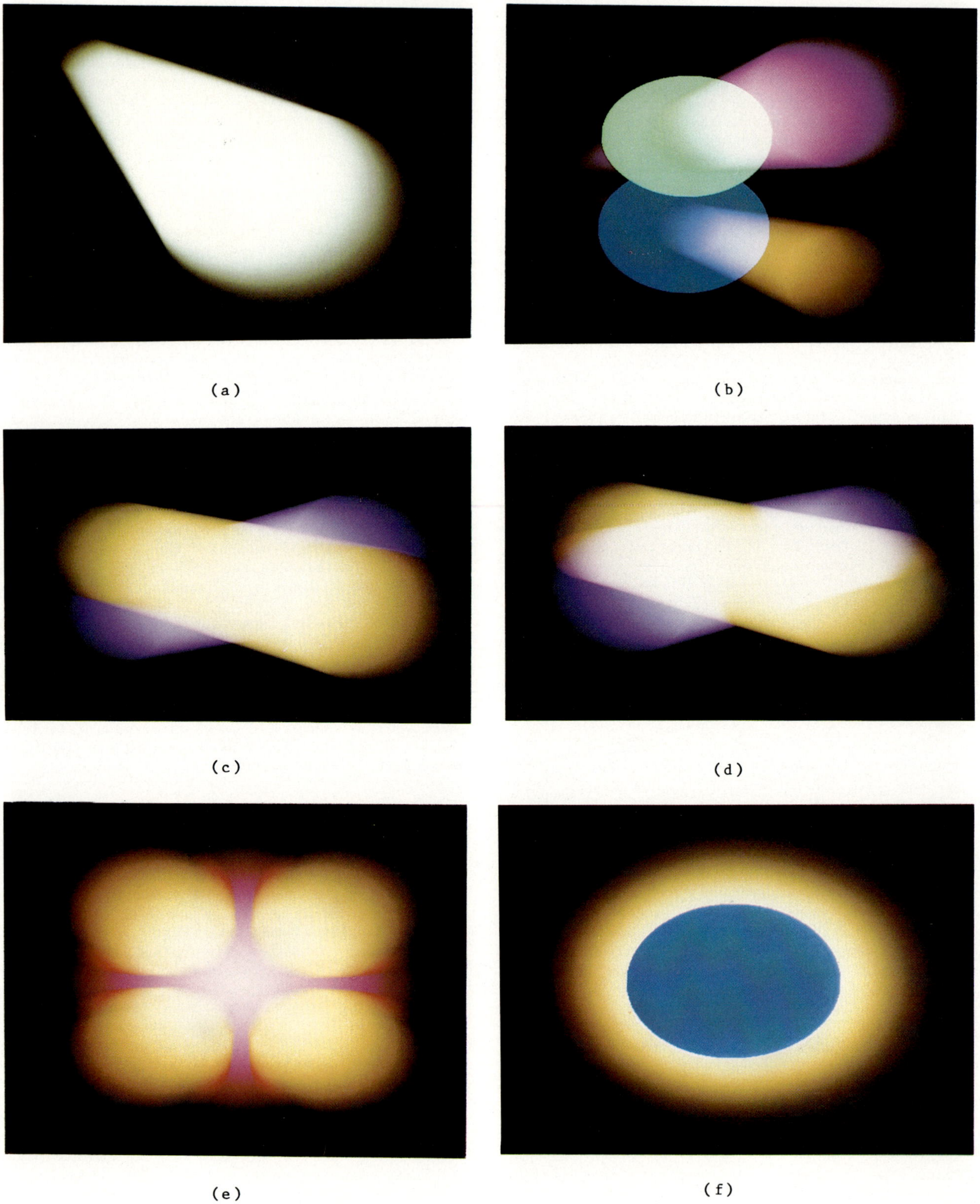

Figure 4

(g)

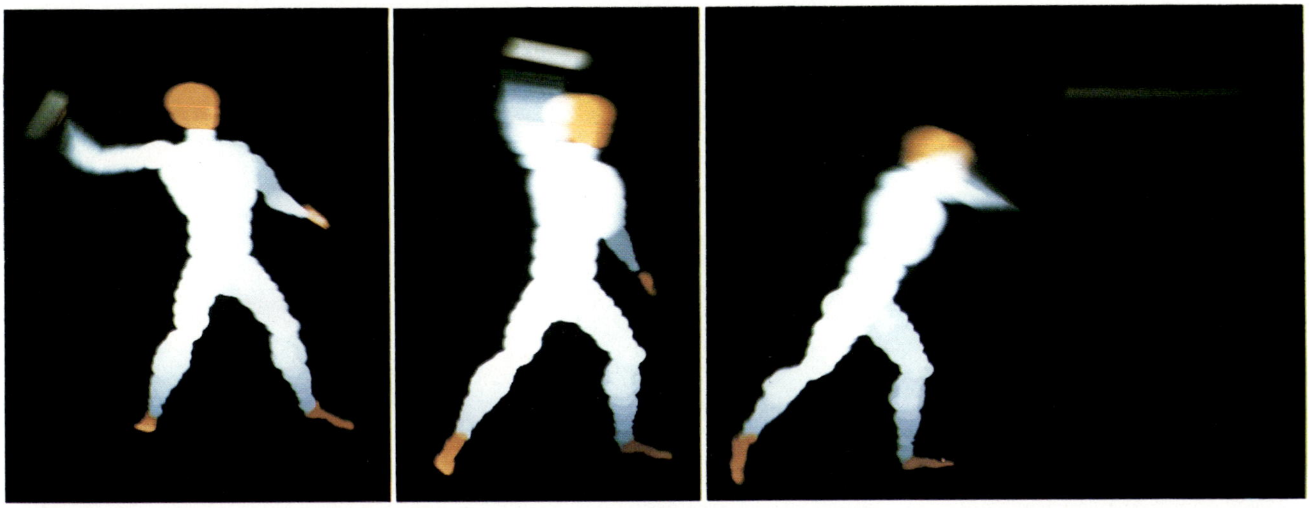

(h)

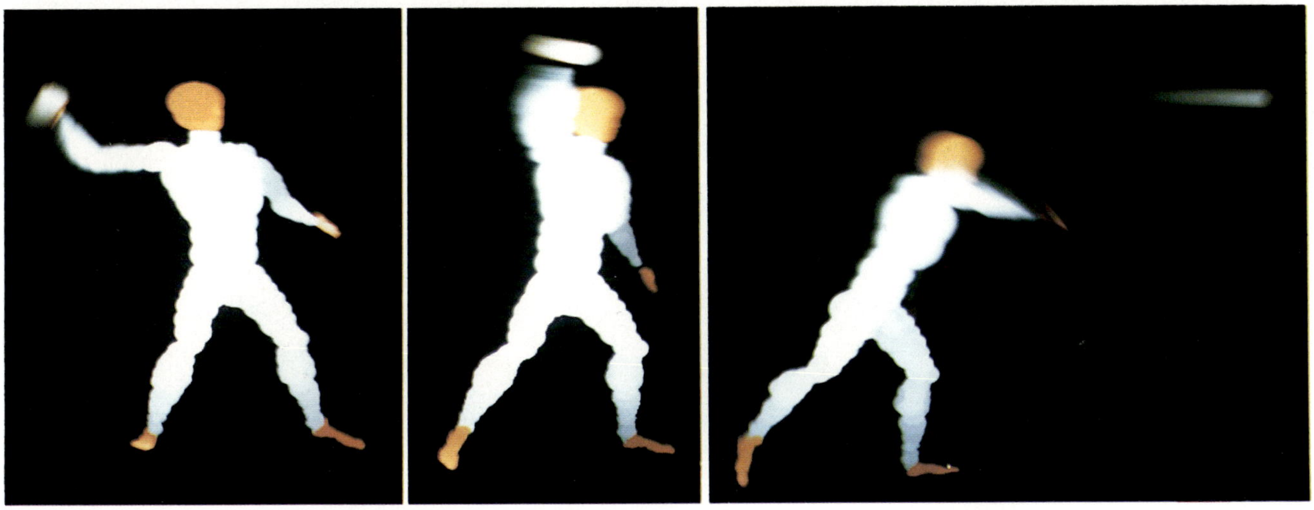

(i)
Figure 4

importance of this consideration. Figure 5 contains examples of pictures in which this technique of temporal anti-aliasing was used.

As can be seen from the examples, there is a problem with this method if objects are thin in the direction of a fast motion. Rather than appearing as a blur, a moving object appears as a sequence of images. This is called the 'spaghetti effect', a name given it by the early cel animators because of the appearance such techniques tended to give the moving object [17] (see figure 1b). While this is useful as a special effect, it may not be desirable as a side effect. There are two ways of dealing with this problem without the gross inefficiency which would be required if enough supersamples were always taken to ensure a smooth blur.

The first is by using a 'skinny' filter, one which covers only a small portion of an output frame interval, and only sampling the image within that subinterval. In this way a higher resolution is achieved under the filtered area, and this can be made dense enough so that the spaghetti effect will not occur. Figure 5b shows a thin filter used with five tightly spaced samples; this may be favorably compared with figure 5a, in which evenly spaced samples and a wide filter function are used.

It is possible to complement this approach by using movement as a determiner of the number of supersamples to create. The animating program is required to make an estimate of the quickest movement occuring in a frame. It sends this estimate to the anti-aliasing program, which

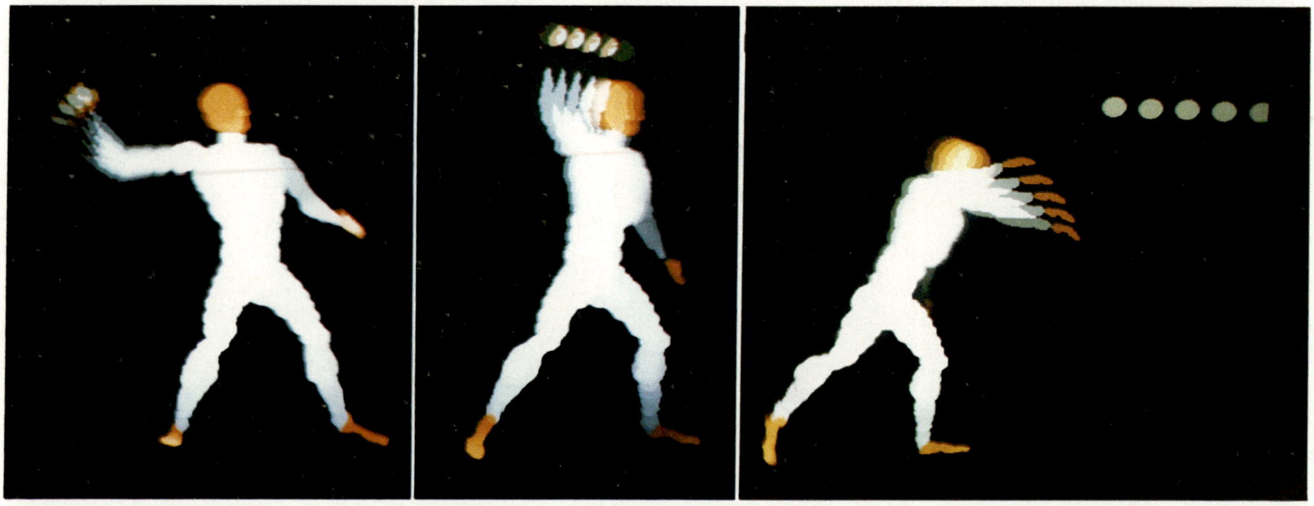

(a)

(b)

Figure 5

calculates the number of supersamples needed for that particular frame. It is also possible to have the anti-aliasing program choose the filter type on the basis of this estimate. This type of program offers an appealing combination of adaptabilty, efficiency, and ease of implementation.

The final modification which might be envisioned in a supersampling program would be utilizing object specific movement, much as was suggested for the continuous algorithm. The animating program determines per object movement, rather than a 'worst case' measure of frame movement. The anti-aliasing program then sends back the number of supersamples of each object to generate. The animation system returns depth as well as intensity images for each object. The anti-aliasing program must perform the hidden surface removal, much as was done in the continuous algorithm, by using the depth samples as piecewise constant functions. Once occluded intervals have been eliminated, the final pixel intensity function can be derived using the sampled intensities. These functions are then filtered and the blurred image output.

Computational efficiency may then be achieved, at the expense of storage efficiency, by subsampling slowly moving or still objects. Because their images are stored, the hidden surface removal algorithm will automatically determine when moving objects, whose projections are sampled at a higher rate, will occlude them. This is quite similar to the use of multiple image planes in cel animation, though it allows much more freedom since the depth of an object is computed separately for each pixel. This method of utilizing frame-to-frame coherence is attractive, but it is expensive in the storage needed and is ineffective in scenes with changing light sources or shadows and reflections.

4. Filters

Various filter types may be used to achieve different special effects in the final image. The standard box filter tends to create an image in which objects are fainter at their extremes in the direction of motion, where they cover pixels for a shorter duration. Gaussian and triangular filters exaggerate this effect. Moving objects can be made to trail faintly away by specifying a filter which increases with time (see figure 4i). Moving objects may be emphasized by considering the length of their covering intervals; this might be a desirable effect, as quickly moving objects thin in the direction of motion tend to all but disappear when a box filter is used.

5. Spatial Anti-Aliasing

Because of the similarity of the problems, it is highly desirable that spatial and temporal anti-aliasing be treated in an integrated fashion. The paper by Norton, Rockwood and Skolmoski [12] is an excellent example of this integration, though their approach treats explicitly defined textures and does not attempt to deal with the hidden surface removal problem. The continuous algorithm described in the current paper intentionally avoids the complexities of this synthesis, though it may point towards future solutions. Once each pixel is treated as an area, covering intervals become covering volumes in a space in which the image forms two dimensions and time the third. The problem may then be restated:

1. Find the covering volumes of each object.
2. If covering volumes intersect determine the visible volume by comparing the corresponding objects' depth functions.
3. Derive the intensity function of the remaining volumes and apply a three-dimensional filter to this function.

The challenge presented by this outline is considerable, but not insurmountable; we feel the design of an efficient algorithm would be a significant advance in the state of the art.

As it stands, the algorithms presented in this paper do not integrate spatial and temporal anti-aliasing. The temporal supersampling approach may be used with any form of spatial anti-aliasing, while the temporal continuous algorithm may only be used with spatial supersampling methods.

6. Efficiency

While no detailed efficiency analyses were done, it is clear that both methods of temporal anti-aliasing are expensive. The times required to generate both the supersampled and continuously anti-aliased bubbleman pictures shown here were between three and ten CPU minutes on a VAX 780. While these times were obtained using very unoptimized Pascal code and could be improved substantially, it is unlikely they could match the ten to thirty seconds needed to create the unblurred pictures. The possibility of decreasing representational complexity in conjunction with the use of temporal anti-aliasing algorithms is being studied.

7. Discussion

This investigation into the temporal anti-aliasing of raster images has led to some definite conclusions and suggestions for future work. Two classes of algorithms have been introduced: those which use continuous approximations of object movement, and those which use discrete object positions sampled at a high rate. The choice between them, as is often the case, depends on the application. If complex object types or rendering techniques are to be used, supersampling has a clear advantage. If considerable anti-aliasing is to be done or a smooth blur is essential, a well designed continuous algorithm streamlined for efficiency is preferable. The integration of continuous spatial and temporal anti-aliasing is seen as the most important area for future research.

8. Appendix : The Temporal Anti-aliasing of Polygonal Objects

The general outline of the continuous algorithm discussed for disks is readily adapted for use with other simple object representations. In particular, polyhedral objects projected with a variety of shading techniques may be effectively anti-aliased within this framework. Again, numerous implementation alternatives are available; the one chosen is a compromise between accuracy and efficiency.

The algorithm described works primarily in object space, though some portions use image coordinates. It will be assumed that each vertex is sampled in object space at appropriate time intervals and that a correspondance is made between the same vertex at succesive sampling times. Information about surface normals must also be supplied, though the location of this information depends on the type of shading used. If the model is strictly polyhedral, the surface normal is associated with each polygon; if the model is actually polyhedra used to represent a curved surface, the normal is associated with each vertex [4,8].

First, the temporal object interpolation functions must be considered. Linear interpolation functions are calculated for each vertex position and for each of the surface normals, whether they be associated with polygons or vertices. The line segment joining corresponding vertex points in succesive sampled scenes plays an important role in the algorithm and will be called the 'vertex path' (see figure 6).

Again, we will examine the rendering of one pixel at this point, though the algorithm may be adapted to scan line methods. It will also be assumed, again to simplify the presentation, that each polygon is sampled only at the beginning and end of the filtered interval. Relaxing this assumption is necessary in practical applications, but while this increases the complexity of the procedures no new conceptual difficulties are introduced.

First the interval during which each polygon covers a given pixel (the 'covering interval') must be found. As with disks, two estimates of the image area swept by a moving object are used to eliminate most polygons from consideration. This is the only portion of the algorithm which operates in image space. The cruder approximation is again the bounding box of two adjacent sampled instances of a primitive object, now a polygon; the more sophisticated estimate is once more the convex hull of these samples. While the latter test is more selective, it will not exclude all uncovered pixels, as will the boundary derived in the moving disk case.

The remaining routines work in object space in order to give more accurate covering interval and surface normal estimates when perspective viewing is used. We define the 'view ray' as the line, in object space, going through the center of projection and a given pixel location on the view plane. To determine the intervals during which the pixel is covered by a given polygon we must first find if it is covered at the beginning of the filtered interval and then find when it is subsequently covered and uncovered. The former can be determined by intersecting the sampled polygon with the view ray; the latter by determining the intersection of the view ray and the polygon's moving edges. These steps are detailed below.

1) Find out if the pixel was covered at the start of the filtered interval. This may be known from calculations performed for the previous frame; otherwise is is necessary to determine if the view ray intersects the initial sampled polygon.

2) Determine the intersection of the the view ray and the polygon's moving edges. The solution is most useful if put in terms of depth along the view ray (d), length along the edge (l), and time (t), rather than object space coordinates. This is done by solving the vector equation

$$R_0 + d(R_1 - R_0) = E_0 + l(E_1 - E_0)$$

where

$$E_0 = E_{00} + t(E_{10} - E_{00})$$

and

$$E_1 = E_{01} + t(E_{11} - E_{01})$$

and, as illustrated in figure 6,

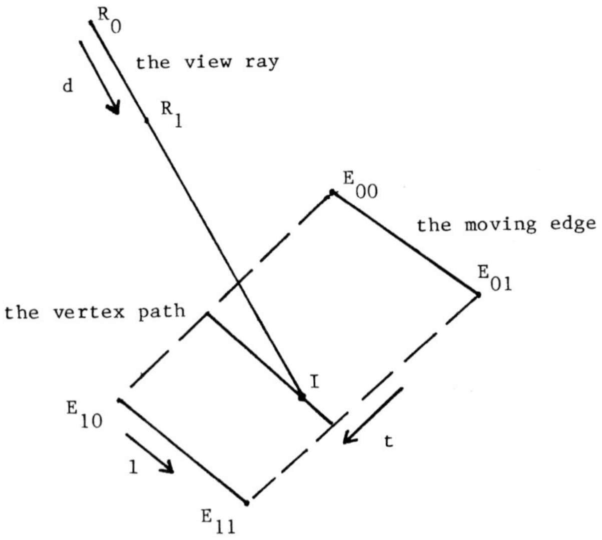

Figure 6. The intersection I between theview ray and the moving edge is most usefully determinedin terms of t, the timeof intersection, d, the depth along the view ray, andl, the length along the edge.

- R_0 is the center of projection,
- R_1 is the pixel point in the view plane,
- E_{00} and E_{01} are an edge's two vertices in the first sample polygon,
- E_{10} and E_{11} are the corresponding vertices from the next sample polygon,
- t is a time parameter used to locate the moving vertices, which are used to define the moving edge,
- l is the length along this moving edge, and
- d is the depth of the view ray from the center of projection.

Determining t, d and l at the point of intersection from the vector quantities, which are known, can be found after straightforward manipulation to require the solution of one quadratic and two linear equations. If this system has a real solution for which t and l are between zero and one and d is greater than one, an intersection of the moving edge and the view ray occurs.

3) As edge intersections are found, they are ordered by time. With each intersecting edge, the status of the pixel's being covered or uncovered by the polygon changes. We may then determine each of the covered intervals within any sampled interval since we have already determined whether or not the pixel is covered at the beginning of each sampled interval.

At this point a depth function must be derived for each of the covering intervals. The parameter d, depth from the center of projection, is the most convenient value to use for this purpose. It is inherently determined when calculating the intersection of the view ray and moving edges, and is easily found when intersecting the view ray with sampled polygons. If these depth samples are linearly interpolated, the visible surface problem presented is the same as in the disk case.

As a shading function we will use a variation of the type derived by Bui-Tuong Phong [4]:

$$i = f(L.N) + s(H.N)^n$$

where

- i is the reflected intensity;
- L is the unit vector to the light source;
- N is the unit surface normal vector;
- H is the unit vector halfway between the viewer and the light source;
- f is the diffuse reflection coeficient;
- s is the specular reflection coeficient;
- n is the specular reflection exponent.

In our case, all vectors are functions of time, but we will restrict H and L to be constant. The determination of the value of N varies depending on whether or not a curved surface is being simulated. If a curved surface is not being represented, the normals of the polygons at the sampled times provide values which can be used in determining the intensity function.

If a curved surface is being approximated, the values of the sampled normals used must be chosen on the basis of where the view ray intersects the polygon. When a covering interval border has been determined by intersecting the view ray directly with a polygon, the normal at that time may be determined by methods adapted from Bui-Tuong Phong [4] and Gouraud [8]. An edge normal function is derived by linearly interpolating the given vertex normals. The plane containing the view ray and its scan line is then intersected with the polygon edges. The normals evaluated for the edges at these intersection points are in turn fitted with a linear interpolation function. Finally, this function may be evaluated at the location of the intersection of the polygon and view ray to determine a final 'curved surface' normal.

The method for calculating normals when a covering interval border is found through the intersection of the view ray with a moving edge is a variation on this theme. A temporal interpolation function is fitted to vertex normals given at adjacent sampling times. These functions may then be evaluated to find the vertex path normals at the time the view ray intersects the moving edge. A spatial linear interpolation function, based on the edge length parameter l, is then fitted to these vertex normal values. This function may then be evaluated at the point of view ray intersection since the value of l at that point has already been calculated.

In either modeling case, we derive accurate samples of the surface normal at the point at which the viewing ray intersects it, despite the fact that this point may be moving both with respect to the world and the surface. We may then estimate and filter the intensity function in a number of ways. The simplest method is to evaluate the intensity function with the average surface normal to determine a constant intensity over each covered interval[1]; using the average of the two normals sampled within each covering interval suffices if a linear normal interpolation function is assumed. If more accuracy is needed, the intensity function may be calculated at several points within each covering interval using such a normal interpolation function. In either case, the resulting intensity function may be filtered discretely [6] or

1. as Blinn [2] did when spatially anti-aliasing perturbed surface normals

continuously, again with the choice reflecting accuracy and efficiency considerations. The most accurate solution would be obtained by representing intensity as a continuous function of the surface normal, rather than sampling the intensity for specific values of the surface normal. Performing a continuous convolution with this function, however, requires symbolic integration (when done for arbitrary specular reflection exponents) and/or numerical integration techniques and will not be discussed.

The method and results of this algorithm are similar to those found in the disk case. The popularity of polygonal representations makes this algorithm more generally useful; as is often true, however, solving a difficult problem within a simple framework has lead to the proper form of solution in a more complex manifestation.

9. Acknowledgements

Special thanks to Jim Korein for our invaluable discussions, Jane Rovins and Jane Korein for their artistic judgements, and Lance Williams for his scribbled insights. We also wish to thank Jeri Brown, Barbara Woolford and Jim Lewis of NASA, whose support and appreciation made this research possible.

10. References

1. Badler, Norman, Joseph O'Rourke, Hasida Toltzis. "A Spherical Representation of a Human Body for Visualizing Human Movement," Proceedings of the IEEE, 67(10), October 1979, pp. 1397-1403.

2. Blinn, James F., Computer Display of Curved Surfaces, University of Utah Doctoral Dissertation, Computer Science Dept., 1978.

3. Bouknight, W. J. "A Procedure for Generation of Half-tone Three-dimensional Computer Graphics Representations," Communications of the ACM, 13(9), September 1970, pp. 527-536.

4. Bui-Tuong, Phong, "Illumination for Computer-Generated Pictures," Communications of the ACM, 18(6), June 1975, pp. 311-317.

5. Catmull, Edwin. "A Hidden-Surface Algorithm with Anti-Aliasing," Computer Graphics, 12(3), August 1978, pp. 6-10.

6. Crow, Franklin. "The Aliasing Problem in Computer-Synthesized Shaded Images," University of Utah Doctoral Dissertation, 1976.

7. Crow, Franklin. "A Comparison of Antialiasing Techniques," IEEE Computer Graphics and Applications, 1(1), January 1981, pp. 40-48.

8. Gouraud, H., "Continuous Shading of Curved Surfaces," IEEE Transactions on Computers, C-20(6), June 1971, pp. 623-628.

9. Gupta, Satish and Robert Sproull. "Filtering Edges for Grey-Scale Displays," Computer Graphics, 15(3), August 1981, pp. 1-5.

10. Lipscombe, James. "Reversed Apparent Movement and Erratic Motion with Many Refreshes per Minute," Computer Graphics, 14(4), March 1981, pp113-118.

11. Knowlton, Kenneth. "Computer-Aided Definition, Manipulation, and Depiction of Objects Composed of Spheres," Computer Graphics, 15(1), April 1981, pp. 48-71.

12. Norton, Alan, Alyn Rockwood and Philip Skolmoski. "Clamping: A Method of Antialiasing Textured Surfaces by Bandwidth Limiting in Object Space," Computer Graphics, 16(3), July 1982, pp. 1-8.

13. Potmesil, Michael and Indranil Chakravarty. "A Lens and Aperture Camera Model for Synthetic Image Generation," Computer Graphics, 15(3), August 1981, pp. 297-305.

14. Potmesil, Michael and Indranil Chakravarty. "Motion Blur in Computer Generated Images," Computer Graphics, 17(3), July 1983.

15. Reeves, William. "Particle Systems - A Technique for Modelling a Class of Fuzzy Objects," Computer Graphics, 17(3), July 1983.

16. Szabo, Nicholas. "Digital Image Anomalies: Static and Dynamic," in Bruce Schachter (ed.), Computer Image Generation, John Wiley and Sons, New York, 1983.

17. Thomas, Frank and Ollie Johnston. Disney Animation: The Illusion of Life, Abbeville Press, New York, 1981.

18. Watkins, G.S. "A Real-Time Visible Surface Algorithm," University of Utah Computer Science Dept., UTEC-CSc-70-101, June 1970.

19. Whitaker, Harold and John Halas. Timing for Animation, Focal Press Ltd., London, 1981.

20. Williams, Lance. "Overview of 3D Animation," Tutorial: Computer Animation Techniques, SIGRAPH '79.

21. Williams, Lance. "Overview of 3D Animation," Seminar: Three Dimensional Computer Animation, SIGRAPH '81.

Modeling Motion Blur in Computer-Generated Images

Michael Potmesil[1]
Bell Laboratories

Indranil Chakravarty[2]
Schlumberger-Doll Research

Abstract

This paper describes a procedure for modeling motion blur in computer-generated images. Motion blur in photography or cinematography is caused by the motion of objects during the finite exposure time the camera shutter remains open to record the image on film. In computer graphics, the simulation of motion blur is useful both in animated sequences where the blurring tends to remove temporal aliasing effects and in static images where it portrays the illusion of speed or movement among the objects in the scene.

The camera model developed for simulating motion blur is described in terms of a generalized image-formation equation. This equation describes the relationship between the object and corresponding image points in terms of the optical system-transfer function. The use of the optical system-transfer function simplifies the description of time-dependent variations of object motion that may occur during the exposure time of a camera. This approach allows us to characterize the motion of objects by a set of system-transfer functions which are derived from the path and velocity of objects in the scene and the exposure time of a camera.

CR Categories and Subject Descriptors: **I.3.7 [Computer Graphics]:** Three-Dimensional Graphics and Realism, **I.4.4 [Image Processing]:** Restoration

General Terms: Algorithms

Key Words and Phrases: Camera Model, Motion Blur, Point-Spread Function, Image Restoration, Digital Optics

1.0 Introduction

The generation of computer-synthesized images with a high degree of realism has been the topic of much current research. The increase in realism in recent years can be attributed mainly to improved shading techniques and to more versatile 3D object modeling techniques that can represent complex objects with great detail. The objective of this paper is to report an image synthesis technique which incorporates the optical effects of a camera in imaging a scene. These optical effects of a camera add another dimension of realism in computer generated images. In this paper we attempt to model *motion blur*, an effect caused by the movement of objects during the exposure time of the camera, and used often to portray to the viewer the illusion of the motion of objects.

In a previous paper [6,7] the authors developed a technique for modeling the effects of a lens and aperture in a camera model for computer-synthesized images. This paper is both an extension and a generalization of the previous paper to incorporate the effects of the camera shutter. In addition, this paper presents the image-generation process in terms of a cascaded optical, system-transfer function which specifies the relationship between object and image points. This formalism allows us to express easily the time-dependent variations of an object's position and provides a more comprehensive approach to synthesizing the effects of motion blur and other camera effects.

The appearance of motion blur in images can occur due to a number of reasons. The primary cause of this blurring is due to the movement of an object's position in the scene during the exposure time of the camera. By *exposure time* we mean the time during which the camera shutter remains open and the film acts as an integrating medium to accumulate the total radiant energy of the objects in the scene. There are two principal reasons for motion blur:

1. Address: Bell Laboratories, Holmdel, NJ 07733
2. Address: Schlumberger-Doll Research Center, Old Quarry Road, Ridgefield, CT 06877

1. Movements of Objects - The motion of objects in the scene is the most common cause for image blurring. The motion of objects can be classified into three categories: motion of the camera and a static scene, motion of objects with a static camera, and finally the simultaneous motion of both camera and objects in the scene.

2. Movement of the Shutter - Film is exposed in a camera by the movement of the shutter across the film plane. The finite opening and closing time of the shutter, the direction of movement of the shutter as well as changes in the shape of the aperture caused by the movement of the shutter may all modify the appearance of motion blur in the image [13]. In this paper we will not be concerned with modeling the blur arising solely from the functioning of the camera shutter.

The problem of characterizing the degradation caused by an optical system has been the topic of extensive research in image processing [1]. The removal of camera degradation to recover the original image based on some a priori knowledge of the degradation phenomenon is called *image restoration.* In synthesizing motion blur the problem is almost inversed, that is, the objective is to generate an appropriate degradation function given an idealized description of the scene. Although one can draw upon the techniques developed for estimating the optical system-transfer function from a degraded image, the synthesis of an optical system-transfer function from a scene description must take into account the individual motion of objects in the scene, the camera path, the occlusion relationships that may vary between the objects during the exposure time, and any optical effects included as part of the camera model.

The generation of motion blur in computer-synthesized images, as described in this paper, consists of two stages: 1) a hidden-surface program generates intensity sample points of an instantaneous image identifying points which are in motion and giving the image path of the projected motion; and 2) a post-processor which blurs the moving points by convolving them with the optical system-transfer functions derived from the image path and merges them with the stationary points into a final raster image.

A ray-tracing program with a recursive shader [15] generates image point samples, keeping intensity contributions due to surface reflections, transparencies and shadows separate. This allows moving objects reflected in mirrors, transmitted through transparent surfaces, and the shadows of such objects to be blurred. For proper merger of moving objects with stationary objects, intensity samples of the stationary surfaces, hiding or hidden by the moving surfaces, are also computed.

The sample points which contain intensity reflected from moving objects are convolved with an optical system-transfer function, derived from the path and velocity of the motion, and the exposure time. The blurred moving objects and the stationary objects are then merged in a time-and-depth buffer into the final image. In this buffer the visibility of a surface point is determined by its depth, and its intensity is modified by the amount of exposure time it remains visible. A hidden-surface program which processes projected surfaces in a back-to-front order [5] can directly convolve each moving object with its optical system-transfer function as it is stored into the output image.

2.0 Image Formation Model

The camera model which underlies the image-formation process, as modeled here, consists of two stages. First, a 3D scene is projected by a geometric transformation into a 2D *image-irradiance plane.* The image-irradiance plane is then further transformed by the optical system-transfer function, also called a *point-spread function* (PSF), into an actual raster image called the *image-output plane.* The image-output plane simulates a film by acting as a medium for accumulating the radiant energy of objects during the exposure time.

The 3D scene is defined in a homogeneous coordinate system $O(x,y,z,w)$ and contains a set of 3D objects represented by $e_i(x,y,z,w)$, $i=1,2,--,n$ as shown in Figure 1. This representation contains both geometrical and optical properties of the objects. This is referred to as the *object-space* coordinate system. A geometrical transformation function $q(x',y'; e_i(x,y,z,w))$ transforms object descriptions from $O(x,y,z,w)$ to $O'(x',y')$ (*image-irradiance plane*) eliminating hidden surfaces of objects and generating the radiant intensity for each visible surface point:

$$f(x',y') = q(x',y'; e(x,y,z,w)) \qquad (2\text{-}1)$$

A discrete formulation of the image-irradiance function is

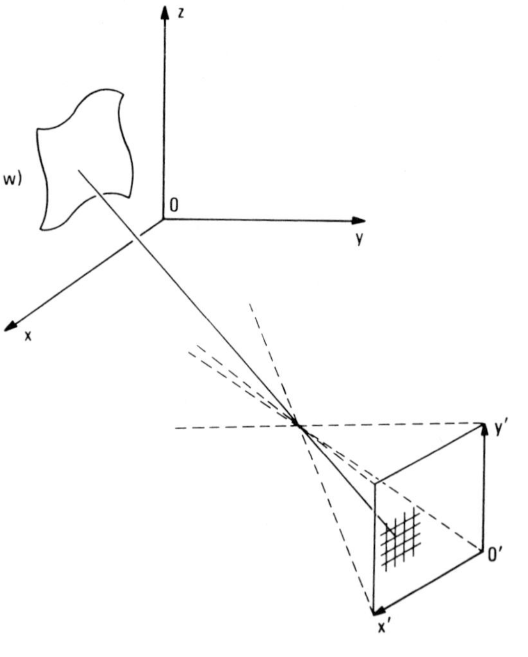

Figure 1 Projection of 3D scene in object space $O(x,y,z,w)$ into image-irradiance plane $O'(x',y')$

equivalent to uniformly sampling the function $f(x',y')$ using a *comb* function (Figure 2) such that

$$f(i\Delta x', j\Delta y') = \sum_{i=0}^{M} \sum_{j=0}^{N} \delta(i\Delta x', j\Delta y')\, f(x',y') \tag{2-2}$$

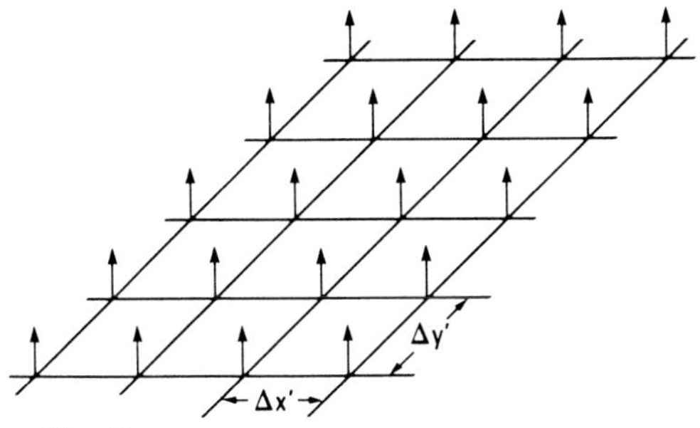

$$\sum_{i=0}^{M} \sum_{j=0}^{N} \delta(x'-i\Delta x',\, y'-j\Delta y')$$

Figure 2 2D comb function of samples of the image-irradiance function in $O'(x',y')$

where $\Delta x'$ and $\Delta y'$ are the sampling intervals in x' and y' directions, respectively. We will assume that the sampling rate is adequate so that we can reconstruct $f(x',y')$ from $f(i\Delta x', j\Delta y')$ by using a suitable interpolating function.

The transformation from the image-irradiance plane $O'(x',y')$ to the image-output plane $O''(x'',y'')$ *(raster image)* incorporates the degradation of the optical system and simulates the imaging medium. We denote this transformation as $h(x'',y''; x',y',f(x',y'))$, and thus we can express the raster image

$$g(x'',y'') = h(x'',y''; x',y',f(x',y')). \tag{2-3}$$

In order to quantify the transformation $h(x'',y''; x',y', f(x',y'))$ we will assume the following properties:

1. The radiant intensity distribution in both the image-irradiance plane and the image-output plane is either positive or zero. This implies that the image-irradiance function (which is a measure of this energy distribution), and any transformations on the image-irradiance function may either conserve the energy or distribute it differently. Thus

$$f(x',y') \geqslant 0, \text{ and } g(x'',y'') \geqslant 0. \tag{2-4}$$

2. The radiant intensity distribution is additive in both the image-irradiance plane and the image-output plane. This superposition property implies that given two points $f_1(x',y')$ and $f_2(x',y')$ and their corresponding mapping $g_1(x'',y'')$ and $g_2(x'',y'')$ then

$$f_1(x',y') + f_2(x',y') = g_1(x'',y'') + g_2(x'',y''). \tag{2-5}$$

Based on these two assumptions we may write the transformation from the image-irradiance plane $O'(x',y')$ to the output-image plane $O''(x'',y'')$ in the spatial domain by:

$$g(x'',y'') = \int_{-\infty}^{\infty} \int_{-\infty}^{\infty} h(x'',y''; x',y',f(x',y'))\, dx'\, dy' \tag{2-6}$$

where $h(x'',y''; x',y',f(x',y'))$ is the optical system-transfer function (PSF) describing the energy distribution between points in the image-irradiance plane O' and the output-image plane O''. This is the most general form for describing the image-formation process.

A number of simplifications can be made to the generalized image formation equation (2-6) described above. If the additive components in the image-irradiance plane relate to the additive components in the image-output plane then the system is said to be linear in which case equation (2-6) can be written in the more familiar form of

$$g(x'',y'') = \int_{-\infty}^{\infty} \int_{-\infty}^{\infty} h(x'',y''; x',y')\, f(x',y')\, dx'\, dy' \tag{2-7}$$

The description of the optical system-transfer function in terms of the all four coordinate variables (x'',y'',x',y') reflects space-variance of the transfer function, that is, the transfer function is allowed to vary with position in both the object space and image space. We define such a transfer function as a space-variant PSF (SVPSF). If we restrict the transfer function to be independent of position, that is, the PSF applies uniformly to all points in the object and image space then it is defined as space-invariant (SIPSF) which can be expressed as

$$h(x'',y''; x',y') = h(x''-x', y''-y'). \tag{2-8}$$

In the space-invariant PSF case, the transformation from the image-irradiance plane O' to the image- output plane O'' can be expressed with the convolution integral:

$$g(x'',y'') = \int_{-\infty}^{\infty} \int_{-\infty}^{\infty} h(x''-x', y''-y')\, f(x',y')\, dx'\, dy'. \tag{2-9}$$

We often denote the convolution operation in the spatial domain by the symbol $*$ so that we may equivalently write equation (2-9) as $g(x'',y'') = h(x'',y'') * f(x',y')$. Finally in the discrete formulation $g(x'',y'')$ can be represented by the convolution summation

$$g(i\Delta x'', j\Delta y'') = \sum_{i=0}^{M} \sum_{j=0}^{N} h(i\Delta x''-i\Delta x', j\Delta y''-j\Delta y')\, f(i\Delta x', j\Delta y') \tag{2-10}$$

The equivalent operation in the frequency domain can be written as the product of the fourier transforms of the image-irradiance plane and the PSF:

$$G(u,v) = H(u,v)\, F(u,v). \tag{2-11}$$

For incoherent image formation systems, such as the ones we are trying to model, we only need to consider the squared magnitude of the PSF [4] in the convolution equations described above. The reason for this assumption is that the intensity (radiant energy) is dependent only on the amplitude and not the phase of a electro-magnetic field distribution.

In many cases it is desirable to simplify the computation of convolution by factoring the 2D PSF into two 1D PSFs. This property is called the separability property of the PSF and can be expressed as follows for the space-invariant case as:

$$h(x'-x'',y'-y'') = h_1(x'-x'')\, h_2(y'-y''). \quad (2\text{-}12)$$

This implies that for an orthogonal coordinate space, the horizontal and vertical transformations can be performed sequentially and independently of each other.

In many instances modeling the camera effects may results in several PSFs cascaded together so that the overall transfer function achieves the desired effect. Given two PSFs $h_1(x'',y'';x',y')$ and $h_2(x'',y'';x',y')$ the overall transfer function $h_{12}(x'',y'';x',y')$ can be expressed as the convolution of the individual transfer functions $h_1(x'',y'';x',y') * h_2(x'',y'';x',y')$. Alternately, in the frequency domain this can be viewed as the product of the two individual transfer functions.

In summary the image formation model can be described by a two stage process as shown in Figure 3. The first is a geometrical transformation which projects the object space onto an image-irradiance plane resolving the hidden surfaces and calculating the radiant intensity for each discrete visible point. We call this process the scene imaging system. An optical system-transfer function (PSF) is then used to transform the image-irradiance plane to the image-output plane. The PSF describes the relationship of the energy distributions between the image-irradiance plane and image-output planes incorporating the effects of the lens, aperture, and shutter. The output-image plane thus acts as an integrating medium accumulating the total radiant energy during the exposure time of the camera.

3.0 Effects of Object Motion and Camera Shutter

3.1 Point-Spread Function of Object Motion

The problem of blurring the output image function $g(x'',y'')$ due to object motion during the exposure time [1,11,12,13] is described in this section. Let the path of the object motion be described in the 3D object coordinate system $O(x,y,z,w)$ as a parametric function of time:

$$\mathbf{r}(t) = \left[\, x(t)\ y(t)\ z(t)\ w(t) \,\right], \quad (3\text{-}1)$$

which is projected into the 2D object coordinate system $O'(x',y')$ as:

$$\mathbf{r}'(t) = \left[\, x'(t)\ y'(t) \,\right] \quad (3\text{-}2)$$

by the geometrical transformation $q(x',y';\, x,y,z,w)$ as in equation (2-1):

$$\mathbf{r}'(t) = q(x',y';\, \mathbf{r}(t)). \quad (3\text{-}3)$$

We assume that all the projected points in $f(x',y')$ of an object are moving along a single projected path $\mathbf{r}'(t)$, that is, $\mathbf{r}(t)$ is projected into a space-invariant $\mathbf{r}'(t)$ in $O'(x',y')$. By this we mean that the blurring is applied uniformly to all points along the projected path of motion.

Suppose that the motion of the object can be stopped at some instant t, and this instantaneous image can be expressed as $g(x'',y'',t)$. Then the recorded image-output function $g(x'',y'')$ during the fixed exposure time interval $[0,T]$ is:

$$g(x'',y'') = \int_0^T g(x'',y'',t)\, dt. \quad (3\text{-}4)$$

This integration is physically performed by the film or other recording medium. It can be described as the summation at image output point (x'',y'') of the intensities of all object points that are mapped onto this image point during the exposure interval. Assuming that energy is conserved by the imaging system at any instant during the exposure, energy radiated by an area element $dx'\,dy'$ of $O'(x',y')$ and collected by an area element $dx''\,dy''$ of $O(x'',y'')$ is described by:

$$g(x'',y'',t)\, dx''\, dy'' = f(x',y')\, dx'\, dy' \quad (3\text{-}5)$$

at instant t. Substituting the path description (3-2) into (3-5) and combining it with (3-4) we obtain the recorded image function:

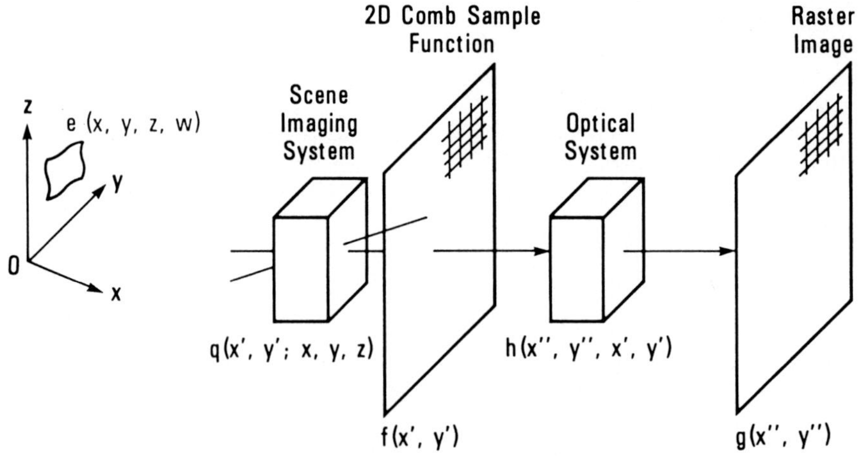

Figure 3 Image-formation system model

$$g(x'',y'') = \int_0^T f(x'(t),y'(t))\, dt. \qquad (3\text{-}6)$$

Given a description of the object motion $\mathbf{r}'(t)$ (3-2) we convert the time integral of the moving object (3-6) into a positional integral over an equivalent stationary object. The elemental length ds of path $\mathbf{r}'(t)$ is given by:

$$ds = \left[\left(\frac{dx'(t)}{dt}\right)^2 + \left(\frac{dy'(t)}{dt}\right)^2\right]^{1/2} dt. \qquad (3\text{-}7)$$

Therefore the time integral in equation (3-6) can be changed into line integral of the form:

$$g(x'',y'') = \int_{\mathbf{r}'(0)}^{\mathbf{r}'(T)} \frac{f(x',y')\, ds}{\left[\left(\frac{dx'(t)}{dt}\right)^2 + \left(\frac{dy'(t)}{dt}\right)^2\right]^{1/2}} \qquad (3\text{-}8)$$

which is a general expression for motion degradation with the linear space-invariant model of equation (2-9). The SIPSF can be identified in equation (3-8) as:

$$h(x'',y'';x',y') = \left[\left(\frac{dx'(t)}{dt}\right)^2 + \left(\frac{dy'(t)}{dt}\right)^2\right]^{-1/2}_{\substack{t = x'^{-1}(\mathbf{r}_x)\\ t = y'^{-1}(\mathbf{r}_y)}} \qquad (3\text{-}9)$$

where $x'(t)$ and $y'(t)$ are valid over the path of the object motion, that is,

$$x'(0) \leqslant x'(t) \leqslant x'(T)$$
$$y'(0) \leqslant y'(t) \leqslant y'(T)$$

and $h(x'',y'';x',y') = 0$ elsewhere. The amplitude of the response is, therefore, inversely proportional to the velocity of the motion of an object point, i.e., as the object moves faster its image spreads over a greater image area with reduced intensity. Since the derived $h(x'',y'';x',y')$ is space invariant, the convolution in equation (2-10) with this PSF can be performed either in the spatial or the frequency domain.

Consider a simple example where $\mathbf{r}'(t) = x_0(t)$ describes planar motion of the object in the x-direction. Using (3-6) we may write

$$g(x'',y'') = \int_0^T f(x'-x_0(t),\, y')\, dt, \qquad (3\text{-}10)$$

and from the frequency-domain relationship in (2-11):

$$G(u,v) = \int_{-\infty}^{\infty}\int_{-\infty}^{\infty} \left[\int_0^T f(x'-x_0(t),\, y')dt\right] e^{-j2\pi(ux'+vy')}dxdy. \qquad (3\text{-}11)$$

By reversing the order of integration and using the shifting property of Fourier transforms $G(u,v)$ can be expressed as

$$G(u,v) = F(u,v) \int_0^T e^{-j2\pi(ux_0(t))}\, dt \qquad (3\text{-}12)$$

Let $x_0(t) = \frac{at}{T}$, and $0 \leqslant t \leqslant T$. Using (2-11) we identify

$$H(u) = \int_0^T e^{-j2\pi x_0(t)}\, dt. \qquad (3\text{-}13)$$

Substituting for $x_0(t)$, we obtain

$$H(u) = \int_0^T e^{-j2\pi\frac{uat}{T}}\, dt = \frac{T}{\pi ua}\, sin(\pi ua)\, e^{-j\pi ua} \qquad (3\text{-}14)$$

Alternatively, one may directly obtain $h(x'')$ by substituting into (3-9)

$$h(x'') = \frac{T}{a}, \text{ where } 0 \leqslant x'' \leqslant a \qquad (3\text{-}15)$$

It is easy to verify that (3-15) is indeed the inverse Fourier transform of (3-14). An example of uniform motion blur is shown in Figure 4. This simulates the motion of a camera viewing a static scene. Figure 4(a) shows the original natural image; the Fourier spectrum of this image is shown in Figure 4(b). This FFT was multiplied by the frequency-domain uniform blur function $x_0(t)$. The convolved image is shown in Figure 4(c) and the inverse FFT producing the blurred image is shown in Figure 4(d).

In a space-variant system where each point of a moving object may follow a different path $\mathbf{r}'(t)$ it is necessary to compute the path $\mathbf{r}'(t)$ and the PSF $h(x'',y'';x',y')$ of the path separately for each moving point in $f(x',y')$. Sawchuk [12] has shown that for a large class of motions it is possible to change a space-variant system by a geometrical coordinate transformation into a space-invariant system.

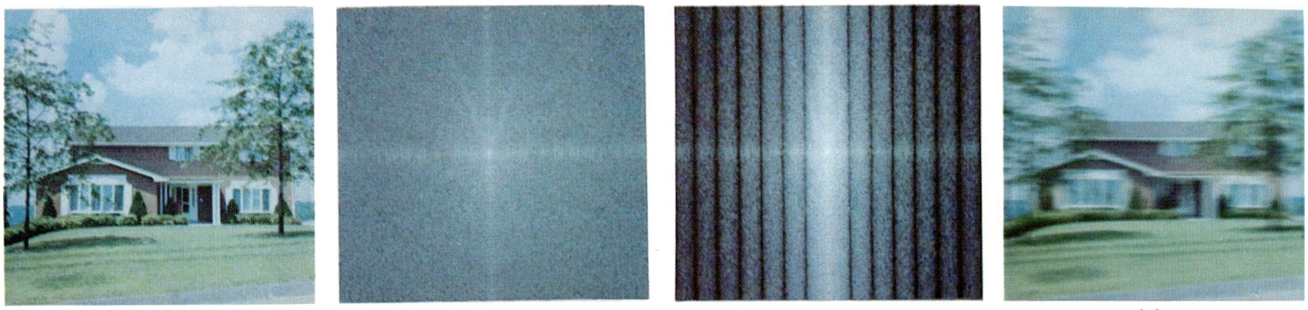

(a) (b) (c) (d)

Figure 4 Uniform motion-blur with frequency-domain computations: (a) original image, (b) FFT of original image, (c) FFT convolved with PSF, (d) blurred image

3.2 Point-Spread Function of Camera Shutter

In the previous section we obtained a PSF due to object motion assuming instantaneous shutter opening at time $t = 0$ and closing at time $t = T$. Most actual shutters, however, are mechanical devices which vary the shape of the aperture during their opening and closing times and therefore further modify the system PSF. Shack [13] derived the shutter PSF's for the two most common types of shutter.

The *focal-plane shutter* is a narrow slit in a curtain which moves across the film frame, slightly in front of the film plane, usually in the x'' (horizontal) direction. The aperture remains open for the duration of the exposure. The exposure is controlled by the speed of the curtain motion and the width of the slit. The PSF for this shutter type is in the frequency domain [13]:

$$H(u,v) = \begin{cases} 1 - \frac{|u|}{d} & 0 < |u| < d \\ 0 & |u| > d \end{cases} \tag{3-16}$$

where d is the ratio of the width of the curtain slit moving in the x'' direction and the radius of the aperture opening.

The *between-the-lens shutter* consists of a usually circular or star-shaped opening made of several blades, placed between lens elements, and similar in construction to the aperture diaphragm. The size of the shutter diaphragm increases as the shutter opens and decreases as the shutter closes. The aperture diaphragm of the lens remains open all the time. The PSF of this shutter type is substantially more complicated [13] than (3-10), and can be best approximated by a PSF of a circular aperture [6,7] whose radius varies with time.

The PSF's due to motion of objects and camera may be cascaded with the PSF due to the shutter into a single system-transfer function [Figure 5].

4.0 Synthetic Image Generation

4.1 Hidden-Surface Elimination

A ray-tracing hidden-surface processor is used to compute the intensity point samples in $O'(x',y')$ from a description of a 3D scene and the camera geometry. The processor uses Whitted's recursive-illumination model [15] to compute intensity-point samples with the following shading equation:

$$f(i\Delta x', j\Delta y') = I_a + I_d + I_s + I_r + I_t \tag{4-1}$$

where

I_a = the ambient light intensity,
I_d = the the diffuse reflection,
I_s = the specular reflection,
I_r = the reflected light intensity, and
I_t = the transmitted light intensity.

This equation can be recursively redefined for I_r and I_t. The intensity change due to a shadow cast by an opaque object is:

$$I_{shadow} = -I_d - I_s \tag{4-2}$$

The hidden-surface program generates a raster image with a pin-hole camera model, and optionally the separate image intensity samples $f(i\Delta x', j\Delta y')$ [6,7]. Each sample consists of the following information obtained from a node of the shading tree at $O'(i\Delta x', j\Delta y')$:

1. the type of intensity information contained in the node: opaque, reflected, transmitted, hidden, or shadow.
2. the (i,j) coordinates of the sampled point,
3. the red, green, and blue intensity values, I_{red}, I_{green}, and I_{blue}, contributed by the measured object point,
4. the z' depth (along the camera's optical axis) of the measured object point (not used for shadows), and
5. the object identification number of the measured point (or object identification number of object casting shadow).

The list of samples of an image frame is then passed to a motion-blur processor together with a list of motion paths of the individual objects, time of the frame exposure t_{frame}, and the exposure duration T_{frame}. In an actual animation system, this information would be provided by an animation processor [2,9,14] which controls the motions of the objects and the camera.

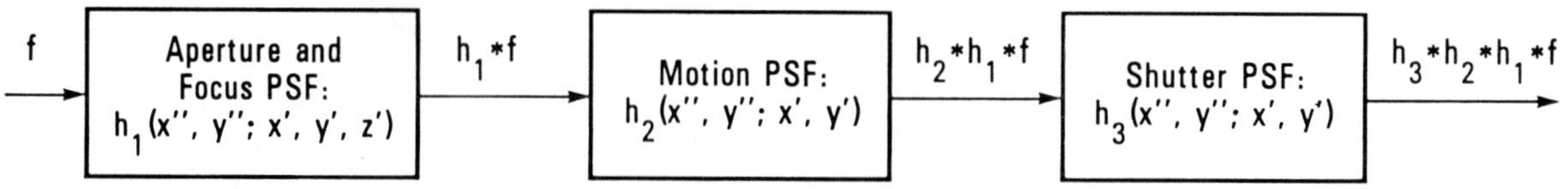

Figure 5 Cascaded system of point-spread functions

4.2 Addition of Motion Blur

Motion blur is generated by a processor shown in the block diagram in Figure 6. This processor separates sample points of a moving object with the same path $\mathbf{r}'(t)$ into a raster image **f**. The motion blur PSF $h(x'',y'';x'y')$ (equation 3-9) is computed from the object path $\mathbf{r}'(t)$, the exposure time t_{frame}, and the exposure length T_{frame} as a raster image **h**. The images **f** and **h** are then convolved into a blurred image **f*h**. This convolution can be performed either directly in the spatial domain, or optionally images **f** and **h** can be converted by FFT into **F** and **H**, respectively, in the frequency domain, multiplied into **F·H**, and then converted back into **f*h** by an inverse FFT. Finally, all blurred images of the moving objects are merged with the image of the stationary objects into the output raster image.

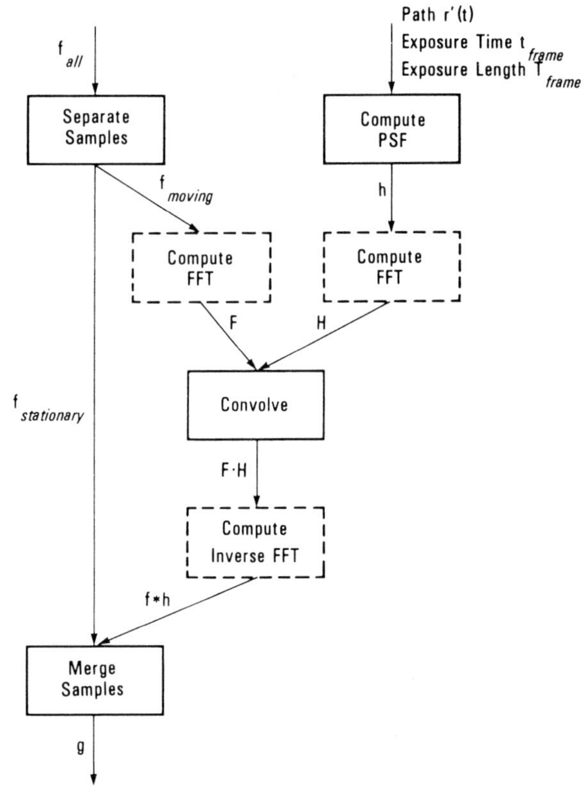

Figure 6 Block diagram of the motion-blur processor

To merge the stationary image with the blurred images of the moving objects, we need to compute in each blurred image the fraction of the exposure length T_{frame} that the moving object overlaps each pixel. From this information we can also determine the amount of time T_{frame} that each pixel in the stationary image is visible. This is accomplished by adding a fourth band (to the red, green and blue intensity bands) to each image **f**. This band contains the exposure length T_{frame} in every pixel that the instantaneous image of the moving object overlaps and 0 elsewhere. This "time" band is convolved with the PSF **h** exactly as the three image intensity bands. In image **f*h** this band, therefore, contains the fraction of timc T_{frame} that the moving object overlaps each pixel. The hidden-surface processor also generates intensity samples of stationary objects hiding or hidden by the moving objects. (Intersections with hidden-surfaces are otherwise used by this program for processing solid objects [10].) The stationary image is an image of the scene without the moving objects, rather than an image with "black holes" in places where the moving objects are missing. The blurred images of the moving objects and the image of the stationary objects are merged in a time-and-depth buffer. In this buffer the visibility of each pixel in the images being merged is determined by its depth, and its intensity by the length of time it remains visible. If a stationary surface is hiding a moving surface, the time exposure and therefore the intensity of the moving surface are reduced to 0. Otherwise, if one or more moving surfaces are hiding a stationary surface, the intensity of the stationary surface is reduced by the amount of time it is invisible which is determined from the exposure time value computed in each blurred image **f*h**. If the sum of the computed exposure times of the moving surfaces exceeds T_{frame} at a given pixel, then the intensity of the blurred moving surfaces is also appropriately reduced, and the stationary surface becomes, of course, completely invisible.

5.0 Results

The image sample functions are generated from a 3D scene description by a ray-tracing program previously described in [6,7]. Moving objects are assigned paths from which the motion-blur PSF's are computed. The motion-blur generation, as described in the previous section (Figure 6), has been implemented in both the spatial and frequency domains.

The first example (Figure 7) illustrates the use of multiple PSFs to describe the motions of several objects in a scene. Figure 7(a) shows an instantaneous image of a magnet and ten metallic balls suspended in air. In Figure 7(b) the balls accelerate along their individual paths toward the magnet during an exposure time T. In Figure 7(c) the exposure time has been doubled to $2T$ with a corresponding increase in the motion blur. In Figure 7(d) the PSF's of the balls have been modified to simulate a multiple exposure. During the total exposure time $2T$ the shutter was opened five times at $0.4T$ intervals, and each time remained open for $0.2T$. Note in the last three images that the intensity of the moving objects diminishes as the velocity of the objects increases.

In the second example motion blur is applied to an image containing reflections and refractions of moving objects. The instantaneous image (Figure 8(a)) consists of a cube with an image of a mandrill mapped on its six sides and three transparent spheres. These four objects are reflected in a planar mirror. The finite-exposure image

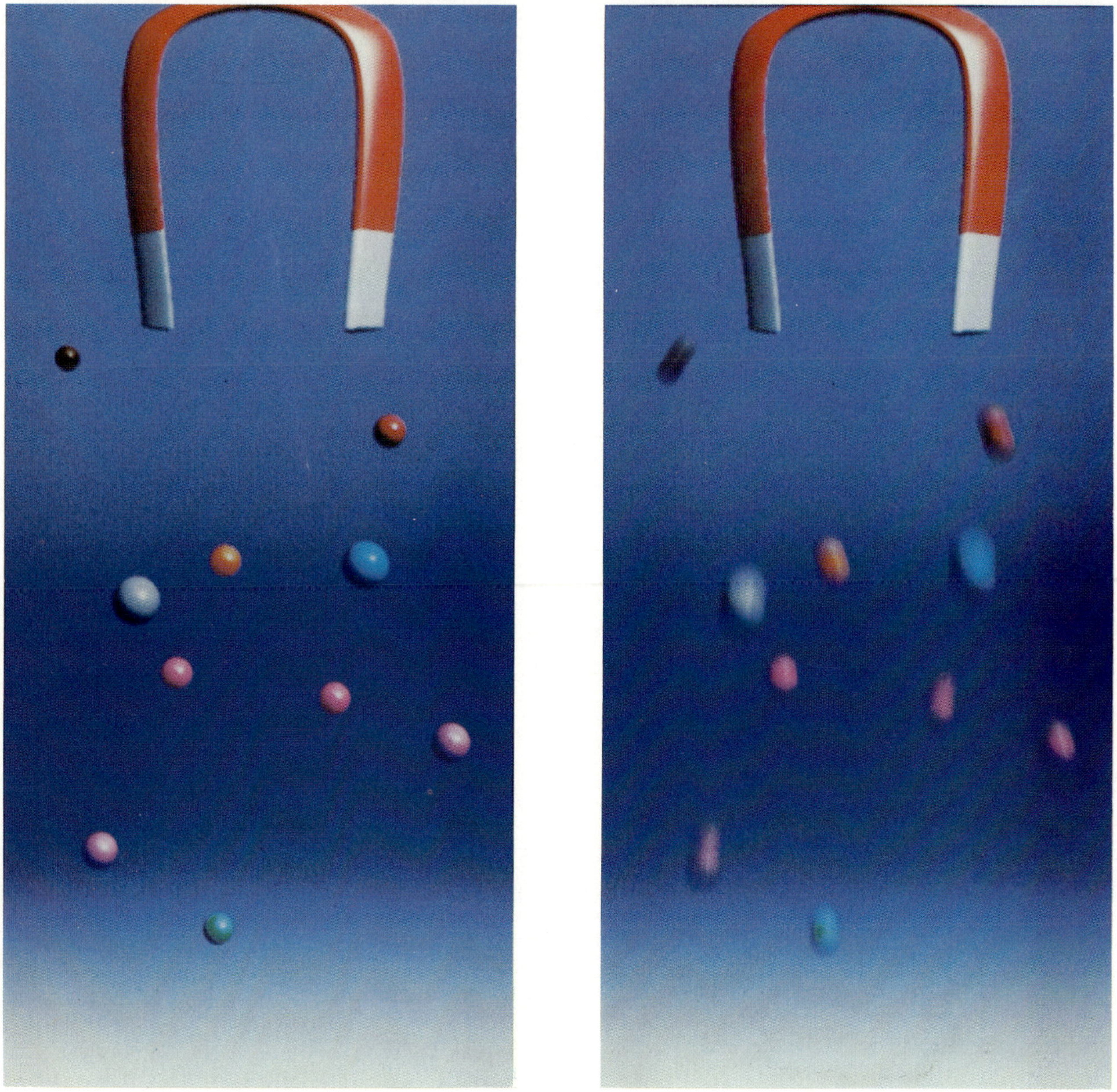

(a) (b)

Figure 7 Magnet attracting metallic balls: (a) instantaneous exposure, (b) finite-time exposure

(Figure 8(b)) shows motion blur of the cube and the three spheres as well as their reflections in the mirror. This is accomplished by convolving the motion blur PSF's of an object with all of its image samples (including reflections and refractions) generated by the hidden-surface program.

6.0 Conclusions

This paper has expanded upon a previously-described model of a camera's optical system [6,7] to include motion blur, that is, the ability to integrate image intensity due to moving objects during the time that a camera shutter remains open.

The camera model has been described in terms of a generalized image-formation system. This has allowed us to express the motion of objects by a set of optical system-transfer functions which are applied to the points in the image exhibiting the same motion, effectively simulating the camera shutter. In addition, this model allows us to cascade several transfer functions where each transfer function contributes one aspect of the overall camera

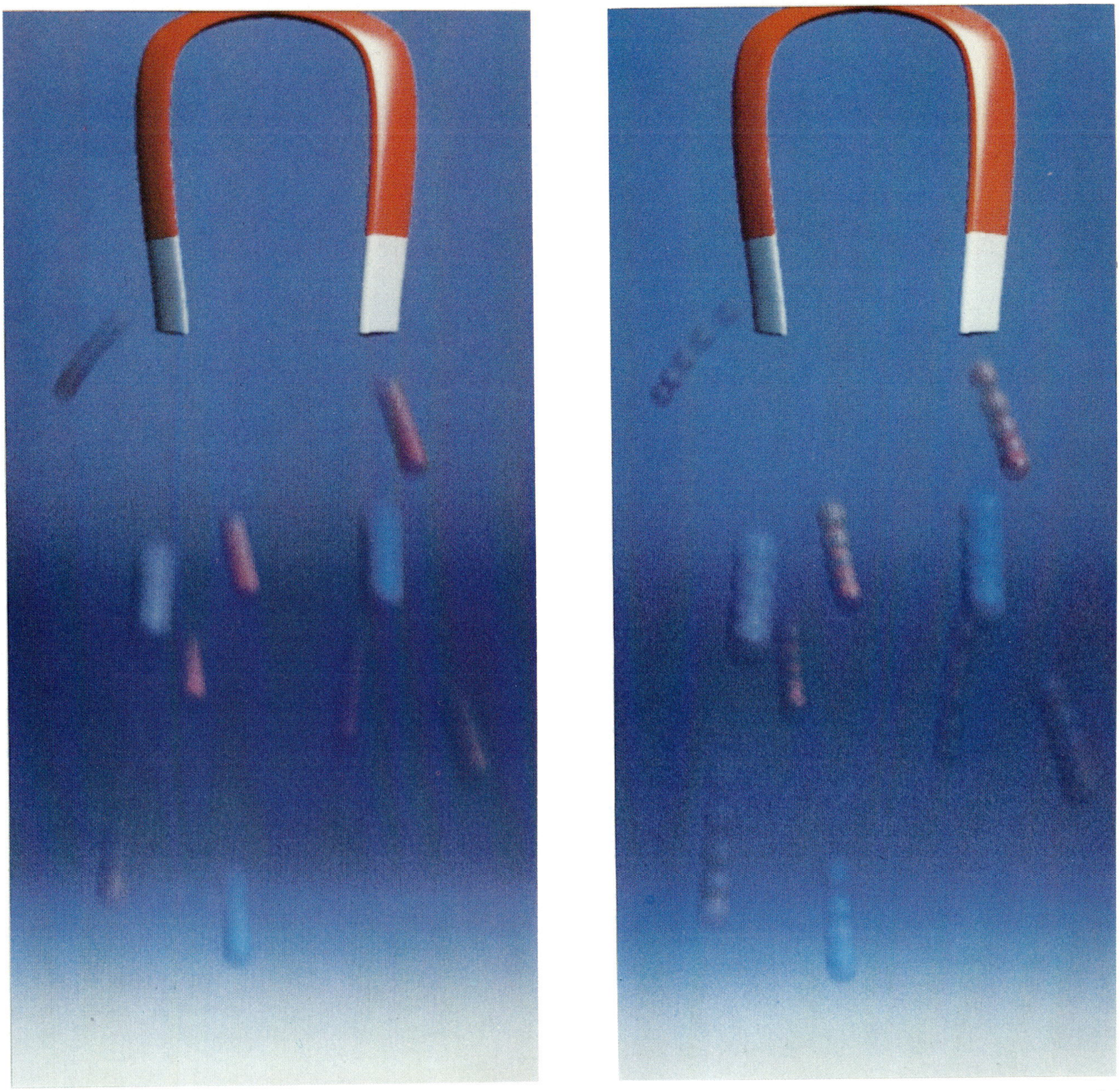

(c) (d)

Figure 7 Magnet attracting metallic balls: (c) extended time-exposure, (d) multiple exposure

model.

The implementation of this procedure has been attempted in both the spatial and frequency domains. A general expression for modeling the PSF of an arbitrary motion has been derived. This model has been applied to a 3D scene with multiple objects, each with its own path and velocity description, to generate images simulating motion blur. Examples of uniform blur due to camera motion and blur of reflected and refracted objects have been also presented. The modeling of motion blur in the most general case can become complicated due to object occlusions that may occur during the exposure time.

In this paper we have considered primarily the camera effects due to the lens, aperture, and shutter and their use in image synthesis. Future enhancements could be in the area of modeling special-effect filters (star, diffraction), the lens transfer function (optical aberrations) and the noise introduced by the optical system and the imaging medium.

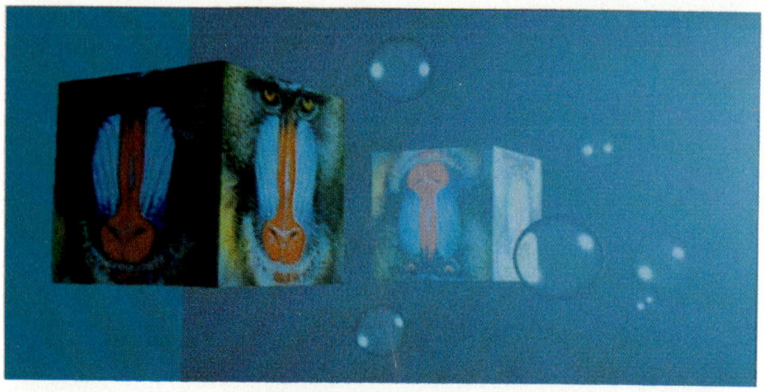

(a)

(b)

Figure 8 Mandrill cube and transparent spheres reflected in a mirror: (a) instantaneous image, (b) finite-time exposure image

7.0 Glossary

Symbol	*Description*
$e(x,y,z,w)$	surface representation in $O(x,y,z,w)$
$f(x',y')$	image-irradiance function in $O'(x',y')$
$f(x',y',t)$	image-irradiance function in $O'(x',y')$ at time t
$F(u,v)$	image-irradiance function in frequency domain
$g(x'',y'')$	image-output function in $O''(x'',y'')$
$g(x'',y'',t)$	image-output function in $O''(x'',y'')$ at time t
$G(u,v)$	image-output function in frequency domain
$h(x'',y'';x',y')$	optical transfer function from $O'(x',y')$ to $O''(x'',y'')$
$H(u,v)$	transfer function $h(x'',y'';x',y')$ in frequency domain
$O(x,y,z,w)$	3D object coordinate system
$O'(x',y')$	2D image-irradiance coordinate system
$O''(x'',y'')$	2D image-output (raster) coordinate system
$q(x',y';x,y,z,w)$	geometrical transformation function from $O(x,y,z,w)$ to $O'(x',y')$
$\mathbf{r}(t)$	object path in $O(x,y,z,w)$
$\mathbf{r}'(t)$	projection of path $\mathbf{r}(t)$ into $O'(x',y')$
t	time parameter
T	exposure time
$\delta(x',y')$	impulse-response function in $O'(x',y')$
$\Delta x'$	sampling distance of input function $f(x',y')$ in x'
$\Delta x''$	pixel size of output function $g(x'',y'')$ in x''
$\Delta y'$	sampling distance of input function $f(x',y')$ in y'
$\Delta y''$	pixel size of output function $g(x'',y'')$ in y''

Abbreviations

FFT	fast Fourier transform
PSF	point-spread function
SIPSF	space-invariant point-spread function
SSIPSF	separable space-invariant point-spread function
SSVPSF	separable space-variant point-spread function
SVPSF	space-variant point-spread function

8.0 Acknowledgments

The authors would like to thank Henry Moreton of Schlumberger-Doll Research for designing the 3D model of the magnet.

9.0 References

[1] Andrews, H. C. and Hunt, B. R., *Digital Image Restoration*, Prentice Hall Inc., New Jersey, 1977

[2] Blinn, J. F., "Systems Aspects of Computer Image Synthesis and Animation", SIGGRAPH 1982 Tutorial Notes

[3] Dainty, J. C., and Shaw, R., *Image Science*, Academic Press, New York, 1974

[4] Goodman, J. W., *Introduction to Fourier Optics*, McGraw-Hill, Inc., New York, 1968, Chapter 4,5

[5] Newell, M. E., Newell, R. G., and Sancha, T. L., "A New Approach to the Shaded Picture Problem", *Proceedings of the ACM National Conference*, 1972

[6] Potmesil, M. and Chakravarty, I., "A Lens and Camera Model for Synthetic Image Generation", *ACM Computer Graphics (Proc. SIGGRAPH 1981)*, *15*, (3), 297-305, August 1981

[7] Potmesil, M. and Chakravarty, I., "Synthetic Image Generation with a Lens and Aperture Camera Model", *ACM Transactions on Graphics*, *1*, (2), 85-108, April 1982

[8] Pratt, W. K., *Digital Image Processing*, Wiley-Interscience, New York, 1978

[9] Reynolds, C. W., "Computer Animation with Scripts and Actors", *ACM Computer Graphics (Proc. SIGGRAPH 1982)*, *16*, (3), 289-296, July 1982

[10] Roth, S., "Ray Casting for Modeling Solids", *Computer Graphics and Image Processing*, *18*, (1), 109-144, January 1982

[11] Sawchuk, A. A., "Space-Variant Image Motion Degradations and Restorations", *Proc. IEEE*, *60*, (7), 854-861, July 1972

[12] Sawchuk, A. A., "Space-Variant Image Restoration by Coordinate Transformation", *JOSA*, *64*, (2), 138-144, February 1974

[13] Shack, R. V., "The Influence of Image Motion and Shutter Operation on the Photographic Transfer Function", *Applied Optics*, *3*, (10), 1171-1181, October 1964

[14] Shelley, K. L., and Greenberg, D. P., "Path Specification and Path Coherence", *ACM Computer Graphics (Proc. SIGGRAPH 1982)*, *16*, (3), 157-166, July 1982

[15] Whitted, T., "An Improved Illumination Model for Shaded Display", *Comm. ACM*, 3, (6), June 1980, 343-349

PANEL

RAMIFICATIONS OF CAD/CAM ON THE AUTOMOTIVE SUPPLIER COMMUNITY

CHAIR: Wayne Hamann, Ford Motor Company
PANELISTS: W. Frankish, Engineering Service, Inc.
M. Glowacz, Revere Mold
T. E. Kelble, Dana Corporation
M. J. Linsell, Ford Motor Company
G. A. MacAlpine, Time Engineering
J. F. Yevitch, General Motors Corporation

CHAIRMAN'S INTRODUCTION

The automotive companies are striving for a totally integrated CAD/CAM environment as a major contribution to improved productivity and product. To the extent that suppliers are involved in the engineering/manufacturing process, they are an essential element of this integration process. Many of these suppliers already have CAD/CAM systems, most do not. From the perspective of the automotive industry, the challenge is to encourage the procurement and utilization of CAD/CAM systems while concurrently factoring in traditional sourcing practices. Suppliers, on the other hand, are often reluctant to make major purchases of CAD/CAM equipment without a commitment from their automotive customers that the equipment will be utilized. There have been instances where suppliers have procured CAD/CAM systems only to find that they were underutilized.

With the migration to electronic format, the problem of data compatibility becomes a major challenge to the supplier who must communicate with a variety of data sources from different automotive customers. Where data translation occurs today between supplier and customers it generally involves simple geometry only using standard formats developed by the major automotive companies. IGES (Initial Graphics Exchange Specification) has capability for much broader translation capability; however, utilization to date has been very limited.

In summary, the two major questions to be addressed in this panel are:

What is the optimum strategy to develop automotive supplier CAD/CAM capability?

What is the optimum strategy to achieve electronic communication of engineering/manufacturing (CAD/CAM) data between suppliers and their customers?

To provide a broad perspective for discussion, the panel members represent a diversity of interests:

James Yevitch, General Motors Corp., and Mick Linsell, Ford Motor Company will provide perspective from the automotive industry.

Bill Frankish, Engineering Service, Inc. and Gordon McAlpine, Time Engineering, will provide the design and tooling design services perspective.

Michaelene Glowacz, Revere Mold & Engineering will give a tooling suppliers perspective.

Tom Kelble, Dana Corporation, will provide a component supplier's perspective.

Panelists will include a brief synopsis on the extent of their involvement in CAD/CAM, what CAD/CAM systems they use, if they have interchanged data with an automotive customer, as well as their views on the issues discussed above.

PANELISTS' ABSTRACTS:

T. E. Kelble, Dana Corporation

Dana Corporation is a Fortune 500 company headquartered in Toledo, Ohio. We provide products and services to everything from the vehicular industry to shelter and security markets. My division is the Spicer Axle Division, which is part of the vehicular segment. We provide driving axles to the automotive and light truck industries. Our customers include American Motors, Chrysler, Ford and General Motors.

The Spicer Axle Division has been using CAD as a productive tool in our Product Engineering area since 1977. In 1977 we installed a Gerber Interactive Design System that is used for product design, drafting, and finite element modeling. In late 1981 the Gerber system was being fully used on three shifts, and we needed additional equipment. A division task force was formed to review what our CAD/CAM objectives should be. After a list of objectives was determined, we evaluated seven CAD/CAM vendors. Of the seven vendors, we benchmarked the three that were best suited to our needs and objectives. Of the three we benchmarked, we ultimately chose the GE/Calma systems. We are currently installing a configuration that will allow us to also integrate CAD/CAM in our manufacturing areas. One of our division objectives is to establish a common data base that can be accessed by all areas.

Part of our division objectives is also the ability to exchange data with both our customers and suppliers. This exchange of data will allow for shortened lead times for new product development, as well as higher quality parts. We are looking forward to exchanging data with both groups of individuals. At the present time, we have exchanged 3D wire frame data with two of our customers. This project was done for another Dana division which produces heavy truck axles. The programs were successful in both cases. It becomes a challenge to fully utilize the CAD data base for its maximum productivity capabilities. One definite area of benefit is clearly between the customer/supplier. It is our intent to develop these links from one data base to another.

Bill Frankish, Engineering Service, Incorporated

The author will present a brief slide presentation on E.S.I.'s experience in CAD/CAM, discussing the kinds of translation tools which E.S.I. utilizes to interchange data between the Ford/Lundy and GM/CGS graphics systems. Within this context, two questions will be addressed:

1. What is the optimum strategy to develop automotive supplier CAD/CAM capability?

2. What is the optimum strategy to achieve electronic communication of Engineering/Manufacturing (CAD/CAM) data between suppliers and their customers?

M. J. Linsell, Ford Motor Company

Ford Motor Company is committed to the implementation of Computer Aided Design and Manufacturing (CAD/CAM) in all activities of the Company. The benefits of increased productivity, improved quality, better and more sophisticated products and shorter product lead times are well recognized. Equally well recognized is the fact that the same benefits that accrue to Ford from the use of CAD/CAM technology can be realized by outside suppliers. To join in the electronic exchange of data, however, suppliers must be able to interface with the hardware and software used by Ford internally.

Over 430 graphics workstations are installed at Ford. Some 360 are the Ford developed Product Design Graphics System which runs on Prime minicomputers and is now being marketed by Prime. The majority of the remainder are Computervision systems. Data has already been exchanged with suppliers for several pilot programs, but on a hand carried tape basis.

Ford is establishing a framework for future exchange by pursuing the following actions:

Limit internal proliferation in the procurement of CAD/CAM equipment. In the near term, the best way to facilitate data exchange is to commonize equipment to the maximum extent practical.

Adopt IGES as a Corporate standard. Ford will adopt IGES as a standard format for communication of geometric data.

Develop common, Corporate standards for the use of graphics data as a means of conveying product design information. Ford is implementing procedures worldwide to commonize design and drafting standards.

Advise suppliers of our CAD/CAM directions and provide information on compatability. Ford will benefit in both lead time and cost if suppliers make effective use of CAD/CAM technology. Information will be provided that will allow them to achieve compatability with Ford. Also, trial programs will continue to be undertaken with selected suppliers to exchange CAD/CAM data on specific components. These will help identify changes needed, both in the company and at the supplier, to support data sharing.

Determine how geometric drawing data and alphanumeric release data should be associated. Work is currently underway to develop the specifications for a new engineering releasing system and will include consideration of the interface with drawing data.

Cumulative Index (SIGGRAPH '74 – SIGGRAPH '83)

Darlene A. Plebon

Computer Graphics Laboratory
Department of Computer Science
University of Waterloo
Waterloo, Ontario, Canada N2L 3G1
(519) 886-1351

SIGGRAPH '74 (Boulder, Colorado)

1. PARKE, FREDERIC I., A Model for Human Faces that Allows Speech Synchronized Animation, 52. (abstract only).
2. PARKE, FREDERIC I., Measuring Three-Dimensional Surfaces with a Two-Dimensional Data Tablet, 52. (abstract only).
3. DEFANTI, THOMAS A., SANDIN, DANIEL J., AND NELSON, THEODOR H., Computer Graphics as a Way of Life, 52. (abstract only).
4. POTTS, JACKIE S., Computer Graphics – Whence and Hence, 52. (abstract only).
5. WRIGHT, THOMAS J., Practical Computer Graphics for Scientific Users, 52. (abstract only).
6. SPRECHER, LEO T., Interactive Computer Graphics for Assisting Human Programmers, 53. (abstract only).
7. STOCKER, FREDERICK R. AND MINSKER, THOMAS, Graphics Geometric Perception and Communication, 53. (abstract only).
8. HOWDEN, WILLIAM E., Solution Plans and Interactive Problem Solving, 53. (abstract only).
9. JARVIS, J. F., A Graphical Display System Utilizing Plasma Panels, 53. (abstract only).
10. JERVERT, J. C. AND DUNN, R. M., Multi-Console Intelligent Satellite Graphics, 53. (abstract only).
11. COHEN, DAN AND TAFT, EDWARD, An Interactive Network Graphics System, 53. (abstract only).
12. COTTON, IRA W., Methodologies for the Cost-Benefit Analysis of Computer Graphics Systems, 53. (abstract only).
13. COTTON, IRA W., Standards for Network Graphics Communications, 54. (abstract only).
14. SMITH, LYLE B., An Example of a Pragmatic Approach to Portable Interactive Graphics, 54. (abstract only).
15. LAWALLEN, RICHARD A., Reducing Graphics Programming Effort through Structured Support, 54. (abstract only).
16. TURRILL, C. NORMAN AND MALLGREN, WILLIAM R., XPLG – Experiences in Implementing an Experimental Interactive Graphics Programming System, 54. (abstract only).
17. DENERT, E., ERNST, G., AND WETZEL, H., Graphical Language Features in ALGOL 68, 54. (abstract.only).
18. FULTON, DAVID L. AND DUQUET, ROBERT T., List Processing Primitives for BASIC, 54. (abstract only).
19. LEWIS, J. W., TREE: An Interactive System for Editing Tree Structures, 55. (abstract only).
20. SCHAEFER, L. J., Implementation of Transform Invoking Elements, 55. (abstract only).
21. KUNII, TOSIYASU L., AMANO, TAKAKO, ARISAWA, HIROSHI, AND OKADA, SACHIKO, An Interactive Fashion Design System "INFADS", 55. (abstract only).
22. ENTWISLE, JEFFREY, An Image Processing Approach to Computer Graphics, 55. (abstract only).
23. EASTMAN, JEFFREY F. AND WOOTEN, DAVID R., A General Purpose, Expandable Processor for Real-Time Computer Graphics, 55. (abstract only).
24. TRIPP, EDWIN R. III AND SUTTLE, JIMMIE R., An Interactive Three-Dimensional Color Graphics System, 56. (abstract only).
25. MCCRACKEN, T. E., SHERMAN, B. W., AND DWYER, S. J., An Economical Tonal Display for Interactive Graphics and Image Analysis Data, 56. (abstract only).
26. RIEBER, JOHN E. AND SHAW, ALAN C., Interactive Picture Generation and Manipulation through Formal Descriptions, 56. (abstract only).
27. EASTMAN, JEFFREY F., An Efficient Scan Conversion and Hidden Surface Removal Algorithm, 56. (abstract only).
28. STAUDHAMMER, JOHN AND OGDEN, DEBORAH J., Computer Graphics for Half-Tone Three-Dimensional Object Images, 56. (abstract only).
29. MORRIS, G. C., Real Time Animation of Dynamic Processes, 56. (abstract only).
30. THOMPSON, F., BIGELOW, R., GREENFIELD, M., ODDEN, J., REECE, D., AND SZOLOVITS, P., The REL Animated Film Language, 57. (abstract only).
31. FUTRELLE, R. P. AND POTEL, M. J., The System Design for GALATEA, an Interactive Real-Time Computer Graphics System for Movie and Video Analysis, 57. (abstract only).
32. BEBB, JOAN, An Interactive Environment for Scientific Development, 57. (abstract only).
33. NEROTH, CHACKO C., A Graphical Programming System with Speech Input, 57. (abstract only).
34. WILLMERT, K. D., Occupant Model for Human Motion, 57. (abstract only).
35. ALEMPARTE, M., CHHEDA, D., DEELEY, D., AND WALKER, W., Interacting with Discrete Simulation Using In Line Graphic Animation, 57. (abstract only).
36. REID, A. C., Searching for Oil through an Interactive Graphic Terminal, 58. (abstract only).
37. LECUREUX, FLOYD AND BURNETT, JAMES, Graphical Methods Used in the Numerical Solution of Jeffrey-Hamel Flow at Fixed Flow Rates, 58. (abstract only).
38. MILLER, IRVIN M., Graphics in Business Decision Making, 58. (abstract only).
39. SOLEM, BARRY J., Graphics in Finance, 58. (abstract only).
40. JOHNSON, THOMAS H., Graphics in Corporate Planning – A Case Study, 59. (abstract only).
41. CHAUHAN, ROHI, Graphics in Business Where We Are and Where We Are Going, 59. (abstract only).
42. WOOD, P. M. AND AUSTIN, D. M., CARTE: A Thematic Mapping Program, 59. (abstract only).
43. HOLMES, H. H., AUSTIN, D. M., AND BENSON, W. H., The MAPEDIT System for Automatic Map Digitization, 59. (abstract only).
44. COLLINS, M. G. AND KANE, G. R., An Interactive Computer Graphics Approach to the Design of Marching Band Routines, 60. (abstract only).

45. STEWARD, DONALD V. AND STEDWELL, MARION J., An Interactive Design System to be Taught 3D Graphical-Mathematical Procedures, 60. (abstract only).

46. SPAHR, HAROLD R. AND SUMLIN, HUGH A., Interactive Computer Graphics Applied to the Theoretical Aircraft/Store Separation Problem, 60. (abstract only).

47. FRITSCH, JOHN M., ELLIS, ROBERT A., JOCOBI, THOMAS A., AND MARSHALL, GRALAND R., A Macromodular Graphics System for Protein Structure Research, 60. (abstract only).

48. STELLMAN, S. D., Application of Three-Dimensional Interactive Graphics in X-Ray Crystallographic Analysis, 60. (abstract only).

49. SIDELL, P. M., ANDERSON, D. U., KNOPP, T. J., AND BASSINGTHWAIGHTE, J. B., Computer Graphics in Simulation of Cardiovascular Transport Phenomena, 60. (abstract only).

50. GUR, YEHUDA AND BIDDLE, CHARLES, Data Management for an Interactive Graphics System Oriented to Planning Applications, 61. (abstract only).

51. MANTEY, P. E., The Design and Evaluation of an Interactive Geo-Data Analysis and Display System, 61. (abstract only).

52. HAMANN, JAY R., A Man-Machine Vehicle Routing and Dispatching System Using Interactive Computer Graphics, 61. (abstract only).

53. SCHNEIDER, J. B., Interactive Graphics for Transportation Systems Planning and Design, 61. (abstract only).

54. WELSCH, ROY E. AND BJAALAND, HELGE, Graphics for Data Analysis, 62. (abstract only).

55. GEVINS, A. S., YEAGER, C. L., AND DIAMOND, S. L., Interactive Analysis and Display of the Electroencephalogram (EEG) in Real Time, 62. (abstract only).

56. SHORE, S., WILSON, J. L., AND SEMSARZADEH, G. A., Interactive Modeling System for Bridges, 62. (abstract only).

57. KING, R. G., GREGORSKI, F. S., AND MARTH, P. C., Traffic Analysis and Display for the San Francisco Vessel Traffic System, 62. (abstract only).

SIGGRAPH '75 (Bowling Green, Ohio)

58. DILL, JOHN C. AND THOMAS, JAMES J., On the Organization of a Remote Low Cost Intelligent Graphics Terminal, 1-8.

59. HAMLIN, GRIFFITH JR. AND FOLEY, JAMES D., Configurable Applications for Graphics Employing Satellites (CAGES), 9-19.

60. STOCKER, FREDERICK R., JOHNSON, GERALD G. JR., AND MCKINSTRY, HERBERT A., The Development of a Dynamic Interactive Computer Graphics Research and Educational Support Environment, 20-31.

61. MAX, NELSON L. AND CLIFFORD, WILLIAM H. JR., Computer Animation of the Sphere Eversion, 32-39.

62. ROBBINS, FRED E. AND GREEN, WILLIAM G., WAVE: Interactive Color Graphics for Waveform Analysis, 40-41.

63. HESSDORDER, R., On CAMS: A Computer Graphics System for the Production of Thematic Maps. (appears elsewhere).

64. KOENIGSBERG, LAWRENCE, MEADS, JON A., SHAW, JOHN, THANHOUSER, NED, AND VOLLUM, STEVEN, A Graphics Operating System, 42-48.

65. TRAMBACZ, ULRICH, Towards Device-Independent Graphics Systems, 49-52.

66. O'BRIEN, C. D. AND BOWN, H. G., IMAGE: A Language for the Interactive Manipulation of a Graphics Environment, 53-60.

67. GILOI, WOLFGANG K., On High-Level Programming Systems for Structured Display Programming, 61-69.

68. SHAPIRO, LINDA G., ESP^3: A High-Level Graphics Language, 70-77.

69. CSURI, C., Current State of the Art in Computer Animation. (panel dicussion, title).

70. BURTNYK, N. AND WEIN, M., Computer Animation of Free Form Images, 78-80. (panel discussion, position paper).

71. LEVINE, S. R., Computer Animation at Lawrence Livermore Laboratory, 81-84. (panel discussion, position paper).

72. TRESSEL, GEORGE W., Effective Application of Computer Graphics, 85-91. (panel discussion, position paper).

73. CSURI, CHARLES, Computer Animation, 92-101. (panel discussion, position paper).

74. POTTER, T. E. AND WILLMERT, K. D., Three-Dimensional Human Display Model, 102-110.

75. WYATT, HARRY J. AND ELLIS, ROBERT A., A Special-Purpose Computer System for On-Line Generation and Display of "Random-Dot" Stimuli for Stereoscopic Vision Experiments, 111-114.

76. WILLIAMS, BEN T., CHEN, THOMAS T., SCHULTZ, DONALD F., AND JOHNSON, ROGER L., A Terminal-Oriented Clinical Record System, 115-135.

77. WARREN, R. B., BARR, R. C., HERMAN-GIDDENS, G. S., AND SPACH, M. S., Display of Electrical Wave Forms from the Heart, 136. (abstract only, complete paper in *Computer Graphics 9,* 3 (Fall 1975), 17-30).

78. DUNN, R. M., Economic Considerations in Computer Graphics Systems. (panel discussion, title only).

79. COLLINS, DONALD WARREN, A Computer Graphics System for Modular Building Elevation Design, 137-147.

80. SIMON, RICHARD L., Computer Aided Design of Sculptured Surfaces, 148-159.

81. ALEXANDER, HOWARD, The Computer/Plotter and the 17 Ornamental Design Types, 160-167.

82. CRAWFORD, B. J., Design Rules Checking for Integrated Circuits Using Graphical Operators, 168-176.

83. JUDICE, C. N., Display of Two-Dimensional Functions Using Grey Scale Simulated on a Bilevel Display, 177-180.

84. STAUDHAMMER, JOHN, Multi-Dimensional Function Display Using a Color Scale, 181-183.

85. JARVIS, J. F., An Area Organized Data Structure for Interactive Graphics, 184-190.

86. STEPHENSON, M. B. AND CHRISTIANSEN, H. N., A Polyhedron Clipping and Capping Algorithm and a Display System for Three-Dimensional Finite Element Models. (abstract only, complete paper in *Computer Graphics 9,* 3 (Fall 1975), 1-16).

87. SCHNEIDER, EDWARD J. AND GOW, DAVID JOHN, Extending the Information Transfer in Multidimensional Analysis through the Use of Interactive Graphics, 191-200.

88. CARDMAN, SAMUEL J., Time Management in a Real-Time Animation/Graphics Environment, 201-207.

89. KACZMAREK, THOMAS AND SMOLIAR, STEPHEN W., An Experiment in Interaction between Independent Music and Graphics Processors, 208-211.

90. GILLENSON, MARK L. AND CHANDRASEKARAN, B., WHATSISFACE: Human Facial Composition by Computer Graphics, 212-221.

91. MOHILNER, PATRICIA R., Implementation of a Simulated Display Processor for Computer Graphics Education, 222-231.

92. WALLACE, V., Human Factors Considerations in Computer Graphics. (panel discussion, title only).

93. WRIGHT, T., Device Independent Graphics. (panel discussion, title).

94. DAVIS, JACK R., Device Independent Graphics Software: Is It Possible?, 232-245. (panel discussion, paper).

95. GEORGE, JAMES E., Algorithms to Reveal Graphic Terminal Characteristics, 246-251. (panel discussion, paper).

96. WRIGHT, THOMAS, A Schizophrenic System Plot Package, 252-255. (panel discussion, paper).

97. THOMAS, R., Manufacturers/Users Discussion Session. (discussion, title only).

98. MOELLERING, HAROLD, At the Interface of Cartography and Computer Graphics: Current Status and Future Prospects. (panel discussion, title).

99. MOELLERING, HAROLD, At the Interface of Cartography and Computer Graphics, 256-259. (panel discussion, position paper).

100. BOYLE, A. R., The Present Status of Automated Cartography, 260-266. (panel discussion, position paper).

101. PEUCKER, T. K., Computer Cartography: Some Critical Comments, 267-269. (panel discussion, position paper).

102. LEUHERMANN, A., Graphics Additions to Languages. (panel discussion, title only).

SIGGRAPH '76 (Philadelphia, Pennsylvania)

103. SONDEREGGER, RICHARD P. JR., TYPER: An Editor for the Online Composition of Text, 1-6.

104. WANG, PATRICK SHEN-PEI AND GROSKY, WILLIAM I., Sequential/Parallel Matrix Picture Languages, 7. (abstract only).

105. MCCAMMON, RICHARD B., An Interactive Computer Graphics Approach for Dissecting a Mixture of Normal (or Lognormal) Distributions, 8-12.

106. THANHOUSER, NED, Intermixing Refresh and Direct View Storage Graphics, 13-18.

107. MORLAND, D. VERNE, Computer-Generated Stereograms: A New Dimension for the Graphic Arts, 19-24.

108. POOCH, UDO W., A User-Oriented Computer Graphics System, 25-31.

109. PARENT, R., A Film Presentation of an Interactive System for 3-D Data Generation. (film only).

110. BAECKER, RONALD M., A Conversational Extensible System for the Animation of Shaded Images, 32-39.

111. NEGROPONTE, NICHOLAS AND PANGARO, PAUL, Experiments with Computer Animation, 40-44.

112. MYERS, ALLAN J., A Digital Video Information and Storage Retrieval System, 45-50.

113. ROSENFELD, A., NEWMAN, W., FREEMAN, H., AND VAN DAM, A., Relationship between Graphics and Image Processing. (panel discussion, title only).

114. BURTNYK, N. AND WEIN, M., Interactive Skeleton Techniques for Enhancing Motion Dynamics in Key Frame Animation, 51. (abstract only, complete paper in *CACM 19*, 10 (Oct. 1976), 564-569).

115. POTEL, M. J. AND SAYRE, R. E., Interacting with the GALATEA Film Analysis System, 52-59.

116. BROWN, MAXINE D. AND SMOLIAR, STEPHEN W., A Graphics Editor for Labanotation, 60-65.

117. RIESENFELD, RICHARD F., A Short Film on Schemes for Interactive Curve Design, 66. (film, abstract).

118. MEADOW, C., NEGROPONTE, N., HEREFORD, A., COTTON, IRA, AND DUNN, R. M., Man-Machine Interaction. (panel discussion, title only).

119. SPEER, RICK AND ELLIS, J., Film Making. (title only).

120. CARLSON, ERIC D., A Summary of Graphics Terminal Requirements Based on Application Studies, 67. (abstract only, complete paper in *Computer Magazine* (Aug. 1976)).

121. WOODSFORD, P. A., The HRD-1 Laser Display System, 68-73.

122. TRIPP, E. R., Slide Presentation on a Full Color Display and Simple Real-Time Animation. (slides only).

123. WEINZAPFEL, GUY AND NEGROPONTE, NICHOLAS, Architecture-by-Yourself: An Experiment with Computer Graphics for House Design, 74-78.

124. MACHOVER, CARL, Automated Drafting Systems – An Effective Person-Machine Interface, 79-81.

125. PERRY, P. F. AND KEENAN, J. D., Interactive Simulation of Network Pumping Policies on a Computer-Based Graphics System, 82-88.

126. WILSON, JOHN L. AND LANSBERRY, CHARLES R., Interactive Computer Graphics for Computer Aided Design in Civil Engineering, 89-96.

127. HEROT, CHRISTOPHER F., Graphical Input through Machine Recognition of Sketches, 97-102.

128. LAFUE, GILLES, Recognition of Three-Dimensional Objects from Orthographic Views, 103-108.

129. KASIK, DAVID J., Controlling User Interaction, 109-115.

130. KAPLOW, ROY AND MOLNAR, MICHAEL, A Computer-Terminal, Hardware/Software System with Enhanced User Input Capabilities: The Enhanced-Input Terminal System (EITS), 116-124.

131. CORNISH, L., Computer Graphic Technology and Its Use at the Census Bureau. (appears elsewhere).

132. SCHNEIDER, EDWARD J., BARGE, SYLVIA, AND MARKS, GREGORY A., Graphics for Social Scientists, 125-131.

133. FOLEY, JAMES D., Specifying Symbol Instances, 132. (abstract only).

134. BERGMAN, S. AND KAUFMAN, A., BGRAF 2: A Real-Time Graphics Language with Modular Objects and Implicit Dynamics, 133-138.

135. PFISTER, G., DALI – A High Level Language Extension for Dynamic Computer Graphics. (appears elsewhere).

136. KELLNER, RICHARD G. AND MAAS, LYNN D., A Developmental System for Microcomputer Based Intelligent Graphics Terminals, 139-142.

137. MILES, JOHN G., A Mobile Remote Data Collection and Graphics Display Station, 143-148.

138. SOWAR, RICHARD M., Animation on a Satellite Graphics System, 149-153.

139. TUERKE, KLAUS, A System for Interactive Acquisition and Administration of Geometric Data for Thematic Map Production, 154-162.

140. CARTER, JAMES R. AND ICOVE, DAVID J., The Application of the Intercolor 8000 Terminal to Thematic Cartography, 163-166.

141. DUEKER, KENNETH J., Cartographic Data Structures: Alternatives for Geographic Information Systems, 167-172.

142. SCHRACK, GUENTHER, On the Semantics of the Assignment Statement of High-Level Graphical Languages, 173-178.

143. LITTLE, W. D. AND WILLIAMS, ROBIN, Enhanced Graphics Performance with User Controlled Segment Files, 179-182.

144. WELLER, DAN AND WILLIAMS, ROBIN, Graphic and Relational Data Base Support for Problem Solving, 183-189.

145. MICHEL, JANET AND VAN DAM, ANDRIES, Experience with Distributed Processing on a Host/Satellite Graphics System, 190-195.

146. HAMLIN, GRIFFITH JR., Configurable Applications for Satellite Graphics, 196-203.

147. MOULTON, SAMUEL D. AND CORMAN, PHILIP J., Remote Programmability of Graphic Interactions in a Host/Satellite Configuration, 204-211.

148. POTOCZNIAK, J., KOSMIN, M., LARKIN, B., CALLAHAN, J., AND DUNN, R. M., Affordability of Computer Graphics for Planning Networks in DOD Program Management, 212-217.

149. CORREA, E. AND DEL PARAL, H. TORRES, Geographic Data Bank. (appears elsewhere).

150. HERMAN, A., Automated Contouring of Vertical Oceanographic Sections Using an Objective Analysis, 218-223.

151. SHEPHERD, WESLEY H., Editing of Digital Data in the Automated Cartography System at the U.S. Army Engineer Topographic Laboratories. (presentation only).

152. PUTNAM, RICHARD E. AND CARMICHAEL, RALPH L., SGP – A Simple Graphics Package, 224-228.

153. BLINN, JAMES F. AND GOODRICH, ANDREW C., The Internal Design of the IG Routines, an Interactive Graphics System for a Large Timesharing Environment, 229-234.

154. BASKETT, FOREST AND SHUSTEK, LEONARD, The Design of a Low Cost Video Graphics Terminal, 235-240.

155. MAX, NELSON L., Computer Rendering of Lobster Neurons, 241-245.

156. ROBB, RICHARD A., RITMAN, ERIK L., GREENLEAF, JAMES F., STURM, RALPH E., HERMAN, GABOR T., CHEVALIER, PETER A., LIU, HSUN K., AND WOOD, EARL H., Quantitative Imaging of Dynamic Structure and Function of the Heart, Lungs and Circulation by Computerized Reconstruction and Subtraction Techniques, 246-256.

157. CAPOWSKI, JOSEPH J., Characteristics of Neuroscience Computer Graphics Displays and a Proposed System to Generate Those Displays, 257-261.

158. LEVIN, JOSHUA Z., A Parametric Algorithm for Drawing Pictures of Solid Objects Composed of Quadric Surfaces, 262. (abstract only, complete paper in *CACM 19*, 10 (Oct. 1976), 555-563).

159. COHEN, EPHRAIM, A Method for Plotting Curves Defined by Implicit Equations, 263-265.

160. BLINN, JAMES F. AND NEWELL, MARTIN E., Texture and Reflection in Computer Generated Images, 266. (abstract only, complete paper in *CACM 19*, 10 (Oct. 1976), 542-547).

161. CLARK, JAMES H., Hierarchical Geometric Models for Visible Surface Algorithms, 267. (abstract only, complete paper in *CACM 19,* 10 (Oct. 1976), 547-554).

162. GONIN, MICHEL-PIERRE AND MOFFETT, THURBER J., ARTES, An Interactive Highway Design Program, 268-274.

163. KOZEMCHAK, E. B., Computer-Aided Integrated Circuit Design – A Distributed Integrated Approach, 275-278.

164. LAVICK, JERRY J., Making Graphics Work, 279-286.

165. CLARK, JAMES H., Three-Dimensional Man-Machine Interaction, 287. (film, abstract).

166. JARVIS, JOHN F., The Line Drawing Editor, An Experiment in Computer Vision, 288-292.

167. HADLOCK, F., PRIMS: An Interactive System for the Design of Hybrid Circuit Layout, 293-301.

168. GEER, RONALD G., Computer-Aided Coarse Grid Layout Technique for Photomasks, 302-307.

SIGGRAPH '77 (San Jose, California)

169. MALLARY, ROBERT AND FERRARO, MICHAEL, ECOSITE: An Application of Computer-Aided Design to the Composition of Landforms for Reclamation, 1-7.

170. TRACY, FRED T., Graphical Pre- and Post-Processor for 2-Dimensional Finite Element Method Programs, 8-12.

171. HAWRYLYSHYN, P. A., TASKER, R. R., AND ORGAN, L. W., CASS: Computer-Assisted Stereotaxic Surgery, 13-17.

172. BERGMAN, S. AND KAUFMAN, A., Association of Graphic Images and Dynamic Attributes, 18-23.

173. EASTMAN, CHARLES AND HENRION, MAX, GLIDE: A Language for Design Information Systems, 24-33.

174. NEWMAN, W., Recent Developments in Raster Scan Graphics. (panel discussion, title).

175. NEWELL, MARTIN E., On the Realism of Digitally Synthesized Images, 34. (panel discussion, abstract only).

176. SZABO, NICHOLAS, Real Time Digital Image Generation, 35. (panel discussion, abstract only).

177. MALESON, JOSEPH T., Raster Displays and Sampled Images, 36. (panel discussion, abstract only).

178. CATMULL, EDWIN E., High Quality Computer Animation, 37. (panel discussion, abstract only).

179. WILLARD, CHRISTOPHER AND HAMANN, JAY R., Interactive Graphics: An Aid to Health Planning and Decision Making, 38-41.

180. RENFROW, NANCY V., Computer Graphics for Facilities Management, 42-47.

181. BENSON, WILLIAM H. AND KITOUS, BERNARD, Interactive Analysis and Display of Tabular Data, 48-53.

182. HACKATHORN, RONALD J., ANIMA II: A 3-D Color Animation System, 54-64.

183. LEVOY, MARC, A Color Animation System Based on the Multiplane Technique, 65-71.

184. POTEL, M. J., Real-Time Playback in Animation Systems, 72-77.

185. HERZOG, B., DUNN, R., EWALD, R., FRYER, R., NEWMAN, W., PUK, R., FOLEY, J. D., AND BERGERON, R. D., Status Report of the Graphic Standards Planning Committee of ACM/SIGGRAPH. (report published in *Computer Graphics 11,* 3 (Fall 1977)).

186. BRASSEL, KURT E., UTANO, JACK J., AND HANSON, PERRY O. III, The Buffalo Crime Mapping System: A Design Strategy for the Display and Analysis of Spatially Referenced Crime Data, 78-85.

187. HEFEZ, E., DROR, L., AND NESHER, P., TRANS – Use of Graphics in the Study of Transformations, 86-89.

188. GREENBERG, DONALD P., An Interdisciplinary Laboratory for Graphics Research and Applications, 90-97.

189. MCCLEARY, LAWRENCE E., Techniques for the Display of Ocean Data on a Raster-Driven Color CRT, 98-101.

190. RUMSEY, JOHN R. AND WALKER, ROGER S., A Practical Approach to Implementing Line Printer Graphics, 102-106.

191. SATTERFIELD, STEVEN G., RODRIGUEZ, FRANCISCO, AND ROGERS, DAVID F., A Simple Approach to Computer Aided Milling with Interactive Graphics, 107-111.

192. CARUTHERS, L. C., VAN DEN BOS, J., AND VAN DAM, A., GPGS: A Device-Independent General Purpose Graphic System for Stand-Alone and Satellite Graphics, 112-119.

193. VICKERS, D. L, SMITH, G. S., LEVINE, S. R., AND CROSS, L. G., Moving, Computer-Generated Images via Integral Holography, 120. (extended abstract, complete paper appears as Two Unusual Three-Dimensional Displays, *Transactions of the American Crystallographic Association 12* (Jan. 1976), 85-101).

194. WOLCOTT, N. M. AND MCCRACKIN, F. L., A FORTRAN IV Program to Draw Enhanced Graphic Characters, 121-127.

195. WRIGHT, THOMAS, Machine-Independent Metacode Translation, 128-130.

196. WU, SHENG-CHUAN, ABEL, JOHN F., AND GREENBERG, DONALD P., An Interactive Computer Graphics Approach to Surface Representation, 131. (abstract only, complete paper in *CACM 20,* 10 (Oct. 1977), 703-712).

197. BREWER, J. A. AND ANDERSON, D. C., Visual Interaction with Overhauser Curves and Surfaces, 132-137.

198. PARENT, RICHARD E., A System for Sculpting 3-D Data, 138-147.

199. EDSON, DEAN T. AND LEE, GEORGE Y. G., Ways for Structuring Data Within a Digital Cartographic Data Base, 148-157.

200. DUTTON, GEOFFREY, An Extensible Approach to Imagery of Gridded Data, 159-169.

201. GOLD, C. M., CHARTERS, T. D., AND RAMSDEN, J., Automated Contour Mapping Using Triangular Element Data Structures and an Interpolant Over Each Irregular Triangular Domain, 170-175.

202. EVANS, D., Graphics Research. (panel discussion, title).

203. WARNOCK, JOHN E., Dynamic Modeling, 176. (panel discussion, abstract only).

204. KNOWLTON, KEN, A System for Interactive Definition and Depiction of Sculptured Surfaces, 177. (panel discussion, abstract only).

205. SHOUP, RICHARD G., Towards a Unified Approach to 2-D Picture Manipulation, 177. (panel discussion, abstract only).

206. PHILLIPS, RICHARD L., A Query Language for a Network Data Base with Graphical Entities, 179-185.

207. BERMAN, RICHARD R. AND STONEBRAKER, MICHAEL, GEO-QUEL: A System for the Manipulation and Display of Geographic Data, 186-191.

208. BLINN, JAMES F., Models of Light Reflection for Computer Synthesized Pictures, 192-198.

209. EARNSHAW, R. A., Line Generation for Incremental and Raster Devices, 199-205.

210. HAMLIN, GRIFFITH JR. AND GEAR, C. WILLIAM, Raster-Scan Hidden Surface Algorithm Techniques, 206-213.

211. WEILER, KEVIN AND ATHERTON, PETER, Hidden Surface Removal Using Polygon Area Sorting, 214-222.

212. TANIMOTO, STEVEN L., A Graph-Theoretic Real-Time Visible Surface Editing Technique, 223-228.

213. PUK, RICHARD F., General Clipping on an Oblique Viewing Frustrum, 229-235.

214. FUCHS, H., KEDEM, Z. M., AND USELTON, S. P., Optimal Surface Reconstruction from Planar Contours, 236. (abstract only, complete paper in *CACM 20,* 10 (Oct. 1977), 693-702).

215. BLINN, JAMES F., A Homogeneous Formulation for Lines in 3 Space, 237-241.

216. CROW, FRANKLIN C., Shadow Algorithms for Computer Graphics, 242-248.

217. HERTLEIN, GRACE C., Computer Art for Computer People – A Syllabus, 249-254.

218. MAGUIRE, R. BRIEN, Automated Display Techniques for Linear Graphs, 255-260.

219. ETRA, W., DEFANTI, T., FELSENSTEIN, L., KATZ, L., MELEN, R., FISCHER, M., BECK, S., AND DOMPIER, S., Low Cost Computer Graphics. (panel discussion, title only).

SIGGRAPH '78 (Altanta, Georgia)

220. CROW, FRANKLIN C., The Use of Grayscale for Improved Raster Display of Vectors and Characters, 1-5.

221. CATMULL, EDWIN, A Hidden-Surface Algorithm with Anti-Aliasing, 6-11.

222. SMITH, ALVY RAY, Color Gamut Transform Pairs, 12-19.

223. JOBLOVE, GEORGE H. AND GREENBERG, DONALD P., Color Spaces for Computer Graphics, 20-25.

224. WHITTED, TURNER, A Scan Line Algorithm for Computer Display of Curved Surfaces, 26. (abstract only, complete paper appears as BLINN, JAMES F., CARPENTER, LOREN C., LANE, JEFFREY M., AND WHITTED, TURNER, Scan Line Methods for Displaying Parametrically Defined Surfaces, *CACM 23,* 1 (Jan. 1980), 23-34).

225. BLINN, JAMES F., A Scan Line Algorithm for Displaying Parametrically Defined Surfaces, 27. (abstract only, complete paper appears as BLINN, JAMES F., CARPENTER, LOREN C., LANE, JEFFREY M., AND WHITTED, TURNER, Scan Line Methods for Displaying Parametrically Defined Surfaces, *CACM 23,* 1 (Jan. 1980), 23-34).

226. FUTRELLE, R. P. AND BARTA, G., Towards the Design of an Intrinsically Graphical Language, 28-32.

227. DEFANTI, TOM, FENTON, JAY, AND DONATO, NOAL, Basic Zgrass – A Sophisticated Graphics Language for the Bally Home Library Computer, 33-37.

228. VAN DEN BOS, JAN, Definition and Use of Higher-Level Graphics Input Tools, 38-42.

229. FREI, H. P., WELLER, D. L., AND WILLIAMS, R., A Graphics-Based Programming-Support System, 43-49.

230. PAVLISCAK, T. J., STOWELL, G. W., AND BAILEY, M. J., A Microcomputer Based System for Automated Pattern Digitization and Editing, 50-53.

231. TOWLE, TOM AND DEFANTI, TOM, GAIN: An Interactive Program for Teaching Interactive Computer Graphics Programming, 54-59.

232. MCINTOSH, JOHN F., The Interactive Digitizing of Polygons and the Processing of Polygons in a Relational Database, 60-63.

233. BURTON, WARREN, A Fixed Grid Curve Representation for Efficient Processing, 64-69.

234. FRANKLIN, WM. RANDOLPH AND LEWIS, HARRY R., 3-D Graphic Display of Discrete Spatial Data by Prism Maps, 70-75.

235. EWALD, ROBERT H. AND MAAS, LYNN D., A High Performance Graphics System for the CRAY-1, 76-81.

236. WEINBERG, RICHARD, Computer Graphics in Support of Space Shuttle Simulation, 82-86.

237. KAUFMAN, ARIE A., System Design and Implementation of BGRAF2, 87-92.

238. DEIMEL, L. E. JR., DOSS, C. L. II, FORNARO, R. J., MCALLISTER, D. F., AND ROULIER, J. A., Application of Shape-Preserving Spline Interpolation to Interactive Editing of Photogrammetric Data, 93-99.

239. GOODMAN, T. AND SPENCE, R., The Effect of System Response Time on Interactive Computer Aided Problem Solving, 100-104.

240. ZIMMERLIN, TIMOTHY, STANLEY, JOHN, AND STONE, WARREN, A Sensor Simulation and Animation System, 105-110.

241. LIEBERMAN, HENRY, How to Color in a Coloring Book, 111-116.

242. SATTERFIELD, STEVEN G., RODRIGUEZ, FRANCISCO, AND ROGERS, DAVID F., A Microprocessor Display Controller for Combining Refresh and Storage Tube Graphics, 117-124.

243. WOETZEL, GERD, A Fast and Economic Scan-to-Line-Conversion Algorithm, 125-129.

244. DUNGAN, WILLIAM JR., STENGER, ANTHONY, AND SUTTY, GEORGE, Texture Tile Considerations for Raster Graphics, 130-134.

245. ROSENFELD, AZRIEL, Algorithms for Image/Vector Conversion, 135-139.

246. SHAPIRO, LINDA G., Data Structures for Picture Processing, 140-146.

247. FU, K. S. AND LU, S. Y., Computer Generation of Texture Using a Syntactic Approach, 147-152.

248. BADLER, NORMAN AND BAJCSY, RUZENA, Three-Dimensional Representations for Computer Graphics and Computer Vision, 153-160.

249. PAVLIDIS, THEODOSIOS, Filling Algorithms for Raster Graphics, 161-166.

250. STAUDHAMMER, JOHN, On Display of Space Filling Atomic Models in Real-Time, 167-172.

251. WEIN, M., TANNER, P., BECHTHOLD, G., AND BURTNYK, N., Hidden Line Removal for Vector Graphics, 173-180.

252. MATHERAT, PHILIPPE, A Chip for Low-Cost Raster-Scan Graphic Display, 181-186.

253. CHRISTIANSEN, H. N. AND SEDERBERG, T. W., Conversion of Complex Contour Line Definitions into Polygonal Element Mosaics, 187-192.

254. TOBLER, W. R., Comparing Figures by Regression, 193-195.

255. SUNGUROFF, ALEXANDER AND GREENBERG, DONALD P., Computer Generated Images for Medical Applications, 196-202.

256. DONELSON, WILLIAM C., Spatial Management of Information, 203-209.

257. HEROT, CHRISTOPHER F. AND WEINZAPFEL, GUY, One-Point Touch Input of Vector Information for Computer Displays, 210-216.

258. BADLER, NORMAN I. AND BADLER, VIRGINIA R., Interaction with a Color Computer Graphics System for Archaeological Sites, 217-221.

259. BRITTON, EDWARD G., LIPSCOMB, JAMES S., AND PIQUE, MICHAEL E., Making Nested Rotations Convenient for the User, 222-227.

260. MOSES, FRANKLIN L. AND MAISANO, RICHARD E., User Performance Under Several Automated Approaches to Changing Displayed Maps, 228-233.

261. HILLYARD, R. C. AND BRAID, I. C., Characterizing Non-Ideal Shapes in Terms of Dimensions and Tolerances, 234-238.

262. ATHAY, RUSSELL J., Object Models for Computer Aided Design: An Overview, 239-244.

263. BLINN, JAMES F. AND NEWELL, MARTIN E., Clipping Using Homogeneous Coordinates, 245-251.

264. BRAID, I. C., On Storing and Changing Shape Information, 252-256.

265. VOELCKER, H., REQUICHA, A., HARTQUIST, E., FISHER, W., METZGER, J., TILOVE, R., BIRRELL, N., HUNT, W., ARMSTRONG, G., CHECK, T., MOOTE, R., AND MCSWEENEY, J., The PADL-1.0/2 System for Defining and Displaying Solid Objects, 257-263.

266. FORREST, A. R., A Unified Approach to Geometric Modelling, 264-269.

267. WILLIAMS, LANCE, Casting Curved Shadows on Curved Surfaces, 270-274.

268. ATHERTON, PETER, WEILER, KEVIN, AND GREENBERG, DONALD, Polygon Shadow Generation, 275-281.

269. PORTER, THOMAS K., Spherical Shading, 282-285.

270. BLINN, JAMES F., Simulation of Wrinkled Surfaces, 286-292.

271. HEILMAN, ROBERT L. AND MARCHANT, JEAN M., TIGS: An Overview of the Terminal Independent Graphics System, 293-297.

272. LEVINE, KEN, Core Standard Graphic Package for the VGI 3400, 298-300.

273. WARNER, JAMES R., POLISHER, MARGARET A., AND KOPOLOW, ROBERT N., DIGRAF – A FORTRAN Implementation of the Proposed GSPC Standard, 301-307.

274. KELLNER, RICHARD G., REED, THEODORE N., AND SOLEM, ANN V., An Implementation of the ACM/SIGGRAPH Proposed Graphics Standard in a Multisystem Environment, 308-312.

275. HAMLIN, GRIFFITH JR. AND CROCKETT, THOMAS, A Microprocessor-Assisted Graphics System, 313-317.

276. HUBBOLD, R. J. AND BRAMHALL, P. J., A Flexible, High Performance Interactive Graphics System, 318-322.

277. HABER, ROBERT, SHEPHARD, MARK, ABEL, JOHN, GALLAGHER, RICHARD, AND GREENBERG, DONALD, A Generalized Graphic Preprocessor for Two-Dimensional Finite Element Analysis, 323-329.

278. BOUQUET, D. L., An Interactive Graphics Application to Advanced Aircraft Design, 330-335.

279. ENGLAND, J. N., A System for Interactive Modeling of Physical Curved Surface Objects, 336-340.

280. BORKIN, HAROLD J., MCINTOSH, JOHN F., AND TURNER, JAMES A., The Development of Three-Dimensional Spatial Modeling Techniques for the Construction Planning of Nuclear Power Plants, 341-347.

281. CATMULL, EDWIN, The Problems of Computer-Assisted Animation, 348-353.

282. HERBISON-EVANS, DON, NUDES 2: A Numeric Utility Displaying Ellipsoid Solids, Version 2, 354-356.

283. KAHN, KENNETH M. AND HEWITT, CARL, Dynamic Graphics Using Quasi Parallelism, 357-362.

SIGGRAPH '79 (Chicago, Illinois)

284. CATMULL, EDWIN, A Tutorial on Compensation Tables, 1-7.

285. SHOUP, RICHARD G., Color Table Animation, 8-13.

286. WHITTED, TURNER, An Improved Illumination Model for Shaded Display, 14. (abstract only, complete paper in *CACM 23,* 6 (June 1980), 343-349).

287. FOLEY, JAMES D., TEMPLEMAN, JAMES N., AND DASTYAR, DARA, Some Raster Graphics Extensions to the CORE System, 15-24.

288. UNO, SAKAE AND MATSUKA, HIDEO, A General Purpose Graphic System for Computer Aided Design, 25-32.

289. BROWN, BRUCE ERIC, Computer Graphics for Large Scale Two- and Three-Dimensional Analysis of Complex Geometries, 33-40.

290. ROESE, JOHN A. AND MCCLEARY, LAWRENCE E., Stereoscopic Computer Graphics for Simulation and Modeling, 41-47.

291. BAECKER, RONALD, Digital Video Display Systems and Dynamic Graphics, 48-56.

292. CAHN, DEBORAH U., JOHNSTON, NANCY E., AND JOHNSTON, WILLIAM E., A Response to the 1977 GSPC CORE Graphics System, 57-62.

293. PRINGLE, ALISON, ROBINSON, PETER, AND WISEMAN, NEIL, Aspects of Quality in the Design and Production of Text, 63-70.

294. BEATTY, JOHN C., CHIN, JANET S., AND MOLL, HENRY F., An Interactive Documentation System, 71-82.

295. SPROULL, ROBERT F., Raster Graphics for Interactive Programming Environments, 83-93.

296. MORSE, ALAN, Some Principles for the Effective Display of Data, 94-101.

297. THORNTON, ROBERT W., The Number Wheel: A Tablet Based Valuator for Interactive Three-Dimensional Positioning, 102-107.

298. FIDDLER, JERRY AND ELISCHER, VICTOR, Graphical Human Interface to a Neutral Beam System, 108-112.

299. ANSON, ED, The Semantics of Graphical Input, 113-120.

300. MONTALVO, FANYA S., LEVINE, STEPHEN R., ANSTIS, STUART, JULESZ, BELA, AND GREGORY, RICHARD L., Special Session on Vision, 121. (special session, introduction).

301. MONTALVO, FANYA S., Human Vision and Computer Graphics, 121-125. (special session, paper).

302. BRASSEL, KURT E. AND FEGEAS, ROBIN, An Algorithm for Shading of Regions on Vector Display Devices, 126-133.

303. RHODES, MICHAEL L., An Algorithmic Approach to Controlling Search in Three-Dimensional Image Data, 134-142.

304. DUNGAN, WILLIAM JR., A Terrain and Cloud Computer Image Generation Model, 143-150.

305. APPEL, ARTHUR, ROHLF, F. JAMES, AND STEIN, ARTHUR J., The Haloed Line Effect for Hidden Line Elimination, 151-157.

306. KAY, DOUGLAS SCOTT AND GREENBERG, DONALD, Transparency for Computer Synthesized Images, 158-164.

307. MAX, NELSON L., ATOMLLL: ATOMS with Shading and Highlights, 165-173.

308. CLARK, JAMES H., A Fast Scan-Line Algorithm for Rendering Parametric Surfaces, 174. (abstract only).

309. FUCHS, HENRY, KEDEM, ZVI M., AND NAYLOR, BRUCE, Predetermining Visibility Priority in 3-D Scenes, 175-181.

310. WRIGHT, THOMAS AND HUMBRECHT, JOHN, ISOSRF – An Algorithm for Plotting Iso-Valued Surfaces of a Function of Three Variables, 182-189.

311. YESSIOS, CHRIS I., Computer Drafting of Stones, Wood, Plant and Ground Materials, 190-198.

312. FOWLER, ROBERT J. AND LITTLE, JAMES J., Automatic Extraction of Irregular Network Digital Terrain Models, 199-207.

313. PALLER, ALAN, D'HONDT, WALTER, DAHL, DAVID, AND DUPREE, ROBERT L., Special Session on Large Scale Applications of Computer Charting and Mapping in Industry, 208-209. (special session, abstract only).

314. PATERNOSTER, R. H., BOUSSE, L. J., AND STEENHAUT, O. L., A Colour Display Unit for a 21-Channel EEG-Monitor, 210-217.

315. MITROO, J. B., HERMAN, NANCY, AND BADLER, NORMAN I., Movies from Music: Visualizing Musical Compositions, 218-225.

316. DALTON, J., BILLINGSLEY, J., QUANN, J., AND BRACKEN, P., Interactive Color Map Displays of Domestic Information, 226-233.

317. PORTER, THOMAS K., The Shaded Surface Display of Large Molecules, 234-236.

318. O'BRIEN, MICHAEL T., A Network Graphical Conferencing System, 237. (abstract only).

319. FLEXER, J. ROBERT AND WIEDERHOLD, GIO, A Building Block Approach to Color Graphics, 238-245.

320. LANG, M. S., COHEN, R. L., ESCHENBERG, K. E., OCHS, J. B., STOCKER, F. R., RANEY, J. L., AND STUCKEY, B. F., Implementation of an Interactive Computer Graphics Environment at NASA/JSC, 246-252.

321. FORREST, A. R., On the Rendering of Surfaces, 253-259.

322. BARROS, JOSE AND FUCHS, HENRY, Generating Smooth 2-D Monocolor Line Drawings on Video Displays, 260-269.

323. DUFF, TOM, Smoothly Shaded Renderings of Polyhedral Objects on Raster Displays, 270-275.

324. SMITH, ALVY RAY, Tint Fill, 276-283.

325. STERN, GARLAND, SoftCel – An Application of Raster Scan Graphics to Conventional Cel Animation, 284-288.

326. CSURI, C., HACKATHORN, R., PARENT, R., CARLSON, W., AND HOWARD, M., Towards an Interactive High Visual Complexity Animation System, 289-299.

327. KAPLAN, MICHAEL AND GREENBERG, DONALD P., Parallel Processing Techniques for Hidden Surface Removal, 300-307.

SIGGRAPH '80 (Seattle, Washington)

328. MARCUS, AARON, KURLANSKY, MERVYN, MARCUS, SUSAN, REINECK, JACK, AND REINECK, GAY, Special Session on Effective Information Presentation Techniques, 1. (special session, abstract only).

329. ARTZY, EHUD, FRIEDER, GIDEON, AND HERMAN, GABOR T., The Theory, Design, Implementation, and Evaluation of a Three-Dimensional Surface Detection Algorithm, 2-9.

330. WEILER, KEVIN, Polygon Comparison Using a Graph Representation, 10-18.

331. MCKEOWN, KATHLEEN R. AND BADLER, NORMAN I., Creating Polyhedral Stellations, 19-24.

332. DE BRUYNE, P., Acoustic Radar Graphic Input Device, 25-31.

333. LIPPMAN, ANDREW, Movie-Maps: An Application of the Optical Videodisc to Computer Graphics, 32-42.

334. BECHTOLSHEIM, ANDREAS AND BASKETT, FOREST, High-Performance Raster Graphics for Microcomputer Systems, 43-47.

335. PARKE, FREDERIC I., Simulation and Expected Performance Analysis of Multiple Processor Z-Buffer Systems, 48-56.

336. FUCHS, HENRY, COHEN, DAN, SPROULL, ROBERT F., CLARK, JAMES H., AND PARKE, FREDERIC I., Trends in High Performance Graphic Systems, 57. (panel discussion, introduction only).

337. TEDROW, LUCKY M. AND HOERAUF, EUGENE A., Atlas Supplement to the 1972 County and City Data Book, 58-62.

338. HEROT, CHRISTOPHER F., CARLING, RICHARD, FRIEDELL, MARK, AND KRAMLICH, DAVID, A Prototype Spatial Data Management System, 63-70.

339. TSURUTANI, TATEYUKI, KASAHARA, YUTAKA, AND NANIWADA, MASARU, ATLAS: A Geographic Database System Data Structure and Language Design for Geographic Information, 71-77.

340. MACHOVER, CARL, TAYLOR, SUSAN, SCHMIDT, ALLAN, BIRKHAHN, PAUL, HAMENT, JUNE, AND QUANN, JOHN, Computer Graphics Moves into the Business World, 78. (panel discussion, introduction only).

341. LAIB, G., PUK, R., AND STOWELL, G., Integrating Solid Image Capability into a General Purpose Calligraphic Graphics Package, 79-85.

342. LEVIN, JOSHUA ZEV, QUADRIL: A Computer Language for the Description of Quadric-Surface Bodies, 86-92.

343. GOATES, GARY B., GRISS, MARTIN L., AND HERRON, GARY J., PICTUREBALM: A LISP-Based Graphics Language System with Flexible Syntax and Hierarchical Data Structure, 93-99.

344. LAKIN, FRED H., A Structure from Manipulation for Text-Graphic Objects, 100-107.

345. FOURNIER, ALAIN AND FUSSELL, DON, Stochastic Modeling in Computer Graphics, 108. (abstract only, complete paper appears as FOURNIER, ALAIN, FUSSELL, DON, AND CARPENTER, LOREN, Computer Rendering of Stochastic Models, *CACM 25*, 6 (June 1982), 371-384).

346. CARPENTER, LOREN C., Computer Rendering of Fractal Curves and Surfaces, 109. (abstract only, complete paper appears as FOURNIER, ALAIN, FUSSELL, DON, AND CARPENTER, LOREN, Computer Rendering of Stochastic Models, *CACM 25*, 6 (June 1982), 371-384).

347. RUBIN, STEVEN M. AND WHITTED, TURNER, A 3-Dimensional Representation for Fast Rendering of Complex Scenes, 110-116.

348. FRANKLIN, WM. RANDOLPH, A Linear Time Exact Hidden Surface Algorithm, 117-123.

349. FUCHS, HENRY, KEDEM, ZVI M., AND NAYLOR, BRUCE F., On Visible Surface Generation by A Priori Tree Structures, 124-133.

350. DESJARDINS, MARY AND HASLER, A. FREDERICK, Stereographic Displays of Atmospheric Model Data, 134-139.

351. TORSON, JAMES M., Application of Graphical Interaction to the Analysis of Radio Astronomy Data, 140-146.

352. HANKLEY, WILLIAM AND WALLENTINE, VIRGIL, Color Graphics for Remote Teaching, 147-153.

353. MARSHALL, ROBERT, WILSON, RODGER, AND CARLSON, WAYNE, Procedure Models for Generating Three-Dimensional Terrain, 154-162.

354. JACKSON, J. H., Dynamic Scan-Converted Images with a Frame Buffer Display Device, 163-169.

355. SHOUP, RICHARD, KLIMEK, TOM, EVANS, LARRY, BLACK, PETER, BLEY, H., AND WEISE, D., Computer Graphics in Television, 170. (panel discussion, introduction only).

356. MAX, NELSON AND BLUNDEN, JOHN, Optical Printing in Computer Animation, 171-177.

357. PARKE, FREDERIC I., Adaptation of Scan and Slit-Scan Techniques to Computer Animation, 178-181.

358. ACKLAND, BRYAN AND WESTE, NEIL, Real Time Animation Playback on a Frame Store Display System, 182-188.

359. BADLER, NORMAN I., O'ROURKE, JOSEPH, AND KAUFMAN, BRUCE, Special Problems in Human Movement Simulation, 189-197.

360. CALVERT, T. W., CHAPMAN, J., AND PATLA, A., The Integration of Subjective and Objective Data in the Animation of Human Movement, 198-203.

361. FUEHRING, GWENDOLYN L., Graphic Analysis and Planning of Electrical Distribution Systems, 204-210.

362. ROGERS, DAVID F. AND SATTERFIELD, STEVEN G., B-Spline Surfaces for Ship Hull Design, 211-217.

363. BLISS, FRANK W., Interactive Computer Graphics at Ford Motor Company, 218-224.

364. ANDERSON, KEN, THOMPSON, MYRL, HARRIS, D. H. W., WILSON, R., CROWLEY, B., BOYD, C., AND WOZNY, M., The User's View of CAD/CAM, 225. (panel discussion, introduction only).

365. ENCARNACAO, J., ENDERLE, G., KANSY, K., NEES, G., SCHLECHTENDAHL, E. G., WIBKIRCHEN, P., AND WEISS, J., The Workstation Concept of GKS and the Resulting Conceptual Differences to the GSPC Core System, 226-230.

366. GURWITZ, ROBERT F., THORNE, RICHARD W., VAN DAM, ANDRIES, AND CARLBOM, INGRID B., BUMPS: A Program for Animating Projections, 231-237.

367. MICHENER, JAMES C. AND CARLBOM, INGRID B., Natural and Efficient Viewing Parameters, 238-245.

368. BONO, PETER, TEN HAGEN, P., CHIN, JANET, ENCARNACAO, J., AND MICHENER, JAMES C., Graphics Standards Status Report, 246. (panel discussion, introduction only).

369. MARCUS, AARON, Computer-Assisted Chart Making from the Graphic Designer's Perspective, 247-253.

370. MEYER, GARY W. AND GREENBERG, DONALD P., Perceptual Color Spaces for Computer Graphics, 254-261.

371. BOLT, RICHARD A., "Put-That-There": Voice and Gesture at the Graphics Interface, 262-270.

372. HANAU, PAUL R. AND LENOROVITZ, DAVID R., Prototyping and Simulation Tools for User/Computer Dialogue Design, 271-278.

373. CATMULL, ED AND SMITH, ALVY RAY, 3-D Transformations of Images in Scanline Order, 279-285.

374. WEIMAN, CARL F. R., Continuous Anti-Aliased Rotation and Zoom of Raster Images, 286-293.

375. FEIBUSH, ELIOT A., LEVOY, MARC, AND COOK, ROBERT L., Synthetic Texturing Using Digital Filters, 294-301.

376. WARNOCK, JOHN E., The Display of Characters Using Grey Level Sample Arrays, 302-307.

377. LELER, WILLIAM J., Human Vision, Anti-Aliasing, and the Cheap 4000 Line Display, 308-313.

378. BAUDELAIRE, PATRICK AND STONE, MAUREEN, Techniques for Interactive Raster Graphics, 314-320.

379. SHANI, URI, Filling Regions in Binary Raster Images: A Graph-Theoretic Approach, 321-327.

SIGGRAPH '81 (Dallas, Texas)

380. GUPTA, SATISH AND SPROULL, ROBERT F., Filtering Edges for Gray-Scale Displays, 1-5.

381. KAJIYA, J. AND ULLNER, M., Filtering High Quality Text for Display on Raster Scan Devices, 7-15.

382. SECHREST, STUART AND GREENBERG, DONALD P., A Visible Polygon Reconstruction Algorithm, 17-27.

383. PAVLIDIS, THEO, Contour Filling in Raster Graphics, 29-36.

384. LEE, D. T., Shading of Regions on Vector Display Devices, 37-44.

385. HUBSCHMAN, HAROLD AND ZUCKER, STEVEN W., Frame-to-Frame Coherence and the Hidden Surface Computation: Constraints for a Convex World, 45-54.

386. WEINBERG, RICHARD, Parallel Processing Image Synthesis and Anti-Aliasing, 55-62.

387. CROW, F. C. AND HOWARD, M. W., A Frame Buffer System with Enhanced Functionality, 63-69.

388. GUPTA, SATISH, SPROULL, ROBERT F., AND SUTHERLAND, IVAN E., A VLSI Architecture for Updating Raster-Scan Displays, 71-78.

389. SPROULL, ROBERT, Custom VLSI Chips for Graphics, 79. (panel discussion, abstract only).

390. CLARK, JAMES H., A System Design Revolution, 79-80. (panel discussion, abstract only).

391. FUCHS, HENRY AND POULTON, JOHN, A VLSI-Oriented Design for a Raster Graphics Engine, 80-81. (panel discussion, abstract only).

392. WHITTED, TURNER, LSI-Enhanced 3-D Raster Display Systems, 81-82. (panel discussion, abstract only).

393. TRUCKENBROD, JOAN R., Effective Use of Color in Computer Graphics, 83-90.

394. EVANS, KENNETH B., TANNER, PETER P., AND WEIN, MARCELI, Tablet Based Valuators that Provide One, Two, or Three Degrees of Freedom, 91-97.

395. GREEN, MARK, A Methodology for the Specification of Graphical User Interface, 99-108.

396. BOLT, RICHARD A., Gaze-Orchestrated Dynamic Windows, 109-119.

397. BAECKER, RONALD, BROOKS, FREDERICK, BUXTON, WILLIAM, AND NEWMAN, WILLIAM, Video Panel Session on Interactive Systems, 121-122. (panel discussion, abstract only).

398. FOLEY, JAMES D. AND WENNER, PATRICIA A., The George Washington University Core System Implementation, 123-131.

399. O'DONNELL, T. J. AND OLSON, ARTHUR J., GRAMPS – A Graphics Language Interpreter for Real-Time, Interactive, Three-Dimensional Picture Editing and Animation, 133-142.

400. GARRETT, MICHAEL T., An Attribute Binding Model, 143-151.

401. DILL, JOHN C., An Application of Color Graphics to the Display of Surface Curvature, 153-161.

402. KINGSLEY, E. C., SCHOFIELD, NORMAN A., AND CASE, K., SAMMIE: A Computer Aid for Man Machine Modelling, 163-169.

403. LIN, V. C., GOSSARD, D. C., AND LIGHT, R. A., Variational Geometry in Computer-Aided Design, 171-177.

404. JOHNSON, L. NEIL, EVANS, DAVID C., HUELSKOETTER, WAYNE R., AND ZAPHIROPOULOS, REN, Presidents' Forum, 179. (panel discussion, introduction only).

405. FEINER, STEVEN, NAGY, SANDOR, AND VAN DAM, ANDRIES, An Integrated System for Creating and Presenting Complex Computer-Based Documents, 181-189.

406. BAECKER, RONALD, MILLER, DAVID, AND REEVES, WILLIAM, Towards a Laboratory Instrument for Motion Analysis, 191-197.

407. FILLIBEN, JAMES J., DATAPLOT – An Interactive High-Level Language for Graphics, Non-Linear Fitting, Data Analysis, and Mathematics, 199-213.

408. DUNHAM, DOUGLAS, LINDGREN, JOHN, AND WITTE, DAVID, Creating Repeating Hyperbolic Patterns, 215-223.

409. TODD, ROBERT AND DESHAZO, PATRICK, Austere C^3 Graphics, 225-232.

410. ROCKWOOD, ALYN P. AND JENSEN, THOMAS W., Two Aspects of Domain Designing: C^∞ Curve Rendering and Blended Map Projections, 233-242.

411. BONO, PETER, PUK, RICHARD, REED, TED, SKALL, MARK, AND WRIGHT, TOM, Panel Discussion on Standards, 243. (panel discussion, abstract only).

412. PLATT, STEPHEN M. AND BADLER, NORMAN I., Animating Facial Expressions, 245-252.

413. WALLACE, BRUCE A., Merging and Transformation of Raster Images for Cartoon Animation, 253-262.

414. REEVES, WILLIAM T., Inbetweening for Computer Animation Utilizing Moving Point Constraints, 263-269.

415. WHITTED, TURNER AND WEIMER, DAVID M., A Software Test-Bed for the Development of 3-D Raster Graphics Systems, 271-277.

416. ATHERTON, PETER R., A Method of Interactive Visualization of CAD Surface Models on a Color Video Display, 279-287.

417. MORAVEC, HANS P., 3D Graphics and the Wave Theory, 289-296.

418. POTMESIL, MICHAEL AND CHAKRAVARTY, INDRANIL, A Lens and Aperture Camera Model for Synthetic Image Generation, 297-305.

419. COOK, ROBERT L. AND TORRANCE, KENNETH E., A Reflectance Model for Computer Graphics, 307-316.

420. MAX, NELSON L., Vectorized Procedural Models for Natural Terrain: Waves and Islands in the Sunset, 317-324.

SIGGRAPH '82 (Boston, Massachusetts)

421. NORTON, ALAN, ROCKWOOD, ALYN P., AND SKOLMOSKI, PHILIP T., Clamping: A Method of Antialiasing Textured Surfaces by Bandwidth Limiting in Object Space, 1-8.

422. CROW, F. C., A More Flexible Image Generation Environment, 9-18.

423. TURKOWSKI, KENNETH, Anti-Aliasing Through the Use of Coordinate Transformations, 19. (abstract only, complete paper in *TOG 1*, 3 (July 1982), 215-234).

424. BLINN, JAMES F., Light Reflection Functions for Simulation of Clouds and Dusty Surfaces, 21-29.

425. STRAAYER, DAVID H., WRIGHT, TOM, SHUEY, DAVID, COHEN, BRUCE, SMITH, BRADFORD M., AND REED, THEODORE N., The Impact of Graphics Standards, 31-32. (panel discussion, introduction only).

426. ROSENTHAL, DAVID S. H., MICHENER, JAMES C., PFAFF, GUNTHER, KESSENER, RENS, AND SABIN, MALCOLM, The Detailed Semantics of Graphics Input Devices, 33-38.

427. REED, THEODORE N., A Metafile for Efficient Sequential and Random Display of Graphics, 39-43.

428. TEN HAGEN, PAUL J. W., Graphics Standardization: Activities of ISO/TC97/SC5/WG2 and their Impact in Europe, 45-46. (abstract only).

429. VAN DAM, ANDRIES, Professional Workstations, 49. (panel discussion, abstract only).

430. CLARK, JAMES H., Workstation Development at Stanford, 49. (panel discussion, abstract only).

431. DUNN, ROBERT M., Improvement Goals for Workstation Facilities, 49. (panel discussion, abstract only).

432. KRILOFF, HARVEY, The Application of Network Workstations to Large-Scale Engineering, 50. (panel discussion, abstract only).

433. NELSON, DAVID, Personal Workstations in a Local Network, 50. (panel discussion, abstract only).

434. SABIN, MALCOLM, Graphics Standards for Three-Dimensional Modelling, 47. (abstract only).

435. MÄNTYLÄ, MARTTI, An Inversion Algorithm for Geometric Models, 51-59.

436. NORTON, ALAN, Generation and Display of Geometric Fractals in 3-D, 61-67.

437. GANAPATHY, S. AND DENNEHY, T. G., A New General Triangulation Method for Planar Contours, 69-75.

438. HANRAHAN, PATRICK M., Creating Volume Models from Edge-Vertex Graphs, 77-84.

439. MACHOVER, CARL, FEDDERSEN, DONALD, LINSALATA, RALPH T., PREUSS, PETER, AND SPANN, RICHARD N., Presidents' Forum: Current Issues in Computer Graphics, 85. (panel discussion, abstract only).

440. WONG, PETER C. S. AND REID, ERIC R., Flair – User Interface Dialog Design Tool, 87-98.

441. KASIK, DAVID J., A User Interface Management System, 99-106.

442. ANSON, ED, The Device Model of Interaction, 107-114.

443. LIPKIE, DANIEL E., EVANS, STEVEN R., NEWLIN, JOHN K., AND WEISSMAN, ROBERT L., Star Graphics: An Object-Oriented Implementation, 115-124.

444. SPANN, RICHARD N., ADLER, FREDERICK R., KURLACK, THOMAS P., MCNAY, JOSEPH C., AND REICHENBACH, MARGARET A., The Graphics CAD/CAM Industry: Financial Perspectives, 125. (panel discussion, abstract only).

445. CLARK, JAMES H., The Geometry Engine: A VLSI Geometry System for Graphics, 127-133.

446. ZYDA, MICHAEL J., A Contour Display Generation Algorithm for VLSI Implementation, 135-146.

447. WHELAN, DANIEL S., A Rectangular Area Filling Display System Architecture, 147-153.

448. MALIN, LEON, BLISS, FRANK, CARMODY, WILLIAM, JOHNSON, ROBERT, SCHLOESSEL, MARTIN, AND SWARBRICK, JOHN, Approaches to Solid Modelling, 155. (panel discussion, abstract only).

449. SHELLEY, KIM L. AND GREENBERG, DONALD P., Path Specification and Path Coherence, 157-166.

450. GOAD, CHRIS, Special Purpose Automatic Programming for Hidden Surface Elimination, 167-178.

451. RABIN, RICHARD, STRASS, ALAN R., ROBILLARD, MARK, SCHEDLER, SUE, AND PETERSON, MATTHEW, Speech Recognition as a Computer Graphics Input Technique, 179-180. (panel discussion, abstract only).

452. FRIEDELL, MARK, BARNETT, JANE, AND KRAMLICH, DAVID, Context-Sensitive, Graphic Presentation of Information, 181-188.

453. MCKEOWN, DAVID M. JR. AND DENLINGER, JERRY L., Graphical Tools for Interactive Image Interpretation, 189-198.

454. FRANK, ANDRE, MAPQUERY: Data Base Query Language for Retrieval of Geometric Data and their Graphical Representation, 199-207.

455. MELKANOFF, MICHEL A., The Challenge of CAD/CAM Education, 209. (panel discussion, abstract only).

456. PUHL, FRANK, Universities' Relationships with Industry, 209-210. (panel discussion, abstract only).

457. LANGER, VICTOR, CADD CAM User Education, 210. (panel discussion, abstract only).

458. GREENBERG, DONALD, Some Problems in CAD Education, 210. (panel discussion, abstract only).

459. SHEPARD, MARK S., CAD/CAM Education in an Engineering Curriculum, 211. (panel discussion, abstract only).

460. REQUICHA, ARI AND VOELCKER, HERB, A Postgraduate Program in "Programmable Automation", 211. (panel discussion, abstract only).

461. MACKAY, STEVEN A., SAYRE, RICHARD E., AND POTEL, MICHAEL J., 3D Galatea: Entry of Three-Dimensional Moving Points from Multiple Perspective Views, 213-222.

462. KAWAGUCHI, YOICHIRO, A Morphological Study of the Form of Nature, 223-232.

463. PITTMAN, JON H. AND GREENBERG, DONALD P., An Interactive Graphics Environment for Architectural Energy Simulation, 233-241.

464. THOMAS, JAMES J., Graphic Input Interaction Techniques, 243. (panel discussion, abstract only).

465. KAJIYA, JAMES. T., Ray Tracing Parametric Patches, 245-254.

466. CARLSON, WAYNE E., An Algorithm and Data Structure for 3D Object Synthesis Using Surface Patch Intersections, 255-263.

467. SCHWEITZER, DINO AND COBB, ELIZABETH S., Scanline Rendering of Parametric Surfaces, 265-271.

468. BLINN, JAMES F., A Generalization of Algebraic Surface Drawing, 273. (abstract only, complete paper in *TOG 1*, 3 (July 1982), 235-256).

469. LUTHER, DAVID, JARETT, IRWIN, JOHNSON, HOWARD, RUSSELL, JACK, AND THOMPSON, JOHN, Business Graphics: What is it?, 275. (panel discussion, abstract only).

470. BEACH, RICHARD J., BEATTY, JOHN C., BOOTH, KELLOGG S., FIUME, EUGENE L., AND PLEBON, DARLENE A., The Message is the Medium: Multiprocess Structuring of an Interactive Paint Program, 277-287.

471. REYNOLDS, CRAIG W., Computer Animation with Scripts and Actors, 289-296.

472. HECKBERT, PAUL, Color Image Quantization for Frame Buffer Display, 297-307.

473. TOMPA, FRANK W., BOTTEN, BRIAN, GODFREY, DAVID, NORTON, JOHN, SCHNEIDER, LOIS, AND VAN DAM, ANDRIES, The Role of Videotex, 309-310. (panel discussion, abstract only).

474. GUIBAS, LEO J. AND STOLFI, JORGE, A Language for Bitmap Manipulation, 311. (abstract only, complete paper in *TOG 1*, 3 (July 1982), 191-214).

475. WARNOCK, JOHN AND WYATT, DOUGLAS K., A Device Independent Graphics Imaging Model for Use with Raster Devices, 313-319.

476. ACQUAH, JAMES, FOLEY, JAMES, SIBERT, JOHN, AND WENNER, PATRICIA, A Conceptual Model of Raster Graphics Systems, 321-328.

477. PARR, WORDIE, Health and Safety Issues in Computer Graphics, 329. (panel discussion, introduction).

478. SLINEY, DAVID, Optical Radiation Emissions from VDTs, 329-330. (panel discussion, abstract only).

479. PETERSON, R. C., Radiofrequency and Microwave Emissions from VDTs, 330. (panel discussion, abstract only).

480. ZUK, W. M., Measurements of X-ray Emission from VDTs, 330. (panel discussion, abstract only).

481. CUSHMAN, WILLIAM H., Human Factors Issues in VDT Workplace Design, 331. (panel discussion, abstract only).

SIGGRAPH '83 (Detroit, Michigan)

482. WILLIAMS, LANCE, Pyramidal Parametrics, 1-11

483. WARN, DAVID R., Lighting Controls for Synthetic Images, 13-21.

484. SCHWEITZER, DINO, Artificial Texturing: An Aid to Surface Visualization, 23-29.

485. FOLEY, JAMES D., BORK, AL, BROWN, MAXINE, KING, ROBIN, VAN DAM, ANDRIES, AND WOZNY, MIKE, Computer Graphics in Higher Education, 31-33. (panel discussion).

486. BUXTON, W., LAMB, M. R., SHERMAN, D., AND SMITH, K. C., Towards a Comprehensive User Interface Management System, 35-42.

487. OLSEN, DAN R. JR. AND DEMPSEY, ELIZABETH P., SYNGRAPH: An Automatic Interaction Generator, 43-50.

488. SINGH, BALDEV, BEATTY, JOHN C., BOOTH, KELLOGG S., AND RYMAN, RHONDA, A Graphics Editor for Benesh Movement Notation, 51-62.

489. SHERR, SOL, CHANG, IFAY, MALONEY, THOMAS, PLESHKO, PETER, SCHLAM, ELLIOT, AND SEATS, PETER, Advances in New Display Technology, 63-64. (panel discussion).

490. FUCHS, HENRY, ABRAM, GREGORY D., AND GRANT, ERIC D., Near Real-Time Shaded Display of Rigid Objects, 65-72.

491. ATHERTON, PETER R., A Scan-Line Hidden Surface Removal Procedure for Constructive Solid Geometry, 73-82.

492. HANRAHAN, PATRICK, Ray Tracing Algebraic Surfaces, 83-90.

493. KAJIYA, JAMES T., New Techniques for Ray Tracing Procedurally Defined Objects, 91-102.

494. STRAAYER, DAVID, BONO, PETER, EHLERS, RICHARD, ENDERLE, GUNTER, REED, THEODORE, SHUEY, DAVID, SKALL, MARK, SONDEREGGER, ELAINE, AND WRIGHT, TOM, Technical Implications of Proposed Graphics Standards, 103. (panel discussion).

495. LOOMIS, JEFFREY, POIZNER, HOWARD, BELLUGI, URSULA, BLAKEMORE, ALYNN, AND HOLLERBACH, JOHN, Computer Graphic Modeling of American Sign Language, 105-114.

496. MYERS, BRAD A., Incense: A System for Displaying Data Structures, 115-125.

497. BEACH, RICHARD J. AND STONE, MAUREEN, Graphical Style – Towards High Quality Illustrations, 127-135.

498. CSURI, CHARLES A., BLINN, JAMES, GOMEZ, JULIAN, MAX, NELSON, AND REEVES, WILLIAM, The Simulation of Natural Phenomena, 137-139. (panel discussion).

499. FIUME, EUGENE, FOURNIER, ALAIN, AND RUDOLPH, LARRY, A Parallel Scan Conversion Algorithm with Anti-Aliasing for a General-Purpose Ultracomputer, 141-150.

500. WHITTED, TURNER, Anti-Aliased Line Drawing Using Brush Extrusion, 151-156.

501. BLOOMENTHAL, JULES, Edge Inference with Applications to Antialiasing, 157-162.

502. GOLDMAN, RONALD N., GOSSARD, DAVID, RIESENFELD, RICHARD, VOELCKER, HERBERT, AND WOO, TONY, Solid Modeling, 163-165. (panel discussion).

503. CAHN, DEBORAH U. AND YEN, ALBERT C., A Device-Independent Network Graphics System, 167-173.

504. DIXON, DOUGLAS F., A Core Graphics Environment for Teletext Simulations, 175-181.

505. SIMONS, RANDALL W., Minimal GKS, 183-189.

506. HERR, LAURIN, AMANO, AKIRA, KATOU, MADOKA, KAWAGUCHI, YOICHIRO, AND OMURA, KOUICHI, Computer Graphics in the World of Japanese Commercial Production for Art, Entertainment and Advertising, 191-192. (panel discussion).

507. BARSKY, BRIAN A. AND BEATTY, JOHN C., Local Control of Bias and Tension in Beta-splines, 193-218.

508. ARNON, DENNIS S., Topologically Reliable Display of Algebraic Curves, 219-227.

509. PLASS, MICHAEL AND STONE, MAUREEN, Curve-Fitting with Piecewise Parametric Cubics, 229-239.

510. KUNII, TOSHIYASU, HERR, LAURIN, IKEDO, TSUNEO, ISHIMURA, KAZUKIYO, IWATA, KANSEI, NAITO, KAZUO, AND SAIMI, SHOHEI, Industrial Strategies of Japanese Computer Manufacturers, 241-242. (panel discussion).

511. SAKURAI, HIROSHI AND GOSSARD, DAVID C., Solid Model Input Through Orthographic Views, 243-252.

512. SCHMANDT, CHRIS, Spatial Input/Display Correspondence in a Stereoscopic Computer Graphic Work Station, 253-261.

513. VANNIER, MICHAEL W., MARSH, JEFFREY L., AND WARREN, JAMES O., Three-Dimensional Computer Graphics for Craniofacial Surgical Planning and Evaluation, 263-273.

514. MARCUS, AARON, COATES, DEL, AND MITCHELL, WILLIAM, Computer Graphics and Visual Designers, 275-277. (panel discussion).

515. MÄNTYLÄ, MARTTI AND TAMMINEN, MARKKU, Localized Set Operations for Solid Modeling, 279-288.

516. CHIYOKURA, HIROAKI AND KIMURA, FUMIHIKO, Design of Solids with Free-Form Surfaces, 289-298.

517. THOMAS, ADRIAN L., Geometric Modelling and Display Primitives Towards Specialised Hardware, 299-310.

518. DIETRICH, FRANK, CUBA, LARRY, GERBARG, DARCY, LIPPMAN, ANDREW, AND SANDIN, DAN, Artists Interfacing with Technology: Basic Concepts of Digital Creation, 311-313. (panel discussion).

519. COWAN, WILLIAM, An Inexpensive Scheme for Calibration of a Colour Monitor in Terms of CIE Standard Coordinates, 315-321.

520. HILL, FRANCIS S. JR., WALKER, SHELDON JR., AND GAO, FUWEN, Interactive Image Query System Using Progressive Transmission, 323-330.

521. PIKE, ROBERT, Graphics in Overlapping Bitmap Layers, 331-356.

522. BLISS, FRANK W., MACHOVER, CARL, SMITH, MAURICE, AND VOGEL, CARL, Solid Modeling: A User Perspective, 357. (panel discussion).

523. REEVES, WILLIAM T., Particle Systems – A Technique for Modeling a Class of Fuzzy Objects, 359-376.

524. KOREIN, JONATHAN AND BADLER, NORMAN, Temporal Anti-Aliasing in Computer Generated Animation, 377-388.

525. POTMESIL, MICHAEL AND CHAKRAVARTY, INDRANIL, Modeling Motion Blur in Computer Generated Images, 389-399.

526. HAMANN, WAYNE, FRANKISH, W., GLOWACZ, M., KELBLE, T. E., LINSELL, M. J., MACALPINE, G. A., AND YEVITCH, J. F., Ramifications of CAD/CAM on the Automotive Supplier Community, 401-402. (panel discussion).

Cumulative Author Index

SIGGRAPH '83

Author Index

Front Cover Credit **Fractal Lunar Mist** by Richard F. Voss, IBM

Exponentially attenuating surface mist, rising above a random cratered non-Gaussian fractal landscape. Fractal characteristics according to "The Fractal Geometry of Nature" by B. Mandelbrot (Freeman 1982). The image was produced with an IBM 4341 Computer/Celco CFR 4000 color film recorder on 4x5 Ektachrome.

Title Page Credit **Road to Point Reyes** directed by Rob Cook, Lucasfilm Ltd.

This landscape was defined using patches, polygons, fractals, particle systems, and a variety of procedural models. The various elements were rendered separately and later composited. Rob Cook designed the picture and did the texturing and shading, including the road, hills, fence, rainbow, shadows, and reflections. Loren Carpenter used fractals for the mountains, rock, and lake, and a special atmosphere program for the sky and haze. Tom Porter provided the procedurally drawn texture for the hills and wrote the compositing software. Bill Reeves used his particle systems for the grass and wrote the modelling software. David Salesin put the ripples in the puddles. Alvy Ray Smith rendered the forsythia plants using a procedural model. The visible surface software was written by Loren Carpenter, and the anti-aliasing software by Rob Cook. The picture was rendered using an Ikonas graphics processor and frame buffers, and was scanned on a COLOR FIRE 240, courtesy of MacDonald Dettwiler and Associates Ltd. The resolution is 4Kx4K, 24 bits/pixel.

Back Cover Credits

1 Time for Computer Graphics

by

Lorraine Prince, Genigraphics

This image was produced with simple primitives on a Genigraphics 100C graphics Console running Genigraphics RSX software. The picture was shot using a modified Forox camera at 4096 lines of resolution at f/8 with the neon glow as a separate exposure.

3 The Skull from GOLGO 13

by

Hitoshi Nishimura and Yoshi Fukushima,
Osaka University Computer Graphics
Research Center

This skull was designed for the animated film "GOLGO 13". The picture was generated by a multi-microcomputer system ("Links 1") consisting of 64 computers (see panel on Japanese Computer Graphics, Part I). Modelled by approximately 600 control points, the skull was rendered with a ray-tracing algorithm. Thanks to the Toyo Links Corporation for the still photograph.

"GOLGO 13"—art direction by Satomi Mikuriya, final design by Shin Matsuoka and final realization by Takashi Fukumoto. Copyright © 1983.

5 Beta-Spline Bottle with Increasing Tension Values and Different Textures

by

Brian A. Barsky, Tony D. DeRose and
Mark D. Dippé,
Berkeley Computer Graphics Laboratory

This array is based on a single Beta-spline bottle with only the tension varying. The tension is increasing from left to right and from top to bottom in an exponential fashion. Each of the tensed bottles has different material characteristics including metallic, dusty and plastic substances. The bias remains fixed throughout. The scene was rendered with a fast subdivision algorithm that converts Beta-splines to polygons, on an Ikonas RDS-3000 raster display attached to a VAX11/750 running Berkeley UNIX.

2 The Gallery

by

Roy Hall, Program of Computer Graphics,
Cornell University

Generated using ray-tracing methods, this scene features focused light sources and a reflection model that simulates metals. The work was computed at 512x512x48 bit resolution on a VAX 11/780 and recorded using a Dunn Instruments camera, model 632. Thanks to Chan Verbeck for technical support.

4 Martini Glass

by

Gray Lorig, Rensselaer Polytechnic Institute
Centre for Interactive Computer Graphics

This image was generated on a Prime 500 using a ray-tracing package based on the super-quadric primitive. The package supports reflection and refraction. The image was displayed on a model one/20 Raster Technologies graphics system and photographed on a Dunn Instruments camera.

6 Cat Clock

by

Glenn Entis, Pacific Data Images, Inc.

The objects in this scene are modelled from anti-aliased polygons. PDI's script system was used to model the objects with various geometric primitives and B-spline based shapes. The three-dimensional scene was then rendered on a VAX 11/750 at 512x486 resolution and matted in the frame-buffer over the sunrise sky and wall gradation. Thanks to Richard Chuang for the bow-tie and the photo.